Canon and (
Christian Theology

To Rachel Roberts

with deep appreciation
for your many gifts
and for your
friendship!

[signature]

09/19/2011

Canon and Criterion in Christian Theology

from the Fathers to Feminism

William J. Abraham

CLARENDON PRESS · OXFORD

1998

Oxford University Press, Great Clarendon Street, Oxford OX2 6DP

Oxford New York

Athens Auckland Bangkok Bogota Bombay Buenos Aires
Calcutta Cape Town Dar es Salaam Delhi Florence Hong Kong Istanbul
Karachi Kuala Lumpur Madras Madrid Melbourne Mexico City
Nairobi Paris Singapore Taipei Tokyo Toronto Warsaw
and associated companies in
Berlin Ibadan

Oxford is a trade mark of Oxford University Press

Published in the United States by
Oxford University Press Inc., New York

British Library Cataloguing in Publication Data
Data available

Library of Congress Cataloguing in Publication Data
Canon and criterion in Christian theology: from the
Fathers to feminism/William J. Abraham.
Includes bibliographical references and index.
1. Bible—Canon. 2. Authority—Religious aspects—Christianity.
3. Knowledge, Theory of (Religion). 4. Theology—Methodology.
I. Title.
BS465.A25   1998   230'.01—dc21   97–47465
ISBN 0–19–826939–0

1 3 5 7 9 10 8 6 4 2

Typeset by Cambrian Typesetters, Frimley, Surrey
Printed in Great Britain on acid-free paper by
Biddles Ltd., Guildford and King's Lynn

To James Barr

ACKNOWLEDGEMENTS

The argument developed in these pages has been germinating in my mind for well over ten years. During that time I have shared varied expressions of it with many people and benefited enormously from their response. It would be impossible to record the debt I owe to all those who have contributed to my reflection. I want in particular to thank William Babcock, Eric Barnes, James Barr, David Beck, Michael Beggs, Clifton Black, Ellen Charry, Keefe Cropper, Cornelia DeLee, Pavel Gavrilyuk, Frank Gourley, Chuck Gutenson, Julie Halstead, Harriet Harris, Jean Ann Karm, Sandy Menssen, Basil Mitchell, Elizabeth Moreau, Russell Pannier, Paddy Roche, Thomas Sullivan, Andrew Walker, and Jerry Walls.

A very special word of thanks goes to the Evangelical Scholarship Initiative for electing me to be a Pew Evangelical Scholar. As a recipient of a fellowship I have been able to garner the time and resources essential to a project of this magnitude. I am grateful beyond words for this invaluable help.

I want also to thank Timothy and Shaun for essential help with the computer. Thanks to Siobhan and Richard for welcome relief in Frederick.

As ever I thank my wife, Muriel, for unfailing support through it all.

W.J.A.

CONTENTS

Orientation: Authority, Canon, and Criterion

The fundamental problems which arise in treatments of authority in the Christian faith stem from a long-standing misinterpretation of ecclesial canons as epistemic criteria.

The former, ecclesial canons, comprise materials, persons, and practices officially or semi-officially identified and set apart as a means of grace and salvation by the Christian community. They are represented by such entities as creed, Scripture, liturgy, iconography, the Fathers, and sacraments. The latter, epistemic criteria, are constituted by norms of justification, rationality, and knowledge. They are represented by such entities as reason, experience, memory, intuition, and inference.

Means of grace presuppose a complex theological vision of creation and redemption. They take as given the existence of God, the estrangement of human agents from their true destiny, and a network of divine action in the salvation of the world. Within this vision means of grace refer to various materials, persons, and practices which function to reconnect human agents with their divine source and origin. They are akin to medicine designed to heal and restore human flourishing; they are akin to various exercises appointed to reorient the whole of human existence to its proper goal. Their natural home is the Church. In fact they are brought into existence by the Church, as she is guided in her pilgrimage into the kingdom of God.

Epistemic criteria belong to a very different arena. Norms or criteria generally arise out of puzzlement about gaining rationality, justified beliefs, and knowledge. Historically they have often arisen out of intellectual curiosity and out of conflict concerning what to believe as true. At their best they are carefully crafted means of articulating the justification of one's beliefs. They are means of demarcating truth from falsehood, reality from illusion, rationality from irrationality, knowledge from opinion. Their natural home is in the discourse and writings of philosophers. In fact, they are discerned and articulated by philosophers as they seek to understand justification and knowledge.

Over a long period of time and due to a great variety of pressures, ecclesial canons, which served in very diverse ways to initiate one into the life of God, were transformed into epistemological categories. The simplest way to record this change is to say that the term 'canon' ceased to be seen as a list of concrete items, such as a list of books to be read in worship, and came to be seen as a criterion of justification in theology. More broadly, Scripture and the tradition of the Church were interpreted as sources of authority. Thus the creeds, a list of doctrines, were treated as a source and warrant of theological claims. Or the canon of Fathers, a list of teachers and theologians, was taken as a graded system of warrant and probability in theological theory building. Most dramatically, the bishop of Rome, one person in a delicate system of oversight adopted by the Church as a whole, was seen as having privileged access to the truth about God. In general, the diverse and complex canonical heritage of the Church was quietly divided up into Scripture and tradition; in the process of abstraction and reduction, these were refashioned as epistemically privileged criteria of truth in theology. This transition had devastating consequences for both sets of concepts. As the canonical materials, persons, and practices of the Church were transformed into norms of epistemology, they were forced into moulds which warped their original use and purpose. At the same time, discussions about epistemology were forced into channels which pictured the justification of theological claims in terms of offering sure and certain foundations upon which everything else could be constructed.

The impact of this development has been so deep that even the effort to describe this transition is treated with scepticism in both philosophy and theology. Our theories of canon have become so encumbered with epistemic overtones that we can no longer recognize the conceptual difficulties from which they have suffered so long. Our theories of justification and knowledge have been so radically divorced from their relation to the history of theology that the idea that theology might throw light on the history of epistemology is treated with incomprehension. Furthermore, even to grasp the issues at stake, much less describe the transition which has occurred, requires a deep rethinking of the very idiom we deploy. The description of what is at stake requires the reworking of standard notions in ways which may initially confuse rather than illuminate. Happily, a number of philosophers have in recent times stressed the significance of historical narrative in appreciating and illuminating certain central difficulties in philosophy.[1] This is precisely so in the case before us, so the difficulties in intelligibility at this level are not entirely unknown. Unfortunately, our narrative in this instance embraces not only philosophy but theology. Hence the difficulties are even more acute than usual.

In order to minimize the confusion, in this opening chapter I shall provide a basic orientation to some of the central issues up ahead. The intention is to open up the arena of enquiry and to provide an initial statement of the core issue at stake. I shall proceed in three steps. First, I shall make a preliminary effort to call into question the long-standing reduction of the canon of Scripture to that of a criterion. Second, I shall show how natural it is to slide into the situation where we confuse the idea of canon with that of a criterion. Within this I shall pause and strengthen our preliminary effort to distinguish between canon and criterion, arguing that it is implausible in the extreme to look upon Scripture as a solution to epistemological questions. In and through this I shall, as a third step, identify the basic strategies which will be deployed in the main argument ahead. I shall end with some notes on the pertinence of our deliberations.[2]

---

[1] For a succinct and incisive example see Charles Taylor, 'Philosophy and its History', in Richard Rorty, J. B. Schneewind, and Quentin Skinner (eds.), *Philosophy in History* (Cambridge: Cambridge University Press, 1984), 17–30.

[2] The argument in this chapter will take the form of a spiral. I shall first stake out a distinction between canon and criterion as applied to Scripture and its use in moral debate, then turn to explain how easy it is to fall into confusing canon and criterion in this arena; I will then return to strengthen the case for a distinction between canon and criterion, proceed to further explanatory remarks on the all too easy confusion of the two. In and through this, at pertinent moments I shall make clear the strategies I shall deploy in the long narrative which follows. Even with this orientation to the argument as a whole, this initial exposition of our thesis may need revisiting. It may be that it is only after the full narrative has been digested that the understandable resistance and puzzlement initially evoked may be addressed and hopefully dissolved. Even then it

Let us begin by examining a relatively simple appeal to the canon of Scripture which most observers will understand, even though they may well reject the material proposals at stake. By examining this appeal briefly, we shall further explore the distinction between canon and criterion which we deem to be so crucial.

Consider the following situation. Christian Jones is remonstrating with Christian Smith about adultery. Smith believes that adultery is a live moral option. Broadly speaking, it is permissible to commit adultery when the partners agree, when proper precautions have been taken, and when no one gets hurt. On this analysis adultery is a serious moral option for Smith. Jones does not agree, and he says so aggressively. 'Look,' says Jones, 'adultery is wrong. The Ten Commandments forbid it, the prophets are against it, Jesus condemns it, and Paul does not countenance it. So the Bible says it is wrong, and that settles it. It does not matter that you feel good about it in experience; your feelings are irrelevant. Nor does reason count at this point, for our reason is unreliable on such matters, as it is apt to be governed by our passions. The Bible is against it, and that settles it. The Bible trumps everything else; that is, the Bible stands in judgement over experience, reason, and Church tradition. Moreover, that is precisely what we mean when we claim that the Bible is canonical.'

This brief conversation captures how some Christians might use Scripture in the domain of sexual morality. It has certainly been common in ethical discussion among Christians to provide brief summaries of biblical teaching in moral and theological arguments. Such usage is representative of the Christian tradition in both its classical expressions and in forms of popular piety. In these circumstances the temptation to see Scripture as an epistemological norm is virtually irresistible. Scripture as canon is, it would appear, a criterion of moral judgement.

It is legitimate to ask, however, whether the appeal to Scripture in this particular instance is best captured by saying that Scripture is an epistemic criterion. It is true that the teaching of Scripture is pitted against experience, reason, and the teaching of

may be helpful to come back full circle and look again at the initial articulation of our central thesis in this chapter. Happily, I can leave this matter to the discretion of the reader.

the community. Moreover, it is used as a kind of trump card. However, when this usage is taken to mean that Scripture as canon is the criterion of moral goodness, or the norm of truth in ethics, then we have moved the whole discussion on to a new plane. We have committed ourselves to a very particular epistemology of morality. Such a move is clearly a major commitment both philosophically and theologically. So we need to stand back and ponder what is at issue.

For the moment it is sufficient to make a simple distinction. It is one thing to say that Scripture is a canon; it is another thing entirely to advance a very particular interpretation of Scripture as canon by insisting that the canonicity of Scripture is constituted by its being a criterion of moral judgement. We cannot automatically assume that because scripture is described as canon or because it functions at times as a criterion in moral theology this means that its canonical status and significance are constituted by its being a criterion or norm.

We might expand on this initial distinction graphically in this way. In appealing to Scripture in moral or theological argument, it is one thing to argue from Scripture, assuming that scripture is a sure and certain foundation of knowledge; it is quite another to argue from Scripture, assuming that Scripture gives us access to special revelation. It is one thing to construe Scripture as a sure and certain foundation of knowledge; it is another to see it as a contingent medium of divine revelation.[3] In turn, both of these need to be distinguished from the idea of Scripture as canonical. We cannot automatically assume that claiming Scripture to be a sure and certain foundation, or declaring that Scripture is a contingent medium of divine revelation, or saying that Scripture is canonical, are all one and the same assertion.

The appeal to Scripture in our brief conversation is really a code for appeal to divine revelation. This is the relevant epistemic concept which is functioning in our conversation. It is only as the Mosaic law, the prophets, Jesus, and Paul are construed as mediating special divine revelation that the appeal to them functions appropriately in a Christian context. The sentence, 'The Bible

[3] Scripture is a *contingent* medium of divine revelation, because there are other ways in which God might have made available his revelation—say, through oral tradition.

says that adultery is wrong, and that settles it', is shorthand for a
deeper appeal to divine revelation. It is not, then, the canon of
Scripture which is functioning *simpliciter* as a norm. In fact, without the context of a whole network of claims about special revelation, the recourse to Scripture collapses. The modern loss of a
working concept of divine revelation makes this patently manifest, for in those theological circles which can make no sense of
any appeal to special divine revelation, Scripture simply becomes
a body of ancient texts whose moral relevance has long since
been abandoned. In classical Christian teaching, as well as in
popular piety, the Mosaic law, the prophets, Jesus, and Paul have
held an epistemically privileged position due to their being seen
as having access to the mind of God. They are believed to mediate divine revelation, and hence a summary of their position set
in the context of a body of background assumptions settles the
matter. Divine revelation is the crucial norm which needs to be
named if we are to capture what is at stake epistemically. Hence
it is misleading to think of the canon being an epistemic concept
in our conversation. Canon and revelation are two different
concepts which need to be distinguished logically even though
materially they cannot in this instance be separated. It is the latter
notion, that of revelation, which is functioning epistemically in
our simple example.

   An additional observation to be made at this point is this.
Construing the canon of Scripture as a criterion may drastically
diminish what it means to perceive Scripture as canonical. The
impression given in this interpretation is that the provision of the
canon of Scripture is the provision of a criterion to settle
contested questions. Properly deployed, that is, in the context of
a serious claim about divine revelation, it can indeed so be used,
or so, at least, it can be legitimately argued. However, even in the
field of morality, this use, if it is deployed exclusively, ignores
important canonical claims about the place of conscience in the
moral life, about the connection between divine commands and
human welfare, and about the relation between obedience and
freedom. More broadly and positively, such a reductionism
ignores the possibility that to have a canon of Scripture is to have
a sophisticated means of grace which is related to formation in
holy living in a host of ways. On this alternative reading,
Scripture functions to bring one to faith, to make one wise unto

salvation, to force one to wrestle with awkward questions about violence and the poor, to comfort those in sorrow, and to nourish hope for the redemption of the world. The interpretation of Scripture primarily or exclusively as an epistemic norm of morality and of theology erodes these crucial dimensions of canonical materials. In short, it ignores the fact that the canon of Scripture might better be construed as first and foremost a means of grace. Indeed, this interpretation may best capture Scripture's status and significance in its original formation, designation, and adoption. Or so I shall argue in what follows, as I seek to articulate our account of the difference between canon and criterion.[4]

The effort to chart and to break out of the confusing of an ecclesial canon with an epistemic criterion and the consequences which this has engendered requires sustained intellectual work on two frontiers simultaneously. At one level we need extended forays into the history of theology and philosophy in order to map the shift from canon to criterion in the Christian tradition. We need a diachronic analysis of the issues which will enable us to see, if only partially and schematically, where, how, and why this shift has occurred. Within this, it will, moreover, be useful to stop and explore synchronic explanations of the interconnections between treatments of canon and criterion in Christian thinkers and movements.

This kind of synchronic and diachronic analysis cannot be performed without also attending to the philosophical sensibilities which both create and explain this shift. The move from canon to criterion is an epistemological development which requires the deployment of relevant philosophical categories and concepts in order even to identify what is at stake. Normative assessment of the various proposals about criterion which emerge in the discussion cannot be made without entering the tangled field of epistemology as it relates to theology. For this reason, standard accounts of the history of Christian doctrine as they relate to the issue of canon have to be consulted with great care. Even where there is scrupulous effort not to import alien descriptive categories into the account, it is almost impossible not to deploy a network of concepts which unintentionally interpret the results in

---

[4] At times I shall speak of 'norm' rather than 'criterion', but nothing hangs on this usage. It is deployed simply for the sake of diversity of expression.

a contested way. In the end it strikes me as impossible to give a
neutral analysis of the historical data available to us. In what
follows I shall be drawing heavily on historical materials, but my
primary aims are to set forth a constructive account of the nature
of canon for Christian theology, to show in great detail the price
that is paid when we insist on developing an epistemology of
theology as constitutive of the canonical heritage of the Church,
and to pave the way for a richer account of the epistemology of
theology than is customary.

The transition from ecclesial canonicity to epistemic normativity is extremely natural. To claim that this transition is natural
does not mean, however, that it is correct. On the contrary, I
think that it has been unwise and unfortunate; so in what follows
I am not endorsing the development I shall schematically trace.
However, it will help give a feel for the tangled issues at stake to
trace how this transition can appear so natural and plausible.
There is an ingrained slide from canon to criterion, even though
it takes really disciplined reflection to detect when it is happening. We can begin to get a hold of these themes by distinguishing
the major issues which arise in the neighbourhood of discourse
about canon and criterion in Christian theology.

In modern theology, the conventional horizon within which
to locate the concepts of canon and criterion is that of authority.
Generally speaking, the topic of canon and criterion crops up
within discussion about what constitutes authority in theology. As
G. R. Evans has noted, 'The theme of Christian authority carries
a great deal on its shoulders.'[5] Within this arena we can detect at
least seven different issues.[6]

First, there is the question of the authority of God for theology
and the Church. Here there is near unanimous agreement that all
authority has to be traced back in some way or another to God. It
is God who provides the ultimate sanction for the authority of
the Bible, holy tradition, the Church, councils, prophets, reformers, bishops, and the like. The claim that God should have
authority is generally taken to be analytic. Given who God is—

[5] See her preface in G. R. Evans (ed.), *Christian Authority: Essays in Honour
of Henry Chadwick* (Oxford: Clarendon Press, 1988), p. v.
[6] For sustained conceptual analysis of the concept of authority see Richard
T. De George, *The Nature and Limits of Authority* (Lawrence, Kan.: University
Press of Kansas, 1985).

that is, all-loving, omniscient, and omnipotent, not to say, our creator and redeemer—it would be a contradiction to deny the authority of God.

Despite the truism embodied in this claim, many moderns have not found it easy to accept that God has such a status. Thus some, like Sartre, have insisted that predicating such authority of God is incompatible with genuine human freedom.[7] More recently, feminist theologians have been very reluctant to speak of the authority of God, and have sought to purge the Christian tradition of those images, like lord and king, which have been used to express the authority of God, because they depict a hier-archical world-view which is morally unacceptable. Clearly, then, there are issues which require attention in any attempt to speak of the authority of God. For the present it is enough to highlight the fact that, conventionally at least, there is a very basic theologi-cal assertion lodged in claims about authority in the Christian tradition: God, and only God, has any ultimate, fundamental authority.

A second crucial theme which is naturally related to the topic of authority is one we have already mentioned: namely, that of divine revelation. General talk about the authority of God remains ethereal and formal if it is not fleshed out in particular claims as to where God's purposes and intentions are made avail-able. These claims have been generally articulated in doctrines which speak of divine revelation, divine dictation, divine inspira-tion, divine speaking, and the Word of God. The assumption driving this transition from God to God's revelation is that in some minimal sense God is a personal agent who makes his will known to human beings.[8] God acts, say, in speaking to a prophet or an apostle, or, say, in becoming incarnate in Jesus Christ; and by having access to these actions, we come to know what God desires. Thus it is through these actions that God's authority is actualized. Without them, whatever we might hold about the

---

[7] For an analysis of this issue see Diogenes Allen, 'The Paradox of Freedom and Authority', *Theology Today*, 36 (1979), 167–75.

[8] This whole topic is pivotal for my project, but it is too complex to take up here. I shall be attending to important aspects of divine agency and divine action in a subsequent volume. I shall in part argue there that we need to explore what these mean in the canonical heritage of the Church as we tackle the issue of an appropriate epistemology of theology.

authority of God formally, there would be nothing material to take as authoritative. Divine authority would simply be a formal reality with no connection to the world. Doctrines of revelation, inspiration, incarnation, and the like provide the crucial materials which specify what God's authority might require. Hence they are never far from the topic of authority.

A similar move takes us to the third theme: namely, that of canon. We automatically think of the canon of Scripture when we begin to unpack the idea of authority in theology. If God has spoken, or in some manner revealed himself, such past actions would need to be identified, described, interpreted, and, above all, passed on to new generations, if they are to be of any effect beyond their original reception. This would seem to be essential if divine revelation has been embodied uniquely in God's past actions in history. Hence it is natural to look for some kind of Scripture, some body of writings, through which new generations can have access to that revelation. It is in this soil that the epistemic conception of the canon of Scripture takes root. Many Christians have taken the bible as authoritative because they look to the Bible as giving access, to a lesser or greater degree, to that revelation which makes available the mind of God for the world. So the topics of canonicity and authority fit snugly together.

Canons of Scripture do not, however, arrive in history like bolts from the blue. Even the strongest doctrines of divine inspiration leave room for the fact that the Scriptures are intimately related to communities. This naturally evokes a fourth topic: namely, the place of community in any account of authority. The Christian Bible arises within the Christian Church; it is interpreted by the Church; it is in some way recognized and authorized by the Church. Hence it is natural to make claims about the authority of the community itself. This in turn leads to proposals about how to locate the authority of the community. Does it reside in the community as a whole, or in its general councils, or in its bishops, or in its chief bishop, or in some combination of these? Moreover, how is the authority of Scripture to be related to the authority of the Church? Is one more basic and authoritative than the other? Or is it wrong-headed to play the authority of the Bible against the authority of the Church? However we resolve these kinds of questions, it is clear that it is initially natural to speak of the authority of the Church once we locate the Bible as intimately related to decisions made within the Church.

Mention of the Church leads naturally into a fifth dimension: namely, the possible authority of the Church's tradition. Over time, members and teachers of the Church develop a body of interpretive material which is evoked by her internal life, by her reception of divine revelation, and by her interaction with intellectual and cultural life. Hence questions naturally arise about tradition. How is tradition to be identified? What forms can it legitimately take? What status is it to receive? What, if any, is its normative force? How is it to be related to the canon of Scripture? How is it related to divine revelation? These are some of the more obvious questions posed by the existence of tradition in the Church.

A sixth dimension to authority lurks in the neighbourhood. Grant that the Bible and tradition exist, and grant that they are intimately related to the life of the Church, then who is to see that the authority of Scripture or the appropriate role of tradition is to be taken seriously and, in cases of rebellion, safeguarded? It would appear that if the Bible is to function appropriately, or if tradition is to have a proper role in the life of the Church, then there must be some kind of oversight. How is this oversight to be implemented? Is it to be left to the judgement of the individual reader, maybe with appropriate help from the Holy Spirit? Is such governance to be left to God's general and providential governance of the Church, perhaps with special intervention here and there, say, by the raising up of prophets and reformers, when their type of witness is essential? Are there institutional mechanisms, like conferences or councils, to deal with questions of oversight? Are there special persons called and equipped by God to exercise authority in the community? Or does the process of oversight call for a balance of some or all of these? However we resolve these questions, there is clearly a distinct kind of social authority or oversight which cries out for attention.

By now we have travelled a long way from the authority of God. We can discern a natural thematic flow from the beginning to the end of our journey. By natural links we have moved from God, to divine revelation, to the canon of Scripture, to the possible authority of the Church and her tradition, and then to the authority of certain persons or social institutions within the Church.

There is, however, one more link to be identified. All of these, either singly or together, prompt the seventh and final element in discussion about authority: namely, how are we going to provide warrants for the claims embodied in any of these proposals? How do we know that God exists in the first place? How do we know where revelation is to be found? How are we to justify the choice of this Scripture over against that Scripture? Why should we acknowledge the authority of the Church? Why should we accept the ruling or judgement of this or that institution or person in the Church? How do we know that any of these claims is in fact true? To what canon or criterion do we appeal in order to resolve disputes and doubts about these various conceptions and proposals regarding authority?[9] What epistemology shall we deploy to under-gird the intellectual quality of our decisions in this arena? In short, what criterion or criteria shall we use to ground any of our claims about authority? With the mention of criteria, the journey which started with mention of canon has ended. The last link in the chain of connections has been reached.

We have just traced a possible journey which naturally connects the idea of canon with the idea of a criterion. We have not, however, endorsed this transition; we have not, that is, agreed that it is wise to think of canon as a criterion. In fact, we wish to resist the move to treat canon in the Christian tradition as a criterion. The deep reason for this judgement is simple: to construe an ecclesial canon, like Holy Scripture, as an epistemic norm is odd in the extreme. It is straightforwardly wrong. A list of religious documents drawn up by a Church is simply not a candidate for a criterion of rationality, justified belief, or knowledge. Within a tradition or a culture accustomed for centuries to think of canon first and foremost as a criterion, pointing this out may be something of a shock. So we need to pause and see why this is so.

Consider the following thought-experiment. Imagine, first, that the only books in the Bible are the books of James and Jude; these constitute our canon of Scripture. Clearly this is an unlikely proposition. However, all we need for the moment is that it is a

    [9] For a marvellous introduction to this topic in the field of epistemology see Roderick M. Chisholm, 'The Problem of the Criterion', in *The Foundations of Knowing* (Minneapolis: University of Minnesota Press, 1982), 61–75.

logical possibility. Then, imagine taking a course in epistemology, where we are exploring what knowledge is and how it is to be related to truth, belief, evidence, justification, warrant, and rationality. Now imagine offering the canon of Scripture—in this case the books of James and Jude—as a serious solution to the kinds of questions which naturally arise in the discussion about the nature of knowledge. Suppose we are worried as to whether knowledge is true, justified belief; or suppose we are puzzled about the reliability of memory or of sense experience or of induction. Appealing to the canon will get us nowhere; the effort simply does not get off the ground. There is something categorically wrong about offering the canon as a serious answer to the questions which crop up in the field of epistemology. It is hard to see how our designated canon can be construed as a criterion of rationality, warrant, justified belief, or knowledge, when we imagine concretely that it is constituted by the books of James and Jude. *Mutatis mutandis* this applies more generally to the collection of books we refer to as the canon of Scripture.

Yet my central thesis, the reader will recall, is that it is precisely this shift which has caused such problems in the discussion about authority. So let us dig a bit deeper to see if we can find further considerations outside the conceptual journey already covered which would make this transition *prima facie* explicable.

One obvious factor fuelling the transition stems from the use of Scripture as a factor in persuasion in the rhetorical practices of the Christian community. As we noted earlier, Christians, because of their background assumptions about special revelation, often use Scripture as a kind of trump card in internal arguments. It is used to overrule intuition, conscience, reason, and experience. Hence it is natural for the unwary to think that the canon is really a grand epistemic norm which can resolve deep problems in the theory of knowledge. Canon appears to belong to the same order of being as intuition, sense experience, memory, reason, and the like.

Another factor that clearly has a role in the transition is the varied way the term 'canon' can be used. Canon, as originally used, had two distinct meanings. The matter is splendidly expressed by Floyd Filson: 'It is not entirely clear whether the first use of the word "canon" to designate the books of the Bible referred primarily to the *list* of them or to the *rule* or *standard* of faith and life which they contained.'[10] At one level, canon simply meant a list of books. Modern usage reflects this when it speaks of the canon of Western civilization and means by this a list of books which from the point of view of the speaker represents a particular set of cultural values and convictions.[11] The canon of Scripture on this analysis is constituted by a set of books which are bound together and treated as one. Moreover, used in this way, the idea of canon is not restricted to Scripture. Edward Reuss captures the issue succinctly: 'It must not be forgotten that the use of the term *canon* has never been restricted to the Bible. There were canons of councils, canon law, the canonical life, canons of cathedrals, etc. All these expressions have at bottom the same origin and are derived from a primitive meaning anterior to our canon of scripture.'[12] However, canon also signifies a standard by which to measure various doctrines, traditions, and actions. Here the concept shifts to that of a norm or a criterion used to measure the rightness of this or that proposal. In this case it is clear that the term has an epistemological ring to it which goes far beyond that represented by usage which more modestly treats canon as simply a list of books. Once we bear this in mind, it is possible to move from talk of canon to talk of criterion relatively easily.

Just how easily this shift can occur is nicely brought out by the recent work of Gamble. Gamble argues convincingly that 'canon' as applied to Scripture meant a list. Yet he cannot accept the implications of his own findings, and readily shifts into construing 'canon' as a norm. Reviewing the debate between Zahn and Beyer, he writes:

---

[10] Floyd V. Filson, *Which Books Belong in the Bible* (Philadelphia: Westminster Press, 1957), 15; emphasis original.

[11] If the speaker is opposed to the values embodied in the canon, the likelihood is that it will be treated not as a canon to be accepted but as an ideology to be rejected. Consider the suggestion of Franz-Xaver Kaufman: 'Whoever commonly speaks of authority intends to show authority or claim authority. Whoever speaks of ideology intends to contest authority. Thus, authority and ideology in everyday language, and above all in political usage, apparently refer to a similar or even to the same content, which in the one case is stated affirmatively and in the other critically. Authority and ideology, therefore, already in their presuppositions are evaluating concepts' ('The Sociology of Knowledge and the Problem of Authority', *Journal of Ecumenical Studies*, 19/2 (1982), 18).

[12] Edward Reuss, *History of the Canon of Holy Scriptures in the Christian Church* (Edinburgh: R. W. Hunter, 1891), 218.

The philological evidence decisively favors the view of Zahn: as applied to a group of writings, 'canon' first of all meant simply a 'list,' specifically a list of those writings generally employed in the Church, and most especially those customarily read in public worship. Thus the term served mainly to signify the actual usage to which these writings were put and not to impute a peculiarly regulative authority to them.[13]

Yet even with such a clear statement of the case for a non-epistemic conception of canon, Gamble cannot give up the quasi-epistemic sense posited by Beyer.

Though it is important to make this distinction, it cannot be absolutized. The writings which were included in the 'list' (or canon) were widely acknowledged as authentic and authoritative and could find a place in the list of books used in worship precisely because of this general recognition of their character. Hence, *even if it was not originally intended by speaking of these documents as 'canonical' in the sense of being 'in the list,'* the idea of their normative status inevitably came to be connoted by the term 'canon,' and all the more so since in previous Christian usage the word had consistently had the sense of 'norm' or 'standard,' albeit in other connections entirely.[14]

A further factor aiding and abetting the shift from ecclesial canon to epistemic criterion is located in the extent to which Scripture is canonized precisely because it is thought to give access to the mind of God. As we shall see, the story of canonization of the Bible is very complex, for the reasons behind the process of canonization are multiple. Yet there is no doubt that from very early times appeals were made to Scripture not just as a source but as a standard of knowledge. Such appeals, in turn, rested almost invariably on theories of divine inspiration and revelation which were often assumed at the outset. With or without the backing of a doctrine of inspiration, the canon of

---

[13] See Harry Y. Gamble, *The New Testament Canon: Its Meaning and Making* (Philadelphia: Fortress Press, 1985), 17–18.

[14] Ibid.; emphasis added. Gamble's reasoning is especially interesting because he goes on to show how difficult it is to sustain the full-blooded epistemic conception of canon he deploys when he discusses the canon as a 'norm'. In fact the concept crumbles in his hands under the weight of historical and exegetical evidence, and he settles in the end for a muddled, compromise position which introduces an entirely new norm more or less out of the blue: the canon is a compromise between the single and specific ground of faith—the Christ event—and the multiplicity of its interpretative appropriations' (ibid. 92).

Scripture was treated as a source of divine revelation, and such
revelation in turn was treated as a norm of truth.[15] This is surely
to be expected, because divine revelation is generally seen as
intrinsically normative. As we noted earlier, that claim can
rightly be construed as analytic. Given who God is, it is not
possible to claim that divine revelation is false. Divine revelation
is an essentially epistemic concept; divinity and knowledge are
logically connected.[16] Buried in the interpretation of the biblical
canon were implicit epistemological moves which easily created
the context for a transition from ecclesial canon to epistemic
criterion.

Particular human claims to be in possession of divine revelation do not, however, carry this kind of cognitive freight. There
is nothing self-contradictory in claiming that Christian avowals
concerning possession of divine revelation are entirely false.[17]
Moreover, different ecclesial groups and different religions make
competing claims about what God has revealed. Hence actual,

---

[15] 'In the second century in the Christian church k. [κανών] came to stand
for revealed truth, *rule of faith*' (William F. Arndt and F. Wilbur Gingrich, *A
Greek–English Lexicon of the New Testament and Other Early Christian Literature*,
(Chicago: University of Chicago Press, 1957), 403). Note here the theologically
loaded way in which canon is defined.

[16] Yet it is an epistemic concept which generally presupposes the reliability
of memory, of sense perception, and inference. Hence in the modern period it
has generally been seen as something of a secondary and even inferior epistemic
notion. In this respect it can usefully be seen as analogous to the concept of
testimony in jurisprudence.

[17] John Locke was especially clear about this issue, characteristically for his
age expressing the point in terms of the relation between revelation and reason.
'Reason must be our last judge and guide in everything. I do not mean that we
must consult reason, and examine whether a revelation from God can be made
out of natural principles, and if it cannot that we may reject it: but consult it we
must, and by it examine, whether it be a revelation from God or no: and if
reason finds it to be revealed from God, reason then declares for it, as much as
for any other truth, and makes it one of her dictates' (*An Essay Concerning
Human Understanding*, ed. Peter H. Nidditch (Oxford: Clarendon Press, 1975),
704). Locke goes on to insist that putative cases of inspiration by the internal
light need to be 'conformable to the principles of reason or to the Word of
God, which is attested revelation' (ibid.). Despite Locke's perspicuity, he does
not seem to note here sufficiently clearly that he is proposing to test revelation
by revelation. What he does grasp is that there is a clear distinction between
divine revelation itself and someone's claim to be in possession of a divine revelation. The authority of the former does not transfer automatically to the latter.

material claims to divine revelation, rather than solving deep
questions about epistemology, are liable to precipitate an acute
epistemological crisis. Given rival claims to divine revelation, one
is immediately tempted to look around for a criterion to sort out
genuine from spurious cases of divine revelation. Immediately
revelation is relegated to the side lines of epistemology.

In these circumstances, the concept of God is easily marginalized and then eliminated. Actual claims about God's intentions
and purposes are themselves a matter of dispute, so appeal to God
or to divine revelation as a way of resolving these deeper disputes
about truth and knowledge is taken to be question begging at
best and logically irrelevant at worst. Consequently, any move to
make God a central category in epistemology becomes implausible. Bringing in God as an essential element in the identification
of justification and knowledge simply prompts one to ask how
one knows that God has such a role in epistemology in the first
place. The upshot of this is that one is prompted to develop epistemological proposals which are entirely secular in content. Few
alternatives meet the conditions for this better than the effort to
think of epistemology as an exercise in discovering the normative
foundations of knowledge. Looking for some kind of criterion of
justification, preferably a criterion which will give absolute
certainty, becomes the central goal of epistemology.

Asking what norm or norms ground our proposals has a devastating impact on the whole discussion. The other six areas we
have identified immediately appear parasitical and secondary.
Somehow, until we deal with the matter of norms, our proposals
on the authority of God, the Bible, the Church, tradition, and
the like lack substance; they fail to connect with truth and reality.
Hence we react with one of two tendencies. On the one side, we
let everything else drop until we can find an answer to the problem of the criterion of truth, as evidenced in the whole train of
discussion initiated by Descartes. Once we become perplexed
about rival claims to authority predicated on rival proposals about
divine revelation, rival canons of Scripture, rival Churches, rival
councils, and rival bishops, then the quest for some criterion of
justification to settle our doubts and difficulties about these
matters may easily become an obsession. The quest became such
an embarrassing obsession for learned Western Christians like
Descartes and Locke that the relation between disputes about

authority within the Church and the origins of modern epistemology have been omitted from the history of philosophy.[18]
Philosophers and students of philosophy for their part are wont to
dismiss any suggestion of a possible relation between the debate
about canon in theology and criterion in epistemology with the
wave of the proverbial hand. They will only allow entry to the
contemporary discussion if the potential partners in the discussion
cast their ideas in ways which fit with certain privileged ways of
conceiving the problems of epistemology. Consequently, there is
a failure to see that current ways of conceiving the issues are in
fact a reflection of older theological questions which have been
suppressed.

On the other side, modern theological students who internal-
ize today's anxiety about the right criterion for theology can
easily become intellectually crippled, often failing to get to grips
with the development of material doctrinal proposals. The initial
temptation is to evade, to turn and run, to change the subject, or
to give up on the question as futile. After all, theologians have to
get on with propounding proposals about God, creation, sin,
salvation, and related topics. Yet to do so without dealing with
the question of truth squarely and honestly leaves those who yield
to such temptation haunted with distress. They find themselves
relentlessly hounded by opponents who press the question of
norm effectively and innocently. The very ideas of being critical,
of being methodologically rigorous and serious in theology, have
hinged on resolving the problem of the fundamental criterion of
justification and knowledge in theology. Hence prolegomena
becomes the centre of gravity in theology.[19]

---

[18] In my own training in philosophy, which I suspect was typical of the
period, Descartes's Christian background was never mentioned, much less taken
seriously. For the most part he was seen as a covert humanist or an outright
atheist. Theological dimensions of his work were totally ignored.

[19] This tendency generally takes the form of a request for appropriate
method in the prolegomena to systematic theology. It is worth noting that in
Roman Catholic theology it was once common to have a whole field of
enquiry devoted to criteriology. See Cardinal Mercier, *A Manual of Modern
Scholastic Philosophy*, trans. T. L. Parker and S. A. Parker (St Louis: Herder,
1953), i. 343–404. Cardinal Mercier writes: 'Criteriology is the *reflex study of our
certain knowledge and of the grounds upon which its certitude rests*. The criterion
(κρίνω, I judge or distinguish) of truth is the test by which we distinguish truth
from error; the word *criteriology* expresses the leading thought, but not the only

In these circumstances it is obvious that one way to deal expeditiously with either the secular or Christian epistemologist in search of a criterion of justification is to think of the canon of Scripture as an epistemic norm. For the modern Protestant, at least, this move keeps intact the appeal to Scripture as a fundamental option in the debate about criterion in theology. On a purely formal level, one has some sort of answer to those who think that there can be no progress in theology until the criterion to which one is appealing to secure the truth of one's claims has been clearly specified. Furthermore, construing Scripture as an epistemic criterion allows one to hold Scripture in the highest possible regard in the debate about authority.[20] Treating Scripture as an epistemic norm has all the features of a godsend which will not just keep the epistemological watch-dog at bay; it can call up in its favour all the weight of Christian history which has resolutely insisted that Scripture is indeed a canon of the faith. In fact, the opponent may well be perplexed at the dexterity of this challenge, for, as we have seen, canon has an epistemological edge to its meaning, and there is no doubt that this move gives the deep appearance of being profoundly Christian.

We can begin to see, then, on a purely conceptual level that buried in the themes which swirl around the idea of authority is the potential for extraordinary intellectual revolutions to take place. Not surprisingly, it can take centuries for these revolutions to work themselves out in the history of theology and philosophy. There is no knowing in advance how these changes will emerge or what shape they will take. Moreover, even with hindsight it is far from easy to map exactly how these revolutions have occurred. There will always be competing narratives available which can provide relatively plausible renderings of the available data. What one can see, however, is that a tradition can begin with a complex network of proposals on canon in the Christian

---

thought of this branch of study. It is also called epistemology (ἐπιστήμη, *scientia*, knowledge), the scientific study of knowledge. Knowledge is knowing with certitude; epistemology is therefore a *theory of certitude*' (ibid. 343; emphasis original).

[20] To speak of an epistemic criterion is something of an oxymoron. I do so deliberately in order to signal the fact that debates about justification are rooted in epistemology. So to construe Scripture in this way drags it inescapably into the domain of philosophy.

tradition at one point in time and end up with a single concept of canon at another point of time. Keeping such possibilities firmly in view is one way to fix some of the boundaries of the disputes which need to be identified and addressed. This is exactly the case, I am suggesting, for the Christian tradition. Naming the transition as a shift from ecclesial canon to epistemic criterion is one illuminating way to organize the debate and work towards a new resolution of old issues.

If we are to make progress in the debate about authority, then, it would help to abandon the assumption that resolving the debate about the right criterion is the first and fundamental issue to get behind us whether in theology or in any other discipline. More radically, it is important to consider that the very framing of the issue of authority or more generally of disputes in epistemology in this way is debatable. Looking for some fundamental criterion of justification is not the innocent affair it is generally perceived to be. On the contrary, it may well be deeply deficient intellectually and spiritually. Of course, saying this is one thing, but showing it is another. Optimally, what one needs to do is to lay out a positive alternative which will simply outshine its rivals by its merits. Yet, looking for some alternative epistemological vision would leave us where we are, for it puts the priority once more on getting one's epistemology straight before settling other important matters related to canon and authority. Hence, while we do not for one moment want to avoid getting into substantial epistemological proposals, we need an alternative strategy.

My strategy in what follows has two components. First, I shall lay out a narrative of canonical development in the early Church. Here the intention is to revise the debate about canon by painting a picture of the internal canonical traditions of the Church. In the process I shall attempt to develop this picture as generously and persuasively as possible. Essential to the attraction of this picture are its complexity and its modesty. I shall seek to develop an account of both the boundaries and the purpose of the canonical heritage of the Church which rivals that currently available in the identification of canon with Scripture and in the interpretation of canon as criterion. Through this historical reconstruction I am therefore proposing a more viable account of canon than has been conventionally available in Western theology. While I shall deploy the language of canon, I want it to be understood from the beginning that my intention is to liberate the Church from its bondage to epistemic interpretations of this notion. I want, that is, to relocate the whole idea of canon within the arena of means of grace within the Church. This is an exercise in revision by retrieval; it is an effort to cure the Church of canonical dyslexia and amnesia.

Second, I shall attempt to show that the inner intellectual harmony of this canonical symphony developed in the early Church was systematically dismantled in the Western Church before, during, and after the Reformation. In particular, the quest for a certain kind of epistemology became so overwhelming that it clouded the perception of Christian intellectuals in the debate about canonical traditions in the life of the Church. This quest also helped precipitate a massive epistemological crisis for Christian intellectuals, which naturally led into Enlightenment theories of knowledge and justification. Equally important, this quest has led to a series of dead ends in modern Christianity, leaving large tracts of it intellectually exhausted and spiritually suffocated.

The argument on this score is extremely long, and it is cumulative in form. I shall seek to show that the great experiments in modern theology represented by John Locke, Friedrich Schleiermacher, John Henry Newman, the great Princeton theologians of the nineteenth and early twentieth centuries, Karl Barth, Schubert Ogden, and representative feminist theologians denote one failed attempt after another to rescue Christian theology from the epistemological captivity to which it has been subject since it lost its moorings in the canonical heritage of the early Church. I shall seek to show that the outcome of these developments over time is the disintegration of the Christian tradition. While we can see such disintegration take place relatively quickly in our narrative, it is graphically visible at the end, when I make manifest the intentional invention of a radically new network of canonical materials, persons, and practices to replace those developed in the early Church.

If I am correct in my analysis, then we have reached the end of the road in the epistemizing of the canonical heritage of the Church. This will undoubtedly appear as grim to many. This is not the response which I want to evoke, however. On the contrary, I invite my readers to be open to a liberation from the inhibiting practices which have grown up around an inadequate vision of canon in the Christian tradition. I shall suggest that the possibility of canonical renewal lies buried in the rubble of its disintegration at the hands of those who have turned the canon into a criterion.

It will become clear, then, from the structure of my narrative that one way to make progress on the issues related to canon lies in a deep internalization of the canonical heritage of the patristic period. Such an internalization cannot be reduced to the simple process of repeating what was said in the past. To think of the issues in these terms is to misrepresent anew the canonical heritage of the Church by treating it as an inert datum to be captured at will rather than as a subtle gift of the Holy Spirit which should be appropriated with skill, humility, and divine guidance. Further, having exposed how precarious and dangerous it is to develop a single epistemology of theology, I shall give some hints as to where we might go to make capital of the problems of the past. In this arena I shall provide a promissory note, drawing attention to epistemic proposals still in the making. In particular, I shall argue that epistemic theorizing be kept in its proper place in any proposal about the nature and content of the canonical heritage of the Church. This accounts for the schematic character of my suggestions on the epistemology of theology. We will not make the kind of progress we can and must make on the epistemology of theology until the painful but liberating lessons unearthed here are heeded. Indeed, internalizing the theological and philosophical narrative which follows is in itself a way of furthering our insight into the epistemology of theology. The narrative is not just a prelude to better things to come; it constitutes a substantial philosophical and theological contribution in its own right.

Equally, it will not be possible to explore adequately the epistemic suggestions I have in mind until we look carefully at the concept of God expressed in the canonical heritage of the Church and until we heed various suggestions which lie buried at an informal level within it. These canonical insights easily become suppressed once the move is made to conceive of canon as a criterion. So it is best for these suggestions to await upon a fuller analysis of divine agency and divine action than can be delineated here. In the course of that story we shall find that previously suppressed ways of conceiving of justification and knowledge are significant resources for the development of a viable epistemology of theology.

It remains to point out in conclusion that the time is now ripe for pursuing these matters. First, it is clear that standard ways of tackling the epistemology of Christian belief have been radically questioned over the last generation. Classical foundationalist epistemologies, which look for some sort of clear, certain, and exclusive norm that will act as a base for all knowledge and justification, have fallen on hard times.[21] This has led some thinkers to panic and reach for some kind of post-modern relativism or epistemic nihilism as the way ahead for theology. In these circumstances we give up the quest for objective truth, for the genuine justification of our beliefs, or for knowledge. On the surface this has all the appearance of leaving the proverbial frying pan for the fire. We might avoid this fate if I am right in my contention that classical foundationalism was developed by theologians before it was secularized by those Christian intellectuals who provided the deep structures of the Enlightenment. Hence, if I am also right in arguing that the whole idea of canon must be extracted from its captivity to such an enterprise, and that such captivity has prevented us from pursuing other epistemic options buried in the canonical heritage of the Church, then we should pause before we reach for one more partnership with the favoured epistemology of the day.

[21] One of the most penetrating attacks has come from the work of Reformed philosophers, especially that of Alvin Plantinga and Nicholas Wolterstorff. See their essays in Alvin Plantinga and Nicholas Wolterstorff (eds.), *Faith and Rationality: Reason and Belief in God* (Notre Dame, Ind.: University of Notre Dame Press, 1983). It should be made clear by way of gentle warning to the unwary that the end of classical foundationalism does not in itself dispose of foundationalism in epistemology. Classical foundationalism means here broadly the view that the foundations of justification and knowledge can only be found in some kind of absolutely certain foundation. Thus the foundations were to consist of those beliefs which are self-evident, say, 'Redness is distinct from greenness', evident to the senses, say, 'There is a tree before me now', or incorrigible, say, 'It seems to me that there is a tree before me now'. It is perfectly possible to reject this view and maintain that justification involves foundations: that is, the view that certain kinds of rational justification end at some point in beliefs not supported by other beliefs. The obvious alternative to foundationalism is prima facie that of coherentism, where one's beliefs are held to be justified by their relation to the rest of one's beliefs.

Moreover, alternative ways of developing an epistemology adequate for Christian belief are currently in the making, and some of these have made the interesting suggestion that Christians should make use of their own theistic commitments to deal with problems of epistemology. This opens possibilities which have not been readily identified in the past. Whether the new insights should be cast in a foundationalist or non-foundationalist form is as yet far from resolved.[22] Equally, whether these new insights will yield a single theory of knowledge which fits theology is a matter which awaits attention.[23]

Second, it is clear that a century of intense ecumenical work has radically altered the climate in which scholars discuss the topic of authority. We have become increasingly aware of the complex alternatives which Christian communities have worked out in the arena of ecclesial canons. More importantly, we can explore these alternatives in a spirit of serious scholarship, cut loose from the polemical warfare which often accompanied disputes about the canonical heritage of the Christian tradition in the past. Such a relaxed atmosphere does not mean that we should approach these matters with diffidence. On the contrary, the freedom to explore radically different possibilities sometimes makes the quest for consensus all the more difficult. Moreover, the very identity of religious communities is bound up with the identity of their canonical traditions. A simple adage applies: change the ecclesial canons of a community, and you change the community. So we can still be propelled by the intensity and seriousness of the issue without yielding to the temptation to engage in fruitless polemics.

A third reason for pursuing the whole question of authority in a fresh way is the fact that the Christian faith has been extensively

[22] Perhaps we should say that they have never really been available in the past. All we may really have had in this arena are fragmentary suggestions rather than systematically developed accounts of the possible role of God in the formation of knowledge.

[23] As is the case generally in epistemology, different theories may work for different tracks of the whole theological enterprise. No single theory may do justice to the complexity and diversity of claims which Christian theologians may need to advance if they are to do justice to the truth about God and his dealings with the world. Similar considerations apply in the case of science, for as yet no agreed theory has emerged to do justice to what scientists claim about the nature of the world.

cut loose and set free from its established place in Western society. As we shall see, canonical disputes have at times been resolved by the state. The social authority internal to the Church was taken over by the political powers of the day. In most places this is a distraction we can now set aside, so the Church is free to recover its own internal authority in matters pertaining to its canonical tradition. In this process it is crucial that the intellectual work related to such action be pursued systematically.

A fourth reason why this work is appropriate at the present time is that many within the Church are extremely dissatisfied with the current canonical heritage of the Church. Among biblical scholars there has been a concerted effort in the last generation to work out a whole new approach to the canonicity of the Bible and to deploy that account for the benefit of the academy and the Church.[24] The proposals are controversial, and there are deep divisions in the debate, but there is no doubt that this development represents a major attempt to think through the meaning of canonicity from top to bottom. There are many as well who are convinced that the classical canonical traditions of the Church as embodied in its scriptures, creeds, and structures need to be modified, reworked, or replaced. One frequent objection in this regard is that the canonical heritage of the Church is oppressive and spiritually damaging. Hence, it is claimed, new, empowering ways of thinking about the canons of the Church and the norms of theology need to be found.[25] Mapping the tangled web of issues which are interconnected in the debate about authority may provide some assistance in making evaluations of such proposals.

A fifth and final reason relates to the profound practical significance of the issues for the life of the modern Church. It is often

---

[24] Particularly noteworthy are the following: Brevard S. Childs, *Introduction to the Old Testament as Scripture* (Philadelphia: Fortress Press, 1979); idem, *The New Testament as Canon: An Introduction* (Philadelphia: Fortress Press, 1985); James A. Sanders, *Torah and Canon* (Philadelphia: Fortress Press, 1972); idem, *Canon and Community: A Guide to Canonical Criticism* (Philadelphia: Fortress Press, 1984); Eugene E. Lemcio and Robert W. Wall (eds.), *The New Testament as Canon: A Reader in Canonical Criticism* (Sheffield: JSOT Press, 1992). For a spirited analysis see James Barr, *Holy Scripture, Canon, Authority, and Criticism* (Oxford: Clarendon Press, 1983).

[25] See e.g. Letty M. Russell, *Household of Freedom: Authority in Feminist Theology* (Philadelphia: Westminster Press, 1987).

thought that issues of canon and criterion are esoteric, intellectual matters which have at best only indirect relevance for, say, the practice of evangelism. This is a mistake. It is becoming increasingly clear, for example, that evangelism properly executed cannot be divorced from the whole process of Christian initiation: that is, from initiation into the kingdom of God and into the Church. In these circumstances, the shape and character of that initiation will be constituted by the formal and material conceptions of canonization deployed. Indeed, we know that in the evangelization of the Roman Empire, one function which creeds fulfilled was that of providing a crucial means of grace for those preparing for baptism. In fact, one reason why creeds were developed was precisely to provide a substantial summary of the substance of the faith which could be grasped and internalized by new believers. There is, then, a clear connection between crucial questions related to canon and the day-to-day life of the Church. Solutions to these questions, therefore, have profound ramifications for the internal life of the Christian community.[26] This constitutes one more reason for pursuing matters related to the canonical heritage of the Church with care and thoroughness.

[26] For a brief but succinct example of this see Geoffrey Wainwright, 'The New Testament as Canon', *Scottish Journal of Theology*, 28 (1975), 551–71. Wainwright takes up the significance of the canon of the New Testament for worship, preaching, evangelism, ecumenism, and ethics.

2

The Emergence of the
Canonical Heritage of the Church

In the course of the Church's history there has been a profound shift in the conception and identification of her canonical heritage. The crucial conceptual shift, as we have seen, is the transition from ecclesial canons to epistemic norms. An ecclesial canon is essentially a means of grace: that is, materials, persons, and practices intended to initiate one into the divine life. By contrast, an epistemic norm is essentially a criterion of rationality, justification, and knowledge. The semantic change from canon to criterion is correlated with a change in the material identification of canonical material. Canon is restricted to Scripture or to other material, often abstractly described as tradition, which can be reconceived in epistemic terms. Indeed, to apply the term 'canon' to anything other than Scripture comes to look inappropriate.

The case for this conceptual and material shift cannot be provided all at once. As we saw in the previous chapter, the argument takes us into complex historical, theological, and philosophical terrain, so it is cumulative in form and force. It has to be built up and developed over time. Its full force cannot be seen until we describe in detail the drastic consequences which our proposed shift evokes in the history of theology and philosophy. In the early phase of this lengthy narrative it is clearly important to lay out the history and grammar of canonization in the early Church, for it is in this period that the crucial initial decisions about canon were made in the Church. With that history in place we can then begin to chart the shift from canon to criterion relatively easily.

Yet, even to frame the issue in terms of a conceptual and material shift is to invite scepticism, for most treatments of canonization interpret the quest for canonization as a quest for an adequate criterion of justification and knowledge and treat canon exclusively as Scripture. In the stretch of the argument already developed, I have tried to show that it is thoroughly implausible to treat the canon of Scripture—that is, a list or *kanon* of sacred books—as a criterion of justification. This is a crucial claim, for it goes immediately to the heart of the conventional way of thinking about canon. Once this high tower of the canonical heritage has been liberated from its conceptual bondage, then the whole castle can be set free. After all, if the canon of Scripture is not best seen as an item in epistemology, then there is hope that other canonical materials can be extracted from their captivity to epistemological categories. Yet, the claim that the canon of Scripture is not an epistemic criterion is a startling one, not least because there are powerful pressures at work to transform the canon of Scripture into a criterion of justification. If we are to withstand these pressures, it is obvious that we need an account of canonization which will, first, bring out the complex, multi-dimensional nature of the Church's canonical heritage; second, show negatively that canonization was not directly the adoption of an epistemology; and third, suggest positively that it is better to think of the process of canonization as the adoption of a complex means of grace. So, in this chapter, after some preliminary comments on canonization, I shall rehearse the history of canonization in the early Church, argue that it is wrong to think of the contents of canon as a criterion of truth, and propose that the multiple materials, persons, and practices which effectively constitute the canonical heritage of the Church were and are intended to function together as complementary means of initiating converts into the life of faith.

As we proceed, it is important to note that one cannot say in advance exactly what form a canonical tradition will take or how it will be transmitted. Had we been present in the Christian community in Jerusalem around AD 40, the only canonical material we might have recognized would have been what is now designated as the Old Testament. Even so, we have no way of knowing the precise content of this canon, for its boundaries were still fluid.[1] Recognizing the existence of this canon would

---

[1] For a useful earlier discussion of the way the Old Testament became canonical for Christians see Albert C. Sunberg, jun., 'The Old Testament of the Early Church', *Harvard Theological Review*, 51 (1958), 205–26.

not have been of much help in predicting what would be the state of canonical affairs in the Church many years later. Making guesses from the various customs and practices of the Church would have been precarious in the extreme. The only way we can find out how canonical material and practices were developed and constituted is by examining what communities actually designated as canonical. The form or forms which canonical material, persons, and practices will take, how they will be received, what their fundamental functions will be—these are contingent matters. There is no prior rational scheme, no prior divine plan known independently of the canonical material itself, no set of agreed sociological laws, and the like, to which we can appeal to settle these matters. We have to piece the story together from the historical record as best we can. Putting the matter theologically, we have to respect the radical freedom of the Holy Spirit to guide the Church into those canonical traditions deemed useful for the community as a whole.

This is another way of saying that canonical material, persons, and practices are fundamentally material, persons, and practices that communities set apart as special, as distinctive, as embodying certain kinds of data or values, or as earmarked for certain kinds of function. We can distinguish at the outset, then, canonical traditions from ecclesial customs or non-canonical traditions. The former are in one way or another distinguished from the latter by the special and even sacred place they occupy in the life of the community. They should not be reduced to that which has generally been designated as orthodox or traditional; nor should they be confused with ecclesial customs. An 'ecclesial custom' picks out material or practices which are generally restricted in time and space, and which are not universally binding; they are not necessarily adopted by the whole Church. The term 'orthodox' identifies material or practices which are deemed right or fitting by most insiders to the tradition. The term 'traditional' sets apart material or practices which are sanctioned by long-standing usage. A 'canonical' tradition picks out material, persons, and practices which are binding on the whole community.

There are no hard and fast rules to distinguish canonical from non-canonical traditions. In some cases the matter is settled by official action, executed in specially designated meetings like ecumenical councils or by specially designated agents of the tradition. In other cases the canonical status of a tradition may be identified more by inference from the universal and pivotal role that the tradition in question plays in the community. In some instances we simply have to reckon with borderline cases which will remain contested. So decisions concerning the canonical status of a tradition are often a delicate affair; they are a matter of judgement. They are not necessarily settled by appeal to some kind of rigid, juridical process. Perhaps the best we can say is that the essential mark of a canonical tradition is that it is that kind of tradition which has been accepted as binding in the community as a whole.

In a real sense canonical material is actually constituted by the community.[2] The two ideas, canon and community, are logically and reciprocally related. A community constitutes its canonical heritage, and in doing so, that community is itself constituted along certain lines. That is one reason why the development of canonical material and its subsequent rejection is so significant for a community. Once a community has formed its canonical traditions, changing, transforming, or rejecting those traditions from within is liable to be a convulsive affair. The canonical heritage is so much a part of the identity and nature of the community that changing that heritage radically changes the community. It is small wonder that disputes about canon are often profoundly unsettling and acrimonious. These disputes cut to the very core of what the community is and how it is to live across the generations. They very naturally lead to the creation of new, breakaway communities which have very tense relations with the parent body. Reunion, in turn, requires the revisiting and resolution of the original canonical disagreements which caused division.

During the early centuries the Christian community developed a very rich network of canonical traditions. These traditions were diverse in character. Some were sacramental, some scriptural, some credal and doctrinal, some liturgical, some institutional and social, and some iconographic. Some were constituted by certain persons who were given a special status as teachers or spiritual exemplars. Some took the form of a list of books, some the form of spiritual and liturgical practices, and

---

[2] The same applies to persons and practices.

some the form of ecumenical councils. Some were identified as Fathers, saints, and teachers, some as epistemic or quasi-epistemic practices, and some as ecclesial regulations; others were identified as rites of initiation, as a body of iconography, and as an accumulation of doctrine gathered together in a single creed.[3] The origins of almost all of these traditions are partly shrouded in mystery; they arise within the community over time here or there. Sometimes they are subject to intense debate as they are disseminated and adopted; sometimes they are accepted with relative ease; eventually they are all approved and used across the face of the Church. The boundaries overall are fluid, but the main outlines of the canonical tradition are not in doubt.

We can helpfully examine the process of canon formation by providing a brief overview of the canonization of the New Testament. We begin here because the story behind this development is relatively familiar[4] and because rehearsing it will bring out how misleading and artificial it is to limit the canonical heritage of the Church to Scripture. The canonization of scripture was part of a wider process of canonization in which the various canonical elements complemented each other in the spiritual direction and pastoral care of the Church.

It is well known that the first reference we have to the list of books currently found in the New Testament is located in the famous Easter Letter of Athanasius in 367. Looking back from the present, given the high status accorded to the New Testament in virtually all forms of Christianity, this is a remarkably late date. Even so, the actual confirmation of the list of books in the canon was not finalized until later. However, it is clear that the widespread use of most of the books of the New Testament was secured much earlier.

---

[3] In briefest form we might say that the canonical heritage is constituted by materials, practices, and persons.

[4] See e.g. H. F. von Campenhausen, *The Formation of the Christian Bible* (Philadelphia: Fortress Press, 1972); W. R. Farmer and D. Farkasfalvy, *The Formation of the New Testament Canon* (New York: Paulist Press, 1983); H. Y. Gamble, *The New Testament Canon: Its Meaning and Making* (Philadelpia: Fortress Press, 1985); B. M. Metzger, *The Canon of the New Testament: Its Origin, Development, and Significance* (Oxford: Clarendon Press, 1987); L. M. McDonald, *The Formation of the Christian Biblical Canon* (Nashville: Abingdon Press, 1988); F. F. Bruce, The Canon of Scripture (Downers Grove, Ill.: InterVarsity Press, 1988); Geoffrey Mark Hahneman, *The Muratorian Fragment and the Development of the Canon* (Oxford: Clarendon Press, 1992).

The initial impetus for usage derives from at least two sources. First, there was the obvious precedent set for the community by its commitment to the Scriptures inherited from the Jewish tradition. The idea of a list or canon of books was not alien to the early Christians; on the contrary, it is likely that the idea of canon played a very significant role in the development of the Christian tradition. Second, it is clear that the first apostles held a special place in the community simply because of their relationship to Jesus. As the apostles moved off the scene, it was only natural that material connected with them would be valued as something very special. Interestingly enough, oral material was initially held in even higher esteem and trust than written material.[5] Papias is a striking witness to this.

I will not hesitate to put down for you along with my interpretations whatsoever things I have learned carefully from the elders and carefully remembered, guaranteeing their truth. For I do not, like the multitude, take pleasure in those that speak much, but in those that teach the truth; not in those that relate strange commandments, but in those that deliver the commandments given by the Lord to faith, and springing from the truth itself. If, then, anyone came, who had been a follower of the elders, I questioned him in regard to the words of the elders,—what Andrew or Peter said, or what was said by Philip, or by Thomas, or by James, or by John, or by Matthew, or by any other of the disciples of

---

[5] Consider the comment of W. D. Davies: 'there was a reserve about the written word among Jews and Greeks alike. This had long come to a clear expression in Plato, who had urged that the invention of writing was a deceptive blessing. For Plato's Socrates, so far from helping the memory, writing militates against it: it is no adequate substitute for living dialogue between teacher and taught. It is as if writing confines or ossifies thought; at best what is written only serves as a reminder of what is already known. The profoundest truth cannot be encapsulated in writing; living thought needs the give and take of speech in dialogue. How widespread such an attitude was among the Greeks is disputed. However, through an emphasis in Plato, it was not a peculiarity of his. This attitude explains why in literary circles in Rome and Alexandria, and probably elsewhere in the Hellenistic age, "publication" did not signify the appearance of a book or volume but of its public recitation. It was this same attitude, along with other probably more important factors, which led in Judaism to the prohibition of the writing of Oral Law. That, like John the Baptist, Jesus did not choose to write, even though he could, may be indicative. For Paul his letters were a necessary, but, by implication, inferior substitute for his presence (Gal. 4: 20; 2 Cor. 13: 10; 1 Cor. 11: 34). The documents of the early Church were only tardily gathered together' ('Canon and Christology', in L. D. Hurst and N. T. Wright (eds.), *The Glory of Christ in the New Testament* (Oxford: Clarendon Press, 1987), 19–20).

the Lord, and what things Ariston and the presbyter John, the disciples of the Lord, say. For I did not think that what was to be gotten from the books would profit me as much as what came from the living and abiding voice.[6]

As time progressed, the written material related to the apostles became even more significant.

While it is clear that the writings of the New Testament played some role in the thinking of the Apostolic Fathers, like Clement of Rome and Ignatius, and also in that of apologists like Polycarp and Papias, they do not initially have a status which could be accurately described as canonical. Their role is significantly altered by crucial developments in the middle of the second century, especially the impetus furnished by Marcion. Even then, we must be careful not to exaggerate the impact of Marcion, for we have Irenaeus as a witness to the delight in oral tradition illustrated from Papias. Irenaeus writes:

I remember the events of those days more clearly than those of recent date, for the things that have been learned from childhood grow up with the soul and become one with it. So I can describe even the place where the blessed Polycarp sat and held discourse, how he came in and went out, his manner of life and personal appearance, the discourse which he delivered to the people, and how he reported his intercourse with John and with the others who had seen the Lord, how he recalled their words, and what he had heard from them about the Lord, His mighty works and His teaching, how, he, Polycarp, had received those things from eyewitnesses of the word of life and reported them all in conformity with the Scriptures. Even then I listened eagerly to these things by the mercy of God which was granted to me, making notes on them not on papyrus but in my heart; and by God's grace I always ruminate on them truly.[7]

Marcion's rejection of the Jewish Scriptures and his rather exclusive attachment to material connected with Paul and Luke may well have encouraged the Church to assimilate more intentionally the material from the Old Covenant. In fact, the very term 'Old Testament' emerges in this period as the Christian way

---

[6] Quoted by Eusebius, *The Ecclesiastical History* (Grand Rapids, Mich.: Beker Book House, 1955), III. 39. 3 f.
[7] Quoted ibid. Eccl. V. 20. 6–7.

to designate and make its own the Jewish scriptural tradition.[8] Likewise, it paved the way for construing the additional material added to the Jewish Scriptures as the New Testament. Perhaps the crucial point to make in addition is that the appearance of a Marcionite canon provided something of a spur and a model in the development of a Christian canon of Scripture. The Church simply fought fire with fire.

Two decades before the end of the second century the special status of the four gospels was secure. In the same time frame, the Pauline corpus was treated as worthy of a distinct place in the life of the Church.[9] Thereafter the story of the acceptance of the other books into this privileged circle is a murky one. From Eusebius we know that around AD330 the books finding the greatest difficulty were the Gospel according to the Hebrews, James, 2 Peter, 2 and 3 John, Jude, and Revelation.[10] The Gospel according to the Hebrews was rejected in the West, as was Revelation at first in the East. The fate of the smaller Catholic epistles is even more difficult to unravel. By the time of Athanasius's Easter Letter, however, the list which was eventually accepted by the Church was complete. It was left for various synods and councils to make the final demarcation.

The process in the various official conferences of the Church left matters somewhat ragged at the edges. Moreover, there was no agreed account as to why the books which achieved canonical status were accepted. Different people and different groups had different rationales for their positions.[11] Yet there is no doubt but that it was

---

[8] The current tendency in some Christian circles to substitute 'Hebrew Bible' as the designation of the Old Testament, whatever its merits, represents in part an interesting dechristianization of the canonical Scriptures. The canonization of the Jewish material required a very particular construal as it passed into explicitly Christian appropriation.

[9] Whether the Pauline corpus was singled out earlier than the gospels is a matter of dispute. R. P. C. Hanson takes this position in *Tradition in the Early Church* (London: SCM Press, 1962), 195–7.

[10] *Hist. Eccl.* III. 25. 1–5.

[11] In some cases the reasons were bizarre. Thus, in the case of the Old Testament some were attracted to the possibility that the number of books in the canon coincided with number of letters in the Hebrew alphabet. In the case of the New Testament, some were attracted to the fact that the number of the gospels coincided with the four seasons. Those who want to make much of there being a theological norm, like the Word of God, or a historical norm, like apostolicity, governing the process of canonization conveniently ignore such embarrassing features of the situation in order to champion their revisionary

the community who decided the final list of books which made it into the canon.[12] The fact that the process was initially informal, that it took centuries to be brought to completion, and that the formal decisions were not altogether tidy does nothing to falsify this claim. The Church deliberately set aside a particular set of books as special and sacred, as the relevant decrees make clear.[13]

What is equally clear is the fact that the Church also canonized a credal statement. It was not content to have merely a list of books. While the canon of Scripture was important in meeting certain needs within the community, it was not on its own deemed adequate to meet other intellectual and spiritual needs of the community. For this reason it is artificial and misleading to hold that the only canonical material adopted by the Church was that represented by the New Testament. Despite the high status accorded the New Testament documents, the community over time took the definite decision to nominate certain doctrinal proposals as canonical alongside the New Testament. This decision has profound implications for our understanding of the canonical process of the Church; these implications become manifest in even the briefest summary of some of the salient historical developments.[14]

It is widely recognized that even in the New Testament there are proto-credal materials.[15] Clearly it is natural for Christian teachers to provide brief, pithy summaries of the heart of the Christian message; anyone acquainted with the history of evangelism will recognize the pastoral need being met by this exercise.

canonical proposals. Communities often reach agreement on the identity of canonical traditions without at all agreeing on why the proposed materials are to be accepted as canonical.

[12] As F. F. Bruce puts it: 'The "canon" of scripture is that "list" of books recognized by the Church as her sacred writings' (*Tradition Old and New* (Exeter: Paternoster Press, 1970), 129). Compare the fact that the canonization of the saints means that 'a Christian has been found worthy to have his or her name placed in the canon, or *list*, of saints remembered by the people of God' (*The Orthodox Church*, 30 June 1994, 1; emphasis added).

[13] The first undisputed decision of a council on the New Testament was at Carthage in 397.

[14] The whole matter of the making of creeds is well covered by J. N. D. Kelly in *Early Christian Creeds* (London: Longmans, Green & Co., 1950). See also John Leith, *Creeds of the Church* (Louisville, Ky.: John Knox Press, 1982).

[15] See Mark 8: 29; 1 Cor. 12: 3; 1 Tim. 3: 16; 1 Cor. 8: 6; 15: 3–7; 11 Cor. 13: 14; 1 Thes. 1: 10; 4: 14; 5: 9.

By the time of Ignatius and Polycarp we can discern the beginnings of a body of catechetical tradition in the making. As with
the canon of Scripture, a highly significant impetus for developing a brief credal statement emerges in the late second century.
This time the stimulus comes not from Marcion but from
Gnosticism.

What is especially significant in this case is that the development of a scriptural canon was utterly inadequate to meet the
challenge posed by the Gnostics. The Gnostics had no difficulty
accepting any canon of Scripture which might be proposed;
being astute in their own way and eclectic in their intellectual
sensibilities, they simply found ways to use Scripture to express
their own theological convictions. This should come as no
surprise to anyone. A list of diverse books merely by the sheer
volume involved is susceptible to a great variety of readings.[16] It is
in the conflict with the Gnostics, then, that various Church leaders, notably Tertullian and Irenaeus, developed what the former
called a 'rule of faith' and the latter a 'rule of truth'. In both cases
what is really at issue is the creation of a summary of Christian
teaching which can be handed over in Christian initiation to the
convert and can be used to identify the boundaries of authentic
Christian teaching.[17]

With appropriate modifications, similar forces play a role in the
eventual outcome of this process in the acceptance of the Nicene
Creed[18] and the famous Chalcedonian Definition. While the
internal debate relative to these momentous summaries of
Christian teaching is intense and prolific, the crucial point to be
made here is that eventually the Church designated these materials as canonical by taking appropriate action as a body. In this case
the process of canonization resulted in very formal procedures for
reaching decisions. In this instance, as in the example of the New

[16] Irenaeus has a very striking image to describe the process. He compares
the activity of the Gnostics to that of those who dismember a mosaic likeness of
the emperor and then reconstruct the various pieces to make a mosaic of a dog
or a fox. See *Against the Heresies* (New York: Paulist Press, 1992), i. 1. 15.

[17] In this context, such teaching clearly functions as a norm; but it functions
not as an epistemic norm, but as a norm of Christian identity. More accurately,
we might call it a norm of orthodoxy and heresy.

[18] Technically, the creed at issue here is the Nicene-Constantinopolitan
Creed. For the sake of convenience I shall simply speak of the Nicene Creed or
the Creed.

Testament, there is no doubt about the canonical status of designated traditions. They are constituted in as juridical a fashion as
can be expected in the circumstances. Even then, material does
not really become canonical until it is accepted by the whole
Church, and this clearly is worked out informally by consensus.

It would, however, be a serious mistake to think that all
canonical tradition has to satisfy such stringent conditions: that is,
the conditions of being agreed on in an ecumenical council and
accepted at large in the Church. We need, therefore, to take note
of other canonical materials which can easily be ignored if we
approach them in this very strict and legalistic fashion. There are
at least six other kinds of canonical tradition which deserve
mention. We recall the pertinent comment of Edward Reuss: 'It
must not be forgotten that the use of the term *canon* has never
been restricted to the Bible. There were canons of councils,
canon law, the canonical life, canons of cathedrals, etc. All these
expressions have at bottom the same origin and are derived from
a primitive meaning anterior to our canon of scripture.'[19] What
follows is a catalogue of the other components of the canonical
heritage in no particular temporal order.

First, there are practices, experiences, and rites intimately
related to baptism and the Eucharist.[20] Second, there are liturgical
traditions concerning the general conduct of worship.[21] Third,

---

[19] Edward Reuss, *History of the Canon of Holy Scriptures in the Christian Church* (Edinburgh: R. W. Hunter, 1891), 218.

[20] See Kilian McDonnell and George T. Montague, *Christian Initiation and Baptism in the Holy Spirit* (Collegeville, Minn.: The Liturgical Press, 1991), for a study of neglected aspects of initiation.

[21] Consider the following famous passage from Basil: 'Concerning the teachings of the Church, whether publicly proclaimed (*kerygma*) or reserved to members of the household of faith (*dogmata*), we have received some from written sources, while others have been given to us secretly, through apostolic tradition. Both sources have equal force in religion. No one would deny either source—no one, at any rate, who is even slightly familiar with the ordinances of the Church. If we attacked unwritten customs, claiming them to be of little importance, we would fatally mutilate the Gospel, no matter what our intentions—or rather, we would reduce the Gospel teaching to bare words. For instance (to take the first and most common example), where is the written teaching that we should sign with the sign of the Cross those who, trusting in the Name of the Lord Jesus Christ, are to be enrolled as catechumens? Which book teaches us to pray facing East? Have any saints left for us in writing the words to be used in the invocation over the Eucharistic bread and the cup of blessing? As everyone knows, we are not content in the liturgy simply to recite the words recorded by S. Paul or the Gospels, but we add other words both

there is a sophisticated iconographic tradition. Fourth, there are ecclesiastical regulations or canons concerning the internal regulation of the life of the Church and its members.[22] Fifth, over time certain leaders and teachers are designated as Fathers, saints, and teachers,[23] thus giving them a special status in the intellectual and spiritual life of the community which is clearly different from that of regular teachers and members.[24]

The sixth and final canonical tradition is sufficiently distinct to be kept separate from the preceding catalogue. It relates to the internal

before and after, words of great importance for this mystery. We have received the words from unwritten teaching. We bless baptismal water and the oil for chrismation as well as the candidate approaching the font. By what written authority do we do this, if not from secret and mystical tradition? Even beyond blessing the oil, what written command do we have to anoint with it? What about baptizing a man with three immersions, or other baptismal rites, such as the renunciation of Satan and his angels? Are not all these things found in unpublished and unwritten teachings, which our fathers guarded in silence, safe from meddling and petty curiosity?' (St Basil, *On the Holy Spirit* (Crestwood, NY: St Vladimir's Seminary Press, 1980), 98–9). Basil goes on to enumerate standing for prayer on Sunday, the season of Pentecost, standing for prayer during the season of Pentecost, and the doxology. This passage completely overturns the view that the early Church was officially or canonically committed to a doctrine of sola scriptura.

[22] For a fascinating case study of a particular canon see J. Wortley, 'The Sixtieth Canon of the Council in Troullo', *Studia Patristica*, 15 (1984), 255–60. For excellent general discussions see Nicholas N. Afanasiev, 'The Canons of the Church: Changeable or Unchangeable?', *St Vladimir's Seminary Quarterly*, 11 (1967), 54–68, and John H. Erickson, 'The Orthodox Canonical Tradition', in *The Challenge of the Past* (Crestwood, NY: St Vladimir's Seminary Press, 1991), 9–21.

[23] In ancient times the word 'Father' was applied to a teacher. Thus Paul in 1 Cor. 4: 15 writes: 'For although you have ten thousand instructors in Christ, yet you have not many fathers. For in Christ Jesus through the gospel I have begotten you.' Cf. Irenaeus *Against the Heresies*, 4. 41. 2: 'For when any person has been taught from the mouth of another he is termed the son of him who instructs him, and the latter is called his father.' Cf. also Clement of Alexandria: 'Words are the progeny of the soul. Hence we call those that instructed us fathers . . . and every one who is instructed is in respect of subjection the son of his instructor' (*Stromata*, 1. 1. 2–2.1).

[24] Quasten notes: 'The first list of ecclesiastical writers who had been approved or rejected as Fathers is contained in the *Decretum Gelasianum de recipiendis et non recipiendis libris*, which belongs to the sixth century' (Johannes Quasten, *Patrology* (Utrecht and Brussels: Spectrum, 1950), i. 10). For an interesting point of entry into this subject see Roger Gryson, 'The Authority of the Teacher in the Ancient and Medieval Church', *Journal of Ecumenical Studies*, 19: 2 (1982), 176–87. See also J. Bentivegna, 'The Times of the Christian Fathers: Theological Attempts at an Ecumenical Definition', *Studia Patristica*, 15 (1984), 268–77.

structures and ordering of the community. We refer, of course, to the whole development of the episcopate as a way of securing the internal supervision of the Church as a whole.[25] Ignatius in his letter to the Ephesians makes clear how early this development was.

> For we can have no life apart from Jesus Christ; and as He represents the mind of the Father, so our bishops, even those who are stationed in the remotest parts of the world, represent the mind of Jesus Christ. That is why it is proper for your conduct to correspond closely with the mind of the bishop. And this, indeed, they are doing; your justly respected clergy, who are a credit to God, are attuned to their bishop like the strings of a harp, and the result is a hymn of praise to Jesus Christ from minds that are in unison, and affections that are in harmony. Pray, then, come and join this choir, every one of you; let there be a whole symphony of minds in concert; take the tone all together from God, and sing aloud to the Father with one voice through Jesus Christ, so that He may hear you and know you by your good works that you are indeed members of his Son's body. A completely united front will keep you in constant communion with God.[26]

As in the case of scriptural and credal tradition, the development of forms of oversight and ministry is convoluted and complex. The striking difference in this instance is the absence of any formal decisions concerning the forms and offices of ministry which eventually became canonical. In this case there is no doubt but that a common pattern of social authority and ministry was adopted throughout the Church, and this pattern simply becomes assumed in the canonical regulations concerning various specific details of Church life which are worked out at synods and councils. The reasons behind the development are not uniform. In some cases the aim was to provide a rejoinder to what were held to be claims to have access to apostolic traditions which were outside the main stream of the Church's life. We can also surmise that some pattern of oversight was essential simply to regulate the life of the Church, as it lived on from generation to generation, and as it sought to uphold the proper deployment of those canonical traditions which gradually emerged over centuries.

Thus far we have sought to provide an appropriate overview of

[25] H. B. Swete (ed.), *Essays on the Early History of the Church and the Ministry* (London: Macmillan, 1918), is still a mine of information on this topic.

[26] *Early Christian Writings: The Apostolic Fathers*, trans. Maxwell Staniforth (New York: Penguin, 1982), 76.

canonical developments in the early centuries of the Church's life. Nothing is new or startling in the information which has been given. What is crucial to our exposition, however, is the claim that canonical material comes in exceedingly diverse forms. Even if we were to restrict the canonical traditions of the Church to its Scriptures, we could confirm this observation. It is a commonplace that a book as big as the Christian Bible has within it a wide variety of materials. When we expand our conception of what is constituted by the canonical traditions of the Church, then the evidence for this claim is overwhelming. Sacraments, doctrinal summaries, particular forms of internal structure, liturgical materials, the designation of certain individuals as Fathers, saints, and teachers, ecclesiastical regulations about fasting—all these constitute canonical material and practice, in that they are acknowledged as binding within the life of the Church across the board.

The pertinent observation to be made now is that it is misleading in the extreme to look upon these ecclesial developments with respect to canon as epistemic in nature. I argued this case with respect to Scripture in the preceding chapter; we now need to extend this observation to cover the rest of the canonical heritage of the Church. None of the constitutive elements we have identified can be accurately described as a criterion of truth. After we have made this negative case, we shall turn and develop a positive, alternative account of the nature and significance of the canonical heritage of the Church.

We need to make the negative case because it is very tempting to seize on talk of 'rule of faith' and 'rule of truth' as showing or implying that the Church was in the business of developing an epistemology. Thus we noted already that Irenaeus spoke of his summaries of the faith as the 'rule of truth'. However, it is misleading to stretch these concepts in this direction, for such language is really a veiled way of insisting that the Church is in possession of the truth when it promulgates its agreed doctrinal proposals. It is not a contribution to epistemology understood as a quest for some way of demarcating, say, knowledge from opinion. It is not a formal norm for measuring truth or falsehood.[27]

---

[27] Later on, theologians distinguish between formal and material norms in theology. Thus, for example, Scripture is treated as the formal norm, and the doctrine of justification by faith the material norm. There are here the seeds of

To treat the Creed as a norm of truth is simply a category mistake. Imagine the impropriety of offering the Creed as a possible norm of truth alongside other candidates such as memory, introspection, sense experience, *a posteriori* reasoning, and the like. It simply does not fit the conceptual bill at stake in the debate. Moreover, to propose the Creed as a norm of truth is to beg the fundamental question of truth at the outset. To be sure, the Church believed the Creed to be true, and it readily used it to make judgements about other claims to truth within and outside the community. Believing the Creed to be true, teachers of the Church naturally rejected material which was incompatible with it. But this only shows such teachers to be intelligent and consistent; it does not show that the Creed is a criterion of truth. Indeed, the Creed itself is subject to truth rather than serving as the ultimate test of truth. Hence adherents of any creed naturally argue for the truth of their Creed when confronted with rival credal proposals.[28]

In fact, when the Church is challenged concerning the truth of its proposals, it cannot simply roll out its 'rule of truth' or 'rule of faith' and leave it at that. The teachers of the Church have to argue for the truth of the Church's doctrine, and they gladly do so in all sorts of ways. For example, a Church teacher may appeal to the historical continuity of the Church's faith with that of the apostles. If that, in turn, is challenged, then appeal may well be made to Jesus Christ. And if that is challenged, the Church teacher as apologist might well offer an account of divine revelation which connects Jesus to the mind of God in such a way that to have access to Jesus is *ipso facto* to know the mind of God. If that in turn is challenged by a determined sceptic, then the reply might well be that in the logic of the situation there can be no

such a move, but it would be anachronistic to attribute such a distinction to Irenaeus. Irenaeus can call his rule a 'rule of truth' because he is convinced that he has possession of the truth. He will naturally, then, use it to rule out other positions as false; but this is only because he assumes his position to be true, rather than because he is assuming that his position is the norm of truth, standing in no need of backing and defence.

[28] One can of course take a fideist line and refuse to argue for the truth of one's creed, but this is not what one generally finds in the patristic tradition. All sorts of arguments were mustered in support of the content of the creeds. It was only later, when the canon became construed as an epistemic norm, that this line became popular.

legitimate appeal beyond the authority of God. The very fact that the Church's teachers are prepared to provide grounds all along the line for their canonical decisions shows that the whole opera-tion of canonical formation is light-years away from some sort of exercise in epistemology.

Similar considerations apply to the canon of Scripture. When pressed to say why the content of Scripture is true, those committed to its canonicity do not simply repeat that the canon is itself the norm of truth. To make that move is simply to argue in a circle. On the contrary, adherents to the canon will tend to argue that the canon is somehow connected to God; that is, that it can be traced back to the apostles, who were connected to Christ, who was in turn uniquely related to God. Alternatively, they will argue that it was inspired by God; or they will argue in both directions at once. Yet the Church nowhere canonized any theory of divine inspiration. It simply allowed a variety of opin-ions to stand side by side in the tradition.[29]

Observe, then, how far removed we are from the field of epis-temology. The case for the wider canonical heritage of the Church in this regard is as compelling as it is in the case of the canon of Scripture. This wider material is not constituted by elements in a theory of knowledge, where we can learn how to distinguish knowledge from mere belief; where we can find the path to true as opposed to spurious certitude; where we can learn appropriate forms of argument for right belief and right action; where we can discern the proper use of sense perception, memory, and the various forms of deductive, abductive, and inductive inference; where we can evaluate the validity or inva-lidity of natural theology; where we can work out how to distin-guish between justification, rationality, and knowledge; where we can discover a norm or criterion of truth, and hence distinguish between truth and error. These matters are not unimportant. Nor is it the case that those who accepted the canons of the Church

---

[29] To speak in these circumstances of there being some kind of Church doctrine of inspiration is historical nonsense. There is no more a single doctrine of inspiration than there is a single doctrine of atonement. Cf. Benjamin Breckinridge Warfield, 'The Church Doctrine of Inspiration', in *The Inspiration and Authority of the Bible* (Philadelphia: Presbyterian and Reformed Publishing Company, 1970), 105–28. See also Brooke Foss Westcott, 'On the Primitive Doctrine of Inspiration', repr. in Everett Ferguson (ed.), *The Bible in the Early Church* (New York and London: Garland Publishing Co., 1993), 2–45.

were indifferent to such concerns.[30] The claim is that the epistemology of Christian belief is not the primary field nor the
primary interest at stake for the Church in the creation of its
canonical heritage.

An ancillary reason which confirms this judgement stems from
a further feature of the situation out of which it arose. One
cannot read far in the literature of the early centuries of the
Church and remain in the dark as to one of the pivotal grounds
for the convictions which are expressed in much of the canonical
heritage. One relevant ground is surely some kind of vision of
divine revelation.

Consider, for example, the following piece of brilliant polemic
from the hand of Ignatius:

> Certain people declared in my hearing, 'Unless I can find a thing in the
> records, I refuse to believe it in the Gospel'; and when I assured them
> that it was indeed in the ancient scriptures, they retorted, 'That has got
> to be proved'. But for my part my records are Jesus Christ; for me the
> sacrosanct records are His cross and death and resurrection, and the faith
> that comes through Him. And it is by these, and by the help of your
> prayers, that I am hoping to be justified.
>
> The priests of old, I admit, were estimable men; but our own High
> Priest is greater, for He has been entrusted with the Holy of Holies, and
> to Him alone are the secret things of God committed. He is the door-
> way to the Father, and it is by Him that Abraham and Isaac and Jacob
> and the prophets go in, no less than the apostles and the whole Church.
> For all these have their part in God's unity. Nevertheless, the Gospel has
> a distinction all its own, in the advent of our Saviour Jesus Christ, and
> His Passion and Resurrection. We are fond of the prophets, and they
> indeed point forward to Him in their preaching; yet it is the gospel that
> sets the coping stone on man's immortality. It is in all these different
> elements together that goodness resides, if you have a loving faith.[31]

This surely makes clear that the ultimate norm in matters of
faith, if we want to use that language, is given in Jesus Christ, who
occupies this place because of his unique relation for Ignatius to
God. Ignatius simply will not allow any other sort of consideration
to displace this. Yet one of the astonishing features of the canonical

---

[30] For a fine treatment of aspects of this subject see Jaroslav Pelikan,
*Christianity and Classical Culture: The Metamorphosis of Natural Theology in the
Christian Encounter with Hellenism* (New Haven: Yale University Press, 1993).

[31] *Early Christian Writings: The Apostolic Fathers*, 114.

traditions of the Church is that she nowhere explicitly or formally canonizes a particular theory of divine revelation.

This point is nicely brought out in A. H. Armstrong's contrast between pagan and Christian intellectual sensibilities in the first three centuries.

We all know that on the Christian side things were very different, at least in the Great Church. The rather Epicurean view of tradition so well expounded by Irenaeus was generally accepted. Sects and heresies there had indeed been, perhaps from the beginning, but the main tradition had always been and remained one, uniform and unchanging. To discover what Christ and his Apostles (between whom difference was inconceivable) had truly meant to teach, one only needed to consult the contemporary teaching of the Churches; and this meant more and more clearly from the second century onwards the teaching of the bishops. There are many ways of looking at and accounting for this much greater emphasis on the community and its continuing tradition in the Christian Church than in the philosophical schools. One reason for it which seems to me important is that for the Pagans God's self-revelation was natural and universal and needed no special body to carry it other than of the cosmos and the whole community of its intelligent inhabitants, especially of course that of Hellenic culture. The great philosopher who was accepted as the authority in a particular school had seen with incomparable clarity what God had to say to men in the universe, but he had seen what in principle what was available to all. But the Christians, as has been said before, were thinking in terms of a special revelation given at one particular time, and such a special revelation requires a particular body to carry it, and special divine assistance and safeguarding to ensure that it continues to be reproduced authentically in each succeeding generation: this is particularly important if the core of the revelation consists in a number of what are asserted to be historical facts, which must not be allegorized away or deprived of their true significance by a too free interpretation.[32]

What is remarkable in the light of Armstrong's accurate observation is that the Church did not canonize a theory of divine revelation. It no more did this than it canonized a theory of the Atonement. Yet a theory of divine revelation, developed as part of a wider vision of how knowledge of God is to be secured, would surely be essential to any epistemology of theology which sought to capture the thinking of the early Church as a whole.

[32] A. H. Armstrong, 'Pagan and Christian Traditionalism in the First Three Centuries', *Studia Patristica*, 15 (1984), 427.

The remarkable fact is that no such theory was canonized. This stark omission stands as a massive road-block in the way of any attempt to argue that the early Church treated its canonical heritage as an epistemology of its theology.

In making this negative claim that the Church did not canonize any theory of divine revelation, I am well aware that discerning the canonical decisions of the Church is often a delicate affair.[33] Promulgation in an ecumenical council and general acceptance in the Church are sufficient but not necessary conditions of canonicity, as I am using that term. Hence it might be argued that a doctrine of revelation is indeed part of the canonical tradition of the Church. If it is, however, it will have to be a secondary or tertiary matter, worked out as a construct from Scripture and other materials. The reason for this bold claim is that we know what doctrines the Church did canonize. The fundamental doctrines canonized are explicitly laid out, for example, in the Nicene Creed and in the Chalcedonian Definition; none amounts to a substantial doctrine of divine revelation of the kind that is common in epistemological debate. It is hard to believe that this kind of omission does not tell us something extremely important about the place of epistemology in the canonical life of the Church in the earliest and most formative period of canonization.

Another way to pursue the central point at issue here is to ask how far the Church canonized a particular philosophy. After all, epistemology is a theme within the wider field of philosophy, so we can tackle our topic usefully from this wider angle. If the Church wanted to adopt a particular philosophy as binding, there

---

[33] Consider in this regard Jaroslav Pelikan's remarks: 'In a remarkable passage in his *Ambigua*, Maximus raised but left to "wise men" to answer, the question "if this dogma [of Θεώσισ] belongs to the mystery of the faith of the church, it was not included with the the other [dogmas] in the symbol expounding the utterly pure faith of Christians, composed by our holy and blessed fathers." The symbol had declared that the Son of God came down "for the sake of us men and for the purpose of our salvation," but it had not specified the content of that salvation as healing, forgiveness, and divinization. Yet this content clearly belonged to the faith and doctrine of the Church. But dogma was not very well equipped to define it: its definition belonged more properly to the worship and piety of the Church. . . . It was through the worship that the Church and its theologians acknowledged "theological mystagogy", which transcended the dogma formulated by the councils' (' "Council or Father or Scripture": The Concept of Authority in the Theology of Maximus the Confessor', in David Nieman and Margaret Schatkin (eds.), *The Heritage of the Early Church* (Rome: Pontifical Institute of Oriental Studies, 1973), 287–8).

is nothing *a priori* to rule this out as a serious possibility. To find out what happened in regard to the Church's appraisal of philosophy, we simply have to come to terms with historical reality. There has long been a tradition in modern scholarship, especially in Protestantism, which interprets the work of the great theologians of the patristic period as founded upon and driven by Greek philosophy. Not surprisingly, this has led generally to the view that, while what they produced may well have been fine for their times, it has only limited value for later generations of Christians, who must think about God in a drastically changed philosophical environment. This vision has cast a deep and negative shadow on the canonical value, for example, of the creeds, for they bear, it is said, the ineradicable imprint of the philosophy of the period. In fact, the natural consequence of this judgement is that fundamental doctrines of the Church have to be reconstructed as changes occur in the philosophical landscape, depending on the philosophical figures or tradition invoked as the relevant foundation.[34]

The thesis developed here rests on a very different historical reading of the relation between philosophy and theology in the early Church. Rather than canonize even indirectly this or that philosophical tradition, the Church permitted its members and teachers to draw eclectically from its intellectual environment. Some, like Tertullian, at times opposed any appeal to philosophical material. Others, like Origen, drew extensively from the philosophical world of his day. Still others, like Augustine and the

---

[34] What is often forgotten in this suggestion is that the very naming and identification of the doctrines to be reconstructed or reimagined are rooted in the structure of the creeds themselves. Systematic theology arose, in fact, as a kind of university-level catechesis which was utterly dependent on the content of the creeds. Sustaining the *loci* of classical Christian theology has no deep warrant outside their rootage in the canonical traditions of the Church. The idea that this structure can be derived from Scripture is impossible to sustain, given the diverse way the books of Scripture can be construed. To be sure, the individual items of the creeds can be argued on the basis of textual evidence from Scripture, and many attempts have been made to do this. However, the creeds are more than the sum of their parts; the idea that the whole structure of the Nicene Creed can be derived from Scripture by deduction from textual evidence is absurd. Textual proof-texting invariably comes in at a later, apologetic stage. Moreover, the warrants for, say, the Trinitarian vision of God embodied in the creeds can in no way be reduced to some process of proof-texting from Scripture. Clearly scriptural materials have a crucial role, but experiential considerations, logical considerations about coherence, theological arguments about divine agency in salvation, and other considerations play a role as well.

Cappadocians, were more circumspect, borrowing, but baptizing, Greek concepts in order to articulate what they were convinced needed to be said about God in the teaching of the Church and in the debate with rival proposals. Hence it is exaggerated and misleading to claim that the Church canonized some particular philosophical position.[35] It left this issue open, so long as the use of philosophical material was not fundamentally incompatible with what was asserted about God in the community. If this is a correct reading, then it is in keeping with the central point made about the nature of canon in our argument to date.

Even though it is the case that the canonical heritage does not in itself constitute an epistemology of theology for the early Church, might it still not be the case that some of the canonical traditions, or even the most central ones, are actually epistemic in character? Moreover, might it not be possible to argue that the process of canonization as a whole has profound epistemological significance, even though canons of the Church as such are not constituted as elements of an epistemological programme? The reason for pressing these questions is that the canonical materials and practices cannot be logically disconnected from knowledge of the divine. There is a real sense in which the canonical tradition mediates knowledge of God, so is it not misleading to say that there is no connection between canonical decisions and epistemological issues? The topic of knowledge of God is there, so to speak, lurking in the neighbourhood of the process of canonization.

We do not, however, have to collapse canonicity into epistemology in order to acknowledge that there is a significant link between the canons of the Church and claims to knowledge of God. The main reason for this assertion is that it is one thing to say that the canonical heritage contains genuine information about God; it is another matter entirely to say that it contains an epistemology of theology. A history text may well contain lots of accurate information about the past, but this does not entail that it contains a theory of historical knowledge. A science text may contain a true account of how the world works in various respects without at the same time containing an epistemology of

[35] Henry Chadwick's *Early Christian Thought and the Classical Tradition* (Oxford: Clarendon Press, 1966), remains a classic on this topic.

science. Likewise, the Scriptures and other canonical material can contain genuine knowledge of and about God without also containing a theory of religious knowledge. It is simply mistaken to confuse knowledge of God with a theory of knowledge of God.

Even if we move beyond knowledge of God to a theory of knowledge of God and explore the possibility of there being a canonized epistemology of theology, we need to be aware of the obvious options open to us. We can think of at least three possibilities:

1 The Church did not canonize epistemic proposals, and the process of canonization does not have epistemic significance. These matters were left as entirely indifferent to the welfare of the Church.
2 The Church canonized a particular epistemology and explicitly interpreted the canonical process as possessing some particular epistemic significance. In this case the epistemology and the epistemic significance were spelled out explicitly and clearly.
3 The Church did not canonize a particular epistemology, but it did happily include epistemic materials within the traditions which it did canonize, leaving these for a variety of reasons in an unsystematic form. In this case the epistemic material and the epistemic significance of the canonical heritage came by way of hints and suggestions, of warnings and insights, of embryonic proposal and counsel.

Let us pursue this matter for a moment. Choosing between these options requires dexterity and sensitivity. Everything initially turns on how we construe epistemology. If we think of epistemology as the quest for absolutely sure and certain foundations of knowledge, then it is very doubtful that we can argue that the Church canonized an epistemology. In canonizing the materials it did, the Church did not set aside a set of criteria of justification or knowledge. However, it is becoming increasingly clear that there are other ways to conceptualize the fundamental issues of epistemology. Thus, in recent years, it has become common in the wake of difficulties in forms of classical foundationalist epistemologies to look for fresh ways to think of the quest for justification and knowledge. Varieties of reliabalism or of virtue theories of knowledge have, for example, been explored. In a virtue theory of knowledge the focus is not on criteria of knowledge but on the proper functioning of the knowing subject.[36] Anyone drawn to this kind of theory will be on the look-out for very different material in the canonical heritage of the Church from that sought when classical foundationalist accounts of knowledge are the model of epistemological success.[37]

It is useful to keep in mind at this point the distinction between an internalist and an externalist vision of justification and knowledge. In the former, internalist case, justification or knowledge is conceived in terms of the agent having internal access to relevant reasons for their beliefs; in the latter, externalist case, we think of justification or knowledge in terms of a reliable belief-producing mechanism. The former naturally drives us to look in the history of theology for relevant criteria, like self-evidence, which will license the move from reason to conclusion. The latter takes us in a radically different direction, driving us to explore the conditions in which belief has been produced. If we bear the externalist option in mind, then it may well be that we will find all sorts of epistemic suggestions, warnings, practices, and insights in the canonical traditions which might otherwise go unheeded. That is, we need to take seriously the third possibility mentioned above and explore how far we may find externalist epistemic material of a greater or lesser degree of formality in the canonical heritage.

The evidence for such a proposal will in the nature of the case be indirect. We will have to ransack and explore the canonical traditions of the Church in order to ferret out material which has for long remained hidden simply because we were unable, due to unintentional intellectual cramp, to pick out relevant items for discussion and reflection. Were we to proceed, there are two sorts of sources we might profitably consult. There is, first, that

---

[36] 'The central idea of virtue epistemology is that justification and knowledge arise from the proper functioning of our intellectual virtues or faculties in an appropriate environment. This idea is captured in the following criterion for justified belief: "(J) S is justified that p if and only if S's believing that p is the result of S's intellectual virtues or faculties functioning in an appropriate environment" ' (John Greco, 'Virtue Epistemology', in Jonathan Dancy and Ernest Sosa (eds.), *A Companion to Epistemology* (Oxford: Blackwell, 1992), 520).

[37] The alternative epistemological vision may remain foundationalist without being committed to classical foundationalism.

material and those practices officially promulgated and accepted by the Church. Hence it would be profitable to search the Scriptures and simply explore its nooks and crannies for epistemic material.[38] Equally, it would be propitious to examine carefully the liturgical and aesthetic practices of the faith to see how far they might be construed as legitimate doxastic practices.[39] Then there is, second, the work of those identified in some way or other as the teachers or Fathers of the tradition. Certainly this material is full of very substantial comments on how knowledge of God is to be attained, on how revelation may function, on the nature of theological discourse, on the right use of philosophical conceptuality and argument in theology, and the like.[40] These considerations alone make it clear that any proposals concerning the canonization of epistemic proposals need to be approached with great caution and care.

On balance, I am prepared to say that the early Church did, indirectly, canonize certain epistemic practices and suggestions. There is a wealth of material in the early canonical heritage related to how knowledge of God is secured, material which is by no means peripheral to the content of that heritage. Certainly this material is undeveloped; it is never pulled together into a systematic whole in the way, for example, the doctrine of God is pulled together in the Nicene Creed. Yet there is just too much scattered material for the serious observer to write it off as marginal or irrelevant. Moreover, a case can be made that certain spiritual exercises or ascetic practices are actually epistemic practices of a certain sort.

This concession does nothing to alter the central claim that it is

---

[38] A model of this kind of enquiry has recently been furnished by James Barr in *Biblical Faith and Natural Theology* (Oxford: Clarendon Press, 1993).

[39] No doubt it will seem odd to ask if spiritual exercises, like prayer and fasting, are epistemic practices. But the shift from an internalist to an externalist epistemology makes possible precisely such questions. Consider the remark of George I. Mavrodes: 'In connection with a rather different sort of revelatory experience of her own, Teresa said, "If anyone thinks I am lying I beseech God, in His goodness, to give him the same experience." *It may be that this prayer is the best epistemic service that we can perform for one another*' (*Revelation in Religious Belief* (Philadelphia: Temple University Press, 1988), 153; emphasis added).

[40] While we are at it, we might also, of course, examine what the Fathers say about knowledge in general. One thinks, for example, of Augustine's ingenious comments on memory as foundational to all knowing in Book X of his *Confessions*.

misleading and inaccurate to look upon the canonical heritage of the Church as an exercise in epistemology. As we have seen, the evidence against this whole way of thinking is compelling. So, if we do not look upon the canons of the Church as epistemic norms, how are we to think of them?

We need at this stage an apt and felicitous way to characterize the process of canonical formation in the Church which will be an alternative to the conventional way of thinking. One route into this is to note how one New Testament writer describes the purpose of canonical material as represented by Scripture. Such a path will continue to undercut the standard epistemic way of thinking about canon with regard to Scripture, and it will provide a suggestive way of thinking about other components of the canonical heritage of the Church.

Consider afresh what the author of Second Timothy says about the Jewish Scriptures:

But as for you, continue in what you have learned and firmly believed, knowing from whom you learned it, and how from childhood you have known the sacred scriptures that are able to instruct you for salvation through faith in Christ Jesus. All scripture is inspired by God and is useful for teaching, for reproof, for correction, and for training in right-eousness, so that everyone who belongs to God may be proficient, equipped for every good work.[41]

We might profitably attend to two features of this description of canon. First, the canon of Jewish Scripture is understood as having come in some sense from God. It is a gift from God. Second, the fundamental purposes of the material are soteriological, pedagogical, and pastoral. In broad terms, the Scriptures are designed for use in the Church to bring people to salvation, to make people holy, to make believers proficient disciples of Jesus Christ, and the like.

It is illuminating to extend this kind of modest proposal to the whole range of canonical material developed in the Church.[42]

---

[41] 2 Tim. 3: 16, NRSV.

[42] Note that the argument here is in no way exegetical. I am simply taking Scripture as a paradigm case of canonical tradition and attempting to see how far characteristics of that paradigm might be usefully applied to other canonical traditions. Consider the following comment of Jaroslav Pelikan concerning Maximus the Confessor: 'And so the attribute "inspired by God [Θεόπνευστoς]," used in the New Testament only once and applied only to

Canonical materials, practices, and structures are the outcome of the work of the Spirit, designed for pedagogical and pastoral purposes in the Church. In one way or another they all arise through the guidance and inspiration of the Holy Spirit. It is simply mistaken to think that the Holy Spirit is confined to the production of the canon of Scripture. The work of the Spirit breathes through the whole life of the Church, guiding and directing it.[43] The various and manifold canonical traditions are gifts of the Spirit; they are to be used under the guidance of the Holy Spirit in the community in order to build up the Church in truth and holiness, in witness and service.

We can spell this out in a number of directions. First, the canonical traditions are best seen as means of grace, as gifts of the Holy Spirit in the Church. They mediate the life of God, bringing healing and salvation to the world. Hence they have to be described in spiritual and theological categories. Construing and interpreting them in purely secular categories will fail to capture the role they have in the economy of God's saving activity in human history. To use a phrase from Gregory of Nyssa, the laws and customs of the Church are the nourishment of the Church's milk. 'By these the soul is nourished, thus being given the means of ascending on high.'[44]

It is tempting to amend this modest description to claim that the canonical heritage of the Church is constituted by means not just of grace but of grace and truth, in that it is clear that one way that the canonical heritage functions is by providing vital information about the nature and purposes of God for the salvation of the world. The objections to this move, however, are obvious. First, while it is appropriate to insist that the canonical heritage

the Scriptures of the Old Testament, could now be applied also to the "inspired fathers" as they explained the meaning of prayer' ('Council or Father or Scripture', 283). I also find it intriguing that Gregory of Nyssa could speak of icons in this way: 'Icons are silent scriptures that speak from the walls' (Leonid Ouspensky, *The Theology of Icons* (Notre Dame, Ind.: Ave Maria Press, 1987), 83–4).

[43] Consider Basil's comment, 'Is it not unquestionably clear that the Church is set in order by the Holy Spirit? God has appointed in the Church first apostles, second prophets, third teachers, then workers of miracles, then healers, helpers, administrators, speakers in various kinds of tongues. This order is established according to the different gifts distributed by the Spirit' (*On the Holy Spirit*, 65–6).

[44] Gregory of Nyssa, *The Life of Moses* (New York: Paulist Press, 1978), 57.

does indeed mediate knowledge, it is odd to speak of all the canonical heritage of the Church functioning in this manner. Thus the canonical practice of oversight is a means of grace not so much by providing knowledge or information but by ensuring that the rest of the canonical heritage is sustained and properly used across the generations. Likewise, it is stretching matters to speak of the sacraments as merely mediating knowledge or information. Second, it is surely the case that one way God works in grace is to give us appropriate kinds of knowledge or information. Hence the phrase, 'means of grace' is broad enough to encompass the provision of relevant truth for the journey of faith. We propose, then, that it is enough to say that the various components of the canonical heritage of the Church are means of grace, given to us by God to initiate us into the divine life, thereby healing us of sin and restoring us to our true destiny as children of God as made visible in his Son, Jesus Christ, through the working of the Holy Spirit.

Second, the canonical heritage of the Church can be evaluated in various ways, with some traditions being more important than others, depending on the scale of values involved and the purposes identified.[45] Hence the Creed is exceptionally useful in catechetical work; the Scriptures are useful in providing agreed texts for preaching; the Eucharist is pivotal in nurturing an intimate communion with the risen Lord; iconography is important in signifying the sanctification of matter; the writings of the Fathers are invaluable in pursuing the implications of the scriptural material and in exploring second-order questions about knowledge and language; the episcopate is vital in dealing with matters of internal order and discipline. Each element in the canonical tradition has its own place to play in the total economy of the community. To ask the sacraments, for instance, to play the role of the Scriptures is to ask for trouble; to ask the Scriptures to fulfil the role of the episcopate is absurd and ludicrous.

Third, the various elements of the Church's canonical heritage will be of little or no value if those who receive them do not

---

[45] What can be said about the whole applies also in this case to what can be said about the various units and books of Scripture. The canon comes already organized in a certain way, with a division between old and new.

approach them in a spirit of repentance and humility. Given their soteriological intention, they presuppose that the ordinary human agent does not fully grasp, if grasp at all, the wounds of the soul which are in need of healing and repair. Without a disposition of radical openness to God and his great acts of deliverance, the canonical traditions can easily be misunderstood. They can readily be used to develop all sorts of proposals which are far removed from genuine salvation and liberation. Moreover, understanding what the traditions mean for human existence may take time and effort. Many insights and discoveries emerge only over time, as the user applies what illumination has already been received in the practice of moral and spiritual virtue through the grace of the Holy Spirit. Hence the reception of the canonical heritage of the Church requires repentance, faith, and obedience to God.

Fourth, so deep is the human predicament from which God delivers through these very means, that no real progress can be made without being personally immersed in the working of the Holy Spirit. The use of the canonical traditions depends crucially on the inner illumination of the Spirit to scatter confusion and darkness and to heal the eyes of the soul. Hence they are not only gifts of the Spirit to be received in humility and joy; they also involve the reception of the Giver of the gifts, the life-giving Holy Spirit who comes to baptize and immerse us into the life of God.

Fifth, the ultimate goal of this whole process, as we have just noted, is to participate in the very life of God, so that the mind and character of Christ may be formed in those who have turned to God for salvation and healing. Hence the canonical materials and practices of the Church are intimately related to the whole sweep of God's action in salvation and sanctification. Properly received and used, they are means whereby we are enabled to love God and neighbour, whereby we are renewed in the image and likeness of God, whereby we become by grace what Christ was by nature, and whereby we are made perfect in holiness. Yet even possessing the mind of Christ or made perfect in love, we are never able to fathom the essence of the divine life. There are real limits to the extent to which one can describe what it is to participate in the life of God, and there are even greater limits to the extent to which we can depict or describe the God in whose life we participate. Human language and intellectual capacity simply fail, and we are lost in a silent wonder of love and praise.

We might sum up by thinking of the varied canonical traditions as different elements in the production of a grand symphony. The music which results is the music of salvation, which naturally transposes itself into hymns of praise. Some of the canonical traditions, like the water, oil, bread, and wine of the sacraments, represent various instruments in the orchestra of the Church. Some, like Fathers and bishops, represent various players. Some, like liturgical material, represent the scores, which are best followed according to the programme notes which accompany them. Everyone involved in the orchestra must approach his or her role in a spirit of humility and dependence, of joy and praise. Most important of all, everyone must heed and be open to the leading of the great conductor, the Holy Spirit, who, through the use of the canonical traditions of the Church, creates within the participants the melody of Christ the Saviour, a music which leads ineluctably into the unfathomable, unspeakable mystery of the living God.

This summary and analogy draws attention to one further feature of the canonical tradition of the Church. From this description it is not difficult to see why the canonical heritage of the Church becomes constitutive of its being and identity. Take away the instruments, the players, and the score, and you take away the orchestra. Remove the various components of the canonical heritage of the Church and you systematically dismantle the life of the Church as a whole. To be sure, there is more to the life of the Church than its canonical heritage, just as there is more to the life of an orchestra than its instruments, its players, and its musical score. Yet the instruments, players, and score are constitutive of the life of the orchestra. Likewise, to remove or to drastically change the canonical heritage once it is up and running will be to reconstitute the Church along radically different lines.

Given that the Church is subject to the actions of human agents, change is surely possible. Moreover, change is also clearly welcome. The canonical heritage of the Church has developed over time. New insights can be derived from its existing canonical heritage, and fresh readings of its materials and practices can and will be creatively advanced and refined. Further, new canonical materials and practices can be developed to enrich the life of faith so long as they fit naturally and appropriately with the canonical tradition already in place. We can envisage this in terms of new players, instruments, and musical scores made available to a great orchestra. However, we can also envisage changes which corrupt the canonical tradition of the Church, or which so radically alter its nature and content that we are confronted either with a reconstitution of the Church or with the wholesale invention of a new religion. In these latter cases we can surely expect intense debate about the nature and boundaries of the canonical life of the Church; we can surely also expect division. Debate and division are also what we find.

3

Canonical Division between East and West

The process of canonization within the great Church of the ecumenical councils was fundamentally a charismatic phenomenon. Over time the Church developed diverse internal canons to be used to initiate its members into the life of God made manifest in Jesus Christ. These canons were seen as derived from the work of the Holy Spirit, hence were gifts of the Spirit, and they were to be accepted and used in a manner appropriate to such sacred gifts. They were to be received in a spirit of repentance, humility, and faith, looking to the ultimate Giver to bestow redemption and new life. In short, they were complex and delicate means of grace.

The canons themselves were extraordinarily diverse in nature. At one level, they involved specific rulings on how to organize the day-to-day life of the community, canons in the narrowest sense; at another level, they involved the reception of a set of sacraments and rites intimately related to a carefully constructed liturgy through which individuals were initiated and sustained in the faith. At one level, they were constituted by a list of scriptural books designated to be read in worship; at another level, they were constituted by a body of Christian doctrine which summarized very carefully the core beliefs to which the Church was committed. At one level, they involved a characteristic way of worship and devotion; at another level, they involved a distinctive manner of participating in the faith by the use of icons. At one level, they were constituted by identifying certain persons as Fathers, who were received as great exemplars and teachers of the faith; at another level, they were constituted by the development of certain offices set aside for the proper functioning of the life and ministry of the Church.

These canonical traditions cohere in a remarkable way. The

scriptural material is both formally and informally divided so as to
construe it fundamentally as giving access to God's saving activity
in Jesus Christ. Thus the Old Testament is carefully folded under
the primacy of the New Testament,[1] and within the New
Testament, the gospels, which focus so specifically on Jesus
Christ, are given a lead place before the crucial letters of Paul. In
turn, the central sacraments, baptism and Eucharist, clearly
involve a recapitulation of the death and resurrection of Jesus
Christ, first in the life of the convert and then in the regular
worship of the community. Properly used, these are meant to
connect the Christian disciple not just to the story of Jesus but to
the risen Lord present mysteriously through the working of the
Holy Spirit. The Nicene Creed dovetails remarkably with these
canonical traditions and practices by spelling out what is believed
ontologically concerning the God encountered in the preaching
of the Gospel, in the Scriptures, and in the sacramental life of the
Church. Overall, it is a portable summary of basic Christian belief
which acts as catechetical material for new believers and a test of
orthodoxy for the community as a whole. The iconography
displays in a visual manner the same content laid out elsewhere in
verbal form, while the Fathers and theologians of the Church
provide extended commentary on the same basic content, exploring the grounds and implications of the faith in a fitting manner
in their context. Finally, the task of the episcopate is to provide
oversight for the whole life and faith of the Church, ensuring
ongoing connection and continuity over space and time.

Such a neat summary cannot begin, of course, to do justice to
the complex origins of this canonical heritage, or to the volatile
and contested character of the process.[2] Nor does this summary

---

[1] The very category, Old Testament, is a Christian invention, required by
the way in which the New Testament is construed. One would dearly love to
know how this quiet conceptual revolution took place.

[2] The chief witness to the deeply contested character of the process is not
just the internal debate about what should be canonized, but the existence of
sects, heretical groups, and the like. Rejection of the letter of the Chalcedonian
Definition led to the formation of the great Oriental churches of the East which
are still in existence to this day. It is only in the last generation that the healing
of this division has become a distinct possibility. Interestingly, this healing has
happened in part because the descendants of both sides have been able to revisit
the original canonical dispute and reach agreement on the congruity of their
canonical commitments.

reflect the fact that the tradition as a whole is intended to be carried across space and time not by books and sacraments but, ultimately, by persons—that is, by Christian believers themselves and by those whom God has called, appointed, and equipped to be responsible for the spiritual welfare of the Church. Yet it does capture the amazing integrity and inner harmony of the tradition. The canonical heritage is like the skeletons, bones, and flesh of a great fish which must ultimately be seen as an organism living and breathing in the ocean. Unless understood as a whole, and unless perceived as utterly dependent on its intimate connection to the life of God, the tradition will be seen in a flat and pedestrian manner.

What is especially striking in reviewing both the canonical material and their history is the reticence in canonizing the particular reasons which can be given for the canonical heritage. Thus it is clear that a vision of divine revelation lies at the base of the whole tradition; yet it is extremely difficult to find an explicit articulation of that vision which is set apart and canonized. Moreover, it is equally clear that initiation into the Christian tradition is construed as involving nothing less than a initiation into knowledge of the triune God; yet no explicitly developed theory of knowledge *per se* is canonized. The best that we have are epistemic hints and suggestions buried in various parts of the tradition.

So long as the Church as a whole remains satisfied with its canonical traditions, and so long as its members and leaders remain in agreement about the material identity of its canons, the Church is well able to sustain its essential unity. There have been, and always will be, internal tensions and even divisions in any community. These can be caused by personality disputes, by differences over this or that issue which may crop up, by disagreements over this or that policy, by political and ethnic strife, and the like. Having a shared canonical heritage will not extinguish internal wars; the canonical arena simply provides one ring in which they can be fought. Furthermore, the canonical heritage has to be received and reaffirmed by each generation. It is not some kind of magical entity or process which protects the Church from its own folly. The canonical heritage has to be interpreted and used by human beings with all the fallible liabilities that come with them.

Moreover, the tradition has to be exercised in new situations which call for discernment and tact. That is one reason why earlier canonical material will be informally adjusted to relate to a new environment, or why the various canons will be found to speak in new and surprising ways to devout Christians in different situations and circumstances. There is no way to say in advance how these kinds of changes will develop or be received. Yet we can say that the canonical tradition as a whole is itself relatively stable. Its main contours are secure, so that if this or that major part is neglected, or if crucial parts are eroded by inappropriate usage or interpretation, alarm bells are liable to go off, and there will be a fresh attempt to appropriate the heritage as a whole or to recover neglected parts of it.

It must also be noted that the canonical process is never formally closed.[3] The canonical heritage already in place arose at a human level because of the vicissitudes of being Christian in the world and because of deep internal disputes about fundamental matters, for example, about doctrine. There is no reason to think that this should suddenly stop. New situations will constantly arise for a missionary faith which cannot remain within the boundaries of its original cultural setting. Even within a single culture and nation, ongoing decisions have to be made about the internal life of the Church; these are recorded in those canons regulating the ongoing activity of the Church.

Yet the really crucial issues have clearly already been decided. There are core canonical traditions, like sacraments, the Creed, the status of Scripture, and others, which are a given. Having been constituted by the community, they become vital in the very identity of the community. To remove or displace these will lead almost inevitably to division. Moreover, new canonical tradition can only be added and absorbed if it is perceived to be substantially in keeping with the core canonical material and the core canonical practices of the tradition. Hence, we can expect that in the history of the Church the really deep divisions are

---

[3] This applies to the biblical canon too. Thus suppose that one of Paul's lost letters were to be found, and suppose it turned out that it was of a quality on a par with that to the Galatians or the Romans. It is hard to believe that this material would not eventually be incorporated into the biblical list. To be sure, there would be plenty of debate, and it is not entirely clear how the lost letter would be officially adopted; but where there is a will, a way can be found.

likely to be focused sooner or later in disputes about canon. Or, to turn this on its head, one good way to get access to disputes about canon is to attend to those divisions which have broken the unity of the Christian community. Clearly, the first major break to be examined and explored from this perspective is that between East and West.[4] In our attempt to examine the shift from ecclesial canon to epistemic norm, we shall see that this was indeed a fateful division.

The canonical division between East and West surfaces in three crucial areas: in the addition of the *filioque* clause to the Nicene Creed, in the articulation of a doctrine of papal infallibility, and in the adoption of a divergent set of approved Fathers and theologians. All three emerge as very significant matters in the thirteenth and fourteenth centuries, although the full impact and development of various aspects of these issues were not fully nailed down until much later. They remain lively points of discussion on the current ecumenical scene.

In identifying these three issues we are not for an instant ignoring the deep cultural and political factors which played a role in the division between East and West. These factors are well documented and well rehearsed in the literature.[5] They cannot, however, erase the claim that matters of fundamental principle were at stake; a clear witness to the place of primordial principle in the division is the fact that the cultural interaction of East and West, which is commonplace in the modern world, has not resolved the long-standing differences which continue to exist.[6] As we pursue these differences, we especially want to explore the way in which they relate to differences concerning the conception and content of the Church's canonical heritage. We may lament these divisions; but we cannot ignore them.

---

[4] I follow at this stage the conventional way of recognizing the first great schism in the Church. For a spirited attack on the conventional way of designating the division in question see John S. Romanides, *Franks, Romans, Feudalism, and Doctrine* (Brookline, Mass.: Holy Cross Orthodox Press, 1982).

[5] Steven Runciman, *The Eastern Schism* (Oxford: Clarendon Press, 1955); Francis Dvórnik, *The Photian Schism: History and Legend* (Cambridge: Cambridge University Press, 1948).

[6] See the irenic analysis of John Meyendorff in 'Rome and Orthodoxy', in Peter J. McCord (ed.), *A Pope for All Christians* (New York: Paulist Press, 1976), 129–47.

On the surface, disputes about the *filioque* clause appear as merely verbal and pedantic. Modern theologians who see the Nicene Creed as a whole as a culturally relative expression of the faith of the Church are sorely tempted to dismiss the whole debate as a verbal quibble. Such a judgement is certainly understandable, for the canonical revolutions which separate us from the faith of the patristic Church have marginalized the Creed, systematically whittling away its significance. Yet, for those who were involved in the debate, the issue was much more than a verbal sophism. The addition of the *filioque* to the Creed had deep theological implications, and, taken with other developments, it had profound canonical consequences for the Church as a whole.

The origins of the move to change the Nicene Creed can be found among the Spaniards and Franks in their battles with Arianism.[7] It was natural to attempt to challenge the Arian position in a clever and tough-minded way by insisting that the Spirit proceeded from both the Father and the Son. By this simple

---

[7] Cf. the comment of Runciman: 'The addition [of the *filioque*] seems first to have appeared in Spain, in the course of the disputes between the Spanish Catholics and the Arian Visigoths. It was inserted in the so-called Athanasian Creed, promulgated by the Spaniards in the seventh century; and when they adopted the Nicene Creed soon afterwards they retained the word. From Spain it found its way to the Carolingian Court and found an eager advocate in Charles the Great, who tried to impose it on the papacy. In 808 the Patriarch of Jerusalem wrote to Leo III to complain that Frankish Benedictine monks on the Mount of Olives were adding the *Filioque* to the Creed. As Charles was paying for these monks, Leo passed the complaint on to him, commenting that while he thought the theological implications of the addition to be unobjectionable and indeed to suit the Western tradition, it was a mistake to depart from the version of the Creed that had been universally accepted by Christendom. When he himself inscribed the Creed on silver plaques round the interior of Saint Peter's he omitted the word. In the course of the ninth century it was generally adopted by the Church in Germany and Lorraine, and by many Churches in France, though Paris retained the original form for another two centuries. German ecclesiastics brought it to Rome, where Formosus, amongst others, accepted it. He in his turn introduced it to Bulgaria, and so to the notice of Photius, who at once protested against it. John VIII took the same line as Leo III. He considered it was impolitic to change the Creed, but he saw no theological objection to the word itself. The revival of German influence at Rome in the late tenth century meant the reappearance there of the *Filioque*, whose insertion came gradually to be accepted as part of the official doctrine. We know that it occurred in the Creed that was formally sung at the coronation of the Emperor Henry II in 1014' (*Eastern Schism*, 29–30).

move, one was able to put the Son on the same ontological level as the Father, and thereby undercut the secondary status accorded the Son by Arianism. Moreover, it was not unknown in the Fathers to speak of some connection between the coming of the Spirit and the activity of the Son; in some cases, the Spirit was in fact described as proceeding from the Father and the Son or from the Father through the Son.[8]

What is clear, however, is that the reasoning which lay behind the move to add the *filioque* clause to the Creed is seriously flawed. The initial attraction of adding the *filioque* clause to the creed displays a superficial grasp of the crucial theological issues at stake. The deep problem at the root of the *filioque* proposal is that it fails to distinguish between the ontological relation between the Spirit and the Son and the joint action of the Father, Son, and implicitly the Spirit in the coming of the Spirit at Pentecost. The sending of the Spirit by the Father and the Son, an action which can be described, albeit dangerously, by saying that the Spirit proceeded temporally from the Father and the Son, should in no wise be construed as a claim about the ontological or 'causal' relation between the persons of the Trinity eternally.[9] Indeed, to confuse them is a category mistake; it construes a thesis about joint action as a thesis about ontological relation.[10] Hence the

---

[8] For an excellent review of the issue, together with his own positive proposals, see Thomas G. Weinandy, *The Father's Spirit of Sonship: Reconceiving the Trinity* (Edinburgh: T. & T. Clarke, 1995).

[9] What is at stake here is the eternal relation between the Spirit and the Father and, depending on our assessment of the *filioque* clause, between the Spirit and the Son. Given the need for appropriate circumspection before this mystery, any predication has to be approached with great care.

[10] Some theologians think that making this distinction 'drives a wedge between the triune being of God in itself (the "immanent Trinity") and the trinitarian activity of God in the history of salvation (the "economic Trinity") (Alisdair Heron, 'The Filioque Clause', *Reformed World*, 39 (1987), 850–1. This is a puzzling comment, offered without support. The activity of all Persons in the Trinity, on the view presented here, is involved in the temporal mission of the Spirit. What this says about the immanent Trinity is an open question; so no wedge has been driven. What is surely obvious is that there is a clear distinction between the *temporal sending* of the Spirit and the *eternal procession* of the Spirit. We can surely insist on this distinction, even without knowing how these concepts are to be further or fully explicated. For a very important discussion of some of the issues at stake here see Philip Cary, 'On Behalf of Classical Trinitarianism: A Critique of Rahner on the Trinity', *Thomist*, 56 (1992), 365–406.

addition of the *filioque* clause is a fundamental matter which strikes at the very identity of the persons of the Trinity. In a real sense it is a radical change in the doctrine of God whom Christians profess to worship, even though many in the tradition would be hard-pressed to explain why this is so.[11]

The acceptance of the *filioque* clause in the West was a fitful affair. Initially the new clause was rejected by the leadership of the Roman Church itself. Thus the Roman Church participated in the Eighth Ecumenical Synod of 879 in Constantinople, which condemned those who either added to or subtracted from the Nicene Creed. The relevant decree did not name the persons involved, that is; it did not single out the Franks, who had added the *filioque* clause, for special condemnation. This may well have been because Pope John VIII persuaded those involved in the decision that the best course in this case would be one of personal admonition rather than official censure. Tougher action could have had serious ecclesiastical and political repercussions. It might well have led to the imposition of the *filioque* clause at Rome by force.

In due course, however, the Franks gained control of the papacy in Rome, and in the first two decades of the eleventh century introduced the use of the *filioque* there for the first time. In 1054 relations became further strained when significant leaders on both sides excommunicated each other.[12] Two centuries later, relationships between Rome and Constantinople reached an all-time low in 1204 with the appalling atrocities connected to the nefarious activity of the crusaders. Two centuries further down the road, at the Council of Florence in 1439, the Roman Church sought to impose the *filioque* on the whole Church.[13] They

---

[11] I am not at all ruling out here that there may well be advances in insight in explicating the eternal relation between the Spirit and the Son. This has long been a matter of serious discussion, and deserves to be pursued with great care. Taking the differences on the *filioque* seriously may continue to lead to gains in this area.

[12] On 7 December 1965 in a common declaration of Pope Paul VI and Patriarch Athenagoras these incidents of 1054 were put to bed when both sides agreed that the sentences of excommunication were directed at particular persons and not at the Churches, and that they were not aimed at breaking ecclesial union between the sees of Rome and Constantinople.

[13] The issue was also on the agenda of the Second Council of Lyons in 1274.

managed to get the leadership of the Eastern Churches to agree to the addition of the *filioque* clause. This, however, was a short-lived affair, for the change was never accepted in the East, and the leadership of the Church readily rescinded their earlier agreement.

It is extremely important not to dismiss this disagreement as a cosmetic affair. In itself, that is, aside from any doctrinal implications which we might want to draw from it, this change in the doctrine of the Trinity is a substantial matter. When we recall the central place that doctrines about God played in the canonical traditions worked out in the early centuries, any change in the details of the Creed has to be seen as a momentous affair. That is precisely why the matter was taken up at the Synod of Constantinople in 897, why the Frankish wing of the Western Churches had such difficulty imposing the addition to the Creed on its Roman neighbours and potential subjects, and why it was a major item of agenda for action at the Council of Florence in 1439. The objections lodged by theologians in the East were very substantial indeed, as the earlier work of Photius on the subject makes abundantly clear. In short, what is at stake in the addition of the *filioque* clause is a major change in a vital canonical organ of the Church. To change the Creed in the way envisaged was to break the canonical tradition of the Church. Or at least, that is how it is seen from the perspective of the interpretation of canonicity laid out heretofore.

Once we have set this in place, we can see that, if this account of the change is to be challenged, then there will have to be, sooner or later, a corresponding challenge to the status of the canonical process which undergirded it. The canonical process which undergirded it was that canonical decisions are in some sense made by the whole Church. Thus the Nicene Creed was canonical because it had been adopted, in this case formally, by the Church as a whole, acting through the agency of an ecumenical council as ratified by the general acceptance in the Church at large. Hence a significant change in the Creed, on this view, would require ecumenical endorsement. In such a case it would not technically matter where the change originated; what would matter was that it be accepted by the Church as a whole. When, the Roman Church in the West adopted the *filioque* clause and changed the Creed, then, it was faced with a choice.

The dilemma was as follows. It could either convince the rest of the Church that the Creed indeed needed to be revised, and hence have the whole Church endorse and accept the Roman adoption of the change as a genuine canonical change according to the conventions which properly delimited canonicity; or it could argue that the Roman tradition had the canonical right to make this change and then require that all other Churches fall into line with the new rule of faith, thereby laying claim to an alternative convention for delimiting canonicity. These are the only genuine, practical alternatives which lay before the Roman tradition.

In the end, it was the latter route that was patiently and persistently pursued by the Roman tradition. The final, official decision was not, of course, taken until the late nineteenth century; but the internal dynamic for that move was already in place during the time of the debate about the *filioque* clause.[14] In fact, the Roman tradition has long argued that its account of the conventions defining and delimiting the canonical heritage of the Church as a whole was in place from the beginning.[15] On this view, all that really happened on 18 July 1870 was that the First Vatican Council defined what had normatively been the case from the time of Christ. Hence the decision of the Council of Lyons in insisting that the Eastern Churches adopt the *filioque* clause was entirely proper. Union in the Church required unity in the Creed. Given that canonicity was really governed, not just by ecumenical consent but essentially by Roman consent or decree, then it was fitting that the Eastern Churches make the required changes in the Creed.

For our purposes, it is not crucial that we decide at this point if this claim is or is not correct. As we might expect, the case for and against the Roman claims has been argued with great skill for centuries. The formal essentials of the Roman claims are very clear. In *Pastor aeternus* the First Vatican Council defined under

---

[14] Officially, the superiority of the Pope even over councils has been maintained since the decree *Exsecrabilis* of 1460. We shall return to this topic when we look at the work of John Henry Newman in ch. 13.

[15] A classic for the conservative position on this is H. E. Manning, *The Oecumenical Council and the Infallibility of the Roman Pontiff* (London: Longmans, Green, 1863). For an alternative reading from the same period see J. J. I. von Döllinger, *The Pope and the Council* (Boston: Robert Brothers, 1870).

anathema that the papacy is of divine institution, that the Pope enjoys a primacy of jurisdiction over all Churches, pastors, and believers, and that, when he speaks *ex cathedra,* as successor of Peter, he is gifted with infallibility. According to this proposal, the Church had from the beginning a particular form of papal oversight. Those committed to this view assume that this was so obvious that it did not need to be stated officially until such times as it became necessary for the life of the Church to do so. The essentials of the Roman claims, it is said, were implicitly present and tacitly operating in the decisions of the Church from the beginning. Clear intimations of the doctrine can be seen, it is argued, in the biblical and patristic materials.[16] Moreover, precursors of this doctrine come to expression quite explicitly at certain moments: for example, in the avowals of Stephen in the third century.[17] Thereafter, the development can be traced through figures like Leo the Great (440–61),[18] Gregory VII (1073–85),[19] and the jurist Popes of the twelfth century.[20]

The alternative reading of the historical narrative, developed by Eastern Christians, is that the Roman claim in its later forms is unfounded. While the Church of Rome was legitimately held in high honour and respect, any claim to special jurisdiction or unique divine inspiration was, and is, false.[21] It is the Church as a whole which is guided by the Spirit.[22] Further, the fullness of the

---

[16] The standard biblical texts used in the debate are Matt. 18: 16–19; John 1: 42, 21: 15–17; and Luke 22: 32.

[17] See e.g. James F. McCue, 'Roman Primacy in the First Three Centuries', in Hans Küng (ed.), *Papal Ministry in the Church* (New York: Herder and Herder, 1971), 42.

[18] Wilhelm de Vries, 'Theoretical and Practical Renewals of the Primacy of Rome, 1. The Development after Constantine', in Kung (ed.), *Papal Ministry*, 49. Cf. J. Michael Miller, *What are they Saying about Papal Primacy?* (New York: Paulist Press, 1982), 5–7.

[19] Horst Fuhrman, 'Theoretical and Practical Renewals of the Primacy of Rome, 2. From the Early Middle Ages until the Gregorian Reform,' in Kung (ed.), *Papal Ministry*, 57–9.   [20] Ibid. 59–61.

[21] A very helpful modern, historical account of the possible origins of papal infallibility which would fit with this reading can be found in Brian Tierney, 'Origins of Papal Infallibility', *Journal of Ecumenical Studies*, 9 (1900), 841–64. See also his *Origins of Papal Infallibility, 1150–1350* (Leiden: E. J. Brill, 1988).

[22] On 6 May 1848 the Eastern Patriarchs, in a reply to an encyclical letter of Pius IX, asserted that 'infallibility resides solely in the ecumenicity of the Church bound together by mutual love, and the unchangeableness of dogma as

Church's life is secured not by a necessary connection with the bishop of Rome but by the eucharistic fellowship of the general episcopate handed down from generation to generation. Moreover, the episcopate is but one movement in a complex symphony of canonical materials and practices put in place by the Church to orchestrate the salvation of the world wrought in Jesus Christ through the working of the Holy Spirit.

It is tempting to be drawn into the complex historical issues related to these competing accounts of the canonical heritage and so miss the really deep issue that separates them. What is at stake is not just a different material account of the canonical heritage of the Church, but radically different conceptions of the canonical heritage. The core issue hangs on how we think of episcopacy as a canonical practice of the Church. On the new reading developed by Rome and the Western half of the Church, episcopacy has been dramatically focused in the bishop of Rome, and the bishop of Rome has been transposed into an infallible belief-producing mechanism represented by the doctrine of papal infallibility. One element in the complex tapestry of canonical tradition has been transformed into an epistemic procedure for securing absolute truth. This constitutes an epistemological shift of the highest magnitude. Special divine assistance in gaining truth about God has been posited for one component of the heritage. It is not in the least surprising that it took centuries for the full implications of this to be worked out and recognized.

A third factor related intimately to canonical division is the divergence in the lists of Fathers accepted as canonical by each side in the Great Schism. In the West, Boniface VIII declared in 1298 that he wished Ambrose, Jerome, Augustine, and Gregory the Great to be known as *egreggi doctores ecclesiae*. These were also designated as great Fathers of the Church. He held that for the 'Greeks' three great Fathers were known: namely, Basil the Great, Gregory of Nazianzus, and St John Chrysostom. Adding Athanasius to this list, he designated these also as Fathers of the Church.[23] Again, over

---

well as the purity of rite are entrusted to the care not of one hierarchy but of all the people of the Church, who are the Body of Christ'.

[23] See Johannes Quasten, *Patrology* (Utrecht and Brussels: Spectrum, 1950), i. 10. For a different and perhaps more comprehensive list in the Roman Catholic tradition see A. M. Henry (ed.), *Introduction to Theology* (Chicago: Fides

time, others were added, most notably Thomas Aquinas. In the East a very different list eventually emerged, with John the Theologian, Gregory of Nazianzus, and Symeon the New Theologian at the pinnacle. In addition, a special place is given to the writings of Gregory Palamas.[24]

What the writings of Symeon and Palamas make clear is that these Eastern Fathers represent a radically different ethos in theology from that which became typical in the West. As the fascinating debate between Palamas and Barlaam the Calabrian shows, the East canonized a way of reaching knowledge of God which is suspicious of deductive reasoning, is essentially rooted in a spiritual life crowned by intimate union with the divine, and is genuinely open to those who have not been initiated into the skills of the philosophers. Whereas in the West, theology moved into the university, where it becomes a specialized science open only to those who are appropriately grounded in philosophy, in the East, theology remained in the monasteries, where it is grounded on a disciplined spiritual life within the Church and is construed as much as a healing art as an academic discipline. Buried in these alternatives are competing accounts of the mystery of God, the relation between reason and revelation, the role of the Holy Spirit in knowledge of God, and the place of philosophical data at the foundation of theology. Varied narratives charting these differences can be constructed and defended,[25] as is the case with all contested accounts of the intricacies of such rich theological traditions: yet there is no denying that the choice of two distinct sets of Fathers in the canons of East and West represents very different sets of proposals in the epistemology of Christian belief. By now the two halves of Christendom have become more and more explicit about the possible theories of religious knowledge which are correlated with their divergent theological traditions. It would be exaggerated to claim that, say, with the arrival of Aquinas and Palamas, we have a fully explicit

Publishers Association, 1954), 342–4. That list begins with Hermas and ends with Theodore Aboukara.

[24] The central doctrines of Palamas were canonized as an authentic expression of Orthodox faith by the Synod of Constantinople in 1351.

[25] One such narrative has been developed by Philip Sherrard in a very penetrating manner in *The Greek East and the Latin West* (London: Oxford University Press, 1959).

epistemology canonically adopted by each side in the schism. However, claims about knowledge of the divine are now developed to a level which goes significantly beyond what was the case prior to the initial divisions. In short, very different visions of authority are in the making, and rival epistemic traditions are now becoming the order of the day canonically.

One way to register this shift is to note the account of the relationship between theology and philosophy proposed by Palamas.[26] Palamas is very wary of those who would attempt to arrive at knowledge of God through sensible things. That wariness is grounded in the fact that those who took this route ended up as polytheists, due in part to what was seen as demonic influence.[27] The intellect of the pagan philosophers is a divine gift 'insofar as it naturally possesses a wisdom endowed with reason. But it has been perverted by the wiles of the devil, who has transformed it into foolish wisdom, wicked and senseless, since it puts forward such doctrines'.[28]

This does not mean, however, that philosophy is to be rejected *in toto*. Palamas uses two very striking images to describe the proper relation between philosophy and theology.

Is there then anything of use to us in this philosophy? Certainly. For just as there is much therapeutic value even in substances obtained from the flesh of serpents, and the doctors consider there is no better and more useful medicine than that derived from this source, so there is something of benefit to be had even from the profane philosophers—but somewhat in a mixture of honey and hemlock. So it is most needful that those who wish to separate out the honey from the mixture should beware that they do not take the deadly residue by mistake. And if you are to examine the problem, you would see that all or most of the harmful heresies derive their origin from this source.[29]

Do you see the swiftest way, full of profit and without danger, that leads to these supernatural and heavenly treasures?

In the case of secular wisdom, you must first kill the serpent, in other words, overcome the pride that arises from this philosophy. How difficult this is! 'The arrogance of philosophy has nothing in common with humility', as the saying goes. Having overcome it, then you must separate and

---

[26] John Meyendorff, *A Study of Gregory Palamas* (Crestwood, NY: St Vladimir's Seminary Press, 1964), remains a classic study of Palamas.

[27] Gregory Palamas, *The Triads* (New York: Paulist Press, 1983), 26.

[28] Ibid. 27.   [29] Ibid. 28.

cast away the head and the tail, for these things are evil in the highest degree. By the head I mean manifestly wrong opinions concerning things intelligible and divine and primordial; and by the tail, the fabulous stories concerning created things. As to what lies in between the head and the tail, that is, discourses on nature, you must separate out useless ideas by means of the faculties of examination and inspection possessed by the soul, just as pharmacists purify the flesh of serpents with fire and water. Even if you do all this, and make good use of what has properly been set aside, how much trouble and circumspection will be required for the task!

Nonetheless, if you put to good use that part of the profane wisdom which has been well excised, no harm can result, for it will naturally become an instrument for good. But even so, it cannot in the strict sense be called a gift of God and a spiritual thing, for it pertains to the order of nature and is not sent from on high. This is why Paul, who is so wise in divine matters, calls it 'carnal'; for, says he, 'Consider that among us that have been chosen, there are not many wise according to the flesh'. For who could better make use of this wisdom than those whom Paul calls 'wise from outside'? But having this wisdom in mind, he calls them 'wise according to the flesh', and rightly too.[30]

Clearly, what is at stake for Palamas here is an epistemology of religious belief which has as one of its central features the purification of 'the cognitive faculty of the soul'.[31] Hence he goes on to identify and explain the significance of the spiritual practices of the Hesychast monks, which convey them to a profound union with God through the illuminating activity of the Holy Spirit. This union leads to a knowledge of God which is of a different order from that which begins with a knowledge of creatures, and from this empirical data moves, by means of analogy, to an inference to the existence of God.[32] In fact, knowledge of God, ultimately, is not reached by sense perception, by reason, or even by the spiritual intellect. True knowledge of God transcends the faculties. Moreover, 'this knowledge, which is beyond conception, is common to all who believe in Christ'.[33] Even then, such knowledge does not pertain to the essence of the divine nature.[34] It reaches only to the action or energies of God. As such, it is made possible through participation in the life of the Spirit who deifies the human subject and thus enables him or her to transcend

---

[30] Ibid. 29. [31] Ibid. 30. [32] Ibid. 61.
[33] Ibid. 67. [34] Ibid.

nature, virtue, and knowledge. Hence, knowledge of God is knowledge of God by grace; it transcends all the normal categories deployed by philosophers to demarcate modes of knowledge derived from or applied to the created order of things.

It is clear here that Palamas is drawing on a tradition of thinking about knowledge of the divine which has its roots in the work of figures like Gregory of Nyssa,[35] Gregory of Nazianzus, Maximus the Confessor, and Dionysius the Areopagite. Equally, although there is no explicit reference to Symeon the New Theologian, there are very substantial affinities to Symeon's thinking on knowledge of God.[36] Hence one can see here the articulation of a very specific epistemic tradition.

Yet it is not easy to know how to categorize this tradition. A fundamental claim of this tradition is that knowledge of God involves a profound transfiguration of human agents which places them on a level above and beyond all ordinary conceptions of knowledge. Hence to speak of the knowledge gained in this state in the same breath as other knowledge—something required of us

[35] See especially his skilful use of analogy in outlining the relation between education in philosophy and the pedagogy of the Church in his *Life of Moses* (New York: Paulist Press, 1978), 56–7: 'Since the daughter of the king, being childless and barren (I think she is rightly perceived as profane philosophy), arranged to be called his mother by adopting the youngster, Scripture concedes that his relationship with her who was falsely called his mother should not be rejected until he had recognized his own immaturity. But he who has already attained maturity, as we have learned from Moses, will be ashamed to be called the son of one who is barren by nature. For truly barren is profane education, which is always in labor but never gives birth. For what fruit worthy of such pangs does philosophy show for being so long in labor? Do not all who are full of wind and never come to term miscarry before they come to the light of the knowledge of God, although they could as well become men if they were not altogether hidden in the womb of barren wisdom? Now after living with the princes of the Egyptians for such a long time that he seemed to share in their honors, he must return to his natural mother. Indeed he was not separated from her while he was being brought up by the princes but was nursed by his mother's milk, as the history states. This teaches, it seems to me, that if we should be involved with profane teachings during our education, we should not be separated from the nourishment of the Church's milk, which would be her laws and customs. By these the soul is nourished and matured, thus being given the means of ascending the height.'

[36] See e.g. Symeon the New Theologian, *The Discourses* (New York: Paulist Press, 1980), chs. 16, 17, 24. See also *The Practical and Theological Chapters and the Three Theological Discourses* (Kalamazoo, Mich.: Cistercian Publications, 1982).

if we are to speak of an epistemology—is to misunderstand the very claim at issue. Further, the knowledge gained, although it is genuine, and although it eliminates doubt of the divine reality, cannot conceptualize or describe the object encountered, for the object is essentially incomprehensible. Hence, not only the means of gaining knowledge, but the very content of the knowledge, takes us right outside the fundamental categories normally deployed in epistemology. Yet, paradoxically, we are dealing here with genuine knowledge, so we are still firmly planted within that sphere normally fenced off for the field of epistemology. So knowledge of God is genuine knowledge, but it cannot be described in modes which are available to, or can be applied to, non-divine reality. In other words, we are confronted here either with sheer unintelligibility, or with a genuine paradox, or with the kind of epistemic puzzle which calls for an intellectual revolution of the whole field which will break and redraw the boundaries of conventional thought in the area.[37]

Whatever we make of this, it is fair to conclude that this approach to knowledge of God is radically different from what we find in figures like, say, Abelard, Aquinas, and Occam.[38] In these primacy is granted to inference to God from the creature and the created order, or from events like prophecy and miracle, or from propositional revelation, or from testimony, and the like. Warranted assertability determined by evidence and inference is at the heart of the epistemic enterprise for them. In the case of Aquinas we encounter a comprehensive theory of knowledge which construes Christian theology as nothing less than divine *scientia*.[39] Moreover, there is a certain reticence about the working

[37] There may be ways to speak about such knowledge available to us now in the field of epistemology which were not available to earlier generations. The very conception of what a mode of knowledge is has had to be reconceived over the last generation in the field of epistemology. A crucial issue in need of further exploration is whether *any* epistemological proposal arrived at through investigation of our knowledge of the created order will really fit the bill.

[38] The sharp theological divergence between these great thinkers is constituted by the relative acceptance of common modes of evidence, rationality, justification, and knowledge derived from reflection on the created order and on divine revelation.

[39] The whole of the next chapter will be devoted to Aquinas. Here I want to provide an initial general description of the difference between East and West.

of the Holy Spirit in coming to knowledge of God.[40] Perhaps
what is especially revealing is Aquinas's claim that one can actually come to know the essence of God in the beatific vision, a
claim clearly rejected by the major figures of the Eastern tradition. This could well be the sign of a very deep cleavage with all
sorts of ramifications.

Yet we must proceed here with great care. It is indeed the
case that Thomas Aquinas at a later stage was assigned an exceptionally high status in the Western Catholic tradition.[41] He was
canonized in 1326, made a doctor of the Church in 1567,
commended for study in *Aeterni Patris* in 1879, and declared
patron of Catholic schools in 1880. This was not just a matter of
romantic idealism directed at the memory of a brilliant thinker
and scholar, for, as Roger Ariew reminds us, 'for the duration
of the Council of Trent (1545–63), his *Summa Theologiae* was
placed next to the bible, on the same table, to help the council
in its deliberations, and so that it might derive appropriate

[40] It would be far too easy to say that this reflects the subordination of the
Spirit to the Son in the *filioque* clause. The role of the Spirit in coming to
knowledge of God in the Western traditions need to be explored with care in its
own right. The issue is not one of either/or but of the weight of emphasis.

[41] For a contemporary expression of this see Aidan Nichols, *The Shape of
Catholic Theology* (Collegeville, Minn.: Liturgical Press, 1991), 51–4. The significance of Aquinas for modern Roman Catholic thought is nicely brought out by
Ralph McInerny in the following thesis propounded on his reception of the
1993 Aquinas Medal: 'Catholic philosophy flourishes only when it is conducted
in response to the church's reiterated directive that we take Thomas Aquinas for
our principal guide. Catholic philosophy falters, and our organizations grow
anemic, to the degree to which Thomism becomes weak. We, our organizations
and institutions, will flourish when there is a renewed sense of the providential
role that Thomas Aquinas is meant to play in the intellectual and cultural life,
not only of the Church, but of mankind generally' ('Second-Hand Straw',
Crisis, 11 (1993), 16). For a more guarded but still thoroughly positive appreciation of Aquinas see A. Liege, 'The Believer and Theological Reflection', in A.
M. Henry (ed.), *Introduction to Theology* (Chicago: Fides Publishers Association,
1954), 277–80. He writes: 'It seems to us that the theological synthesis of Saint
Thomas, to the extent that its rational contribution is situated upon a truly
metaphysical and universal plane, remains open to perpetual enrichment, first,
by a return to the sources of living faith, and then through an acceptance of
contributions from different theological systems or attempts. *But a theological
system would certainly cease to be true to the degree in which it was elaborated in using
intuitions and elementary principles radically different from that used by Saint Thomas*'
(p. 280; emphasis added).

answers'.[42] However, various options in philosophy were tolerated within the West.[43] Moreover, there are also figures in the West, like John of the Cross, who develop accounts of knowledge of God which have clear affinities with the themes which crop up in Symeon, Palamas, and the like.[44] On the other side, the Eastern tradition has been well able to tolerate large doses of Aristotle, as the work of John of Damascus makes evident.[45] Hence efforts to draw very neat boundaries and demarcate rigid differences are doomed to failure. Yet, despite these reservations, the main point stands: East and West were systematically canonizing different epistemological strategies.

Thus far we have plotted how shifting positions on the *filioque* clause of the Nicene Creed, papal infallibility, and the canonization of lists of Fathers both bring about and constitute a major canonical break in the fabric of the Church's early canonical heritage. The first represents a change in the rule of faith, the second a break in the canonical arrangements related to episcopacy, and the second and third taken together provide clear indications of a divergence in the epistemology of religious belief. We could also, of course, pursue differences which crop up in the area of liturgy and iconography. Hence it is clear that in the West

[42] Roger Ariew, 'Descartes and Scholasticism', in John Cottingham (ed.), *The Cambridge Companion to Descartes* (Cambridge: Cambridge University Press, 1992), 62–3. The encyclical letter of Leo XIII which commended 'the restoration of Christian philosophy according to the mind of St. Thomas Aquinas', expresses this effusively: 'But we come now to the greatest glory of Thomas—a glory which is altogether his own, and shared with no other Catholic Doctor. In the midst of the Council of Trent, the assembled Fathers so willing it, the *Summa* of Thomas Aquinas lay open on the altar, with the Holy Scriptures and the decrees of the Supreme Pontiffs, that from it might be sought counsel and reasons and answers.' See St Thomas Aquinas, *Summa Theologica* (Westminster, Md.: Christian Classics, 1920), i. p. xvi.

[43] Augustine's relation to Neoplatonism is parallel to Aquinas's relation to Aristotle. We need also to bear in mind that there were significant elements of Neo platonism in the thinking of Aquinas.

[44] The commitment of John of the Cross to a Thomistic framework is, of course, generally well recognized.

[45] See 'Philosophical Chapters of John of Damascus', *Writings* (Washington, DC: Catholic University of America Press, 1958). The translator, Frederick H. Chase, describes this work in the introduction as 'the last work of any theological importance to appear in the East' (p. v). Thankfully, the significance of later Eastern thinkers is now taken more seriously than this in the West.

both the number and the specific understanding of the sacraments is formalized and canonized in a way that never happened in the East. Moreover, one suspects that the debates over the proper nature and use of icons would provide further grist for the canonical mill.

Charting the changes in liturgy and iconography would not, however, alter the primary thesis presented so far in this chapter. The differences between East and West, I have argued, can legitimately be described as canonical differences. More precisely, division between East and West is constituted by irreconcilable readings of the canonical arrangements of the patristic period. It is not that the process of canonization comes to a halt in the period of the Church of the ecumenical councils. On the contrary, the reception of the earlier canonical heritage and its creative continuation breaks in two, with both sides claiming ownership of the earlier tradition and both sides mounting arguments as to the legitimacy of their ownership and the illegitimacy of the alternative. In this process the very history of the canonical tradition is reconceived to keep in step with the reading of the heritage on offer.

This is extremely fertile ground for epistemic deliberation and innovation, something we have seen in our brief review of the different epistemic proposals emerging in the competing canons of Fathers. In other words, canonical crises precipitate epistemic speculation and theorizing. After all, if there is a dispute about the canons of the Church, this is not exactly like a dispute about the weather. Canonical disputes revolve around a rich network of materials and practices which are constitutive of Christian identity; even more importantly, they concern those means of grace which mediate that knowledge of God which bring salvation. Hence differences regarding canon call forth second-order disputes about the status of this or that canon and how to interpret it. In turn, given that these canons are treated as giving access to the divine order, these second-order disputes push the participants to develop accounts of how God is known and as to how knowledge of God is related to the canonical heritage of the Church, as conceived by the competing parties. The slide into epistemology is virtually inevitable. The only way to call a halt to this is to set severe limits on the very idea of epistemology in the case of divine reality, something which is clearly happening in the work of Palamas.

This perhaps explains why the debate between East and West has for so long remained for the most part at the canonical level. One side tends to accuse the other of schism and call for its repentance.[46] This happens because it is really the only common playing-field available to the combatants. To pitch the debate at the level of epistemology would be either to lose the game at the outset, because one would have allowed the other side to set up an alien set of rules to judge the outcome of the game, or to beg the question *ab initio* against the other side by requiring that the matter be decided by the epistemic or quasi-epistemic rules enshrined in one's own canonical traditions. So the simpler strategy in debate is to stick to the canonical dispute from the outset and focus on those canonical issues like the *filioque* and papal infallibility which can be handled without getting bogged down in abstruse debates about epistemology.

A splendid example of this can be found in the brilliant polemical work of Aleksey Khomiakov in the Russian tradition in the nineteenth century. The crux of the issue between East and West, as he saw it, was that Rome had broken the canonical traditions of the Church. Roman Christians, when they added the *filioque* clause, were really the first Protestants.

Having appropriated the right of independently deciding a dogmatic question within the area of the Ecumenical Church, private opinion carried within itself the seed of the growth and legitimation of Protestantism, that is, of free investigation torn from the living tradition of unity based on mutual love. Thus at its origin, Romanism manifested itself as Protestantism.[47]

According to Khomiakov, what had originally belonged to the whole Church—namely, the right to decide dogmatic questions—was now claimed by one part of the Church. To support this, a monopoly of inspiration was predicated of the Roman tradition. The Romans, he insisted, are those 'who have anointed themselves with the chrism of infallibility'.[48] In turn, this claim to a special chrism fitted nicely with the infallibility of the Pope,

---

[46] In more recent times this has publicly been replaced by displays of affection and prayers for reconciliation.

[47] Aleksey Stepanovich Khomiakov, 'On the Western Confessions of Faith', in Alexander Schmemann (ed.), *Ultimate Questions* (New York: Holt, Reinhart, and Winston, 1965), 47–8.   [48] Ibid. 63.

who became a kind of oracle whose effectiveness did not depend
on ethical considerations. Hence an external law took over and
disrupted the delicate intellectual life of the Church as a whole.
The bond between knowledge and inner perfection of soul was
broken. Rome 'gave free reign to reason while at the same time
trampling it under foot'.[49] Rationalism, understood as seeking
guarantees of the spirit of love beyond hope and faith, was now
the hallmark of the Church.[50] The way forward in disputes with
Rome, then, was not to have a seminar on epistemology, important as that might have been to Khomiakov, for his essay is laced
with the epistemic suggestions we have already encountered in
Palamas. Nor was the way forward to hold a great ecclesial council to resolve the differences, for the principles on which a
council operates have already been breached by Roman practice
and theory. What was needed was for Rome to condemn its own
infringement of the council principle and all the consequences
stemming from this infringement. In other words, Rome must
return to the original Creed and submit its opinion, by which the
Creed was impaired, to the judgement of the ecumenical faith.[51]

The problem with this solution, of course, is that Rome does
not believe that it has departed from the ecumenical faith. On the
surface, the claim to have departed from the ecumenical faith
looks like a simple historical matter which can be resolved by
appeal to historical evidence. That is why so much of
Khomiakov's argument was historical in character. He thought
that he could show that Rome had departed from the ecumenical
faith of the Church. Much better historians than Khomiakov
have already attempted this; the results have not been encourag-
ing. Compelling presentations of the evidence which might plausibly be thought to falsify the claim that Rome has always had a
special gift of infallibility within her possession fail to persuade
sophisticated and mature adherents of the Roman position. In
short, Rome has a strategy of its own to counter Khomiakov's
reading of the relevant history.

[49] Khomiakov, *Ultimate Questions*, 51.
[50] 'Where, then, will we find a guarantee against error in the future? There
is only one answer to this question: Whoever seeks beyond hope and faith for
any guarantee of the spirit of love is already a rationalist. For him the Church,
too, is unthinkable, since he is already, in his whole spirit, plunged in doubt'
(ibid. 54).   [51] Ibid. 63.

A pertinent recent example can be seen in the response to the work of Brian Tierney.[52] Tierney has argued with great erudition that the doctrine of papal infallibility was really invented in the thirteenth century in the debates about the place of poverty in the Franciscan tradition. Cardinal Alfons Stickler undercuts the whole foundation of Tierney's argument by simply insisting that the issue at hand is clearly a theological matter which must be settled by 'the rules proper to the science of theology'.[53] Tierney reads this as meaning that 'he should have accepted the truth of the current teaching of the Church and limited himself to explaining how the final form of the doctrine evolved from its initial expression in the early sources of revelation'.[54] This is indeed a correct reading of Stickler's position. Stickler is splendidly clear on this issue.

Theology deals with revealed data, and all scholarly research in *theology*, therefore, must begin with the acceptance of a valid revelation even when it exceeds rational verifications, and it must accept as its own scientific criteria not only the written revealed truths but also their cognitive development and their binding definitions through the living magisterium supported by a tradition which is likewise under the guidance of a higher revealed light. If, therefore, a historian sets up criteria of research, with the results derived therefrom, of a purely rational nature, he is not a historian of theology.[55]

What Stickler's move exposes is that the development of a doctrine of infallibility brings with it a certain reading of the canonical heritage of the Church. Seen from the perspective of canonicity laid out in the last chapter, it amounts to a quiet revolution in the conception of canon. Now one of the canons—namely, that related to episcopal oversight—has become a foundation for everything else. It has become a norm of truth which can be assumed in the pursuit of knowledge, and in this

---

[52] Tierney, *Origins of Papal Infallibility*.

[53] Alfons M. Stickler, 'Papal Infallibility—A Thirteenth-Century Invention? Reflections on a Recent Book', *Catholic Historical Review*, 60 (1974), 437.

[54] Tierney, *Origins of Papal Infallibility*, 300.

[55] Stickler, 'Papal Infallibility', 437; emphasis original. The methodological position so superbly stated here does not, of course, inhibit or prevent Stickler from seeking to overturn Tierney's arguments on Tierney's own grounds as a historian.

instance historical knowledge.[56] It is not the case, of course, that the other canons will be ignored or set aside. Scripture and the other traditions of the Church were used and appealed to by the Pope himself in the articulation of what is to be believed or practised. However, what these mean, and how they are to be worked out in the present, are to be determined finally through the appropriate determination of the Pope. In this way doubt about the truth can be eliminated, the unity of the Church can be secured on pertinent matters of faith and morals, and ordinary believers can have a secure source of sacred knowledge. Nothing less than certain knowledge has been attained.[57]

Another way to state this thesis is that a particular account of divine inspiration, or divine assistance, or divine intellectual oversight, has achieved canonical status as a foundation for everything else.[58] A particular mode of knowing the divine mind has been canonized. A norm has been introduced which can be appealed to as a criterion of truth to settle disputes about the identity or meaning of the other canons or about other crucial matters of faith and morals. At this point it does not matter how often this is or is not invoked. Nor is it crucial that there can be continued

---

[56] 'If the (Catholic) science of historical theology recognizes a *dogma*, certainly such, as an unquestionable point of reference even for historical research, it is not engaging in apologetics nor is it renouncing the historical method, but rather it is trying to explain *in the light of the certainty attained* what is possibly left obscure or disputed. But it cannot reject a *truth now theologically certain* because of obscurity in the knowledge of its development, or difficulties of explanation, or of different opinions of the doctrine in the past or in present-day theology' (Alfons M. Stickler, 'A Rejoinder to Professor Tierney', *Catholic Historical Review*, 61 (1975), 277; emphasis added).

[57] In fact, a very complex scale of theological notes, which delineates the cognitive weight to be assigned to Roman claims, is worked out. For an excellent description of this scale see Robert J. Dionne, *The Papacy and the Church* (New York: Philosophical Library, 1987), 23–5. The highest note is *de fide divina*, which means that the doctrine is clearly contained in the sources of revelation; the lowest note is *tuta*, which means that it would not be imprudent to believe this doctrine.

[58] It is not easy to capture exactly the divine assistance granted. It does not require divine revelation or divine intervention, for the Pope in the process of coming to a decision will think about the issues, read various texts, ponder the problem in his heart, consult relevant experts, and so on. The guarantee is that God will ensure that he does not fall into error on those occasions when a formal definition or pronouncement is delivered.

discussion about the exact identity and meaning of the relevant pronouncements. What is critical is that a fundamental epistemic source which, by definition, serves as a norm of truth has been posited.

In turn, the other canons of the faith, like Scripture or the various traditions of the Church, also become norms which can be used to settle intellectual debates about theological matters. Yet these other canons are carefully subordinated to the canon of papal infallibility. One can see this very clearly in the way Thomas Aquinas uses the authority of the Roman Pontiff in his arguments on the *filioque* clause. Responding to those who claim that the Church was wrong to add to the Creed, he says: 'The authority of the Roman Pontiff sufficed for this addition; by this authority too, all the ancient councils were confirmed.'[59] There is an ultimate or final norm available in principle for resolving disputes which cannot be settled by appeal to the other norms. Even non-ecclesial norms—say, reason or sense experience—although they can have a role in theological argument, must ultimately be made subordinate to this working norm. Indeed, in due course canonical decisions on how reason is to relate to faith are formally promulgated.[60]

There is no way to remain neutral on these matters. The very description of canon which one uses to lay out the history of canonicity gives the game away.[61] In the preceding chapters I

---

[59] *Summa Contra Gentiles*, trans. C. J. O'Neil (Notre Dame, Ind.: University of Notre Dame Press, 1957), iv. 25, p. 142. Here the authority of Scripture is subordinated to the infallibility of the Pope; yet it can equally be argued, as we shall see in the next chapter, that the infallibility of the Pope is circumscribed by what can be derived from Scripture. We have in fact a carefully constructed doctrine of double infallibility. There is infallibility of the foundations, ultimately represented by Scripture; and there is an infallibility of interpretation represented by papal infallibility. Both are essential to provide the kind of certainty desired. Aquinas discusses papal infallibility in *Summa Theologiae*, II-II, q. 1, a. 10. For a useful discussion of Aquinas's views and their significance see Hans Küng, *Infallible?* (London: Collins, 1971), 95–8.

[60] A useful selection of some of the relevant material can be found in *The Church Teaches* (St Louis: Herder, 1955), 11–39.

[61] As Newman was to argue, a doctrine of development is absolutely essential to the Roman Catholic position. In the present instance, this permits the redescription of a 'canon' as a 'norm' in the following way. For a long time, the story runs, the teachers of the Church may well have deployed a rather loose and even meagre conception of canon, using it, for example, to denote simply a

proposed that in the early days of the Church, canons were not epistemic norms. They were means of grace given by the Holy Spirit to bring order to the life of the Church and to mediate salvation to those who would use them in a way appropriate to their nature. Although salvation was in no way possible without knowledge of God, and although all sorts of epistemic materials are buried in the canonical traditions, no particular theory of knowledge was canonized. A variety of arguments was used to defend this or that theological position, and in these arguments one can detect a vision of divine revelation which can function as a warrant for various theological claims; but no theory of revelation was systematized and canonized.

From this perspective, the division between East and West involves on the part of the West a revolutionary reconceptualization of canon in the Western Church. Changes in the canonical heritage related to the *filioque* clause, papal infallibility, and the canon of the Fathers in themselves look as if they are a matter of simple addition to what has gone before. Certainly these are additions, and they are extremely significant additions, not least because they lead to a profound division in the Church as a whole. However, there is much more here than meets the eye of the historian who focuses merely on the rearrangement of the ecclesiastical furniture. Implicit in these changes are significant epistemic shifts which have profound consequences for the life of the Church. Within only two centuries they precipitated a convulsive canonical and epistemic crisis in the Church in the West.

We might capture the main point accurately by saying that developments in the articulation of a doctrine of papal infallibility in the West opened up a second front in the war about an appropriate epistemology for the life of the Church. The first front was located in the material developed by the competing lists of Fathers canonized. The contrast between Aquinas and Palamas best shows what was at stake for the divided sections of the Church. In the schism a second front appeared in the articulation

list of books or Fathers. However, over time a tacit understanding of canon as a norm of truth not reflected in this usage, but still present in a hidden way in the mind of the Church, was made explicit and accepted as canonical. From then on, canons are naturally reconceived to bring one's perspective into line with the truth about canon now made available to the Church as a whole. As has long been recognized, this is an ingenious move.

of a doctrine about the unique capacity of the bishop of Rome to mediate the truth about God, and thereby provide an ultimate test of God's will for the Church as a whole. The attraction of this was obvious: it provided one secure locus of epistemic authority to settle matters of substance. In certain instances it furnished for scholars and intellectuals a certain and infallible foundation from which to begin their enquiries, even though the material implications of this foundation for their studies may have to be worked out using the most delicate judgement imaginable. For the ordinary convert, on the other hand, it provided a peace and certainty that he or she would not forfeit for the world. As one modern American convert expressed it: 'In order to accept God's truth men must first know in an absolutely certain way what it is.'[62]

As we all know, a war on two fronts can be a costly affair, unless the two fronts can be co-ordinated in a single strategy which hangs together coherently. In the rich intellectual heritage of Roman Christianity in the West there has been no shortage of attempts to provide such a coherent epistemology. One of the most thorough and comprehensive was that provided by the great Thomas Aquinas. What is especially interesting is the fateful consequences which his views entail for the Western interpretation of Scripture. To those views we now turn.

---

[62] Oliver Barres, *One Shepherd, One Flock* (New York: Sheed and Ward, 1956), 146. Compare the scathing comment of Döllinger: 'It [Papal Infallibility] seems to attain, by the shortest road, in the simplest way, and with the least waste of time, what the Ancient Church expended so much trouble upon, with so many appliances, and for so long a time. But, if once finally accepted as a rule of faith, it becomes not only a soft cushion on which the wearied or perplexed mind, as well of the layman as of the theologian, may repose softly, and abandon itself to undisturbed slumber, but it also supplies to the intellectual world in religious matters what our steam conveyances and electrical wires supply to the material world in the saving of time and labor. Nothing could be more economical or better adapted to save study and intellectual toil even for Rome herself; for the inevitable result of the principle would speedily bring to this point, that the essence of Infallibility consists in the Pope's signature to a decree hastily drawn up by a congregation or single theologian. The remark has frequently been made that it is chiefly converts, with little theological cultivation, but plenty of useful zeal, who surrender themselves in willing and joyful mental slavery to the infallible ruler of souls; rejoicing and deeming themselves fortunate to have a master, visible, palpable, and easily inquired of ' (*Pope and Council*, p. xxv).

4

Canon and Scientia

The division in the Christian tradition between East and West represents two very different ways of receiving the canonical heritage of the early and patristic Church. That heritage was a complex entity embodying a variety of materials and practices. As the canonical heritage was constructed, it is impossible to find an explicit account of its overall nature and boundaries. In some cases the canonical practices, best exemplified in the sacraments, were in place from the outset. These were received from the apostles and handed down to those appointed to care for the life of the Church. The practice of teaching and oversight, another canonical practice, was also in place from the beginning; yet the form it took developed over time, until it became relatively settled in character. The adoption of a canon of books, the Bible, ultimately decided for the most part on the basis of usage, but officially and explicitly carried out in a Church council, was also drawn out over time, and even then there were loose edges which were not tied up. The drawing up of a list of Fathers was relatively informal, as the teaching and sanctity of the various Fathers impressed themselves on the Church as a whole. The adoption of the Nicene Creed, of the Chalcedonian Definition, of standard forms of iconography—these required extensive debate and discussion in the councils of the Church. The adoption and adaptation of various kinds of regulations covering the ongoing affairs of the Church was a very subtle process.

It would have been very difficult for any comprehensive vision of these diverse materials, practices, and persons to be available in the course of their being adopted and developed. There was no committee at work, presenting a commanding and agreed theory which would make sense of the canonical process as a whole. Nor did that process capture the sustained attention of any individual. In fact, one can only see what was happening by looking back over time and observing the complex interconnections which held the whole process together. The Church, relying on the guidance of the Holy Spirit, proceeded, however, with confidence, assured that God would provide what was needed for its pilgrimage. It neither sought nor needed a formal analysis of its internal developments, being more interested in the use of this heritage to initiate people into the healing life of God than in a comprehensive, second-order account of it.

Yet various parts of the total heritage and tradition of the Church were subject to interpretive analysis. Thus, as the Church settled on the canon of Scripture, various teachers in the Church made efforts to provide theories of Scripture which would capture its nature and significance. Likewise, efforts were made to identify Rome as not just the primary see of the whole Church but also as possessing special authority in the episcopal practices of the tradition. These theories were never adopted initially as binding on the whole Church. On the contrary, competing and conflicting accounts were allowed to coexist in the Church as a whole. Moreover, in some cases, even though there was agreement that the Church utterly depended on divine revelation at the very heart of its existence, no particular theory of revelation of the kind which would become fashionable later was ever formally adopted. Revelation was left to be carried in an indirect way in the bosom of the Church, mediated by the various canonical materials already in place.

This situation changed with the arrival of substantial and serious division between East and West. The adoption of the *filioque* clause in the Creed in the West and claims about papal infallibility caused extensive debate about the status of various components of the Church's canonical heritage. Such developments, joined with earlier efforts to provide theories of the status of various elements of the tradition, precipitated a deep debate about the epistemic commitments of the Church as a whole. In this context there developed in the West a concerted effort to epistemize the canonical heritage of the church. By 'epistemize' I mean the process of interpreting and perceiving that heritage in epistemic categories. Thus a particular account of divine revelation, which granted an epistemic privilege to the Roman see in the adjudication of ecclesial disputes, became normative. In this case a particular ecclesial institution or practice was vested with epistemic significance. The East rejected these claims, developed its own account of the canonical heritage received from the Fathers, and cultivated its own rather modest epistemic proposals.

Nowhere is the move to construe the canonical heritage of the Church in epistemic categories more visible than in the theology of Thomas Aquinas. In Aquinas we see the development of a comprehensive account of *scientia*[1] in which various aspects of the canonical heritage are located in its proper place in the epistemic scheme of things.[2] Especially important in this programme was the place which Aquinas gave to the canon of Scripture. With Aquinas we move from a situation in which the Church in the West lived with a relatively modest set of epistemic proposals to one in which it developed and adopted a carefully constructed, comprehensive epistemology. To be sure, Aquinas's own position represented for a time only one possible option. The medieval intellectual world was fecund in the area of epistemic speculation, so Aquinas was not the only option in his day; indeed, some elements of his teaching were placed under condemnation for a short, three-year period, beginning in 1277. Eventually, however, it became the model, if not the actual content, of Roman Catholic accounts of religious knowledge. His status as the angelic doctor of the Church is relatively secure.[3]

It is crucial to bear in mind that Aquinas saw himself first and foremost as a theologian of the Church, and that theology was for him a form of catechesis in which the Church was fed and nurtured.

---

[1] This is a technical term in Aquinas which is best left untranslated; it should not be confused with the modern term 'knowledge'. We might construe it as demonstrative knowledge.

[2] Compare the judgement of Thomas Gilby that the *Summa Theologiae* 'represents the first completed attempt to establish Christian theology as a scientific discipline, and students who start from inside the Christian tradition recognize that it is one of the few masterpieces of its kind, though not all would agree that it is the kind of thing that should be done'. See his introduction to Thomas Aquinas, *Summa Theologiae* (Garden City, NY: Image Books, 1969), i. 12.

[3] See above, p. [74], for the official status of Aquinas's work. We shall note difficulties later in the position accorded to Aquinas. See below, pp. [102–7].

Since the teacher of Catholic truth has not only to develop advanced students but also to shape those who are making a start, according to St. Paul, *even as unto babes in Christ I have fed you with milk and not meat*, we propose in this work to convey the truths which are part of the Christian religion in a style serviceable for the training of beginners.

For we have in mind how much newcomers to this teaching are hindered by various writings about it, partly by a swarm of pointless questions, articles, and arguments, partly because essential points are treated according to the requirements of textual commentary or of academic debate, not to those of a sound educational method, partly because repetitiousness breeds boredom and muddle in their minds.

Eager, therefore, to avoid these and other like drawbacks, and trusting in God's help, we shall try to pursue the truths of Christian theology, and, so far as the subject permits, to be concise and clear in the process.[4]

Aquinas perceived his work as providing a form of schooling in well-being which involved access to special divine revelation.[5] What is fascinating is the way that he integrated this conception of theology, one which saw theology as logically dependent on faith, into an account of theology as *scientia*. As Gilby felicitously writes, 'Christian theology derives from faith and yet is truly science.'[6]

The claim that theology is truly a science comes across as anomalous to modern sensibilities. We naturally take science to be an academic discipline, represented paradigmatically by the natural sciences, and therefore marked by such constitutive elements as hypotheses, general laws, predictions, falsifiability, crucial experiments, confirmation, probability, naturalism, paradigm shifts, and the like. Theology simply does not fit into this way of thinking. This observation alerts us immediately to the fact that Aquinas was not operating in the intellectual world which has become so commonplace for us. For Aquinas theology was *scientia*, not in the modern sense of 'science'[7] but in the Aristotelian sense: that is, the area of belief demarcated by

---

[4] See the foreword to the *Summa Theologiae* (hereafter *ST*). Aquinas's whole career as preacher, exegete, and theologian bears out the claim that he was deeply committed to the formation of Christians.

[5] *ST* IA. I. I.

[6] Gilby, introduction to *ST*, i. 22.

[7] It should be remembered, of course, that what we now call 'science' was once housed in the field of natural philosophy.

demonstration and certainty, as contrasted with *opinio*, the area
demarcated by appropriate authorities and probability.[8]

This proposal of Aquinas required several ingenious moves
which the sure-footed prose of the *Summa Theologiae* can easily
conceal from the unwary reader. *Scientia* for Aquinas, if taken
pretty much intact from Aristotle, would require that the single
science of theology advance from self-evident principles, that it
not be concerned with individual causes or events, that it treat
one class of subject-matter, that it not be based on authority, and
that it not use texts which offer various meanings.[9] Aquinas's
resolution of the difficulties which these requirements posed for
theology depended in part on a very precise way of construing
the canon of Scripture, as well as the received teaching of the
Fathers and councils of the Church. It also required a theory of
divine revelation which made special revelation virtually identical
with the content of the Bible.

Aquinas's account of Scripture was located firmly within a
vision of *scientia*, which was in turn located within his wider epistemology. Contrary to what has often been believed in philosophical circles, it would appear that Aquinas was not a classical
foundationalist.[10] Moreover, it is clear that his epistemology

[8] It needs to be borne in mind throughout that Aquinas did not have access
to modern conceptions of probability. Probability meant for Aquinas: approved
by authority. For an important discussion see Ian Hacking, *The Emergence of
Probability: A Philosophical Study of Early Ideas about Probability, Induction, and
Statistical Inference* (Cambridge: Cambridge University Press, 1975). For the
concept of probability in Aquinas see Edmund F. Byrne, *Probability and Opinion:
A Study in the Medieval Presuppositions of Post-Medieval Theories of Probability* (The
Hague: Martinus Nijhoff, 1968).

[9] These are the central questions which Aquinas takes up in the very first
question of the *Summa Theologiae*.

[10] See e.g. the account of Alvin Plantinga in 'Reason and Belief in God', in
Alvin Plantinga and Nicholas Wolsterstorff (eds.), *Faith and Rationality: Reason
and Belief in God* (Notre Dame, Ind.: University of Notre Dame Press, 1983),
39–63. Plantinga is well aware of the possibility of another reading of Aquinas
based on various texts which do not quite fit his interpretation: see ibid. 47. For
a different account, which argues that Aquinas was not a foundationalist, see
Eleonore Stump, 'Aquinas and the Foundations of Knowledge', *Canadian Journal
of Philosophy*, supp. vol. 17 (1900), 125–58. See also Scott MacDonald, 'Theory
of Knowledge', in N. Kretzmann and E. Stump, *The Cambridge Companion to
Thomas Aquinas* (Cambridge: Cambridge University Press, 1993), 160–95.
MacDonald argues that Aquinas was a foundationalist.

cannot be divorced from his theology. In fact, Aquinas's episte-mology was profoundly theocentric, for God represented not just the paradigm knower for Aquinas; rather, God's knowledge was the standard of excellence and the goal of all that human agents know or seek to know. Only by participation in the life of God in the beatific vision will human beings achieve the kind of perfect knowledge of which they are capable of knowing.[11] This meant that for Aquinas all human knowing this side of eternity, when compared to the knowledge which God has, was imper-fect. No matter how high it reached, even in the case of *scientia*, it fell short of what it can be and will be for the saints in heaven. This shortfall is due to the fact that such knowledge depends for its existence on a discursive movement from principles to conclu-sions.

Given this important qualification, what did Aquinas mean by *scientia*? We can explore this briefly by identifying the positive marks of *scientia* and by indicating the characteristics of the lesser form of knowledge we find in Aquinas: namely, *opinio*.[12]

Those propositions which constitute *scientia* have three charac-teristics: they are universal, necessary, and certain. They are universal, in that they apply to every member of the class repre-sented by the grammatical subject of the proposition. Such knowledge arises through the senses, but, by means of abstraction, following Aristotle, we can arrive at the universal. They are necessary, in that what is asserted in *scientia* cannot be other than what it is. This does not mean that there cannot be *scientia* of the contingent, for Aquinas held that there can be necessary aspects of what is otherwise contingent. Finally, they are certain in that they are arrived at by demonstration. Working from ineluctable first principles, one arrives by way of syllogism at the conclusion, which, while less certain than the premisses on which it is based, still yields certainty.

All knowledge which does not fall into the category of *scientia* is *opinio*, or non-demonstrative knowledge. In the case of *opinio*,

---

[11] This is well brought by Byrne, *Probability and Opinion*, ch. 6. I am much indebted to Byrne for the exposition of Aquinas's epistemology which follows.

[12] Again we will simply stick with Aquinas's own terms. It should also be noted that Aquinas used other terms which were closely related to *opinio*, like *aestimatio, existematio, sententia*. The differences between them do not alter the main point at issue here.

the human agent adheres to the relevant proposition based on criteria other than strict demonstration. Hence it has less rationality than *scientia*. It is reasonable in the light of the authorities and the arguments which lie behind it, but it is not rational in an unqualified sense. We have in this case a less perfect cognition; it represents a domain of fallibility strictly speaking not occupied by *scientia*. In the case of *opinio*, arguments proceed by testing the consistency or compatibility of a proposition with other propositions which are accepted as true for one reason or another. The aim is analysis rather than demonstration. One relies extensively on authority. Probability in this scheme means, in fact, approved by various authorities, who are graded in various ways, and whose views are taken not as truth itself but as a sign or pointer to the truth. By means of dialectic and disputation one digs deeper than mere authority, believing that there is ultimately a truth to be discovered, and that this truth will eventually be brought to light by means of forms of argumentation which result in demonstration. Disputation is the necessary probing of opinion, which, while it can only in itself lead to probability, clears the way for the possible attainment of truth in demonstration. Disputation presents as well as is humanly possible the reasons for adhering to opinions. In fact, if an opinion is in some way probable—that is, approved—it cannot be totally devoid of truth. Probing opinions is indispensable, then, as a kind of preliminary operation to the identification of the truth contained within them.

It is God who knows all truth. God knows absolutely everything in one simple intuitive glance which transcends all time. God's knowledge is comprehensive. Humans know things because they exist; the ultimate reason why things exist in the first place is because God knows them. Hence, for us, things are the measure of truth; whereas for God, the measure or standard of things themselves is God's knowledge of them. God has certain and causal knowledge of all things; God alone has wisdom. God knows perfectly and completely whatever is or can be, whatever was or might have been, whatever will be or could be. Below God in a descending hierarchy of capacity stand the angels, who exist with a full supply of principles together with all knowledge which is implied in them. The angels do not have errors to dispel; nor do they have to overcome dispositions which hinder clear thinking. Anything new is supplied directly from God or another angel. Yet they know the infinite in a finite way. They do not have God's simultaneous intuition of all things all at once and as one.

There are, however, cases in the human domain where the knowledge gained is superior in its excellence to what is characteristically the case in the human sphere. Thus, in the case of prophecy, certain human beings gain knowledge which is remote from the prophet himself, as when he sees a distant land—knowledge which is inaccessible because of the deficiency of human knowledge, as in the case of the mystery of the Trinity and knowledge which concerns future contingents. Also, in the obvious case of Christ, his knowledge encompassed everything of which humans are theoretically capable. Then, by way of supernatural, infused knowledge, he knew all singulars, past, present, and future. He had certitude about all things, not needing to reflect, deliberate, or ponder possibilities; hence, he had no opinions. In addition, there were, and are, those humans who possess charismatic knowledge. These, through supernatural gifts, share some of the intellectual superiority of Christ, so that they may teach others. Supernatural gifts aid in the task of persuading others of the truth of divine revelation. As a consequence of this help, they better know themselves, they are better able to confirm what they say, and they are able to present their material in a manner appropriate to their listeners.

Given these deep contrasts between God and virtually all human beings and between *scientia*, constituted by universality, necessity, and certainty, and *opinio*, constituted by probability, how could Aquinas claim that theology was a divine science?[13] This is how he answers:

Christian theology should be pronounced to be a science. Yet bear in mind that sciences are of two kinds; some work from premises recognized in the innate light of intelligence, for instance arithmetic, geometry, and sciences of the same sort; while others work from premises recognized in the light of a higher science, for instance optics starts from

[13] 'Thomas modifies Aristotle's rigorous conception of science in a variety of ways. But . . . the modifications are due not so much to reflection upon the nature of science as to what Thomas considers to be the exigencies of the Christian faith', Byrne (*Probability and Opinion*, 76).

principles marked out by geometry and harmony from principles indicated by arithmetic.

In this second manner is Christian theology a science, for it flows
from founts recognized in the light of a higher science, namely God's
very own which he shares with the blessed. Hence, rather as harmony
credits its principles which are taken from arithmetic, Christian theology
takes on faith its principles revealed by God.[14]

This science of theology is a single science, for its object is
God and creatures in relation to him; thus it has unity by treating
one class of subject-matter. Angels, human beings, and any other
topics are examined theologically only in so far as their relation to
God is at issue. As such, it is more theoretical than practical, since
it is mainly concerned with the divine things which are, rather
than with human acts. Yet it deals with human acts in so far as
these acts prepare human agents to achieve that knowledge on
which eternal bliss reposes. Moreover, theology ranks above all
other sciences, practical or theoretical.

It ranks above other practical sciences because it aims at eternal
happiness, the final end which governs all the practical sciences. It
ranks above other theoretical sciences in the certitude attainable
and in the value of the object studied.

As to certitude, because theirs comes from the natural light of reason
which can make mistakes, whereas sacred doctrine's is held in the light
of divine knowledge which cannot falter. As to worth of subject,
because their business is only things underneath reason, whereas sacred
science leads to the heights the reason cannot climb.[15]

Such objective certainty predicated of the content of divine
science does not mean that the content will be subjectively certain
to human subjects. Doubt arises because human understanding is
feeble and because of the disability of our minds. Nevertheless,
'the slenderest acquaintance we can form with heavenly things is
more desirable than a thorough grasp of mundane matters'.[16]

---

[14] *ST* IA. 1. 2. It may well be misleading, despite the tenor of this quotation, to say that sacred doctrine is a subalternate science. The latter suggests that
it is somehow inferior to other *scientia*, whereas, for Aquinas, given that sacred
doctrine draws its first principles from divine revelation, it is higher than other
scientia. It is important to avoid futile verbal disputes on this issue, for the main
contentions of Aquinas's position are clear.   [15] *ST* IA. 1. 5.
   [16] *ST* IA. 1. 5.

Moreover, theology can borrow from the other sciences, not because it needs to beg from them, but for the purpose of greater clarification of the things conveyed.

For it [theology] takes its principles directly from God through revelation, not from other sciences. On that account it does not rely on them, as though they were in control, for their role is subsidiary and ancillary; so an architect makes use of a tradesman as a statesman employs soldiers. That it turns to them in this way is not from any lack of sufficiency within itself; it is the more readily guided into the world above reason, set forth in holy teaching, through the world of natural reason from which other sciences take their course.[17]

The gift of such revelation is essential for human happiness and salvation. God has destined human beings for an end beyond the grasp of human reason; hence, if they are to stretch out and exert themselves for it, they will need to be able to recognize and possess truths surpassing reason signified through divine revelation. Even in the case of theological truth where human reason is able to investigate, divine revelation is essential.

For the rational truth about God would be reached only by a few, and even so after a long time and mixed with many mistakes; whereas on knowing this depends our whole welfare, which is in God. In these circumstances, then, it was to prosper the salvation of human beings, and the more widely and less anxiously, that they were provided for by divine revelation.[18]

Given that theology directs human acts to their highest end, that it considers the first and final cause of the whole universe, and that it is derived not just by means of knowledge of creatures but from what God alone knows and yet discloses for others to share, it is wisdom in the highest degree.[19] Theology is exclusive

[17] *ST* IA. 1. 5.   [18] *ST* IA. 1. 1.

[19] In light of this, I am not convinced by the 'transmutation thesis' of Wolterstorff and others that natural theology in Aquinas transmutes the belief of the believer into sight. See Nicholas Wolterstorff, 'The Migration of the Theistic Arguments: From Natural Theology to Evidentialist Apologetics', in Robert Audi and William J. Wainwright (eds.), *Rationality, Religious Belief, and Moral Commitment* (Ithaca, NY: Cornell University Press, 1986), 78. The believer, by definition, is one who believes that the Scriptures are from God, and therefore has already obtained certain knowledge; otherwise Scripture could never be the foundation for sacred *scientia*. It is in fact difficult to see how natural theology is of any cognitive benefit to believers, given that they believe

in its status as knowledge, for it is about truth which comes
through revelation rather than through natural reasoning. Its
status is so high that anything encountered in the other sciences
which is incompatible with its truth should be completely
condemned as false. Moreover, this wisdom can be gained by
humans either directly through the gift of the Holy Spirit or indirectly by study, reasoning from premises held on the basis of
divine revelation.

Theology's derivation from divine revelation also ensures that its
content cannot be considered merely probative, as its reliance on
authority might lead one to conclude. If it were based merely on
human authority, this would follow; but the unique feature of
Christian theology is that it is based on the authority of God. This
does not derogate from the dignity of theology, 'for though weakest
when based on what human beings have held, the argument from
authority is most forcible when based on what God has disclosed'.[20]
Hence it can proceed from the known, given in divine revelation,
and work to bring out other things in its field by inference. Faith
rests on unfailing truth; hence alleged proofs against faith are not
demonstrations but merely charges which can be refuted. Yet the
authority of the philosophers who have been able to perceive the
truth by natural reasoning can be used as a form of assistance.

Yet sacred doctrine employs such authorities only in order to provide as
it were extraneous arguments from probability. Its own proper authorities are those of canonical Scripture, and these it applies with convincing
force. It has other proper authorities, the doctors of the Church, and
these it looks at as its own, but for arguments that carry no more than
probability.

that they already possess divine revelation. Moreover, as I go on to point out
here, the knowledge derived from Scripture is of greater value than any other
knowledge, even of *scientia* derived from non-revelatory sources. What happens
in the case of the believer from a cognitive point of view is that there is a deepening of understanding and an increase in knowledge through sacred doctrine.
This is taken into a new and ultimate stage in the beatific vision. Wolterstorff's
essay is a very stimulating overview of the whole sweep of religious epistemology from the medieval period to the Enlightenment. Like most treatments in
the history of philosophy, it gives little or no attention to the role of thinking
about canon and criterion in either medieval or Reformation thinkers. This
ignores the extent to which the whole epistemological endeavours of these periods were intimately linked to a host of theological issues, most especially to that
of canon, as we shall see as we proceed.   [20] *ST* IA. 1. 8.

For our faith rests on the revelation made to the prophets and Apostles who wrote the canonical books, not on a revelation, if such there be, made to any other teacher. In this sense St. Augustine wrote to St. Jerome; *Only to those books or writings which are called canonical have I learnt to pay such honour that I firmly believe that none of their authors have erred in composing them. Other authors, however, I read to such effect, that no matter what holiness and learning they display, I do not hold what they say to be true because these were their sentiments.*[21]

We have now reached the point where we can see very clearly the place that the canon of Scripture held in Aquinas's vision of both theology and the Christian life. In the enclosed quotation we encounter an informal effort in a letter on the part of Augustine to treat Scripture as an epistemic norm. Aquinas has taken this idea, transposed it into formal theory, transferred it into a carefully constructed epistemological scheme, and then locked it into place. The canon of Scripture has been set apart in a radical way from the rest of the Church's canonical heritage.[22] The Fathers are converted into doctors of the Church, ready now to serve not as spiritual friends and directors, who, guided by the Spirit, will lead us to Christ and to the life of holiness made manifest in him, but as authorities who can secure variable

---

[21] *ST* IA. 1. 8.

[22] There is a striking similarity here between the position of Aquinas and that of the Reformers. 'Reading what St. Thomas writes on the relation between Scripture and revelation, one gets the impression that both are put by him on a par, or at least that he considers Holy Scripture as the only existing source of revelation. In this he seems not to be alone; a certain number of texts of Fathers of the Church give the same impression and the reformers of the sixteenth century cited them in confirmation of their doctrine of the *sufficientia Sacrae Scripturae*. Moreover, does not St. Thomas say explicitly that all that is necessary for faith can be read clearly and in the literal sense in the Bible? Is this not the Protestant doctrine of *perspicuitas* of Holy Scripture, and does this not practically exclude tradition as a source of revelation?' (J. Van Der Ploeg, 'Holy Scripture in the Theology of St. Thomas', *Thomist*, 10 (1947), 417–18). Van Der Ploeg nicely answers this by showing that Aquinas clearly relied on the faith of the whole Church, although the position on this issue changed somewhat after the Council of Trent. The close similarity between Aquinas and the Reformers is also recognized by Norman Geisler, *Thomas Aquinas: An Evangelical Appraisal* (Grand Rapids, Mich.: Baker Book House, 1991), 48–9. See also Heiko Augustus Oberman, *Forerunners of the Reformation: The Shape of Medieval Thought, Illustrated by Key Documents* (New York: Holt, Rinehart and Winston, 1966).

degrees of probability. Above them rank the councils and the Popes whose interpretations, illumined by the Holy Spirit, explain infallibly the sense of the sacred text. In short, the canon of Scripture is now put to work to secure the epistemic status of theology as the highest form of *scientia* in the university.

This had immediate consequences for Aquinas's vision of Scripture. Clearly Scripture could not perform the role now assigned to it in the field of epistemology if its meaning was equivocal, for in such a case we could not draw inferences from it for our demonstrations in theology.[23] Theology would immediately crumble at the foundations.

Allow a variety of readings to one passage, and you produce confusion and deception, and sap the foundations of argument; examples of the stock fallacies, not reasoned discourse, follow from the medley of meanings. Holy Scripture, should effectively display the truth without fallacy of any sort. One text, therefore, should not offer various meanings.[24]

Aquinas faced a very serious problem here, for he confronted the prospect of having to eliminate any spiritual reading of Scripture, together with his authorities who had argued for multiple senses of Scripture for centuries in the Church. His solution was to insist generally on one and only one literal meaning of Scripture, to permit another spiritual sense,[25] and to tie demonstration to the literal meaning only. It certainly was the case that, as God was the author of Scripture, he could have intended more than one literal sense. Prima facie, this could pose an enormous threat to the whole enterprise of sacred science, for if God meant more than one meaning, then one might worry about how to discern such meanings, and one might wonder about which one to use as the foundation for inference.

Aquinas could surely reply to this threat that he nowhere claimed that exegesis was easy, and if more than one meaning is

---

[23] Aquinas faced a similar problem from the use of metaphor in Scripture, for symbols and metaphors, for him, obscured the truth. See *ST* IA. 1. 9. For the most part he treats this as a pedagogical issue. However, the crucial move he makes is to say that 'truths expressed metaphorically in one passage are more expressly explained elsewhere'.   [24] *ST* IA. 1. 10.

[25] Within this category, Aquinas distinguished between the allegorical, the tropological or moral, the anagogical, and the parabolic. These are based on, and presuppose, the literal sense.

intended by God, this simply enriched the field of theology by enlarging the foundation a little. Moreover, this doctrine provided a splendid way of dealing with cases of conflict generated by contradictions between the various fields of knowledge and theology.

For, the dignity of divine scripture is such that in one expression (*sub una littera*) many meanings are contained. As a result, so suited is Scripture to diverse intellectual milieux that any given individual is surprised to find the truth which he knows contained therein. This makes our defense against unbelievers easier. For if the manner in which someone interprets Sacred Scripture appears false, he can have recourse to some other meaning thereof. Whence the following is believable: God granted it to Moses and to the other authors of Sacred Scripture that whatever truths men might be able to learn they themselves knew, and that these (truths) they would express in one writing (*sub una serie littera*). Thus, any one (of these truths) is the meaning of the author. Whence, even if the interpreters of Sacred Scripture relate to the letter some truths which the (human) author did not know, those truths were surely known to the Holy Spirit, who is the principal author of divine Scripture. Accordingly, any truth which, taking into account the context, can be related to divine Scripture is the meaning thereof.[26]

The consequences of Aquinas's epistemology reach beyond their implications for his understanding of the literal sense of Scripture. Given his overall confidence about the status of theology, it is not surprising that he had little patience with those who did not accept the Western position on the *filioque*. Confronted with the claim that the Holy Spirit does not proceed from the Son, Aquinas was convinced that he could show that the Spirit does indeed proceed from the Son.[27] In the opening section of his treatment of the procession of the Spirit, Aquinas confidently marshalled a series of arguments from Scripture, the Doctors of the Church, the Fifth Ecumenical Council, and Augustine. He

---

[26] Quoted in Byrne, *Probability and Opinion*, 137. It should be noted that Aquinas has several strategies for dealing with such conflict. Given his account of theology as *scientia*, he clearly needs every strategy he can find. For a clever defence of Aquinas see Eleonore Stump, 'Revelation and Biblical Exegesis: Augustine, Aquinas, and Swinburne', in Alan G. Padgett (ed.), *Reason and the Christian Religion* (Oxford: Clarendon Press, 1994), 161–97.

[27] See *Summa Contra Gentiles* trans. C. J. O'Neil (Notre Dame, Ind.: University of Notre Dame Press, 1957), IV. 24–5, pp. 133–41.

then turned to straight reasoning: that is, various arguments from the logic of differentiation and identity. A potential exegetical objection, based on the *locus classicus* of John 15: 26, was swept aside as frivolous, and the appeal to the prohibition of some councils to add anything to the Creed was dismissed by claiming that the *filioque* was already implicit in it. As a penultimate nail in the coffin of the opposition, Aquinas added: 'And the authority of the Roman Pontiff sufficed for this addition; by this authority, too, all the ancient councils were confirmed.'[28] A final duo of arguments against his position which appeal to the simplicity of the Spirit were dispatched with the confident claim that they 'are easy to resolve, even if one is a little skilled in theological matters'.[29]

This extraordinary confidence of Aquinas in the rightness of his own position was no accident. Whatever qualifications he tendered concerning the feebleness of the intellect in understanding divine revelation, he was very sure of his ground most, if not all, of the time. This derived in part, surely, from the sense of his own prodigious gifts as a thinker and scholar. However, it also surely stemmed from his confidence in theology as *scientia* and from his positive assessment of the ability of theologians to demonstrate from Scripture and elsewhere the truth of his theological beliefs.[30]

It is in this context of Aquinas's deep confidence that we must also draw attention to the crucial place that the beatific vision played in his epistemology and to the daring claim that we will perceive at that time the very essence of God. This vision was not a pious afterthought in Aquinas. Nor was it construed simply as a gracious blessing poured out on the saints from the bounty of

---

[28] *Summa Contra Gentiles*, 140.   [29] Ibid. 141.

[30] Applied to the *filioque* phrase, it might be easy to dismiss this as a minor matter touching only the outskirts of the doctrine of the Trinity. However, it is very natural to ask whether this kind of confidence does not cut to the very heart of the Christian tradition, for it spilled over into his Christology as well. Byrne's brutal comment, while surely exaggerated, is worth pondering: 'As a matter of fact, Thomas's idealization of the Man of Sorrows tends to make of the latter a rather unapproachable God-machine. Faithfully grinding out the conclusions of his rigid Christological presuppositions, Thomas produces the apocryphal gospel of the intellect—not a baby Jesus who turns clay into pigeons, but a fully turned out Aristotelian wise man superendowed with layers of supernatural cognition to fill in the gaps' (*Probability and Opinion*, 91).

grace and mercy. The beatific vision, in which we see the essence of God, was needed to round off the epistemic pilgrimage which Aquinas had constructed.

Since it is impossible for a natural desire to be incapable of fulfillment, and since it would be so, if it were not possible to reach an understanding of divine substance such as all minds naturally desire, *we must say that it is possible for the substance of God to be seen intellectually*, both by the separate intellectual substances and by our souls.[31]

After showing how this was so, Aquinas without a pause identified this claim with the Pauline promise that we will one day see 'face to face'.[32] A catena of other texts were similarly assembled to establish that we will one day see God without a medium in the way God sees himself.[33] At that point *scientia* will be transposed into the possession of divine wisdom itself, and the epistemic journey will be over, swallowed up in the timelessness of eternity.

There are at least two other areas where we can see very clearly the consequences of epistemizing Scripture and locating it within *scientia*: namely, Aquinas's attitude to the creeds and his concern with prophecy and inspiration.

With respect to creeds, Aquinas's disposition is remarkably casual. The articles of faith for Aquinas are to be located first and foremost in the words of Scripture. Within this, Christ is seen as the first and chief teacher of the faith, for, being divine, he knows divine truth without the need for revelation. Alongside Christ, there are the prophets, apostles, and evangelists, from whom, taken all together, the matter or content of divine revelation is to be derived. The Christian creeds represent a restatement of what is in Scripture, 'a pocket Bible, so to speak', as Davies describes it.[34] The creeds are needed for pedagogical purposes, so that the truth can be made accessible in summary form to those who need it. The creeds add nothing to what is already contained in

---

[31] *Summa Contra Gentiles*, trans. Vernon J. Bourke, bk. III, pt. I, ch. 51, p. 175; emphasis added. Note here how the essential incomprehensibility of God has been abandoned. [32] 1 Cor. 13: 12.

[33] This is a startling claim which it would be easy to miss in reading Aquinas. Aquinas employs an ingenious interpretation of the Eucharist, borrowing from Prov. 9: 5 ('Eat my bread and drink the wine which I have mingled for you') to develop this point (ibid. 177).

[34] Brian Davies, *The Thought of Thomas Aquinas* (Oxford: Clarendon Press, 1992), 12.

Scripture. The truth of faith is sufficiently plain in the teaching of Christ and the apostles. It is only because 'wicked men have wrested apostolic teaching and the other scriptures to their own destruction, [that] declaration of the faith against those impugning it is needed from time to time'.[35]

This is a remarkable vision of the credal heritage of the Church. It makes no significant distinction between canonical and non canonical creeds, playing down the significance of the formal adoption of the Nicene Creed and the Chalcedonian Definition. Moreover, it gives the impression that the contents of the creeds are easily derivable from Scripture, a very precarious proposal which ignores the complex intellectual, experiential, and spiritual process which actually lay behind their creation. Yet the thoroughly secondary role assigned to the creeds falls into place, once we note that Scripture has been transposed to fit the epistemology worked out by Aquinas. Rather than seeing Scripture as a pivotal means of grace, Aquinas construed Scripture as the foundation of divine *scientia*; thus Scripture's pedagogical purpose in the liturgy, which it shared with the Creed, was superseded and systematically played down. In the process Aquinas failed to see that reading Scripture on its own, even after all the strenuous study he recommends, does not lead to the creeds as obviously as his account of them suggests. The Church, in developing its canonical heritage, found that it needed besides Scripture a rule of faith, a set of separate articles, which, of course, were intimately related to the substance of Scripture, but which were both more and less than a pocket Bible. They were more, because the creeds offered a vision of God which drew on Christian experience, as much as they drew on special divine revelation. They were less, because there was a host of materials in Scripture, which did not begin even to be echoed in the creeds.

With respect to Aquinas's interest in prophecy and inspiration, it is in these areas that he worked out his theory of revelation without which the whole programme would have collapsed immediately. Thus Aquinas had to secure a theory of the production of Scripture which would ensure that it would provide a text which had God as its author. In many ways Aquinas's position in this domain was less developed than one might expect. He was

---

[35]   *ST* 2a2ae. 1. 9. ad 4.

happy to posit that God is the author of Scripture,[36] to provide a
very substantial account of prophecy,[37] and to leave the details of
the divine activity constituted by inspiration to be worked out by
posterity. What are paramount are the first and second of these.
So long as Scripture is authored by God, then it is written by
God, and the words of Scripture, suitably interpreted, constitute
the teaching of God. Equally, what matters in prophecy is that
the prophet reproduces the content of the divine mind.

. . . prophecy is a knowledge which divine revelation engraves in the
mind of the prophet, in the form of teaching. Now the truth of knowledge is the same in disciple as in master. The disciple's knowledge is, in
effect, a reproduction of that in the master, just as in natural realities the
form of engendered creature is in some sense a likeness of the generator.
That is why Jerome speaks of prophecy as *a seal of the divine
foreknowledge.* Thus the truth of prophetic knowledge and prophetic
proclamation must needs be the same as that of divine knowledge. And
falsity . . . cannot creep into prophecy.[38]

Taken together, these two claims concerning divine authorship
and prophecy secured the truthfulness of the premises of divine
scientia as highly as possible; for, given God's position as the fountain of knowledge, nothing will ever match what God has to say.
Material which contradicts Scripture, even if derived from
another *scientia*, must be false, even though we may not at the
moment be able to see that this is the case. This is so because
divine *scientia* is unsurpassed, given that it is derived from God.[39]
   In these circumstances, a complex theory of divine revelation
and inspiration becomes absolutely essential for the welfare of
theology and the Church. In fact, such theories will become
canonical, for they are constitutive of the very interpretation of
Scripture as canonical. To deny these theories, or to provide
significantly different accounts of the role of God in the production of Scripture, will destroy the whole theological operation as

---

[36] *ST* IA. 1. 10.
[37] All of ST 2a2ae, q. 171–5, is devoted to this. For a very interesting
commentary and discussion see Paul Synave and Pierre Benoit, *Prophecy and
Inspiration* (New York: Desclee Company, 1961).
[38] *ST* 2a2ae, q. 171. 6.
[39] In the light of the foregoing, it should come as no surprise that Aquinas
should be admired and championed by astute and combative modern fundamentalists like Norman L. Geisler.

envisaged by Aquinas. Furthermore, anyone who challenges such theories will be deemed heretical. Thus, in his commentary on Job, Aquinas declares that 'it is heretical to say that any falsehood whatsoever is contained either in the gospels or in any canonical Scripture'.[40]

As we have explored the ramifications of Aquinas's position, it is clear that his wider epistemological commitments and, within this, the tightening of the epistemic noose around Scripture, had far-reaching consequences. It led to a very particular view of the literal sense, a cavalier attitude to those who refused to take the Western line on the *filioque*, a particular reading of the eschato-logical promises of the Gospel, a casual attitude to the Nicene Creed, and a distinctive vision of divine revelation. These were not accidental developments. They were required by the episte-mology which was developed by Aquinas. Difficulties in the region of these proposals travel back up the line into the very foundations of his whole theory of divine *scientia*.[41]

By far the most interesting problem generated by this proposal arises from the need to show that Christians do have in fact access in their Scriptures to divine revelation. Let us grant, for the sake of argument, that there is such an epistemic genus as divine *scien-tia*, and that the corollaries required to make this operate in regard to Scripture actually hold. Aquinas clearly has to show that the Scriptures are indeed the place where the mind of God is actually disclosed. He must establish, over against competing claims—say, from the Islamic tradition—that the Christian Bible, rather than the Koran, is the Word of God. Note well that this must be established in some sort of necessary fashion; for without this kind of strong claim, the foundational and demonstrative

---

[40] *Commentary on the Book of Job*, 13, lect. 1: quoted in Geisler, *Thomas Aquinas*, 47.

[41] I will not pursue these difficulties here, as my intent is to provide a picture of what happened to canon in the hands of Aquinas, when the drive to develop an epistemology was fully at work in the life of the Western Church. One obvious difficulty, which I have discussed elsewhere, is the tendency to interpret the concept of divine inspiration in such a way as to ensure the epis-temic results required by the theory (see my *The Divine Inspiration of Holy Scripture* (Oxford: Oxford University Press, 1981)). Here Aquinas's own very fruitful theory of analogy, which could have been valuable in its own right and which could have prevented various unnecessary difficulties, was left entirely idle.

character of theology will be immediately forfeited. In other words, it is not enough to show that divine revelation would constitute the foundations of divine *scientia*; that claim is agreed, on the grounds that what God reveals is true. What has to be verified is the Christian claim to have secured, as a matter of necessity, the location of divine revelation in its sacred Scriptures.

Aquinas is certainly aware of this issue. Hence he attempted to show that it was reasonable to believe that Christians possess divine revelation in their Scriptures and that Muslims do not.

It [the divine Wisdom] reveals its own presence, as well as the truth of its teaching and inspiration, by fitting arguments; and in order to confirm those truths that exceed natural knowledge, it gives visible manifestation to works that surpass the ability of all nature. Thus, there are wonderful cures of illnesses, there is the raising of the dead, and the wonderful immutation in the heavenly bodies; and what is more wonderful, there is the inspiration given to human minds, so that simple and untutored persons, filled with the gift of the Holy Spirit, come to possess instantaneously the highest wisdom and the readiest eloquence. When these arguments were examined, through the efficacy of the above mentioned proof, and not the violent assault of arms or the promise of pleasures, and (what is most wonderful of all) in the midst of the tyranny of the persecutors, an innumerable throng of people, both simple and most learned, flocked to the Christian faith. In this faith there are truths preached that surpass every human intellect; the pleasures of the flesh are curbed; it is taught that the things of the world should be spurned. Now, for the minds of mortal men to assent to these things is the greatest of miracles, just as it is a manifest work of divine inspiration that, spurning visible things, men should seek only what is visible. Now, that this has happened neither without preparation nor by chance, but as a result of the disposition of God, is clear from the fact that through many pronouncements of the ancient prophets God had foretold that he would do this.[42]

[42] *Summa Contra Gentiles*, trans. Anton C. Pegis (Notre Dame, Ind.: University of Notre Dame Press, 1975), I. 6. 72. Aquinas continues the same chapter by arguing that Muhammad proceeded in a way that was opposite to this. 'The point is clear in the case of Mohammed. He seduced the people by promises of carnal pleasure to which the concupiscence of the flesh goads us. His teaching also contained precepts that were in conformity with his promises, and he gave free rein to carnal pleasure. In all this, as is not unexpected, he was obeyed by carnal men. As for the proofs of the truth of his doctrine, he brought forward only such as could be grasped by the natural ability of anyone with a very modest wisdom. Indeed the truths which he taught were mingled with

The heart of this argument is the principle that a visible action which can only be divine reveals an inspired teacher of truth. Thus the presence of prophecy, miracles, and holiness establishes that the Christian Scriptures are divine in origin.[43]

The crucial difficulty with this claim is not that there are problems in the intrinsic logic of the position,[44] nor that Aquinas shows no interest in the whole question of the reliability of the witnesses,[45] but that it is not at all clear how we could ever have a sacred *scientia* which was so crucially dependent on this kind of argument. Aquinas envisaged us arriving at the conclusion that the Scriptures are of divine origin by combining a major premiss, embodying the principle that a visible action which can only be divine reveals an inspired teacher of truth, with a minor premiss that agents A, B, and C, or events X, Y, and Z, can only be divine. The argument would be as follows:

1. A visible action which is explicable only as divine reveals an inspired teacher of truth.
2. The actions and behaviour of X, or the events associated with X, are explicable only as divine.
3. Therefore, X is an inspired teacher of truth.

fables and with doctrines of the greatest falsity. He did not bring forth any signs produced in a supernatural way, which alone fittingly give witness to divine inspiration; *for a visible action which can be only divine reveals an invisibly inspired teacher of truth.* On the contrary, Mohammed said that he was sent in the power of his arms—which are signs not lacking even in robbers and tyrants. What is more, no wise men, men trained in things divine and human, believed in him from the beginning. Those who believed were brutal men and desert wanderers, utterly ignorant of all divine teaching, through whose numbers Mohammed forced others to become his followers by the violence of his arms' (ibid., p. 173, emphasis added).

[43] It would appear that they also somehow confirm the truth of the doctrines promulgated.

[44] The argument is in fact a kind of teleological argument which deserves to be evaluated on merit when read in this fashion. I have discussed this elsewhere in *Divine Revelation and the Limits of Historical Criticism* (Oxford: Oxford University Press, 1982).

[45] This is, of course, where Hume made his decisive move against the argument from miracles.

The crucial problem is that the second premiss will always be contingent and non-necessary.[46] One can clearly be mistaken in one's judgement about the relevant actions, behaviour, and events. This introduces a non-necessary element into the arguments which are needed to secure the foundations of divine *scientia*. Aquinas may have missed this because he was so taken with the fact that what God reveals must be true that he transferred the necessity attached to that judgment to the necessity attributed to the judgement that he actually possessed in the scriptures a divine revelation. He took his own judgement about the divine origin of Scripture to be itself of divine origin.[47]

This latter claim suggests an additional argument which might be lodged in Aquinas's argument: namely, that Christians believe that the Scriptures are of divine origin because this belief has been implanted in them by the Holy Spirit.[48] However, this does not

[46] It should be noted that the first premiss is almost certainly false. Thus we might agree that certain actions, behaviours, and events related to X were divine, but infer that these showed that X was merely highly favoured by God or the instrument of God's purposes, and the like. It is even conceivable that there be a visible divine action and that that action not be revelatory. It is certainly not a necessary truth that all visible actions, even of the deity, are revelatory.

[47] There may well be a way to circumvent the argument I have just deployed against Aquinas. We can catch the gist of it by considering an analogy with a mathematical proof. Suppose for the moment that Andrew Wiles has solved Fermat's famous fourth theorem. Suppose now that person P believes the content of Fermat's Fourth Theorem on the authority of Professor Wiles. P believes a mathematical proposition on the basis of testimony; he takes it on Professor Wiles's word. However, Professor Wiles could be wrong. It is a contingent truth that Wiles's word is reliable. Yet the mathematical proof believed is not a contingent truth; it remains a necessary truth, even though believed on the basis of a contingent proposition. We can go further. We have no proof that the foundations of mathematics are foundational. We simply have to take them as given axioms. Now in the case here, Aquinas is in a better position than is normally the case with *scientia*. After all, he can give reasons for his foundational axioms, for he can argue that God would not speak falsely, and he has arguments for saying that he possesses a divine revelation. However, the problem still remains: namely, that there is a crucial non-necessary element in the chain of argument, and this immediately undercuts the construal of theology as *scientia*.

[48] For Aquinas, divine grace is essential for belief, even in those cases where there is the presence of miracle, functioning as evidence. 'The act of believing is an act of intellect assenting to the Divine truth at the command of the will moved by the grace of God' (*ST* II–II, q. 2, art. 9, resp.). 'As regards . . . man's

resolve the dilemma; for in this case also, the judgement that the relevant belief is caused by God could well be false. This judgement will not yield the necessity required for *scientia*. It could well be the case that the Christians are mistaken and that the Muslims are right about the location of divine revelation. Even if either side is right, the judgement at issue will not be a necessary proposition, and the consequences for divine *scientia* are obvious.

Another interesting problem generated by Aquinas's general proposal relates to the place of Aristotle in the canonical heritage of the Faith, if, for the sake of argument, we were to grant that Aquinas was correct in his analysis of the canon of Scripture. How far would agreeing with Aquinas involve the adoption of the work of a particular philosopher into the very heart of the Faith?

On the surface, it would appear that Aristotle stays outside the boundaries of the Faith, for, according to Aquinas, it is Scripture, not natural theology or the philosophy of Aristotle, which is the foundation of theology. Natural theology or human reason come into the picture only to confirm those truths attainable by reason, or to refute objections which would contradict or call into question the articles of faith. Hence Aquinas would appear to provide a thoroughly autonomous position for the canon of Scripture. This judgement could then be augmented very easily by pointing out that Aquinas, in developing his notion of divine *scientia*, has

---

assent to the things which are of faith, we may observe a twofold cause, one of external inducement, such as seeing a miracle, or being persuaded by someone to embrace the faith; neither of which is a sufficient cause, since of those who see the miracle, or hear the same sermon, some believe, and some do not. Hence we must assert another internal cause, which moves man inwardly to assent to matters of faith. The Pelagians held that this cause was nothing else than man's freewill. . . . But this is false, for since man, by assenting to matters of faith, is raised above his nature, this must needs accrue to him from some supernatural principle moving him inwardly; and this is God. Therefore faith, as regards the assent which is the chief act of faith, is from God moving man inwardly by grace' (*ST* II–II, q. 6, art. 1, resp.). For a fine discussion of these suggestions see Eleonore Stump, 'Intellect, Will, and the Principle of Alternative Possibilities', in Michael D. Beatty (ed.), *Christian Theism and the Problems of Philosophy* (Notre Dame, Ind.: University of Notre Dame Press, 1990), 254–85. In the argument currently under consideration I am positing the logically possible case in which there is no evidence at all, just the working of the will, the intellect, and divine grace.

made major adjustments in the account of *scientia* found in Aristotle. He has, as it were, baptized the use of Aristotle, rather than simply adopted him without change in theology.[49]

This initial appearance is misleading, however. Aquinas was clearly a theologian who deployed philosophical argument and material in order to develop an orderly theological system. However, the fundamental character of that system is determined by his commitment to an Aristotelian conception of *scientia*.[50] This is not an optional extra for Aquinas, which can be discarded and replaced by some other epistemological scheme. Lose this epistemic scheme, and the whole system collapses and forfeits its identity. In this regard Aristotle is not just one philosopher among many; he is, as we read again and again, 'the Philosopher'. Even Plato was to be received through Aristotle.[51]

Another way to record this point is to note that the fundamental epistemic system deployed by Aquinas was not derived from Scripture. Nor was it even derived from the insights and suggestions of the early Christian Fathers. Its basic elements were taken from Aristotle. Moreover, the vision of Scripture developed was dictated by those elements as reworked by Aquinas. Hence the conception of canon deployed by Aquinas was not derived from a study of what canonization may have meant in the patristic period, or from diligent observations regarding the nature of Scripture itself. It was derived from the epistemic theory which was developed by Aristotle and from Aristotle. The obvious problem in this is that the canon was made captive to Aristotle. Despite protestations to the contrary, Aristotelian convictions about knowledge determined at a basic level the inner structure of the Christian tradition. That all this could be presented in a

---

[49] Aquinas once suggested that those who 'use philosophical texts in teaching, by subjugating them to faith, do not mix water and wine, but turn water into wine' (quoted in Mark D. Jordan, *The Alleged Aristotelianism of Thomas Aquinas* (Toronto: Pontifical Institute of Medieval Studies, 1992), 33). Jordan's book is an erudite account of the limited place of Aristotle in Aquinas which fails to see the consequences of the adoption of Aristotle's epistemology for the construal and character of Scripture and Christian tradition.

[50] We leave aside the whole question of the Neoplatonic elements present in the thought of Aquinas.

[51] See Byrne, *Probability and Opinion*, 110, who writes that Aquinas tells us 'in his commentary on the *Politics*, that the opinions of Plato are known only by way of Aristotle'.

way which insisted on the autonomy of theology in the strongest terms possible and which gave to Scripture the most exalted position imaginable in the life of the Church is truly amazing and ironic.

Once Aquinas himself was canonized and identified as a doctor of the Church, if not *the* doctor of the Church, then Aristotelian convictions became canonical in a different sort of way. In the first instance, crucial elements of his thinking were put to work in the interpretation of one part of the canonical heritage: namely, its scriptural component. Once Aquinas's work was in turn added to the canonical heritage, then the role which Aristotle plays in that new corpus was set apart and sanctified. The degree to which Aristotle was constitutive of the thought of Aquinas was the degree to which Aristotle was canonized by the Church in the West. Even on the least estimates, we must reckon this as no mean achievement for a pagan philosopher.

Before providing a final summary, it is worth ruminating on the remarkable events which are associated with the death of Aquinas. It has been claimed that before he died Aquinas had a vision of God, in which he is reported to have told his long-serving companion, Reginald of Piperno, that he could not return to his work as a theologian: 'Reginald, I cannot, because all that I have written seems like straw to me.'[52] Were this experience and comment to be interpreted as confirmation of the claim that encounter with God is not a deepening of *scientia* but total and absolute silence in the mysterious presence of God, it could also be taken as a repudiation of the whole import of Aquinas's teaching. One would have expected as honest and careful a scholar as Aquinas to have made this known to us if it were so. The more likely explanation is that Aquinas was perfectly able to accommodate his experience to the epistemology which he had so carefully developed.

We know that this incident, this mystical experience, if it happened, took place while Aquinas was on his way to the Council of Lyons, one of the two unity councils summoned to deal with the division between East and West. Even the least curious must wonder if his presence there might have made any difference to the fateful discussions which took place. It would be

---

[52] Davies, *Thought of Thomas Aquinas*, 9.

nice to believe that he might have at least toned down the opposition clearly visible in his treatment of those who did not share
his judgement on the *filioque* clause. Yet it is difficult to believe
that Aquinas would have been anything but a formidable opponent of those who came from the East. He was too committed to
theology as *scientia*, too confident about the status of Aristotle in
any accurate analysis of human reasoning, and too sure that the
Church in the West was right, for anyone to expect the outcome
to have been radically different from what it was. Even if we are
wrong in these speculations, it now no longer matters. The ink
has been spilt, and it cannot be gathered up again. The Church in
the West canonized not the mystical experience of Aquinas but
the writings which had preoccupied him during his demanding
and saintly life. Even if his work is attacked by theologians of his
own tradition, even if it suffers the more deadly fate of icy indif-
ference, it still stands as a monumental achievement in Christian
theology. In addition, it still stands as canonical for many Western
Christians.

The import of the developments brought about by Aquinas are
by now clear. He inherited a tradition which had already moved
to treat the complex canonical heritage of the Church in normative, epistemic categories. The papacy, representing the see of
Rome, had been proposed as a crucial epistemic institution
which, under appropriate circumstances not yet fully worked out,
settled crucial disputed matters in the Church, not just from the
point of view of governance but from the point of view of truth
itself. Behind this lay a complex theory of divine revelation
which began informally and without any official sanction to treat
the Scriptures as identical with the written words of God and
therefore foundational for everything else in theology. Aquinas
gathered these up and placed them in a brilliant network of
formal, epistemic theory which attempted to show that the
Church had access to the only knowledge really worth having,
God's own knowledge. The Church could have in its teaching
nothing less than divine *scientia*. Within this he developed a
correlative account of the canon of Scripture. Scripture became
the foundation of sacred *scientia*, which, given its special origins in
God, could stand up to any and all criticism. Other canonical
material which did not fit this scheme, such as iconography,
simply dropped quietly out of sight and was relocated elsewhere,

or, like the Creed, was suitably reconstituted as mere summaries of the Scriptures, or, like the Fathers, were transposed into special authorities called Doctors. Even obscure eschatological material—namely, the experience of the beatific vision—was interpreted to serve the epistemic ends engendered by the deep Aristotelian themes and convictions which had been borrowed to construct the epistemic theory desired.

If treated as a speculative epistemological suggestion, which the Church might draw on to fulfil its intellectual responsibilities at a fascinating juncture in its pilgrimage in the thirteenth century, this would be a jewel in the crown of its intellectual endeavours. In time, the harmful consequences for the canonical heritage of the Church could be repaired. Other epistemic proposals could be offered. A different vision of divine revelation, which would make sense of the crucial place of Scripture in the total life of the Church, yet without jeopardizing other elements of the canonical heritage, might be pursued. But Aquinas's proposals were not received in this manner. Aquinas acquired a canonical status which ensured that his work would be construed as more than epistemic speculation. It became a model for the Christian theologian and, in the hands of the leadership of the Western Church, became constitutive of the intellectual identity of the Christian faith. The difference all this made for the division and history of the Church has been incalculable.

5

Theological Foundationalism

By the time of the Reformation in the Western Church the biblical and patristic heritage of the early Church was received and construed in significantly different ways. The external expression of this divide was the explicit and official schism between East and West. The internal manifestation was constituted by radical differences in the interpretation and identification of the canonical heritage of the Church.

Canonical division in no way suggests, of course, that there were not significant areas of agreement between the two halves of the Christian tradition. On the contrary, there was much in common. Both sides shared the same Scriptures, the same sacraments, many of the same dogmas, many of the same councils, many of the same Fathers, common monastic traditions, similar tacit convictions about the cruciality of divine revelation as the primary ground of the whole Christian scheme of things, and the like. They also shared many of the same problems, not least of which was the deep entanglement of the political powers in the life of the Church. Yet the differences were deep enough to cause a break which has not yet been resolved, despite strenuous efforts on both sides to heal the breach.

I have named the crucial differences as canonical in character because they involve competing accounts of the canons of the Church. The canons of the Church, we proposed, began life as relatively informal, non-theoretical affairs. Thus the sacraments, canonical practices *par excellence*, were clearly present in the Church from the beginning, handed down through the apostles from generation to generation. The separate books that made up the canon of the New Testament were written relatively early on, but their collection into a single canon, or list, took centuries to be worked out. It was likewise with the Creed and the Chalcedonian Definition, the development of the liturgy, the appearance of iconography, the tacit acceptance of the internal structures of the Church in councils and offices, the canonization of saints and teachers, and the development of various regulations governing the internal life of the Church as a whole. In the end, a delicate synthesis of canonical materials, persons, and practices was elaborated.

It is far from easy to know precisely how best to describe these complex canonical traditions as they were understood in the patristic period. Nowhere are we given an explicit account of the internal components of the Church's life as a whole. It is doubtful if such an account could have been given in the patristic period, for one can only really see what is at stake by standing back and reviewing the development as a whole, and this cannot be done while the canonical materials are themselves being identified and articulated.

In attempting to give a tacit account which would fit with the writings and practices available, my favoured category is that of means of grace. Thus the sacraments, the Scriptures, the Creed, the canon of Fathers, and the like, I am suggesting, were construed as materials and practices which fed the soul, which mediated the life of God, which returned human beings to their true destiny as children of God, and which ultimately led to a life of sanctity. Alternatively, we might say that they were seen as gifts of the Holy Spirit in the life of the Church, intended to bring about participation in the life of God through the working of the same Spirit, who guided the Church in their selection and use.

This account is at once substantial and modest. It is substantial because it has profound consequences as to how these practices and materials were received and used. Thus they were approached in a spirit of humility and faith, accepted gratefully as medicine to heal the sickness of the world. It is modest because it leaves open a host of questions which can take a lifetime to unravel, much less resolve. Thus, although virtually everyone held that canonical materials, especially the Scriptures, were divinely inspired, no particular doctrine of inspiration was canonized. Moreover, the canons did not in themselves provide explicit answers to the deep questions about divine revelation and knowledge which their content and their actual use naturally evoked. Hence, although the use of the early canons in the Church clearly involved a coming to know God in a very deep way in the life of the Church, the canons were relatively reticent about how we are to think of it and about how we might relate this knowledge to other species of knowledge we might want to identify. In short, they did not generally supply any kind of explicit epistemology, not even an explicit religious epistemology.

Yet there were clearly tacit commitments to some kind of vision of divine revelation undergirding the canonical materials and practices of the Church, and there were all sorts of epistemic suggestions and practices lying in wait to be articulated and developed. Moreover, the central content of the canonical materials themselves and the appearance of sharp canonical disagreement in the Church were liable to cause all sorts of epistemological theorizing and speculation. Both ordinary Christian and advanced teachers of the tradition found it difficult to avoid reflecting on what they were convinced they had come to know in the canonical life of the Church. The canonization of Fathers late on in the canonical developments of the Church bears witness both to the secondary, yet inevitable, nature of this kind of deliberation. In the end, deep questions about the nature of knowledge of the divine could not be avoided. They were intrinsically interesting, as one can see very powerfully in the writings of Augustine;[1] and they were essential to the welfare of the Church, for doctrines about knowledge and related topics can have profound consequences, if only in a negative way, for the central claims made in the Scriptures, the creeds, the liturgy, and the like, as the writings of Gregory the Theologian readily display.[2]

This interpretation of the canonical heritage of the Church is offered primarily as a hypothesis about the interpretation of that heritage prior to the schism between East and West. It seeks to articulate a tacit understanding of the canonical heritage, as that heritage was developed and adopted. Secondarily, I am proposing that this account, at the very least, is compatible with the canonical vision owned by the Eastern wing of the Church during and

---

[1] Augustine's *Soliloquies* (Warminster: Aris and Phillips, 1990) are a marvellous example of this spirit.

[2] Most especially his *Theological Orations*, in Edward R. Hardy (ed.), *Christology of the Later Fathers* (Philadelphia: Westminster Press, 1954), 128–214.

after the schism.[3] In fact, it was this vision, or one very similar to
it in crucial respects, which, even though tacitly accepted, made
it impossible for the Eastern Churches to accept the canonical
changes gradually developed and articulated in the Roman tradition.[4] Moreover, both the continuing reception of the canonical
heritage of the patristic period in the Eastern Churches and the
additions made to that heritage were in keeping with the canonical vision of the early Church. Whether they lived up to this
vision is another matter entirely, of course; more often than not,
there is a wide gap between canonical aspiration and ecclesial
reality. By contrast, the Western Church articulated and developed the canonical heritage of the early Church in a very different way.

The initial canonical changes were changes in the material
content of the canonical heritage. The most conspicuous instance
of this was the addition of the *filioque* clause to the Creed. In
itself, given certain subtle interpretations of it, such a change
could well have been accommodated without schism.
Appropriate actions could have been taken in a general council of
the Church to reach agreement on this complex matter, but
efforts to this end failed on several occasions. However, for various reasons, this change was accompanied by concomitant
changes in the canons concerning the deep internal regulation of
the life of the Church. The fundamental issue which eventually
surfaced was the primacy and infallibility of the Roman see in
adjudicating disputed questions. The East took up a sophisticated
conciliar view, which gave authority to the Church as a whole
acting in a general council.[5] The West took an equally sophisti-

---

[3] Note that I am not making the stronger claim that this vision was in fact
the vision of the Church in the East. I suspect that many of the leaders of the
Church in the East were much more concerned to maintain the actual canonical
traditions of the Church rather than sustain any particular vision of the canonical
tradition as a whole. Many observers have been struck by the reticence of the
Church in the East to engage in second-order analysis of the tradition. Certainly
this is how it strikes me. If this observation is true, then it fits with the reticence
to deal formally with epistemological questions. This is often seen as a serious
weakness; if my longer argument holds good, it may well be extraordinarily
wise.

[4] I am not here denying that other very human factors were also involved.

[5] This possibility keeps recurring in the West, but it has never been able to
win the day.

cated position which rested ultimate authority in the appropriate judgement of the Pope of Rome. Both of these positions involved a contested claim about the locus of divine guidance in the Church. The East located divine guidance in the ultimate judgement of the whole Church, the West in the ultimate judgment of the Pope.

The articulation and deployment of a doctrine of papal infallibility had profound consequences for the canonical heritage of the Church. Whether seen positively or negatively, papal infallibility introduced the idea of one privileged locus of epistemic authority: namely, that of the magisterium of the Roman tradition.[6] Once papal infallibility was enunciated, there was now available, for those who accepted it, one place where all crucial matters of faith and practice could be ultimately resolved with certainty. Previous decisions of the Church could be confirmed, old disputes could be definitively determined, and new problems could be resolved. This was, and is, the deep attraction of the Roman tradition. There is now a living foundation which can be relied on to get things right for the faithful. Even the most complex epistemological questions about the relationship between faith and knowledge can in principle find a working resolution.[7]

On this analysis the institution of the papacy can, of course, be construed as a wonderful means of grace. Through appropriate decisions of the Pope, definitive answers can be given to controverted questions which have a bearing on the ultimate quest for holiness. However, the papacy represented much more than a means of grace; it represented also a kind of epistemic mechanism which could in principle be utilized to arrive at genuine knowledge. It provided not just a means of grace, but a norm of knowledge, a criterion of truth. Hence it introduced a whole new conception of one of the canonical components of the Church as a whole. It took what was originally a complex canonical practice, that of oversight exercised in the Church through council,

[6] Note that I am not claiming that there was only one locus of authority. This would completely misrepresent the subtlety of the Roman position.

[7] This does not entail that the Roman Church claims to be a philosophical magisterium. There are hosts of philosophical questions which lie outside the boundaries of those philosophical queries which impinge on matters of faith, which the Church leaves open.

episcopate, Fathers, and the like, and after focusing the work of all these in one person, transformed certain of his intellectual acts into a criterion of truth.

Another way to express this claim is to say that the deployment of papal infallibility transformed what was originally a tacit claim about divine guidance in the Church as a whole into an explicitly formulated canon of divine revelation which gave precedence to the Pope in resolving crucial disputes about the very content and meaning of divine revelation itself. Thus two canonical changes were really taking place at once. A complex practice was transformed into a norm of truth, which was constructed by making what was originally one part of a tacit vision of divine revelation into an explicit and canonical theory of special revelation. This complex development represented a radical reconception of the canonical heritage of the Church. It constituted a deep epistemizing of the canons of the Church.

From this point on, the very description of the canonical heritage as a whole was changed to fit this new interpretation. The debate in the West now centred on the relative merits of such entities as Scripture, tradition, and Western magisterium. It became increasingly difficult to recall that the canonical tradition was a complex and subtle configuration of Scripture, liturgy, sacraments, iconography, Fathers, the Creed, the Chalcedonian Definition, Church councils, bishops, sundry regulations on the internal ordering of the life of the Church, and the like. These materials, holy persons, and practices, with all the rough edges which go with their reality and their enumeration, were suitably divided up into manageable epistemic entities like revelation, tradition, Scripture, teaching magisterium, so that they could be discussed as solutions to problems in religious epistemology. Moreover, the tacit counsels on the usage and reception of the canonical heritage were subordinated to the supposedly deeper concern to have at hand the appropriate foundations of a theological science.

This process was accompanied in the Western Church by a concomitant alteration in the list of Fathers to be identified as the great teachers of the Church. Thus Augustine, whose own theological speculations about, say, the *filioque* were never intended to be anything other than ingenious speculation, became an oracle, displacing the other great Fathers of the early Church from their rightful place in the economy of the Church. Brilliant efforts to turn theology into a special kind of science, as represented by Aquinas, became canonical for the Church as a whole. Consequently, the pressure to develop theology as the queen of the sciences in the university fostered the interpretation of the canons as the foundations of truth. Mystical and experiential elements in the acquisition of knowledge of God, which were tacitly crucial to the early teachers of the faith, while not utterly rejected, tended to be held in suspicion or systematically marginalized. Furthermore, the ultimately mysterious character of the divine life tended to be treated as a challenge to be overcome intellectually by the skill of the human mind working from divine revelation, rather than as a final barrier whose outskirts, where they could be engaged at all, could be reached only by a divine transformation of the whole human person bathed in a spirit of complete repentance and humility.

Seen from this angle, the canonical proposals of the Reformers represent a flowering of the canonical developments in the Church of the West. The changes introduced by Luther and Calvin were sufficient to precipitate a further schism in the Church and to evoke profound theological consequences in their own right; yet in their formal nature they did not alter the fundamental conception of canon which was already taking shape in the Roman tradition. In fact, they only cemented and solidified the radical epistemizing of the canons of the Church already developing. In short, the Reformation kept in place the fundamental conception of canonicity already at work in the medieval tradition. It was neither a radical break from the fundamental canonical vision of the Church in the West nor a radical return to the canonical paradigm of the early Church.[8]

[8] There is a very strong tendency among scholars to lump together the patristic and medieval visions of canonicity in the Church, as if these visions represent a single paradigm of canonical development and understanding. Thus Gerrish sees the patristic and medieval Church as inheriting a kind of Jewish biblicism in the form of a theory of divine inspiration which was qualified by the growth of allegorization and by the development of ecclesiastical hierarchy. See e.g. B. A. Gerrish, *The Old and New Protestantism* (Edinburgh: T. & T. Clark, 1982), 51–3. Gerrish maintains this view despite the fact that he informs us in a footnote that there were actually two strikingly different theories of inspiration prevalent in the early Church (ibid. 290). Gerrish's analysis is typical in that (a) it presupposes that canonicity in the early Church was exclusively a

This may come as a surprise to those observers who hold to the popular and conventional accounts of the changes associated with the Reformation.[9] On that account the Reformation made a complete canonical break with the Roman tradition. Yet, it is now increasingly realized in narratives of the Reformation that the continuity between the Reformers and the medieval tradition at a deep structural level is very considerable.[10] The main burden of the argument which follows is to show that, material differences notwithstanding, the adoption of the canon of Scripture as the sole source and ground of theology does not constitute at all a radical formal break from the Roman tradition. It simply represents a particular rendering of the epistemizing of the canonical life of the Church in the Protestant traditions. In what follows I shall discuss the relevant issues as they occur in Luther and Calvin, and then very briefly in the Reformation Confessions. Thereafter, I shall stand back and draw attention to the significance of the whole Reformation enterprise.

The crucial factor which holds all these traditions together is that they involve an appeal to *sola scriptura* as the ultimate norm of truth and propriety for the life and faith of the Church.[11] This

matter of the canonicity of the Bible, and (b) it sets enormous store by theories of inspiration in working out an analysis of canonicity in the early Church. Both these assumptions are very seriously misleading in any attempt to get as clear a picture as we can of canonical developments in the early Church. They betray the effects of later theories of canon on our contemporary reading of the materials.

[9] The heart of these accounts is that the Reformers developed a wholly different canonical vision from that available in the Roman Catholic tradition. In what follows I shall argue that the changes are purely material in nature: that is, they revolve around what *counts* as canon. They do not revolve around how we are to *construe* the canon. Canon, however materially identified, continues to be construed fundamentally as a norm of truth: that is, as an item in epistemology.

[10] See e.g. Heiko Augustinus Oberman, *The Harvest of Medieval Theology* (Durham, NC: Labyrinth Press, 1983), 361–422.

[11] 'Without exception, the early sixteenth century reformers appealed to Holy Scripture as the ultimate authority for the faith and life of the Church. Based on this authority, they did not hesitate to criticize ecclesiastical tradition or authority where they felt such criticism was needed. In theory as well as in practice, Holy Scripture was the supreme canon' (Ralph Arthur Bohlmann, 'The Criteria of Biblical Canonicity in Sixteenth-Century Lutheran, Roman Catholic, and Reformed Theology' (Ph.D. thesis, Yale University, 1968), 99). This thesis is a very valuable discussion of the canonicity of Scripture in the sixteenth century. David W. Lotz also stresses the epistemic conception of

began life as a proposal, and ended as a carefully developed principle in most of the Confessions of the Reformation Churches.

Luther began his work as a relatively conservative, medieval Roman Catholic. He did not believe that his struggle to reform the Church of his day required him to depart in any serious way from the canonical heritage of the Church.

I was so drunk, yes, so submerged in the pope's dogmas, that I would have been ready to murder all, if I could have, or to co-operate willingly with the murderers of all who would take but a syllable from obedience to the pope. So great a Saul was I, as are many to this day.[12]

Provoked by Eck at a debate in Leipzig during the summer of 1519, he denied that the Pope was head of the Church by divine right.[13] In due course he moved beyond this to claim that the Scriptures alone constituted the norm of truth in theology. In and around this claim Luther developed extensive proposals concerning the nature of the Gospel, the location of the Word of God, and the boundaries of Scripture.

His appeal to Scripture against the received tradition of the Church is nicely illustrated in one of his arguments in *The Babylonian Captivity of the Church*:

Some time ago, when I was drinking in scholastic theology, the learned cardinal of Cambrai gave me food for thought in his comments on the fourth book of the *Sentences*. He argues with great acumen that to hold that real bread and real wine, and not merely the accidents, are present on the altar, would be much more probable and require fewer superfluous miracles—if only the church did not decree otherwise. When I learned later what church it was that decreed this namely the Thomistic—that is, the Aristotelian church—I grew bolder, and after floating in a sea of doubt, I at last found rest for my conscience in the above view, namely, that it is real bread and wine, in which Christ's real

canon for Luther: 'For present purposes, therefore, I shall take for granted the indisputable fact *that* Luther insisted upon Scripture's sole normative authority for Christian faith and life. My intent, rather, is to show *why* Luther ascribed such authority to the Bible' ('Sola Scriptura: Luther on Biblical Authority', *Interpretation*, 35 (1981), 260).

[12] 'Preface to the Complete Edition of Luther's Latin Writings', in Theodore G. Tappert, *Selected Writings of Martin Luther, 1517–1520* (Philadelphia: Fortress Press, 1967), i. 18.

[13] The significance of the Leipzig debate for the development of Luther's position is well brought out by Gerrish (*Old and New Protestantism*, 54).

flesh and blood are present in no other way and to no less a degree than others assert them to be under their accidents. I reached this conclusion because I saw the opinions of the Thomists, whether approved by pope or by council, remain only opinions, and would not become articles of faith even if an angel from heaven were to decree otherwise [Gal. 1: 8]. *For what is asserted without the scriptures or proven revelation may be held as an opinion, but need not be believed.*[14]

What this might suggest is that Luther looked for a revelation outside Scripture. This is not the case. The content of divine revelation is constituted by Christ. Indeed, the very boundaries of Scripture are determined by what Christ preaches to helpless sinners, making possible their justification by faith alone. Before we explore these themes, it is worth noting Luther's fuller exposition of his vision of Scripture in his treatise *On the Councils and the Church*.

Luther held the Fathers and the councils of the early Church in extremely high regard.[15] Yet his reservations expose a mind-set which clearly sees them in predominantly epistemological categories. Thus it is clear that he was profoundly unhappy with the various councils, because their proposals could no longer be followed in his day[16] or because, taken over time, they contradicted each other. In line with this, his more positive account of the councils reveals that he construed them in a juridical fashion, with Scripture functioning as the law to which exclusive and final appeal is made.

A council, then, is nothing but a consistory, a royal court, a supreme court, or the like in which the judge, after hearing the parties, pronounces sentence, but with this humility, 'For the sake of the law,' that is, 'Our office is *anathematizare*, "to condemn"; but not according

---

[14] Tappert, *Selected Writings*, 380–1; emphasis added.
[15] '[T]he writings of all the holy fathers should be read only for a time so that through them we may be led into the Scriptures. As it is, however, we only read them these days to avoid going any further and getting into the Bible. We are like men who read the signposts and never travel the road they indicate. Our dear fathers wanted to lead us to the Scriptures by their writings, but we use their works to get away from the Scriptures. Nevertheless, the Scripture alone is our vineyard in which we must all labor and toil' (ibid. 341).
[16] Luther wittily points out that if they were to follow the Council of Jerusalem, then German Christians would be forbidden from eating *Blutwurst* and from trapping rabbits by snares.

to our whim or will, or newly invented law, but according to the ancient law, which is acknowledged as the law throughout the entire empire.' Thus a council condemns a heretic, not according to its own discretion, but according to the law of the empire, that is, according to Holy Scripture, which they confess to be the law of the holy church. Such law, empire, and judge must surely be feared on pain of eternal damnation. This law is God's word, the empire is God's church; the judge is the official or servant of both.[17]

Such is Luther's confidence in God's word, that its possession constituted the first and, if need be, the exclusive sign of the existence of the Church, the holy Christian people.

Now, whenever you hear or see this word preached, believed, professed, and lived, do not doubt that the *ecclesia sancta catholica*, 'a Christian holy people' must be there, even though their number is very small. For God's word 'shall not return empty,' Isaiah 55 [: 11], but must return at least a fourth or a fraction of the field. And even if there were no other sign than this alone, it would suffice to prove that a Christian, a holy people must exist there, for God's word cannot be without God's people, and conversely, God's people cannot be without God's word. Otherwise, who would preach or hear it preached, if there were no people of God? And what could or would God's people believe, if there were no word from God?[18]

For Luther that word from God had a very particular content. At one level it can accurately be described as Jesus Christ, the eternal Word of God. Yet for Luther Christ is not simply some past historical figure, divorced abstractly from the message he embodies. Jesus Christ stood as a kind of cipher for the message of justification by faith, for in encountering Christ in Scripture Luther had found a saviour who received him as a sinner in mercy, independently of any works on his part. This word Luther received as profoundly liberating and transforming for his own life and for that of the Church as whole. Moreover, the gospel of Christ was not something received in a purely human way; it was received in the power of the Holy Spirit, who was intimately involved in the origin and reception of the Scriptures, the written Word of God. Hence Luther had a very comprehensive doctrine

[17] *On the Councils and the Churches*, in Theodore G. Tappert (ed.), *Selected Writings of Martin Luther, 1539–1546* (Philadelphia: Fortress Press, 1967), iv. 325. [18] Ibid. 342.

of canonical authority, even though in constructing it we have to pull together a body of unsystematic materials.

We might summarize the central components of Luther's vision of canon as follows. First, Luther received the canon more or less as it had been bequeathed to him by the Church of his day. Even though he excluded some of the books accepted in the current Vulgate and German editions, he did not offer a reconstruction of the canon as a whole. He was on the whole a traditionalist on the extent of the canon.[19]

Second, within the canonical books received he distinguished between those which were biblical and those which were scriptural. Thus Luther could say that 2 Maccabees was 'the most inferior and contemptible book in the whole Bible' and is not to be counted 'among the books of Holy Scripture'.[20] Here we have at work a distinction between biblical books and scriptural books. Thus for Luther, for a time at least, 'bible' was a wider concept than 'scripture'.[21] Here, in all probability, he was drawing on a distinction which had a long pedigree, reaching back as far as Jerome, whose influence in the Western Church as a whole on issues of canon had been phenomenal.[22] That distinction was between those books which were useful and good to read and those books which were useful as a basis for dogma, for convinc-

---

[19] The details of Luther's account of the extent of the canon are well laid out in Bohlmann, 'Criteria of Biblical Canonicity', 100–18.

[20] Ibid. 104.

[21] This kind of distinction was not entirely foreign to the theologians of the early sixteenth century. Cardinal Cajetan developed a double concept of canon which was closely parallel to that of Luther. Thus the Septuagint additions to the Old Testament 'are not canonical, that is, they are not normative for confirming those things which are of faith. Nevertheless they can be called canonical, that is, normative for the edification of the faithful' (quoted in Bohlmann, 'Criteria of Biblical Canonicity', 88). We can see here the epistemizing of the concept of canon as applied to Scripture take place before our very eyes.

[22] In Jerome the distinction is well made in the following passage: 'As, then, the Church reads Judith, Tobit, and the books of Maccabees, but does not admit them among the canonical Scriptures, so let it read these two volumes for the edification of the people, not to give authority to doctrines of the Church.' (Henry Wace and Philip Schaff (eds.), *A Select Library of Nicene and Post-Nicene Fathers of the Christian Church* (14 vols., New York: Charles Scribner's Sons, 1917), 2nd series, vi. 492.)

ing a gainsayer, or for proving a point in theological debate.[23] It was the latter books which were scriptural. What we see here is that Luther was clearly enunciating a thoroughly epistemic conception of the canon. Scriptural material is demarcated by its epistemic properties: it is material which is useful as a basis for dogma. Even as Luther pursues this line, we can see peeping through from behind the scenes another conception of canon, here captured by his concept of Bible, which has not yet reduced it to epistemic proportions.

Third, in resolving the canonical status of disputed books, Luther decided this on the ground of apostolicity; but apostolicity was not a purely historical designation. It was, in fact, a dogmatic criterion constituted by what preached Christ clearly.

All the genuine sacred books agree in this, that all of them preach and inculcate (*treiben*) Christ. And that is the true test by which to judge all books, when we see whether or not they inculcate Christ. For all the Scriptures show us Christ, Romans 3 [: 21]; and St. Paul will know nothing but Christ, 1 Corinthians 2 [: 2]. What does not teach Christ is not apostolic, even though St. Peter or Paul does the teaching. Again, what preaches Christ would be apostolic even if Judas, Annas, Pilate, and Herod did it.[24]

It was this conviction which allowed Luther to accept the canonicity of 2 Peter and 2 and 3 John but led him to challenge the canonical status of James and Revelation.[25] Implicit in this proposal is the conviction that, practically speaking, the historical apostles did in fact preach Christ clearly. Hence Luther can move

---

[23] This distinction is pivotal for a host of theologians. Bohlmann supplies evidence that it occurred in Hugo of St Cher, William of Occam, Nicholas of Lyra, Wyclif, Alphonsus Tostatus, John Froben, and Erasmus ('Criteria of Biblical Canonicity', chs. 1 and 2).

[24] *Preface to the Epistles of St. James and St. Jude*, in *Luther's Works* (St Louis: Concordia Press, 1955), xxxv. 396.

[25] Luther's objection to James was that it mentioned Christ but failed to preach him: that is, present him as saviour from sin. It is for this reason that Luther wants to dismiss James as a letter of straw. 'One of these days I'll use Jimmy to light the fire!' (see Gerrish, *Old and New Protestantism*, 55). There is an amusing proposal in Karlstadt, one of Luther's colleagues, that Luther's opposition to James was designed to keep students away from Karlstadt's course on James. Karlstadt claimed that Luther would have challenged the canonicity of Matthew if he had taught a course on it. See Bohlmann, 'Criteria of Biblical Canonicity', 82.

from a core set of texts in Paul and John, which he sees as both apostolic and clear in their presentation of Christ, to include other material as properly canonical.[26]

This move had the further consequence of rejecting the Church as the criterion of canonicity. Canonical books were not canonical because the Church set them apart as such; they were canonical because they preached Christ, the eternal Word of God, who had become incarnate in the flesh for the salvation of sinners. For Luther to have accepted that the Scriptures were canonical because they were canonized by the Church would have been to interpret the Church's judgement as more foundational than that of Scripture itself. It would have undermined the whole point of his appeal to Scripture as the ultimate norm of all theological judgements, putting the norm precariously back into the hands of humans.

Fourth, the eternal Word encountered in the apostolic Gospel was at work through the Holy Spirit in the production of the written word. The ultimate author of the written word was God, or the Holy Spirit. Hence Scripture was reliable and inerrant in what it said.[27] Not surprisingly, Luther deploys here a doctrine of inspiration which construes the divine activity involved as that of divine speaking.[28] He puts the matter succinctly: 'Holy Scripture

---

[26] This is brought out most clearly in Luther's prefaces to his German New Testament. In a section entitled 'Which are the true and noblest books of the New Testament', he says that 'St John's Gospel and St Paul's epistles, especially that to the Romans, and St Peter's first epistle are the true kernel and marrow of all the books'. He later includes Ephesians and Galatians in this group. See Bohlmann, 'Criteria of Biblical Canonicity', 114.

[27] Many modern interpreters of Luther have been embarrassed by this component in Luther's account of the authority of Scripture. For an unsuccessful attempt to eliminate this line of argument in Luther see Lotz, 'Sola Scriptura', 267–9. Lotz's aim here is to drive a deep wedge between Luther and his later 'scholastic' followers and thereby create room for an appeal to Luther which would underwrite an account of Scripture more 'existentialist' and doxological in character and thus immune to objections derived from historical criticism. Aside from the historical difficulties in Lotz's argument, this whole operation depends on treating Luther as a kind of new Father of the Church; only this time he is a Protestant Father whose canonical theory has absolutely no room for such a canon.

[28] It is this kind of confusing talk which paves the way for the construal of divine inspiration as a form of divine dictation. Those sympathetic to Luther and the other Reformers who held such a view generally see this as an improvement

has been spoken by the Holy Spirit.'[29] Not surprisingly, Luther
also attributes deep significance to the exact details of the biblical
text. He can do this because he will not allow human judgement
or reason to act as any kind of ultimate norm in theological
matters. The truth by which we are to be governed is located in
the wisdom of God, which has been delivered in the divine
Scriptures.

We can see in all of this an integrated account of canon,
gospel, apostolicity, salvation, divine speaking, and truth which is
clearly taking a foundationalist direction. Luther is proposing to
ground all of Christian life and thinking exclusively on the canon
of Scripture. His position is nicely laid out in this way:

All Scripture is to be understood alone through that Spirit who wrote it.
This Spirit you cannot find more securely present and active anywhere
than in these Sacred Scriptures, which He Himself wrote. Our endeavor
must, therefore, not be to put aside Scripture and to direct our attention
to the merely human writing of the fathers. On the contrary, putting
aside all human writings, we should spend all the more and all the more
persistent labor on Holy Scriptures alone. . . . Or tell me, if you can, who
is the final judge when statements of the fathers contradict themselves? In
this event the judgment of Scripture must decide the issue, which cannot
be done if we do not give scripture the first place . . . so that it is in itself
the most certain, most easily understood, most plain, is its own interpreter, approving, judging, and illuminating all the statements of all men.

on later theories of 'mechanical' dictation, which everyone takes pains to exco-
riate. This is an absurd line of reasoning. Later theories abandoned theories of
dictation in favour of a complicated theory of divine concurrence, which at least
recognized that it is a serious conceptual mistake to think of divine inspiration as
a form of divine dictation. The whole problem lies precisely with the
Reformers' marriage of a particular vision of divine inspiration, an integral part
of their theology, to the determination to see Scripture straightforwardly and
primarily as an epistemic norm for theology. The Reformers were not the first
to confuse divine inspiration with divine speaking or divine dictation, but they
certainly gave this whole way of reading Scripture an enormous shot in the arm.
I have discussed this matter at some length in *The Divine Inspiration of Holy
Scripture* (Oxford: Oxford University Press, 1981).

[29] Quoted in Gerrish, *Old and New Protestantism*, 55. Gerrish provides an
excellent rendering of Luther's position on this highly charged issue (ibid. 54–7.
Richard A. Muller also provides a valuable service in seeking to do justice to the
various dimensions of Luther's position on Scripture. See his *Post-Reformation
Reformed Dogmatics*, ii: *Holy Scripture: The Cognitive Foundation of Theology* (Grand
Rapids, Mich.: Baker, 1993), 53–7.

. . . Therefore nothing except the divine words are to be the first principles (prima principia) for Christians; all human words are conclusions drawn from them and must be brought back to them and approved by them.[30]

It is a small step from this to a full-blown, exclusivist theological foundationalism which would insist that the Christian can attain certainty in those beliefs and only those beliefs which can be derived from Scripture.

Is it appropriate to attribute such a position to Luther? Luther probably never explicitly or formally committed himself to this doctrine. However, Luther did express himself at times in such a way as to make this at the very least a possible reading of his position. We can identify several claims in his writings which, when taken together, support such a reading.

To begin, Luther clearly believes in the attainment of truth and the rejection of scepticism.

Not to delight in assertions is not becoming to a Christian heart. Nay, a man must delight in assertions, or he is no Christian at all. But (lest we play with words) I call an assertion a constant adhering, affirming, confessing, defending, and invincibly preserving. . . . Furthermore, I am speaking about the asserting of those things which have been divinely delivered to us in Holy Writ. . . . Far removed be skeptics and academics from us Christians. But there may be with us more asserters who are twice as stubborn as the Stoics. . . . But why is it necessary to multiply words? Nothing is better known and thought among Christians than a firm assertion. Take assertions away, and you have taken Christianity away.[31]

A Christian rather says this: I so strongly dislike the sentiments of skeptics that, wherever the weakness of the flesh does not hinder me, I will not only constantly, everywhere, and in all parts adhere to Holy Writ and assert it, but I also desire to be as certain as possible in matters that are not necessary and lie outside Scripture. For what is more miserable than uncertainty?[32]

---

[30] *Assertio Omnium Articulorum M. Lutheri per bullam Leonis X, in D. Martin Luther's Werke* (Weimar: H. Bohlau, 1883), vii. 96–8; emphasis added. The translation used here is that found in *What Luther Says*, compiled by Ewald M. Plass (St Louis: Concordia Press, 1959), 87–8. This latter volume constitutes a remarkable collection of Luther's ideas which not only gathers up Luther's thoughts on various topics but also bears witness to one significant way in which Luther has been received in the Lutheran tradition.

[31] *The Bondage of the Will*, in *Luther's Works*, xxxiii. 19–20.

[32] Ibid. 22.

The Holy Spirit is no skeptic, nor has he written doubts and mere opinions into our hearts. He has written assertions more certain and firmer than life itself and all human experience.[33]

Where can this certainty be found?[34] In the following passages Luther's answers are very suggestive of theological foundationalism: that is, the view that theological claims are true if and only if they are grounded in, or proved from, Scripture. Thus, speaking of the Emperor Charles concerning his certainty about the persecution of Protestants, he writes:

We are not bound to believe that he is sure, for he goes his way against the Word of God, and we have the Word of God. Rather it is his duty to recognize the Word of God and further it with all his powers, as we do. It would mean nothing if a murderer or an adulterer were to pretend: I am right; therefore you must sanction my deed because I am sure of my case. *It is his duty to produce a clear word of God as a proof of his undertaking.*[35]

Speaking of the need for the individual to be sure of his grounds he writes:

Everyone must take care to be certain and sure of the doctrine by himself and must not found his certainty on what other people have determined and concluded. If you do not do this, the Holy Spirit is bound soon to let you suffer a humiliating defeat. If you are to be saved, you must personally be so certain of the Word of grace that though all human beings were to speak differently, nay, all angels were to say no, you could stand alone and say: Nevertheless, I know this word is right.[36]

---

[33] Ibid. 24.

[34] The issue of certainty had become an important matter as a result of disputes in the medieval period which called into question the identity of the boundaries of Scripture and the identity of the Pope. Joseph Lortz describes the situation as follows, albeit with a Roman Catholic gloss: 'Thus we can sum up: There existed in the late Middle Ages a dangerous theological uncertainty of such a degree that it was relatively easy for a theologically independent man to become a heretic' (*How the Reformation Came* (New York: Herder and Herder, 1964), 63).

[35] Letter to Melanchthon, 8 Sept. 1530, in the Weimar edition of the letters, *Briefe* (Weimar: Böhlau, 1883), 614–15. The translation used here is from Plass (comp.), *What Luther Says*, sec. 4488; emphasis added.

[36] From a sermon of 1524, in *D. Martin Luther's Werke*, xv. 582. The translation used here is from Plass, *What Luther Says*, sec. 4490; emphasis added.

In his comment on Matthew 7: 15 he gives the following advice:

Everyone should see to it, above all, that he is sure of his cause and his doctrine. In his heart he should be so well grounded in it that he can stick to the doctrine even though he sees everyone on earth teaching and living the contrary to it. Anyone who wants to move along in safety simply dare not pay attention to any of the outward masks of Christendom and guide himself by them. He must pay attention only to the Word, which shows us the right way of life that avails for God.[37]

The crucial test of the grounding of our beliefs and convictions will come at death. So Luther says:

See to it that you are well armed and fortified so that you are able to stand before God and the world when you are assailed, and especially when the devil attacks you in the hour of death. It is not enough to intend to say: This man and that have done the same thing. . . . I followed the crowd, as the provost, Dr. Carlstadt, Gabriel, or Michael preached. No! Everyone must stand on his own feet and be prepared to give battle to the devil. *You must ground yourself on a strong and clear passage of scripture with which you may stand the test. If you do not possess it, you cannot stand the trial.* Then the devil will pluck you like a withered leaf.[38]

The only options that Luther seriously considers here as possible grounds for belief are tradition, human reasoning, and Scripture. The first two are unreliable; hence certainty can be attained only by deriving one's beliefs and convictions from the word of Scripture. If one does not derive one's beliefs from Scripture, then one will not have attained the truth about God. There is, then, only one foundation for the truth about God, and it is one's epistemic duty, as well as the only safeguard for one's spiritual salvation, to be sure that all one's beliefs are properly grounded on this foundation.

It should come as no surprise in the light of this that Luther insists that the message of Scripture is clear, for obviously a foundation which was essentially obscure in its content would be useless in resolving disputed questions.

---

[37] From *The Sermon on the Mount*, in *Luther's Works*, xxi. 254. The translation is from Plass, *What Luther Says*, sec. 4499; emphasis added.

[38] From the 'Third *Sermon*, 11 March 1522 Tuesday after *Invocavit*', in *Luther's Works*, li. 79–80. The translation is from Plass, *What Luther Says*, sec. 4501; emphasis added.

Holy Scripture must certainly be clearer, plainer, and more explicit than the writings of all others, because by it, as by a writing clearer and more reliable, all teachers prove their statements. And they all want their writing to be confirmed and clarified by it. But surely no one can prove an obscure statement with a more obscure statement. Therefore we must needs turn to Scripture with the writings of all teachers and from that source get our judgment and verdict concerning them. For Scripture alone is the true lord and master of all writing and teaching on earth.[39]

No clearer book has been written on earth than the Holy Scripture. It compares with other books as the sun with other lights. . . . It is a horrible shame and crime against the Holy Scripture and all Christendom to say that Holy Scripture is dark and not so clear that everybody may understand it in order to teach and prove his faith.[40]

If one does come across obscure passages, then the solution is to turn to the clear ones.

It is indeed true that some passages of Scripture are dark; however, they contain nothing but precisely that which is found at other places in clear, open passages. But now the heretics come on, understand the dark passages according to their own mind, and contend with them against the clear passages, the foundation of our faith.[41] Then the fathers fought them with the clear passages, threw light with these on the dark passages, and proved that the dark passages taught precisely the same thing as the clear passages.[42] . . . Be sure and do not doubt that nothing brighter exists than the sun, that is, the Scripture. But if a cloud has drifted behind it, there, after all, is nothing else behind it but the same

[39] From 'An Argument in Defence of all the Articles of Martin Luther Wrongly Condemned in the Roman Bull', in *Works of Martin Luther* (Philadelphia: A. J. Holman, 1915–32), iii. 16; quoted in Plass, *What Luther Says*, sec. 226; emphasis added.

[40] From 'Exposition of Psalm 37', in *D. Martin Luther's Werke*, viii. 236. The translation is from Plass, *What Luther Says*, sec. 222.

[41] Notice how the norm of truth is now shifting from the actual canon designated by Luther to another norm identified by what Luther takes to be the clear message of Scripture. Later scholastic Protestantism took this up and construed this material technically as a foundation within the foundation. See Muller, *Post-Reformation Reformed Dogmatics*, 211.

[42] Luther shows here that he is living in a fantasy land. The whole point of the 'rule of faith' was to act as a rebuttal to the heretics who twisted Scripture for their own purposes. It was precisely because the appeal to Scripture failed that other canonical material was in part developed, as I have already argued. The relationship between this material and Scripture is far more complex than Luther envisages here.

bright sun. Therefore if you come upon a dark passage in Scripture, do not doubt that it surely contains the same truth that is clearly expressed at other places; and whoever cannot understand the dark passage should stay with the clear ones.[43]

These observations are meant to draw attention to the fact that Luther clearly steps into the arena of epistemology when he begins thinking through his account of canonicity. To be sure, he is not interested in epistemology *per se*; nor does he provide a comprehensive account of knowledge. However, he is well aware of the possibility of scepticism in theology, and he provides an account as to how that scepticism is to be combated.[44] We see, then, how Luther's proposals about canon not only have an epistemic cast to them, but, placing them alongside his worries about scepticism, also how they fit into a deeper epistemic framework as to how the truth of God is to be attained. Luther was clearly looking for a foundation that would stand secure, that would settle contested questions, that would be the basis for any and every article of faith. And he was convinced that he had found it in the canon of Scripture, or at least in a canon of clearly demarcated material within the canon of Scripture. Here and only here could one rebuild the ruins of the Christian Church which in the West had been held captive by Rome.

John Calvin shared a similar interest in finding a way to provide adequate foundations for the life of the Church he felt called to rebuild. The continuities between Calvin and Luther are well known. Both rejected the authority of the Church; both had no confidence in the deliberations of natural reason; both saw the content of Scripture as intimately related to Christ and the promise of grace embodied in his death and resurrection; both insisted on the working of the Holy Spirit as essential to the hearing of the

---

[43] 'Exposition of Psalm 37', as translated and quoted in Plass, *What Luther Says*, sec. 229.

[44] Luther even took care of possible doubts about the capacity of the agent to read Scripture aright, a possibility which arose because of his doctrine of the effects of sin on human perception. 'If you speak of internal clearness, no human being sees one iota of Scripture unless he has the Spirit of God. All men have a darkened heart, so that even if they know how to tell and present all that scripture contains, yet they are unable to feel and truly know it. . . . For the Spirit is required to understand the whole of Scripture and every part of it' (*Bondage of the Will*, 28; quoted in Plass, *What Luther Says*, sec. 230).

Word; and both held a very exalted view of Scripture in the economy of coming to know God. Two elements in Calvin's position are of particular interest to us. First, Calvin developed a more rounded account of knowledge of God, within which he located his account of the authority of Scripture. Second, he provided an intriguing account of the internal witness of the Holy Spirit as absolutely essential to his account of the normative status of Scripture.

Scripture played a pivotal role in Calvin's theology in part because of the inadequacy of other ways of coming to know God in his grace and mercy. Hence he was thoroughly opposed to attempts to arrive at knowledge of God from observation of, or inference from, the natural order. Although human beings have a natural awareness of God, an implanted understanding of God's majesty, they do not foster this understanding, repelling all remembrance of God from their minds.[45] Not even the continued testimonies of God's wisdom avail to remedy human ignorance; on the contrary, they are met with ingratitude and with a tendency to twist the truth by the ravings or evil imaginations of our flesh, corrupting by vanity the pure truth of God. Without access to God's own self-designation, 'only the bare and empty name of God flits about in our brains, to the exclusion of the true God'.[46]

In response to this, God in the Scriptures has provided a way to come to knowledge of the truth.

. . . it is needful that another and better help be added to direct us aright to the very Creator of the universe. It was not in vain, then, that he added the light of his Word by which to become known unto salvation; and he gathered as worthy of this privilege those whom he pleased to gather more closely and intimately to himself. For because he saw the minds of all men tossed and agitated, after he chose the Jews as his own very flock, he fenced them about that they might not sink into oblivion as others did. With good reason he holds us by the same means in the pure knowledge of himself, since otherwise those who seem to stand firm before all others would soon melt away. Just as old or bleary-eyed men and those with weak vision, if you thrust before them a most beautiful

---

[45] This has very serious consequences for Calvin in that proper human self-understanding is logically related to knowledge of the divine.

[46] John Calvin, *Institutes of the Christian Religion*, ed. John T. McNeill, 2 vols., (Philadelphia: Westminster Press, 1960), I. xiii. 2.

volume, even if they recognize it to be some sort of writing, yet can scarcely construe two words, but with the aid of spectacles, will begin to read it distinctly; so Scripture, gathering up the otherwise confused knowledge of God in our minds, having dispersed our dullness, clearly shows us the true God. This therefore is a special gift, where God, to instruct the church, not merely uses mute teachers but also opens up his own most hallowed lips. Not only does he teach the elect to look upon a god, but also shows himself as the God upon whom they are to look. He has from the beginning maintained this plan for the church, so that beside these common proofs he also put forth his Word, which is a more direct and certain mark whereby he is to be recognized.[47]

Hence, if we are to learn about God, the place to which to turn is the Holy Scripture. 'Now, in order that true religion may shine upon us, we ought to hold that it must take its beginning from heavenly doctrine and that no one can get even the slightest taste of right and sound doctrine unless he be a pupil of scripture.'[48] It is here that we will find the 'rule of eternal truth'.[49] If we ignore this rule of truth, we will stagger about in vanity and error.

The question which naturally arises at this point is this: Why should we accept this rule of truth? There are in fact two distinct questions buried in this, as Calvin's discussion implicitly acknowledges, even though he did not formally distinguish them very carefully. We can take it as a question as to why we should believe God when he speaks to us or, more accurately, when he has spoken to us in his word, the Scriptures. Calvin's answer to this question is justly famous for its directness and candour.

When that which is set before us is acknowledged to be the Word of God, there is no one so deplorably insolent—unless devoid also both of common sense and of humanity itself—as to dare impugn the credibility of Him who speaks. Now daily oracles are not sent from heaven, for it pleased the Lord to hallow his truth to everlasting remembrance in the scriptures alone [cf. John 5: 39]. Hence the Scriptures obtain full authority among believers only when men regard them as having sprung from heaven, as if there the living words of God were heard.[50]

Calvin's view is entirely correct here. Given his view of Scripture—that is, that Scripture is the equivalent of hearing the

---

[47] John Calvin, *Institutes of the Christian Religion*, I. vi. 1.
[48] Ibid. I. vi. 2.   [49] Ibid. I. vi. 3.   [50] Ibid. I. vii. 1.

living words of God—then it should be believed immediately, for God on this analysis does not lie.[51] But this is only half the problem at issue. Everything hinges on what is acknowledged to be the Word of God. If we get the acknowledgement wrong, then we are still in the dark. So we have a second query on our hands: namely, how does Calvin know that the Christian Scriptures, and these alone, are indeed the Word of God?

We can recognize immediately from Calvin's answer that this is a new formulation of an older question about canon. That question is this: How do we identify the canonical heritage of the Christian tradition? The answer which one naturally expects is that this is a historical matter that can be resolved only by finding out what the Church has in fact canonized. By now, however, the canon has been transposed into an eternal rule of truth, identified as the Word of God. Once that shift has been made, it is useless to answer the new question in terms of the decisions of the Church.[52] If we say we know that Scripture is the Word of God because the Church tells us so, then we immediately want to know how the Church managed to get the right answer to such a pivotal question. Anyone who, like Calvin, is setting out 'to banish all doubt'[53] will find it thoroughly unsatisfactory to be told that the Church must decide this issue. It will mean that the Word of God rests in a deep way on the testimony of unreliable human agents; the whole appeal to divine revelation will have been vitiated. We will not have been lifted out of the ravings of our depraved judgement.

The crux of Calvin's answer to this question of the proper locus of the divine Word is to be found in his appeal to the internal witness of the Holy Spirit.

---

[51] This line of development is entirely in keeping with Calvin's account of the origins of Scripture which he is bold enough to describe in the language of dictation. This is an inescapable part of Calvin's position which was reworked into a complex doctrine of divine inspiration by his later followers. Attempts to see Calvin as committed to a dynamic view of Scripture which merely witnesses to the Word of God or which becomes the Word of God founder on this rock.

[52] Calvin recognizes the legitimacy of this question, but runs it without distinction or discrimination into the primary question: namely, 'Who can convince us that these writings came from God?' (ibid. I. vii. 1). No doubt, Calvin's opponents on the Roman Catholic side, committed to the same process of epistemizing the canons of the Church, aided and abetted him in this confusion.   [53] Ibid. I. vii. 1.

What Calvin exactly means by this is notoriously difficult to determine, but there is no doubting its central place in his epistemology. We know it does not rule out the use of arguments to establish that Scripture is truly the Word of God. Calvin himself outlines a whole series of considerations which give good grounds for believing that Scripture is such. He claims, in fact, that 'if we wished to proceed by arguments, we might advance many things that would easily prove—if there is a god in heaven—that the law, the prophets, and the gospel come from him'.[54] However, the deep ground for the resolving doubts about the authorship of Scripture lies outside the bounds of reason.

If we desire to provide in the best way for our conscience—that they may not be perpetually beset by the instability of doubt and vacillation, and that they may not also boggle at the smallest quibbles—we ought to seek out our conviction in a higher place than human reason, judgments or conjectures, that is, in the secret testimony of the Holy Spirit.[55]

Yet they who strive to build up firm faith in Scripture through disputation are doing things backwards. . . . But even if anyone clears God's Sacred Word from man's evil speaking, he will not at once imprint upon their hearts that certainty that piety requires. Since for unbelieving men religion seems to stand by opinion alone, they, in order not to believe anything foolishly or lightly, both wish and demand rational proof that Moses and the prophets spoke divinely. But I reply: the testimony of the Spirit is the more excellent than all reason. For as God alone is a fit witness of himself in his Word, so also, the Word will not find acceptance in man's heart before it is inwardly sealed by the inward testimony of the Spirit. The same Spirit, therefore, who has spoken through the mouths of the prophets must penetrate into our hearts to persuade us that they faithfully proclaimed what had been divinely commanded.[56]

Calvin uses two kinds of description to fill out what he means by the inner testimony of the Holy Spirit. The first is perceptual, the second affective.

. . . illumined by his power, we believe neither by our own or by anyone else's judgment that Scripture is from God; but above human

---

[54] Ibid. I. vii. 4. The whole of I. viii is devoted to this. Calvin takes up there such matters as the unique majesty and impressiveness of Scripture, its antiquity, the confirmation by miracle, the simplicity and heavenly character of the New Testament, and the like.   [55] Ibid. I. vii. 4.

[56] Ibid. I. vii. 4.

judgment we affirm with utter certainty (*just as if we were gazing upon the majesty of God himself*) that it has flowed to us from the very mouth of God by the ministry of men. . . . we feel that the undoubted power of his divine majesty lives and breathes there. By this power we are drawn and inflamed, knowingly and willingly, to obey him, yet also more vitally and effectively than by mere human willing or knowing. . . . Such, then, is a conviction that requires no reasons; such a knowledge with which the best reason agrees—in which the mind truly reposes more securely and constantly than in any reasons; such, finally, *a feeling that can be born only of a heavenly revelation.* I speak of nothing other than what each believer experiences within himself—though my words fall far beneath a just explanation of the matter.[57]

These last remarks suggest that, in essence, appeal to the inner testimony of the Holy Spirit is an appeal either to an internal divine revelation or to the personal experience of the believer. No reasons can be given, for what is at stake is a personal direct experience in which one comes to see that Scripture is from God. It is a matter of inner vision, rather than discursive argument. In this fashion Calvin clearly is convinced that he knows for certain where the Word of God is to be found. He has secured the foundation of his whole theological edifice. He has found a canon, an eternal rule of truth, witnessed to by the Church over the years, but clearly independent of its judgement.

It remains to mention that what was initially developed by Luther and Calvin found its way by diverse routes into the Confessions of the Protestant Churches.[58] The Confessions develop the theological convictions of the various Lutheran and Reformed communities which are either implicitly or explicitly derived from the canon of Scripture. Our interest here is the fact that the appeal to the canon of Scripture we have seen worked out in Luther and Calvin is repeated again and again.

The Preface to the Augsburg Confession offers and presents 'a confession of our pastors' and preachers' teaching and of our own

---

[57] Ibid. I. vii. 5; emphasis added.

[58] The way in which the revised account of canon in the Western Church is developed in Protestant scholasticism is extensively and carefully worked out in Muller, *Post-Reformation Reformed Dogmatics.* Muller's account is exceptionally good in bringing out the way in which the epistemic consequences of the Reformers' position is elaborated and incorporated into the whole fabric of systematic theology.

faith, setting forth how and in what manner, *on the basis of the Holy Scriptures*, these things are preached, taught, communicated, and embraced in our lands, principalities, dominions, cities, and territories'.[59] The Second Helvetic Confession is much more forthright: 'in controversies of religion or matters of faith, we cannot admit any other judge than God himself, pronouncing by the Holy Scriptures what is true, what is false, what is to be followed, or what to be avoided'.[60] Finally, the Westminster Confession is by far the most comprehensive and concise:

> The whole counsel of God, concerning all things necessary for his own glory, man's salvation, faith, and life, is either expressly set down in Scripture, or by good and necessary consequence may be deduced from Scripture: unto which nothing is at any time to be added, whether by new revelations by the Spirit, or the traditions of men.[61]

It is clear from the foregoing exposition that the Reformers brought about a major canonical change in the Church in the West. Their clear intent was to recover the gospel of grace, as they found it in their encounter with crucial parts of the received Scriptures. As they proceeded, they were forced by degrees to provide a serious intellectual justification for departing in what was perceived as a radical way from the Church as a whole. This they did by developing an epistemic principle which located all theological authority in the canon of Scripture. The canon alone, *sola scriptura*, was designated as the norm of all theological proposals.

The crucial difference from the received position was that this excluded any foundational appeal to the tradition of the Church, or to the teaching magisterium of the Church, as a foundation of matters of faith. Church tradition itself had to be tested by Scripture. Any appeal to tradition could only be heuristic and secondary. Moreover, Church bodies, deliberating in the present, had to test all theological proposals by the text of the Bible.

The continuity with the received tradition with regard to the canonical heritage of the Church is also clear. Both sides to this debate thought of canon primarily in epistemic categories. Where Reformers appealed to the authority of Scripture, their opponents

[59] John H. Leith, *Creeds of the Churches* (Louisville, Ky.: John Knox Press, 1982), 65; emphasis added.   [60] Ibid. 136.
[61] Ibid. 195.

did not oppose this in itself; they simply insisted that the appeal to Scripture alone did not represent the position of the early Church, and that it was also permissible to appeal to the tradition of the Church, as interpreted by an infallible magisterium. Hence the centre of gravity in their thinking about canon lay in the epistemology of Christian belief. Ultimately, they were utilizing another norm, which in a curious way was at once both above and below Scripture. The norm of the teaching magisterium, of papal infallibility, was below Scripture in that for matters touching the deep content of Christian belief conclusions had to be drawn either from Scripture or from Scripture interpreted in the light of tradition. Yet the norm was above Scripture in that the magisterium was the ultimate norm for disputes about the identity and interpretation of Scripture and of tradition.

For the Reformers the appeal to Scripture was, of course, located in the context of piety or spirituality, for they were profoundly concerned about coming to know God, receiving the gift of eternal life, living a godly life, and entering final glory. Hence salvation and knowledge of the true God were inextricably connected. Knowledge of God was located in Scripture, rather than in religious experience, natural reason, the ancient tradition of the Church, or its current teaching. The Bible provided the norm of all claims about the identity, character, and action of God.

I have described this position as one of theological foundationalism. We might also call it 'canonical foundationalism'. A person, on this view, is rationally entitled to his beliefs about God in so far as they can be shown to be expressly set down in Scripture or by good and necessary consequence be deduced from Scripture. We might also designate this as a form of canonical internalism. A person, that is, is justified in holding her theological beliefs in so far as she has access to the relevant evidence for those beliefs in Scripture and in so far as she is aware that evidence supports the beliefs that she has. If this is not an accurate description of the actual position the Reformers held, it is certainly the position that they aspired to, or that they held as the ideal for their best theological endeavours. Such a policy, they thought, would lead to certainty in theological matters. Such a policy also entailed the duty to test all one's theological beliefs by this norm. As Luther put it bluntly and succinctly: 'Everyone must take care to be certain and be sure of the doctrine by himself and must not found his certainty on what other people have determined and concluded.'[62] The only qualification to this was that in some circumstances concerning the worship of God and the government of the Church, matters were to be ordered by the light of nature and Christian prudence, but even these deliberations were to be according to the general rules of the Word, which are always to be observed.

[62] See n. 36 above.

6

The Epistemic Fortunes of Sola Scriptura

The major divisions which have arisen in the Church over the centuries have been intimately tied to canonical convictions which have gripped some section of the Church. Thus the split between East and West revolved around the *filioque* clause of the Nicene Creed, the place of papal infallibility in the economy of divine revelation, and competing lists of Fathers deemed to have special insight into theological method and proposals. The split within the West, between Roman Catholics and Protestants, began as a debate about the place of pious works in the gaining of salvation, quickly spread to disagreements about papal supremacy, and ended with rival accounts of the normative status of Scripture in the grounding of theological belief. In both cases doctrinal disputes, in the one case about the *filioque*, in the other about justification, required the respective protagonists to develop theories concerning how they were to justify the intellectual merits of their proposals in the teeth of hostile opposition. Moreover, in both cases the move was made very early on to settle all intellectual disputes in the neighbourhood of the original dissension in terms of a foundation, a canon, a norm, which would, by right and by nature, be beyond question. There had to be an ultimate foundation where argument ceased, where truth was secured, and where certainty was attained.

The seeds of both the Roman Catholic position and that of the Reformers can be found in the writings of the Fathers. Hence it is not surprising that both sides claimed to represent the mind of the Church in the patristic period. Thus in various conflicts in the early Church it was perfectly natural that protagonists would appeal to Rome in order to obtain her blessing. Rome, for her part, was apt to use such situations to advance her own claims to supremacy among the major sees. Yet it would be forced to claim that this constituted proof of papal jurisdiction and papal infallibility. The more reasonable reading is that the deliberations of general councils, for example, were ultimately deemed authoritative because they were accepted *de facto* by the whole Church rather than because they were confirmed *de jure* by the Roman see.

Likewise, in the case of the appeal to Scripture many Church Fathers used Scripture epistemically. They appealed to Scripture proof-texts to support their proposals; they made explicit statements about the normative role of Scripture in their theological deliberations; and they attempted to provide criteria of canonicity which would enable them to demarcate canonical from non-canonical texts. However, it would be exaggerated to claim that all these together add up to the assertion that the Church as a whole canonized an epistemic conception of the Scriptures.

Thus, the primary purpose in canonizing Scripture was to provide an authorized list of books for use in worship. The primary setting envisaged for the use of Scripture was not that of the science of theology, or that of the debates of scholars, but the spiritual nourishment of the people of God. This cannot be emphasized too heavily. Further, the really astute theologians of the patristic period, like Gregory of Nazianzus, were well aware that their theological proposals went significantly beyond the text of the Scriptures. Their proposals involved an appeal to non-scriptural axioms, to various empirical considerations, to human insight, to developments of biblical ideas, and to the mystical experience of believers. Moreover, no theory of canon, no criterion of canonicity, carried the day. Aside from the fact that some of the theories were patently daft, resting on bizarre numerological speculation which showed only that the decision to include an item in the canon was already thoroughly secure, the factor which ultimately carried the day was actual usage in the Church.[1]

---

[1] The comments of Edward Reuss are appropriate here: 'If, after all, there was agreement towards the end of the second century only regarding what had been already sanctioned by usage, it is because the canon, whether in earliest times or later, was formed only by this ecclesiastical usage, in part local and accidental, and was not formed according to scientific principles and methods, nor by the ascendancy of a primordial and pre-eminent authority' (*History of the Canon of Holy Scriptures in the Christian Church* (Edinburgh: R. W. Hunter,

That is the main reason why the edges of the canon remained ragged and unsettled for centuries.

The Scriptures and the Creed were indeed a kind of standard or norm; but they were essentially a standard of teaching and instruction for the Church in its worship, its catechesis, and the direction of its spiritual life. Equally we might say that they provided standards for demarcating orthodoxy from heresy. That they were not proposed as epistemic norms of truth is revealed by the fact that the Church's teachers defended their content in a host of ways. The arguments in the case of New Testament material revolved around the possible apostolicity of the material, the intimate relation between the apostles and Christ, the locus of special divine revelation in Christ, and the possible divine inspiration of the various writers. These in turn make visible tacit epistemological commitments, say, to the reliability of testimony and memory, the intrinsic truthfulness of divine revelation, the reliability of divine inspiration, and the like. Yet these kinds of proposals remained undeveloped, and it is fair to say that they were never canonized by the Church.

What is crucial to note about the patristic developments is that the Scriptures found a home alongside and within a whole series of canonical materials and practices. Even as a list of books, held in the highest esteem within the life of the Church, Scripture was never intended to function on its own in the spiritual nourishment

1891), 183). 'The usage of the readings had consecrated writings which had not been composed by apostles properly so called: other books which might claim such a title—at least in the opinion of more than one theologian—had not had the advantage of being known soon enough or widely enough, to obtain general acceptance without great difficulty. As theology could not establish a rule to decide the choice, or rather as it was entirely dependent on a tradition which had arisen and gained strength in complete independence of all theological formulae, theologians had soon to face numerous difficulties. . . . Theory aspired towards a rigorous selection, and from its own point of view was perfectly right, for it was a matter of much moment to purify from all alloy the texts which alone were to have an indisputable authority in the ever-widening discussions of theological questions. Practice sought everything suitable to its purpose, and was particularly afraid of divesting itself of any one means of action—i.e. of any book used in popular instruction, which, perhaps, was not of the number of those extolled by theory, but had the immense advantage of being already familiar to the class least easy to initiate into abstract theories' (ibid. 214–15). Reuss in the interests of a truly 'scientific' account of the canon opts in the end for a Lutheran solution to this theoretical concern.

of the people of God. In fact, experience had shown that it was an inadequate bulwark against the infiltration of foreign material into the bloodstream of the Church. It needed to be read and pondered in the context of worship, sacramental practice, credal summary, pedagogical expertise, devout commentary, and iconographic display.[2] This setting in turn required that it be received as a gift of the Holy Spirit, who acted in both its origin and in its current use to bring people to salvation in Christ.

To transpose Scripture, one element in the canonical tradition of the Church, which was to be used with other canonical materials and practices, into the single norm of theological truth, which was to be used on its own as the foundation for argument, was to reconceive the whole scope and character of the complex canonical heritage of the Church. It meant, for example, recasting that heritage in terms of a doctrine of revelation which in the very transposition gave that doctrine of revelation canonical status, something this kind of doctrine never had in the actual canons of the Church's life. In turn, that required the reclassification of the canonical heritage into categories which were amenable to epistemic discourse. Hence the rather loose designation of a variety of canons, themselves never ironed out into a comprehensive theory but left in a relatively confused yet stable form, was replaced by a neat array of canonical entities labelled respectively as Scripture, tradition, and teaching magisterium. These were batted about between the various theorists as complementary or competing epistemic norms which were to provide a foundation for permissible theological belief.

In this process the older notion was not entirely eliminated of course. It was simply displaced. The new use still permitted the canons to be placed in the context of worship and spiritual direction, but piety or spirituality was constantly in danger of being tied to the adoption of the epistemic proposals which had been smuggled into the heart of the Church. Rejection of the favoured criterion was perceived as tantamount to spiritual damnation or blasphemy. Guarding the new conceptions of the canons was interpreted as a pious act on a par with defending the honour of God and the Gospel. So spirituality was itself reinterpreted to fit

---

[2] The reverse also applied: that is, each of these had to be considered in the light of the canon of Scripture.

the new theory. Acceptance of the relevant canon or canons and bowing to their deliverances was construed as the first step, or as an essential step, in the gaining of that knowledge deemed necessary for salvation.

These changes were exacerbated by other developments which took place in the Church after Christianity became the religion of the Roman Empire. Two in particular deserve mention.

First, there was the breakdown of substantial forms of Christian initiation. The earlier discipline constitutive of initiation was impossible to sustain; the increase in the numbers of new converts put an intolerable strain on the resources of the Church. Yet it was in the context of Christian initiation that so much of the rich canonical heritage we have identified found its most natural home. Once the canonical materials were extracted from this and used extensively for purposes other than those of the evangelization and spiritual direction of those seeking union with God, it was easy to miss their delicate but pivotal place in the life of faith. It was easy to use Scripture, Creed, or sacramental usages as weapons with which to score points against opponents or as elements in theological debate very far removed from any desire to deepen knowledge and love of God.

Second, the status and responsibilities of the episcopal leaders of the Church changed significantly. The forms of ministry which eventually became canonical in the early Church were entirely understandable. Moreover, there is no reason to deny that they were guided by the working of the Holy Spirit. There was surely a need for the community to develop ways to hand on the faith across the generations, and the offices which emerged to make this possible can, from a Christian perspective, be seen as genuine gifts of the Holy Spirit. However, when bishops, clergy, and other Church leaders were called upon to assist in the administration of the Empire, it was inevitable that their primary task as shepherds of the flock would be eroded and compromised.

The great danger which emerged from these developments was that the spiritual life of the community did not get the attention it constantly needed and deserved. Yet without systematic attention to the life of the Spirit in the Church, the canons of the Church become removed from their natural setting, and are received and used in a way that distorts their proper function. Rather than being the means of ascent to a life of fellowship with

God, they become predominantly quarries for clever arguments about doctrinal matters; or they get used in a purely formal manner, disconnected from the life of the Spirit who inspired them in the first place. It is hard to deny that such was a besetting temptation in the Church from its earliest times. The marriage between Church and State intensified the likelihood of Church leaders and teachers yielding to this temptation.

Proper usage of the canonical traditions did not, of course, die out in the Church. It is clear that the various monastic developments represented a constant effort to renew the Church in accordance with its primitive standards and practices. However, the monastic traditions were often an élite affair, whose very existence made manifest the breakdown in serious initiation for most believers. In addition, monastic communities very easily got caught up in those intricate webs of political activity both within and outside the Church which greatly enhanced the development of papal infallibility.[3]

Any deep account of the canonical revolution which took place at the Reformation must acknowledge that one important factor in its origins and development was a thirst to find the God of the canonical traditions.[4] The canonical heritage was *de facto* in such disrepair that the Reformers entered into a revolt against the prevailing heritage of the West in order to recover a living faith in God and to renovate the tradition along different lines from those which they had inherited. Yet they received not just the material proposals about canon which had developed in the West; they also came to possess the concept of canon which had

[3] Within the Church renewal movements were intimately related to the development of papal supremacy. See David L. d'Avray, 'Papal Authority and Religious Sentiment in the Late Middle Ages', in Diana Wood (ed.), *The Church and Sovereignty c. 590–1915* (Oxford: Blackwell, 1991), 393–408. Consider in this regard Steven Runciman's comment on the reform at the abbey of Cluny: 'The Cluniacs continually found their efforts thwarted by local interests. They therefore placed their Order under the direct control of the Bishop of Rome. It was in consequence essential to them that the authority of the Pope should override all other ecclesiastical authorities' (*The Eastern Schism* (Oxford: Clarendon Press, 1955), 28–9).

[4] 'Protestantism was born, after all, in reaction to failing spiritual leadership and church piety. In their place the reformers attempted to create a simple and effective alternative' (Steven Ozment, *Protestants: The Birth of a Revolution* (New York: Doubleday, 1992), p. xiii).

become normative in the West. Hence the changes they proposed perpetuated the departure from the tacit conception at work in the patristic period. The Reformers did not change the formal properties of the canonical tradition: they simply substituted a different canonical content.

Part of the attraction of their proposal was its simplicity. In place of a triumvirate of Scripture, tradition, and teaching magisterium, which in practice needed to be suitably ranked in significance, they insisted on one and only one foundation.[5] There was one canon, which was the only rule of truth in faith, which was

---

[5] In a fascinating revisionist reading of the doctrine of Trent, George Tavard has argued that the Council permits the claim that Scripture is the sole source and norm of Christian doctrine. On this reading, Trent did not resolve the question of the norms of Catholic doctrine; it simply stated that the Gospel was contained in both the Scriptures and in unwritten traditions preserved in the Church. See his important book, *Holy Writ or Holy Church* (London: Burns and Oates, 1959). A similar position is developed by Josef Rupert Geiselmann in 'Scripture, Tradition, and the Church: An Ecumenical Problem', in Daniel J. Callahan *et al.*, (eds.), *Christianity Divided* (New York: Sheed and Ward, 1961), 39–72. A significant challenge to this view is given by Heiko Augustus Oberman in 'Quo Vadis Petre? Tradition from Irenaeus to Humani Generis', in *The Dawn of the Reformation* (Edinburgh: T. & T. Clark, 1986), 269–96. The theological consequence of Tavard's view is also challenged by Maurice Bevenot, in 'Tradition, Church, and Dogma', *Heythrop Journal*, I (1960), 34–47. Both Tavard and Geiselmann in their eagerness to point out that Trent did not use the formula, *partim . . . partim*, which was in the original draft for the Council, miss entirely the fact that the traditions of the Church, like the Scriptures, are depicted as spoken by Christ or dictated by the Holy Spirit. The final draft reads: 'Following the example of the orthodox fathers, the council accepts and venerates with a like feeling of piety and reverence all the books of both the old and the new Testament, since the one God is the author of both, as well as the traditions concerning both faith and conduct, *as either directly spoken by Christ or dictated by the Holy Spirit*, which have been preserved in unbroken sequence in the catholic church' (Norman P. Tanner (ed.), *Decrees of the Ecumenical Councils*, vol. ii: *Trent to Vatican II* (Washington: Georgetown University Press, 1990), 663; emphasis added). If the traditions are either spoken by Christ or dictated by the Holy Spirit, it is hard to see how this does not entail that the tradition provides as strong a warrant as Scripture for any theological proposal. Doctrines of divine speaking and divine dictation are pivotal for Protestant doctrines of the authority of Scripture; here they apply *mutatis mutandis* to tradition. Hence the attempt to argue that Trent leaves open the possibility of a doctrine of *sola scriptura* is ingenious but unconvincing. In either case, it is clear that the canonical traditions within and outside Scripture are cast in epistemic categories. Whoever embraces a doctrine of *sola scriptura,* whether Protestant or Roman Catholic, faces formidable difficulties, as I shall argue below.

clear in what it affirmed, which secured certainty for one's beliefs, and which one had a duty to consult on every significant theological issue. This simple notion was like a crowbar which appeared to smash down the door of the castle of the enemy with ease.

Again, we need to stress that moving to construe the canon as a norm of truth did not mean that piety was cast aside. On the contrary, the new theory of canon enunciated by the Reformers was at one level an expression of deep spirituality. For both Luther and Calvin the whole content of the canon was summed up by the gospel of grace, by the offer of salvation, by the very name of Jesus Christ as gracious saviour for lost sinners. Moreover, the right hearing of Scripture was possible only when the human capacity for hearing had been suitably cleansed and refurbished by the Holy Spirit. This introduced an externalist component into the edges of their epistemology. That is, it drew attention to the importance of both human faculties and divine repair of those faculties in the perception of truth about the human situation and its divine context. This important insight was, at the very least, an echo of the epistemic suggestions of many of the Fathers. However, the epistemic centre of gravity was located in the provision of a secure foundation for belief, which could not be gainsaid because it was constituted by special divine revelation of the highest order.

Apart from its simplicity, there were other dimensions of the position of the Reformers which proved to be highly attractive and which are still pertinent to the life of the Church today. The emphasis on justification as an act of God, acquitting the sinner here and now, independently of merit, was a profoundly liberating notion.[6] This doctrine was set in a theocentric and Trinitarian account of salvation, which provided great depth to the Reformers' vision as a whole. Further, the Reformers recovered a lively sense of the place of preaching in the ministry of the Church; they made the scriptures and the liturgy available in the vernacular; they aquired extensive skill in studying the Scriptures

---

[6] There has been much debate about the extent to which Luther's particular doctrine of justification was something radically new in the history of the Church. For a concerted effort to show that it was in fact new, see Alistair McGrath, 'Forerunners of the Reformation? A Critical Examination of the Evidence for Precursors of the Reformation Doctrines of Justification', *Harvard Theological Review*, 75 (1982), 219–42.

in the original languages; they made room for the vocation of laity in the Church; and they fostered personal responsibility to seek and find the truth about God for oneself. There is, then, a very rich spiritual and intellectual legacy which gained currency as a result of the life and work of the great Reformers.

By far the most conspicuous virtue in the work of the Reformers with respect to the canon of Scripture was their concerted effort to reconnect the Bible to the spiritual formation of the individual. They intuitively grasped that the purpose of Scripture was intimately bound up with the sharing of the Gospel, so that people might find the favour and mercy of God for themselves. This represents a conception of the Scriptures as food for the soul, or as medicine which heals the human person through deep exposure to the Good News made manifest in Jesus Christ. This surely accounts for Luther's proposal to isolate what preaches Christ as the genuine mark of canonical material. He was reaching to recover one of the fundamental purposes of the canonical heritage of the Church. Very naturally, however, he was not able to extract this crucial insight from his particular doctrine of justification by faith, or from the particular epistemic categories in which Scripture was already embedded in the theological tradition he inherited.

Our goal here is to reach an extended assessment of their contribution to the discussion on the nature and significance of the canonical heritage of the Church. As a slogan intended to highlight an important aspect of the place of Scripture in the life of the Church, the principle of *sola scriptura* was entirely salutary. It raised up the crucial place of Scripture in the economy of the Church's life, which rightly awakened the Church to hear this material ever and anew in its preaching, its theological reflection, and more broadly in its spiritual direction. Whenever the Scriptures become buried beneath a weight of ecclesiastical tradition and practice which prevent them being heard, we can expect someone somewhere to recover their treasures and in the excitement to insist that scripture alone should capture all our attention. *Sola scriptura* is a fine rhetorical device to arouse our interest and to drive us to examine the Scriptures with fresh eyes; it is another matter entirely when it is offered as an exclusive foundational principle for ordering the whole of the Christian life and theology. The problems that arise are manifold.

To begin, the sharp reduction of the total canonical heritage of the Church to that of Scripture leaves the Church deeply impoverished. It cuts the Church off from a vast body of materials and practices which have their inimitable place to play in the life of the Church. Thus it gradually erodes the place of the Fathers, of the early liturgical treasures of the faith, of the Creed, of the regulatory canons, and of iconography. In fact, only those materials which can be recast in epistemic categories can effectively survive, and then only in so far as their delicate function in the economy of the spiritual life is displaced. It is no accident that over time replacements for virtually all of these canonical traditions were developed by the Reformers and their followers, albeit with a cloak of silence about their significant role in the Church. Perhaps the most ironic of these developments was the informal canonization of the founders of the Reformation as the true interpreters of Scripture and the norm of theological developments. Also ironic was the extraordinary dependence of the theologians of the Reformation traditions on the structure and content of the creeds. Having rejected the Nicene Creed as normative, they happily used its themes as the normative loci of their systematic theology, albeit suitably transposed to incorporate their epistemological interests, reflected very conspicuously in the increased attention and content of the prolegomena.[7]

A further problem in the implementation of *sola scriptura* is the fact that its use puts in doubt within the very heart of the Church the content of basic Christian doctrines and fundamental Christian practices. Crucial Christian doctrines, like that of the Incarnation and the Trinity, have to be proved ever anew to ensure that they are properly derived from the appropriate foundation. They can no longer be construed as constitutive of the Christian tradition. The same applies *mutatis mutandis* to sacramental practices.

Over against such doctrines as those of the Trinity and the Incarnation, doctrines of inspiration and revelation become pivotal and mandatory; for, without these, the appeal to Scripture as the foundation of all theology becomes entirely arbitrary.

---

[7] This is well brought out by Richard A. Muller in *Post-Reformation Reformed Dogmatics*, vol. i: *Prolegomena to Theology* (Grand Rapids, Mich.: Baker Books, 1987).

Hence the very kind of material which the early Church left implicit in its canonical traditions was made explicit and set in place as the foundation of everything else. In time, doctrines of divine inspiration, down to the inspiration of the vowel points in the Hebrew of the Old Testament, became vital to the maintenance of sound theology.[8]

Moreover, revelation and inspiration became so much identified with divine communication of the divine Word that the revelation of God in history, both in Israel and in the Incarnation, became marginal to revelation. The very term 'revelation' became defined in terms of the supernatural communication of supernatural information. Emphasis on the communication of propositions displaced the teaching of Scripture on divine revelation, where such a notion captures only one dimension of the topic.[9] All sorts of crucial epistemic ideas and suggestions did not begin to receive the attention they merit because the epistemic questions, which are engendered by Christian theology, and which are present in the Scriptures and the Fathers, had already been decided in terms of a doctrine of canonical foundationalism. Paradoxically, while doctrines of divine revelation were canonized and thus given a whole new status in the canonical heritage of the Church, epistemic considerations of an externalist rather than an internalist kind, which were clearly manifest in the Church's canons, were neglected, if not completely ignored.

In addition, the adoption of *sola scriptura* led to a thoroughly profane vision of the life of the Church. The Church *qua* institution was seen as a purely human body, bereft in any substantial way of the leading of the Holy Spirit. The chief attitude directed to the Church was, therefore, one of criticism and suspicion. Governance and oversight within the Church were construed primarily in secular terms which left no real space for the working

---

[8] 'The problem of the vowel points, noted tangentially in several of the previously offered examples of debate over the purity and perfection of the text of the Old Testament, occupied the Protestant orthodox during the whole course of the seventeenth century' (Richard A. Muller, *Post-Reformation Reformed Dogmatics, Theology*, vol. ii: *Holy Scripture: The Cognitive Foundation of Theology* (Grand Rapids, Mich.: Zondervan, 1993), 426).

[9] Even then we are being very generous in our assessment, as divine speaking more often takes the form of promise and warning than of assertion.

of the Holy Spirit in the Church outside the reception of the Word and the reception of salvation by the individual.[10]

Concomitant with this, a tremendous burden was placed on the individual as the locus of discernment and insight. Only the individual could be the subject of divine inspiration and direction. This too came under a cloud, because, once it was permitted that the individual could be led and guided by the Holy Spirit, this opened the door for the Church too to be led. If the Church was guided by the Spirit, then the tradition of the Church would have to be taken very seriously. In later generations divine inspiration of the individual would be dismissed as 'enthusiasm'. Further, the individual was removed from the rich formation and support mediated by the Church. The Church, rather than providing indispensable guidance and formation, became a likely source of corruption and misdirection for the individual. So the idea of human agents as persons, intimately and necessarily related to others in a fellowship of faith, was displaced by that of human agents as individuals, who are indeed utterly dependent upon God and upon divine revelation, yet who are effectively cut off from the nurture and corrective of the Christian community.[11]

Some of the most serious difficulties related to *sola scriptura* arise from the epistemological problems which are connected to it. It is worth pausing to identify these with care.

To begin, the appeal to Scripture as the foundation of theology required that the Bible be unequivocal in its teaching. The Bible must exhibit the kind of clarity and distinctness in its message which all can grasp on their own with relative ease. In short, the Reformers assumed an exegetical optimism which is precarious in the extreme. They wrongly believed that we can piece together the overall message of Scripture, and they convinced themselves that they could derive more extended theological conclusions from Scripture than is warranted. The early history of canonization makes this clear, in that the debate with Gnosticism in the second century revealed that the Church needed both a canon of

[10] A place was also assigned for the work of the Holy Spirit in the sacraments, but this was subject to considerable slippage.
[11] The Reformers ran the risk here of fostering a thoroughly impoverished notion of the self.

Scripture and a rule of faith if it was to preserve the distinctive intellectual core of the Christian message. It was precisely because *sola scriptura* was inadequate that Irenaeus insisted that the Church also needed a rule of faith. The Reformers ignored this aspect of canonical history.

Moreover, Luther's attempt to develop a canon within the canon—that is, to isolate and make normative that material which clearly preached Christ—should have alerted everyone to the fact that the Scriptures, as we actually have them, are not as clear as Luther's theory of canon requires. They are a very rich and diverse treasure of materials which cannot be reduced to a formula. There is far more to Scripture than what preaches Christ or what can be captured in any doctrine of justification by faith through grace. Pushing these themes in the way they were developed by Luther leads either to the elimination of vast tracts of the Bible or to the awkward attempt to force crucial parts of Scripture to say things their authors or editors never intended to say in the first place. Either way, the spiritual and theological life of the Church was in the long run impoverished in the name of a doctrine which was supposed to give Scripture a pivotal place in the life of the Church.

In addition, the Christian Church cannot survive merely on doctrines of salvation and justification, no matter how richly articulated by the Reformers or others. As the Reformers themselves were well aware, these doctrines make sense only within a whole body of teaching about God, sin, Jesus Christ, the Holy Spirit, the sacraments, and the like. Both Luther and Calvin were also convinced that doctrines about the nature of the will and about predestination were crucial to the full exposition of their particular proposals.[12] It was not long, then, before the Reformers themselves began developing radically different proposals—for example, about the sacraments—which were entirely incompatible with the claim that the teaching of Scripture was clear on these matters either in itself or derivatively. Their exegetical optimism was utopian and unrealistic. David Steinmetz's comment on this matter is accurate:

---

[12] Both Calvin and Luther draw heavily on certain readings of Augustine on these subjects. Their proposals are not simply an exegesis of Scripture, as the later challenge from Arminius makes clear.

Both Luther and Calvin reflect the exegetical optimism which marked early Protestantism. For a brief period of time, Protestants thought it would be possible to write a theology which was wholly biblical and excluded all philosophical and speculative questions. It became clear within a decade that such a hope was not well-founded. Nevertheless, Protestants remained optimistic about the clarity of Scripture and the simplicity and persuasive power of the truth which it contained. Protestants were not well-prepared for the internal disagreements within Protestantism when the careful exegesis of one group of godly and learned men clashed with the exegesis of another group equally learned and godly.[13]

The deep problem here is not simply that the Reformers disagreed on fundamental matters, or that their disagreements called into question their claims about the clarity of Scripture, or that insistence on clarity has deep repercussions for the status of the mysteries of the faith;[14] it is that the clarity of Scripture was absolutely essential to their epistemology of divine revelation. Once the clarity of Scripture, in the terms in which they framed it, was called into question, then their whole proposal about canon was in serious trouble.

Furthermore, there is a deep incoherence in the efforts of the Reformers to find a way to provide a rationale for the authority of Scripture. By far the most interesting and influential rationale is that provided by Calvin. Luther, for his part, simply took what he heard as preaching Christ as a yardstick for canonicity; that is, he adopted a dogmatic criterion of canonicity. This has two obvious problems. First, his own theological norm nowhere says that such a dogmatic criterion should be used as the hallmark of canonical material. Scripture nowhere teaches that the criterion of canonicity

---

[13] David C. Steinmetz, 'Luther and Calvin on Church and Tradition', in *Luther in Context* (Bloomington, Ind.: Indiana University Press, 1986), 96.

[14] It is not clear, for example, how long one can maintain a heavy stress on the clarity of Scripture and equally maintain a serious place for the doctrine of the Trinity in one's theology. Luther clearly holds to the doctrine of the Trinity, and he is well aware of the mysteries surrounding this pivotal doctrine, but he fails to see the discrepancy between this commitment and his doctrine of the clarity of Scripture because he has already decided that the heart of the Scriptures is not the doctrine of the Trinity but the doctrine of justification by faith, a doctrine which in his eyes is clear. In his embrace of the Trinity, Luther borrows lavishly from a tradition which his own theory of Scripture does not really permit.

is what preaches Christ. Hence, it is unsupported in terms of his own theory.[15] Second, in the end we simply have to take Luther's word that his criterion of canonicity is the correct one. We rely on a fallible human judgement to decide these matters, something that Luther rejected when he refused to allow the Christian community to have a decisive role in determining what constitutes its canonical materials.

Calvin's appeal to the inner witness of the Holy Spirit as the ground for his canonical decision fares no better than Luther's proposal. Recall that the prime consideration for Calvin in designating Scripture as the Word of God, and therefore as canonical, was not the properties of scripture but the fact that the inner witness of the Holy Spirit in the minds of Christian believers proved Scripture to be the Word of God. The difficulties with this claim are as follows.

1. This is not a doctrine which is itself taught in Scripture. There is, of course, a doctrine that the Father will bear witness to Christ;[16] but this is a far cry from a doctrine that proposes that the Father will tell us that Scripture alone is the Word of God in written form. Equally, there is a very important doctrine of the inner witness in Paul;[17] but this doctrine concerns how the Holy Spirit bears witness in the hearts of believers that they are children of God. It has nothing to say about a doctrine of Scripture or about the boundaries of the biblical canon. Calvin and his followers have in all probability extrapolated from these materials to develop an extended inner witness of the Spirit to support their doctrine of Scripture; but they have no warrant in their own norm of theological reflection for such a move.

2. It is untrue to say that the experience of Christian believers actually confirms Calvin's claim that they accept the canon because the Spirit bears witness to them inwardly in the way required. Calvin claims to speak of 'nothing other than what each believer experiences within himself'.[18] However, there is no

[15] Paul's proposal in Galatians 1 about the proper measure of other gospels is not addressed to the issue of what constitutes the content or boundaries of the Christian canon. Paul's canon was clearly that bequeathed to him by the Jewish tradition; it was only much later that Christians had to face questions about their own canon as distinct from that of Judaism.

[16] See John 8: 18.   [17] See Rom. 8: 15–17.

[18] See above, p. [135].

consensus on that to which Christians bear witness at this point. Thus Reuss, in exploring what it was that led Christians to distinguish canonical from non-canonical texts, asks pointedly:

Was it really in virtue of the sovereign principle of the inward testimony of the Holy Spirit? Would it be quite true to say that the first Protestant theologians, while unmoved by the enthusiastic eloquence of the author of Wisdom, so much extolled by the Alexandrians, felt the breath of God in the genealogies of Chronicles, or the topographical catalogues of the book of Joshua? Did they really find so great a difference between the miracles of the Chaldean Daniel and those of the Greek Daniel, that they felt bound to remove the first two chapters from the volume which bears Daniel's name? I have some difficulty in believing that they arrived at the *distinction* they drew by any test of that kind.[19]

If we were to follow what the experience of believers tells us, then it is not very likely that we would arrive at the canon identified by Calvin. Moreover, it is not at all clear that the experience of believers actually underwrites Calvin's very specific claim about the canon: namely, that in the Bible and in the Bible alone we hear the Word of God. The religious experience of believers rarely addresses such a question.

3. The really deep problem with the appeal to the inner witness in Calvin is that either it is circular, or it shifts the foundations of Christian belief from Scripture to religious experience. Everything hinges here on which reading of Calvin we deploy.

On one reading, the appeal to the inner witness is an appeal to an inner revelation to the individual, wherein God tells that individual that his Word is located in Scripture. If this is correct, then Calvin has really proposed that the test of genuine revelation is another revelation. However, if one is following the logic of Calvin's position, this leads only to the obvious question: How do we know that the Spirit has truly spoken to us in our hearts? Once we ask this, we are off again in search of a further criterion of genuine divine revelation. On another reading, we might take Calvin as asserting that the divine Word in Scripture is grounded in the experience of Christian believers. They experience Scripture, it might be said, as being a divine Word. If this is correct, we now have another foundation for theology outside that of the canon of Scripture: namely, religious experience.

[19] Reuss, *History of the Canon*, 312.

Scripture no longer operates as the foundation for all theological proposals. So, depending on the option taken, we either beg the question by positing another revelation, or we introduce a whole new foundation for Christian theology, which is explicitly repudiated by Calvin.

In these circumstances it is not surprising that many Protestants have not been happy to follow Calvin in his account of the warrant for the canonicity of Scripture. Some have reinterpreted the doctrine of the inner witness as a doctrine of self-authentication in which no reasons are permitted for the norm of Scripture; Scripture authenticates itself as normative. Others have developed an appeal to Christ as the warrant for the normative status of Scripture, arguing that to reject the canon as norm is to reject the authority of the Son of God. Yet others have worked out complex combinations of these kinds of claims.[20]

All of these in one way or another, like their mentors in the Reformation period, persistently eschew any kind of appeal to the decisions of the Church in arriving at the boundaries of the canonical tradition. To appeal to the Church is unacceptable because it makes the Church the foundation of theology and of the Church's life. The doctrine of *sola scriptura* was intended to overturn precisely this sort of move. This doctrine continued to be maintained even while the Reformers and their followers appealed to the Jewish community's decisions on the canon when it came to deciding the boundaries of the Old Testament. Somehow it was all right to appeal to the Jewish community to determine the boundaries of the Old Testament, but it was not appropriate to appeal to the Christian community concerning the boundaries of the New Testament. Few appear to have been aware of the obvious inconsistency in these deliberations.

---

[20] The doctrine of the inner witness, as applied to the canon, is, in Reformed theology, like a moveable feast that we can shift around at will. Thus Paul Helm in a charming essay has suggested that we should construe the internal testimony of the Holy Spirit as the discovery in experience that the promises of God in Scripture are true. See his 'Faith, Evidence, and the Scriptures', in D. A. Carson and John D. Woodbridge (eds.), *Scripture and Truth* (Grand Rapids, Mich.: Zondervan, 1983), 312–13. The primary argument, for Helm, for the claim that the sixty-six books of the bible are God's Word is from the authority of Christ: 'It is because He endorses the Old Testament and makes provision for the New that both the Old and New have this authority' (ibid. 311).

By now we can see the deep reason why it became impossible to appeal to the Church to settle questions about the limits of the scriptural canon. Between the patristic period, on the one hand, and the late medieval and Reformation period, on the other, there had been a sea change in the way the canon of Scripture was construed. Originally, for a whole host of reasons, the Church identified a list of books to be read in its liturgical gatherings, chiefly for the purposes of celebration, catechesis, and spiritual direction. In making this decision, the Church did not *per se* become some sort of norm. On the contrary, the Church had various reasons for the inclusion of this body of material rather than another body of material. These reasons might then be examined, of course, in order to extract from them the possible norms which may have informed their decisions. Thus we might come up with such norms as divine inspiration, divine revelation, apostolicity, the experience of the community in its use of this material over time, the prior decisions of the Jewish tradition, and the like. Only someone with an eye and an ear for certain kinds of epistemological theories would be interested in such matters. Certainly, several of the Fathers and teachers of the Church, who had a role in the discussions which were in the neighbourhood of the canonization of the Scriptures, were interested in these kinds of issues. However, they were mostly a secondary concern, and the Church left these matters unresolved. The Church was interested primarily in singling out medicine for the soul. In making its decisions about the canon of Scripture, the Church was neither setting itself up as a norm of epistemology nor advocating any particular norm as governing its decisions. Certainly it believed that it was guided and directed by the Holy Spirit, but this in no way amounts to an epistemic claim about its own authority; on the contrary, it points away from itself to the activity of God as the ultimate source of its confidence and of truth.

By the end of the medieval period there were many in the Western division of the Church who had come to believe that the Church was indeed a norm of truth. When the Roman Catholic Church through its appropriate channels spoke, then God spoke. To know the mind of this Church was *ipso facto* to know the mind of God, and hence to know the truth. Indeed, the Roman Church constituted a kind of epistemic mechanism

by means of which one could locate the truth about God's definitive revelation in history. This was perceived by many Christians
in the West as tantamount to the claim that the Roman Church
was the ultimate foundation of truth in theology. Even though
the Roman tradition might claim that its own norm of truth was
the Scriptures, the proper interpretation of the truths available in
Scripture, either expressly stated therein or somehow drawn from
there by reason and the working of the Spirit in the Christian
community down through the centuries, was to be found in the
teaching magisterium of the Roman see. Hence, however we fill
out the details, the crucial norm of theological truth was the
appropriate deliberations of the Church of Rome. The Church
was the foundation of truth. In these circumstances it was impossible for the Reformers to permit the Church to be decisive in
the debates about the content and boundaries of the canon. They
were so convinced from their own experience of its mistakes and
follies that this would have opened the floodgates to error and
falsehood. At best the Church could be a witness to the truth.
Given their convictions about the errors and failures of the
Church, the foundation of truth had to be located elsewhere.

It was this epistemic claim that the Church was a norm of
truth that the Reformers rejected. As an alternative they proposed
that the Scriptures alone constituted the norm of theological
truth. In making this move, they shared the implicit claim with
Rome, over against the witness of the patristic Fathers, that the
Church must have an agreed, foundationalist epistemology of
religious belief. They agreed that there needed to be one ultimate
norm of religious belief. They proposed that the canon of
Scripture should be that single, clear, definitive norm. From this
starting-point, they sought to rebuild the whole of Christian
practice and teaching on a sound base. The epistemizing of the
Church's canonical life had by then moved into its second major
phase.

Two observations reinforce the perception of a deep gap
between the Reformers and the early Christian heritage. The
writer of the Epistle to the Hebrews was clearly interested in the
image of the building of foundations for the Christian faith. What
for the writer are these foundations? They are constituted by basic
Christian teaching: that is, 'repentance from dead works and faith
toward God, instructions about baptisms, laying on of hands,

resurrection of the dead, and eternal judgment'.[21] The Reformers are also interested in the foundations of the faith, but for them this eventually means some norm of theological truth, which, once in place, will deliver the truth. The image of a building and its foundation has travelled a long way in its use and content between the Epistle to the Hebrews and the Reformers.

The other observation concerns the change which has overtaken the notion of the 'rule of faith' or 'rule of truth' which we met in Tertullian and Irenaeus. For them the 'rule of faith' was a substantial summary of the actual beliefs about God's mighty acts in Jesus Christ for the salvation of the world. The rule was a short, relatively informal creed. By the time of the Reformation, the rule had ceased to be a summary of Christian belief and had become a norm of Christian belief. The rule of faith was no longer a creed; it was the canon of Scripture, understood as a norm for testing all theological proposals for their truth. It no longer tells us what Christians actually believe; it tells us how to work out for ourselves what Christians ought to believe, if they are to be rationally responsible in their beliefs.

By the time of these profound changes, any alternative reading of the patristic heritage on canon had long been forgotten or excluded from the conversation. The Eastern wing of the Church, which might have offered a different reading of the canonical traditions of the Church, had been cut off from the West, dismissed as schismatic, and in all probability construed as theologically uncreative and stubborn. Yet there was one very interesting development which bears mention. Between 1573 and 1581 there was a serious attempt on the part of the Lutherans to enter into conversation with the Orthodox tradition as represented by Constantinople.[22]

The first two efforts by the Lutherans to make contact with the patriarch of Constantinople failed, mostly, it would appear, because of misadventure rather than failure in diplomacy. Then in

---

[21]   Compare at this point how the image of foundations is deployed by the author of Hebrews. See Heb. 6: 1–3.

[22]   An extended review and assessment of this dialogue can be found in John J. Zoppi, 'The Correspondence of 1573–1581 between the Lutheran Theologians at Tübingen and the Eastern Orthodox Patriarchiate at Constantinople, on the Dispute concerning Sacred Tradition', *Patristic and Byzantine Review*, 4 (1985), 175–95; 5 (1986), 5–18, 139–46, 207–21.

1573 a group of Lutheran theologians at Tübingen, led by Jacob Andreae, managed to open a dialogue with Patriarch Jeremias II and his advisers. Andreae's objective was in part to spread the Reformation abroad; so he sent various letters, homilies, and a copy of the Augsburg Confession in Greek to the patriarch. Over time the patriarch and his advisers provided a response covering areas of agreement and disagreement. As the dialogue progressed, it became clear that a critical factor in the disagreements concerned the opposing views on the relation between Scripture and tradition. The Lutherans took the position that the traditions of the Church could well be wholesome, but that it was dangerous to accept something which was not explicitly witnessed to by Scripture.

When we say that only those things by necessity should be believed and done which have been proposed by the Sacred Scriptures, we do not demand that those very same words and syllables be read in the Scriptures, but that we gladly retained everything which can be logically deduced from the Scriptures, even when these words cannot be found in them. Thus concerning the Son of God, we gladly accept the word 'homoousion,' even though this word is not found in the Sacred Books. Moreover, we accept it not because it is found or ratified by the Synod in Nicaea, but because the sense (or meaning) of this word is expressed in many places in the Scriptures.[23]

They also insisted that in cases where the meaning of Scripture was obscure then Scripture must be used to interpret Scripture, rather than there being an appeal to the interpretation of the Scriptures found in the explanation and commentaries of the Fathers.

The patriarch and his advisers did not accept the Lutheran approach to Scripture and tradition. The patriarch's response focused on the need to accept the tradition of the Church and give up the attempt to rationalize its content.

Therefore, brethren, let us stand on the rock of faith and on the tradition of the Church, and not remove the boundaries which our Holy Fathers have set. Thus we will not give the opportunity to those who wish to innovate and destroy the edifice of the holy, catholic and apostolic Church of God. For if permission is granted to everyone who wants it, little by little the whole body of the Church will be destroyed.[24]

---

[23] Ibid. 10.   [24] Ibid. 13.

Let us accept, then, the tradition of the Church with a sincere heart and not a multitude of rationalizations. For God created man to be (morally) upright; instead they (humans) sought after diverse ways of rationalizing. Let us not allow ourselves to learn a new kind of faith which is condemned by the tradition of the Holy Fathers.[25]

We do not know enough from the record to be able to delineate a clear account of the Eastern vision of the canonical heritage of the Church at this time. What little we do have shows that Eastern theologians were exceptionally perceptive in their assessment of the Lutheran position. Thus they grasped that the Lutheran proposal would put the future of the Church and its heritage into the hands of the individual Christian, who would now accept or reject this or that part only in so far as it came up to the standard of his or her interpretation of the supposedly clear passages of the Bible. This manifestly would eliminate the ecclesial boundaries which the Church as a whole had set. The Eastern theologians were also uneasy with the Lutheran policy of treating both the Scriptures and the tradition primarily in epistemic categories. Thus, the Fathers were rejected by the Lutherans because they contradicted each other, and the Scriptures were described by the Lutherans as a measure and norm of doctrine and practice.[26] We can see, then, that little if any attention was paid by the Lutherans to the possibility that the Church had canonized a whole network of materials, including its biblical materials, for purposes other than that of being an epistemic norm. Moreover, they did not consider the possibility that those purposes might well best be served by having canonical materials which would never satisfy those who want their canonical heritage to be first and foremost a quarry for argument and evaluation.

It would be easy to dismiss the patriarch's reference to a multitude of rationalizations as anti-intellectualism, as an expression of a traditionalism which refuses to face tough questions about truth

---

[25] Zoppi, *Patristic and Byzantine Review*, 13.

[26] 'There is, indeed, no more sure, nor truer, nor better standard rule for judging all dogmas, all institutes, and usages of faith and human traditions and works, than the Word of the Almighty God of all; the Word, which has been revealed to the human race by the Prophets and Christ and the Apostles and written in the Old and New Testament for the benefit and salvation of the entire Church' (ibid. 9).

and evidence, as a sign of epistemological failure of nerve when it comes to the foundations of the Faith. But it can also be taken as a sign that the canonical heritage of the Church need not be seen as the provision of a religious epistemology, even though there are epistemological questions to be resolved in their own time and place.

7

Initiation into the Rule of Truth

It is patently clear that the Protestant Reformers of the sixteenth century were driven not just by pious concerns to save their souls but also by epistemic convictions concerning the true source and ground for all theological claims. Over time they became deeply interested in questions about the origin, extent, and certainty of their theological convictions about God and his relation to the human creation. Their proposals on these matters proved extraordinarily influential on the subsequent history of Christianity in the West.

Their interest in these epistemic questions stemmed initially from the failure of the received tradition to deliver a satisfactory answer to their spiritual needs. For good or ill, the Church in which they had been baptized failed to enable them to come to know the true and living God of the Gospel. In coming to know God, Calvin and Luther found themselves in a storm of debate. In this debate they forged a new vision of how God was known. The heart of that new vision was that the Scriptures constituted the only valid canon of Christian doctrine. The non-scriptural traditions of the Church and her current teachings were acceptable only in so far as their content could be found expressly stated in Scripture or be validly deduced from Scripture. Scripture was the foundation of theological reflection. Constituted as it was by the Word of God, it was a reliable test of all theology. Theological claims based on human reason or on Church tradition were not an adequate basis for faith. It was Scripture alone which could provide clarity and certainty.[1]

---

[1] For this reason it is deeply mistaken to accuse the Reformers of choosing some sort of inner, subjective, or personal criterion of truth to replace that of the Church. For the Reformers the norm was clearly objective and external in character, as objective and external as the Bible itself.

This epistemic policy became the hallmark of Protestant thought and practice. On this foundation the Reformers and their followers set out to reconstruct the life of the Church. Within a very short time, a decade at the most, the exegetical optimism which accompanied this revolution had clearly failed in practice. The Reformers very quickly found that they reached radically different theological conclusions regarding the sacraments, Church order, the place of predestination in the scheme of things, the Trinity, and the like. In no way did this blunt their commitment to *sola scriptura*. Epistemic proposals run so deep in our thinking that they are not normally given up at the first sign of trouble. The Reformers simply divided into various schools, developed their own Confessions of faith, and set up their own Churches.

In their own way the Reformers recapitulated the early history of the Church. Proclaiming a gospel of grace, and entering into their own encounter with God, they found that, whatever they might say in theory about *sola scriptura*, they needed another 'rule of faith' to construct and keep their communities together. They met in councils, synods, and assemblies to debate and hammer out areas of agreement. Once they had reached agreement, and once they had established their Churches, they developed means of oversight to preserve the Faith across the generations.[2] They also developed the catechetical practices essential for teaching the Faith to young and old.

The effects of these developments on the unity of the Western Church were devastating. The Church in the West was split in two, between Roman Catholicism and Protestantism, and Protestantism was in turn split along several lines: notably, Lutheran, Reformed, Anglican, and Anabaptist. The political, economic, and social consequences of these divisions have long occupied the minds of historians. Clearly the Reformation presented several crises, which took years to be worked out in

---

[2] In most cases they never really managed to reach agreement. In all the main examples, Lutheran, Reformed, and Anglican, the matter of doctrinal agreement was closely tied to the authority of the State. In this respect the Anabaptists were at a distinct disadvantage, for they rejected on principle the role of the State in matters of Christian faith and practice. The latter only really came into their own in North America, where they have flourished in a situation where the State is prohibited from establishing any religion.

detail. The shadows of the theological and political crises of the Reformation still linger on like an incurable disease in the north-western outskirts of modern Europe.

One crisis, however, deserves very special attention in any narrative of the canonical heritage of the Church. The Reformation effectively created a massive epistemological crisis for the whole of Western culture.[3] On the one hand, the Reformers challenged and broke the tenuous theological unity of the Church in the West. The relatively secure appeal to the Church as the ultimate norm of theological reflection was now opposed by appeal to a rival canon which the Church itself had identified and created: namely, Holy Scripture. This in itself was a division of enormous proportions. On the other hand, the promise of the new religious epistemology did not quite work out as expected. Protestant failure to agree on the teaching of Scripture might not matter to those who were so buried in their own squabbles that they could not see beyond their narrow sectional interests. It was another matter entirely for those who might be concerned to reach the truth for themselves. For them the canonical crisis of the Church, a crisis about the ultimate foundation of theological truth and doctrine, became a comprehensive epistemic crisis about the ultimate foundation of all truth and doctrine. What began as a regional problem became a universal problem.

The intellectual genius who best captured the deep implications

---

[3] For various reasons this fact has not been adequately registered in accounts of the origins of epistemology in the modern period. The great exception to this is the remarkable work of Richard H. Popkin, most notably in *The History of Skepticism from Erasmus to Spinoza* (Berkeley: University of California Press, 1979). Popkin's carefully argued account of the relationship between the Reformation, scepticism, fideism, and other developments in epistemology has not begun to receive the attention it deserves. E. M. Curley in *Descartes against the Skeptics* (Cambridge, Mass.: Harvard University Press, 1978), 10–20, gives brief attention to the issue. The significance of the divisions of the Church for general intellectual developments in the sixteenth and seventeenth centuries is well brought out by Robert Mandrou, *From Humanism to Science, 1480–1700* (New York: Penguin, 1978), although Mandrou shows little interest in developments in epistemology. An extremely important interpretation of Descartes and his place in the stream of epistemology in the modern world is given by Jeffrey Stout in *The Flight from Authority: Religion, Morality, and the Quest for Autonomy* (Notre Dame, Ind.: University of Notre Dame Press, 1981).

of the epistemic crisis which lay at the heart of the divisions within Western Christianity was René Descartes.[4] In a series of brilliant moves Descartes set out to resolve the impasse which had developed at the Reformation by constructing a whole new way of construing the foundations of knowledge. In turn, this solution was taken up by John Locke, suitably expanded into the realm of theology, transposed into a new key, and then made available to the culture as a whole. In this chapter we shall explore the remarkable symmetry which exists across these massive changes in the field of epistemology. Despite the changes in content concerning the criteria of knowledge, Descartes, whom we shall take as a crucial figure in the transition to modernity, kept intact the epistemic structures of the Christian tradition he inherited.

If we are right about this, then the Enlightenment, which figures like Descartes and Locke helped to create, together with the acute difficulties it has thrown up for the credibility of Christian doctrine in the modern world, were in part a Christian creation. The Enlightenment was not merely a secular revolt against the authority of the Church or tradition or Scripture; it was a movement created by Christian intellectuals to resolve deep canonical problems which Christians themselves had unwittingly created. It was in part a Christian heresy. Hence, the attack on the credibility of Christian tradition which eventually emerged was not the alien invention of outside enemies. It was the revolt of Christian offspring. Using the brilliant epistemic weapons of their parents, invented in all good faith to save the tradition, they undermined from within the whole Christian enterprise. Christians in effect reaped the deep consequences of the canonical sins which they had committed in the initial division between East and West and the ensuing divisions within the West, and

---

[4] I am not at all seeking to deny the fact that other elements played a very significant role in the origins of Descartes' thinking. Clearly the breakdown of scholasticism and the rise of the new science were also involved in precipitating a deep sceptical crisis for Descartes. The comment of E. M. Curley is apt: 'To the average intelligent nonscientist, accustomed, as nonscientists generally are, to being guided by the consensus of the learned, the destruction of a scientific world view which had nearly universal acceptance for over a thousand years was deeply disturbing. It seemed to illustrate nothing so well as the skeptical position that for any given proposition counterarguments can be found as forceful as any of the arguments in its favor' (*Descartes against the Skeptics*, 10).

consisted in transforming the canons of the Faith from spiritually effective means of grace into dubious norms of truth.

The obvious epistemic problem which was in part precipitated by the Reformation was the problem of the criterion. Clearly, Christians were deeply divided in what they claimed about salvation, the sacraments, the Church, the nature of the human will, and so on. How, then, should we decide which of their claims is ultimately true? Different groups of Christians proposed different answers to this question. Some said we should appeal to the infallible teaching of the Church, some to the infallible teaching of Scripture. We now have at least two different criteria being invoked. This simply generated a further question: Which of the criteria on offer is the right one? But this generates yet another question: What criterion shall we use to decide the debate about the criterion, for there are bound to be rival alternatives on the criterion question itself? This in turn will lead to a further question about the rightness of this criterion. And so on, *ad infinitum*. Hence the problem of the canon in theology naturally generated a more general query about the criterion of truth.

Calvin was aware of this problem. His insistence that the Word of God was to be believed merely because it was the Word of God was his way of stopping the infinite regress. Given who God is, it is strictly irrational not to believe what God says. However, both sides in the debate about canon could agree on this. The problem was that they disagreed on where to locate the Word of God. Was it in the Bible alone, or was it in the Bible appropriately interpreted by the teaching magisterium of the Church? Calvin's doctrine of the internal testimony of the Spirit was his way of responding to this issue. One knew where the Word of God was because the Spirit told one. This, however, opened up an acute dilemma. On the one side, this was simply another appeal to the voice of God; one decided what was revelation by appeal to another revelation. In this new case of the alleged inner voice, one wanted to know how one could know that this was God speaking rather than, say, one's imagination, and the whole problem came back on the table. Alternatively, one could say that the internal testimony was a special kind of religious experience, and now one found that experience had displaced Scripture as the ultimate norm of theological debate. Clearly the epistemic consequences, either way, were unpalatable.

Several leaders of the Counter-Reformation in France were fully aware of the epistemic vulnerability of the Reformers' position and were ready to press this kind of case against them. Drawing indirectly on the work of Michel de Montaigne, they were able to cause severe difficulties for their Protestant opponents. St Francis de Sales, for example, exposed the difficulty of appealing to the inner witness as follows:

Now let us see what rule they have for discerning the canonical books from all of the other ecclesiastical ones. 'The witness,' they say, 'and inner persuasion of the Holy Spirit.' Oh God, what a hiding place, what a fog, what a night! We are not in this way very enlightened in so important and grave a manner. We ask how we can know the canonical books. We would very much like to have some rule for detecting them, and we are told of what takes place in the interior of the soul that no one sees, no one knows, except the soul itself and its Creator.[5]

In other words, we really need to know that this inner persuasion is caused by the Holy Spirit, something Calvin and his followers have failed to show.

On this analysis the whole foundation of the Reformers' case was in trouble. The superstructure was also faulty. Articles of faith are, according to the Reformers, either plainly readable in Scripture, or they can be derived from it by logical inference. However, the rule to read difficult passages of Scripture through plain passages of Scripture was not itself given in Scripture. If we appeal to the inner witness to support this rule, then we face the same difficulties already encountered on this score. Moreover, any alleged reading of Scripture may be mistaken, unless there is an infallible rule for interpretation. Hence we cannot gain assurance by relying on the Reformers' reading of Scripture. Certainly, if the whole Church has erred, then it is likely that the parochial Protestant minister or the local cobbler may also have erred. Furthermore, Scripture does not itself state any rule of logic, or that we can derive true articles of faith by rules of logic. If it said that we are given rational faculties to discern such laws of

---

[5] Quoted in Popkin, *History of Skepticism*, 71.

logic, then reason has become the judge of religious truths, and we have really abandoned Scripture as the norm of truth.[6]

These sorts of arguments could very easily escalate into full-scale scepticism, as the Reformers in their counter-attacks were quick to realize. If, for example, one could not rely on inference, then the whole Catholic appeal to the Fathers and councils could easily be undermined, for questions could always be raised about the authenticity, meaning, and significance for faith of these writings too. Some Roman Catholic intellectuals, notably Montaigne, from whom these sorts of arguments were quarried, may well have been prepared for this kind of consequence. In this case we have a fully developed scepticism which is construed as a kind of preparation for the infusion of divine revelation. On this analysis, Pyrrhonism was a splendid human achievement.

There is nothing in man's invention which has so much verisimilitude and usefulness. It presents man naked and empty, acknowledging his natural weakness, fit to receive from some outside power; stripped of human knowledge, and all the more apt to lodge divine knowledge in himself, annihilating his judgment in order to make room for faith; neither disbelieving nor setting up any doctrine against the common observances; humble, obedient, teachable, zealous; a sworn enemy of heresy, and consequently free from the vain and irreligious opinions introduced by the false sects. *He is a blank tablet prepared to take from the finger of God such forms as he shall be pleased to engrave on it.*[7]

The problem with this, of course, is that it takes us right back to the problem of the inner witness. How are we to know who has true access to the engraving of the finger of God? What do we do when the alleged finger tells some to consult the infallible Bible and others to consult the infallible Church of Rome? We now have a criterion which yields to two competing norms of theological truth.

---

[6] A whole barrage of arguments like these were marshalled by François Vernon. See ibid. 71–2. Popkin tells us that 'Vernon became so good at debating and demoralizing Protestants, that he was freed of his duties as a teacher, and later from those of his order, so that he could be the official arguer of the Faith for the King of France. He was given free rein to attend Calvinist meetings and services, and to debate with Reformers, anywhere and anytime always with the King's protection. Thus he rapidly became the scourge of the French Protestants who tried desperately to avoid him and his attacks' (ibid. 70).

[7] Ibid. 47; emphasis added.

Descartes must surely have been well aware of the deep epistemic problems which had been thrown up by the divisions within the Christian West. He was certainly well aware of the ancient sceptical traditions which had been resurrected by the French attack on the Reformers.[8] In addition, as a leading figure in mathematics and in the developing natural science of his day, he was acutely aware of the need for a better way to secure the foundations of beliefs about the world. It was the search for the latter that led him to devise his remarkable epistemic proposals. In all probability, he did not see the serious consequences which these views could have for the epistemology of theology, for he was a sincere Catholic,[9] a reclusive figure who was prudent in staying out of trouble from the authorities,[10] and generally uninterested in the details of theological problems.[11] Yet Descartes was bold enough to offer his proposals not just as a foundation for knowledge but as an aid to the theologians.[12]

---

[8] It cannot be stressed enough that the revival of scepticism went hand in hand with an attack on the new epistemic proposals of the Reformers. The full Latin edition of Sextus Empiricus's work was published by the French Counter-Reformer Gentian Hervet in 1569. Popkin tells us that Hervet found a manuscript in the library of the Cardinal of Lorraine when he was worn out from his work in the Counter-Reformation and in the Church Fathers. 'He took the manuscript to read as a divertissement while traveling. Then, he reported, when he had read it with unbelievable pleasure, he thought it was a most important work, since it showed that no human knowledge can resist the arguments that can be opposed to it' (ibid. 34).

[9] I agree with A. D. Lindsay in his claim that Descartes was 'a sincere and devout son of the church'. See his introduction to *A Discourse on Method* (New York: Dutton, 1978), p. xii. For a useful discussion of Descartes's religious background see Herman R. Reith, *René Descartes: The Story of a Soul* (Lanham, Md.: University Press of America, 1986), 2–4. 'There is no question but that Descartes had difficulties with the literal sense of Scripture at times and that he took the trouble to wear a mask in order to stay out of trouble' (S. V. Keeling, *Descartes* (Westport, Conn.: Greenwood Press, 1970), 20–1).

[10] Descartes was well aware of the fate of Galileo, abandoning the initial publication of *Le Monde* because of this.

[11] The clear exception to this was his proposal on transubstantiation, although even then, this arises as a consequence of his philosophical views.

[12] There is a tendency to dismiss Descartes's 'Dedication' to *Meditations on First Philosophy* as a kind of prudent window-dressing, to mask his unbelief. It is much more plausible on both internal and external grounds to see it as an effort to get the endorsement of the distinguished theologians of his day, made in good faith and without dissimulation. All in good time Descartes's arguments

Descartes's confident suggestions are an ingenious network of ideas.[13] In the *Discourse on Method* they come across at times with all the force of a religious testimony or conversion narrative. The main outlines of his proposals begin with the acknowledgement that he had accepted many opinions as true which had turned out to be false. Given such an unsatisfactory state of affairs, he determined to rid himself of all his opinions and begin afresh from the foundations. The general destruction of all one's former opinions is a tough assignment, even for one who has waited for the maturity to carry this out, and who has found the time and place to do it. Descartes's strategy was developed by deploying a method of doubt. If there was the slightest ground for doubt for any of his opinions, then he would reject them. More drastically, he would seek to bring down the foundations on which his opinions had been based; for, if he destroyed the foundations, then the edifice would fall with them. Two sorts of foundations were forthwith demolished: namely, the foundations of the senses and the foundations of his reasoning faculties. The first was destroyed by the dream argument, which posited that the deliverances of his senses might well be illusions, the second was overturned by pursuing the possibility that he was being deceived by a demon, who had interfered in the working of his cognitive capacities.

The beauty of Descartes's material strategy here is that he has entered as deeply as is possible into the territory of the sceptic. By invoking the possibility of demonic deception, he has gone beyond the standard sceptical arguments which focus on lack of consent, cases of illusion, instability in our sensory experience,

---

were taken up and used by both Catholics and Protestants in the foundations of their theology. For reaction to Descartes's philosophy within and outside theology see Nicholas Jolley, 'The Reception of Descartes' Philosophy', in John Cottingham (ed.), *The Cambridge Companion to Descartes* (Cambridge: Cambridge University Press, 1992), 393–423. Descartes's views were to cause such a stir among Dutch Calvinists that at one point the usual Sunday afternoon sermon on the Heidelberg Catechism was replaced by sermons on the dispute between Cartesians and anti-Cartesians. See Ernestine Van Der Wall, 'Orthodoxy and Skepticism in the Early Dutch Enlightenment', in Richard Popkin and Arjo Vanderjagt (eds.), *Skepticism and Irreligion in the Seventeenth and Eighteenth Centuries* (Leiden: E. J. Brill, 1993), 125.

[13] Descartes's most cherished conclusions had actually been reached before along different lines by Hagues de Saint-Victor in the twelfth century. See Keeling, *Descartes*, 51.

and the like. In short, he has stated the opponent's position even better than the opponent has stated it to date. He has carried his scepticism right into the very core of his cognitive capacities. If he were now to beat the opponent, he would achieve a masterly victory; if he were to lose, then, unfortunately for him, he would have extended the power of the sceptical enemy. Furthermore, in setting an extraordinarily high standard of acceptance—that is, in treating the slightest ground of doubt as sufficient for the rejection of any belief—he had set himself the high goal of winning in the best possible way, rather than just accepting some kind of minimal victory.

Pursuing this carefully orchestrated strategy of doubt, he hit upon a truth which cannot be doubted, even if he conceived himself as being in the grip of a powerful, cunning, evil demon. He found himself assured that, whatever the demon might do, he could not deceive him about his own existence.

I had persuaded myself that there was nothing at all in the world: no sky, no earth, no minds or bodies; was I not, therefore, also persuaded that I did not exist? No indeed; I existed without doubt, by the fact that I was persuaded, or indeed by the mere fact that I thought at all. But there is some deceiver both very powerful and very cunning, who constantly uses all his wiles to deceive me. There is therefore no doubt that I exist, if he deceives me; and let him deceive me as much as he likes, he can never cause me to be nothing, so long as I think I am something. So that, after having thought carefully about it, and having scrupulously examined everything, one must then, in conclusion take as assured the proposition: *I am, I exist,* is necessarily true, every time I express it or conceive it in my mind.[14]

Descartes's discovery was unearthed by intuition, not by inference; hence it did not depend on the reliability of his reasoning faculties.[15] He had now to hand one truth, which he was absolutely sure of, which had withstood the ravages of total doubt. In its vicinity, he quickly discovered a further truth: namely, that he was constituted as a thinking substance, for in thinking of his own existence, while he could easily conceive of

---

[14] René Descartes, *The Meditations* (London: Penguin, 1968), 103.
[15] For an interpretation of Descartes in keeping with this see Peter A. Schouls, *The Imposition of Method: A Study of Descartes and Locke* (Oxford: Clarendon Press, 1980), ch. 4.

himself without his body, he could not conceive of himself as not thinking.

What am I? A thing that thinks. What is a thing that thinks? That is to say, a thing that doubts, perceives, affirms, denies, wills, does not will, that imagines also, and which feels. Indeed this is not a little, if all these properties belong to my nature. But why should they not so belong? . . . For it is so self-evident that it is I who doubt, who understand and who wish, that there is no need here to add anything to explain it. . . . From this I begin to know who I am, a little more clearly and distinctly than hitherto.[16]

Having found the truth about his existence and about his nature, Descartes paused to reflect on the significance of this for a rule of truth. What is it that enabled him to distinguish true opinions from all the others that occured to him? The answer was simple:

Now I shall examine more closely if perhaps there is not to be found in me other knowledge that I have not observed before. I am certain that I am a thinking being; but do I not therefore likewise know what is required to make me certain of something? In this first knowledge, there is nothing except a clear and distinct perception of what I affirm which would indeed not be sufficient to assure me that my assertion were true, if it could ever happen that a thing I perceived to be thus clearly and distinctly true were found to be false. And consequently it seems to me that I can establish a general rule that all the things we conceive very clearly and distinctly are true.[17]

Here we see Descartes working as a particularist, rather than a methodist, in this stretch of his epistemological journey.[18] Knowing a certain proposition to be true, he tried to arrive at the characteristic marks of that proposition which make it true. Clarity and distinctness of conception constituted the relevant marks. With these in his possession he could then proceed systematically to arrive at other truths which lay buried among the mass of ideas which occupied his mind. Relatively quickly

---

[16] Descartes, *Meditations*, 107.   [17] Ibid. 113.
[18] A particularist initially takes a proposition to be true and then, from this, if he or she thinks a method is worth having, seeks at a theory of the marks of truth. A methodist knows something to be true only after he or she has found the right method for demarcating propositions. I am not at all denying here that in general Descartes is a methodist in his epistemology.

Descartes moved to establish the existence of God by appealing to the clear and distinct principle that there must be at least as much reality in the efficient and total cause as in its effect. It was clear to Descartes that only a perfect being could be the cause of his idea of a perfect being. Then, after a digression on the aetiology of error, he returned to the idea of a perfect being, and provided this time not a causal but an ontological argument for the existence of God, deploying the notion that existence is logically inseparable from the idea of perfect existence. This conclusion in turn gave him a stability in the beliefs already acquired, and provided a true and certain knowledge of the rule of truth he had arrived at when he carefully inspected the first truth which emerged from his initial session of radical doubt.[19] Furthermore, having established the existence of God, he proceeded to show that he could rely on his senses and on his nature in certain crucial respects, for a perfect being would not have created him so that he was constantly deceived about what he came to believe through his senses and through nature.[20] Thereby he arrived at substantial conclusions both about the material world and about the interaction between minds and bodies. Having taken away everything with his method of doubt, he gave it all back again to us, more or less, with his rule of truth.

The aim of this brief exposition of Descartes has been to display, if only in a minimum of terms, the sheer ingenuity of his proposals. There is here an intellectual depth, seriousness, elegance, and rigour which deserve our lasting admiration. It is small wonder that Descartes, whether his ideas are loved or hated, is generally seen as a heroic figure in the history of modern philosophy, and that his slender body of meditations have become part of the canon by means of which students are initiated into the field of epistemology, if not the whole field of philosophy itself.

The naturalness of thinking of Descartes as a hero and his

---

[19] In this exposition of Descartes I have expressed his position in such a way that he is not obviously open to the standard charge of circularity. For a splendid discussion of the debate about circularity in Descartes see George Dicker, *Descartes: An Analytical and Historical Introduction* (New York: Oxford University Press, 1993), 119–41.

[20] It would be fair to say that Descartes is less sure of the testimony of his senses than he is of his logical faculty.

meditations as a canon prompts us to pursue this question: How far can we see in Descartes the transposition of the canonical heritage of the Church, as that had been reconceived at the Reformation? In asking this question, we are deliberating relocating the Cartesian project within the field of Christian theology. Several distinct considerations are pertinent at this point. We shall explore in turn three issues: the theological design of Descartes's work, the remarkable symmetry between his general epistemological proposals and those of the epistemology of theology worked out by the Reformers, and the intriguing way in which his views echo the catechetical tradition of the early Church.

There is, first, the matter of how far we are to view Descartes as a Christian intellectual. Suppose we take seriously Descartes's own comments about the theological significance of his work, together with his brief comment on the theology of the day. What do these suggest? In the preface to the *Meditations*, dedicated to the very sage and illustrious, the dean and doctors of the very sacred Faculty of Theology of Paris, Descartes made it clear that he thought his work was very significant for the fate of theology in the modern world.

I have always been of the opinion that the two questions respecting God and the soul were the chief of those that ought to be determined by help of philosophy rather than theology; for although, to us, the faithful, it be sufficient to hold as matters of faith, that the human soul does not perish with the body, and that God exists, it yet assuredly seems impossible ever to persuade infidels of the reality of any religion, or almost any moral virtue, unless, first of all, those two things be proved to them by natural reason . . . and although it is quite true that the existence of God is to be believed since it is taught in the sacred Scriptures, and that, on the other hand, the sacred Scriptures are to be believed because they come from God (for since faith is a gift of God, the same Being who bestows grace to enable us to believe other things, can likewise impart of it to enable us to believe his own existence), nevertheless, this cannot be submitted to infidels, who would consider that the reasoning proceeded in a circle. . . . I have, therefore, thought that it would not be unbecoming in me to inquire how and by what way, without going out of ourselves, God may be more easily and certainly known than the things of the world.[21]

---

[21] Lindsay, *A Discourse on Method*, 65–6.

In this passage Descartes is reproducing the standard line on the relationship between philosophy and theology as that had been developed by Aquinas and the conventional teaching of the Church. On the basis of divine revelation, mediated and identified by the teaching magisterium of the Church, the ordinary Christian, including Descartes, was entitled to hold that God exists and that the human soul does not perish with the body. Otherwise expressed, we might say that the Sacred Scriptures of the Church teach that God exists and that the soul is immortal; in turn, the Scriptures are to be believed because they come from God. Hence Christians will hold to propositions on faith, a gift from God, or because God has enabled them by grace to believe them. Descartes registered here no dissatisfaction concerning the epistemic position of the believer. However, this kind of epistemic strategy was useless in attempting to deal with the epistemic concerns of the unbeliever, for the unbeliever was worried about the status of the proposition that God exists, and appealing to Scripture or the teaching of the Church will not work in this instance. It was at this level, the level of persuasion of the outsider, that the value of his work was to be judged.

Descartes was extremely confident that his services in this regard were unsurpassed. He was convinced that he had supplied a demonstration for both the existence of God and the continued existence of the soul after the dissolution of the body. Indeed, his demonstrations were 'of the highest certainty and evidence'. They were such that 'there is no way open to the mind of man by which proofs superior to them can ever be discovered'.[22] To be sure, they are not immediately comprehensible to everybody, but that is due to human prejudice and distraction, rather than any weakness in the arguments themselves. Moreover, the propensity to doubt everything, common in philosophy, made it all the more imperative that the arguments developed gain the prestige that the backing of the Church and of the current Faculty of Theology in Paris would secure for them. Hence, properly contextualized and used, his work would be of great value in bringing everyone to believe in the existence of God and to accept the real distinction between mind and body. On this

---

[22] Ibid. 67.

analysis, Descartes was simply helping out in the field of apologetics; he was not securing the primary epistemic status of belief in
the existence of God or in the continued existence of the soul
beyond death.

The problem with this claim, so clearly laid out here by
Descartes himself, is that it does not at all fit with some of the
content of his first attempts at his epistemic vision as we find
them in the *Discourse on Method*; nor does it square at all well with
whole tone and emphases of the *Meditations* themselves. In a
telling autobiographical comment on his assessment of theology
Descartes had this to say:

> I revered our theology and aspired as much as anyone else to gain
> heaven; but having learnt as a certain fact that the path thither is open
> no less to the most ignorant than to the most learned, and that the
> revealed truths which lead to it are beyond our understanding, I would
> not have dared submit them to my weak powers of reasoning, and, in
> my opinion, to undertake the examination of them, and succeed, one
> would need some special grace from heaven and to be more than a mere
> man.[23]

This passage occurs in the opening discourse, where
Descartes is reviewing the failure of all his studies to provide an
adequate foundation for gaining truth. He tells us that he was
already 'assailed by so many doubts and errors that the only
profit I appeared to have drawn from trying to be educated,
was progressively to have discovered my ignorance'.[24] Despite a
splendid education by the Jesuits, Descartes does not strike us
here as having really accepted the status of theology as
presented by the Church; that is, as underwritten by divine
revelation. In fact, there is a note of ironic disdain in the
comment that for a mere man, like Descartes himself, there is
not much hope that he will understand any revealed truth at
all. It is hard to imagine Aquinas, for whom theology was the
highest truth possible, expressing such a low view of the status
of the Faith.

In addition, it is obvious that when Descartes launched his
whole programme, the goal was to clear away absolutely everything, together with the foundations which go with his current

---

[23] Descartes, *Discourse on Method* (London: Penguin, 1968), 32.
[24] Ibid. 29.

opinions, and then to build everything up from new and sound foundations. Nowhere in the midst of this massive reconstruction of the path to truth did Descartes pause to make any exceptions to the general rule for truth, which he developed from his discovery of the *cogito*. On the contrary, the whole tenor and emphasis of his revisionist programme leaves no exception for theology whatsoever. Making an exception for theology would have ruined the whole enterprise as it stood. Hence Descartes's claim that he was merely offering appropriate, divinely sanctioned apologetic help does not fit with the content and tenor of his new epistemology.

There is no need to see this as an instance of bad faith on Descartes's part. The more likely and generous possibility is that Descartes failed to see the consequences for theology of the position he developed with such care in the *Meditations*. Clearly, if we cannot trust our senses until they are secured in Cartesian fashion, we cannot believe what we hear from the Church, for we need our senses to obtain access to the teaching of the Church in the first place. The same applies to the teaching of Scripture; being taught by the Scriptures presupposes that we can rely on our senses and on our cognitive capacities. Similar considerations apply to beliefs supposedly implanted in us by grace. It is obvious that we can be easily mistaken in the identification of those propositions implanted by grace; hence these propositions do not survive the onslaught of Descartes's radical doubt. The whole programme of the *Meditations* insisted that we were not rationally entitled to construe any of the conventional beliefs of the Church as true until they had been fitted into the whole new system of knowledge worked out by Descartes.

Furthermore, Descartes at no point stopped to ask whether his actual theological beliefs fitted with the canonical teaching of the Church. He assumed that his general theism and that his dualistic anthropology were what the Church believed and taught. Nowhere did he pursue the possibility that both the doctrine of God and the doctrine of human beings actually held by the Church might run into serious difficulties once they were subject to the stringent cognitive requirements laid down in his rule of truth. In the one case where he was faced with a serious problem—that is, with respect to transubstantiation—he made a rather half-hearted attempt to deal with it.[25] All this suggests that his real confidence stemmed from the proper application of his epistemology applied across the board, with no exception for theology.[26]

The second line of enquiry worth pursuing concerns the remarkable symmetry that exists between Descartes's epistemological programme and the canonical programme of the Reformers. The former appears as if it were a remarkable transposition of the latter.

Consider the following features of the canonical vision of the Reformers:

1. Individuals must take responsibility for their own theological convictions.
2. All the past traditions of the Church must be set aside, for they are liable to error and corruption.
3. In the search for God one finds oneself believing with certainty that the Scriptures are the Word of God.
4. This certainty is derived not from argument but from the inner light and testimony of the Holy Spirit, who tells us that the Christian scriptures are indeed the Word of God.
5. There must be one single, solid foundation for everything which is to be believed. That foundation is the Word of God, written in the Scriptures, the rule of faith.
6. The teaching of the rule of faith is constituted by clarity.
7. Only those articles of theology are to be believed which can be shown to be built on this foundation, as expressly stated in it, or derived from it by deductive inference.

[25] For a discussion of the importance and complexity of Descartes's views on transubstantiation see Richard A. Watson, 'Transubstantiation among the Cartesians', and Ronald Laymon, 'Transubstantiation: Test Case for Descartes's Theory of Space', both in Thomas M. Lennon, John M. Nicholas, and John W. Davis (eds.), *Problems of Cartesianism* (Kingston and Montreal: McGill–Queen's University Press, 1982), 127–48, 149–70.

[26] This fits with the judgement of Watson: 'In fact, Descartes was not himself inclined to develop a Cartesian theology. He was preoccupied with setting out his metaphysical position, and with its implications for natural science, in such a way as to avoid sharing Galileo's fate. What he rather hoped for was that some theologians, preferably of the dominant Jesuit sect, would base a solid theological structure on Cartesian principles, just as Thomas Aquinas had on Aristotelian principles. Descartes's arrogance was to see himself not as another Thomas Aquinas, but as a modern Aristotle' ('Transubstantiation', 128).

8. The truth of the rule of faith, the Scriptures, is secured by its having God as its author, a being who cannot lie.
9. Given our fallibility, it is appropriate to check again and again that the articles are actually built on the scriptural foundation.

It is intriguing that many of these themes show up in the Cartesian project, but their content applies not to theological truth but to truth in general.

1. Individuals must face the disquieting reality of diverse opinions and take responsibility for finding the truth for themselves. One cannot rely on past tradition, on the untested opinions of others, on hearsay, and the like.
2. All that has been previously believed must be courageously eradicated in order to prepare for the building of a new foundation.
3. In the ruthless search for truth, one finds oneself believing with certainty in one's own existence.
4. This certainty is not secured by inference; it is a matter of intuition; it is set apart in one's experience by its clarity and distinction. It is marked by the presence of a natural light and by a compulsion to believe it on beholding its content.
5. There can only be one rule of truth, one rule for determining true beliefs.
6. Clarity and distinction of conception are the marks of this belief; these marks constitute the rule of truth.
7. By this rule all other truth is to be identified and built up systematically.
8. Our confidence in the rule of truth is strengthened by the fact that we are created by a perfect being, who would not deceive us concerning our intuition of the truth of what is clear and distinct.
9. From time to time it is essential to check that the beliefs one holds as true actually conform to the rule of truth.

There is no claim here that this in any way shows that Descartes was intentionally drawing on the debates about canon in the Church in order to construct his epistemological programme. The fact that a whole raft of similar themes show up could be purely accidental. The only connection we have sought to point out to date between the canonical debate and the Cartesian project has been indirect. Thus I have suggested that the canonical disputes led to sceptical overtones among some theologians, and that they precipitated the quest to quarry the ancient sceptical traditions for ammunition against one's opponents in the storm about the rule of truth in Christian theology.

Yet the similarities in theme and structure are extraordinarily striking. It is hard to believe that the connections are entirely accidental. After all, Descartes was formed in the cognitive womb of the Church; he was intellectually nourished by those who were in the vanguard of the Counter-Reformation; and he was operating in a context where the canonical division of the Church had got so out of hand that it had led to war. Hence it is not at all fanciful to surmise that there is here, not in intention but in historical effect, a transposition of elements in the debate about canon into the debate about the foundations of truth.[27] At the very least, the position of Descartes in general epistemology is foreshadowed in the epistemology of theology as held by the leading Reformers. At the root of both is a claim to have access to the light of God: in one case the light of the Holy Spirit, in the other the natural light of God shining in human reason. Does not the light of reason play a role in Cartesian epistemology that is structurally analogous to the role played by the Holy Spirit in the epistemology of theology of the Reformers? Might it not be that the testimony of the Holy Spirit has been naturalized into the light of reason? Might it be no accident that the movement which looked back to Descartes as its founding father came to be known as the Enlightenment, echoing the original enlightenment of the Holy Spirit in salvation? More boldly and graphically, may we not ask if the light of nature in Descartes does not represent the secularization of the internal witness of the Holy Spirit? Did this move constitute the first step in a wave of demythologization, which centuries later would become a major school of Christian theology?

I am not alone in this kind of conjecture. Popkin raised a similar

---

[27] For an account which rightly sees the significance of the ecclesial and social context for the interpretation of Descartes but which does not reckon with this possibility see Stephen Toulmin, *Cosmopolis* (Chicago: University of Chicago Press, 1990).

kind of possibility in his suggestion that Descartes followed the same path as the Reformers. After pointing out that the Reformers sought to link their subjective assurance about the rule of faith to an objective 'skyhook' which would transform it into an objective feature of the world, he wrote:

In Descartes's answer to skepticism one finds the same sort of Reformation development, and the same attempt to objectify subjective certitude by attaching it to God. The Cartesian 'voie d'examin' is the method of doubt, the examination of what we believe. By moving from the partial Pyrrhonism of doubting the reliability of our senses, to the metaphysical Pyrrhonism of the dream hypothesis, doubting the reality of our knowledge, to the total Pyrrhonism of the demon hypothesis, doubting the reliability of our rational faculties, we finally discover the *cogito*, a truth so subjectively certain that *we* are incapable of doubting it at all. This is the first aspect of the illumination—there is truth. The second is the realization of the source of truth, of the guarantee of truth. The *cogito* leads to the rule of truth, the rule to God, and God provides the objective assurance of our subjective certitude. Having started on the way to truth by experiencing the illumination of the *cogito*, one ends by realizing that the indubitability of all clear and distinct ideas is a God-ordained fact, and hence objectively true.[28]

If there is any truth in this surmise, then we can begin to see the deeper consequences, for theology and for the life of the Church, of the move to treat Scripture as a norm of truth, rather than, more modestly, as one of a rich set of canonical materials bonded together in a network of canonical practices. The rule of faith has travelled from a modest creed, summing up basic Christian doctrine, to a criterion of truth for theology, constituted by the Bible, to the one and only rule of truth, construed as clarity and distinction in conception as perceived by intuition. Once the Church changed the canon into a norm of truth, it had cast its nets out into the sea of epistemology. All sorts of fish would now be hauled on board and served as food to the crew or converted into medicine for passengers. Like it or not, it did not have a committee of angels to sort out the good into vessels and throw the bad away. Epistemologists like Descartes cannot be disposed of that easily once the Church has raised the stakes by epistemizing its canonical heritage.

---

[28] Popkin, *History of Skepticism*, 191.

The Church found itself officially and constitutively landed with the job of articulating its epistemic proposals in a thorough and responsible manner. It now had to become an expert not just on salvation and holiness but on theories of knowledge. It now staked its very existence not just on its claims about the Trinity, the Incarnation, the nature of salvation, and the like, but on the correctness of the epistemic theories of its teachers. It claimed not only to know the truth about God; it claimed to know with certainty, and in some cases with infallibility, how it knew what it knows about God. It knew that it knows through the canon of Scripture, through the teaching magisterium of the Church, and the like. Moreover, it knew these kinds of truth, in turn, through the secret revelation of the Spirit or through the writing of the finger of God on the human heart.

The circularity of these claims and the contradictory conclusions spawned by such epistemic theorizing within the Church created a cognitive accident which was waiting to happen. Part of the genius of Descartes was that he was one of the first to see that these debates could not be settled on the grounds which Christian intellectuals and teachers had staked out for themselves within theology. If serious thinkers could not agree about the foundations of the truth about God, then the only way to tackle this problem, given the terms in which the debate had been conducted, was to go back and raise questions about the foundations of any and all truth. Descartes, like his predecessors, was confident that he should stick to the image of sure and certain foundations in his thinking about the pathway to truth, and he was equally confident that he could secure as certain the actual foundations of all truth that was worth having. This confidence was misplaced. His proposals have sparked centuries of debate, which have exposed the fault-lines which run through his system.

Thus, to express our judgement briefly, Descartes was working with geometry as the paradigm of knowledge, an assumption which he nowhere establishes as indubitable. The claim that clarity and distinction in conception are sufficient to secure truth is highly questionable, however certain it may appear phenomenologically to Descartes.[29] Descartes cannot secure the continued

---

[29] Some claims which initially appear clear and distinct to us turn out to be false.

existence of himself beyond the time he is reflecting on his own thinking activity.[30] The causal principle that only a perfect being could cause human agents to have the idea of a perfect being is false. His ontological argument for the existence of God is questionable, if not invalid; for it is possible that existence is not essential to perfection. It is true that the power and agency of God can explain the reliability of our senses and cognitive capacities, but this claim has to be argued in its own right;[31] it will not yield certitude, and it is a matter of substantial debate if it will help us in our epistemic endeavours. Notoriously, there is a host of problems related to the dualism worked out by Descartes, and some of his claims about the actual nature of the physical world as mediated through the senses are thoroughly questionable. Finally, the Cartesian project set up a model for success in securing truth which was difficult to reconcile with a whole range of truths to which Christians were committed if they took the historic canonical tradition of the Church seriously. That model allowed one to hold only those beliefs which one had shown to be derived from absolutely certain foundations: 'whether we are awake or asleep, we should never let ourselves be persuaded except on the evidence of our reason.'[32] As Descartes himself was aware, this required that one pass through a process of cognitive cleansing or therapy which was demanding in the extreme.

This theme of cognitive therapy takes us into our third and last topic related to the ecclesial and theological significance of Descartes's vision. We noted in our account of the canons in the patristic Church that they were intimately related to the catechetical activity of the Church. Thus the Scriptures and the creeds were used in the spiritual direction which the Church's evangelists and teachers gave to those who were coming to faith and entering the life of holiness. The various canonical materials and practices were joined together to enable the humble and the repentant to be immersed in the life of God and thereby be healed and morally transformed and make manifest the holiness of God. The demands

---

[30] As it has again and again been pointed out, the most that Descartes has secured is 'I thought, therefore I was'.

[31] The form that the argument needs to take is that of an argument to the best explanation or some version of a teleological argument for the existence of God.   [32] *Discourse on Method*, 59.

that this laid on the seeker, convert, and believer were anything but easy. It meant struggle against sin, warding of the demonic, joining in the fellowship of the Church, meditating on the great events and truths of the Gospel, submission to the direction of the elders and Fathers, waiting patiently on God, trusting that the seed of the Gospel would bear abundant fruit, and the like.

An attentive reader, aware of the massive conceptual shift on canon which developed in the Church in the split between East and West, and which was deepened by the divisions at the Reformation, cannot but notice that there is in Descartes more than an echo of the catechetical tradition of the early Church. It cannot be an accident that he casts his work in the form of a series of discourses, which read at times like a religious testimony, and in a serious of essays classified as 'Meditations'.[33] Nor can it be accidental that he sets his sights on the ordinary people of the world, writing in French, so that the priesthood of true believers can be established. Nor can it be an accident that, like the monks of old, he finds a place of solitude where he could be as withdrawn as 'in the most remote of deserts'.[34] Nor that he devises a set of simple rules to give himself direction;[35] nor that he sets out to eradicate error as whole-heartedly as a Christian should eradicate sin;[36] nor that he calls for constant practice, vigilance, and repeated meditation to get his mind fixed on the task in hand;[37] nor that success in gaining truth 'so filled my mind that nothing else mattered to me';[38] nor that he was convinced that following this path would be the means of 'acquiring all the true goods which would ever be in my power', including all the virtues and happiness;[39] nor that he could look to imagination, 'a mode of thinking peculiar to material objects', and to preoccupation with worldly pursuits as the chief barrier to success in his programme;[40] nor that he should be so occupied with the subject of the soul, for, 'after the error of those who deny the existence of God . . . there is nothing which leads feeble minds more readily astray

---

[33] It is intriguing that the literary model on which the *Meditations* was based in part was the *Spiritual Exercises* of St Ignatius Loyola. See Z. Vendler, 'Descartes' Exercises', *Canadian Journal of Philosophy*, 19 (1989), 193–224.

[34] *Discourse on Method*, 52.

[35] See the four famous rules in Discourse Two, ibid. 41.

[36] Ibid. 37.   [37] Ibid. 48.   [38] Ibid. 49.

[39] Ibid.   [40] Ibid. 57.

from the straight path of virtue than to imagine that the soul of animals is of the same nature as their own, and that, consequently, we have nothing to fear or hope for after this life than flies or ants';[41] nor that by keeping his directions to himself he might sin against the general good of his neighbours;[42] nor that through his cognitive regime he was seeking perfect peace of mind.[43] Descartes had developed a scheme of initiation into his rule of truth, a pale shadow and substitute for the original initiation into the rule of God performed out by the Church.[44]

Descartes in a remarkable way was setting forth a whole way of life for human beings conceived fundamentally as thinking substances.[45] He had a whole plan of salvation which would not

[41] Ibid. 76.   [42] Ibid. 78.   [43] Ibid. 88.

[44] It should be borne in mind at this juncture that Descartes believed himself to have a divine mission to found a new philosophical system. During the night of 10 Nov. 1619, Descartes, then 23, experienced three troubling dreams, accompanied by earnest prayer for light, which ended with a vow to make a pilgrimage to Our Lady of Loretto, which he probably fulfilled the following year. The spiritual significance of such dreams in the Jesuit tradition is well brought out by Reith, *René Descartes*, 5. For a fine summary of the dreams and their significance for Descartes, see John Cottingham, *Descartes* (Oxford: Blackwell, 1986), 9–10. For an extended discussion of these dreams see Gregor Sebba, *The Dream of Descartes* (Carbondale, Ill.: University of Illinois Press, 1987).

[45] Compare the comment of Jacques Maritain: 'Let us try to find the right names for things: The sin of Descartes is the sin of *angelism*. He turned Knowledge and Thought into a hopeless perplexity, an abyss of unrest, because he conceived human Thought after the type of angelic Thought' (*Three Reformers: Luther–Descartes–Rousseau* (New York: Charles Scribner's Sons, n.d.), 54; emphasis original). As Maritain goes on to show, there are fascinating affinities between Descartes's conception of human beings and that of angels in medieval philosophy and theology. 'The angel knows himself immediately by his substance, in a perfect intuition which yields him the ground of his being. His natural cognizance of God is consummated not only in his beholding external objects, but primarily and above all in beholding himself, in the most pure mirror of his own essence. His own essence is the first object of his intellection, and he is always in act of intellection of himself. Everything he knows, he knows by first being cognizant of himself and by a sort of prolongation of his cognizance of himself. All that appears again, transposed and lessened, in Cartesian thought' (ibid. 77). This whole essay brings out astutely and suggestively the potential spiritual significance of the Cartesian revolution and its aftermath. It is true that the later writings of Descartes provide a richer account of the human situation than that captured by the notion of spiritual substance. Descartes wants to do justice to the emotions and passions. However, this addition does not alter the main point made here.

just put the academic world in working order and provide an adequate basis for the new sciences, but would also rid the world of error and sin.[46] In this scheme there was room for a general theistic deity, but the deity was not really worshipped and glorified for his own sake or for the mighty works he had done for the healing of the world. This deity was lauded primarily because he could deliver us from scepticism by strengthening our confidence in our intuitions and by delivering us from the darkness of the senses to which the method of doubt had doomed us.

This vision of humanity and salvation, when compared to the vision of the great Christian teachers and Fathers, is thin and emaciated. It cuts us loose from the riches of tradition and Scripture. It substitutes rationality for holiness. It eliminates the secret working of the Spirit, reducing it to the natural light of creation. It separates us from Church and neighbour—unless, that is, we can find artisans or such people as we can pay to do our wonderful scientific experiments for us.[47] For all its confessions of ignorance and error, and for all its sense of dependence on God, it fosters arrogance and pride. Yet crucial elements of this vision have become the air we breathe in the Western world. Descartes has been one of the great heroes of high modernism, and his writings have become an integral part of the canons of modern educational institutions.[48] It is ironic in the extreme that an ingenious Roman Catholic intellectual, unwittingly representing in a radically transposed form the canonical and epistemic revolution of Protestants, and echoing the spiritual direction of the early Fathers, should have contributed so much

[46] In the Fourth Meditation, systematically neglected in much of the modern commentary on Descartes, intellectual error is analysed in terms of a particular conception of sin. 'Whence then my errors? From this fact alone, that the will being much more ample than the understanding, I do not contain it within the same limits, but extend it also to things I do not understand, and the will being of itself indifferent to such things, very easily goes astray and chooses the bad instead of the good, or the false instead of the true, which results in my falling into error or sinning' (*Meditations*, 137).

[47] Descartes is scathing in his comments about the trouble caused by volunteers who would cost so much precious time (*Discourse on Method*, 87).

[48] I leave aside the tangled question of how far the Cartesian project was under fire from the outset and how far it can survive the current drive towards post-modernity.

to the intellectual secularization of modern Western culture. It is also ironic that Descartes should have initiated a tradition which aggressively repudiates all tradition, and that he should be one of the founding fathers of a movement which aggressively rejected the very concept of Fathers. In this he was not alone, as our continued journey through the history of canonization will disclose.

8

Canonical Synthesis:
The Anglican Via Media

The inherent difficulties which lie buried in the Continental Reformers' proposals concerning the canonical heritage of the Church and which did so much to precipitate the characteristically modern approach to knowledge in Descartes become readily apparent in the fascinating developments which constitute the bedrock of the Church of England. In this case the endemic confusing of canon and criterion, of means of grace and epistemic theorizing, is clearly visible. We are even given a handy conventional formula which is presented as the genius of theological method, but which carries an unmistakable message for those who have eyes to see; theological disputes are to be settled, it is proposed, by an appeal to Scripture, tradition, and reason. Here *in nuce* we see the mixture of canonical apples and epistemic oranges which, presented as the essence of tolerance and sweet reasonableness, will create unending doctrinal chaos in the life of the Church. Four centuries later, the pietistic offspring of the Anglican tradition in the New World, the United Methodists, took this proposal to its logical conclusion and attempted to establish a new Church on the basis of Scripture, tradition, reason, and experience.[1] Not surprisingly, both traditions, the sedate mother and the rich but diminishing daughter, are now in serious internal disarray. Even so, they are not without their devout and learned advocates. However, we must not get too far ahead of ourselves too quickly. There is a story to be unfolded whose plot is pivotal in marking a transition in the narrative of canon and criterion in the Christian tradition.

---

[1] I have dealt with the value of the Methodist quadrilateral in *Waking from Doctrinal Amnesia: The Healing of Doctrine in The United Methodist Church* (Nashville: Abingdon Press, 1995).

The most striking feature of the Anglican experiment in canon and norm is its attempt to break loose from the canonical foundationalism inherited from the Continental Reformation. This claim about the nature of the Anglican tradition stands, despite the fact that it would be easy to dismiss the Anglican theological and ecclesial arrangements as first and foremost a political settlement determined predominantly by secular rather than theological constraints.

To be sure, there is no denying the deep political constraints and considerations which lie at the base of the Anglican experiment. The various phases of the English Reformation are shot through with political ideology and interests at every turn. Yet the modern distinction between secular and religious is anachronistic when applied to the Reformation in England. All sides to the disputes in the sixteenth century were committed to the concept of a national Church; the idea of a separation of Church and State would have appeared thoroughly unchristian and inappropriate. Moreover, the kings and queens who were involved in the various settlements were Christian laity who took a deep interest in theology. Henry VIII earned the title of 'Defender of the Faith' for his work on the sacraments,[2] while recently, albeit somewhat in jest, Elizabeth I has been nominated by one modern Anglican for a place in a canon of Anglican divines.[3] Political decisions were influenced, then, by theological constraints.

More important still, whatever role purely political factors may have played, Anglicanism eventually emerged with its own theological interpreters who provided their own inimitable rationale and account of the arrangements which eventually won the day. Within these there developed a characteristic way of thinking about canon and criterion which has outlived the particular political circumstances in which it came to birth and which still has its advocates today. The heart of the Anglican proposal is that theological claims are to be justified by a complex appeal to Scripture, tradition, and reason.

This attractive triad emerged over time as part and parcel of an

---

[2] This was the title given by Leo X to Henry VIII for his work *Assertio Septum Sacramentorum*.

[3] See the suggestion of John Booty in 'Standard Divines'. in Stephen Sykes and John Booty (eds.), *The Study of Anglicanism* (London: SPCK, 1988), 163–74.

effort to develop a middle way between the rival alternatives of Roman Catholicism and a native English version of the Calvinistic tradition. Initially the break with Rome was so tied to Henry VIII's marital concerns that a Catholicism without the Pope constituted the first phase of the Reformation in England. From the latter part of his reign to the opening of that of Elizabeth, no fewer than six varieties of Christian faith and practice successively prevailed. Cranmer, the first great architect of the Church of England, whom Henry appointed as archbishop of Canterbury, was deeply tinged with Lutheranism, both through his studies at Cambridge and his stay in Germany, where he married the niece of Andreas Osiander. Under Edward VI, in a short, six-year period, a whole series of significant changes were introduced. In turn, a book of Homilies, a series of Books of Common Prayer, an ordinal, a catechism, and a set of forty-two Articles were promulgated. The reforms introduced the doctrine of justification by faith, stressed the importance of Bible reading, allowed for the possibility of married priests, and eliminated the idea of transubstantiation from the Eucharist.

Contrary to initial appearances, the reforms were gradualist and pragmatic, with the acceptance of one reform leading to the introduction of another. All these changes were swept aside, however, when Mary Tudor, gaining the throne in 1553, repealed the relevant laws and revived the old heresy laws against the Reformers. Three hundred people were martyred, and eight hundred fled to foreign lands. In turn, these changes were reversed when Elizabeth I came to the throne in 1558. Within one year a process of consolidation and stability was introduced which secured the Reformed character of the Church of England.[4]

Henceforth the crucial debates centred not so much on the break with Rome as on the positive character of the changes which were to be made and institutionalized. It was in this context that Richard Hooker, while not exactly holding the place

---

[4] Whatever may be said later about the Reformation among Anglicans inclined towards Rome, there is no denying the Reformed character of the Church in its formative developments under Edward VI and Elizabeth I. For a good discussion see William P. Havgaard, *Elizabeth and the English Reformation: The Struggle for a Stable Settlement of Religion* (Cambridge: Cambridge University Press, 1968), esp. ch. 6.

that Luther and Calvin occupied for their followers in the Continental Reformation, earned a unique place in the history of the Church of England as apologist and theorist.[5] We shall turn shortly to explore the crucial moves he made in the debate about canon and norm in Christian thinking.

Before taking this up, it is worth drawing attention to the fact that in time the Church of England developed a comprehensive vision of Christian corporate thought, life, and practice. Thus, not only did it procure its own translation of the Bible under King James I, it also put formally in place a form of corporate prayer and worship, incorporating the two sacraments of baptism and Eucharist, a book of Homilies, a set of Thirty-Nine Articles to which the clergy were required to subscribe, an episcopal system of ecclesial oversight, and a tradition of canonical regulation. It solved the vexed question of royal supremacy by giving the occupant of the throne a position as supreme governor of the Church, and it also kept in place the book of Homilies as a standard of preaching and theological competence. Securing this kind of comprehensive settlement was not, to put it mildly, an easy affair. There were periods of savage torture and execution and times when tender consciences found themselves shut out from the subtle comprehensiveness which was sincerely sought by many in high places. Final arrangements took almost two centuries to be consolidated; they were dramatically interrupted by an alternative experiment with a Presbyterian form of the Church in a stormy period in the 1650s.[6] Despite these difficulties and changes, a form of classical Anglicanism emerged which has endured and thrived across the generations.

Our interest here is in how early Anglicanism resolved the vexed issues related to canon and criterion in the Christian tradition. The core of the tradition can best be summarized initially as a careful attempt to preserve a primary appeal to Scripture as the norm of Christian belief and practice but to supplement the limitations of this proposal by appeal to early tradition and reason.

---

[5] Commentators have rightly stressed the fact that no one person was the architect of the Church of England. Yet there is no denying the pivotal role played by Hooker in articulating the Anglican position and in setting the model for later expositions of the tradition.

[6] The crucial figure here, of course, is Oliver Cromwell, who favoured first Presbyterianism and then Independency.

We can see this solution beginning to emerge in the work of Thomas Cranmer before it flowered in the work of Richard Hooker. We can then detect a natural transition to the proposals of John Locke, whose innovations radically transformed the foundations embedded in the initial forms of the tradition and whose thinking I shall consider in a separate chapter. Once I have completed our descriptive survey of the terrain, I shall stand back and provide an extended evaluation.

Clearly the first move in the tradition was to work with the standard appeal to *sola scriptura* as the warrant for the changes introduced by those committed to reform of the medieval English Church. There is little if any intrinsic interest in religious epistemology; the Anglican Reformers simply inherited a very strong commitment to the authority of Scripture from the Continental Reformation and set about making the changes they deemed essential. We can see this in the thinking of Cranmer, the primary architect of the Homilies, in the Book of Common Prayer, and in the Articles of Religion.

One of the best places to catch the drift of the initial Anglican position is in the two homilies devoted to Scripture.[7] Four points deserve mention. First, while it is certain that a conventional account of Scripture as the oracles of God lies behind the ideas in the sermons, the stress is on the adequacy and sufficiency of Scripture to achieve the deep spiritual purposes intended for them by God.

Unto a Christian man there can be nothing either more necessary or profitable than the knowledge of holy Scripture; forasmuch as in it is contained God's true word, setting forth his glory and man's duty. And there is no truth nor doctrine necessary for our justification and

---

[7] The fact that a set of homilies was produced and authorized is testimony to the deep influence of Luther, who had recalled the Church to the work of preaching and had authorized a collection of his own sermons for reading in parish churches. There were two books of homilies presented eventually. Useful background can be found in Peter Toon, 'The Articles and Homilies', in Stephen Sykes and John Booty (eds.), *The Study of Anglicanism* (London: SPCK, 1988), 133–43. There are two homilies on Scripture: 'A Fruitful Exhortation to the Reading and Knowledge of Holy Scripture', attributed to Cranmer, and 'An Information for them which take Offence at Certain Places of Holy Scripture', attributed to John Jewell. I have drawn from the following edition: *Certain Sermons or Homilies Appointed to be Read in Churches in the Time of Queen Elizabeth of Famous Memory* (London: SPCK, 1890).

everlasting salvation, but that it is or may be drawn out of that fountain and well of truth.[8]

Let us diligently search for the well of life in the books of the New and Old Testament, and run not to the stinking puddles of men's traditions, devised by men's imaginations, for our justification and salvation. For in Holy Scripture is fully contained what we ought to do and what to eschew, what to believe, what to love, and what to look for at God's hands at length.[9]

Second, Scripture fulfils its function of healing and nurturing people into a life in God only when it is approached in a spirit of humility and when the reader is guided and assisted by the Holy Spirit.

And, if you be afraid to fall into error by reading of holy Scripture, I shall shew you how you may read it without danger of error. Read it humbly with a meek and lowly heart, to the intent you may glorify God, and not yourself, with the knowledge of it; and read it not without daily praying to God, that he would direct your reading to good effect; and take upon you to expound it no further than you can plainly understand it. For as St. Augustine saith, the knowledge of Holy Scripture is a great, large, and a high palace, but the door is very low; so that the high and arrogant man cannot run in it, but he must stoop low and humble himself that shall enter into it. Presumption and arrogancy is the mother of all error: and humility needeth to fear no error.[10]

The Holy Ghost is the Schoolmaster of truth, which leadeth his scholars, as our Saviour Christ saith of him *into all truth*. And whoso is not led and taught by this Schoolmaster cannot but fall into deep error, how goodly soever his pretence is, what knowledge and learning soever he hath of all other works and writings, or how fair soever a shew-face of truth he hath in the estimation and judgment of the world.[11]

Third, it is clear that the truth of Scripture will often appear unacceptable to 'carnal' reason; hence, when moral and other problems arise, reason is to give way before the wisdom of God.

Thus, if you will be profitable hearers and readers of the holy Scriptures, you must first deny yourselves, and keep under your carnal senses, taken by the outward words, and search the inward meaning; reason must give place to God's Holy Spirit; you must submit your worldly wisdom and judgment unto his divine wisdom and judgment. Consider that the

[8] *Certain Sermons or Homilies*, 1.   [9] Ibid. 2.
[10] Ibid. 7.   [11] Ibid. 390.

Scripture, in what soever it be pronounced, is the word of the living God . . . the God of gods and Lord of all lords, yea, God that is God alone, incomprehensible, almighty, and everlasting, he hath spoken it: it is his word. It cannot therefore be but truth; it cannot but be wisely and prudently commanded, what Almighty God hath devised; howsoever, through want of grace, we miserable wretches do imagine and judge of his most holy word.[12]

Fourth, while Scripture is entirely sufficient in itself, it is legitimate to appeal to ancillary arguments to confirm its claims.

You have heard, well beloved, in the first part of this Homily, the doctrine of the word of God against idols and images, against idolatry and worshipping of images, taken out of the Scriptures of the Old Testament and the New, and confirmed by the examples as well of the Apostles as of our Saviour Christ himself. Now, although our Saviour Christ taketh not nor needeth not any testimony of men, and that which is once confirmed by the certainty of his eternal truth hath no more need of confirmation of man's doctrine and writings, than the bright sun at noon tide hath need of the light of a little candle to put away darkness and to increase the light; yet, for your further contentation, it shall in this second part be declared . . . that this truth and doctrine concerning the forbidding of images and worshipping of them, taken out of the holy Scriptures as well of the Old Testament as the New, was believed and taught by the old holy fathers and most ancient learned doctors, and received in the old primitive Church, which was most uncorrupt and pure. And this declaration shall be made out of the said holy doctor's writings and out of the ancient historical ecclesiastical to the same belonging.[13]

The main point to be gleaned from this material is that there is considerable reserve about the place of reason and tradition as a warrant for theological claims. A doctrine which posits Scripture as spoken by God combined with a second doctrine which stresses the carnality and weakness of human reason puts the brake on any overly optimistic evaluation of reason and tradition. In Richard Hooker we can see that brake begin to be loosened up considerably.[14]

---

[12] *Certain Sermons or Homilies*, 399.

[13] 'An Homily against Peril of Idolatry', ibid. 194–5. This sermon is usually attributed to Bishop Ridley, with additions by Bullinger.

[14] This is close to the view developed by Stephen Carter in 'The Protestant Doctrine of Scripture in the Church of England, 1547–1553' (M. Phil. thesis, University of Oxford, 1990). Carter brings out succinctly the appeal to tradition in Cranmer. See esp. 42 f.

By Hooker's time, it is clear that the opponent to be faced was no longer Rome but the more radical kind of Reformer, whether Presbyterian or Separatist,[15] who was convinced that the Church of England had settled for less than the best in the arena of worship and Church order. This conviction was fuelled by a particular reading of the *sola scriptura* formula of the Continental Reformation. All theological issues, it was averred, should be determined by appeal to Scripture; that is, only those things sanctioned by the manifest meaning of Scripture or deducible therefrom were to be permitted in the Church. Some, following this principle, even gave the impression that virtually every belief had to be determined by Scripture; hence they rejected logic and rhetoric in the exposition of Scripture. It fell to Hooker to provide a devastating critique of this position. In the course of this he developed an alternative epistemology for theology.

In doing so, Hooker took for granted the bedrock doctrines of the Christian faith contained in the patristic creeds, and he happily expounded the Reformation doctrine of salvation by grace through faith in Jesus Christ. Indeed, Hooker's epistemological doctrines are very clearly embedded in a theistic and trinitarian metaphysical vision. Moreover, one can hear throughout the echo, if not the exact thinking, of Aquinas.

Hooker's deep concern was as much pastoral and political as epistemic. He clearly had his eye on the social consequences of the doctrines he was seeking to attack and replace, and he had a keen nose and a warm heart for the problems which those doctrines would naturally engender in those of tender and weak conscience. In this arena he was in fact remarkably prescient, anticipating the kind of social chaos and violence which would ensue once the canonical foundationalism of his opponents was to win the day. A splendid reasonableness, affection for tolerance, and desire for peace breathe through his work.

The initial arena of dispute between Hooker and his opponents was remarkably narrow. The issue was this: How should the Church resolve disputed questions concerning the exact character

---

[15] The highways and byways of the debate between Presbyterians and Separatists is nicely covered in W. A. C. Tovey, 'Forms of Authority in the Theology of the Elizabethan Separatists' (BD thesis, University of Oxford, 1991).

of its internal order, its worship, and its rites and ceremonies? Should it resolve these by appeal to Scripture alone? Or should it resolve them by appeal to reason and Church consensus? The crucial subject was one not so much of belief as of action. In the neighbourhood, there was the additional question of social authority and discipline in the Church: that is, how are the decisions in this arena to be enforced?

What emerged in Hooker's answer was a very firm commitment to the use of human wisdom, law, judgement, or reason in the life of the church.[16] Hooker uses these terms interchangeably to identify a capacity to judge and reason which is given by God and which is to be used in its appropriate place and manner. Part of the proper use of human wisdom is to examine the contrary claim that Scripture is the only touchstone of wisdom in the life of faith. Here Hooker was relentless and devastating in his criticisms. Three in particular which are general in scope will suffice to give the gist of his case.

One line of argument exploited by Hooker was simply that the claim that Scripture alone is to decide all matters of faith and practice cannot itself be based on an appeal to Scripture.

We all believe that the Scriptures of God are sacred, and that they have proceeded from God; ourselves we assure that we do right well in so believing. We have for this point a demonstration sound and infallible. But it is not the Word of God which doth or possibly can assure us, that we do well to think it is his word. For if any one book of Scripture did give testimony to all; yet still that Scripture which giveth credit to the rest, would require another Scripture to give credit unto it; neither could we ever come unto any pause whereon to rest our assurance this way: so that unless beside Scripture, there were something which might assure us that we do well, we could not think that we do well; no, not in being assured that Scripture is a sacred and holy rule of well-doing.[17]

A second argument developed by Hooker is drawn from the fact that any appeal to Scripture requires in itself an appeal to human authority.

But for the most part, even such as are readiest to cite for one thing five hundred sentences of Holy Scripture; what warrant have they, that any

---

[16] Given Hooker's concern for peace and order in Church and State, it is not surprising that his favoured term for the use of reason is the 'law of reason'.

[17] *The Works of Richard Hooker* (Oxford: J. Vincent, 1843), *Laws*, II: iv. 249.

one of them doth mean the thing that it is alleged? Is not their surest ground, most commonly, either some probable conjecture of their own, or the judgment of others who take the Scriptures as they do? Which notwithstanding, to mean otherwise than they take them, it is not still altogether impossible. So that now and then they ground themselves on human authority, even when they most pretend divine.[18]

Finally, it is worth noting the intellectual and pastoral consequences Hooker saw as flowing from a wrong rendering of the appeal to Scripture:

But admit this [that all things to be done are comprehended in the Scripture], and mark I beseech you what would follow. God in delivering his Scripture to his Church should clean have abrogated amongst them the law of nature, which is an infallible knowledge imprinted in the minds of all the children of men, whereby both general principles for directing human actions are comprehended, and conclusions from them; upon which conclusions groweth in particularity the choice of good and evil in the daily affairs of this life. Admit this, and what shall the Scriptures be but a snare and torment to weak consciences, filling them with infinite perplexities, scrupulosities, doubts insoluble, and extreme despairs? Not that the Scripture itself doth cause any such thing . . . but the necessities of this life urging men to do that which the light of nature, common discretion, and judgment of itself, directeth them unto; on the other side, this doctrine teacheth them so to do were to sin against their own souls, and that they put forth their hands to iniquity whatsoever they go about and have not first the Scripture of God for direction; how can it choose but bring the simple thousand times to their wits' end? how can it choose but vex and amaze them? For in every action of common life, to find out some sentence clearly and infallibly setting before our eyes what we ought to do, (seem we in Scripture never so expert) would trouble us more than we are aware. In weak and tender minds we little know what misery this strict opinion would breed, besides the stops it would make in the whole course of all men's lives and actions. Make all things sin which we do by direction of nature's light, and by the rule of common discretion, without thinking at all upon Scripture: admit this position, and parents shall cause their children to sin as oft as they cause them to do anything before they come to years of capacity, and be ripe for knowledge in the Scripture.[19]

Moving to the positive doctrines developed by Hooker, it is clear that his commitment to reason was deeply undergirded by

---

[18] Ibid. II. vii. 277. [19] Ibid. II. viii. 282–4.

his theism. Human beings are made by God to operate according to certain laws. Included in these laws is the law of reason, which is given by God, sustained continually by providence, and restored by grace. Hooker was acutely aware of the way the law of reason can be corrupted and misused; even the most brilliant minds can be misdirected by sloth and pride.

If it here be demanded, by what means it should come to pass (the greatest part of the moral Law being so easy for all men to know) that so many thousands of men notwithstanding have been ignorant, even of principal moral duties, not imagining the breach of them to be sin: I deny not but lewd and wicked custom, beginning perhaps at the first among few, afterward spreading into greater multitudes, and so continuing from time to time, may be of force even in plain things to smother the light of natural understanding, because men will not bend their wits to examine whether things wherewith they have been accustomed be good or evil.[20]

Yet, rightly ordered, reason functions to lead us to goodness and truth, both of which are constituted by the very being of God, so that reason, rightly used, will lead us to God, in whom we will find our highest felicity, something no one can reasonably reject.[21] We might say that at this level Hooker was committed to a version of virtue epistemology. In using their cognitive capacities in the way intended by God, human agents arrive at and are drawn to the truth.

This provided the obvious warrant for Hooker's relative optimism about knowing which was pivotal to his rejoinder to the canonical foundationalists inspired by Calvin. It was clear to him that human agents can know in some measure what is right and wrong without consulting scripture, and, after consulting scripture, they are still required to use their reason to resolve those matters not determined by scripture. This does not mean that divine revelation is superfluous. On the contrary, given the human predicament of sin and given the nature of the truths needed for human beings to achieve their true destiny, revelation

---

[20] *Laws*, I. viii. 194. It is worth noting that it would not take much to redeploy this explanation of human error and use it against the tradition of the Church—indeed, against all tradition.

[21] Hooker is well aware of the difficulties this creates for any analysis of the Fall and sin, and he has his own way of responding to these problems.

is absolutely essential.[22] There is a supernatural law which can only be attained through the voice of Scripture. Where God has spoken, where we have divine oracles, nothing can overthrow the truths thereby made available.[23] Yet the appearance of new truth about salvation from God does not entail the rejection of truth found through the right use of reason.

Yet great care must be taken to bear in mind precisely why God has spoken. God's intention in speaking was to make available what was essential to salvation. God has graciously made available those truths which are needed to reverse the effects of the Fall and to bring human agents to their ultimate destiny of union with the divine. Initially, what was spoken was recorded and written down in order to overcome the limitations of human memory and transmission. This means that Scripture must be read and understood within the framework intended for it by God.[24] It was precisely this teleology, so characteristic of all God's activity and doings for Hooker, which is either overlooked or scorned by the canonical foundationalists.[25] Indeed, Scripture itself was by divine intention a mixture of natural and supernatural law which required human judgement if it was to be identified and read

---

[22] 'The schools of Rome teach Scripture to be insufficient, as if, except Traditions were added, it did not contain all revealed and supernatural truth which absolutely is necessary for the children of men in this life to know, that they may in the next be saved' (ibid. II. viii. 283).

[23] 'Scripture by Christian men being received as the Word of God; that for which we have probable, yea, that which we have necessary reason for, yea, that which we see with our own eyes, is not thought so sure as that which the Scripture of God teacheth, because we hold that his speech revealeth there what he himself seeth, and therefore the strongest proof of all, and the most necessarily assented unto by us, (which do thus receive the Scripture,) is Scripture' (ibid. II. vii. 272). There are close affinities here to the position of Aquinas.

[24] Within this framework it is nothing less than perfect for Hooker. 'Howbeit, that here we swerve not in judgment, one thing especially we must observe, namely, that the absolute perfection of Scripture is seen in relation unto that end whereto it tendeth' (ibid. II. viii. 281).

[25] 'Again, the scope and purpose of God in delivering the Holy Scripture, such as do take more largely than behoveth, they on the contrary side, racking and stretching it further than by him was meant, are drawn into sundry as great inconveniences. These, pretending all the Scripture's perfection, infer thereupon, that in Scripture all things lawful to be done must needs be contained. We count those things perfect which want nothing requisite for the end whereto they were instituted' (ibid.).

aright. Christians believe in divine revelation because there is evidence for believing in the existence of such revelation;[26] with good reason they reject the Roman claim that there is additional revelation in Church tradition; and they depend on human reason to interpret Scripture, to gather up its meaning as a whole, and to apply it to the changing circumstances of life. Even a supernatural divine law may not be immutable, and where it is, judgement is needed to work out its implications and usage.

These considerations provided the warrant for Hooker's insistence that Scripture did not furnish the criterion for deciding for one system of Church order and worship over against another. To appeal to Scripture alone in this instance was to misunderstand the function of Scripture in the divine economy. Scripture was given to repeat what could be known by the law of reason, to clear up what yet remained dark and cloudy after the use of reason, and above all to provide a clear and adequate account of the essentials of salvation.[27] Hence, as human judgement or reason was intended by God to be relied on prior to the arrival of Scripture, so too it was to be used after the arrival of Scripture to work out what was required in the area of worship, ceremony, and Church order.

[26] Hooker shows little interest in the whole issue of credentials for divine revelation. There are hints that he implicitly follows Aquinas in believing that signs and miracles constitute the evidence for special revelation. This becomes a very important issue in later generations, as we shall see.

[27] 'The first principles of the Law of Nature are easy; hard it were to find men ignorant of them. But concerning the duty which Nature's Law doth require at the hands of men in a number of things particular; so far hath the natural understanding even of sundry whole nations been darkened, that they have not discerned, no, not gross iniquity to be sin. Again being so prone as we are to fawn upon ourselves, and to be ignorant as much as may be of our own deformities without the feeling sense whereof we are most wretched; even so much the more, because not knowing them, we cannot so much as desire to have them taken away; how should our festered sores be cured, but that God hath delivered a law as sharp as the two-edged sword, piercing the very closest and most unsearchable corners of the heart, which the Law of Nature can hardly, human laws by no means possibly, reach unto? Hereby we know even secret concupiscence to be sin, and are made fearful to offend, though it be but in a wandering cogitation. Finally, of those things which are for direction for all the parts of our life needful, and not impossible to be discerned by the light of Nature itself; are there not many which few men's natural capacity, and some which no man's hath been able to find out' (ibid. I. xii. 221).

We are now in a position to note how Hooker deployed his appeal to the consensus of the early Church. This in fact is a minor motif in Hooker; it can easily be accommodated within his appeal to reason.[28] For Hooker, consensus was virtually a mark of truth.[29] So, given how human agents are intended to function, universal consent is a sign of truth. Moreover, not all human beings have the same degree of wisdom. Hence, as far as the life of the Church is concerned, it is very important to consult what those who have given themselves to holiness and study have agreed on. While there is no guarantee that such a consensus is infallible, it does constitute evidence in favour of the position actually agreed on. Therefore, the decisions of the General councils of the Church have a special place in any decision concerning the worship and structure of the Church.

A thing whereof God's own blessed Spirit was the author; a thing practised by the holy Apostles themselves; a thing always afterward kept and observed throughout the world; a thing never otherwise than most highly esteemed of, till pride, ambition, and tyranny began, by factious and vile endeavours, to abuse the divine intention unto the furtherance of wicked purposes.[30]

Further, the mere fact that a custom had been agreed on and established provided a warrant for its acceptance. If the consensus in mind did not contradict the clear teaching of Scripture, if it constituted a genuine consensus which had been in place for some time, it merited acceptance unless and until it was changed by appropriate authority after relevant argument and reason.[31] This in a nutshell was the reasoning which lay behind Hooker's defence of episcopacy as the right form of government for the Church of England.

[28] Technically, Hooker in fact held to the twin appeal to reason and revelation. 'There are but two ways whereby the Spirit leadeth men into all truth; the one extraordinary, the other common; the one belonging but unto some few, the other extending itself unto all that are of God; the one, that which we call by special divine excellency Revelation, the other Reason' (ibid., preface, iii. 124).

[29] 'The general and perpetual voice of men is as the voice of God himself' (ibid. I. viii. 187). [30] Ibid. I. x. 210.

[31] 'As for the orders which are established, sith equity and reason, the law of nature, God and man, do all favour that which is in being, till orderly judgement of decision given against it' (ibid., preface, vi. 140).

Hooker had a very astute eye for the constraints of social and political life in this arena. Once he had rejected the view that these matters could be decided by Scripture, he needed to provide an alternative which could command the assent of reason and which would work in practice. Here he rightly noted that some kind of social authority was essential in the life of the Church. It was not enough to have an agreed form of prayer, or agreed structures of order, or even an agreed canon of Scripture which taught the essentials of salvation. Much less was it enough to have a splendid theory which would articulate and defend a sophisticated account of the appropriate weight to be assigned to the law of reason, special revelation, and the consensus of the Church. There was also the need for the exercise of authority by appropriate persons within the community.

Authority is a constraining power, which power were needless if we were all such as we should be, willing to do the things we ought to do without constraint. But because generally we are otherwise, therefore we all reap singular benefit by that authority which permitteth no man, though they would to slack their duty. It doth not suffice, that the Lord of an household appoint labourers what they should do, unless he set over them some chief workmen to see they do it.[32]

Taken as a whole, what is striking about the Anglican synthesis is its ambivalence. The Anglican *via media,* as represented by Hooker, was a valiant attempt to retrieve a patristic alternative to the canonical foundationalism of the Continental Reformers which failed because it did not really come to terms with the damage already done to the tradition from within. To put the matter sharply, there is an incoherence which is rarely faced and overcome. There are three main observations to be made here initially.

First and foremost, there is the ambivalence in the position taken on Scripture. On the one hand, there was a splendid recovery of the primary function of Scripture as that was originally conceived in many of the Fathers. Thus Scripture was seen at one level in soteriological categories which highlighted its spiritual purpose in mediating divine revelation and in bringing salvation to the recipient. Scripture was seen at times, then, as a pivotal

---

[32] *Laws*, VII. xviii. 335.

means of grace. On the other hand, the effects of epistemizing the concept of Scripture are equally visible. Even though the appeal to Scripture was expressed at times in a negative way, the idea of deriving the content of the creeds from Scripture alone remained substantially intact.

Holy Scripture containeth all things necessary to salvation: so that whatsoever is not read therein, nor may be proved thereby, is not to be required of any man, that it should be believed as an article of the Faith, or be thought requisite or necessary for salvation.[33]

The Three Creeds, Nicene Creed, Athanasius's Creed, and that which is commonly called the Apostle's Creed, ought thoroughly to be received and believed: *for they may be proved by most certain warrants of holy Scripture.*[34]

Perhaps one of the best illustrations of this strategy is the determined attempt by the learned Bishop Pearson, almost a century after Hooker, to provide scriptural warrant for the clause on the descent into hell in the Apostles' Creed.

I observe again that whatsoever is delivered in the Creed, we therefore believe because it is contained in the Scriptures, and consequently must so believe it as it is contained there; whence all this exposition of the whole is nothing else but an illustration and proof of every particular part of the Creed by such Scriptures as deliver the same, according to the true interpretation of them and the general consent of the Church of God. Now these words, as they lie in the Creed, *He descended into hell*, are nowhere formally and expressly delivered in the Scriptures; nor can we find any one place in which the Holy Ghost hath said in express terms, that Christ as he died was buried, so *he descended into hell.* Wherefore being these words of the Creed are not formally expressed in the Scripture, our inquiry must be in what Scriptures they are contained virtually; that is, where the Holy Spirit doth deliver the same doctrine, in words whatsoever, which is contained, and to be understood in this expression, *He descended into hell.*[35]

---

[33] Article VI.

[34] Article VIII; emphasis added. See also Article XX: 'On the Authority of the Church; Article XXI: 'Of the Authority of General Councils'; and Article XXIV: 'Of the Traditions of the Church'. All stress the normative role of Scripture.

[35] John Pearson, *An Exposition of the Creed* (Oxford: Oxford University Press, 1847), 269. This was first published in 1659. There follows a lengthy chase for appropriate proof-texts.

So long as everything had to be tested again and again by appeal to Scripture, then the commitment to the doctrinal material enshrined in the creeds together with the sense of the creeds as a whole remained extremely vulnerable to erosion. With Hooker this was not a problem, for most of the marrow of the canonical doctrines of the Church was built into the very foundations of his epistemology. Moreover, he was sufficiently steeped in the Fathers to be able to mediate that component of the heritage with ease. Once his epistemic proposals are adopted, and once they are allowed to displace this significant canonical material, however, then it is far from clear that these components can be sustained.[36]

Second, it is surely questionable whether we can reduce Scripture to a kind of handbook on the essentials of salvation. The very notion of the essentials of salvation is thoroughly ambiguous. It is derived in part from the Continental Reformers' attempt to secure a clear component of Scripture which will not need the interpretative tradition of the Church in order to be understood. An echo of it also shows up as a rhetorical device in the preaching of St John Chrysostom, and is picked up from that arena in the Homilies.[37] As a rhetorical device it is entirely salutary as a way of highlighting certain aspects of the composite biblical tradition or as a fundamental part of the Christian tradition as a whole which deserves particular emphasis at a particular moment in the history of the Church. Pushed to carry more than originally intended in a homiletical context, however, it runs into obvious difficulties.

Does it mean those doctrines which are to be believed as essential to the Christian faith? Does it mean those components of the Christian life, such as repentance and faith, justification and sanctification, which the Reformers took as crucial to any

[36] 'Today Anglicanism cannot justify its adherence to the doctrines of the Trinity and the incarnation unless it is prepared to accord an authority to the church as "witness and keeper of Holy Writ" (Article XX). It is on the authority of the church of the early centuries, not of the Bible alone, that Anglicanism upholds them' (R. H. Fuller, 'Scripture' in Sykes and Booty (eds.), *Study of Anglicanism*, 88). Note here how the quest for adequate epistemic foundations still haunts the discussion.

[37] 'A Fruitful Exhortation to the Reading and Knowledge of Holy Scripture', in *Certain Sermons*, 3.

true account of salvation? Does it mean those things essential to the whole economy of salvation from the first movements of grace in the human soul to the final glorification in the life to come? How we answer this will have significant consequences for our appropriation of Scripture. Hooker was, of course, right overall in his case against his more Protestant opponents; but, by making the notion of the essentials such a pivotal matter for his theory, he ran the distinct risk of losing the great doctrines of the Faith and of reducing Scripture to a short list of doctrines which cannot begin to do justice to the full riches of the biblical heritage.[38] Any attempt to isolate the essentials in a hard and fast manner will lead to a systematic ignoring of other parts of the tradition. Alternatively, it will lead to extensive efforts to force the non-essentials into some sort of artificial

[38] This certainly happens in the case of Locke, as we shall see. To be fair to Hooker, he has a splendid sense of the great complexity of the biblical materials and of the many ways they work in the life of faith. 'By Scripture, it hath in the wisdom of God seemed meet to deliver unto the world much, but personally expedient to be practised of certain men; many deep and profound points of doctrine, as being the main original ground whereupon the precepts of duty depend; many prophecies, the clear performance whereof might confirm the world in belief of things unseen; many histories, to serve as looking-glasses to behold the mercy, the truth, the righteousness of God towards all that faithfully serve, obey and honour him; yea, many entire meditations of piety, to be patterns and cases in like nature; many things needful for explication, many for application unto particular occasions, such as the providence of God from time to time hath taken, to have the several books of his holy ordinance. Be it then, that together with the principal necessary laws of God there are sundry other things written, whereof we may haply be ignorant and yet be saved: what? shall we hereupon think them needless? shall we esteem them as riotous branches, wherewith we sometimes behold most pleasant vines overgrown? Surely, no more than we judge our hands or our eyes superfluous, or what part soever; which if our bodies did want, we might, notwithstanding any such defect, retain still the complete being of men. As therefore a complete man is neither destitute of any part necessary, and hath some parts, whereof though the want could not deprive him of his essence, yet to have them standeth him in singular stead in respect of the special uses for which they serve; in like sort, all those writings which contain in them the Law of God, all those venerable books of Scripture, all those sacred tomes and volumes of Holy Writ, they are with such absolute perfection framed, that in them there neither wanteth any thing, the lack thereof might deprive us of life, nor anything in such wise aboundeth, that as being superfluous, unfruitful, and altogether needless, we should think it no loss or danger at all, if we did want it' (*Laws*, I. xiv. 224).

relationship with the essentials, in order to keep them from not being used at all.[39]

This point can be worked up from the other side of the categories deployed by Hooker. For Hooker, Scripture is concerned with matters essential to salvation. Reason and tradition take care of matters like Church order and worship, presumably issues which are not essential to salvation. But does this not underplay the spiritual significance of such matters as the number of sacraments made available in the Church, whether the magistrate has a right to intervene in the reform of the Church, whether the offices of evangelist, apostle, and prophet have ceased in the Church, whether the extraordinary gifts of the Spirit are still available, how and when discipline is to be exercised, whether Christians should obey the law if it goes against conscience, how the Church is to relate to the State, how clergy are to be appointed, the sexual orientation and gender of ordinands, and the like? It would not be difficult, given certain accounts of salvation, to argue that these issues lie well outside the boundaries of the essentials of salvation. Yet, despite the efforts to take the Church seriously, this way of dividing up the life of faith fails to take it sufficiently seriously. The Church is more intimately related to the experience of salvation than this picture suggests or really allows. Once again, epistemic theorizing is having subtle yet profound effects on the life of faith which were probably never intended by those who invented it.

Another angle on the same point is this. It is surely altogether artificial to divide matters into the essentials and non-essentials of salvation and then claim that God gives very special help with the former, leaving the rest more or less to our own devices. It is as if God has a policy of dictating the answers to the required questions on the syllabus and providing no help at all on the optional questions.[40] Hooker has a keen sense of God as an agent acting intentionally and wisely in all his acts of creation, providence, and

---

[39] It is tempting to believe that the whole idea of working with merely the essentials of salvation is a covert way to hold on to the idea of Scripture as a criterion when it has failed to live up to its expectations in certain areas of Church life.

[40] The deep insight which Hooker and those he is following has captured is, of course, that very significant divine help is needed, not least that of God speaking to us in no uncertain terms.

salvation. Yet it is difficult to make sense of the policy attributed to God in drawing a contrast between Scripture and the other components of the canonical heritage of the Church. It is certainly as cogent to think of God providing help all along the line and to think of human agency at work in response and participation all along the line too. This certainly applies to the Scriptures; there is both divine and human involvement. Likewise, we might think of the worship and orderly life of the Church as involving both divine guidance and human reflection. This will surely appear appropriate to those who rightly insist that the action of grace is needed in human hearts and wills in response to the Gospel. It is odd to let grace in to the working of the soul but keep it out in the ordering of the life of the Church.

Third, the warrants on episcopacy worked out and adopted officially in the Anglican tradition were hopelessly compromised, displaying a kind of double-mindedness about the commitment to *sola scriptura*. Hooker was consistent on this matter. He rigorously tried to keep Scripture in its proper place as mediating the essentials of salvation; here he was able to keep the *sola scriptura* principle intact. Yet others really wanted more. They wanted episcopacy to be grounded in a stronger divine warrant than human reason as represented in the consensus of the Church. Indeed, one suspects that some believed that consensus itself was in place because it had stronger divine sanction in the apostles and Scriptures. Thus the Preface to the forms of ordination reads: 'It is evident unto all men diligently reading holy Scripture and ancient Authors, that from the Apostles' time there have been these Orders of Ministry in Christ's Church: Bishops, Priests, and Deacons.'[41]

Perhaps we can see here the great difficulty in countenancing a genuine role for the guidance of the Holy Spirit above and beyond reason in the development of the complex canonical life of the Church. Once the more modest conception of canon had been abandoned and Scripture was considered only in categories of divine speech, the possibility of a genuine inspiration, which would be short of divine speaking but more than the mere exercise of

[41] Book of Common Prayer. Compare the comment of Fuller: 'Today Anglicanism can justify adherence to episcopacy only by appealing to post-New Testament developments' (*Scripture*, 88).

reason operating in the canonical life of the Church was completely overshadowed. The idea of genuine inspiration as applied to the order and worship of the early Church was completely forgotten. The only alternatives available for thinking about episcopacy were these: (1) episcopacy was grounded directly in Scripture, the oracles of God; or (2) episcopacy was worked out by human reason; or (3) episcopacy was dictated by the Holy Spirit in the Church.

Undoubtedly the fear of falling into the arms of the Roman opponent had a blinding effect even on the judicious Hooker at this point.[42] The Reformers had no real alternative to the strong Tridentine claim of divine dictation as applied to Church tradition other than to reject it outright. Anglicans who wanted to resort to the tradition of the early Church were especially vulnerable, because this claim to dictation was always lurking at the door, once they made any appeal to tradition. Construing the development of episcopacy as one part of the wider canonical heritage of the Church inspired by the Holy Spirit would have provided a genuine alternative and would have brought the admirers of tradition much closer to the actual position sought by the Anglican Reformers. It would also have fitted very neatly with the strong stress on the teleology of God's provisions for the life of holiness that one finds in Hooker.

A fourth element takes us to a more general level. When one looks at the more obviously canonical material put in place by the Anglican Reformers, it is striking how much their position mirrors that of the patristic Church. Thus they adopted the Scriptures,[43] various creeds, sacraments and ceremonies, a specific

---

[42] It is not a little notorious that Pusey in his masterly preface to his edition of *Hooker's Laws* has to go to considerable length to excuse Hooker for his lapses on the true doctrine of episcopacy as divinely given. What is needed here is a real doctrine of divine guidance married to Hooker's fine sense concerning the possible flexibility and adaptability of divine action in the economy of salvation in the means of grace. When faced with special circumstances in the history of the Church with respect to the orders which develop, it is rash to adopt a wholly exclusivist account of the guidance of the Holy Spirit. At any rate, the debate needs to be conducted in terms of divine guidance rather than in terms of a rather crude juxtaposition of direct divine decree over against the deliberations of human reason.

[43] It is interesting how deliberate they were in spelling out the content of the canon of Scripture and how careful they were to retain the Old Testament despite the Christocentric focus of their soteriology.

liturgy, an episcopal form of Church government, and a network of canonical regulation.[44] What is missing here, of course, when compared with the comprehensive developments of the earlier tradition, is a canon of Fathers and iconography.[45]

Alongside these materials there emerged, as we see in the case of Hooker, a characteristic way of thinking about the justification of these components in the life of the Church. It was in this context that the triad of Scripture, tradition, and reason arose. This might be better described, as we have already seen, as a dyad of revelation and reason. What is puzzling is how the triad comes to be identified with the core identity of the tradition.

There is in fact enormous confusion at precisely this point in the exposition of the tradition, which is clearly visible in the modern texts on the subject.[46] Thus a section is devoted to questions related to authority, and extended attention is given to the relative merits of Scripture, tradition, and reason. These are treated as the standards or norms of Anglican faith and practice. Then, without any explanation or warning, this is followed by another section devoted to Anglican standards of faith, and here attention is given to such matters as the creeds, antiquity and tradition, ordinals, the Homilies, catechisms, councils, the Book of Common Prayer, and the Thirty-Nine Articles. What is fascinating is the

---

[44] It is clear in Anglicanism that much of the spirit of the early Fathers was captured as regards how the canonical material was to be received. We have already noted the stress on humility, on the need for the cognitive faculties to be transformed by the Holy Spirit, the strong stress on Scripture as a means of grace intended to bring salvation and initiate union with the divine, and the like. There is also an apophatic strain which deserves further study.

[45] It is a measure of the lack of serious attention to the appeal to the consensus of the Church that Anglican apologists are so inconsistent in this appeal. They stop abruptly at the fourth or fifth century, and fail to carry through to the full number of ecumenical councils. Some may have been influenced by the romantic notion, attributed to Pope Gregory the Great, that four councils were sufficient because there were four canonical gospels. See Henry Chadwick, 'Tradition, Fathers and Councils', in Sykes and Booty (eds.), *Study of Anglicanism*, 58. This very incomplete appeal to consensus shows that the real interest lay elsewhere: that is, in the appeal to reason, with consensus merely a subplot in this line of development.

[46] This is true of the two splendid texts which serve to introduce the Anglican tradition to the contemporary reader: Paul Elmer More and Frank Leslie Cross (eds.), *Anglicanism* (London: SPCK, 1951), and Sykes and Booty, (eds.), *Study of Anglicanism*.

conceptual disarray which is on display here. No serious effort is made to explain why, given that the issue of the standard and rule of faith has already been addressed in the section on Scripture, tradition, and reason, the whole matter of standards is taken up all over again. The obvious explanation is historical. What we have is the carry-over of earlier distinctions between canon and norm, or between means of grace and epistemological theory. In this instance they are garbled together indiscriminately. Moreover, it is clear from the priority assigned to Scripture, tradition, and reason that these have gained the ascendancy over creeds, articles, liturgy, and the like. In short, the epistemological theory has become the primary focus of identity.

This was achieved without there being any serious attempt to canonize a list of Anglican Fathers. Clearly this failure to canonize a list of teachers or authoritative interpreters fits with the great reserve shown towards tradition as a whole. Whatever the reasons, it certainly was the case that the Anglicans emerged with an implicitly canonized epistemology: that is, Scripture, tradition, and reason. In time this became the primary carrier of their identity.

This shift in priority could be explained by saying that the latter identity—that is, an identity located in theological method rather than in confessional commitment—is really a modern ideological device to secure a certain interpretation and working out of modern Anglican theory and practice. Thus the insistence, heard often among contemporary Anglicans, that they are not committed to any Confession, but that they are committed to a particular theological method, is really a way of coming to terms with perceived difficulties in the creeds in the modern period and a means of keeping alive a rigorous engagement with the intellectual forces of modern culture.[47] There is almost certainly some warrant for this, for serious engagement with new developments of thought is inescapable and has long been one of the great virtues of Anglican theology.[48]

However, the move to secure identity by means of the triad of

[47] One way to pursue this issue would be to examine carefully the fortunes of subscription to the creeds and to the Thirty-Nine Articles within Anglicanism.

[48] This stands despite the fact that Anglicans characteristically develop a love for historical learning over against speculative genius.

Scripture, tradition, and reason may in fact reflect a very basic perplexity which was a marked feature of the identity of the tradition from the beginning. For once Scripture was cast in the form of a norm of justification and knowledge, it was entirely natural, given the kind of epistemology developed by figures like Hooker, that Scripture should be linked with other epistemic notions like reason and wise consensus, and for the whole identity of the tradition to be relocated in a particular brand of religious epistemology. Once Scripture was seen as a warrant for the essentials of salvation, which then needed to be supplemented by reason, if the system as a whole was to make sense and be defended, then the tacit patristic understanding of the canonical heritage had been turned inside out. Material which had been carefully kept at a distance and included more by way of suggestion than explicit theory was now brought front and centre stage. Hence, *de facto*, figures like Hooker became the fathers of the tradition, and the identity of the tradition was relocated in this more epistemic component of the heritage.[49]

The haphazard way in which this is carried out is reflected in internal squabbles about identity which refuse to disappear. Thus it is characteristic of Anglicans to divide into various parties which look to different elements in the heritage to provide continuity

---

[49] A very significant attempt to get away from an account of identity which on the surface seems to eschew epistemic commitments is provided by Paul Avis in *Anglicanism and the Christian Church* (Edinburgh: T. & T. Clark, 1989). Yet it is interesting how far Avis ends up with an account shot through with epistemic overtones. He calls his account the 'baptismal paradigm', contrasted with the Erastian and apostolic paradigm. 'The baptismal paradigm, as I understand it, involves a mystical perception of (that) fundamental ecclesial reality. It is response to the transcendent mystery of the God who may be loved and not thought, as *The Cloud of Unknowing* puts it. It takes that love of God in Christ as the central Christian phenomena, and doctrines and dogmas as necessary and valid ways of discerning the mystery, provided we never forget that they are human productions, essentially personal and existential statements. The pluralism of belief and practice in world Christianity represents human perceptions of the many-faceted truth of God in Christ, as that is refracted through diverse cultures and life-forms. Where these come into conflict it is neither desirable nor possible for a central authority (magisterium) to pronounce on their authenticity. Instead through the conflictual process itself—through argument, criticism and attempts to understand one another on the basis of respect and acceptance— beliefs may be refined and agreement perhaps discovered' (R: 310). Avis begins here with clouds and mysteries, and ends with arguments and criticism.

and legitimacy. Thus an evangelical wing stresses the *sola scriptura* of the Reformation, wedded to a Calvinistic articulation of the doctrinal heritage. A high, or Anglo-Catholic, wing focuses on the patristic legacy of the creeds, the historical episcopate, and the authority of the early tradition. A broad Church movement takes up and develops the theme of reason and credibility. The divisions are not meant to signify some kind of exclusive appeal to merely one side of the tradition; rather, they reflect deep differences of tone and emphasis, although there is indeed a tendency for the various parties to pit one element of the tradition against another.

The presence of such vigorous groups certainly provides lots of stimulus for extended study and research, for intellectual debate and probing criticism, and for tolerance and forbearance within the Church. This is extremely healthy and invigorating. Moreover, this kind of intellectual stimulus dovetails with the fact that the triad of Scripture, reason, and tradition is a most valuable pedagogical device in theology. The triad opens up lines of enquiry which would otherwise be neglected. It also draws attention to the fact that theological claims may often take the form not of necessary truths, or of truths supported by deductive proof, but of truths supported by a network of signs, testimonies, intuitions, expressions of conscience, and factual material, which cannot be reduced to a single category of evidence. That is, it captures the great significance of cumulative case arguments in theology.[50] This notion is surely in part a by-product of launching an appeal to Scripture, tradition, and reason. Furthermore, the Anglican triad provides a methodological agenda which can be a useful first word. On the theory in hand, however, it also functions too often as the last word.

As we shall see in the next chapter, taken simply as an epistemic proposal, this position is inherently unstable and incoherent. Here

---

[50] It is surely no accident that cumulative case arguments become the hallmark of religious epistemology in the Anglican tradition. One thinks immediately of a line of great figures: Richard Hooker, William Chillingworth, John Locke, Bishop Butler, John Henry Newman, William Tennant, J. R. Lucas, Basil Mitchell, and Richard Swinburne. Just as there is a distinctive Reformed epistemology and a distinctive Roman Catholic epistemology, there is also a distinctive Anglican epistemology. The full sweep of this tradition awaits careful historical exposition which would attend to its continuities and diversity.

I want to press its religious and spiritual inadequacy as a rendering of the canonical heritage of the Church. At one level it fails in consistency because it does not line up with its profession to represent the canonical heritage of the patristic Church. It is not a retrieval of the canonical heritage of the first five centuries. It is a novel canonical arrangement which has its own dynamic and ethos, which has its own virtues and vices, and which has its own way of being renewed and replenished.

The deep problem identified here, however, is not its inconsistency, but its inherent tendency to put epistemic materials at the very heart of the Church. There is nothing wrong with developing epistemic theory. Indeed, in its proper place it is a very valuable and indispensable asset. In the long run and at certain levels of enquiry, it is inescapable in the life of the mind. However, ecclesial commitment, like Christian commitment generally, has its own appropriate mode. It is one thing, for example, to be committed to the Trinity and to the incarnation of God in Christ; it is another to be committed to Scripture, tradition, and reason. Christians rightly pray that, should the time of testing come, they will be prepared to die for the Trinity and the Incarnation. It is ludicrous from a spiritual point of view even to think of dying for the Anglican triad.

Yet the fact that we can conceive of such a possibility is the deep consequence of the canonical shift represented by the move to epistemize the canonical heritage of the Church. Much as we can admire those who were martyred at the hands of their epistemic enemies, it is surely a sign of the intellectual corruption of the Church that the possibility of death and martyrdom for rival types of epistemic schemes was even considered in the volatile events that constituted the various phases of the Reformation and Counter-Reformation in England in the sixteenth century. Except perhaps in cases long debated and contested within the canonical heritage of the Church, Christians have no business killing their enemies. Nor have they any business *qua* Christians dying for their epistemic theories. Yet there is a place, surely, for dying for the canonical faith of the Church. Pondering this distinction will help confirm that it was a sorry day when theologians turned the canonical faith of the early Church into a half-baked exercise in religious epistemology.

This interpretation of the situation is borne out by the enormous impact which John Locke had on the Anglicanism of his day, for what we see in Locke is a radical working out of the position of Hooker in such a way as to secure tolerance and bring the canonical wars of the Church to halt. In Locke's case the epistemic tradition bequeathed to him was also reworked in order to fit with the perceived new developments in natural science ushered in by Newton and others. The result was a reversion to a rigorous form of epistemic foundationalism, comparable to what we have seen in a theological form in the Continental Reformers and in a secular form in Descartes.

In the course of this the difficulties in speaking of a triad of Scripture, tradition, and reason were laid bare. In turn, the vestiges of the patristic canonical tradition represented by such doctrines as the Trinity and the Incarnation became thinner and thinner. The complex material of the canonical heritage of the Church, which had been identified as the core of the tradition, but which had initially been elbowed out by an epistemic heritage of no mean proportion became less and less visible with Locke. His own epistemic proposals in time paved the way for their total dismantling at the hands of Hume and Kant.

9

The Rule of Reason

The Anglican ecclesial and theological experiment represents a brilliant attempt to break loose from the limitations of the canonical foundationalism of the Reformation. By means of an appeal to early tradition and reason, it sought to recover crucial components of the patristic heritage. In recovering tradition, it sought to recall and put in place precious components of the Faith which were far from easy to establish merely on the basis of Scripture. By insisting on the use of reason, it sought to be more faithful to the deep ethos of the theology of the Fathers and to introduce a sense of order and rational deliberation into the supervision of the Church and the articulation of her doctrines.

Yet, from the outset, the tradition was marked by tension and strain. Most notably in this regard, tradition was uncertain and insecure. Tradition was constantly overshadowed by Scripture and reason. It is true, for example, that the creeds were kept intact. In fact, much of the credal material, having been rehearsed no fewer than three times in the Apostles', Nicene, and Athanasian versions, was repeated again in the Thirty-Nine Articles. Yet there was tremendous reluctance to jettison the notion of *sola scriptura*, so that the place of the creeds and the wider tradition in which they were embedded was constantly at risk. The principle of *sola scriptura* was kept intact, but its application was carefully limited to the essentials of salvation. Clearly this was a device for protecting the principle of *sola scriptura;* for one way to keep it afloat is to restrict its range of application. Applying the rule only to the essentials of salvation is a natural way to proceed if protecting the rule is one's goal.

From the beginning it was uncertain whether these essentials were constituted by soteriological doctrines like, say, justification by faith alone, or by the great Christological doctrines which were naturally linked to the doctrine of the Trinity.[1] Hence there was plenty of room for doubt down the road as to what exactly in the credal tradition might or might not be secured from Scripture. What was not secured under the rubric of the essentials of salvation had to be secured by rational arguments, showing that credal tradition was a secondary notion which was really at the mercy of reason. Hence what was effectively operating was a dyad of Scripture and reason, as a reading of Hooker makes clear.

What can be said here about the creeds applies *mutatis mutandis* to liturgy, canon law, sacraments, iconography, episcopacy, the Fathers and Teachers of the Church, and the like. These did or did not survive, depending on what one judged to be the essentials of salvation, and what one judged to be the outcome of reason in theology.

Moreover, it was clear from the outset that questions had been raised as to how one identified divine revelation at all. It was natural, given the rival claims about the location of divine revelation posed by the Reformers, for theologians to ask how they knew that the Scriptures really were the Word of God. Not that one needed another canonical crisis to ask that question, for it is one that naturally occurs to the enquiring mind. The only two options already allowed to deal with this matter were an appeal either to revelation or to reason. It was obvious, given that to appeal to revelation simply begged the question, that the only alternative was reason. Hence, built into the Anglican experiment was a propensity to lurch into a straight appeal to reason as the ultimate foundation of faith.

Given the assumptions in place and the logic of the alternatives implicit in the appeal to Scripture, tradition, and reason, the stage was set for the emergence of a whole new version of foundationalism. A Reformation which began with a canonical foundationalism, which insisted that only Scripture could be used in theology, shifted, through an unstable *via media* which appealed to Scripture, tradition, and reason, to an epistemic foundationalism which insisted that reason, and reason alone, was the only legitimate foundation of theological belief. We have, then, a repeat performance of what we saw happen in the case of the

---

[1] The tension is clearly visible in the theology of John Wesley. While he is resolutely committed to the doctrine of the Trinity, it has been displaced by his doctrine of the Christian life in the analogy of faith.

Cartesian revolution. This time, while the language of the final script was very similar, the content was radically different; the same epistemic tune was played, but the verse had a different message, and the accent was decidedly English. The relevant difference is that now sense experience is taken as the foundation, even though intuition and demonstration still have a crucial role. Reason is seen as sense experience plus the intellectual capacity of the mind to identify knowledge and make judgements of probability.[2] The aim of this chapter is to chart this development in the Anglican tradition, as we find it in John Locke, and to reflect on its significance as an account of the canonical tradition of the Church.

John Locke did not, of course, stand alone in the complex canonical and epistemic developments of his time. He clearly built on the fascinating deliberations of William Chillingworth, whom he greatly admired,[3] and he was followed by more radical disciples who developed his suggestions and principles in directions which would probably have surprised him. Yet he gained in the Anglican world of the eighteenth century, not to speak of the wider world, the status of intellectual mentor and hero. This is entirely fitting given the great range and depths of his writings and the Protestant cast of his outlook.[4] Thankfully, in Locke's case, by contrast with that of Descartes, there is a general recognition of the religious content of his work, for this is amply manifest in his early initiation into the Protestant tradition,[5] in his own

[2] The continuity between Descartes and Locke is well brought out by Peter A. Schouls, *The Imposition of Method: A Study of Descartes and Locke* (Oxford: Clarendon Press, 1980).

[3] This is well brought out in Robert R. Orr's fine study of Chillingworth: *Reason and Authority: The Thought of William Chillingworth* (Oxford: Clarendon Press, 1967), 178. The significance of Chillingworth for developments in epistemology is explored in a very illuminating fashion by Henry Van Leeuwen, *The Problem of Certainty in English Thought, 1630–1690* (The Hague: Martinus Nijhoff, 1963).

[4] For a fascinating essay on Locke as a Protestant philosopher see John T. Noonan, 'The Protestant Philosophy of John Locke', in John K. Ryan (ed.), *Philosophical Studies in Honor of The Very Rev. Ignatius Smith, O.P.* (Westminster, Md.: Newman, 1952), 92–126.

[5] 'One permanently formative part of his upbringing was his induction into his parents' determined Protestant faith; this led him in his manhood to be contemptuous and distrustful of religious enthusiasts, Catholics, and atheists' (N. P. Nidditch, introduction to John Locke, *An Essay Concerning Human Understanding* (Oxford: Clarendon Press, 1975), p. x.

spiritual pilgrimage,[6] and in the extraordinary amount of biblical commentary and exegesis in his writings.[7] In the light of Locke's interests, his material proposals on a wide range of issues, and his subsequent reception within theology, it is no exaggeration to construe Locke as first and foremost a Christian intellectual who valiantly sought to resolve the tensions bequeathed to him by the Anglican tradition he inherited.[8]

Locke was deeply concerned by the failure of Protestants to reach agreement on theological and moral issues.[9] This was not

---

[6] Locke seriously thought of becoming an Anglican priest, and spent the last years of his life working on the writings of St Paul. The standard account of Locke's last hours is worthy of any Protestant divine. 'The day before his death, Lady Marsham being alone with him, and sitting by his bed, he exhorted her to regard this life only as a state of preparation for a better; and added, that he had lived long enough, and thanked God for having passed his life so happily, but that his life appeared to him a mere vanity. He had not slept that night, but resolved to try to rise next morning, as he did. He was carried into his study, and placed in an easy chair, where he slept a considerable while at different times. Seeming to be a little refreshed, he would be dressed as he used to be. He then desired Lady Marsham, who was reading the Psalms low, while he was dressing, to read aloud: she did so, and he appeared very attentive, till the approach of death preventing him, he desired her to break off, and a few minutes later expired, on October, 28, 1704, in the seventy third year of his age' (John Head, 'The Life of the Author', in *The Works of John Locke* (London: Rivington Press, 1824), pp. xxviii–xxxix).

[7] Biblical commentary and exegesis occupy large portions of *Two Treatises of Government*, *The Reasonableness of Christianity*, the *Letter on Toleration*, and the *Paraphrases of St. Paul*. The exception to this is *An Essay Concerning Human Understanding*.

[8] A fine discussion of Locke's personal faith and theology is found in John Marshall, *John Locke in Context: Religion, Ethics, and Politics* (Cambridge: Cambridge University Press, 1994).

[9] Hans Aarsleff sums up well the immediate reality for the vast majority of men and women: 'It was a time of violence, death, rape, war, and devastation on a vast scale. It was years of religious strife caused by sectarian disputes over the right reading of Scriptures and the flaunting of royal despotism justified by the doctrine of the divine right of kings. It was a world of constant religious and political intolerance and repression, and of ensuing dislocation that made fugitives wander across the lands of Europe in search of peace and security. England had its share of this reality in the religious enthusiasm and apocalyptic promises of life in an egalitarian society that largely caused the disorders and violence of the 1640s and 1650s' ('Locke's Influence', in Vere Chappell (ed.), *The Cambridge Companion to Locke* (Cambridge: Cambridge University Press, 1994), 254).

merely a theoretical issue for him. It was a personal matter which he had experienced at first hand working with a group of friends, and it was a very serious moral and political matter which was brought to a head for him in and around the issue of toleration in Church and State. Hence it is not implausible to see his epistemological deliberations and his discussion of the reasonableness of Christianity as directly rooted in the inability of English Christians to solve the problems which divided them by appeal to the canonical proposals in hand. Locke was effectively seeking to heal the illness in the canonical tradition he had inherited.[10] In fact, the very writing of the *Essay Concerning Human Understanding* was precipitated by the breakdown of the first principles currently in use.[11] Locke recognized, if only implicitly, that the issue would have to be pursued at a deeper, epistemic level, if he and his friends were to get beyond the impasse they had encountered. His epistemic interests were in turn reinforced by his ready acquaintance and interest in the new developments in the physical sciences, whose foundations also required extensive exploration, given the inadequacy of the scholastic proposals currently available.[12]

[10] The relation between Locke's philosophy of religion and the general fracturing of tradition in the seventeenth century is splendidly brought out by Nicholas Wolterstorff, 'Locke's Philosophy of Religion', in *Cambridge Companion to Locke*, 172–98. My concern in what follows is to bring out the close connection between the proposals already at work within the epistemology of Protestant theology and the inner structure of Locke's general epistemology.

[11] This actually happened in a discussion group at which Locke was present. We know from the notes in the margin of the *Essay* written by one of the six present at the historic meeting that they had reached a standstill on 'the principles of morality and revealed religion' (James Gibson, 'John Locke', *Proceedings of the British Academy*, 19 (1933), 16).

[12] Locke trained as a doctor, practised medicine for a time, was a member of the Royal Society, and was intimately acquainted with several of the great scientific virtuosi of his day, like Boyle, Sydenham, Huygens, and Newton. His self-deprecating comparison is nicely stated: 'The commonwealth of learning is not at this time without master-builders, whose mighty designs in advancing the sciences will leave monuments to the admiration of posterity; but everyone must not hope to be a Boyle, or a Sydenham; and in an age which produces such masters as the Great Huygenius and the incomparable Mr. Newton, with some other of that strain, 'tis ambition enough to be employed as an underlabourer in clearing ground a little, and removing some of the rubbish that lies in the way to knowledge' (*Essay*, 10). There is a tendency in some interpretations of Locke to ignore the role of theological factors underlying his philosophical deliberations, and

Locke's background interests in theology and ethics emerged immediately in the task he set for himself in *An Essay Concerning Human Understanding*. As the title suggests, his plan was to provide an adequate account of the nature and extent of human understanding.

Were it fit to trouble thee with the history of this Essay, I should tell thee that five or six friends meeting at my chamber, and discoursing on a subject very remote from this, found themselves quickly at a stand, by the difficulties that rose on every side. After we had a while puzzled ourselves, without coming any nearer a resolution of those doubts which perplexed us, it came into my thoughts, that we took a wrong course; and that before we set ourselves upon enquiries of that nature, it was necessary to examine our own abilities and see what objects our understandings were or were fitted to deal with. This I proposed to the company, who all readily assented; and thereupon it was agreed, that this should be our first enquiry.[13]

The implication is that with this in hand we would know how we know what we know, and we could then, in turn, resolve the disputes in theology and morality which could not be adequately addressed with current principles. Locke, then, clearly wanted to move from epistemology to theology and ethics; or, more accurately, theology and ethics were to be relocated within a more general epistemological theory. Once we get a clear picture of what we can genuinely know, then we can work out what is in fact the case in theology and morality, and we can spare ourselves the effort of engaging in the kind of fruitless investigation which will not lead to truth. Suitably applying the account of knowledge to theology, we could then

hence to exaggerate the role of the quest for adequate foundations for the new science as virtually the sole occasion of his thought. See e.g. Isaiah Berlin's lucid and illuminating commentary in *The Age of Enlightenment* (New York: Mentor, 1956), esp. 11–29. Compare the comment of Ryle: 'It is likely that in Locke's mind and in the minds of his contemporaries, no more important or urgent question was discussed in the whole *Essay* than the question of the nature and certainty of the propositions of theology' (Gilbert Ryle, *John Locke on the Human Understanding* (Oxford: Oxford University Press, 1933), 36–7). My claim here is that Locke's theological and moral interests are, at the very least, as significant as his scientific interests. Moreover, Locke is more than able to kill two birds with the one stone.

[13] *Essay*, 7.

implicitly resolve the problems which were currently at a standstill.[14]

Locke's account of knowledge and understanding was subtle and complex. Rejecting both the general version of scholasticism he was taught at Oxford and the proposals he found in Descartes, he sought to work out a radically new account of the foundations of knowledge.[15] His purpose was 'to enquire into the original certainty and extent of human knowledge, together with the grounds and degrees of belief, opinion, and assent'.[16] At its core Locke's account involved the claim that all knowledge and judgements of probability must be traced back to what was given to the individual in experience.

Locke's way of working out this proposal positively and materially was by insisting that all cognition was related to the ideas present in the mind through experience. 'Since the mind, in all its thoughts and reasoning, hath no other immediate object but its own ideas, which it alone does or does not contemplate, it is evident that our knowledge is only conversant about them.'[17] The term 'idea' is something of a technical term for Locke. Where for us, it stands for one item in consciousness, for Locke, as for his predecessors and successors, it was used as a general term to designate all items of consciousness.

[14] This comes out clearly in the structure of the *Essay*. Books I and II clear the decks by disposing of innate ideas and showing how the origins of our ideas are to be analysed; book III further clears the decks by providing an account of the relation between ideas and language. It is then that Locke is in a position to give his general account of knowledge and understanding, which is climaxed by an account of the relation between revelation and reason. The nature of morality, the other major concern of Locke, is also dealt with in a general way in book IV. Locke refused to spell out his account of morality on the grounds that this was already adequately dealt with in Scripture and that he did not have the ability to execute this task. He did, however, find time to deal at length with the content of divine revelation and with the hermeneutics of Scripture, as we shall see.

[15] Locke brings out the importance of the image of foundations in a delightful passage at the end of Book I: '[I]n the future part of this discourse, designing to raise an edifice uniform and consistent with itself, as far as my own experience and observation will assist me, I hope to erect it on such a basis that I shall not need to shore it up with props and buttresses, leaning on borrowed or begged foundations; or at least, if mine prove a castle in the air, I will endeavour it shall be all of a piece and hang together' (*Essay*, I. 4. xxv).

[16] Ibid. I. 1. i.   [17] Ibid. IV. 1. i.

Every man being conscious to himself that he thinks, and that which his mind is applied about whilst thinking being the ideas that are there, it is past doubt that men have in their minds several ideas, such as those expressed by the words 'whiteness,' 'hardness,' 'sweetness,' 'thinking,' 'motions,' 'man,' 'elephant,' 'army,' 'drunkenness,' and others.[18]

All such ideas fall into one of two classes, sensation and reflection. The former are constituted by sensations like hardness, coldness, and bitterness, the latter by operations of the mind like thinking, doubting, and willing. All these ideas are discovered in a broad sense by experience. Hence, given that knowledge reaches no further than our ideas, all our knowledge and warranted conclusions are derived from experience. There are no innate ideas; the mind is like an empty box in interaction with an external world in which various granules of sand are deposited to be received or arranged in various combinations by the mind itself. Initially Locke tells us that the only operation employed by the mind is that of combination, but as he proceeds this is stretched to cover a greater range of mental activity: namely, comparing and abstracting.[19]

Ideas then provide the basic raw materials of knowledge. The actual scope of knowledge is severely limited. It is constituted by a hierarchy which begins with intuition, where what we know is given immediately, and descends by way of what is known by demonstration to our knowledge of those things actually present to the senses. It is clear that knowledge for Locke was constituted by absolute certainty and universality. Only those propositions which can legitimately be seen as certain and universal count as knowledge. What is surprising is that Locke combined this claim with the conviction that there can be degrees of knowledge. Yet, given his attempt to track all knowledge back to experience, this makes sense; for it is clear that demonstration goes beyond intuition by relying on memory, and knowledge of things given through the senses is much more complex than what is given in intuition and demonstration. Thus sensitive knowledge involves a complex causal account of how the world interacts with the mind

---

[18] Locke, *Essay*, II. 1. i.

[19] For a fine exposition of Locke and the difficulties he encounters see James Gibson, *Locke's Theory of Knowledge* (Cambridge: Cambridge University Press, 1968), ch. 3.

to produce some qualities which mirror it and other qualities which, while caused by the world, do not represent the way the world actually is.

Contrasted with the realm of knowledge was the realm of belief, assent, and faith. In this case what are attained are judgements of probability based on observation and experience or on human testimony. Here assent or degree of belief is to be proportioned to the level of evidence. A properly functioning intellect will in fact find itself making appropriately scaled judgements, for the will does not determine directly what beliefs the agent holds. Beliefs arise naturally, and are not under the direct control of the will. What is under the control of the will is whether we are prepared to make relevant enquiries and whether we are prepared to keep our interests and passions in check.[20] Locke was adamant that everyone should make the pursuit of truth a ruling passion which would displace those passions which all too readily prevent us from attaining knowledge and good judgements of probability. Thus Locke was an evidentialist who insisted that we have no right to convictions which cannot be traced back to experience in the correct way and to the right degree.[21]

The general picture which emerges here is rightly seen as foundationalist and empiricist in character. While it does not exactly fit the kind of textbook description of empiricism which understandably operates as a heuristic summary of a complex configuration of epistemic proposals, Locke's account resolutely seeks to make certain units of experience perceived in various ways by the understanding of the foundation to which all knowledge and all judgements of the intellect are to be answerable. Any claim which does not meet these standards is to be rejected. Assurance of the truth of one's proposals is to be regulated in an aggressive fashion by these strictures. The individual is to take responsibility for her convictions and beliefs, determining for herself the truth of the matter in hand and refusing to submit blindly to the will and dictates of others.

[20] For a lucid account of the relation between belief and will in Locke, see J. A. Passmore 'Locke and the Ethics of Belief', in Anthony Kenny (ed.), *Rationalism, Empiricism, and Idealism* (Oxford: Clarendon Press, 1986), 23–46.

[21] This did not apply across the board, but it did apply to religious matters. For a fine summary of Locke's position see Wolterstorff, 'Locke's Philosophy of Religion', 183–5.

These standards apply to theology as much as they do to any other field of discourse, like mathematics or ethics. In fact, Locke was convinced that God had made us to operate according to these standards, so that to breach them was not just an infringement of proper epistemic policy, but also a failure to accept our proper position in the created order.

When applied to Christian theology, they lead to a fascinating two-stage operation. In the first stage one establishes the existence of God as an item of knowledge, for the existence of God can be known as a matter of demonstration. Here Locke deployed his own version of the cosmological argument, using the intuitive knowledge of his own existence as one of the crucial premisses. So belief in the existence of God, understood in general theistic categories, clearly satisfied Locke's epistemic requirements. In the second stage, one appeals to original divine revelation attested by miracles to arrive at judgements concerning, say, the existence of angels or the fact and nature of life after death. Here Locke was very keen to ensure that we have a proper account of what is and is not acceptable.[22]

Crucial to Locke's thinking at this juncture is his distinctions between truths according to, above, and contrary to reason.

1. According to reason are such propositions, whose truth we can discover, by examining and tracing those ideas we have from sensation and reflection; and by natural deduction, find to be true or probable. 2. Above reason are such propositions, whose truth or probability we cannot derive from those principles. 3. Contrary to reason are such propositions, as are inconsistent or irreconcilable to our clear and distinct ideas. Thus the existence of God is according to reason; the existence of more than one God contrary to reason; the resurrection of the dead, above reason.[23]

For Locke, revelation could only be used as a means of support where the purported truth was above reason. Revelation cannot be used, for example, to support a doctrine of transubstantiation, for this claim is contrary to reason, while it can be used to

---

[22] Locke was well aware that a distinction had to be made between original revelation, accompanied by miracles, and traditional revelation, which need not be. Clearly the latter posed a problem, in that Locke would have to appeal to testimony to secure the claim that the original revelation was faithfully recorded in the traditional revelation.   [23] *Essay*, IV. 13. xxiii.

support, say, a doctrine about the existence of angels. Moreover, the claim that revelation has actually occurred has itself to be supported, and given the kind of support potentially available on Locke's epistemic principles, the content of revelation must be believed with a degree of assent appropriate to judgements of probability as opposed to knowledge. The evidence for original revelation is generally to be found in the presence of accompanying miracles. And the assurance attached to a doctrine based on revelation cannot be greater than the evidence used to support that revelation in the first place. This is so despite the fact that any proposition revealed by God must of necessity be construed as certainly and infallibly true, for the whole strength of the assent depends in this case on the strength available to ascertain the existence of the revelation itself. It is precisely this consideration which is systematically ignored by the 'enthusiast' who appeals to personal inspiration or revelation without adducing relevant external proof and who expects others to accept his proposals with a degree of commitment which is completely unwarranted.

We are fortunate in having access to Locke's material deliberations concerning the actual content of divine revelation.[24] Against the incipient deism of his day, Locke was convinced that God had given special revelation to the world, adequately supported by miracle. What he was at great pains to determine was what God actually required us to believe if we are to be saved. For Locke, while all of Scripture is indeed true, all that God requires for salvation is captured by belief in Jesus as the Messiah, accompanied by repentance.[25] Here Locke set aside assent to the traditional creeds or Articles of Religion, and resorted to his own independent reading of the Scriptures as determined by a natural, historical reading of the relevant texts. Thus the individual was to determine for him or herself what was required for salvation and not rely on Church authority, tradition, or others.

We have now before us sufficient material to discern how

[24] These are laid out most clearly in *The Reasonableness of Christianity as Delivered in the Scriptures*, ed. with an introduction by George E. Ewing (Washington: Regnery Gateway, 1965).

[25] For Locke, belief in the proper sense was not just a matter of bare assent but of assent accompanied by reliance and obedience. Locke clearly adhered to a classical Protestant account of the doctrine of justification by faith. See e.g. *Reasonableness*, para. 229.

Locke has received and transformed the canonical traditions handed over to him in his day. The most conspicuous matters are these:

1. Epistemology is logically the primary issue to be resolved and settled before everything else. Before one can make any deep progress in faith, one must have to hand a relatively comprehensive account of the boundaries of human understanding. Knowing how one knows takes precedence over everything else. We find here the same ordering of priorities which was developed at the Reformation in the place given to the doctrine of Scripture as the norm of doctrine, where all other doctrines had to be derived from this source, and which was transposed in the Cartesian project into secular form. The crucial difference between Locke and Descartes is not in the place assigned to epistemology but in the content of the epistemology to be espoused. Where Descartes distrusts the senses, Locke makes the senses the foundations of all claims to truth.

2. The internal structure of the epistemology mirrors that found in the theology of the Reformers and in the Cartesian project. In each case, all claims to truth are ultimately to be traced back to a single foundation, represented in this case in the content of the mind as ideas. Anything which does not fit this scheme is to be rejected. The concepts of rationality, justification, and knowledge are most naturally interpreted within this horizon.

3. The foundations posited by the theory are clear and distinct, or, as Locke prefers to say, determinate. Hence elements of mystery have to be dismissed as out of court from the beginning.

4. In arriving at truth, the individual is self-sufficient in himself or herself. There is no need for any kind of special grace; one can rely on the abilities given in creation by a benevolent deity.[26]

5. In seeking the truth, one should not trust to tradition, to religious communities, or the like, as there is no guarantee that these have arrived at the truths they proclaim in the correct way. The individual is basically an isolated epistemic unit, operating effectively on his own.

6. In holding to the truth, one must be careful to proportion one's commitment to the relevant weight of evidence available.

---

[26] There are scattered references in Locke to the working of the Holy Spirit, but they are exceptionally underdeveloped.

In the case of knowledge one naturally assents with certainty, for knowledge by definition involves certainty. In the case of belief, the level of assent should not go beyond that required by the evidence in hand, for judgements of probability are a matter of degree.

7. Theological beliefs are subject to these general rules. Belief in God is a matter of demonstrative knowledge, as opposed to intuitive or sensitive knowledge. Other more specific theological claims can only be a matter of probability, as they are only legitimately derived from divine revelation, and support for divine revelation can, in turn, only be a matter of probability. Even the certainty which, for Locke, is logically connected to the content of divine revelation is displaced by the probability which is attached to a person's identification of a putative divine revelation.

Taking these proposals as a whole, we witness the continued erosion of the patristic conception of canon as represented by the rich and varied ways it is applied to diverse materials and practices. The Nicene Creed, the Chalcedonian Definition, the liturgy, iconography, and the Fathers are not just missing; they are treated with distaste because, both in fact and in principle, any use of them is ruled out by the strictures of the favoured epistemology. The very notion of the Church as an extended historic community, bound in some sense by its canonical history, is replaced by a vision of the Church as a voluntary association of individuals held together by their own independent judgement concerning the correctness of the doctrine of justification by faith as established from the Scriptures.[27] In fact, all that is left is the residue of the canon of Scriptures completely transposed into a theory of divine revelation and in practice reduced to the barest minimum of theological content in order to satisfy Locke's Protestant conviction about the essentials of salvation.

Even then, Scripture is carefully subordinated to the requirements of reason as spelled out in the essentials of his epistemology. The rule of faith, originally applied to the proto-creeds of

---

[27] 'A church I take to be a voluntary society of men, joining themselves together on their own account in order to the public worship of God, in such a manner as they judge acceptable to him and effective to the salvation of their souls' (*First Letter on Toleration*, in *Works*, v. 13).

the early Church, transposed in time into the rule of Scripture, has now become transposed in a complex way to the rule of reason cast in incipient empiricist categories. What began among the Anglicans as an appeal to Scripture, tradition, and reason has become by degrees a straight appeal to reason. 'Reason must be our last judge and guide in everything.'[28]

There is little chance of escaping this development once the canonical tradition of the Church is cast in the kind of epistemic categories which the history of the Western Church engendered. Four crucial considerations drive the engine which is at work. First, the canonical heritage is reduced to Scripture. Tradition is quietly dropped, or, more likely, becomes subject to hostility. Second, Scripture is construed *simpliciter* as divine revelation rather than in more complex terms as an inspired means of grace. The crucial epistemic category deployed is that of propositional revelation, and the content of that revelation is limited to the essentials of salvation. Both these moves were already more or less complete by the time Locke was initiated into the Christian tradition.

Third, Locke rightly noticed that there were, and are, competing claims to divine revelation and competing accounts of the interpretation of the divine revelation actually accepted by Western Christians. Disputes over which revelation or interpretation to accept cannot be resolved by a further appeal to divine revelation, for any such appeal will only compound the dilemma in hand. Locke, like Aquinas before him, insisted that there must be some kind of exterior evidence to warrant assent, and he found this, again like Aquinas, in miracle. But whether the miracles actually occurred, and hence whether the putative revelation is genuine, is now taken to be determined by a judgement of probability. It is this proposal, which Aquinas merely mentions, which Locke pressed with determination. Fourth, there is the foundationalist structure embedded in the epistemic policy deployed. A person's beliefs are to be arranged in a hierarchy in which priority is assigned to those that are closest to the original input of evidence. Hence the specifically Christian beliefs held, even though they are derived from propositional revelation, are ruled in a very strict sense by those below them in the hierarchy

---

[28] *Essay*, IV. 19. xiv.

which supports them. Reason, understood in terms of evidence traced to the senses, is, therefore, the ultimate rule of theology. 'Reason must be our last judge and guide in everything.'

There is surely considerable attraction in taking the line developed by Locke. The picture of knowledge and warranted belief designed by Locke provides a clear method for dividing up and resolving intellectual disputes which can be taken up and pursued with diligence by the individual. The promise is that one can build up an edifice of justified claims by beginning with the input from the senses and by appropriate steps reach all the way up to the existence of God and the Last Judgement. This can be done with appropriate labour, it can be checked by others for accuracy; and it can be applied in fields as diverse as mathematics and ethics.

Moreover, Locke's strategy promises to bring to an end the babel of voices which occupy the contested field of religion in general and Christianity in particular. Thus it furnishes a demonstration for the existence of God; it articulates a clear concept of propositional revelation; and it identifies the relevant evidence for adjudicating competing claims to special revelation. In addition, it provides a warranted account of the actual revelation made available in the Christian tradition, specifying precisely what should be believed and done to gain eternal salvation. Hence the canonical crisis of the Western Church can be objectively and dispassionately resolved in a way that safeguards the authority of divine revelation and the essentials of salvation. Besides, there is available the foundation for a policy of mutual respect and tolerance in Church and State. Human beings are intended to operate according to the epistemic policies delineated here. Hence, with a few understandable exceptions, individuals are to be persuaded by reason, rather than coerced by the threat of violence, and they are to be permitted to approach membership in the Church in terms of their own voluntary commitment. Given all these attractions, it is small wonder that Locke became the mentor and hero of those who wanted to build a new world in the West.

Whatever else we may say, there is no gainsaying the need to pursue the kinds of questions pursued by Locke. One great virtue of Locke's work is that it exposes the extent to which there is a field of enquiry wherein we are forced to pursue a series of questions which perplex, if not torture, the very best of human minds. Many commentators have rightly insisted that the catalogue of issues unearthed by Locke is exceptionally impressive. Both the main road of his enquiry and the many byways he tracks down on his journey deserve to be frequently traversed. It is noble to develop a theory of human understanding which will enable us to know what are the contours and limits of its capacities. It is important to think through the relation between experience, knowledge, and justified belief, to explore the nature of language and its relation to sense experience, to pursue such concepts as probability, personal identity, substance, causality, personhood, and the host of others which crop up almost incidentally in our intercourse with the world and each other. It is intrinsically worthwhile to face the dilemmas posed by the existence of different interpretations of the divine, to explore the provinces of faith and reason, to examine the proposal that the justification of claims to knowledge and warranted belief is best pictured in terms of foundations, and to investigate the place of mystery in our understanding of the world.

Locke is correct to insist that pursuing these issues is not antithetical to a robust religious faith. On the contrary, the quest for a worthy doctrine of creation will foster such enquiries; for an account of human understanding can legitimately be construed as much as an analysis of our divinely given capacities,[29] represented by, say, memory and judgement,[30] as an analysis of the complex concepts and criteria deployed to make sense of such notions as knowledge, justification, rationality, and evidence. Within this there is room to think of the epistemic responsibilities of the individual as much as the possible role of tradition and community. Further, appeal to divine revelation, rather than leading us to reject reason, forces us to delineate its nature, for the alternative to the deployment of some form of rationality in the face of competing claims to revelation is not a deeper faith but an arbitrary one. Locke's worries about the dangers of 'enthusiasm' are entirely salutary.

The strength of our persuasions are no evidence at all of their own rectitude; crooked things may be as still and inflexible as straight; and men may be as positive and peremptory in error as in truth. How come

---

[29] Locke refers to our understanding as the most excellent part of God's workmanship (ibid. IV. 18. v).

[30] Locke's discussion of the nature of judgement as it relates to the place of the syllogism in reasoning is exceptionally insightful (see ibid. IV. 17).

else the untractable zealots in different and opposite parties? For if the light, which everyone thinks he has in mind, which in this case is nothing but the strength of his own persuasion, be an evidence that it is from God, contrary opinions may have the same title to be inspirations; and God will not only be the Father of lights but of opposite and contradictory lights, leading men contrary ways; and contradictory propositions will be divine truths, if an ungrounded strength of assurance be an evidence, that any proposition is a divine revelation.[31]

We can go further. Even Locke's mistakes do not diminish the stature of his accomplishments. On this topic Berlin has the matter straight.

[Locke's] own theories are often fanciful enough; he is guilty of many inconsistencies and obscurities and lapses into modes of thought which he is supposing himself to combat. Nevertheless, his ideas, or at least the effects of his skill in presenting them (the literary taste of the latter part of the seventeenth century and the whole of the eighteenth century is clearly different from our own) were genuinely revolutionary. His view that many cardinal errors are due to the mistaking of words for things; that minds—or their thoughts—are capable of having their natural histories written no less than plants or animals, with equally startling and fruitful results; that the findings of philosophers must not depart too widely from the beliefs of balanced common sense (Locke must almost be said to have invented the notion of common sense); that philosophical problems are as often as not due to confusion in the mind of the philosopher rather than the difficulties inherent in the subject—all these transformed the ideas of men.[32]

What is at stake, however, is not the stature of Locke's proposals, but their significance for the canonical traditions of the Church. The obvious question to ask is whether they resolve the canonical crisis of the Church which had done so much to motivate Locke's endeavours. Does it really help to shift, say, from a body of specific doctrines and practices, agreed on by the Church for a host of reasons, to a theory about the sources and norms of all knowledge and all judgements of probability? Will such a move liberate us? Will it secure consensus? Is it the only one which will engender tolerance in the social and political arena? There are several considerations which deserve attention at this juncture.

---

[31] Ibid. IV. 19. xi.   [32] Berlin, *Age of Enlightenment*, 31.

First, Locke's epistemic proposals, while they may profess to be grounded simply on experience and observation, are deeply indebted to the communities and traditions in which he lived. To take an obvious example, Locke's conception of knowledge was more or less borrowed from the scholastic and the Cartesian tradition. Locke from the outset was working with a conception of knowledge which identified it with absolutely certain and universal propositions. Hence, rather than see belief as contained within the concept of knowledge, belief is contrasted with knowledge in a way which is at odds with our everyday use of the term. Equally, the whole picture of the attainment of knowledge as a building with solid foundations is brought to the table at the outset, rather than derived from sense experience.[33] We might also add to this list of intellectual debts his deployment of the distinction between primary and secondary qualities, some of his notions of substance, the normative status of Scripture, the idea of essentials of salvation, the attributes of God, the conception of philosophy as a kind of introspective science, and many others. All these have been gained by way of tradition, a tradition which in turn is enriched by Locke's own variations on these themes.

It is true that Locke could well acknowledge this possibility, for he has an acute sense of the place of opinion and tradition in life generally. Moreover, this observation about the origins of various elements in his proposals does nothing in itself to undermine the normative claim that all our concepts and beliefs should be constructed and arrived at in the way required by Locke's empiricism. Theoretically, Locke could well be right; we do not know in advance of serious philosophical investigation if his empiricist programme fails. However, it was Locke himself who insisted on the value of the genetic method, and if central

---

[33] Locke himself recognized this when he asked the reader to allow him to deploy his own fundamental claim about the nature of knowledge from the beginning. 'I warn the reader not to expect undeniable cogent demonstration, unless I be allowed the privilege, not seldom assumed by others, to take my principles for granted; and then I doubt not but that I can demonstrate too. All that I can say for the principles I proceed on is that I can only appeal to men's own unprejudiced experience and observation, whether they be true or no; and this is enough for a man who professes no more than to lay down candidly and freely his own conjectures concerning a subject lying somewhat in the dark, without any other design than an unbiased enquiry into truth' (*Essay*, I. 4. iv).

components of his position are better explained as derived from tradition rather than experience, then his whole position, like that of the believer in innate ideas whom he attacks in book I, is in serious trouble. Locke's dogmatic opposition to tradition and community served him badly at this point. He had cut himself off from the resources essential to understanding central elements in his own position, and he had failed to recognize the extent to which he was indebted to tradition in epistemology.

Second, this second-order tradition about the nature of knowledge and justification is no more intellectually secure than the canonical traditions of the Church which it seeks to replace. If anything, it may be even less secure, if we pursue it on both formal and material grounds.

Formally, theories of knowledge and probability are philosophical proposals subject to appropriate scrutiny and criticism. On Locke's own theory they will have to be based on experience and observation, for these are the only canons allowed to be operative. If anything is clear, however, epistemological theories are not determined in this way. They are not straightforwardly verifiable or falsifiable by sense experience. In fact, one task of an epistemological theory is to enquire into the status of experience and observation in knowledge and justification. Furthermore, it is extremely likely that one test of a good epistemic theory will be its ability to cope with ordinary, first-order claims to knowledge and justification. It can be argued that claims about how we know what we know are to some degree parasitic on simple claims to know this or that proposition, so that on purely formal grounds, the former will always be less secure than the latter. Claims about the methodology of knowledge and justification, on this view, are dependent on particular judgements of knowledge and justification.[34]

Materially, it will suffice to draw attention to the widely recognized problem in Locke's representative theory of perception.

[34] This suggestion is often missed when the primary aim of epistemology is taken to be the call to answer the sceptic. However, there is nothing sacrosanct about the honoured place of the sceptic in the field of epistemology. We have as much right to be particularists as to be methodists. For the importance of this distinction see Roderick M. Chisholm, 'The Problem of the Criterion', in *The Foundations of Knowing* (Minneapolis: University of Minnesota Press, 1982), 65–7.

Thus we are told initially that all we can really know are the contents of our ideas and their internal relationships to each other. Yet Locke claims to be able to reach beyond this to an external world in causal interaction with our ideas which in some cases mirror the nature of external reality and in other cases do not. As Berkeley was quick to point out, these claims are incompatible.

Turning to his philosophy of religion, it is surely false to claim that logical properties attached to reliance on testimony transfer to the content of the proposition presented in testimony. Thus, if I rely on the testimony of learned mathematicians that Andrew Wiles has solved Fermat's fourth theorem, and as a consequence I believe the content of that theorem, what I believe is necessarily true, even though my belief rests on fallible human testimony. Also, Locke is altogether too cavalier on how to resolve puzzles about the relationships between beliefs which are divinely revealed, contrary to reason, and above reason. Thus, because he was convinced that the doctrine of transubstantiation is contrary to reason, he held that it could not be construed as revealed by God. However, if the doctrine is revealed by God, it is equally appropriate to claim that it must be above reason rather than contrary to reason, even though we may not be able to show that it is not contrary to reason.[35] Furthermore, Locke's claims that we cannot lack a clear proof of God 'as long as we carry ourselves about us',[36] and that the appropriate evidence for divine revelation is constituted exclusively by miracles, are highly dubious.

It follows from these observations that it is profoundly mistaken to believe that these epistemic proposals are somehow an improvement on the central canonical beliefs of the Church enshrined, say, in the Nicene Creed. Such doctrines as the Trinity and the Incarnation are indeed disputed; they are far from easy to articulate succinctly; and they can sometimes appear remote from the problems of our daily lives. To a great extent

---

[35] Copleston's comment is appropriate: 'Catholic theologians would not deny that reason is capable *in principle* of distinguishing between propositions which are contrary to reason and propositions, the truth or falsity of which cannot be decided by reason without the aid of revelation. But in particular cases we may, when left to our own devices, confuse the latter with the former' (Frederick Copleston, *A History of Philosophy* (New York: Image Books, 1964), v. 233; emphasis original).   [36] *Essay*, IV. 10. i.

these pedestrian truths about the doctrines of the Trinity and the Incarnation are handed over in the very transmission of this material in the life of the Church. However, it is far from clear what is gained by replacing the canonical tradition with a commitment to epistemic policies which exaggerate the significance of epistemology and in some cases are manifestly absurd. Yet commitment to a highly dubious epistemology is ultimately what the Lockean project involved. It constituted a profound reconstruction of the Christian tradition wherein methodological considerations replaced the concrete particularities of a comprehensive religious tradition. But the former are no more secure than the latter.[37]

Third, a further factor at stake in the Lockean project depends on a failure to grasp the potential place of epistemic material in the economy of the Christian tradition. Theoretically, it is perfectly possible for epistemic proposals to be incorporated into the canonical tradition of the Church. This can be done by canonizing the particular figure or teacher who developed or summed up the relevant epistemic theory, as happened in the case of Aquinas. Alternatively, it can be done by adopting with varying degrees of formality the favoured epistemic theory, as happened in Reformation Confessions on the place of Scripture in the construction of doctrine. So Locke can have his day in ecclesiastical court, so to speak. It is entirely feasible for his admirers to argue the case that he or his views should be formally adopted as canonical.[38]

[37] Another way to make the same point is to say that Locke is dramatically changing the place of philosophy in the economy of theology and the life of the Church. Following his predecessors in the intellectual tradition of the Western Church, he has made philosophy master in the Church. Where before there was some kind of minimal check from revelation, this last wall of protection has now been dismantled. Despite all Locke's sincere protestations about the status and significance of Scripture, he has simply ignored the caution and warnings of the scriptural writers on the perils of philosophy.

[38] This is not a merely speculative possibility. '*The Reasonableness of Christianity*, with its rejection of creeds, its affirmation of the sole and plenary authority of the Scriptures, its careful distinction between the covenants, its exhaustive and even tedious juxtapositioning and comparison of related passages, and its insistence upon the rational approach to the Scripture, sets forth a theological view with an intrinsic exegetical method–call it Socinian, Lockean, or Campbellian. This method later gained wide acceptance in America with the rise of the Disciples of Christ, the Church of Christ, and other "fundamentalist" groups, which are among the fastest growing religious bodies today' (George E. Ewing, introduction to his edition of *Reasonableness of Christianity* (p. xvi).

Locke was so convinced that he was right about the nature of knowledge and probability, and that every right-thinking person, having consulted experience, would agree with him, that he scarcely stopped to reckon with such a possibility. Indeed, he did not even begin to investigate whether it was appropriate to have this kind of canonical material at all. Perhaps epistemic material by Christian intellectuals should be left to the side, neither adopted nor rejected, say, on the grounds that salvation does not depend on holding a correct epistemic theory. Certainly, if an epistemological theory is to be adopted, then, at the very least, a case needs to be made that it is essential to the welfare of the Church. Locke showed no interest in these matters. He took it as given that his epistemic proposals should be consulted as the ultimate norms of theological judgement. In addition, with his stress on the ultimate authority of the individual, Locke had virtually no sense of the Church as a historic community stretching across time and committed to handing on its hard-won treasures from generation to generation; so the very concept of a canonical decision probably eluded him.[39]

Clearly, any epistemic proposals should be compatible with, and integrally related to, the existing canonical tradition of the Church, or, if new material is incompatible with older material, this discrepancy should be addressed. Locke did in fact address this matter, albeit indirectly. His general hostility to the canonical doctrines of the Church is unmitigated.

If schisms and heresies were traced up to their original cause, it would be found that they spring chiefly from the multiplying of articles of faith, and narrowing the bottom of religion by clogging it with creeds and catechisms and endless niceties about the essences, properties and attributes of God.[40]

More specifically, it is hard to see how Locke, given the way he understood the concepts of substance and person, could leave

---

[39] Locke does at one point define a church as 'a convention of clergymen making canons' (*First Letter on Toleration*, in *Works*, v. 13). However, he has no desire to explore this notion. It would be interesting to extrapolate in a speculative manner from his social philosophy to explore exactly what social concepts would be available to Locke in the field of ecclesiology.

[40] Quoted in Noonan, 'Protestant Philosophy of Locke', 120.

much room for the doctrine of the Trinity.[41] It can be no accident that he studiously avoided the subject as best he could.
Further, Locke's own central article of faith, the Messiahship of
Jesus, is a pale alternative to the canonical doctrine of the
Incarnation.[42] Thus, *prima facie*, Locke surely would have an interesting dilemma on his hands were he to pursue the possibility of
the canonization of his proposals.

Fourth, Locke's claim to be offering an objective, unprejudiced, plain reading of Scripture is difficult to sustain. Locke has a
clear sense of the hermeneutical procedures to be deployed in
reading Scripture. The words of Scripture are to be understood

as they may be supposed to have been used in the mouths of the speakers who used them according to the language of that time and country,
wherein they lived, without such learned, artificial, and forced senses of
them as are sought out and put on them in most of the systems of divinity, according to the notions that each one has been bred up in.[43]

The reader is to set aside preconceived opinions, to avoid piece-
meal readings or citations, and to compare text with text.[44]

Yet Locke himself approached Scripture as a unity and as a
medium of divine revelation, so much so that he could claim that
the New Testament 'has God for its author, salvation for its end,
and truth without any admixture of error for its matter'.[45] In his
ecclesiology he also approached Scripture as a voluntarist who

[41] For an exceptionally important essay on this topic see William S.
Babcock, 'A Changing of the Christian God: The Doctrine of the Trinity in the
Seventeenth Century', *Interpretation*, 45 (1991), 133–46. There is also a useful
discussion in John Redwood, *Reason, Ridicule and Religion* (London: Thames &
Hudson, 1970), ch. 7.

[42] These comments in no way suggest that Locke was a deist. On the
contrary, Locke clearly intended *Reasonableness* as a rejoinder to the deists of his
day. 'But if there be a great number of deists, and that the preventing their
increase be not worth every true Christian's care and endeavours, those who
have been so loud against them have been much to blame, and I wish to God
there were no reason for their complaints. For these, therefore, I take the liberty
to say, as I did before, that I chiefly designed my book' (*The Works of John Locke*,
vii. 265). Locke's commitment to special revelation and miracle is enough to
undermine any charge of deism.

[43] Quoted in Noonan, 'Protestant Philosophy of Locke', 118.

[44] *An Essay for the Understanding of St. Paul's Epistles by Consulting Paul
Himself*, in *Works*, vii, p. x.

[45] Letter to R. King, 25 Aug. 1703, in *Works*, ix. 306.

held that the teaching of the Church should be ignored. He was even convinced that what God revealed in Scripture must be plain to all. 'It would be strange indeed, if God, who made the tongue and orders of speech, who gave us all the use of language, cannot be understood, when he declares his will to man, who must thus know the thoughts of God better than God himself.'[46] For Locke, Christianity was a 'plain, simple, reasonable thing'.[47] It was absurd that one be asked to believe 'things not plain, not clear, not intelligible to common apprehensions'.[48] This should come as no surprise, for Locke's whole epistemology requires that everything be ultimately reducible to clear and distinct ideas.

What this displays is that once we adopt the fundamentals of Locke's epistemology, then consequences show up in the most unexpected places. The theory so colours everything the minds of its adherents touch that even when Locke is self-consciously and officially on guard, as he is in his hermeneutical comments and his summary of the teachings of Scripture, it prevents him seeing its effects. The theory becomes so constitutive of claims to knowledge and rationality that opponents are liable to be defined out of the conversation. That it is accompanied by protestations of tolerance, good sense, and intellectual virtue only compounds the problem.[49]

Fifth, and finally, provided the Church as a whole has a robust sense of the complexity and peculiar value of her canonical heritage, she can easily survive the potential erosion engendered by this or that epistemic proposal put forward by Christian intellectuals. Locke appeared when there was deep confusion about the canonical heritage of the Church and when the primary lens for reading the canonical heritage had become profoundly epistemic in nature. Moreover, he wrote to win the allegiance of the

---

[46] Quoted in Noonan, 'Protestant Philosophy of Locke', 117.

[47] Ibid. 121.   [48] Ibid.

[49] It is tempting to hold that at the end of his life Locke was pessimistic about the possibility of attaining agreement on the simple, plain meaning of the Scriptures. In a letter he wrote to Anthony Collins two months before his death, he said: 'If there be need for authentic interpreters in the word of God, what is the way to find them out? This is worth your thinking of, unless you would have everyone interpret for himself, and what work would that make? Betwixt these two, find something if you can; for the world is in want of peace, which is much better than everlasting Billingsgate' (Letter to A. Collins, 1 Oct. 1703, in *Works*, ix. 207).

common people of his day, and he sincerely believed that his proposals would provide a whole new way of thinking about knowledge and judgement which would terminate the endless disputes about the content of true Christianity. Once his views became widely disseminated and accepted, there was a price to be paid when the internal difficulties of his epistemology were exposed. Thus, when Bishop Berkeley took Locke's empiricism and laid bare the flaws in his theory of perception, it was natural for him to argue that his own more radical, revised version of empiricism, complete with its idealistic ontology, should be accepted as the only true philosophy which could safeguard the riches of the Christian faith. Philosophy and faith had once again become so entangled that a crisis in philosophy seemingly put at risk the whole content of the Faith. So faith needed a new philosophy if it was to survive. The only alternative to idealism, as Berkeley saw it, was atheism.

The most telling developments, however, came from the hands of the great David Hume. Adhering faithfully as a philosopher, but not as a plain citizen, to Locke's empiricism, he drew the drastic consequences for which he is now justly famous. On a strictly empiricist account of rationality, it was impossible to believe in the external world, in the self, and in causality. Locke's God and the special revelation attributed thereto were also summarily and brilliantly disposed of by undercutting Locke's natural theology and by challenging the credibility of any historical testimony for those miracles which were the warrants for special revelation. The blow delivered caused a devastating crisis for Locke's revised account of the canonical heritage of the Church.[50] Much modern theology can legitimately be seen as a series of failed attempts to recover from the indirect consequences of the continued reworking of the canons of the Church as epistemic norms so superbly, but tragically, represented by Locke. Locke was really the last great Christian intellectual in the West to win the mind of the culture. Consequent on his labours, the Christian intellectual has been playing ball at the defensive end of the field.

[50] I take the story of the impact of Hume and Kant on the whole tradition of natural theology and of appeal to miracles to be well enough known not to require further exposition here.

Theology within the Limits of Experience Alone

One of the remarkable features of the epistemology of theology in the West is the late arrival of the appeal to experience as the foundation for religious belief. Experience shows up in an oblique way in the appeal to the inner witness of the Holy Spirit in Calvin, but it figures not at all, say, in Aquinas, Descartes, Hooker, and Locke. The non-appearance in Locke is certainly a surprise, for Locke is a foundationalist who clearly believes that knowledge and judgements of probability are to be derived from sense experience. Moreover, it is not in the least surprising that Jonathan Edwards and John Wesley, who were both deeply influenced by Locke, should have explored the role of experience in any true knowledge of God.[1] Yet the persistent Protestant convictions of Edwards and Wesley clearly kept the appeal to experience subordinate to the rule of Scripture.[2] Hence, it was not until the more general epistemology of Locke, represented by his natural theology and his account of divine revelation, were thoroughly undermined by the philosophers who succeeded him that appeal to experience became the rule of truth in theology.

When it did, a whole new era of theology was inaugurated.

---

[1] For important reservations concerning Edwards as a Lockian see Norman Fiering, 'The Rationalist Foundations of Jonathan Edwards's Metaphysics', in Nathan O. Hatch and Harry S. Stout (eds.), *Jonathan Edwards and the American Experience* (New York: Oxford University Press, 1988), 73–101.

[2] Wesley even tries to find biblical warrant for his Lockean sensibilities. See my 'The Wesleyan Quadrilateral', in Ted Runyon (ed.), *Wesleyan Theology Today: A Bicentennial Theological Consultation* (Hashville: Kingswood Books, 1985), 119–26. For a perceptive summary of Wesley's epistemology see Mitsuo Shimizu, 'Epistemology in the Thought of John Wesley' (Ph.D. diss., Drew University, 1980). For a fine analysis see Rex D. Matthews, ' "Religion and Reason Joined": A Study in the Theology of John Wesley' (Th.D. diss., Harvard University, 1986).

The crucial figure who made experience the foundation of theology was Friedrich Schleiermacher. Our aim in this chapter is to chart the development of this move and show how it altered the standard Protestant appeal to scripture. As in earlier instances, we shall indicate how epistemological proposals, while offered as liberating replacements of the canonical heritage of the church, turn out to be dubious. In the case of Schleiermacher they also appear to be fragments of the pietist traditions of his parents.

A useful point of entry is to note briefly the significance and consequences of Locke's replacement of the canon of Scripture by the rule of reason. Once this shift became part of the general consciousness of Christian leaders and intellectuals, the Church became hostage to the fortunes of the material epistemological proposals developed by Locke. Should they triumph in the academy and culture, then all would be well. Should they fall into disfavour, then Christianity itself would be at a crossroads. The basic alternatives facing Christian intellectuals and leaders in the latter case were these. First, they could make an effort to rescue the Lockian proposals and regain intellectual respectability that way. Thus they might rebut the objections made against Locke, or they might find an alternative version of natural theology and special revelation to rebuild the Lockian strategy. Second, they could accept that Locke was wrong, construe Locke's vision of reason as the only viable conception of reason available, and then argue that faith and reason were antithetical. Faith was founded on, say, divine revelation, which was opposed to reason.[3] Third, they could accept the criticisms levelled at Locke and find an entirely different way to secure the intellectual respectability of the Christian heritage by deploying an entirely altered set of philosophical and epistemological proposals.[4]

Much modern theology since Schleiermacher can be understood as a series of salvage operations which have deployed the third alternative as the way out of the dilemma bequeathed by the

[3] There is a whole line of figures in a Protestant underworld of counter-Enlightenment thought, paradoxically inspired in part by Hume and represented by Hamann and Kierkegaard, who take this line. See e.g. Isaiah Berlin, *The Magus of the North, J. G. Hamann and the Origins of Modern Irrationalism* (New York: Farrar, Straus & Giroux, 1993).

[4] Clearly, for Protestants in the Reformed, as opposed to the Anglican, tradition, resorting to the Roman tradition was still not an attractive alternative.

Lockian tradition.[5] Thus, in Schleiermacher, in the great
Princeton tradition of the nineteenth century, in John Henry
Newman, in Karl Barth, and in the revival of Liberal
Protestantism represented by Schubert Ogden, concerted efforts
have been made to secure the ongoing fortunes of the Christian
faith by appeal to this or that epistemic construction.[6] At times
the appeal to epistemology has been masked by a repudiation of
philosophy or by hiding its light under a theological bushel. Yet
in each case the framework created by the shift from canon to
criterion has controlled the fundamental grammar of the debate.
The content of the Christian tradition and the nature of Christian
identity have been cast in categories which are logically determined by the requirements of epistemic theory. More particularly, the canon of Scripture has been interpreted in terms which
dovetail with the epistemic proposals on offer.

On the surface this interpretation does not seem to apply to
Schleiermacher. What strikes one initially in Schleiermacher is
the effort he made to cut the Christian faith loose from the philosophical commitments in which it had become entangled. It is as
if he forswore any appeal to philosophy, much less epistemology,
as essential to Christianity, seeking to recover its pristine essence
in a living experience of God, as mediated through Jesus Christ in
the Christian community.[7] However, it becomes clear, once one
pursues his position in any depth, that his whole understanding of
the Christian faith was dependent on extraordinarily subtle and
complex ontological and epistemic theory. Thus, from the outset,
one is confronted with a paradox. A position which was proffered
as a recovery of the heart of true religion, uncontaminated by
speculative metaphysics and natural theology, turns out to be

---

[5] Generally speaking, the great difficulty with the second option was that it
was paradoxical in the extreme to claim that faith was both *founded* on divine
revelation and *opposed* to reason. Besides, appeal to divine revelation, if it was
not to be seen as arbitrary, required some account of how one was to decide
between various claimants to revelation, how one was to interpret revelation,
and how one was to face the battery of questions raised by historical criticism.

[6] I indicate here the map we shall be following over the next five chapters.

[7] 'I have said repeatedly that Christian doctrine must be set forth in
complete independence of each and every philosophical system. . . . I could
never allow that my faith in Christ came from philosophy' (quoted in H. R.
Mackintosh, *Types of Modern Theology* (London: Collins, 1937), 42).

unintelligible outside the parameters of a lavish ontological drama cast in virtually inaccessible jargon and laden with a network of epistemic conviction.[8]

Yet the apparent primacy of piety over philosophy is not in the least surprising given the contours of Schleiermacher's spiritual and intellectual pilgrimage. His life began and ended as an expression of Christian piety. Brought up in a Christian home, where his parents had been converted to a living Christian faith by the Moravians, he was intensely initiated into the spirituality of that— so much so that at the age of 14 he underwent a conventional, datable conversion at school, and as a 16-year-old student he sincerely composed a conventional Moravian poem for the birthday of his sister, Lotte, on the assigned biblical text of the day.[9] At the other end of his life, on his deathbed, he exhibited a moving commitment to the value of the Eucharist, celebrated in his home with the adult members of his family.[10] Between these two poles

---

[8] Gerrish's amusing comment is appropriate: 'Even the tough Scots who translated the book [*The Christian Faith*] apparently hesitated over some of the centipede words in the original German, and to be on the safe side they retained them in parentheses along with the best English equivalents they could manage' (B. A. Gerrish, *A Prince of the Church: Schleiermacher and the Beginnings of Modern Theology* (London: SCM Press, 1984), 4). It is important to realize that this does not apply to Schleiermacher as a preacher. His sermons are extraordinarily lucid, substantial, and inspiring. See Friedrich Schleiermacher, *Servant of the Word* (Philadelphia: Fortress Press, 1987).

[9] Rom. 4: 25. 'Behold him there upon the cross, And thus be blessed by satisfying hours, the martyred one beloved by us, the sacred Lord now wounded. Beloved, that is blessedness, the highest good in all the earth. And even in eternity, none greater could be given, he washed me there in his blood, from each and every sin, and gave forgiveness with his death, and showed me peace and rest. He led me also to his fold, that I might be secure, from all the evil of this world, with his own people sure' (Martin Redeker, *Schleiermacher: Life and Thought* (Philadelphia: Fortress Press, 1973), 11–12).

[10] 'On the last morning, Wednesday, Feb. 12th, his suffering evidently became greater. He complained of a burning inward heat, and the first and last tone of impatience broke from his lips: "Ah, Lord, I suffer much!"—The features of death came fully on, the eye was glazed, the death-struggle was over! At this moment, he laid the two fore-fingers upon his left eye, as he often did when in deep thought, and began to speak: "We have the atoning death of Jesus Christ, his body, and his blood." During this he had raised himself up, his features began to be reanimated, his voice became clear and strong; he inquired with priestly solemnity: "Are ye one with me in this faith?" to which we . . . who were present, and myself, answered with a loud *yea*. "Then let us receive

his life was a massive effort to find an appropriate intellectual setting and content for his faith. Finding it impossible to accept the orthodox doctrines held by the Moravians who nourished him in the Faith[11] and rejecting the standard foundations of faith available to him in the culture, he turned to an intense study of Plato, Kant, and other luminaries of his day. It was partly in encounter with these that he found the bricks to rebuild the house of faith.[12]

Schleiermacher was well aware of the empiricism of Locke and the epistemology of theology which accompanied it. His rejection was emphatic and scathing.

Those proud islanders whom many among you venerate so unduly, know no other watchword than to profit and enjoy. Their zeal for the sciences, for the wisdom of life and for holy freedom, is merely an empty sham battle. Just as the most inspired champions of freedom among them do nothing but defend the national orthodoxy with rage and delude the people with miracles so that superstitious devotion to old customs might not vanish, so they are no more serious with all the rest that goes beyond the sensual and nearest immediate use. Thus they seek knowledge; their wisdom is only directed toward a lamentable empiricism, and thus religion can be nothing else for them than a dead letter, a holy article in the constitution in which nothing is real.[13]

the Lord's supper! but the sexton is not to be thought of: quick, quick! let no one stumble at the form; I have never held to the dead letter." ' After sharing Communion, in which Schleiermacher movingly professes that the words of institution were the foundation of his life, he requested that his position in the bed be changed. 'After a few minutes he said: "Now I can hold out here no longer," and then "lay me in a different posture." We laid him on his side—he breathed a few times,—and life stood still!' More than 20,000 turned out for his funeral three days later. The report given here is by his wife. See 'Introduction by the Translator', in Friederich Schleiermacher, 'On the Discrepancy between the Sabellian and Athanasian Method of Representing the Doctrine of the Trinity in the Godhead', *Biblical Repository and Quarterly Review*, 5 (Apr. and July 1835), 62–3.

[11] Schleiermacher's personal journey is poignant in the extreme; the anguish and honesty displayed by him are very moving. Schleiermacher could no longer believe, for example, in the divinity of Christ or the vicarious atonement. See Gerrish, *Prince of the Church*, 11–12.

[12] For a superb account of the crisis concerning the viability of reason in German thinking at the end of the eighteenth century, see Frederick C. Beiser, *The Fate of Reason: German Philosophy from Kant to Fichte* (Cambridge, Mass.: Harvard University Press, 1987).

[13] Friedrich Schleiermacher, *On Religion: Speeches to its Cultural Despisers* (Cambridge: Cambridge University Press, 1988), 85.

While Schleiermacher himself could be classed as an empiricist,[14] he was averse to the general overtones of British empiricism, and he accepted the standard objections to a Lockian natural theology developed by Kant and others. In addition, he found the conception and defence of special revelation accepted by Locke untenable, not least because it could not withstand the kind of critical enquiry which had become relatively commonplace in academic biblical studies.[15] Given that he considered it essential that religious belief be defended against the objections of many in the cultural élite of his day, he was driven to find a whole new way of interpreting the rational viability of Christianity.[16] Kant, another product of pietism who found its beliefs and epistemology seriously flawed, attempted to resolve this problem by making religion subordinate to morality. Schleiermacher saw this compromise of the autonomy of religion as no more adequate than attempts to make it subservient to natural theology.[17] His own positive proposals were worked out and refined across a lifetime.[18]

The crucial theses which best serve to introduce Schleiermacher's

[14] Richard Brandt, *The Philosophy of Schleiermacher: The Development of his Theory of Scientific and Religious Knowledge* (New York: Harper and Row, 1941), 315.

[15] Schleiermacher provides a carefully argued rejection of the appeal to miracle as a warrant for revelation in *The Christian Faith* (Edinburgh: T. & T. Clark, 1928), sec. 14, postscript.

[16] Schleiermacher was not an evidentialist. The ordinary believer does not need to engage in some kind of conceptual analysis or appeal to rational arguments to secure the rationality of his faith. Indeed, Schleiermacher purposefully displays the believer as rightly distrustful of such endeavours as a distraction from the heart of true faith. This is wonderfully brought out in the figure of Joseph in the final scene of Schleiermacher's discussion of the meaning of Christmas. See Friedrich Schleiermacher, *Christmas Eve: Dialogue on Incarnation* (Richmond, Va.: John Knox Press, 1967), 85–6.

[17] Schleiermacher saw the Kantian position as inconsistent. A pure morality would be contaminated by any appeal to happiness, not to speak of the happiness in an afterlife made possible by God, as postulated by Kant. For a brief summary of the argument see Louis Dupré, 'Towards a Revaluation of Schleiermacher's *Philosophy of Religion*', *Journal of Religion*, 44 (1964), 99.

[18] We do not need to cover here the full narrative of Schleiermacher's philosophical and theological pilgrimage. Brandt, *Philosophy of Schleiermacher*, remains a splendid tour of the territory. A fine exposition and critical assessment of Schleiermacher from a philosophical point of view can be located in Wayne Proudfoot, *Religious Experience* (Berkeley: University of California Press, 1985).

final judgement on both the heart and foundation of religion are laid out early on in his systematic account of the Christian faith.

The piety which forms the basis of all ecclesiastical communions is, considered purely in itself, neither a Knowing nor a Doing, but a modification of Feeling, or of immediate self-consciousness.[19]

The common element in all howsoever diverse expressions of piety, by which these are conjointly distinguished from all other feelings, or, in other words, the self-identical essence of piety, is this: the consciousness of being absolutely dependent, or which is the same thing, of being in relation with God.[20]

The immediate impression given by these theses is that religion in general and Christianity in particular are very far removed from knowledge. The popular conception of feeling as a kind of episodic mental event does nothing but add to this impression. Yet Schleiermacher is adamant that piety involves a kind of cognition which is of the highest importance. We can begin to explore how this is so as we seek to articulate the core components of his proposals.

One route which Schleiermacher uses to bring out the cognitive significance of piety is that of introspection. Consulting our own inner consciousness, we find two distinguishable elements. We find a self-caused element and a non-self-caused element. The former is represented by a sense of freedom, a sense of self-determination; the latter by a sense of constraint, a sense of being determined by and dependent on the things around us. Our consciousness is in fact characterized by a succession of these two 'feelings'. We interact with that which is not ourselves in such a way that we constrain and are constrained by our environment. There is both a sense of freedom and a sense of dependence; there is both an active and a receptive aspect of existence. The degree of freedom and dependence we experience depends on the nature of that with which we interact. In the case of our interaction with a relatively small finite object, such as a tool, the feeling of freedom predominates over the feeling of dependence. In the case of a larger finite entity, such as the nation, the feeling of dependence predominates over the feeling of freedom. Suppose now we think of relating not just to this or that finite

[19] *Christian Faith*, sec. 3.   [20] Ibid., sec. 4.

object, however large or small, but to the whole of finite existence, including ourselves as part of all finite reality. In this case, says Schleiermacher, the sense of freedom totally recedes, and we are left with a feeling of absolute dependence. There arises at this moment a new determination of consciousness, a sense of the transcendental condition of all active and receptive existence, which is the source of the feeling of absolute dependence. In this transcendental condition all antithesis between one individual and another is done away with; there is simply the 'Whence of the Whole', namely, God.[21]

Laid out conceptually, the feeling of absolute dependence appears somewhat theoretical, abstract, and dry. It was anything but this to Schleiermacher. An early depiction of the feeling which was reworked and toned down in later life captures in unforgettable imagery its vividness for him. In this account Schleiermacher uses the language of both intuition and feeling to capture the experiential and cognitive dimensions of the feeling of absolute dependence.[22]

That first mysterious moment that occurs in every sense perception, before intuition and feeling have separated, where sense and its objects have, as it were flowed into one another and become one, before both turn back to their original position—I know how indescribable it is and how quickly it passes away. But I wish you were able to hold on to it and also to recognize it again in the higher and divine religious activity of the mind. Would that I might express it, at least indicate it, without having to describe! It is as fleeting and transparent as the first scent with which the dew gently caresses the waking flowers, as modest and delicate

---

[21] This is in fact how God is defined by Schleiermacher. 'As regards the identification of absolute dependence with "relation to God" in our proposition this is to be understood in the sense that the *Whence* of our receptive and active existence, as implied in this self-consciousness, is to be designated by the word "God," and that this is for us the original signification of that word' (*Christian Faith*, sec. 4.4). Although in the first edition of the *On Religion*, it was difficult to distinguish between his position and that of pantheism, it is very clear that this cannot be said of his more mature period. 'In this connexion we have first of all to remind ourselves that . . . this "Whence" is not this world, in the sense of the totality of temporal existence, and still less is it any single part of the world' (ibid.).

[22] Later, as we see in the material just quoted from *Christian Faith*, he dropped talk of intuition and deployed the language of feeling. The reasons for this change are discussed by Brandt, *Philosophy of Schleiermacher*, 145–99. Cf. Richard Crouter, 'Introduction', in *On Religion*, 55–73.

as the maiden's kiss, as holy and fruitful as a nuptial embrace; indeed not *like* these, but *is itself* all of these. A manifestation, an event develops quickly and magically into an image of the universe. Even as the beloved and ever-sought-for form fashions itself, my soul flees to it; I embrace it, not as a shadow but as the holy essence itself. I lie in the bosom of the infinite world. At this moment I am its soul, for I feel all its powers and its infinite life as my own; at this moment it is my body, for I penetrate its muscles and its limbs as my own, and its innermost nerves move according to my sense and my presentiment as my own. With the slightest trembling the holy embrace is dispersed, and now for the first time the intuition stands before me as a separate form; I survey it, and it mirrors itself in my open soul like the image of the vanishing beloved in the awakened eye of a youth; now for the first time the feeling works its way up inside and diffuses itself like the blush of shame and desire on its cheek. This moment is the highest flowering of religion. If I could create it in you, I would be a god; may holy fate only forgive me that I have had to disclose more than the Eleusian mysteries.[23]

This experience of absolute dependence was the 'natal hour of everything living in religion'.[24] Whatever doctrines a person may believe, if this were missing, then the soul had never been conceived. If we must speak of revelation, this constitutes the original revelation of God to humanity. It is logically distinct and prior to any previous knowledge about God. Particular religious experiences, insights, doctrines, and the like, as embodied in Christian or other religious self-consciousness, presuppose this feeling, and without it they would necessarily be incomplete.

This feeling of absolute dependence is an essential element in human nature. Everyone participates in the feeling of absolute dependence. This does not mean, however, that everyone is at all times conscious of a feeling of absolute dependence.[25] At the

---

[23] *On Religion*, 112–13.   [24] Ibid. 113.

[25] There is a radical difference here between Schleiermacher and Locke. For Locke there could not be consciousness without immediate knowledge of that consciousness. Here Locke is close to the common sense conviction that one cannot have a feeling of any kind without being conscious of that feeling. As we shall see later, the language of feeling is a deep snare in the interpretation of Schleiermacher. If we think of feeling as the equivalent of apprehension, then it is possible for there to be an apprehension of 'x' without there being a concomitant conscious awareness of 'x'. This takes us deep into areas in the philosophy of mind which cannot be pursued here, but it is important to realize that Schleiermacher's position is more coherent than may appear on first reading.

conscious level, the feeling can vary in strength. 'Indeed, there will naturally be moments in which a man is not directly and definitively conscious of such a feeling at all.'[26] Nor does this mean that the feeling of absolute dependence comes to consciousness independently of our everyday sensible consciousness of finite reality, as if it were consciously experienced on its own. Rather, the feeling of absolute dependence can be kindled and awakened. In fact, it is awakened by a definite causal process. 'As regards the feeling of absolute dependence in particular, everyone will know that it was first awakened in him in the same way, by the communicative and stimulative power of expression or utterance.'[27] Moreover, it is known in and through our everyday consciousness of the finite world. '[I]n its actual occurrence it is never separated from the lower, and through its combination therewith in a single moment it participates in the antithesis of the pleasant and the unpleasant.'[28] The sensible self-consciousness and the feeling of absolute dependence are, then, logically distinct, but contingently inseparable. There is a reciprocal relation, a coexistence, but no fusion between the two. Thus experienced, the feeling of absolute dependence is accompanied by 'an immediate self-consciousness expressive of certainty and conviction'.[29]

A further feature of the religious self-consciousness is that it necessarily leads in its developments to fellowship or communion with others. The crucial reasons for this are that such a movement is constitutive of what it is to be human, that the inward necessarily expresses itself in the outward, that the outward expression naturally evokes imitation in others, thus drawing the person ineluctably into relationship with others.[30] By a kind of inner agitation, a quest for satisfaction, a person 'steps forth beyond the limits of his own personality and takes up the facts of other personalities into his own'.[31] The bounds of this communion are variable and fluid, yet human agents find themselves drawn together in families by congruity, kinship, and religious

---

[26] *Christian Faith*, sec. 5. 5.   [27] Ibid., sec. 6. 2.
[28] Ibid., sec. 5.   [29] Ibid., sec. 5. 2.
[30] Schleiermacher insists that his claims fall at this point into the domain of 'a scientific theory of morals' (ibid. sec., 6. 2). He clearly thinks that it is established by some kind of introspection. His claim really belongs in the philosophy of mind.   [31] Ibid.

emotion. In turn we find families 'standing collectively in distinctively defined combinations, with common language and customs, and with some knowledge or inkling of a closer common origin'.[32] Coming together in this manner, they constitute a religious communion.

Every relatively closed religious communion, which forms an ever self-renewing circulation of the religious self-consciousness within certain definite limits, and a propagation of the religious emotions arranged and organized within the same limits, so that there can be some kind of definite understanding as to which individuals belong to it and which do not—these we designate a *Church*.[33]

Given such developments, it is obviously important to find a way to demarcate the identity of one religion over against another.[34] Such judgements are more than empirical description; they involve a judgement as to what constitutes the essence of a particular religion.[35] Each form of religion or communion has a distinctive unity.

---

[32]   *Christian Faith*, sec. 6. 4.   [33]   Ibid.; emphasis original.

[34]   Differences in religion arise because the feeling of absolute dependence must first unite itself with a sensible stimulation of self-consciousness, and 'these sensible stimuli must be regarded as infinitely various' (ibid. sec. 9. 1). Schleiermacher provides a careful, evaluative taxonomy of religions which we need not pursue here.

[35]   Such judgements Schleiermacher allocates to the field of philosophical theology, drawing on philosophy of religion. See *Brief Outline on the Study of Theology* (Richmond, Va.: John Knox Press, 1966), secs. 23, 24. However we label these judgements, it is clear that Schleiermacher is deeply indebted to his hero Plato in his quest for the essence of religion. He describes the general issue at stake in this way: '[E]very species has the same characteristics as every other species of its genus, and everything which is really additional is merely accidental. But the discovery of this differentiating matter in any individual existence is a task which can never be perfectly, but only approximately, discharged in words and sentences . . . But if we must make an attempt at some kind of general statement . . . we should be content with saying this: in every individual religion the God-consciousness, which in itself remains the same everywhere on the same level, is attached to some relation of the self-consciousness in such an especial way that only thereby can it unite with other determinations of the self-consciousness; so that all other relations are subordinate to this one, and it communicates to all others its colour and its tone' (*Christian Faith*, sec. 10. 3). Schleiermacher is attempting here to provide an analysis of the concept of religion. The best solution to this problem, in my judgement, has been provided by W. B. Gallie through his articulation of the idea of essentially contested concepts. See W. D. Gallie, 'Essentially Contested Concepts', in *Philosophy and*

Each particular form of communal piety has both an outward unity, as a fixed fact of history with a definite commencement, and an inward unity as a peculiar modification of that general character which is common to all developed faiths of the same kind and level; and it is from both of these taken together that the peculiar essence of any particular form is to be discerned.[36]

Applied to Christianity, this principle of demarcation entails that the constitutive feature which distinguishes it from all other faiths is the fact that everything in it is related to the redemption accomplished by Jesus of Nazareth. This is the element which 'remains constant throughout the most diverse religious affections within this same communion, while it is absent from analogous affections within other communions'.[37] Materially, this element is constituted not by a set of doctrines or precepts handed down by Jesus to his followers, or by a sense of forgiveness to be alleviated, say, by penances and purifications. It is identified by a consciousness that redemption—a redemption which presupposes an incapacity to deliver oneself from God-lessness or God-forgetfulness—has been brought about by Jesus.

In the first place, in Christianity the incapacity and the redemption, and their connexion with each other, do not constitute simply one particular religious element among others, but all other religious emotions are related to this, and this accompanies all others, as the principal thing which makes them distinctively Christian. And secondly, redemption is posited as a thing which has been universally and completely accomplished by Jesus of Nazareth.[38]

The Christian communion is picked out from other faiths, then, first by identifying those who lay claim to a process of redemption through Jesus of Nazareth, rather than, say, a process of redemption not related to Jesus, or a relation to Jesus not constituted by a process of redemption; and second by the colouring of everything else by that very particular consciousness of redemption. Christians are those who claim that they have

---

the Historical Understanding (London: Chatto & Windus, 1964), 157–91. I have attempted to exhibit the great value of this solution as applied to forms of the Christian tradition in *The Coming Great Revival: Recovering the Full Evangelical Tradition* (San Francisco: Harper and Row, 1984).

[36] *Christian Faith*, sec. 10. [37] Ibid., sec. 11.

[38] Ibid., sec. 11. 3.

been redeemed by Jesus of Nazareth through the mediation of the Christian Church as a matter of contingent historical fact.

The reference to redemption is in every Christian consciousness simply because the originator of the Christian communion is the Redeemer; and Jesus is Founder of a religious communion simply in the sense that its members become conscious of redemption through him.[39]

Christianity is that communion in which a consciousness of redemption which is posited as emanating exclusively through Jesus of Nazareth has become the central or governing point of the whole. 'In Christianity . . . the redeeming influence of the Redeemer is the primary element, and the communion exists only on this presupposition, and as a propagation of that redeeming activity.'[40]

The means of that propagation is preaching. Such preaching takes the form of testimony to one's own experience of redemption through faith in Jesus as the redeemer, and this preaching can arouse in others the desire to have the same experience. Thereby the very same impression which was received directly from Jesus has been received in the Church down through history. Thus, originally through Jesus, and subsequently through the testimony of those who had directly or indirectly come to experience redemption through him, there came into existence a communion of people whose feelings of absolute dependence on God, together with the affections or emotions accompanying that feeling, were mediated through him. The God-consciousness of Christians, which by definition remains the same everywhere within the Christian religion, is, then, attached to a consciousness of redemption through Jesus of Nazareth, which communicates its colour and tone to all other relations within it. Christian consciousness is constituted by the set of specific affections or emotions shaped in this very particular way. Christian doctrines, in turn, are 'accounts of the religious affections set forth in speech'.[41]

The term 'doctrine' is misleading here, for it suggests that all religious discourse takes the form of carefully formulated teaching intended to express the mind of the Church. We naturally think

---

[39] *Christian Faith*, sec. 11. 3.   [40] Ibid., sec. 11. 4.
[41] Ibid., sec. 15.

of the doctrines of, say, the Trinity or the Incarnation. What Schleiermacher has in mind is simply the expression of Christian self-consciousness brought forth in any kind of speech, as contrasted with symbolic action.[42] The inward life of piety, stimulated, for example, by interaction with its already existing outward expression in the Christian community, comes naturally to outward expression in speech, because each person becomes an object to him or herself and finds ways to express in language what is otherwise expressed by facial expression, modulation of voice, and gesture. Such speech is poetical when it has come purely from within; it is rhetorical when it is elicited by a perceived need and directed to a definite end; and it is descriptively didactic when it goes beyond these two forms to become instructive, as most closely represented by Christian doctrinal confession.[43] It is within this third class that Schleiermacher locates dogmatic propositions.

Such propositions are not merely carefully constructed confessional statements. They may well take that form, but that is not their defining characteristic. Dogmatic propositions are those descriptively didactic propositions 'in which the highest possible degree of definiteness is aimed at'.[44] Thus, on the one hand, they express a religious affection, and, on the other, they are carefully constructed with maximum precision and with maximum fruitfulness in pointing to other dogmatic propositions. Thus dogmatic doctrines and propositions are distinct from poetical and rhetorical doctrines and propositions. Dogmatic propositions often grow out of the contradictions within poetic and rhetorical forms of expression, yet they are logically distinct from those propositions, given their intention and form. Dogmatic theology, in turn, is 'the science which systematizes the doctrine prevalent in a Christian Church at a given time'.[45]

It is clear from the preceding account that Schleiermacher provides a very sophisticated account of the nature, origin, and discourse of the Christian tradition. One of the most perplexing questions which that account poses is how we are to capture the

[42] Doctrine might also be contrasted with the expression of religious consciousness in music, a theme which was significant to Schleiermacher.

[43] Schleiermacher operates here by means of elimination. Such speech as is not poetic or rhetorical is descriptively dogmatic (ibid., secs. 15 and 16).

[44] Ibid., sec. 16.   [45] Ibid., sec. 19.

epistemic claims which are clearly embodied within it.[46] Critics have often complained that all Schleiermacher can really offer is an account of the religious emotions and affections, so that at the outset his claim to give an account of objective reality is compromised. Schleiermacher was, in short, a subjectivist. While I cannot here provide a detailed defence of a contrary view, I can express my rejection of this interpretation and criticism of Schleiermacher by indicating the epistemic options open to us in reading Schleiermacher.

Part of the problem at this juncture is that Schleiermacher is badly served by the language of feeling.[47] Much of the standard criticism of his work stems from the fact that reports of feelings are generally seen as simply reports of a person's psychological states which in themselves tell us nothing about a world logically external to the human agent. However, there is a very different possibility, which has long been canvassed in the literature.[48] Thus the language of feeling, while it is often used to describe inner states, can also be used to express judgements about objective reality. The relevant distinction is between the cognitive or intentional use of the word and the qualitative or non-intentional use.[49]

The latter is represented by such sentences as 'I feel happy', 'I feel overjoyed', or 'I feel sleepy'. What we have in these cases are reports of various emotional or psychological states. Although they make manifest those states, they do not purport to give us information about any reality outside those states. It is this usage which the critics are fastening on in their censure of Schleiermacher as a subjectivist. Schleiermacher is taken as claiming that religion expresses merely subjective human emotions or feelings and nothing more. 'Feeling' is taken in a qualitative or

---

[46] It is worth pointing out that it is useless to deal with this issue by claiming that Schleiermacher was a mystic or advocated mysticism. All this does is shift the problem to the potential epistemic significance of mysticism. On Schleiermacher as a mystic, see Brandt, *Philosophy of Schleiermacher*, 101–4.

[47] In German 'das Gefühl der schlechthinnigen Abhängigkeit'.

[48] See e.g. *Philosophy of Schleiermacher*, Brandt, 106–9.

[49] For a catalogue of the use of emotion terms see William P. Alston, 'Emotion and Feeling', in Paul Edwards (ed.), *The Encyclopedia of Philosophy* (New York: Macmillan, 1967), ii. 479–86. Alston outlines no fewer than nine uses in all.

non-intentional sense. However, this is a tendentious and narrow reading of Schleiermacher. It is much more likely that 'feeling' should be taken in a cognitive or intentional sense.[50] This usage is captured by such sentences as 'I feel that the Cowboys will win the Superbowl', 'I feel that peace will ultimately come to Northern Ireland', or 'I feel that mercy is of greater value than justice'. In this usage the feeling is a mode of awareness of some other putative fact. We might say that the agent apprehends what is the case external to himself or claims to perceive a truth which goes beyond the reporting of some inner emotional state. Used in this way, Schleiermacher is entitled to claim that the feeling of absolute dependence is indeed cognitive.

Another way to pursue the cognitive use of 'feel' is to draw on Chisholm's distinction between the comparative and epistemic use of 'appear' words. In one case, we report a mental state; in the other, we express what we are inclined to believe about the world. Thus, when I say that the table appears to me elliptical, even though I believe it really to be round, I am using 'appears' comparatively, and am thereby reporting a mental state. I am saying that the table looks to me as it would look were it elliptical and were it to be observed under standard conditions. Alternatively, were I to say simply that the table appears round, I am using 'appears' epistemically; I am reporting what I am inclined to believe about the world on the basis of my present sensory experience. Stretched to apply to Schleiermacher's feeling or sense of absolute dependence, we might interpret this claim in an epistemic way rather than a comparative way to report a belief about the nature of ultimate, objective reality. To lay claim to a feeling of absolute dependence is to be taken as a claim regarding what the agent believes about the relation between creation and the divine on the basis of his or her experience rather than a report of the inner state of the agent.

Yet another way to try and capture what Schleiermacher is saying is to posit a unique mode of awareness of ultimate reality which cannot be assimilated to our normal modes of apprehension

---

[50] Even with reference to subjective states, 'feeling' can, of course, be used in a cognitive and intentional sense. Consider, for example, 'I feel that I am tired'. This utterance is clearly cognitive. The crucial difference, however, is that between claiming something to be the case with respect to our emotional states and claiming something to be the case about the world. Schleiermacher should be read as insisting on the latter.

or perception. Thus Schleiermacher might say that what is at stake is a kind of human faculty which is *sui generis*. The appeal to intuition in the first edition of *On Religion*, even though it is dropped later, would provide some warrant for this interpretation.[51] In this case we have a logically primitive ability to recognize what is the case concerning the conditions governing reality as a whole, analogous to what intuitionists have claimed when they insist that we intuit the first principles of morality.

A further alternative available to us in interpreting Schleiermacher is to invoke a causal theory of knowledge. In this case the fundamental claim is that in our encounter with the whole, somehow the sense of absolute dependence is brought about by transcendental conditions of the whole and, in the absence of good reason to the contrary, is to be considered as appropriate to that reality. All sense and speech causally generated by that reality depicts that reality. Thus in religion the human agent is subject to the influence and energy of ultimate reality; the reception and comprehension of that reality is in accordance with its distinctive nature.[52] In the case of the Christian religion that reality is appropriately represented in the feeling of absolute dependence which is mediated by Christ through the Church and brought to expression in Christian speech or doctrine. Thus, although Christian doctrine is twice removed from God, it is yet causally dependent upon, and hence appropriate to, the divine world which underlies it. Doctrine expresses not just mental states; it also appropriately depicts the reality of God because it arises on account of a causal process which leads from God to the appropriate doctrine.[53]

---

[51] It is worth remembering that Schleiermacher used a variety of terms to capture his central thesis: *Anschaung, Denken, Ansicht, Wahrnehmung, Sinn*, and the like. The importance of this for the interpretation of his work is well brought out by Van Austin Harvey, 'On the New Edition of Schleiermacher's *Addresses on Religion*', *Journal of the American Academy of Religion*, 39 (1971), 488–512.

[52] Charles E. Scott captures this point nicely by saying that for Schleiermacher 'the criterion of religious truth is conformity to the presence of the unconditioned' ('Schleiermacher and the Problem of Divine Immediacy', *Religious Studies*, 3 (1968), 507).

[53] Throughout this exposition of the possible epistemic significance of Schleiermacher's position I am indirectly calling into question the widely accepted view, worked out in the influential work of George Lindbeck in *The Nature of Doctrine* (Philadelphia: Westminster Press, 1984), that Schleiermacher

We have, then, at least three ways to delineate the possible epistemic position adopted by Schleiermacher in his account of religion: namely, by reference to apprehension or perception, by resort to a special faculty of cognition, or by drawing on the resources of a causal theory of knowledge.[54] All three fit with Schleiermacher's rejection of proofs in religion and with his appeal to experience as the bedrock foundation of religion. They cohere, that is, with his repudiation of natural theology and his elimination of special revelation as a distinctive warrant for Christian doctrine, and they fuse with his conviction that Christian doctrine is yet fully an expression of reason.

We entirely renounce all attempt to prove the truth or necessity of Christianity; and we presuppose, on the contrary, that every Christian, before he enters at all upon inquiries of this kind, has already the inward certainty that his religion cannot take any other form than this.[55]

The whole process of formulating our expressions concerning the religious self-consciousness is just as much a rational process as in the case of Nature; and the difference is merely that this objective consciousness is given at first hand only to him who is affected by Nature, while that (Christian) self-consciousness is given only to him who is affected by the Redeemer in the manner which is peculiar to His followers. Now this itself makes plain what we are to think of the prevalent view that Christian doctrine consists partly of rational and partly of supra-rational dogmas. It is, indeed, of itself obvious that this can be no more than a juxtaposition, and that these two kinds of dogmas cannot form one whole. Between the rational and the supra-rational there can be no connexion. This further becomes pretty clearly evident in all treatises upon Christian doctrine which divide themselves into a natural theology,

---

provides merely an expressivist interpretation of Christian doctrine. For an incisive critique of Lindbeck on this score see George Behrens, 'Schleiermacher *Contra* Lindbeck on the Status of Doctrinal Sentences', *Religious Studies*, 30 (1994), 399–417. It should also be clear that my account of Schleiermacher immediately undercuts the criticism that Schleiermacher sees religion as purely anthropocentric. On the contrary, it is clear that human agents are utterly unable to originate their capacity for religion. That Schleiermacher insisted that absolute dependence is pivotal for religion should be enough to dispatch this old saw. The standard version can be found in Karl Barth, *Protestant Theology in the Nineteenth Century* (London: SCM Press, 1972), 458–9.

[54] We need not worry at this stage that these ways of construing Schleiermacher may well overlap.

[55] *Christian Faith*, sec. 11. 5.

purely rational and thus valid only within it, but also outside of Christianity, and a positive supra-rational theology, valid only within the compass of Christianity. For then the two remain separate from each other. The apparent practicality of a union of the two arises from the fact that there are, of course, Christian dogmas in which the peculiarly Christian element retreats considerably into the background, so that they may be taken to be purely rational in those respects in which the others are recognized as supra-rational. But if that peculiarly Christian element was not in them at all, they would, of course, not be Christian dogmas. Hence the truth of the matter is as follows. In one respect all Christian dogmas are supra-rational, in another they are all rational. They are supra-rational in the respect in which everything experiential is supra-rational. For there is an inner experience to which they may all be traced: they rest upon a *given*; and apart from this they could not have arisen, by deduction or by synthesis, from universally recognized and communicable propositions. If the reverse were true, it would mean that you could instruct and demonstrate any man into being a Christian, without his happening to have had any experience. Therefore this supra-rationality implies that a true appropriation of Christian dogmas cannot be brought about by scientific means, and this lies outside the realm of reason; it can only be brought about by each man willing to have the experience for himself, as indeed it is true of everything individual and characteristic, that it can only be apprehended by the love which wills to perceive. In this sense the whole of Christian doctrine is supra-rational. It may, however, be further asked whether the dogmas which give expression to the religious affections of the Christian and their connexions are not subject to the same laws of conception and synthesis as regulate all speech, so that the more perfectly these laws are satisfied in such a presentation, the more will each individual be constrained to apprehend correctly what is thought and intended, even if he cannot, for lack of the fundamental inward experience convince himself of the truth of the matter. It must be answered that in this sense everything in Christian doctrine is entirely according to reason. Accordingly, the supra-rationality of all particular Christian dogmas is the measure by which it can be judged whether they succeed in expressing the peculiarly Christian element; and again, their rationality is the test of how far the attempt to translate the inward emotions into thoughts has succeeded.[56]

---

[56]   *Christian Faith*, sec. 13, postscript; emphasis original. The same point can be expressed in terms of a doctrine of the Holy Spirit. 'But however great a difference we make between this supra-rational and the common human reason, it can never, without falling into self-contradiction, be set up as an *absolutely* supra-rational element. For the highest goal that is set for these workings of redemption is always a human state which would not only obtain the fullest

The question which naturally arises at this stage concerns how Schleiermacher dealt with the canon of Scripture. On the surface it would appear that Schleiermacher had no need whatsoever to appeal to Scripture as a warrant for the truth of Christian doctrine. There is, after all, no kind of special revelation embodied in Scripture, as held, say, by Locke and Aquinas. Thus the rationality of Christian doctrine is not to be proved by appeal to biblical texts construed as expressions of propositional revelation and guaranteed by miracle. That rationality is secured by Christian experience in the same way as truths about the world are secured by experience of nature; or rather, rationality is secured by the causal relation existing between God and the Christian consciousness, which is paralleled by the causal relation between nature and perceptual consciousness. The fact that Schleiermacher placed his main discussion of Scripture under the topic of ecclesiology, and hence all of 600 pages into *The Christian Faith*, bears out the claim that appeal to Scripture would appear to be entirely redundant as a warrant for the truth of Christian doctrine.[57] Yet what is fascinating is that Schleiermacher continued to construe Scripture in quasi-epistemic categories.

Schleiermacher was very clear that the authority of Scripture cannot, on his analysis, be the foundation for faith in Christ. On the contrary, faith in Christ is presupposed before any peculiar authority can be granted to Scripture.[58] His argument for this manifests the breakdown in the appeal to the canon of Scripture which became prevalent after the Reformation.

recognition from the common human reason, but in which also it is impossible always to distinguish, even in the same individual, between what is effected by the divine Spirit and what is effected by the human reason. Inasmuch, then, as the reason is completely one with the divine Spirit, the divine Spirit can itself be conceived as the highest enhancement of the human reason, so that the difference between the two is made to disappear. But further: even at the very outset, whatever opposes the movements of the divine Spirit is the same as what conflicts with human reason; for otherwise there could not exist in man (as there does), before the entry of those divine influences, a consciousness of the need of redemption, which these very influences set at rest. If then, the human reason itself in a sense contains that which is produced by the divine Spirit, the latter does not in this connexion, at least, go beyond the former' (ibid., sec. 13. 2; emphasis original).

[57] The issue is also picked up very early on, however, in sec. 27.

[58] Ibid., sec. 128.

If faith in Jesus as the Christ or as the Son of God and the Redeemer of men is to be based on the authority of scripture, the question arises how this authority itself is to be based; for obviously the thing must be so done as to impress the conviction on unbelieving hearts, so that they too may by this path come to faith in the Redeemer. Now if we have no point of departure but ordinary reason, the divine authority of Scripture to begin with must admit to being proved on grounds of reason alone; and against this two points must be kept in mind. First, this involves a critical and scientific use of the understanding of which not all are capable; on this theory, therefore, only those so gifted can attain to faith in an original and genuine way, while all others would merely have faith at second hand and on the authority of experts. . . . Secondly, if such a proof could be given and if faith could be established in this fashion—if, that is to say, faith, given a certain degree of culture, could be implanted by argument—then on such terms faith might exist in people who feel absolutely no need of redemption, that is quite apart from repentance and change of mind; which means that having origi- nated in this way, it would not be genuine, living faith at all.[59]

So true faith exists independently of any doctrine of Scripture. It is from within a faith already formed that we arrive at an acceptable account of the nature of Scripture and of the state of mind which produced it. The importance of Scripture is not that it provides a foundation for faith but that it 'gives expression to an original and authentic element in Christian piety'.[60] A doctrine does not belong to Christianity because it is in Scripture; it is in Scripture because it belongs to Christianity.

The obvious difficulty with this claim is that Scripture contains the Old Testament, material which is anterior to the rise of Christianity and which, therefore, cannot be an expression of Christian piety. Schleiermacher's solution to this difficulty is consistent and radical. The Old Testament is not canonical; only the New Testament is canonical. The latter is the first in a series of expressions of piety; hence all other expressions must be homogeneous with it in form and content. As a norm of Christian identity, Scripture is canonical. It was an original and authentic expression of Christian piety, so that later expressions, if they are to count as authentic and truly Christian, must be in continuity with the New Testament. The various books 'must become the regulative type for our religious thinking, from

---

[59] *Christian Faith*, sec. 128. 1.   [60] Ibid., sec. 128. 3.

which it is not of its own motion to depart'.[61] The appeal to
Scripture 'can directly prove only that a proposition which has
been set up is Christian'.[62]

More precisely, it is those elements in the New Testament
which truly reflect the living intuition of Christ, as opposed to
what is apocryphal, which are canonical.[63]

If we figure that the normative character of particular propositions
includes perfect purity on the one hand and, and on the other the fullness of inferences and applications which may develop from them, we
have no reason to suppose that the first attribute will exist, absolutely,
anywhere but in Christ alone, and must concede that, as to the second
attribute, natural imperfection could operate obstructly in all others but
not in him.[64]

At the beginning, Church presentations of Christianity contained
elements which imperfectly represented true piety, for they were
subject to influences which were foreign.[65] As time passed, these
influences were gradually eliminated, because in the development
of the Christian Church redemption was ever more completely
realized in time. Moreover, each age has had its own original
contribution to make to the content of Christian thinking. Even
so, it was only through the Scriptures that the Church was able to
ward off the derivative and foreign elements from its midst.
Through our use of the Scripture, 'the Holy Spirit can lead us
into all truth, just as it led the Apostles and others who enjoyed

[61] Ibid., sec. 131. 2. '[T]he interpretation of Christian faith which validates
itself in each age as having been evoked by Scripture is the development, suited
to the moment, of the genuine original interpretation of Christ and His work,
and constitutes the common Christian orthodoxy of that time and place' (ibid.).
It is interesting to note that Schleiermacher insists that a modern dogmatic
theology could not give rise to new heresy: 'For new heresies no longer arise,
now that the church recruits itself out of its own resources' (ibid., sec. 21. 2).

[62] Ibid., sec. 27. 1.

[63] The apocryphal signifies for Schleiermacher those 'Christian writings
from the time of the canon to which we deny normative value' (*Brief Outline*,
sec. 109).

[64] Ibid., sec. 108. It is clear that Christology is pivotal for Schleiermacher at
this point. Given the purity and perfection of God-consciousness in Christ,
Christians attribute redemption to him. See *Christian Faith*, secs. 93–4, 98.

[65] Schleiermacher is especially adamant in insisting on the radical divergence
between Judaism and Christianity and in eliminating any Jewish influence
(*Christian Faith*, secs. 12 and 129. 2).

Christ's direct teaching'.[66] Hence the New Testament, critically received and interpreted, has a special, normative status as the first in the series of expressions of Christian piety.

Given their place in the stream of the Church's life, we can also say that the individual books are divinely inspired; and the collection of these books into a single canon was done under the guidance of the Holy Spirit. We trust the universal Christian experience as the testimony of the Holy Spirit 'that the Canon we have received from the Church tradition has not by deceit or ignorance had introduced into it such constituent parts as belong either to an apocryphal or heretically suspect zone of Christianity', even though not all the books are 'equally fitted, by content and form, to vindicate their place in the Canon'.[67]

We might summarize the crucial elements in Schleiermacher's account of canon and criterion in two main points. First, Christians do not need to support their doctrines by appeal to the proofs of natural religion or to special revelation. Christian belief is constituted by a sense or feeling of absolute dependence which, although present to every human being, is mediated through Jesus of Nazareth as a consciousness of redemption through him, and is brought naturally to expression in symbol, gesture, and speech. This feeling is a cognitive state or process which provides the warrant for claiming that Christian belief is in accordance with reason. Christian doctrine is rationally justified because it is rooted causally in ultimate reality; it is naturally accompanied by a conviction of certainty. Second, a particular doctrine is Christian if it is an expression of Christian piety. Because Christian piety is derived from a sense of redemption, as evoked and fulfilled by encounter with Jesus of Nazareth and his followers in history, and because an expression of that original and authentic piety has

---

[66] *Christian Faith*, sec. 131. 2.

[67] Ibid., sec. 131. 1. '[T]he judgment of the Church is only approximating ever more closely to a complete expulsion of the apocryphal and the pure preservation of the canonical' (ibid., sec. 130. 4). 'Hence even though the Canon is fixed in many Confessions of our Church, this ought not to prevent further unrestricted investigation of the matter; critical inquiry must ever anew test the individual writings of Scripture with a view to decide whether they rightly keep their place in the sacred collection' (ibid.). Schleiermacher is very adamant about the difficulty of fixing the boundaries of the new canon he has posited. See his *Brief Outline*, secs. 103–9.

been suitably expressed in the New Testament, the canon of the New Testament is the norm through which we identify any proposed doctrine as authentically Christian.

What Schleiermacher has done is to develop a distinction between the epistemology of Christian doctrine and the canon of Scripture. In his epistemology, he has rejected evidentialism: that is, the thesis that for a doctrine to be believed to be true it must be supported by propositional evidence, derived, say, from the premises of natural theology or from the oracular deliverances of special revelation, or even from an authentic Christian doctrine. Yet he has retained a foundationalist structure by insisting that every single doctrine be traced in an appropriate manner to a foundation in Christian experience and by holding that such experience is causally related to an objective divine reality which transcends the world.

He has also developed a radically reconstructed canon of Scripture, reworked in both content and concept. He discarded the Old Testament, looking instead to the New Testament alone. He construed the New Testament not as a canon of truth or justification, but as a norm of the Christian identity of doctrine. If a doctrine is canonical, it is Christian. A canonical or Christian doctrine also happens to be rationally justified. However, it is not justified because it is canonical; it is justified because it is an expression of piety, and because piety, in turn, is a valid apprehension of objective reality.

We have now before us a relatively full account of Schleiermacher's proposals on Scripture and on the epistemology of religious belief. How should we gauge their significance in the debate about canon and norm in the Christian tradition? How far was Schleiermacher a revolutionary figure? Or better, if Schleiermacher was a revolutionary, what kind of revolutionary was he?

There is no denying the profound changes which Schleiermacher inaugurated in the history of theology. We need to be cautious, however, in trying to determine the precise nature of the changes he launched. We shall discover that Schleiermacher was a very special kind of revolutionary. Materially, he introduced deep changes in the self-understanding of the Christian tradition in the West; yet the formal nature of the root causes which brought about those changes were nothing

new. Schleiermacher pursued a line which had long been operative; and even the deep structure of his position had been around
for centuries. His status rests on the pioneering nature of the
change he introduced at that formal level and on the thoroughness with which he pursued the implications of that change for
theology and the life of the Church.

At one level, Schleiermacher was still attempting to resolve the
epistemic crisis which Christian intellectuals had created for
themselves when they epistemized the canonical heritage of the
Church. Having transposed the canons of the Church into
elements of epistemology, it was inevitable that the Church in the
West would find itself taken hostage by crises in epistemology.
Once a crucial canon in the Church—say, Scripture—was taken
to be a criterion of truth or knowledge, then, when a full-scale
debate developed on the nature of knowledge and related
concepts, that debate with all its problems would be transposed
into the very core of the Church's life. Given the crucial role of
the canons of the Church in delineating the content of Christian
belief, in shaping the character of Christian life, and in articulating Christian identity, sooner or later, replacing proposals about
canon by proposals about epistemology would absolutely transform everything. It fell to Schleiermacher to make this truly visible. Consequently, he is rightly seen as the founder of an epoch
in the history of Christian theology.

Schleiermacher inherited and experienced in his own mind
and soul the internal struggles of the Christian culture of his time.
For centuries Christian leaders and intellectuals had insisted that a
theory of the intellectual foundations of Christian belief and life
was constitutive of ecclesial identity. They came to believe that
the Church needed an account of the foundations of its faith as
indispensable to its very existence. Protestants located this originally in Scripture; Roman Catholics located it in the Church or
in a variation of this position spelled out in a doctrine of Scripture
plus tradition. The failure to resolve this debate on the terms
initially accepted by the protagonists caused its most perceptive
participants and observers to develop general theories of knowledge. The twin pillars of those theories were developed by
Descartes and Locke, who sought by appeal to reason and experience to provide a universally valid theory of cognition which
would once and for all give the truth about everything essential

to human life in the world. The assumption behind this strategy was that we could come to know what was the case with respect to God and salvation if we could come to know what it was to know anything at all. Once we knew the true nature and boundaries of reason and experience, then we could apply this knowledge about knowledge to theology, and all would be well.

Being committed Christians, Descartes and Locke were supremely confident that their respective versions of the Christian tradition would win the epistemic race which had been set before them. Descartes clearly hoped to become a new Aristotle who would in time find his new Aquinas. Locke was confident enough to try his hand in his later work at being his own Aquinas; he gave his own account of the essentials of the Christian faith by reducing it to an emaciated version of the Protestant heritage. Descartes and Locke were laymen. Even though their proposals became extraordinarily influential in the general culture, they could be ignored if one so desired. Moreover, in Roman Catholicism there were ecclesial procedures for keeping Descartes in his place. Meanwhile, in the Anglican version of the Protestant tradition there was a sufficient recovery of the canonical beliefs and practices of the patristic period to provide a bulwark against the full impact of the Lockian position.

Within Protestantism, such an arrangement was a mere stopgap. Pasting together Scripture, tradition, and reason constituted an unstable adjustment which was destined to disintegrate under pressure. The pressure was applied to the relevant spot: that is, to the epistemology which Locke had so carefully constructed. Over time it became clear that his natural theology and his proposals on the warrants for special revelation were inadequate. Perceptive radicals, like Hume, adopted his general epistemology and used it to destroy the foundations of the faith which Locke had built for himself and his friends.

In the mean time other Christians who were in search of a living relationship with God and whose interests in epistemology were marginal gathered together in small groups and communities among the Moravians and Methodists to find their own way to God. The heavy appropriation of Locke in the Church was complemented by the emergence of forms of underground Protestantism which had discovered that experience of God was

pivotal for their pilgrimage. Only the kind of intelligent, independent pietist we find in John Wesley could dare to try to hold
together in his own person, as a 'reasonable enthusiast,'[68] both
Locke's philosophy and direct experience of God a project which
Locke would have found ridiculous. It fell to Schleiermacher to
resolve the crisis created by the failure of Locke and his allies by
reworking the pietist emphasis on experience to construct a
whole new epistemology of religious belief. He could assume this
role because both these elements, the crisis and the experience,
were ingrained in his mind and soul from his teenage years; he
had inherited and made his own the inchoate struggles of a
Christian culture. The work which resulted from this is that of a
genius who attempted to return to first principles.

The continuity with the earlier epistemic tradition is manifest
in the following features of his position:[69]

1. Schleiermacher continued to take epistemology as the
fundamental point of departure and the critical field of enquiry.
Hence he perceived the deep problem as the collapse of the
Lockian and Cartesian appeal to reason as applied to the foundations of theology and Christian existence. The failure of natural
theology and the emergence of biblical criticism especially called
into question the Lockian project. Schleiermacher was convinced
that the ensuing vacuum needed to be filled with appropriate
material.

2. Schleiermacher kept intact the assumption that the fundamental structure for any acceptable epistemology be
foundational.[70] Thus his solution postulated one single source

---

[68]   This is the felicitous term employed by Henry Rack to describe the core
of Wesley's project. See his *Reasonable Enthusiast: John Wesley and the Rise of
Methodism* (Nashville: Abingdon Press, 1993).

[69]   A valuable discussion of the place of Schleiermacher's epistemology in the
history of modern epistemology is available in Laurence Philip Barnes,
'Religious Experience, Philosophical Foundationalism and the Quest for
Certainty in Modern Theology' (Ph.D. thesis, Trinity College, Dublin, 1992).

[70]   It is often thought that a foundationalist epistemology insists that the
foundations be neutral, self-evident, and universally available. We have seen,
however, that this is a derivative doctrine and represents a very particular species
of foundationalism mostly found among secular thinkers or those whose thought
has been thoroughly secularized. The crucial notion at stake in foundationalism,
over against coherentism, is that there is a privileged class of experiences or
propositions which are the basis for others.

from which all Christian doctrines were to be derived. Experience, understood in a particular way, replaced reason and sense experience as the foundation.[71] As in the case of Locke, this removed any kind of cumulative appeal to Scripture, tradition, and reason. The appeal to experience, aside from being more economical and elegant, removed any potential conflict which might arise between Scripture, tradition, and reason.

3. Schleiermacher continued the fundamental method of turning inward to find the foundation which would do the epistemic work which was sought. This is the truth which lies behind those criticisms which focus on an anthropocentric turn in Schleiermacher and which accuse him of subjectivism in a pejorative sense. Like Descartes and Locke, he turned to the inner content of the mind, or to the inward, private experience of the self. Where Descartes and Locke found 'ideas', Schleiermacher found 'feeling', or awareness. All three were profoundly committed to the value of introspection, and all of them attended to the psychological in what they found through that process.

4. Schleiermacher retained the fundamental quest for certainty as the goal of his epistemic endeavours. He appropriated the view that, ideally, rationality should be crowned by the attainment of certainty. It was no accident that Descartes, Locke, and Schleiermacher were naturally drawn to the language of intuition. They all sought the certainty which accompanies direct sight over against derived information. Anything short of this was inadequate at the foundations of knowledge.

5. Schleiermacher continued to uphold the tradition of metaphysical realism and objectivism. Thus he rejected scepticism, and he held that it was possible for human agents to come to know an objective reality which was logically distinct from themselves. More specifically, human agents can discern the truth about a divine reality upon which the whole universe depends unconditionally and absolutely. Hence Schleiermacher displayed a serene confidence about the critical enterprise and its application to the whole range of intellectual endeavour. Philosophy, history, and the natural sciences, for example, were

---

[71] Like Locke, Schleiermacher saw experience under certain descriptions simply as reason. The term 'reason' is, of course, elastic enough to make this possible in both cases.

worthy of the fullest cultivation; they would provide invaluable resources for the life of faith and culture.

6. Schleiermacher perpetuated the claim that the ultimate truth about reality could be expressed propositionally with clarity and precision. Religious discourse need not, of course, be expressed in this fashion. The religious affections could be expressed in music, ritual, gesture, facial expression, and the like. However, given sufficient skill, time, and effort, they could also be expressed in dogmatic propositions, one of whose marks was precision of the highest order. What in Descartes' and Locke's case was referred to as clarity and distinctness was transferable to the propositions of the scientific or systematic theologian.[72]

Given these commitments, it is clear that Schleiermacher was markedly conservative and traditionalist.[73] This was masked by two factors. First, he saw his own vocation as that of a theologian, and, within that, he saw himself less as advocating a particular philosophy than as cleansing Christianity of its entanglement with a speculative rationalism and a barren empiricism. Hence he comes across at times as rescuing the Christian faith from its captivity to the prevailing philosophical traditions. However, he does not himself escape the entanglement with philosophy. His work as a theologian is located within a network of epistemological proposals which are comprehensive and determinative.

The second factor which masks the conservative character of Schleiermacher's achievement is constituted by the genuine changes he introduced into religious epistemology. The most conspicuous change is the resort to experience as the foundation of theology. Here Schleiermacher was a pioneering figure. To be sure, one can find this proposal in some of the early Fathers, and it had a prominent role in the remarkable vision of Symeon the New Theologian in the East. Schleiermacher, however, took the standard line that Eastern Christianity had become intellectually

[72] This is marvellously evident in the very form of systematic theology as developed by Schleiermacher. The material is laid out in terms of a series of precise propositions accompanied by extended commentary and argument.
[73] For a fascinating essay on the continuity between Schleiermacher and Calvin, see B. A. Gerrish, 'Theology Within the Limits of Piety Alone', in *The Old and New Protestantism* (Edinburgh: T. & T. Clark, 1982), ch. 12. See also the incisive comments in Van Austin Harvey, 'A Word in Defence of Schleiermacher's Theological Method', *Journal of Religion*, 42 (1962), 166–8.

moribund after the patristic period,[74] and the reception of the patristic heritage in the West made it generally unlikely that anyone would have turned to the Fathers for insight into epistemology. Thus his appeal to experience as a way out of the crisis of credibility is a truly original suggestion. It is astonishing that only isolated and marginal figures in the past had hit upon this hypothesis. It is not surprising that once Schleiermacher had opened this door, generations would happily follow his lead.

Schleiermacher's true identity as a revolutionary lies in the way he pursued the implications of this for theology and the life of the Church. He embarked on a bold experiment. He sought to provide a normative account of the intellectual content of Christianity that would be credible in his cultural setting. Hence he proposed a whole new rendering of the Christian doctrines which would be traceable to their source in the religious experience of the Church. He hoped to articulate a system of doctrine which would be integrated, precise, and comprehensive, and which would serve the needs of Church leaders in their tasks of preaching and teaching. In all of this he wanted a faith which would be religiously adequate and intellectually credible, which would be warm at heart and be sound of mind.

The chief problem with Schleiermacher's revolution is that, like the work of his predecessors, it was built on shifting sand. He no more resolved the problems he had inherited than Locke did before him. What Schleiermacher may have gained by way of supposed theological rigour and comprehensiveness, he lost by way of epistemic default. Furthermore, he continued to perpetuate the fanciful illusion that somehow his own putative insights into the essence of religion, or into the cognitive inner workings of the self, or into the true relationship between faith and reason, were better attested than the canonical heritage of the Church. Where Locke was a layman and an amateur in his efforts to work out the theological implications of his appeal to experience, Schleiermacher was truly a professional. In the case of Locke, the ordinary seeker or Christian could still gain access to the canonical heritage of the Church and see for him or herself what was available. He or she could treat Locke's reduced, emaciated Protestantism as Locke's private affair. With Schleiermacher, all

---

[74] He describes the Eastern tradition as 'torpid' (*Christian Faith*, sec. 23. 1).

that was changed, for he insisted that the theological consequences of his epistemology should become nothing less than the scientific standard of the Church's preaching.

The difficulties in his position become immediately visible in his treatment of the canon of Scripture. By the strike of a pen the Old Testament was eliminated.[75] Even the content of the New Testament, whose origins and collection Schleiermacher construed as divinely inspired and guided, was rendered thoroughly ambivalent, because it is really only canonical in so far as it truly expresses authentic and original elements of Christian piety. How these elements are to be properly identified was left unanswered.

Moreover, it is not at all clear why any appeal to Scripture should be deployed. The true basis for doctrine is to be found in the religious affections; this was the explicit canon for dogmatic statements for Schleiermacher.[76] To speak of the authority of Scripture in these circumstances is totally redundant. The very use of the language of authority is a hangover from an earlier period in Protestantism when Scripture was seen as a canon of truth. Schleiermacher's transposition of this into a norm of Christian identity is the kind of brilliant invention which displays the bankruptcy of the doctrine he had inherited. He preserved the quasi-epistemic discourse of canon, all the while gutting it of epistemic content. He kept afloat the epistemizing of the canon of Scripture, only now the amount of epistemological work has been reduced virtually to zero.[77]

A further problem emerges in the way in which Schleiermacher's proposals play themselves out in his Christology. Consider the following claims about Jesus of Nazareth: 'The Redeemer . . . is like all men in virtue of the identity of human nature, but distinguished from them all by the constant potency of His God-consciousness, which was a veritable existence of

[75] Although Schleiermacher was happy to retain the Old Testament as a kind of useful appendix to the New Testament (ibid., sec. 132. 3).

[76] See e.g. ibid., sec. 99. 1, where he refers the reader back to the crucial enunciation of this claim in sec. 29. 3.

[77] It goes virtually without saying that Schleiermacher accepts the tradition of the Church only in so far as it can survive being tested by his own norm of theological adequacy. 'The ecclesiastical formulae concerning the Person of Christ need to be subjected to continual criticism' (ibid., sec. 95). The second unit of this section shows supreme self-confidence in the primacy of his epistemology over the teaching of the Church.

God in Him';[78] 'Christ was distinguished from all other men by
His essential sinlessness and His Absolute perfection.'[79] The crucial
problem to be noted is that it is hard to see how one could arrive
at these assertions merely on the basis of religious experience.
How are we to move from the consciousness of Christian believers to the conclusion that such a figure lived such a life 2,000
years ago? That things appear this way to Christians is certainly
not adequate warrant. Nor can such a claim be secured by historical investigation, for the historian does not begin to have sufficient evidence to support these claims. Nor can it somehow be
inferred from the fact that Christians claim on the basis of experience to need such a redeemer, or claim, again on the basis of
experience, that such a figure must have existed because they
now derive such satisfaction from internalizing the reports about
such a redeemer as preached in the Church. The obvious explanation is that Schleiermacher has smuggled into his consciousness
a radically revised edition of the canonical faith of the Church
and has relied on this to determine the content of his historical
beliefs. How that canonical faith or its revision is to be secured is
a total mystery, given Schleiermacher's official epistemology.

A similar difficulty surfaces as Schleiermacher begins to work
out the consequences of his position for the doctrine of the
Trinity. This doctrine shows up virtually as an appendix in his
systematic theology, and he very naturally argues that all we can
know of God is God as he is related to us through redemption.
Thus nothing can be posited of the eternal, ontological nature of
God.[80] In technical terms, the immanent Trinity is reduced to

---

[78] Ibid., sec. 94.   [79] Ibid., sec. 98.

[80] Schleiermacher's position went beyond the positive employment of his
epistemic principles. He went so far as to claim that not even revelation could
overcome the gap between the human and the divine at this point. '[C]omplete
truth would mean that God has made Himself known as He is in and for
Himself. But such a truth could not proceed outwards from any fact, and even if
it did in some incomprehensible way come to a human soul, it could not be
apprehended by that soul, and retained as a thought; and if it could not be in
any way perceived and retained, it could not become operative. Any proclamation of God which is to be operative upon and within us can only express God
in his relation to us; and this is not an infra-human ignorance concerning God,
but the essence of limitedness in relation to Him' (ibid., sec. 10, postscript). One
would dearly love to know how Schleiermacher was initiated into such epistemic secrets. To any robust theist, these must appear as extraordinary claims.

the economic Trinity. However, the obvious question is why
any talk of Trinity should be preserved in these circumstances.
There is no warrant for retaining the language once the epistemology has been adopted. Again we see the shell of the canonical language of the Church being deployed, but now deprived of
its content and merely idling. The best we are offered is a
promissory note whose fulfilment failed to take care of our
objection.[81]

A further difficulty surfaces in Schleiermacher's more general
doctrine of God. Relying on the feeling of absolute dependence,
Schleiermacher defines God as the unconditional Whence of all
finite existence, of all knowing and doing. Leaving aside the
coherence and intelligibility of this idea of God, it is hard to see
how such a deity could enter into any kind of real relation to the
world. The sense of absolute dependence, as opposed to a sense
of relative dependence, requires that the creature have no effect
on the creator. Hence for God genuinely to respond to the needs
of his creatures is impossible. In this case Schleiermacher swallowed the consequences and denied that God is merciful: 'To
attribute mercy to God is more appropriate to the language of
preaching than to the language of dogmatic theology.'[82] We are
here surely far removed from the living God so beloved of
Schleiermacher's pietist forebears.[83]

Perceptive admirers of Schleiermacher have noted that one
way to resolve the dilemma I have identified is to use his
methodological tools more consistently.[84] Thus, while he may
have failed here or there, the underlying assumption about the
warrant for Christian doctrine is secure. No doubt such an
undertaking would have radical consequences for the content
of Christian belief, and it would displace even more of that

[81] The note is delivered in *On the Discrepancy between the Sabellian and Athanasian Method*.   [82] *Christian Faith*, sec. 85.

[83] Schleiermacher's stance on this issue explains the uncharacteristically
direct comment of Mackintosh: 'It is painful to watch this extraordinarily gifted
man, who lacked nothing but a touch of childlike and unreserved trust in the
Father, expound as the Christian view of salvation what too often is but the
attenuated creed of idealistic Monism' (*Types of Modern Theology*, 100).

[84] For a fascinating move in this direction see Van Harvey, 'A Word in
Defense of Schleiermacher's Theological Method'. Harvey has since abandoned
this project.

canonical and conventional language which Schleiermacher managed to retain in poetic and symbolic form. However, if his epistemology is correct, there is everything to gain in the search for truth and nothing to lose by way of Christian identity. We reach here the final component in our critique of the great experiment initiated by Schleiermacher.

Let us suppose for the moment that Schleiermacher is correct in his religious epistemology. The very least that we can ask of him and his followers is that in their zeal to replace the canonical heritage of the Church they should have the courtesy to bring their proposals into the councils of the Church. Canonical decisions are characteristically taken by the whole Church. They require extended discussion to guarantee that they are not simply imposed from on high and to ensure that they contribute to the welfare of the community as a whole. The kind of change envisaged by Schleiermacher, even by his own lights, is so significant that it should not be adopted without being generally agreed on by the Church through appropriate channels.

Schleiermacher was well aware of this as it applied to the canon of Scripture, and he was thoroughly informed about the way the old Confessions of the Protestant faith had been thrashed out and adopted in the Lutheran and Reformed traditions. Somewhere in the mists of the Protestant past this insight about the nature of canon had been lost. We may chalk it up to historical amnesia; we may explain it as the exercise of covert power in the Church; we may treat it as one more consequence of the epistemizing of the canonical heritage of the Church. However we explain the phenomenon, the fact is that Schleiermacher simply pressed on and insisted that the Church work henceforth on the basis on his epistemic principles.

To be sure, he would protest against this kind of accusation, for even in his lifetime he eschewed the cultivation of a body of disciples or a party within the Church.[85] Whatever his intentions and avowals, the effect was clear. Those modern Protestants who followed his lead were equipped with a whole new canonical tradition whose essence was epistemological to the core. By proposing that there be a new office in the Church, that of a

---

[85] Schleiermacher protests against even the idea that he should be the founder of a new school (*The Christian Faith*, p. viii).

prince of the Church, he was even institutionalizing the change.[86] Henceforth the Church would be captive to its theological experts as appointed by the professional guild of the university. Their authority would be grounded less on such factors as their holiness, their knowledge of God, or their commitment to the Church than on their position as experts in the science of theology.

The larger problem is, of course, one of philosophical substance, rather than ecclesiastical arrangements. After all, we can imagine, albeit with considerable difficulty, Schleiermacher and his admirers bringing their new proposals to the Church and securing their subsequent adoption as the new canon. Why should we not welcome this?

The material reason is that Schleiermacher's religious epistemology is both underdeveloped and insecure. As a network of epistemic proposals almost every item is open to objection. The kind of foundationalist structure posited is in need of detailed defence. The radically inward turn within the self is poorly placed to deal with the public character of our discourse about ourselves and the world. The quest for certainty is but a marginal component of any adequate theory of knowledge. The notion of a preconceptual experience, which is not logically dependent on prior conceptual formation, is disputable. The concept of God as the Whence of all finitude is thoroughly opaque, if not vacuous. The idea that all religious language is fundamentally expressive or descriptive of inward affections does not begin to do justice to the extraordinarily diverse ways that language is used in religion. The general appeal to 'feeling', to a 'sense' of the divine, can be made minimally coherent, but much more epistemological work needs to be done before its credentials and proper deployment will have been secured. Any one of these considerations should make us pause before we officially adopt Schleiermacher's programme. Taken together, they add up to an overwhelming case against the motion.

---

[86] 'If one should imagine both a religious interest and a scientific spirit conjoined in the highest degree and with the finest balance for the purpose of theoretical and practical activity alike, that would be the idea of a "prince of the church" ' (*Brief Outline,* sec. 9). It is clear that Schleiermacher intends his princes to take the place of the Fathers. 'It does seem more suitable than the term "Church father," which is already used for a special category of men' (ibid.).

The other reason is simpler. The official adoption of this kind of material is not essential to the welfare of the Church or its identity. To the contrary, it is likely to be a snare and a distraction. The Church exists as the Body of Christ to make known the good news of the kingdom of God and to initiate people into salvation. It cannot do this adequately if it does not preserve the riches of the Faith as embodied in its complex canonical heritage, most especially that enshrined in its Scriptures. As originally conceived and transmitted, great care was taken to keep epistemic material on the margins or outside of the canonical tradition altogether. Even when these materials were epistemized, they were sufficiently resilient to survive their misinterpretation and abuse. When they were almost completely absorbed in a network of epistemic theory, alarm bells went off. Since Schleiermacher, the alarm bells have never stopped ringing.

The Canons of Common Sense

The most conspicuous feature of the epistemology deployed by Friedrich Schleiermacher is that it was conservative and traditionalist. Schleiermacher's deliberations in the theory of knowledge resulted in an outlook which was foundational in its basic structure, turned inward into the self for its raw materials, continued to seek certainty, and looked for clarity and precision in expression as the ultimate goal. These components of epistemological theory had been in place for centuries; they were neither new nor revolutionary. It is, therefore, ironic in the extreme that Schleiermacher should be seen primarily as a revolutionary figure, and that his opponents should be cast in the role of traditionalist conservatives. Yet this is exactly what happened. Thus one distinguished network of Schleiermacher's opponents, the great Princeton theologians of the nineteenth century, have been regularly put on display as theological dinosaurs.

Schleiermacher was, however, a revolutionary figure; for he transposed the contents of the coveted foundations to experience, and he worked out the consequences of this shift for the content of theology with a thoroughness and a brilliance which are startling. Hence at this level he is rightly construed as anything but a conservative and a traditionalist; and those who oppose him are bound to appear as reactionary to those who share his vision.

The writings of Schleiermacher's Princeton opponents and of the populist allies who used their work later throw fresh light on the debate about canon and norm which has not been adequately articulated and elaborated to date. Over the next two chapters I shall seek to show that they represent a fascinating effort to respond to the same crisis which faced Schleiermacher. That the Princeton theologians ultimately failed, not least because they shared the same epistemological sensibilities of Schleiermacher and his predecessors, does nothing to detract from the rigour and originality of their deliberations.

Originality is not, of course, a feature of theological life which the great Princeton theologians would want in any way to claim for themselves. In a celebrated comment, Charles Hodge at the semi-centennial observance of his election as professor in 1872 said: 'I am not afraid to say that a new idea never originated at this Seminary.'[1] Two years earlier he had written: 'Whether it be a ground of reproach or of approbation, it is believed to be true, that an original idea in theology is not to be found on the pages of the *Biblical Repertory and Princeton Review* from the beginning until now. The phrase "Princeton Theology," therefore, is without distinctive meaning.'[2] From the beginning, the Princeton tradition was conceived and executed as a return to the Calvinist heritage in all its glory and fullness. As B. B. Warfield summed it up in 1904: 'Calvinism is just religion in its purity. We have only, therefore, to conceive of religion in its purity, and that is Calvinism.'[3] Like his predecessors Archibald Alexander (1772–1851), Charles Hodge (1797–1878), and A. A. Hodge (1823–86), Warfield (1851–1921) devoted his prodigious gifts to the restatement of the Augustinian and Calvinist heritage. In this chapter we shall trace the work of Archibald Alexander and Charles Hodge; in the next we shall look at that of Warfield.

The strategy of the Princeton theologians was on the surface relatively simple. They set out to articulate and defend the faith once and for all delivered to the saints. They did this not just to counter the influence of Schleiermacher, as that drifted across the Atlantic, but also to respond to the several challenges they encountered within and outside their beloved Presbyterian tradition on

[1] Quoted in A. A. Hodge, *Life of Charles Hodge* (New York: Charles Scribner, 1880), 521.

[2] Charles Hodge, *Biblical Repertory and Princeton Review*, index volume (1870–1), 1. 11. More graphically, Hodge once remarked: 'A man behind the wall of Gibraltar, or of Ehrenbreitstein, cannot, if he would, tremble at the sight of a single knight, however gallant or well appointed' (quoted in Sydney Ahlstrom, 'The Scottish Philosophy and American Theology', *Church History*, 24 (1955), 265.

[3] B. B. Warfield, 'What is Calvinism?', in John E. Meeter (ed.), *Selected Shorter Writings of Benjamin B. Warfield* (2 vols., Phillipsburg, NJ: Princeton and Reformed Publishing Company, 1970), i. 389.

the home front. Chief among these were the rise of Unitarianism, of frontier revivalism, and of the higher life movements.

This self-presentation of traditionalism and lack of originality is, however, a façade. The really deep issue facing the Princeton theologians was the same as that which confronted Schleiermacher. The crisis they faced was the collapse of the Lockean synthesis of faith and reason at the hands of Hume and the subsequent attractions of deism, atheism, and secularism. Noll's comment is accurate.

Even simple chronological conjunctions show us that the Princetonians were children of their age who responded to issues that also troubled others in the Western world. Thus, to note that Alexander published his *Thoughts on Religious Experience* (3 eds., 1841–1844) in the same decade that Søren Kierkegaard wrote *The Sickness Unto Death* (1848) suggests that Princeton shared a widespread concern to maintain authentic spirituality in the midst of enthusiasm, nascent rationalism, and creeping modernization. Or to see Hodge's *Systematic Theology*, a massive exposition of theology based on a Calvinistic conception of biblical authority, as belonging to the same era as the First Vatican Council (1870), the great Catholic effort to shore up ecclesiastical authority, is to realize that Princeton too was addressing the issue of religious certainty when most of the West was rethinking that matter.[4]

The solution to this crisis they found in the work of the great Scottish philosopher Thomas Reid and the tradition which arose in, around, and after him.[5] The position they developed can be

---

[4] Mark A. Noll (ed.), *The Princeton Theology, 1812–1921* (Grand Rapids, Mich.: Baker, 1983), 34.

[5] It is only in recent years that the stature of Reid as a philosopher has been recognized. This delay is in part due to the failure of Kant to appreciate the philosophical nature of his proposals. Kant, like many others who followed his lead, saw Reid simply as an apologist for common sense, rather than as offering a genuinely philosophical response to the challenge of Hume. Kant's disparaging remarks can be found in the *Prolegomena to Any Future Metaphysic of Morals* (Indianapolis: Bobbs-Merrill, 1950). Kant only knew Reid second-hand through the reports of Reid's philosophical enemy, Joseph Priestley. Reid had a profound indirect influence on G. E. Moore, and he is a major figure behind the development of reliabilism in recent years. For a fine discussion of the impact of Reid see Keith Lehrer, 'Scottish Influences on Contemporary American Philosophy', *Philosophical Journal*, 5 (1968), 34–42, and *idem*, 'Reid's Influence on American and British Philosophy', in Stephen F. Barker and Tom L. Beauchamp (eds.), *Thomas Reid: Critical Interpretations* (Philadelphia: Philosophical Monographs, 1976), 1–7.

spelled out both in terms of a general epistemology and in terms of a philosophy of science.[6]

The crucial feature of Reid's work, which best introduces us to his rebuttal of Hume, is this. Whereas Hume tended to overthrow his ordinary beliefs about the existence of minds, the external world, and causality by invoking a general empiricist principle which they failed to satisfy, Reid reversed this by appealing to ordinary beliefs to overthrow the acceptance of Hume's epistemic principle. Reid saw Hume's views as leading to unwelcome consequences.

---

[6] In Reid these two enterprises are virtually identical. The task of the epistemologist was precisely that of the scientist who engages in careful, inductive study of the human intellect in order to determine its workings and nature. In Reid's day the natural scientist was construed as a natural philosopher, a fact which is still enshrined in the designation of chairs of science in the older universities in England. Reid himself, as regent of the University of Aberdeen, taught a full round of subjects. Thus he taught natural science, mathematics, logic, metaphysics, political philosophy, and ethics. For a set of orations which nicely bring out Reid's construal of his work see *The Philosophical Orations of Thomas Reid* (Carbondale and Edwardsville, Ill.: Southern Illinois University Press, 1989). Like Locke and Hume, Reid was convinced that the philosophy of human nature would make no progress until it adopted the procedure utilized by Newton. This whole way of thinking has become foreign to modern sensibilities, which tend to separate science off as a radically different enterprise from philosophy. What we call 'natural science' began life within philosophy as 'natural philosophy' and only gradually became separated from its parent body. It is fascinating that Reid's chosen field of study, human nature, was itself a part of the field of pneumatology, a field which covered the study of spirits: divine, angelic, and human. On the latter see the fascinating essay of Charles Stewart-Robertson, 'Thomas Reid and Pneumatology: The Text of the Old, the Tradition of the New', in Melvin Dalgarno and Eric Matthews (eds.), *The Philosophy of Thomas Reid* (Boston: Kluwer Academic Publishers, 1989), 389–412. Given this sort of background, it is not in the least surprising that the Princeton theologians of the nineteenth century should have been convinced that theology was a true science. Nor is it surprising that the twentieth-century defenders of the Princeton doctrine of Scripture should find that commitment troublesome. Thus Balmer and Woodbridge confess: 'Their [the Princetonians] discussion of theology as a science is unnerving' (John D. Woodbridge and Randall H. Balmer, 'The Princetonians and Biblical Authority: An Assessment of the Ernest Sandeen Proposal', in D. A. Carson and John D. Woodbridge (eds.), *Scripture and Truth* (Grand Rapids, Mich.: Zondervan, 1983), 410 n. 180). As we shall see, the attempt to preserve the Princetonian account of canon and criterion while ditching the philosophy which undergirds it is a major cause of acrimonious friction within strands of the Reformed tradition in North America.

The theory of ideas, like the Trojan horse, had a specious appearance both of innocence and beauty; but if those philosophers had known that it carried in its belly death and destruction to all sciences and common sense, they would not have broken down their walls to give it admittance.[7]

The way to rebuild the walls was to start again from a radically different set of foundations constituted by the very beliefs which Hume had called into question.

This was truly a revolutionary procedure. Rather than begin from a general commitment to a method or criterion for accepting or rejecting a particular belief, Reid insisted that any theory about epistemic method or criterion must be tested by the particular beliefs which were generally accepted as correct. Thus, rather than say that we should give up our belief in the external world because that belief failed to satisfy the canon that all our beliefs be derivable from immediate sense experience, we should appeal to our general belief in the existence of the external world to access the validity of the epistemic claim that all our beliefs be derivable from immediate sense experience. In this particular case the material empiricist principles enunciated by Locke and Hume were to be rejected.[8]

Pursuing this line of enquiry, Reid posited a network of faculties which lay behind the general commitment to the deliverances of testimony, memory, perception, inference, intuition, and the like. These faculties were conceived as natural endowments given to human agents by God. The task of philosophy, in part, was to provide a detailed and coherent account of these faculties, the first principles which governed them, their internal phenomenology, their psychological mechanisms, the belief dispositions and feelings

[7] Quoted by A. C. Fraser, *Thomas Reid* (Edinburgh: Oliphant, Anderson, and Ferrier, 1898), 41.

[8] Reid's position is subtle, in that he relies on observation of human nature, and hence stays within the contours of the empiricist tradition, to establish certain truths which are not based on the existence of inner 'ideas' as happens in the case of Locke, Berkeley, and Hume. Reid considered the positing of inner ideas as representations, say, of the external world as the fatal mistake in Locke which needed to be overcome. His arguments on this score are remarkably incisive. In this regard some of his claims are very similar to those of Aquinas. See John J. Haldane, 'Reid, Scholasticism and Current Philosophy', in Dalgarno and Matthews (eds.), *The Philosophy of Thomas Reid*, 285–306.

which accompanied them, and the like. In this regard Reid stood firmly in the tradition of Locke and Hume, for he continued to see epistemology as a quasi-descriptive enterprise which relied on introspection and which construed philosophy as a form of science modelled on the work of Bacon and Newton.[9] He differed from Locke and Hume by deploying the assumption that the acceptance of particular beliefs as rationally justified is logically prior to the elucidation of general epistemic principles and by arriving at a broader set of governing principles.

The basic beliefs which Reid took as embedded in the philosophy of Common Sense are not difficult to identify. Chief among them were the claims that there is an objective world of material objects in space and time, that reality is knowable by the human mind, that human beings are personal agents with free will, that the fundamental requirements of morality are intuitively discernible, and that such knowledge is a sound guide to human action, collectively and individually. It is more difficult to identify the marks of these truths of Common Sense.[10] Overall, Reid held that these truths were self-evident, universally accepted, irresistible, unprovable, yet capable of being confirmed.[11] Consequently, we might say that they are built into the very constitution of human nature. We might also say that they are given to human agents by God in creation. This does not mean, as might at first appear, that their truth was guaranteed by appeal

[9] For a fine discussion of the relation between Reid and Newton, see L. L. Laudan, 'Thomas Reid and the Newtonian Turn of British Methodological Thought', in R. E. Butts and W. Davis (eds.), *The Methodological Heritage of Newton* (Oxford: Blackwell, 1970), 103–31.

[10] It is common to prefer to speak of the criteria of these truths of Common Sense, but this is very misleading. If we speak of criteria, this means that the truths of Common Sense are only true because they satisfy a set of general criteria and are shown to be so by relevant inspection. What are at issue, however, are the identifying marks of such truths—that is, the common features of these basic truths. The goal under this description is not to establish the first truths of Common Sense, but rather, having already identified these truths, to examine whether they fall into a discernible pattern or under a general set of rules. This is a crucial distinction. Some in the Common Sense tradition see them as laws of belief.

[11] It is clear that Reid is a foundationalist, yet the last mark introduces into his epistemology a coherentist dimension which is easily missed. For a useful discussion see Daniel Schulthess, 'Did Reid Hold Coherentist Views?', in *The Philosophy of Common Sense*, 193–204.

to the goodness and power of God. On this view, they could only be accepted if we could first establish the truth of theism. On the contrary, this order was turned on its head. Working from the unproved but entirely rational acceptance of these truths and principles, we argue to the rationality of belief in God. Thus Reid emphatically rejected the arguments from the veracity of God to the reliability of the senses as circular, as laid out in Descartes, and he was wholly committed to the validity of natural theology.[12]

A rendering of many of these fundamental ideas was embedded in the very fabric of the Princeton tradition.[13] Their specific application, however, was shaped in interesting ways by confessional and apologetic constraints which played next to no role in the work of Reid.[14] Hence one can trace a fascinating inner development in the Princeton tradition in epistemology which can be charted by showing where its theologians locate the place of natural theology within the contours of the general Reidian strategy. One can also use this

---

[12] For a very good treatment of the conflicting interpretations of Reid, and one which supports this reading, see Paul Vernier, 'Thomas Reid on the Foundations of Knowledge and his Answer to Skepticism', in Barker and Beauchamp (eds.), *Thomas Reid: Critical Interpretations*, 14–24. Given these moves, it is not surprising that Reid's work was embraced by moderate Calvinists and Unitarians. This is nicely brought out by Sydney Ahlstrom, 'The Scottish Philosophy and American Theology', *Church History*, 24 (1955), 257–72.

[13] The connection between the Princeton tradition and Scottish Common Sense Realism goes beyond the general cultural impact of that tradition on North American life and thought, broad and deep as that impact was. The Scottish Common Sense tradition was deliberately imported no less than twice into Princeton in the persons of John Witherspoon (1723–94) and James McCosh (1811–94). One of the best accounts of the relationship between Scottish Common Sense Realism and the Princeton tradition is to be found in Harriet Anne Harris, 'The Banner of Truth: Fundamentalism and its Influence on Evangelicalism' (D.Phil. diss., University of Oxford, 1994), 103–67.

[14] Reid's work stands apart in spirit from that of other figures in the Common Sense tradition and in the theological traditions he inspired, most especially the tradition at Princeton. Reid clearly followed out the alternatives he rejected as living options which he had actually embraced or could be persuaded to embrace. He felt deeply indebted to Hume for awakening him to the consequences of his Berkeleyan commitments and as a model of philosophical temper. This is one reason, but clearly not the only or best reason, why he receives deep attention and respect in current discussions of the history of epistemology.

procedure to expose and explain the theological innovations and inner tensions of the tradition. Some of these innovations involved a subtle reworking of the doctrine of inspiration which is pivotal for grasping the adjustments on the canon of Scripture which developed. Their relevance for our general project is therefore self-evident. We shall explore these outgrowths by looking now at the work of Archibald Alexander and Charles Hodge.

It would be difficult to improve on the summary of the epistemological theory which Archibald Alexander laid out in his opening lecture to theological students at Princeton. Virtually all the themes of Scottish Common Sense Realism were presented with astonishing clarity and succinctness. Clearly Alexander had done his philosophical homework. Thus theology was seen as a science; the case for the claim that human agents can have real knowledge was skilfully marshalled; and the cavils of sceptics and objectors were summarily overcome. Human knowledge, for Alexander, is structured in such a way that all claims to truth are ascertained either by showing that they are self-evident or that they are appropriately derived from self-evident truths. Human faculties, although subject to development from infancy and in need at times of internal correction, are inherently reliable. The exact number of self-evident truths cannot be ascertained, but those we can ascertain fall into several distinct classes. These are:

1. The Existence of objects of sense and consciousness.
2. Necessary truths, such as Mathematical axioms.
3. Philosophical principles, such as 'Every effect must be produced by some cause,' etc.
4. Moral truths, as for instance, that there is an essential difference between moral good and evil; that benevolence is better than malevolence, etc.
5. Facts, reported to us by a sufficient number of competent witnesses, past or present, as that such men as Caesar and Pompey did once exist; that there was a beautiful building formerly in Jerusalem called the Temple, etc.
6. Truths founded on uniform experience as that the sun will rise tomorrow, that fire will burn the next hour as well as the present.
7. Memory.[15]

---

[15] Archibald Alexander, 'Nature of Evidence and Truth', in Noll (ed.), *Princeton Theology*, 68.

Alexander had his epistemic wits about him. Although Hume was not mentioned by name, Alexander attempted a brief refutation of his objections to miracles. Both Locke and Descartes were taken to task with skill and fervour. Alexander's reiteration of Reid's position on the relationship between the reliability of the senses and theism is a model of philosophical argument.

To prove that our faculties are not so constituted as to misguide us, some have recourse to the *goodness* and *truth of God*, our creator, but this argument is unnecessary. We are as certain of these intuitive truths as we can be. No supposition of the possibility of deception shakes in the least my belief that I exist, and that the world exists; and if it did this argument or any other would be unavailing; because, if I supposed that my faculties were deceptions, I should have as much reason to doubt of their correctness in forming such an argument, as in any other case. Besides we must be sure that we exist, and that the world exists, before we can be certain that there is a God, for it is from these data that we prove his existence.[16]

What is interesting here is that the proposition 'God exists' is not taken as a self-evident truth; on the contrary, the existence of God must be proved at the outset.[17] Alexander was a typical natural theologian who had to tread a fine line between those who claim too little for reason by saying that the existence of God is self-evident, hence not in need of demonstration, and those who claim too much for reason by insisting that there is no need for revelation on the grounds that agents have sufficient knowledge for life and salvation. The key to getting access to divine revelation was testimony.

As we naturally are disposed to credit the testimony of our fellow creatures, much more will we be under a necessity of believing the testimony of God, if he should deign to speak to us in such a way that we should be certain that it was indeed he who was speaking whether mediately or immediately. We need no arguments that God will speak the truth. This we [take] as a self-evident truth. The only use of argument in the relation to testimony of God is to prove that what is alleged

---

[16]   Archibald Alexander, *Princeton Theology*, 65; emphasis original.

[17]   After a standard deployment of the argument from design complete with watch and steam-engine, Alexander concludes: 'Reason, then, clearly indicates that this universe is not God, but is the work of God, and that he must be a being of transcendent perfection' ('The Bible and the Natural World', in Noll (ed.), *The Princeton Theology*, 96).

to come from him is really his word. The Israelites who stood at the foot of Mt. Sinai and saw the symbols of his majesty and glory and heard his awful voice stood in no need of reasoning or argument to convince them that what was spoken was true.[18]

This is an intriguing passage, for Alexander insisted that the claim to possess a revelation had to be supported by argument, and yet he immediately eschewed the need for argument in the case of the Israelites at Mt. Sinai. The obvious way to resolve this conflict is to assume that Alexander believed that the various events in and around Sinai constituted good evidence for the Israelites.

This reading is in keeping with the extended treatment of evidence which Alexander affixed to his treatment of the authority of Scripture. Alexander was as confident as Locke in his appeal to reason in this arena.

In receiving . . . the most mysterious doctrines of revelation, the ultimate appeal is to reason: not to determine whether she could have discovered these truths; not to declare whether considered in themselves they appear probable; but to decide whether it is not more reasonable to believe what God speaks than to confide in our own crude and feeble conceptions. . . . If . . . we receive the witness of men in matters above our comprehension, much more should we receive the witness of God, who knows all things, and cannot deceive his creatures by false declarations.[19]

Alexander's marshalling of the relevant evidence to establish that revelation is necessary, that it is likely to take place, that it is not available outside the Christian canon of Scripture, and that it is actually available within the Christian canon, was a *tour de force*. Concerning the latter, he led with a network of external evidence which essentially appealed to human testimony, to miracles, to prophecies, and to the rapid and extensive spread of the Gospel through few and feeble instruments. A major effort was made to refute in detail the famous claims of Hume concerning miracles.[20] After working through the external evidence, Alexander laid out a brief catalogue of the internal evidence for revelation by citing

---

[18] Noll (ed.), *Princeton Theology*, 71.
[19] Archibald Alexander, *Evidences of the Authenticity, Inspiration and Canonical Authority of the Holy Scriptures* (Philadelphia: Presbyterian Board of Publication, 1836), 11. [20] Ibid., ch. 6.

the splendour of the Bible's depiction of God, the impossibility of it being written by impostors, the way its account of the origins of human beings accords with reason and experience, the fact that it gives knowledge essential to human welfare, its moral excellence, its depiction of the person of Christ, and its salutary effects on people.[21] Alexander believed that such evidence was internal not in the sense that it appealed only to Christian believers but in the sense that it was drawn from within the Scriptures themselves. Indeed, 'more instances have occurred of skeptical men being convicted by the truth of Christianity by the internal than by the external evidences'.[22] Yet, in striking the balance between the appeals to these two kinds of evidence, one needed to attend to the importance of a docile and candid disposition, if the internal evidence was to strike home.

It is admitted that a revelation from God would have internal evidence of its origin, but this does not strike the attention at once. It requires time before it can be perceived; but in the first establishment of a revelation, there is need of some evidence which is obvious to the senses and level to the capacities of all. Just such an evidence are miracles. Moreover internal evidence requires, in order that it may be perceived and appreciated, a certain favourable state of the moral feelings, without which it is apt to be overlooked, and produces no conviction; whereas, external evidence is not only level to every capacity, but adapted to bring home conviction to every description of men, to the bad as well as the good.[23]

It was at this level, that of securing the right moral feeling, that Alexander invoked the relevance of the working of the Holy Spirit, for even the serious mind may fall into doubt about divine truth. The remedy for this is divine illumination.

The mind may be in such a state that it is rather perplexed, than relieved, by mere human reasoning; but at such times a lively impression made by the Spirit of truth banishes all doubt and hesitation; and then the same texts or arguments which were before unavailing to our conviction and satisfaction exhibit the truth in a light as clear as demonstration. This

[21]   Archibald Alexander, *Evidences of the Authenticity, Inspiration and Canonical Authority of the Holy Scriptures*, ch. 13.
[22]   Ibid. 187. In his *Thoughts on Religious Experience* (Philadelphia: Presbyterian Board of Publication, 1844), Alexander recounts the 'remarkable conversion of a blind infidel from hearing the Bible' (ch. 7).
[23]   *Evidences*, 64.

may appear to some to savour of enthusiasm. Be it so. It is, however, an enthusiasm essential to the very nature of our holy religion, without which it would be a mere dry system of speculation, of ethics and ceremonies. But this *divine illumination* is its *life*, its *soul*, its *essence*.[24]

Alexander was clear about the possibility of certainty for religious belief. This is a recurring refrain in his work. Working through his remarks in the vicinity of this subject exposes tensions which become especially conspicuous later on in the work of Warfield. It is clear, first, that Alexander coveted the possibility of certainty for the model religious believer: 'To affect the conscience and influence the heart, it is highly important that religious truth should be attended with certainty, and should be felt to possess the sanction of divine authority.'[25] It is clear that this is something he wanted for himself and others, so much so that there is virtually a moral presumption that it will be supplied by a benevolent deity. Thus in respect to the immortality of the soul, 'this, of all others, is the point, on which we want certainty—absolute certainty'.[26] However, little light is available even to the powerful intellects of Socrates, Plato, and Cicero. So, 'from the very nature of the case, no one can give us an absolute assurance of our future and immortal existence, but God alone'.[27] Yet this quest for absolute certainty is threatened by the feebleness and fallibility of human reasoning. Thus, after cataloguing a series of unacceptable yet common views about the origins of the universe, he averred: 'From what has been said, it is evident that the human intellect is prone to wander from the truth; and that reason is liable to be perverted, even in matters of the highest importance; and in which the light of evidence seems to us to shine most clearly.'[28] Moreover, despite the great strength of

[24] Archibald Alexander, 'Inaugural Address', in Noll (ed.), *The Princeton Theology*, 86; emphasis original. Alexander is speaking specifically of the theologian, but the main point has a wider application. See e.g. *Evidences*, 189.

[25] *Evidences*, 35.   [26] Ibid. 40.

[27] Ibid. 41. Alexander applies the same reasoning to the knowledge of human origins: 'We know that man must have had a beginning, and consequently a Creator; but reason could not inform us, how, in what circumstances he commenced his existence: that, therefore, *which we wish to know, and need to know*, is distinctively revealed and plainly recorded in the Bible', 'Bible and Natural World', 101; emphasis added.

[28] 'Bible and Natural World', 95.

reason in proving the existence of God, the human race really depends on divine revelation for sustaining the truth of pure theism: 'There is not now in the world an individual who believes in one infinitely perfect God, whose knowledge of this truth may not be traced directly or indirectly to the Bible.'[29]

The problem in this is that the more Alexander exalted the role of revelation, the less need there was for reason. Given his intuitions about the cruciality of revelation as a source of absolute certainty, it is not surprising that he began to waver in his allegiance to the place of reason in his system as a whole. There is no doubt where his heart finally lay. God had acted in revelation to provide a clear demonstration of his character, and he had acted in inspiration and continuing revelation to ensure that certainty concerning such revelation is attainable. By this time, even though Alexander still needed the veracity of human testimony to ensure the credibility of the testimony of the apostles as historians, his intellectual nerve failed him, while the quest for absolute certainty remained undiminished.

Thus he began his discussion of inspiration with the platitudes of the Common Sense tradition.

The gospel history may be established on the common principles of human testimony, in the same manner as any other history. Indeed, this must be done, in the order of proof, before any convincing argument can be formed in favour of divine revelation. Accordingly, all judicious writers on the Evidences of Christianity first attempt to establish the facts recorded in the Gospels, by an appeal to mere human testimony.[30]

Alexander was well satisfied with the results attained in this manner. 'The authenticity of the facts is sufficient to demonstrate that the Christian religion is of divine origin.'[31] There was, in the neighbourhood, however, another issue: namely, that of inspiration. This topic, while not so vitally important as the authenticity of facts, was of great moment, and deserved 'a serious and impartial consideration'.[32]

---

[29] *Evidences*, 191.
[30] Ibid. 222. It is odd here for a devotee of the Common Sense tradition to speak of 'mere' testimony, as if this was somehow an inadequate basis for a claim about the past. It is for that tradition virtually as solid as appeal to perception itself.
[31] Ibid. 223.   [32] Ibid.

It was at this stage that Alexander summoned the resources of divine illumination in order to relieve any doubt in the mind of the reader of Scripture and evoked divine inspiration in order to eliminate any doubt about the veracity of the writers of Scripture. Illumination enables the soul spiritually to apprehend truths already revealed, while inspiration directs or strengthens the faculties of the mind so that 'it is enabled to communicate with *unerring certainty*, truths before unknown'.[33] Understandably, Alexander proceeded immediately to spell out his material theory of divine inspiration, depicting the latter in terms of superintendence, suggestion, and elevation. This kind of inspiration, merely by definition, secured precisely such certainty. The crucial self-revelation came at the end of his exposition. 'It certainly is a matter of no consequence how our knowledge is obtained, *if it is only rendered infallibly certain.*'[34] Clearly, absolute certainty had to be secured somehow. Inspiration was tailor-made to supply it.

Once this goal of absolute certainty was posited, it became so attractive that anything less would appear radically inadequate. After all, it furnished nothing less than the kind of certainty we associate with demonstration. Speaking of plenary inspiration, Alexander remarked: 'No thing can be conceived more satisfactory. Certainty, infallible certainty, is the utmost that can be desired in any narrative; and if we have this in the sacred Scriptures, there is nothing more to be wished in regard to this matter.'[35] For Alexander the certainty secured by inspiration was of the kind we gain from the intuition of first principles.

Suppose a man by a constant plenary inspiration to be made absolutely sure of the truth of certain propositions, so that he could not entertain any doubt respecting them, in what respect would there be any difference between this and the intuitive perception of self-evident principles, which every rational man by nature possesses?[36]

[33] Ibid. emphasis added.
[34] Ibid. 227; emphasis added. It is interesting that even in the body of his exposition Alexander betrays the need and how it must be met: '[N]o man can avoid mistakes in a narrative of facts, long past. If it is important that such a narrative be exempt from error, the writer must be inspired' (ibid.). This reverses the way the argument usually runs and the way it tended to run hereafter in the Princeton tradition. Rather than argue from inspiration to inerrancy, inerrancy is said to require inspiration.
[35] Ibid. 230.   [36] Ibid. 228.

There are at least three possible sources for this line of argument. It could be a recovery of the medieval notion of the
Scriptures as the first principles of a divine *scientia*, which thus
furnish premisses which are self-evidently secure. It could be a
carry-over of the eighteenth-century conviction of rationalist
theologians that theological propositions, unlike the contingent
truths of history, must be necessary truths. Either of these would
yield the kind of certainty Alexander was seeking. The most
likely possibility, however, is simply that he construed the prod-
ucts of divine inspiration as worthy of the same kind of
certainty as that which the Common Sense Realists predicated
of the first principles of truth. These truths were intuitively
certain, even though the human agents who held them were
not infallible. When assisted by divine inspiration, the human
agent was raised from a position of fallibility to one of infallibility, and the resulting certainty would then be infallible and
absolute. There was no higher level of certainty to attain at this
point.

Once this kind of possibility was broached, mere human
veracity would appear less than what was required and wanted.
Or, as Alexander suggested, 'it would be less than satisfactory'.[37] A
record which merely gave substantially the facts of the witness
was not enough.

Such a record would lose a portion of that reverence which it ought to
possess, in order for it to give a commanding authority over the
conscience, and make it a solid foundation for unshaken confidence. In
regard to the mysterious and sublime doctrines which the apostles teach
in their epistles, if once we admit the idea they were fallible men, we
shall continually be liable to doubt: we shall be afraid they have misap-
prehended, or forgotten what they heard; or that, under the bias of prejudice and inclination, they may have been led insensibly to give a
distorted view of the truths which they inculcate.[38]

[37] *Evidences*, 236.
[38] Ibid. It should be noted that this is not a slip by Alexander. This was the
second time that this worry was expressed within two pages. 'The end of revelation is to convey to men a certain knowledge of truth, to guide their faith and
practice. But if the book which contains such a revelation is composed by
erring, fallible men, we never can be sure, in any particular case, that we are in
possession of the truth revealed. The men may be honest and faithful, but we
know that all men are liable to errors and mistakes; and that all men are more or
less under the influence of prejudices and prepossessions. It is evident, therefore,

What is especially significant about this comment is the deep scepticism concerning the status of the human faculties which runs through it. When Alexander opposed the sceptical tradition, he was a great champion of reason. Reid would have been proud of his North American disciple in his defence of the certainties of Common Sense. However, when he put reason to work in the field of theology, he ultimately withdrew to a much less secure position regarding the reliability of the human faculties. Even though Alexander had argued that the witnesses were reliable enough to secure nothing less than the divine origin of Scripture, in this passage he represents the typical sceptic. All the arguments of the sceptic are marshalled against the veracity of the apostles: their fallibility, the possibility of a single doubt opening up an abyss of complete doubt, the possibility of misapprehension, the unreliability of memory, and the distorting effects of the passions and prejudice on the intellect. This is an extraordinary turn-around for one so intelligent as Alexander. It is a bizarre proce-dure for a devotee of Common Sense and the inductive method to adopt. Clearly the desire for a 'commanding authority' and a 'solid foundation for unshaken confidence' has completely smoth-ered his Common Sense sensibilities. He has reverted to the position of the sceptic who is profoundly dissatisfied with the ordinary operations of perception, memory, testimony, and the like.

It is no surprise, then, that Alexander immediately set out to prove by a whole battery of arguments that the Scriptures were divinely inspired in the required sense; that is, in the sense that they would yield the kind of absolute certainty which Alexander desired. He proposed that there was clear and abundant proof from the promises of Christ to the apostles, from the prophetic character of various parts of the New Testament, from the attest-ation of the Church, from miracles, and from the style of the writ-ings and other internal evidences. Alexander was well aware that these arguments would only hold up once the initial premisses were granted; so he carefully limited their efficacy to those who were already Christian believers. Even then, he did nothing to

---

that the purpose of giving a revelation would be in a great measure defeated, unless inspired men were employed to make the record by which it is transmit-ted to the various nations of the earth and posterity' (ibid. 235).

show that they secured the kind of absolute certainty which he had posited. He did not seem to realize that this kind of *ad hominem* argument was totally useless to overcome the sceptical epistemology which by now was driving the argument as a whole.

It is no accident that in a crucial part of the argument from the avowals of the apostles concerning their own inspiration, Alexander had to assume the veracity and integrity of their testimony. Speaking of Christian believers in contrast to infidels, he wrote:

Now, as these persons admit that the apostles and evangelists were men of veracity and integrity, their testimony on this subject ought to be decisive. If they claim inspiration, we cannot deny it to them, without invalidating all the strongest arguments of the truth of Christianity. Why were they endowed with the power of working miracles, but that full credence might be given to what they testified? And when they declare that they were moved by the Holy Ghost, and that what they delivered was not the word of men, but the word of God received by divine revelation, do not these miraculous powers they possessed, as fully confirm what they wrote as what they spoke?[39]

Alexander worked here from the assumption that it was already believed that the apostles and evangelists were credible witnesses; the old confidence in the reliability of testimony has fallen by the wayside. Once he had secured the initial testimony, he could then argue to the credibility of the miracles, and from the miracles he could move to the apostles and evangelists being credited by God, and from their being credited by God he could move to their being infallible in what they write or speak, and from their infallibility in what they write and speak, he can move to their being inspired by God. Hence a denial of their inspiration required a break somewhere in the chain of inference. On pain of contradiction, either the veracity of God or the credit-giving property of miracles would have to be abandoned. Either move would undermine Alexander's proposals concerning the evidence for Christianity, for these were constituted by appeal to the veracity of God and the credit-giving properties of miracles. Aside from the precarious status of his claim about the avowals of the apostles and evangelists, and aside from the assumption that

---

[39] *Evidences*, 240.

miracles underwrite the total credit of those they accompany, this is a complete reversal of the earlier position. In the earlier position one secured the credibility of the witnesses to miracles on the ground of the general credibility of human testimony, as manifest in this case by the apostles and evangelists. Here Alexander worked from the particular veracity of the apostles and evangelists. The general veracity of testimony had been abandoned, so one had to assume the specific veracity of the apostles and evangelists in order to secure the veracity of the miracle reports. Once the veracity of these reports was in place, the argument could then proceed down the deductive line to the conclusion that the apostles and evangelists were actually inspired by God. Not long afterwards Alexander again reversed his earlier position by insisting that 'if inspiration be denied, the authenticity of the miracles and prophecies will soon be abandoned'.[40] Once inspiration, as he understood it, was abandoned, then miracles and prophecies, he believed, would go too. Here Alexander has lost all confidence in his earlier arguments about the reliability of testimony. This convoluted argument recurred at a crucial point in the apologetic of Warfield, where it exposes a similar fault-line in the whole appeal to the reliability of human cognition. We shall revisit the issue more formally in the next chapter.

Another matter worth observing is that Alexander wavered in working out the full consequences of his position. If inspiration were sufficiently efficacious to secure the kind of certainty we associate with intuitive truths, it would be natural to argue that the inspiration would extend to the very words of Scripture. Yet Alexander shrank from such a conclusion. After suggesting that those for and against the inspiration of the words have some merit on their side, he concluded:

But as in the narration of well-known facts, the writer did not need a continual suggestion of every idea, but only to be superintended, as to be preserved from error; so in the use of language in recording such familiar things, there existed no necessity that every word should be inspired; but there was the same need of a directing and superintending influence as in regard to the things themselves. Here, then, we see that the language of the sacred writers might be preserved from impropriety and inaccuracy, and yet all the characteristics of style peculiar to each be retained.[41]

[40] Ibid. 243. [41] Ibid. 226–7.

Given that Alexander secured the kind of inerrancy he coveted, and given that there appears to be here a distinction without a difference, for directing and superintending are more or less how he generally construed inspiration, not much hangs on this passage materially. Yet there is clearly a minor piece of unfinished business which needed the labours of Warfield two generations later to resolve.

The central claims advanced so far in this chapter concerning the work of Archibald Alexander are these. First, Alexander adopted and applied the general epistemology of Reid to articulate a comprehensive case for the rationality of Christian belief. Second, in that application he adopted Reid's own position on the need for, and the legitimacy of, natural theology as a preamble to special revelation. Where he may well have gone beyond Reid is in the use of the general appeal to testimony to secure the historical reliability of the Scriptures and to mount a case for the existence of divine revelation on the basis of various external and internal arguments. Third, in the actual reception of evidence he appealed to the inner illumination of the Holy Spirit as a way of removing emotional or moral barriers to the discernment of the force of evidence. Fourth, while Alexander was ordinarily committed to the general reliability of our faculties, he was not satisfied with the level of certainty this might provide in the case of any record of special revelation. Paradoxically, at this point he went over to the sceptical side, insisting that there had to be a totally infallible and absolutely certain foundation for faith. This certainty was supplied by a theory of the divine inspiration of the Scriptures which was purposely designed and developed precisely in such a way that it would supply the required foundation.[42] In this arena Alexander departed from his original epistemological orientation.

Alexander's case, then, reveals both his dependence on, and independence of, the epistemology of the Common Sense tradition. We can perceive a similar pattern in the work of Charles

---

[42] Note that I am not claiming that Alexander developed this theory from scratch. He drew massively on earlier tradition, and would have been shocked to think that he was party to any kind of innovation. My aim here is to bring out the way in which the epistemology is driving his theory of inspiration. I shall take up the exact nature of the innovation in the Princeton tradition in the next chapter.

Hodge. As there is considerable continuity right through the long life of the Princeton tradition, we can concentrate here on three factors: the role of argument in natural theology and in securing the existence of divine revelation, the relation of the Holy Spirit to argument, and the nature of theology as a science. The crucial surprise in Hodge is that he departed radically from Alexander in the way he deployed the resources of the Common Sense tradition.

One way to expound that tradition is by means of the notion of properly basic beliefs. A properly basic belief is a belief which one is rationally entitled to hold without evidence. The obvious examples are such beliefs as 'There exists an external world', 'There is a desk before me now', 'There is a past', 'Other minds exist', and the like. These are precisely the kind of beliefs which Reid took as foundational. As such, they were the deliverances of reason; they cannot be proved, in the sense that any evidence adduced in their favour would be no better warranted than they are; and they arise naturally in the human mind under certain circumstances. For both Reid and Alexander, belief in God was not a properly basic belief. It required to be proved by reason, and they were convinced that such a proof was relatively easily furnished. Moreover, Alexander held that belief in special divine revelation was not properly basic. God's revelation in Scripture needed to be established by reason, and appropriate reason was furnished by a combination of external and internal evidence. What is fascinating about Hodge is that he rejected this whole way of proceeding and took belief in God and belief in the inspiration of the Bible as properly basic beliefs. While staying within the boundaries of the Reidian epistemology, he relocated two of the fundamental pillars of his theism in the foundations of the Christian's cognitive structures.

Take, first, the matter of belief in God. Hodge's claim that this is a properly basic belief emerged most conspicuously in his discussion of the origin of the idea of God.

Innate knowledge is the kind of knowledge which arises when the soul sees certain things to be true immediately in their own light, without any proof or argument. 'These immediate perceptions are called intuitions, primary truths, laws of belief, innate knowledge, or ideas.'[43] These intuitive truths fall into various

---

[43] Charles Hodge, *Systematic Theology* (3 vols., Grand Rapids, Mich.: Eerdmans, n.d.), i. 191.

classes. There are intuitions of sense perception, the understanding, and morality. Thus human agents immediately acknowledge
the existence of material objects, the axioms of geometry, the
necessity of causal relations, and such moral truths as that right is
distinct from wrong. These truths, if they are seen at all, are seen
as immediately true, without the intervention of proof. Not all of
these truths may be self-evident to everyone, and the power of
the mind to perceive may be greater in some people than in
others; yet, within this general class of truths there are some
which are marked by both universality and necessity. 'What all
believe, and what all men must believe, is to be assumed as unde-
niably true.'[44] The mind necessarily assents to such truths when
they are presented to it; they are part of the very constitution of
human nature.

Belief in God is precisely such a belief; it is marked by universality and necessity.

When it is asked, Whether the existence of God is an intuitive truth,
the question is equivalent to asking, Whether the belief in his existence
is universal and necessary? If it be true that all men do believe there is a
God, and that no man can possibly disbelieve his existence, then his
existence is an intuitive truth. It is one of those given in the constitution
of our nature; or which, our nature being what it is, no man can fail to
know and acknowledge.[45]

Hodge's answer to his own question was unequivocal: the
knowledge of God is universal, belief in God is necessary, and the
knowledge of God is not due to a process of reasoning.[46]

The one caveat which Hodge allowed is that the idea of God
which is entertained by all may not, of course, be that 'sublime
idea of God' held by Christians. Nevertheless, God has not left
himself without a universal witness. Common opinion, Scripture,
and the evidence of the history of religions, he believed,
supported his contention. Furthermore, it was no objection to
argue that belief in God is on a par with two plus two equals
four. Mathematical necessity represents but one kind of necessity.
Nobody can deny that they have a body, but this is not a matter
of mathematical necessity. If some for a while deny the existence
of God either because of the grip of some metaphysical theory or

---

[44] Charles Hodge, *Systematic Theology*, 193.   [45] Ibid. 194.
[46] These are three of the section titles which follow Hodge's question.

because of moral corruption, as soon as these are banished, belief in God naturally returns to the mind. Moreover, the fact that belief in God arises among those who are incapable of arguments attests to its intuitive character. The inescapably religious character of human beings ensures that they believe in the existence of God, just as nature ensures that they believe in the existence of the external world.

Adam believed in God the moment he was created, for the same reason that he believed in the external world. His religious nature, unclouded and undefiled, apprehended the one with the same confidence that his senses apprehended the other. It is of great importance that men should know and feel that they are by their very nature bound to believe in God; that they cannot emancipate themselves from that belief, without derationalizing and demoralizing their whole being.[47]

. . . so long as men are moral creatures, they must believe in the existence of a Being on whom they are dependent, and to whom they are responsible for their character and their conduct. To this extent, and in this sense, therefore, it is to be admitted that the knowledge of God is innate and intuitive; that men no more need to be taught that there is a God, than they need to be taught there is such a thing as sin. But as men are ignorant of the nature and extent of sin, while aware of its existence, until instructed by the Word of God, and enlightened by His Spirit; so they greatly need the same sources of instruction to give them any adequate knowledge of the nature of God, and of their relations to Him.[48]

Does this then mean that natural theology is invalid? Does it mean that the existence of God cannot be proved? Not at all. Hodge was convinced that there are perfectly good arguments for the existence of God. The purpose of these arguments is not to supplant the innate knowledge of God but to confirm, illustrate, and strengthen it. To set these two kinds of knowledge of God against each other was sophistical. 'Although all men have feelings and convictions which necessitate the assumption that there is a God; it is, nevertheless, perfectly legitimate to show that there are other facts which necessarily lead to the same conclusion.'[49]

---

[47] Ibid. 200–1.   [48] Ibid. 198–9.

[49] Ibid. 202. Not surprisingly, Hodge proceeded almost immediately to discuss virtually all the standard arguments for the existence of God. The same point about the compatibility of intuitive knowledge of God and proof of God is made at ibid. 23.

It is equally wrong-headed to set innate knowledge of God or the knowledge gained from natural theology against knowledge gained from divine revelation. Like Alexander, Hodge held that divine revelation was essential for salvation. This claim takes us naturally to the question of the role of argument in establishing the existence of such revelation. How do we know that there is such a revelation in the Scriptures of the Christian Church? The pattern just established for innate knowledge of God held also for the case of revealed knowledge of God. This emerged in Hodge's account of the various strands of evidence for the claim that Christian Scripture constitutes special revelation.

For Hodge, Scripture was to be believed because it is the inspired Word of God. In this he was a stalwart, traditionalist Protestant. 'The infallibility and divine authority of the Scriptures are due to the fact that they are the word of God; and they are the word of God because they were given by the inspiration of the Holy Ghost.'[50] The obvious question which Hodge had to face, given this commitment and given its denial by others, was how he knew that Christian Scripture was indeed the word of God. Alexander's answer took the form of an extended deployment of external and internal arguments, accompanied by the work of the Holy Spirit in illumination in those cases where the moral feelings failed to perceive the value of the relevant evidence. Hence one was permitted to believe that Scripture was the word of God because there was good evidence for it. Hodge did not share this view. Christians were entitled to believe because of the internal witness of the Holy Spirit which accompanied the perception of varied features of the content of Scripture, the internal evidence, and then that perception and the beliefs it evoked could be strengthened by appeal to external evidence.

Hodge's position can be misleading on this score because of the rather loose way he spoke of evidence and knowledge[51] and

---

[50] Charles Hodge, *Systematic Theology*, 153.

[51] Thus Hodge sometimes appealed to internal evidence as proof, and his comments on knowledge at times are inconsistent. Compare: 'Knowledge is the persuasion of what is true on adequate evidence' (ibid. 1) with 'Knowledge is perception of the truth' (ibid. 360). It is interesting that there is a similar problem in Reid with respect to the equivocal way in which he speaks of evidence: '[P]erception is most properly applied to the evidence which we have of external objects by our senses' (Reid, *Essays on the Intellectual Powers of Man*, in *Works*,

because he did not fully work through his thoughts on the issues.[52] Yet the case for this reading of his position is strong. The best summary is as follows:

We believe the external evidence of the Bible to be perfectly conclusive; we believe its internal evidence (that is, its majesty, its purity, its consistency, its manifold perfections,) to be no less satisfactory; but we believe also, that the ultimate foundation of the Christian's faith, is the testimony of the Holy Spirit, by and with the truth in our hearts.[53]

Hodge rejected the claim that the ordinary believer is dependent on the evidence from, say, miracles, or from learned disquisitions on the historical origins of the Bible. This would leave the poor and the illiterate at the mercy of scholarly research.

It is a monstrous idea, that the thousands of illiterate saints who have entered eternity in the full assurance of hope, had no better foundation than the learned to the truth of the Bible. Let the advocates of such an opinion ask the true Christian, why he believes the word of God, and they will find he can give some better reason for the hope that is in him than the faith or testimony of others. Let them try the resources of their philosophy, empirical or transcendent, on a faith founded on the testimony of the Holy Spirit by and with the truth, let them try the effect of demonstrating that such and such doctrines cannot be true; they will assuredly meet with the simple answer, 'One thing I know, whereas I was blind, now I see.'[54]

Hodge drew a set of parallels between belief in God, belief in Christ, and belief in the Scriptures as the infallible Word of God.

It is the experience of Christians in all ages and nations that their faith is founded on the spiritual apprehension and experience of the power of truth. There are multitudes of such Christians, who, if asked why they

---

ed. Sir William Hamilton (2 vols., Edinburgh: James Thin, 1895), i. i). For a perceptive analysis see William P. Alston, 'Reid on Perception and Conception' in Dalgarno and Matthews (eds.), *Philosophy of Thomas Reid*, 35–48.

[52] The difference of emphasis in Hodge between his earlier and later work could well be accounted for in terms of the different readers he intended to reach. Despite the great appearance of being thorough and systematic in his thinking, Hodge was often quite undiscerning in the way he presented some of his material.

[53] Charles Hodge, 'The Latest Form of Infidelity', in *Essays and Reviews* (New York: Robert Carter and Brothers, 1856), 94.

[54] Ibid. 92.

believe the scriptures to be the word of God, might find it difficult to give an answer, whose faith is nevertheless both strong and rational. They are conscious of its grounds though they may not be able to state them. They have the witness in themselves, and know they believe, not because others believe, or because learned men have proved certain facts which establish the truth of Christianity. They believe in Christ for the same reason that they believe in God; and they believe in God because they see his glory and feel his authority and power.[55]

In keeping with the letter of the Westminster Confession of Faith, Hodge made the work of the Holy Spirit the foundation. In fact, some of his very language was taken straight from the Confession.[56] Later, in his *Systematic Theology*, he spoke of the work of the Spirit in terms of the demonstration of the Spirit.

Besides this external supernatural testimony, the Bible, is everywhere attended by 'the demonstration of the Spirit,' which gives to its doctrines the clearness of self-evident truths, and the authority of the voice of God; analogous to the authority of the moral law or the natural conscience.[57]

Although Hodge did not at that point elaborate, concentrating in that section on the various internal and external proofs, there is no evidence that he changed his mind on this matter.[58]

Furthermore, over against Alexander, who tended to give equal weight to external and internal evidence, Hodge clearly preferred the value of internal evidence, not least because he wanted to safeguard the believer from dependence on learning or scholarship. This is a surprise coming from a scholar who seemed

[55] Charles Hodge, *The Way of Life* (Philadelphia: American Sunday School Union, 1841), 63. This quotation makes clear that for Hodge there was an intimate connection between the apprehension of God's existence or of the Scriptures as the Word of God and the data which form the basis of various arguments for the existence of God and for the divine origin of Scripture. There are deep epistemic subtleties here which Hodge did not explore.

[56] Hodge quoted it exactly (ibid. 9) and picked up the last crucial phrase: 'yet not withstanding, our full persuasion and assurance of the infallible truth and divine authority thereof, is from the inward work of the Holy Spirit, bearing witness *by and with the truth in our hearts*' (emphasis original).

[57] *Systematic Theology*, i. 39.

[58] In speaking against a form of rationalism which he defined as dogmatism, Hodge wrote: 'In thus shifting faith from the foundation from divine testimony, and making it rest on rational demonstration, it is removed from the Rock of Ages to a quicksand' (ibid. i. 46).

never to be content unless he had provided an exhaustive, ency-clopeadic treatment of any issue. Speaking of the internal evidence, he wrote: 'it is obvious that this evidence, in all its full-ness and force, may be exhibited to a man, who knew nothing from others of the origin of the scripture, even to one who should read them for the first time in a desert island.'[59]

This in no way lessened the validity of various proofs for the divine origin and infallibility of Scripture, however. Hence Hodge laid out a whole battery of arguments which were intended to strengthen the commitment of the believer by disposing of various objections and to win over adherents to less adequate conceptions of canon and authority in the Christian tradition. Once the divine origin and infallibility of Scripture were secured, he then argued that Scripture alone ultimately furnished the content of Christian belief. It was the only canon of faith and practice. Even the initial perceptions of the divine given through nature and through the inner witness of the Holy Spirit given in experience had to be tested and filled out by the content of this single norm.

Hodge put this claim formally by insisting that theology was an inductive science. By this he meant that the Bible contained all the facts which the theologian was to consult in order to provide an orderly and systematic account of the content of the Christian faith. It is at this point that we can perceive exactly the same fault-line which we encountered in Alexander. Whereas both initially had enormous confidence in reason, whether conceived as furnishing properly basic beliefs or beliefs appropriately founded on evidence, somehow they ended up radically dissatis-fied when it came to the actual content of theology. Thus Hodge, after confessing his faith in the platitudes of the Common Sense tradition, suddenly insisted on the authentication of what-ever facts he had already perceived or established by intuition or experience.

. . . all the truths taught by the constitution of our nature or by religious experience, are recognized and authenticated in the Scriptures. This is a safeguard and a limit. We cannot assume this or that principle to be intuitively true, or this or that conclusion to be demonstrably certain, and make them a standard to which the Bible must conform. What is

---

[59] 'The Ground of Faith in the Scriptures', in *Essays and Reviews*, 192.

self-evidently true, must be proved to be so, and is always recognized in the Bible as true. Whole systems of theology are founded on intuitions, so called, and if every man is at liberty to exalt his own intuitions, as men are accustomed to call their strong convictions, we should have as many theologies in the world as there are thinkers. The same remark is applicable to religious experience. There is no form of conviction more intimate and irresistible than that which arises from the inward teaching of the Spirit. All saving faith rests on his testimony or demonstrations (1 Cor. ii. 4). Believers have an unction from the Holy One, and they know the truth, and that no lie (or false doctrine) is of the truth. This inward teaching produces a conviction which no sophistries can obscure, and no arguments can shake. Two things, however, are to be borne in mind. First, That this inward teaching or demonstration of the Spirit is confined to truths objectively revealed in the Scriptures. It is given, says the Apostle, in order that we may know things gratuitously given, i.e. revealed to us by God in his Word (1 Cor. ii. 10–16). It is not therefore a revelation of new truths, but an illumination of the mind, so that it apprehends the truth excellence, and glory of the things already revealed. And second, This experience is depicted in the Word of God. The Bible gives us not only the facts concerning God, and Christ, ourselves, and our relations to our Maker and Redeemer, but also records the legitimate effects of these truths on the minds of the believers. So that we cannot appeal to our feelings or inward experience, as a ground or guide, unless we can show that it agrees with the experience of holy men as recorded in the Scriptures.[60]

This is an extraordinary passage for someone committed to the epistemology of the Scottish Common Sense tradition.[61] The obvious problems it exposes in Hodge's position are these. First, earlier what was self-evidently the case was taken at face value, whereas, now the self-evident must be proved to be self-evident by appeal to Scripture.[62] Second, earlier, intuition and experience

---

[60] *Systematic Theology*, 1. 15–16.

[61] Hodge was aware of the possible charge of inconsistency in his position, for he opened this paragraph with the bold claim that his position was indeed consistent. Hodge's wavering commitment to the Common Sense tradition is well brought out by John H. Gerstner, 'The Contributions of Charles Hodge, B. B. Warfield, and J. Gresham Machen to the Doctrine of Inspiration', in Gordon R. Lewis and Bruce Demarest (eds.), *Challenges to Inerrancy: A Theological Response* (Chicago: Moody Press, 1984), 347–82.

[62] This proposal is odd in the extreme. The very reading of Scripture itself depends on relying on the self-evident testimony of the senses, a matter Hodge himself fully acknowledged elsewhere (see *Systematic Theology*, i. 59–60).

were taken as reliable, whereas now they are seen as opening the door to all sorts of arbitrary convictions and theologies. Third, earlier the testimony of the Spirit was the real foundation for faith in the Scriptures, whereas now the testimony, construed in generic terms as religious experience, has to be validated by checking it against the experience of holy persons as recorded in Scripture.[63]

A plausible explanation for this amazing shift is that Hodge, like Alexander, was ultimately dissatisfied with anything less than complete and infallible certainty on every 'fact' about God. Theological 'facts' could not in the end stand on a par with other facts; they had to be grounded in a flawless foundation which transmitted the kind of knowledge which God possessed.[64] By drawing on the epistemic resources of Common Sense Realism, Hodge constructed a ladder up to heaven; having reached up into the skies he discovered another, flawless ladder coming down to earth in the opposite direction. In his excitement he then threw away the old ladder for a time, jumped on the new one coming down from heaven, and dragged it back down to earth.

Not everyone agreed with the supposedly flawless character of Hodge's new ladder. Suppose Scripture appeared to have this or that flaw in it. What then? Or suppose modern scientific discovery did not agree with Scripture. What then? Hodge was well aware of these issues, and he gladly spent time attempting to show that many supposed flaws were not genuine flaws and that genuine scientific fact, over against speculative scientific theory, did not contradict Scripture. Beyond these moves he was prepared, like Alexander, to make minor concessions on the flaws, and, unlike Alexander, he deployed a crucial methodological strategy.

The concession is now justly famous.

[63] This proposal is thoroughly obscure, if not incoherent. First, Hodge nowhere tells us how this checking of experience against the record of experience is to be articulated and applied. Second, it is difficult to see how the experience of the holy men of Scripture is the same experience to which Hodge has appealed. The latter is an experience of the believer in encountering the full canon of Scripture; it is difficult to see how such an experience can be predicated of anyone before the appearance of the actual canon of Scripture.

[64] There is not in Hodge the same recurring concern about certainty that one finds in Alexander. Hodge may well have been driven by his opposition to the Roman Catholic view of tradition. 'If it be proved that tradition is untrustworthy, human, and fallible, then the Scriptures by common consent stand alone in their authority' (ibid. 183).

The errors in matter of fact which skeptics search out bear no proportion to the whole. No sane man would deny that the Parthenon was built of marble, even if here and there a speck of sandstone should be suspected in its structure. Not less unreasonable is it to deny the inspiration of such a book as the Bible, because one sacred writer says that on a given occasion twenty-four thousand, and another says that twenty-three thousand were slain. Surely a Christian may be permitted to tread such objections under his feet.[65]

The methodological strategy was this:

. . . it is unwise in theologians to array themselves needlessly against the teachings of science. Romanists and Protestants vainly resisted the adoption of the Copernican theology of our solar system. They interpreted the Bible in a sense contradictory to that theory. So far as in them lay, they staked the authority of the Bible on the correctness of their interpretation. The theory proved to be true, and the received interpretation had to be given up. The Bible, however, has received no injury, although theologians have been taught an important lesson; that is, to let science take its course, assured that the Scriptures will accommodate themselves to the well-authenticated scientific facts, as they have in time past.[66]

It is admitted that the theologians are not infallible, in their interpretation of scripture. It may, therefore, happen in the future, as it has in the past, that interpretations of the Bible, long confidently received, must be modified or abandoned, to bring revelation into harmony with what God teaches in his works. This change of view as to the true meaning of the Bible may be a painful trial to the Church, but it does not in the least impair the authority of the Scriptures. They are infallible; we are merely convicted of having mistaken their meaning.[67]

[65] *Systematic Theology*, 170. Note how Hodge loads the dice tendentiously by attributing the identification of the difficulties to sceptics. His sceptics include large numbers of those committed to the platitudes of Common Sense Realism. In fact, their concern about certain matters of fact arose precisely because they were committed to a reliabilist epistemology. No wonder Hodge wanted to sweep such problems under his feet; it was from under his own feet that they originated. It is also worth noting that later descendants of the Princeton tradition were embarrassed by this concession. John H. Gerstner finds 'Hodge napping as far as *inerrancy* is concerned' in this passage ('The Contributions of Charles Hodge', 351; emphasis original).

[66] *Systematic Theology*, i.

[67] Ibid. 59. A view remarkably similar to this has been developed of late by Richard Swinburne in *Revelation* (Oxford: Clarendon Press, 1992). Hodge was now fully back into his Common Sense commitments. The ambivalence which haunted the Princeton tradition is clearly visible here. It is also fascinating to

We can see from this exploration of Hodge that the Common Sense tradition lent itself to considerable adaptation as it was mediated through a second generation of Princeton theology. Hodge differed from Alexander in the status he gave to natural theology and in the role he attributed to external as against internal evidence in debates about the rationality of belief in divine revelation. Yet he shared Alexander's ambivalence concerning the ultimate status of the platitudes of Common Sense Realism in theology. Both preferred and vehemently argued for a higher foundation for their theological proposals, even though this entailed a scepticism which they generally repudiated with vigour. This creates an interesting question, as we turn to look at the work of Warfield. Did Warfield develop the fideist position bequeathed by Hodge, or did he revert to the earlier evidentialist tradition of Alexander? Once we have explored this issue and one response it evoked, we shall be in a position to lay out the significance of the Princeton tradition for the discussion on canon and criterion.

note how different this strategy was to that of Alexander. '[E]very particular passage of scripture should be interpreted according to the peculiar circumstances of the case: the literal should be considered as the true meaning, unless some remoter sense be indicated by some peculiar aptitude, correspondence, or fitness, *in the words and ideas of the text*; or unless it be referred to *something else in the Scriptures themselves*. Good sense and the analogy of faith are the guides which we should follow in interpreting the Bible' ('Inaugural Address', 82–3; emphasis added). Alexander was very keen to draw on material from science. Such material made it possible for students of Scripture to solve difficulties and repel the assaults of adversaries. It also enabled the theologian to 'maintain his standing as a man of learning' (ibid. 84).

The Rough Intellectualist Road of a Sound Epistemology

The epistemology of the Scottish Common Sense tradition was a godsend to the great theologians of the Princeton tradition of the nineteenth century. Faced with the powerful attack on the Lockean tradition by Berkeley and Hume, the work of Reid provided a rejoinder which spoke directly to the scepticism which threatened to undermine the intellectual foundations of the Christian tradition. Reid furnished a basic epistemological strategy which secured the actuality of knowledge. He tried to show how one could overcome the difficulties unearthed by Hume, not by meeting Hume on his own ground, but by challenging the underlying assumption that one must first have a criterion or theory of knowledge before one could claim to have knowledge. Theories of knowledge were conceived as essentially second-order operations; one began with what one took to be various instances of knowledge, and from these examples developed an account of the marks of knowledge.

It was Charles Hodge who made the most original and indeed revolutionary use of this strategy. He interpreted the twin pillars of his theism, belief in the existence of God and belief in the existence of special divine revelation, as properly basic beliefs on a par, say, with belief in the existence of the material world or belief in various moral truisms. Within this deployment of Common Sense Realism, natural theology and the traditional arguments for divine revelation were construed as arguments to fend off objections and to provide supplementary support to the original pillars of Christian theism. Yet despite such support, Hodge still insisted that all the truths of theology were really to be found within Scripture, for Scripture provided an infallible source which eliminated any residue of doubt about the foundations of the Christian faith.

This strategy appeared to provide a threefold chord of support for traditional Christian theism. It is difficult to conceive of a stronger case for theism. This case began with a basis in intuition, drove it home by means of various proofs, and then nailed it down once and for all with an infallible canon of Scripture. On the scales of Hodge's epistemic weighing machine, each of these in itself provided certainty, so presumably with three of them, the results were trebled. Paradoxically, however, buried within it was a deep sceptical impulse which went unnoticed. In all likelihood, the primary motivation for positing a totally infallible canon of Scripture arose from a nagging anxiety that the truths of divine revelation, if they were to provide infallible and absolute certainty, had to be transmitted by a form of inspiration which would secure precisely this result.

That nagging anxiety signalled the existence of a surreptitious scepticism. The first two-thirds of Hodge's work was undergirded by a Common Sense Realist epistemology, the last third was driven by a sceptical epistemology. The first two elements in the chord, intuition and proof, posited the general reliability of human perception, memory, ratiocination, and the like; the last element was introduced because of the general unreliability of these very same capacities. It was because human beings were all too liable to make mistakes, to be distorted by their passions and prejudices, to substitute their own subjective proposals in the place of God's Word, that there was a need for a totally infallible record of divine revelation furnished by divine inspiration. Once this need had been identified, then one turned to history in order to ascertain if it had been met. Both Alexander and Hodge triumphantly insisted that it had been abundantly supplied in the Scriptures of the Christian Church. Both also agreed that once we had Scripture in hand, it was possible for theology to be a science. Scripture provided a storehouse of facts which needed to be arranged in an orderly system in the same way that the facts of nature had to be arranged by the natural sciences.

It was left to Benjamin Breckinridge Warfield to uphold this great tradition, to tighten up its loose ends, and to defend it against its critics. Such had been the success of Charles Hodge in developing a truly scientific theology that in that department there was nothing left to be done.[1] So not surprisingly, Warfield never wrote a systematic theology. Moreover, he was reluctant to publish his own work so long as it might interfere with the sales of Hodge's writings. Yet he left behind a massive body of rigorous material which has had an enormous impact at a popular level. We shall look in turn at his general epistemology, his positive apologetics, and his doctrine of Scripture.

One way into Warfield's position is to note that he sided with Reid and Alexander over against Hodge in the place he assigned to argument in attaining the truth about God. He rejected the view that assurance was an immediate matter, insisting that we

assure ourselves that there is knowledge of God in the Scriptures. And before we do that, we must assure ourselves that there is a knowledge of God in the world. And, before we do that, we must assure ourselves that a knowledge of God is possible for man. And, before we do that, we must assure ourselves that there is a God to know. And in working thus back to first principles, we exhibit the indispensability of an 'Apologetical Theology'.[2]

Warfield had a masterly grasp of the current literature on apologetics. In his own proposals he made it abundantly clear that the provision of evidence was essential to the foundations both of faith and of theology as a science. Apologetics was not just the defence of the faith, as in the case of his Dutch Calvinist counterparts; it was basic and primary.

If it is incumbent on the believer to be able to give a reason for the hope that is in him, it is impossible for him to be a believer without a reason for the faith that is in him; and it is the task of apologetics to bring this reason clearly out in his consciousness, and make its validity plain.[3]

---

[1] Warfield expressed his allegiance very graphically: 'Though the power of Charles Hodge may not be upon me, the theology of Charles Hodge is within me, and . . . this is the theology which, according to my ability, I have in my heart to teach to the students of the coming years. Oh, that the mantle of my Elijah might fall upon my shoulders; at least the message that was given to him is set within my lips' (*The Idea of Systematic Theology as a Science* (New York: Anson Randolph & Co., 1888), 5–6).

[2] Introduction to Francis R. Beattie, *Apologetics or the Rational Vindication of Christianity* (Richmond, Va.: Presbyterian Committee of Publications, 1903), 24.

[3] 'Apologetics', in *Studies in Theology* (New York: Oxford University Press, 1932), 4.

This thesis dovetailed with Warfield's account of theology as a genuine science; for once we claim that theology is a science, then we must begin by establishing the facts on which it is based. Apologetics lays the foundations on which the temple of theology is built and by which the whole structure is determined. Without this preliminary work, the whole system would be up in the air. Just as for astronomy there have to be various heavenly bodies, a mind capable of comprehending relevant natural laws, and a means of observing various structures and movements, so for theology there must be a God to constitute its subject-matter, a capacity of the human mind to apprehend and so far comprehend God, and some media by which God is made known to human beings. It is not enough to assume these realities in theology. 'That a theology, as the science of God, may exist, therefore, it must begin by establishing the existence of God, and the capacity of the human mind to know Him, and the accessibility of knowledge concerning Him.'[4] Fully worked out, this will encompass working through the topics of God, religion, revelation, Christianity, and the Bible.

Warfield did not mean that the theologian establishes the separate truths of Christianity individually. The argument proceeds by stages. First, one establishes the existence of God. Second, one establishes the religious nature of human beings and the validity of their religious sense. Third, one establishes the nature of God's relation to the world and the fact of revelation as the condition of all knowledge of God, 'who as personal Spirit can be known only so far as He expresses Himself'.[5] Fourth, one establishes the divine origin of Christianity as the religion of revelation in the sense just specified. Fifth, one establishes the trustworthiness of the Christian Scriptures as the documentation of the only revelation of God for the redemption of sinners.

We can detect in this list the confidence and some of the language of the Scottish Common Sense tradition. We can also detect a contradiction, for the third claim is incompatible with the second. The second posits the validity of a religious sense, thus allowing that religious experience or direct perception of the divine is veridical, so that it furnishes knowledge of the divine, whereas the third restricts knowledge of God to divine revelation. This has

⁴ Ibid. 11.   ⁵ Ibid. 13.

far-reaching consequences for Warfield's doctrine of Scripture, as
we shall see, while it also raises the question of how far the platitudes of the Common Sense tradition remain intact in this arena.

Warfield was not, of course, arguing that skill in formal apologetics was essential to becoming or being a Christian. Yet he is
insisting that evidence of some kind is essential, even as he
equally insisted that the work of the Holy Spirit is absolutely
necessary for a saving faith.[6]

Whenever a sinner accepts Jesus Christ as his Saviour, there is implicated
in that act a living conviction that there is a God, knowable to man, who
has made Himself known in a revelation of Himself for redemption in
Jesus Christ, as is set down in the Scriptures. It is not necessary for his act
of faith that all the grounds of his conviction should be drawn into full
consciousness and given the explicit assent of his understanding, though
it is necessary for his faith that sufficient ground for his conviction be
actively present and working in his spirit. But it is necessary for the
vindication of his faith to reason in the form of scientific judgment, that
the grounds on which it rests be explicated and established.[7]

The task of the Holy Spirit, in turn, depended on the very existence of compelling reasons.

Though faith is the gift of God, it does not in the least follow that the
faith which God gives is an irrational faith, that is, a faith without
cognizable ground in right reason. We believe in Christ because it is

---

[6] It is profoundly misleading to think that Warfield denied the work of the
Holy Spirit in the origination of a saving faith. His position was very similar to
that of Alexander on this issue. He described, on at least one occasion, the 'felt
presence of the Holy Ghost' as 'a fundamental truth of the first importance'
('The Latest Phase of Historical Rationalism', in *Studies in Theology*, 620). There
follows a marvellously eloquent summary of the working of the Holy Spirit in
the Christian life. In their important study, Rogers and McKim mistakenly lump
together Warfield and Hodge in their account of the relation between evidence
and the working of the Holy Spirit in the Princeton tradition. See Jack B.
Rogers and Donald K. McKim, *The Authority and Interpretation of the Bible* (San
Francisco: Harper and Row, 1979), 331–2. They ignore here crucial differences
between Warfield and Hodge in their appropriation of the Common Sense
tradition.

[7] 'Apologetics', 16. Note the double necessity, that for the believer and
that for the theologian. Warfield saw the scholastics of the Middle Ages as especially effective; Augustine and Eusebius were the greatest apologists of the patristic age; but it was in his own day that the apologetics had at last come into its
own. Warfield indulged in a Whig interpretation of the history of apologetics.

rational to believe in Him, not even though it be irrational; but that is not because faith is not the result of evidence, but because a dead soul cannot respond to evidence. The action of the Holy Spirit is not apart from evidence, but along with evidence; and in the first instance consists in preparing the soul for the reception of evidence.[8]

There are no surprises in Warfield's account of the relevant evidence which is available for the Holy Spirit to use. In the case of the existence of God, Warfield looked to the traditional evidence furnished by natural theology. In the case of authentication of the divine revelation vouchsafed to the apostles, the relevant evidence was furnished by miracles. Miracles, in fact, had such a constitutive role in the validation of the apostles that Warfield was utterly convinced that they had ceased with the death of the last apostle. Hence he argued strenuously against the conventional claim that miracles extended into the third or fourth century of the early Church and against alleged miracles in the modern world.[9] Miracles were performed by God to show that the apostles had the right to impose new books in the received canon of Scripture. 'The authority of the apostles, as founders of the Church by divine appointment, was embodied in whatever books they imposed on the Church as law, not merely in those which they themselves had written.'[10]

Much of Warfield's attention was given to articulating the nature of the divine inspiration which brought these books into existence and to defending inspiration against the rising tide of critics who attacked it. He held that the way to proceed in understanding inspiration was to be inductive. This meant examining to the actual character of the writings designated as inspired,

---

[8] Ibid. 15. Elsewhere Warfield wrote: 'Does God the Holy Spirit work a blind and ungrounded faith in the heart? What is supplied by the Holy Spirit in working faith in the heart surely is not a ready-made faith, rooted in nothing and clinging without reason to its object; nor yet grounds of belief in the object presented; but just a new power to the heart to respond to the grounds of faith, sufficient in themselves, already present in the mind' (John E. Meeter (ed.), *Selected Shorter Writings of Benjamin B. Warfield* (Phillipsburg, NJ: Presbyterian and Reformed Publishing Company, 1970), ii. 116). Warfield's essay 'On Faith in its Psychological Aspects', in *Studies in Theology*, 313–42, is a sophisticated and thorough elaboration of his position.

[9] *Counterfeit Miracles* (London: Banner of Truth, 1972). Warfield comes across as unbelieving as the vulgar rationalists he elsewhere excoriates.

[10] 'Latest Phase of Historical Rationalism', 645.

most especially to what was said therein concerning the nature of inspiration. One of his favourite ways of expressing his views was in terms of historical theology.

The Church, then, has held from the beginning that the Bible is the Word of God in such a sense that its words, though written by men and bearing indelibly impressed upon them the marks of their human origin, were written, nevertheless, under such an influence of the Holy Ghost as to be also the words of God, the adequate expression of His mind and will. It has always recognized that this conception of co-authorship implies that the Spirit's superintendence extends to the choice of the words by human authors (verbal inspiration), and preserves its product from everything inconsistent with a divine author-ship—thus securing, among other things, that entire truthfulness which is everywhere presupposed in and asserted by the Biblical writers (inerrancy).[11]

Suppose, however, that there appeared to be errors in the text. Given his Common Sense commitments to the general validity of the human cognitive faculties and operations in those who read the text, Warfield had to deal with observations which conflicted with the inferred effects of inspiration. Hodge had dismissed these as mere specks of sandstone which could be set aside. Warfield had a much more comprehensive defence. He pushed the standards of observation as high as possible, so that the possibility of a conflicting observation would be reduced to a minimum. The critical investigation had to be made, and all had to abide by the ensuing results, but the results were likely to come out on Warfield's side. He laid down three conditions of proof:

(1) . . . let it be proved that each alleged discrepant statement certainly occurred in the original autograph of the sacred book in which it is said to be found. (2) Let it be proved that the interpretation which occasions the apparent discrepancy is the one which the passage was evidently intended to bear. It is not sufficient to show a difficulty which may spring out of our defective knowledge of the circumstances. The true meaning must be definitively and certainly ascertained, and then shown to be irreconcilable with other known truth. (3) Let it be proved that

[11] 'The Real Problem of Inspiration', in *The Inspiration and Authority of the Bible* (Philadelphia: Presbyterian and Reformed Publishing Company, 1948), 173.

the true sense of some part of the original autograph is directly and necessarily inconsistent with some certainly-known fact of history or truth of science, or some other statement of Scripture certainly ascertained and interpreted.[12]

Not surprisingly, Warfield concluded that the case against his position had never been successfully prosecuted.

In the essays related to inspiration Warfield's mind was like a steel trap. Sometimes drawing on the exact arguments of his predecessors, he would lure the opponent into the premises of his position and relentlessly draw him within the boundaries of the consequences. Equally thoroughly, he staked out a defence which was designed to be impregnable. Yet, as happened in the case of Alexander and Reid, his deliberations rested at one crucial point on a general scepticism which was never recognized. Thus at one moment he claimed that inspiration was an incidental feature of the Christian faith on which nothing rested intellectually. In the very same essay he reversed himself to insist that a departure from his theory of inspiration would undercut all the relevant evidence there is for the Christian faith. Unravelling this shift is crucial to showing that the fault-line he inherited from Alexander and Hodge had reached breaking-point.

The initial claim was this:

Let it not be said that thus we found the whole Christian system upon the doctrine of plenary inspiration. We found the whole Christian system on the doctrine of plenary inspiration as little as we found it on the doctrine of angelic existences. Were there no such thing as inspiration, Christianity would be true, and all its essential doctrines would be credibly witnessed to us in the generally trustworthy reports of the teaching of our Lord and of His authoritative agents in founding the Church, preserved in the writings of the apostles and their first followers, and in the historical witness of the living Church. Inspiration is not the most fundamental of Christian doctrines, nor even the first thing we prove about the scriptures. It is the last and crowning fact as to the Scriptures. These we first prove authentic, historically credible, generally trustworthy, before we prove them inspired. And the proof of their authenticity, credibility, general

---

[12] 'Inspiration', in Mark A. Noll (ed.), *The Princeton Theology, 1812–1921* (Grand Rapids, Mich.: Baker, 1983), 232. This paper was jointly written with A. A. Hodge, but the material in question was by Warfield.

trustworthiness would give us a firm basis for Christianity prior to any knowledge on our part of their inspiration, and apart indeed from the existence of inspiration.[13]

Immediately, Warfield proceeded to turn this on its head by insisting that giving up inspiration would entail giving up the evidence on which our trust in Scripture rests.

We do not think that the doctrine of plenary inspiration is the ground of Christian faith, but if it is held and taught by the New Testament writers, we think it an important element in the Christian faith; a very important and valuable element; an element that appeals to our acceptance on precisely the same ground as every other element of the faith, viz., on the ground of our recognition of the New Testament as trustworthy witnesses to doctrine; an element of the Christian faith, therefore which cannot be rejected without logically undermining our trust in all other elements of distinctive Christianity by undermining the evidence on which this trust rests. We must indeed prove the authenticity, credibility and general trustworthiness of the New Testament writings before we prove inspiration; and even were they not inspired this proof would remain valid and we should give them accordant trust. But just because this proof is valid, we must trust these writings in their witness to their inspiration, if they give such witness; and if we refuse to trust them here, we have in principle refused them trust everywhere. In such circumstances their inspiration is bound up with their trustworthiness, and therefore all else that we receive from them.[14]

The difficulty in these passages is that Warfield has denied and then affirmed that the central doctrines of Christianity and inspiration are logically separable from the point of view of the evidence available for them. In one breath, one can have all the central doctrines of Christianity without even the existence of inspiration; in the next breath, if we reject inspiration, we cannot have the central doctrines.

The bridge which links inspiration and the central doctrines is the trustworthiness of the apostles. How can we interpret Warfield's use of this notion to unravel the difficulty? Perhaps the argument was this. Given the trustworthiness of the apostles, we read that they teach central Christian doctrines, and we believe these central Christian doctrines. We then discover that they also teach that they themselves are inspired. If we have accepted their trustworthiness on the general doctrines, we must now trust them in respect of their inspiration. Hence, if we reject their inspiration, we have to reject their general trustworthiness. If we reject their trustworthiness, we have lost the evidence for general Christian doctrines and must abandon them.

Aside from the dubious assumption that the witnesses teach their own inspiration in the sense required and enunciated by Warfield, the problem with this construction is that it is unconvincing.[15] First, it is not essential to the general reliability of a witness that the witness be infallible or absolutely, 100 per cent reliable. All that is required is that the witness be overall reliable; a single mistake does not negate that general reliability; otherwise we could not rely on any witness, for no witness is completely reliable. Hence it is entirely consistent theoretically to reject the claim concerning inspiration and retain the general reliability thesis.

Second, the whole procedure of dividing up Christianity into subsets of doctrine cuts across Warfield's general strategy in his apologetics. That strategy was to take Christianity as a whole and establish its basis in divine revelation, rather than argue for its essential doctrines as a separate item over against divine inspiration. Indeed, Warfield expressly repudiated this latter option.

In establishing the truth of Christianity, it has been perennially asked, are we to deal with all its details (e.g. H. B. Smith), or merely with the essence of Christianity (e.g. Kübel). The true answer is neither. Apologetics does not presuppose either the development of Christianity into its details, or the extraction from it of its essence. The details of Christianity are all contained in Christianity: the minimum of Christianity is just Christianity itself. What apologetics undertakes to establish is just this Christianity itself—including all its 'details' and involving its 'essence'—in its unexplicated and uncompressed entirety,

---

[15] There are, in fact, very deep questions about this whole strategy which the Princeton theologians never faced. First, they nowhere show how trustworthiness as historical guides can underwrite the theological and doctrinal claims of the Christian tradition. Historical claims do not in themselves establish theological claims. All that the Princeton tradition had to offer here was the conventional argument from miracle. Second, the later Princeton tradition never grasped the logic of the objections developed by Ernst Troeltsch, who insisted that the very logic of historical investigation undermined traditional theological claims about divine action. Both issues needed to be addressed if the Princeton tradition was to withstand scrutiny.

as the absolute religion. It has for its object the laying of the foundations on which the temple of theology is built, and by which the whole structure of theology is determined.[16]

Clearly something has gone astray here, for Warfield is much too systematic and careful a thinker to suffer such a lapse unless something really crucial were at stake. The claim that the central doctrines can be established independently of divine inspiration may well have been an unconscious attempt to draw the opponent into a trap. As every component of the Faith stood or fell together for Warfield, then, once commitment to the central doctrines was secured, the commitment to his account of inspiration would necessarily follow, once the full force of the position had been registered. Hence it was distinctly to Warfield's apologetic advantage to concede that it was possible to have the central doctrines without inspiration. Alternatively, Warfield may have been trying to stave off a charge of having begged the question by suggesting that the divine inspiration is established not by appeal to Scripture itself but by a set of independent considerations which also establish other doctrines of the Faith.

Yet this could only be a temporary manœuvre, for there is a much deeper issue lurking in the wings.[17] There are two clues which bear pursuit. In a footnote related to the passage on the significance of inspiration, Warfield drew attention to two things.

---

[16] 'Apologetics', 9.

[17] The dilemma is missed by David Kelsey's reading of Warfield. Kelsey takes Warfield to be claiming that 'the doctrine of inspiration is *methodologically indispensable* for doing theology Warfield's way, but *logically dispensable* so far as the explication and defense of other doctrines' (*The Uses of Scripture in Recent Theology* (London: SCM Press, 1921); emphasis original). Kelsey misses Warfield's second claim that plenary inspiration is an element of the Christian faith 'which cannot be rejected without *logically undermining* our trust in all the other elements of distinctive Christianity *by undermining the evidence* on which this trust rests' ('The Real Problem of Inspiration', 212; emphasis added). Kelsey also suggests that Warfield's construal of Scripture is really based on his and the Church's experience of the Scripture as a religious object (*Uses of Scripture*, 24). This ignores Warfield's distinction between the Church's experience as a witness to the inspiration of the Bible down through history and the Church's experience as the basis of the Church's doctrine of inspiration. This matter is forcefully discussed in a remarkable essay of Warfield, 'Augustine's Doctrine of Knowledge and Authority', in *Studies in Tertullian and Augustine* (New York: Oxford University Press, 1930), 183–225.

First, he insisted that inspiration was '(1) that element which gives detailed *certitude to the delivery of doctrine* in the New Testament, and (2) the element by which the individual Christian is brought into *immediate relation with the revelation of truth* through the prophets and apostles'.[18] Second, he quoted a version of the classical slippery slope argument from Hodge. Once inspiration was abandoned, averred Hodge, then 'a wet sponge was passed over all the doctrines of redemption and their outlines obliterated'.[19] If one abandoned inspiration, then eventually all the central doctrines would also be abandoned. What connects these two observations is the quest for certainty. In the last analysis, as we saw in the case of Alexander and Hodge, Warfield really rested his doctrines on the doctrine of inspiration. Inspiration provided a divine guarantee; it gave detailed certitude to the believer; it entailed that all the historical critics must be wrong in relying on their witnesses against the divine authority of Scripture.[20]

We can approach the issue from a slightly different direction. For Warfield it was essential that there be divine revelation, if certain crucial elements in his theology—say, the terms on which a person is justified or the nature of life after death—were to be secured. Neither natural theology alone, nor religious experience alone, nor a combination of the two together could underwrite the specific doctrines held by Christians on these issues. Revelation gave crucial knowledge which was not otherwise available. Revelation constituted an indispensable external authority in religion. For this reason Warfield was an implacable enemy of rationalism and mysticism.[21]

It was his contention that the need for the provision of this revelation had been graciously supplied by God. He was equally convinced that there was good evidence that this provision was

---

[18] 'Apologetics', 212; emphasis added.　　　　　　　　　　　[19] Ibid.

[20] Warfield is very clear that among the features that put the science of theology beyond all comparison to all other sciences is 'the certainty with which its data can be determined' ('The Idea of Systematic Theology', in *Studies in Theology*, 68). Furthermore, he argued that the certainty of faith was on a par with the certainty of sight. See 'Herman Bavinck', in Noll (ed.), *Princeton Theology*, 306–7.

[21] For Warfield, mysticism differs from technical rationalism 'only in a matter of temperature, the feelings and not cold reason alone being involved' ('The Latest Phase of Historical Rationalism', 590).

materially given in Christianity, more specifically in the Bible. Up to this point he was a Common Sense Realist.

He then proceeded to argue that an infallible record of that revelation must also be available if rationalism and mysticism were to be avoided. This does not follow. All that is needed to secure his position is reliable access to divine revelation. Given the platitudes of Common Sense Realism, he can legitimately claim that human agents are capable of identifying, understanding, and recording the revelation. These acts can be done without any absolute assurance of infallibility; all that is needed is a reliable capacity to get the job done. However, in all likelihood, Warfield thought that the absence of infallibility entailed the embrace of either rationalism or mysticism, positions which on his analysis he had already quite rightly rejected. It was this confusion which created the crack in the door for the entry of scepticism. Being rightly sceptical of the resources of rationalism and mysticism, he transferred that scepticism to the gap between a reliable and an infallible record of revelation. This in turned required that he attack his earlier commitments to the reliability of the recorders of revelation. Consequently, he could not be satisfied with anything less than a divinely revealed record of the original revelation. Anything less would spell disaster for theology by driving us into the arms of rationalism or mysticism.

The significance of this is simple. Despite the whole structure of his positive epistemology, Warfield was a sceptic about human cognitive capacities when it came to recording the content of divine revelation. Despite all his positive talk about the cruciality and reliability of objective evidence, there was a failure of nerve when it came to the justification of theological claims. The only adequate foundation, the only resting-place, for securing the certainty he required lay with an infallible, divine inspiration.

His own version of the wet sponge argument revealed the truth of the matter. It began with his characteristic epistemic optimism:

Without any inspiration we could have had Christianity; yea men would still have heard the truth, and through it been awakened, and justified and sanctified and glorified. The verities of our faith would remain historically proven to us—so bountiful has God been in his fostering care—even had we no Bible; and through these verities salvation.[22]

---

[22] 'Real Problem of Inspiration', 211.

It then passed immediately into unmitigated scepticism.

But to what uncertainties and doubts would they be prey!—and to what errors, constantly begetting worse errors, exposed!—to what refuges, all of them refuges of lies, driven! Look but at those who have lost the knowledge of this infallible guide: see them evincing man's most pressing need by inventing for themselves an infallible church, or even an infallible pope. Revelation is but half revelation unless it be infallibly communicated; it is but half communicated unless it be infallibly recorded. The heathen in their blindness are our witnesses of what becomes of an unrecorded revelation. Let us bless God, then, for His inspired word! And may He grant that we may always cherish, love and venerate it, and conform all our life and thinking to it! So may we find safety for our feet, and peaceful security for our souls.[23]

One can only marvel at this development. To finish out the development of his argument, Warfield should have called not just for an infallible revelation, an infallible record, and an infallible communication. He should also have summoned up the resources of an infallible listener to receive them, an infallible interpretation to understand them, an infallible memory to retain them, and of an infallible insight to apply them aright to life. Given the litany of uncertainties, doubts, errors, and lies, how else can poor sinners find safety for their feet? However, the great logician drew back in silence. It was perhaps well that he did, for his own discourse would then have exposed the deep hiatus in his epistemic commitments. He appealed to objective historical evidence to secure the trustworthiness of his witnesses to doctrinal truth, and thereby revealed his commitment to the platitudes of the Common Sense tradition. However, his arguments on the cruciality of divine inspiration manifest a scepticism about the validity of those same platitudes. If he had followed through fully in the expression of his scepticism, the platitudes of Common Sense would have publicly disintegrated.

What Warfield failed to see was quickly identified and pursued by others in the Calvinist tradition. Inspired by a very different epistemological trajectory in Holland, they pressed home the sceptical consequences of their Calvinism by arguing that the difference between the redeemed and the unredeemed stretched right down to the very presuppositions of what counted as factual.

---

[23] *Inspiration and Authority of the Bible*, 422.

It would be a distraction here to enter into a mapping of this some-what remote but fascinating epistemological planet, but the criti-cism registered there against Warfield was on target.[24] At the very least he had provided a point of entry for the Calvinists into the consistency of his position. It is bad enough that human agents are naturally subject to error and liable to entertain lies and falsehood. The epistemic predicament is immeasurably worse if Calvinism is true. If human agents are as sinful as Calvin and the Westminster divines have shown, if regeneration creates an epistemic divide between the redeemed and the unredeemed, if recognition of the canon of Scripture as the Word of God is a matter of the inner testimony of the elect, then the darkness is indeed great. There is no neutral, objective, non-person-relative fact or reason to which to appeal. Everything, including the very laws of logic, will be justifiable only by means of grace and revelation. Reason will be within the limits of double predestination alone.[25]

To be sure, there are mitigating factors at work to soften the consequences, and Warfield was adept at exploiting some of them in debates with his Dutch opponents.[26] On the one hand, there

[24] Some of the major figures in this territory are Abraham Kuyper, Herman Bavinck, Herman Dooyeweerd, Cornelius Van Til, and Gordon Clark. For a fine discussion of the logic of this tradition see Harriet Anne Harris, 'The Banner of Truth: Fundamentalism and its Influence on Evangelicalism' (D.Phil. diss., Oxford, 1994), 234–315. For a very good review of the possible logical relations between Common Sense Realism and Calvinism see Paul Helm, 'Thomas Reid, Common Sense and Calvinism', in Hendrik Hart, Johan Van Der Hoeven, and Nicholas Wolterstorff (eds.), *Rationality in the Calvinian Tradition* (Boston: University Press of America, 1983), 71–92.

[25] In its own way this competing Calvinist tradition may be in the neigh-bourhood of two crucial problems in the Reidian position. First, Reidians tended to be too quick to appeal to psychological factors like prejudice, bad education, and passion to deal with those who did not find the platitudes of Common Sense compelling. Second, Reidians were never really able to show why one could not be a sceptic about the platitudes of Common Sense at the level of epistemology while remaining committed to them in everyday life as a set of heuristic commit-ments. This was more or less the position of Hume. There are ways to address these issues, but Reid's depth and philosophical acumen, despite serious lapses here and there on his part, were not always matched by his successors.

[26] See e.g. 'Herman Bavinck', 303–7. For a wonderfully measured statement of the presuppositionalist position as contrasted with the position held by a scholar whose position was close to, if not identical with, that of Warfield, see George Marsden, 'J. Gresham Machen, History, and Truth', *Westminster Theological Review*, 42 (1979–80), 171–3. Marsden presents a thoroughly sensible mediating position.

was common grace at work to explain how the unredeemed shared the beliefs of the redeemed. On the other hand, there was enough continuing sin in the redeemed to explain why the elect were subject to the same epistemic stresses and strains as the non-elect. So various components of the Calvinist vision could be deployed to smooth the rough edges of the initial dichotomies.

Yet even the most cursory summary of this reversal of the Princeton tradition on the relation between faith and reason displays once more the price which is paid when Christian intellectuals insist on treating the canons of the Church as an epistemic foundation *tout court*. Reacting against the invasion of the Church by alien theories of knowledge, it is not surprising that other intellectuals decide to fight fire with fire. How better to do this than to reverse the whole operation. Rather than make the canons of the Church subservient to an independent epistemology, why not make epistemology dependent on the canons of the Faith? The reverse strategy is to make access to Scripture a presupposition of genuine epistemology, and, if need be, build this thesis into the very confessional commitments of one's institutions and Churches. The reliability of the senses, the laws of logic, intuition, memory, and the like is now dependent on Holy Scripture. The unbeliever, of course, will rely on these cognitive capacities and processes. This is precisely how God has made them to operate. The ultimate validity of these capacities and operations depends, however, on the creative activity of God; hence a whole new negative apologetic can be developed to show that the unbeliever has no epistemic right to them unless they convert to theism.

We have already begun to trespass into an evaluation of the whole Princeton tradition. Thus, in the case of Alexander, Hodge, and Warfield we have detected a deep ambivalence about the place of reason in their account of the foundations of theology. On the one side, they want to rely on reason to provide the evidence for the pillars of their theistic commitments. The peculiar position of Hodge, by contrast with Alexander, and Warfield does not alter this judgement. All three were committed to the platitudes of Scottish Common Sense Realism which presupposed a bedrock commitment to the reliability of our cognitive capacities and practices. On the other side, they were convinced that the only satisfactory foundation for theology was the divine inspiration of the Scriptures, for this provided absolute certainty that the ultimate source of theological proposals came with immediate divine assurance.

They were equally convinced that dropping this specific foundation would spell an end of the Faith. To say that they were afraid and that they trembled at the ark of faith at this point would be an understatement. This fear and trembling was driven by a profound scepticism about human reason. Even though reason had provided the evidence for the existence of God and for the location of divine revelation, it could not be trusted to make a fair evaluation of the Scriptures on the basis of the very same cognitive capacities and processes which had been agreed to be so trustworthy in the initial construction of their system. Hence the Princeton tradition found itself cornered. It could stick to its general epistemic principles and maintain the trustworthiness of human cognition, or it could rework its epistemic position by seeking to find a different way of dealing with the scepticism lurking in its own bosom. The crisis which this choice precipitated broke the tradition in two. Eventually, the more radical alternative found a home at Westminster Seminary.[27] A crisis in epistemology, masked as a problem concerning a pivotal canon of the Church, the Holy Scriptures, had led once more to a deep split in the body of the Protestant heritage.

We need now to broaden our evaluation in order to provide a more comprehensive account of the significance of the deployment of the epistemic resources of Common Sense Realism in response to the ongoing canonical crisis of the Church in the West. In a rare moment of levity Charles Hodge made the following comment on the work of a rival adherent to the Reidian tradition, Charles Finney: 'It is like one of those spiral staircases, which lead to the top of some high tower, without a landing from the base to the summit; which if a man has once ascended, he resolves never to do the like again.'[28] Ironically, that appears to have been the fate of the great Princeton theologians. Despite the extraordinary range and depth of their learning, the

[27] An intriguing figure who held the line on the platitudes of the Common Sense tradition was Gresham Machen, but his position was supplanted at Westminster by that of Cornelius Van Til.

[28] 'Finney's Lectures on Theology', in Noll (ed.), *The Princeton Theology*, 167.

genuineness of their piety, the thoroughness of their arguments, their persistent pursuit of the good of the Church, and the sheer magnitude of their writings, they are rarely given the attention they deserve. The problems they tackled were central in their day, and the intellectual energy they expended to resolve them was formidable. They were brilliant polemical writers, and their work as a whole bears fitting testimony to the perennial intellectual fecundity of the Reformed tradition.

It is quite unsatisfactory to dismiss them as reactionary scholastics who were out of touch with the trials of modernity. On the contrary, they were figures whose fundamental work cannot be understood outside the contours of the Enlightenment traditions which they inherited and internalized. They perpetuated the same underlying obsession with the epistemic status of theology that is visible in Schleiermacher. They were haunted by a Cartesian anxiety which would be satisfied by nothing less than the attainment of absolute, infallible certainty. They shared the same foundationalist sensibilities within and outside their theology that has been a central mark of the modern period. In their own way they looked to philosophy for the salvation of the Faith.

The two basic moves they made are thoroughly modern. First, the attempt to secure the epistemic status of theology by arguing that it is a genuine science is a recurring one. The current work of such figures as Richard Swinburne and Michael Banner repeats the same tune with a different verse.[29] Second, they drew heavily on the work of Thomas Reid. Attending to the work of Reid as an inspiration for new vistas in epistemology which have special relevance for theology is a full-scale industry. So there is ample cause to look carefully at the insights and difficulties of the Princeton tradition.

The crucial insights which they worked with were surely these:

1. The Christian tradition in its historic form is deeply dependent on divine revelation in history which can only be reached through the relevant testimony. There is, therefore, dependence on an authoritative tradition which is inescapable. No matter

[29] Richard Swinburne, *The Existence of God* (Oxford: Clarendon Press, 1979); Michael C. Banner, *The Justification of Science and the Rationality of Religious Belief* (Oxford: Clarendon Press, 1990).

how narrowly or widely understood, reason alone cannot directly supply the content of the faith. This was a bedrock concern of the Princeton theologians.

2. The careful, self-critical study of the canons of the Church, most especially the Scriptures, will always be a marked feature of the Christian Faith. The Princeton concern with induction, despite its naïve form, will always be attractive, because, as applied to the texts of the tradition, this is one way to safeguard access to the manifold riches of the heritage as a whole. Comprehensive study of the biblical material, using all the relevant tools at the disposal of scholarship, is essential to the health of the Christian faith.

3. The adequate articulation and defence of the Christian tradition in its cultural setting make it inevitable that Christian intellectuals will be called upon to provide relevant responses to the epistemic questions which arise within and without. Princeton was typical in its concern with this arena. Within it Christians will very naturally be drawn to the exploration of the human mind itself and of its complex operations, because these are not perceived in a neutral fashion but as a gift from God. The relationshp between theology and epistemology, between nature and grace, is a crucial matter which deserves close attention.

4. Princeton theologians were consistently committed to the view that genuine human knowledge of God and his nature is possible. Such knowledge has a vital role to play in salvation, hence some kind of access to a real world which is logically independent of the human subject is essential. Moreover, crucial knowledge of God is mediated in historical events; hence reliable testimony about such events is equally essential.

5. Another issue which played a central role in the Princeton trajectory was that of the place and ground of certainty in faith. Clearly the work and witness of the Holy Spirit need extended exploration in relation to this topic. The differences within the Princeton tradition on this matter suggest that there is much unfinished business in this field.

6. The perpetuation of the Princeton tradition across a full century is standing testimony to the significance of the handing over of the treasures of the Christian faith across space and time. There is a moving story of the aged Alexander, shortly before

his death in 1851, handing over a carved, white bone walking-stick to Charles Hodge, instructing him to leave this cane 'to your successor in office, that it may be handed down as a kind of symbol of orthodoxy'.[30] This is not quite what one expects from great stalwarts of the Reformed tradition, yet it bears eloquent testimony to the role of leaders and institutions in the continuation of the Faith.[31] This social component is a vital feature in the continuity of the canonical traditions of the Church.

The pursuit of these insights and topics should not blind us, however, to the severe difficulties which are embedded in the great Princeton experiment. We shall look now at some of the consequences of the Princeton position by reviewing a brief cata-logue of significant issues. We shall begin with a comment on the prospects for theology as a science, drawing on the latest Princeton articulation of this. In the course of our short journey we shall draw attention, where appropriate, to the impact of epis-temology on the life of the Church.

One of the major problems in the Princetonian proposal that theology should be construed as an inductive science is that it is quite impossible to execute. Consider what is needed. Granting for the moment that scripture contains all the facts that need to be covered,[32] the theologian has first to carry out the task of exegeti-cal theology, interpreting every text according to appropriate hermeneutical procedures. When that is done, then the theolo-gian has to engage in biblical theology.

The task of Biblical Theology, in a word, is the task of coordinating the scattered results of continuous exegesis into a concatenated whole, whether with reference to a single book of Scripture or to a body of related books or to the whole Scriptural fabric. Its chief object is not to find differences of conception between the various writers, though some recent students of the subject seem to think this is so much their duty, that when they cannot find differences they make them. It is to reproduce

[30] Quoted in John C. Vander Stelt, *Philosophy and Scripture* (Marlton, NJ: Mack, 1978), 120.

[31] The place of institutions in the perpetuation of the Princeton tradition is well brought out by Noll in 'Introduction', in *The Princeton Theology*, 18–24.

[32] Warfield, following the lead of Hodge, provides a lucid account of his reason for this claim in 'Idea of Systematic Theology', 61.

the theological thought of each writer or group of writers in the form in which it lay in their own minds, so that we may be enabled to look at all their theological statements at their angle and to understand all their deliverances as modified and conditioned by their own point of view.[33]

This then provides the raw material for systematic theology. The systematic theologian takes this material and brings it into a more complex arrangement.

The immediate work of exegesis may be compared to the work of a recruiting officer; it draws out from the mass of mankind the men who are to constitute the army. Biblical Theology organizes these men into companies and regiments and corps, arranged in marching order and accoutered for service. Systematic Theology combines these companies and regiments and corps into an army—a single and unitary whole, determined by its own all-pervasive principle. It, too, is composed of men—the same men which were recruited by the Exegetics; but it is composed of these men, not as individuals merely, but in their due relations to the other men of their companies and regiments and corps.[34]

Exegetical theology and biblical theology furnish the direct materials related to systematic theology. The indirect materials which have a bearing on it are encompassed by all the data bearing on its problems supplied by all the sciences and by the material supplied by natural and comparative theology, as gathered up in apologetics.

This is a preposterous undertaking. It is ludicrous to think that this kind of territory can be studied, critically examined, and worked up into a coherent system with any measure of success. One would have to be virtually omniscient to execute such a project.[35] Yet Warfield believed that the results of such work were essential to the attainment of holiness. He held that such knowledge was an essential prerequisite for a sanctified character.[36] It was not even enough to know the separate doctrines which emerged from such research. The internal relation to other

---

[33] Warfield, 'Idea of Systematic Theology', 65–6.   [34] Ibid. 67–8.

[35] I am not here claiming that no good is to be gained from engaging in the development of 'biblical theology'. There can well be a place for this kind of work in the economy of scholarship and in the life of the Church. What is at stake here is the precariousness of such work in itself and the oddity of making this work essential to the very existence of systematic theology. We need an entirely different way of conceiving the relationship between biblical material and systematic theology.   [36] Ibid. 80.

doctrines in the total system needed to be known, if the full effect in life was to be gained.[37] All Warfield's efforts to secure the Faith for the ordinary believer by means of his doctrine of inspiration are dissipated at one stroke by this thesis.

It is not surprising, given the contingent impossibility of this methodological proposal, that Warfield was profoundly dependent on the tradition of the Church in the actual articulation of any system of doctrine. It was the tradition of the Church which actually furnished him with his specific doctrines. Despite intense avowals about developing a biblical theology, he was captive to his native Presbyterian confessions of faith[38] and to his own list of Fathers.[39] It was these prior commitments, along with his prior convictions about the unity of the biblical material derived from his doctrine of inspiration, which controlled his reading of Scripture. The supreme irony is that Warfield was forced to impose upon Scripture his own subjective requirements. He could not let Scripture be itself, but constantly interpreted it so that it harmonized with his prior methodological constraints. Eventually this also spilled over into his handling of historical theology.

Especially interesting in this context is the way that his epistemological requirements constrained his interpretation of Scripture. The obvious case is his treatment of miracle. Given that miracle must function as a credential for divine revelation,

[37] Ibid. 83. It is interesting that Warfield embraced a coherentist account of truth at this point.

[38] Professors at Princeton were restricted by oath from teaching or insinuating anything contrary to the Westminster Confession of Faith or the Catechisms. See General Assembly of the Presbyterian Church in the USA, *The Plan of the Theological Seminary* (Philadelphia: Aitken, 1816), 11. Thomas Reid was also severely bound by oath. 'I, in the presence of the omniscient and all-powerful God, vow and swear that I will sincerely profess the doctrine and faith of the Scottish Church (inasmuch as it plainly sets forth teachings taken from the pure word of God), the one and only orthodox church, right to the last breath of my life, standing in strong abhorrence of all heresies of popes and of any others.' (*The Philosophical Orations of Thomas Reid* (Carbondale and Edwardsville, Ill.: Southern Illinois University Press, 1989), 39). Despite this, Paul Helm has questioned Reid's commitments to Calvinism. See 'Thomas Reid, Common Sense and Calvinism', 81.

[39] 'Augustine determined for all time the doctrine of grace, Anselm the doctrine of atonement, Luther the doctrine of forensic justification' ('Idea of Systematic Theology', 78).

and given that divine revelation is confined to the canon, Warfield's whole apologetic would collapse were miracles to happen beyond the lives of the apostles. Warfield's solution was simple.[40] Alleged miracles after the time of the apostles were counterfeit.[41] Like with some of his Calvinist forebears, Warfield was forced to make a distinction between the ordinary and the extraordinary working of the Spirit and to argue that only the former is present in the Church today. In such a fashion was the meaning and significance of the Scriptures set aside in order to accommodate Warfield's epistemological requirements.

By far the most blatant effects of this in his historical theology cropped up in the very core of his position: that is, in his doctrine of inspiration. The crux of the matter is this. Warfield presented his interpretation of inspiration as both biblical and historical. He never tired of pointing out that he was simply presenting the doctrine of the Church as it had been held throughout the ages. However, he systematically and conveniently ignored the plain historical facts. First, the Church never at any time prior to the Reformation adopted a canonical account of inspiration. In fact, the early Church never even sanctioned a doctrine of divine revelation, content to leave this matter in the Scriptures and in the writings of the Fathers in an informal state.

Second, and much more important, Warfield's own predecessors more often than not held to a doctrine of divine dictation, the precise doctrine which Warfield rejected. Thus, to go no further than Turretin, whose massive text in systematic theology was used for a generation at Princeton before it was replaced by the work of Charles Hodge, we find the following comment: 'Nor can we readily believe that God, who dictated and inspired each and every word to these inspired (*theopneustois*) men, would not take care of their entire preservation.'[42] Warfield was so blinded by his own theorizing that he totally ignored this material. Charles Hodge before him went so far as to express agreement with a theory of

---

[40] Alexander takes a similar, although much less developed, position to that of Warfield. See the curt dismissal in *Evidences of the Authenticity, Inspiration and Canonical Authority of the Holy Scriptures* (Philadelphia: Presbyterian Board of Education, 1836), 186.

[41] This is the central thesis of *Counterfeit Miracles*.

[42] Francis Turretin, *Institutes of Elenctic Theology* (Phillipsburg, NJ: Presbyterian and Reformed Publishing Company: 1992), i. 71.

dictation and apparently not notice what he was doing. Referring to the doctrine of the Scriptures, he wrote:

On this subject Romanists agree with Protestants, (1.) In teaching the plenary inspiration and consequent infallible authority of the sacred writings. Of these writings the Council of Trent says that God is their author, and that they were written by the dictation of the Holy Spirit ('Spiritu sancto dictante').[43]

What Warfield failed to recognize was that his doctrine of inspiration, while it fastened on various aspects of the work of a host of writers on the topic, represented a remarkable reconstruction of that material in order to ensure that he could have the kind of foundations which he considered essential for theology. He brought together a theory of divine agency, a doctrine of providence, a battery of favoured biblical texts, a carefully selected network of historical materials, and the common modes of inference. Once assembled, he shielded his theory from criticism come hell or high water. The standards of proof he deployed were a carefully fabricated, impregnable wall of defence.

This was one more point at which any commitment to the Reidian tradition was abandoned. Reid was extremely wary of these kinds of constructions. He was exceptionally sensitive to the way human agents could ignore the facts to suit themselves. 'When a man has, with labour and ingenuity, wrought up an hypothesis into a system, he contracts a fondness for it, which is apt to warp the best judgment.'[44] 'When a man has laid out all his ingenuity in fabricating a system, he views it with the eye of a parent; he strains phenomena to make them tally with it, and makes it look like the work of nature.'[45] 'These facts are phenomena . . . of nature, from which we justly argue against any hypothesis, however generally received. But to argue from a hypothesis against facts, is contrary to the rules of true philosophy.'[46] All the transgressions mentioned here by Reid can be found in Warfield's handling of the biblical and historical materials.

[43] Charles Hodge, *Systematic Theology* (3 vols., Grand Rapids, Mich.: Eerdmans, n.d.), i. 194.

[44] Reid, *Essays on the Intellectual Powers of Man*, in *Works* ed. Sir William Hamilton (2 vols., Edinburgh: James Thin, 1895), i. 250.

[45] Ibid. 472.

[46] Reid, *An Inquiry into the Human Mind*, in *Works*, i. 132.

The net effect of Warfield's epistemological proposals on the reading of Scripture and tradition is that they are spiritually and intellectually suffocating. One of his critics, Thomas Lindsay, astutely drew attention to this feature of the Princeton doctrine of inspiration.

Now I ask, is this a theory which can be called religious in the deepest sense of the word? Inerrancy makes no appeal to heart or conscience. It cannot touch the deep springs of sinful human nature. I do not mean to discuss the question of fact. For my own part, I do not care to use 'error' as applied to the Bible, but this whole question of the formal inerrancy of Scripture seems to me to be trivial in the extreme. My sense of the infallibility of the Bible is in no way affected by the knowledge that while the author of the Second Book of Samuel says that David bought the threshing floor and oxen of Ornan for fifty shekels of silver, the author of the First Book of Chronicles says that the price was 600 shekels of gold. I say simply there is some discrepancy here; how the mistake arose I do not know and I do not much care . . . I do not go to Scripture to learn the price of threshing floors and oxen. I go to learn God's wonderful dealings with David, to see the sins, and repentance, and faith, of the man after God's own heart.[47]

It is because I believe that the Bible as we now have it is the inspired and infallible Word of God that I can take it as my guide for this life and the life beyond; that I can preach from it; that I can put it in the hands of unbelievers and heathen. And if I am asked why I receive Scripture as the Word of God and as the perfect rule of faith and life I do not answer: Because it is the slightly imperfect copy of original autographs, which, if I could only get my hands on them, I should show you to be absolutely errorless writings. I answer—Because the Bible is the only record of the redeeming love of God, because in the Bible alone I find God drawing near to man in Christ Jesus, and declaring to us in Him His will for our salvation.[48]

The problem with the Princeton tradition at this juncture is not the use of the term 'inerrancy' in rendering its doctrine of Scripture. Even Warfield could concede that 'the inerrancy of the original autographs' was not an altogether happy phrase 'to express the doctrine of the Scriptures as given by God'.[49] Equally, as the Princeton theologians often pointed out, hosts of great

---

[47] Thomas Lindsay, 'The Doctrine of Scripture: The Reformers and the Princeton School', *The Expositor*, 14 (1895), 287.   [48] Ibid. 293.
[49] Warfield, 'The Inerrancy of the Original Autographs', in Noll (ed.), *Princeton Theology*, 270.

theologians and ordinary Christians have believed in the 'inerrancy' of Scripture. There are perfectly respectable ways of deploying that term to good effect even today.[50] The problem goes much deeper, as we can see if we compare their account of canon with the subtleties of the original canonical arrangements of the Church. Drawing the doctrine of inspiration into the very foundations of the canonical life of the Church overturns the delicate internal ordering of the full canonical heritage of the Church. It radically alters that heritage by making epistemology a central element in the working canons of the Faith. Consequently, the Creed, the sacramental practices, the episcopal oversight, and the like are removed and are now subject to endless dispute in an absurd process of theological construction. They can never again be a fundamental feature of the life of faith. They are derivative, secondary, and discretionary.

Another way to approach this matter is to note how the Princeton theologians, in making the need for a certain kind of absolute assurance paramount in their theology, undermined the sovereign freedom of God in his works of salvation and displaced crucial aspects of the working of the Spirit. Because of their scepticism, the Princeton theologians made it mandatory on God to provide a specific kind of record of revelation if the Church was to survive. Fear replaced faith. Rather than humbly and self-critically enquire of the past and the Church what God had actually done in preserving the treasures of the Faith, they made a certain kind of text an essential condition of divine success. Consequently, God's sovereign freedom was radically compromised.

Moreover, having fastened on the need for a certain kind of certainty, they interpreted the witness and testimony of the Spirit in the light of that requirement. For Alexander, the work of the Spirit was characteristically tied to making the evidence for the canon compelling. Hodge valiantly tried to make the work of the Spirit more foundational in his doctrine of Scripture.[51] Warfield

---

[50] See e.g. Daniel P. Fuller, 'Benjamin B. Warfield's View of Faith and History', *Journal of the Evangelical Theological Society*, 11 (1968), 75–83. See also Eleonore Stump, 'Revelation and Biblical Exegesis: Augustine, Aquinas, and Swinburne', in Alan G. Padgett (ed.), *Reason and the Christian Religion* (Oxford: Clarendon Press, 1994), 161–97.

[51] It is notorious that Hodge devoted a mere thirteen pages to the formal doctrine of the Holy Spirit in his *Systematic Theology*.

reverted to the position of Alexander, pushing it to the edges of his theory by making it totally subservient to the enlivening of the force of relevant evidence. It becomes natural to ask why the work of the Spirit is at all necessary if the evidence is as compelling as the Princeton theologians claimed it was. Perhaps there is something wrong with the evidence if it is so ineffective. Clearly the next step is to eliminate the appeal to the inner witness altogether. This is exactly what happened in the tradition two generations later.[52]

What this whole line of development ignored was that the assurance originally predicated of the inner witness of the Holy Spirit had nothing to do directly with decisions as to which books truly belonged in the canon or concerning debates about how to resolve disputes about which books truly embodied divine revelation. The inner witness gives a certainty not about such matters but about the believer's relation to God.[53] Hence the whole subject of certainty has been removed from where it truly belongs in the first place. Crucial epistemic material embedded in the Scriptures has been summarily cast aside and replaced by the dictates of human need.

Taken in the round, the difficulties in the Princeton tradition are formidable. It is conspicuous that the attempt to shore up the foundations of the Christian faith by initial deployment of the Scottish Common Sense tradition filled the Princeton theologians with great hope in the work of handing over the faith of the Church from one generation to another. They set enormous store by the fortunes of an epistemological tradition, looking to it to stem the tide of the destructive criticism which they believed was at work on every side within and outside the Church. To use

[52] Harold Lindsell is a perceptive observer of the difficulties in the appeal to the inner witness of the Spirit. 'Perhaps a third possibility should be explored—namely that the Holy Spirit bears witness with our spirits that this is the word of God which should be trusted. But this presents its own difficulty, since there are those who claim to be Christians who would say that the Holy Spirit has not witnessed to them in that way. And some might even claim that the Spirit has witnessed to them that there are errors in the Word of God' (*The Battle for the Bible* (Grand Rapids, Mich.: Zondervan, 1976), 183). The problems with the Princeton tradition stretch right back to Calvin himself, where the inner witness easily becomes transposed into a claim about divine revelation or about religious experience.

[53] The crucial text is Rom. 8: 16.

Warfield's apt phrase, they had 'an old-fashioned prejudice for reasoned views of truth'.[54] To cite J. Gresham Machen's adroit expression, they were obliged to keep to 'the high, rough intellectualistic road of a sound epistemology'.[55]

This was indeed a rough road, for this strategy only partly served their purposes. They departed from the Reidian position and embraced scepticism at one crucial moment in their work on the foundations of the Christian faith. They were driven at that point by a conviction that human beings could not be trusted to receive and retain the treasures of divine revelation. Given this pessimistic view of the Church and of redeemed human nature, it is comical to think of the future of orthodoxy hanging on the handing over of a carved white bone walking-stick by a dying seminary professor. Yet what else is there to rely on if the canons of the Church are hostage to the epistemological crises of the Western world? In the next chapter, as we turn to the thought of John Henry Newman, we shall take a step back in time and look at the proposals of a theologian who wanted a lot more than a white bone walking-stick.

[54] Warfield, 'William Newton Clarke', in Noll (ed.), *Princeton Theology*, 310.
[55] J. Gresham Machen, 'The Relation of Religion to Science and Philosophy', *Princeton Theological Review*, 24 (1926), 66.

More Light Amid
the Encircling Gloom

Few people tackled the canonical crisis of the Church in the West as it emerged in the nineteenth century with greater originality and seriousness than John Henry Newman. His place in our narrative is secured by the intrinsic interest and depth of his proposals. It is sealed by the fact that in his extraordinary and torturous pilgrimage he experienced no fewer than three conversions, all of which were accompanied by intense epistemological reflection. Thus he was converted to a form of Evangelicalism in his teen years; in his twenties and thirties he was converted to a version of Anglicanism which he virtually invented for himself; finally he converted to Roman Catholicism, and became a champion of moderate ideas concerning papal infallibility.[1] Even this summary is inadequate, for we also know that Newman was for a time attracted to Liberal Protestantism, so much so that liberalism became a kind of shadow against which he reacted with passion and dexterity.

My aim here is not to try and cover all the nooks and crannies of Newman's thought, but rather to illustrate how the epistemizing of the canonical life of the Church bore fruit in one of the great theological and philosophical minds of the nineteenth century. Moreover, reviewing and evaluating the relevant developments in Newman's life and work allows us to take fresh stock of the way the problem of canon and criterion has played itself out in Anglicanism and in Roman Catholicism.

---

[1] Ian T. Ker, *John Henry Newman* (Oxford: Clarendon Press, 1988), is an invaluable intellectual portrait of Newman. Louis Bouyer, *Newman, His Life and Spirituality* (New York: Meridian, 1988), and Sheridan Gilley, *Newman and his Age* (London: Darton, Longman and Todd, 1990), are also very helpful. Robert Pattison, *The Great Dissent: John Henry Newman and the Liberal Heresy* (Oxford: Oxford University Press, 1991), is a refreshing, iconoclastic essay.

We begin by setting the scene. There are two crucial features of the Anglican settlement which need to be mentioned immediately. When it became clear to the established powers in post-Reformation England that the appeal to Scripture was, practically speaking, an inadequate norm for resolving theological disputes within Protestantism, much less a viable blueprint for ecclesiastical existence, this precipitated a twofold crisis. First, how were the English to resolve *de facto* the need to have some kind of agreed Church structure? Second, how was the problem of criterion in theology to be met? The first problem was solved quite simply by political power, and where necessary, brute force. As a result, Anglicanism became the established Church of the land, backed up by law, privilege, power, patrimony, and the like. England became a confessional state with carefully managed loopholes for those who disagreed with the system as a whole.[2] The second problem was solved by reworking the appeal to Scripture in such a way that it permitted a judicious additional appeal to the universal tradition of the early Church and to reason. So the social arrangements essential to preserving the canonical heritage of the Church were taken care of by action of the State, while the epistemological problems generated by the doctrine of *sola scriptura* were resolved by working out a complex appeal to Scripture, tradition, and reason.

By the time we get to Newman neither of these solutions was really working. On the political front, the reforms of the 1820s and 1830s made it clear that the State would no longer protect the hegemony of the Anglican tradition. The effect of this on many loyal and devout Anglicans, as we can see in the case of the famous Assize Sermon of Pusey, was dramatic. Clearly, the whole internal life of the Church now appeared to be at the mercy of the political masters of the day.[3] While this was true in principle from the beginning, the stark consequences of this arrangement

[2] J. C. D. Clark, *English Society, 1688–1832, Ideology, Social Structure and Political Practice during the* Ancien Régime (Cambridge: Cambridge University Press, 1985), is a contested but very interesting account of the situation.

[3] Newman expressed the matter caustically as follows: 'In truth, we have had enough, if we would be wise, of mere political religion; which, like a broken reed, has pierced through the hand that leaned upon it' (*The Via Media of the Anglican Church*, ed. H. D. Weidner (Oxford: Clarendon Press, 1990), 66).

were brought home by harsh political realities as represented by repeal of the 'Test Act' and 'Corporation Act' in 1828 and by the Reform Bill of 1832. The quasi-political nature and identity of Anglicanism were now publicly exposed to view.

On the epistemological front the crisis was no less serious. The triad of Scripture, tradition, and reason is an inherently confused and unstable one. While it has long been attractive as a subtle and sensible solution to debates on the epistemology of theology, it has obvious difficulties below the surface which over time became visible. Coined in a world which wanted one single and certain ground for theological truth, its adherents invariably gravitated to one or other of its components. The result was a clash of parties in the Church. Evangelicals generally focused on Scripture, High Church Anglicans on tradition, and Latitudinarians on reason. If need be, the other two components could be manipulated or finessed to fit the favoured locus of authority. This epistemic dispute inevitably took its toll on the material doctrines and practices of the Church. Each party had its characteristic and competing version of the Christian faith. Not surprisingly, there was intense internal animosity and disagreement.

Newman himself was very much a partisan in these internal disputes. He emerged from his Evangelical phase with two enduring gifts: a deep personal relationship with Christ as his judge and saviour, and a lively sense of the perduring sense of Christianity as a religion with essential and non-negotiable doctrine or dogma.[4] It is frequently insisted that he did not undergo a typical conversion experience as a way of playing down his Evangelical commitments, but this is an entirely secondary matter. It is doubtful that there was one agreed model of conversion among the Evangelicals of his day, despite our temptation to find or invent one. What is fascinating is that Newman emerged from his experience convinced of the epistemic significance of the experience of self and of conscience. This became pivotal in his reworking of natural theology.

What is equally fascinating, but less surprising, is that he found

---

[4] The deep break with Evangelicalism emerges most clearly in *Lectures on Justification* (1838), although the break took place a decade and more earlier. For a valuable discussion of Newman and Evangelicalism see Thomas L. Sheridan, *Newman on Justification: A Theological Biography* (New York: Alba House, 1967).

Evangelicalism unable to sustain the dogma which it bequeathed to him. A simple appeal to *sola scriptura* was not adequate, for example, to sustain the doctrine of the Trinity, a component of the Faith stoutly maintained within Evangelicalism;[5] nor could it uphold the Calvinistic doctrines which had long been typical of the Evangelicalism into which he was initiated.[6] It is small wonder that Newman was tempted to some version of Liberal Protestantism, for this tradition resolved the second dilemma by rejecting the whole idea of enduring dogma and held common ground with Newman by making as much theological hay as possible out of experience. We can usefully see his proposals to reform the Anglican tradition and his ultimate conversion to Roman Catholicism as his escape route from Liberal Protestantism. The great merit of this approach to our exposition is that it brings out the crucial role that epistemological issues played in his second and third conversions.

There is, of course, a measure of contortion here, for Newman never used the term 'Liberal Protestantism'; hence we are importing concepts which run the risk of distorting what is at stake. Yet Newman himself made it abundantly clear that his chief adversary was theological liberalism, and there is no doubt but that he was well aware of the Liberal Protestant alternative which had emerged in his day.[7] In any case, it is not difficult to discern what he meant by liberalism and why he was so resolutely opposed to it.[8] There

[5] See 'Holy Scripture in its Relation to the Creed', in *Discussion and Arguments on Various Subjects* (New York: Confucian Press, 1981; original edition by Basil Montagu Pickering, 1873), 113, 144. Throughout this piece, written in 1838, Newman is engaged in a clever exercise of moving those committed to Scripture and the Creed to accept the wider Catholic doctrines to which he was becoming attached.

[6] Newman over time found some of the central Calvinistic doctrines detestable. See his *Apologia pro Vita Sua* (London: Sheed and Ward, 1945), 3.

[7] Newman's acquaintance with scholarship beyond the English scene was limited, but he did have some acquaintance with the work of Schleiermacher. For brief discussion of this see Stephen Thomas, *Newman and Heresy: The Anglican Years* (Cambridge: Cambridge University Press, 1991), 132–9.

[8] Liberalism for Newman is one of a cluster of terms and ideas, like private opinion, scepticism, and infidelity, which are closely interrelated. He provides a very important note on liberalism at the end of the *Apologia pro Vita Sua*, 191–200. For a brief discussion see Marvin R. O'Connell, 'Newman and Liberalism', in Stanley L. Jaki (ed.), *Newman Today* (San Francisco: Ignatius Press, 1989), 79–93.

are two elements which need to be unpacked initially. The first pertains to the relationship between reason and revelation, the second to the relationship between reason and assent; both are in different ways derived from Locke.[9]

For Locke there was no question but that Christianity depended on special revelation from God as mediated through prophecy, through Christ the Messiah, and through Scripture. The actual content of the revelation given by God was above and beyond reason; yet it was not contrary to reason, and its identity as divine revelation was vouchsafed by miracle and hence validated by reason. This is a complex doctrine, which was easily transposed by Locke's disciples in such a way as to make revelation redundant. For, if the content of revelation is subject to evaluation by reason and the source of revelation has to be validated by reason, it is a simple, if mistaken, step from this to the claim that reason and reason alone is sufficient in theology. This is exactly what Newman found so troubling in the liberal circles of his day. In essence, liberalism entailed the introduction of the rationalistic principle into theology, a principle which meant the end of divine revelation as an indispensable warrant for Christian doctrine.[10] And once revelation was abandoned, then the only real alternative, given certain assumptions about the limits of reason, was chaos or scepticism. The canonical doctrines of the Church were acceptable only in so far as they were warranted by the evidence of reason and experience. Furthermore, once reason was given a free hand to examine the content of revelation, the dimension of mystery in divine revelation was immediately put at risk.

The other problem bequeathed by Locke needed no transposition, for it was there in Locke himself. If revelation is tested and validated by reason, then the measure of assent given to any doctrine derived from divine revelation must match the level of evidence vouchsafed by reason. This immediately called into

    [9] The importance of Locke in providing the background to Newman is well brought out by Basil Mitchell, 'Newman as a Philosopher', in Ian T. Ker and Alan G. Hill (eds.), *Newman after a Hundred Years* (Oxford: Clarendon Press, 1990), 222–6.
    [10] See his 'The Introduction of Rationalistic Principles into Revealed Religion', in *Essays Critical and Historical* (2 vols., London: Longmans, 1910), I. 30–99.

question any idea of unconditional assent or of any assent which went beyond the relevant degree of support. Thus it directly set a question against any notion of infallible doctrine or of absolute certainty in faith. Indirectly, it challenged the whole idea of secure dogma in the life of the Church. Given that human beings are fallible, that there will always be the need to check the evidence available, and that everyone has to work things out personally and privately for themselves, the notion of a constitutive body of Christian dogma or doctrine is incoherent. The only alternative is tolerance and pluralism within and outside the Church.

Newman tackled this manifold challenge with characteristic thoroughness. To begin, he was resolutely opposed to the application of evidentialism to the life of the mind; that is, he rejected the view that we are only entitled to our beliefs if we have gone through a process of validating them for ourselves. In Newman's view, we are rationally entitled to our beliefs in the absence of consciously examined evidence. This does not mean that there is no evidence for our beliefs. On the contrary, there is a wealth of relevant evidence; but we do not need to consciously base our beliefs on that evidence for our beliefs to be rational. Thus ordinary religious believers have every right to hold to what they believe without having gone through some sort of evidentialist calculus. Moreover, wide tracts of Christian belief are not directly based on reason at all, for they rest on divine revelation. Thus they are not worked out by inference from data generally available, but are derived from special revelation given in history. They rest directly on divine testimony and indirectly on human testimony. Indeed, to look to reason for the source and ground of these truths would be disastrous. They have been, and ever shall be, a matter of faith; that is, they rest on the Word of God.[11]

It is their grounding in divine revelation which renders these truths infallible. Since God is infallible, and since they are given by special divine inspiration, they are irreformable. But how do

---

[11] Newman lays out his position with consummate skill in sermons IX and X, 'Faith and Reason Contrasted as Habits of Mind,' and 'The Nature of Faith in Relation to Reason', in *Sermons Chiefly on the Theory of Religious Belief Preached before the University of Oxford* (London: Rivington Press, 1844), 167–93, 194–214.

we know that God exists in the first place? And how do we know that we are in possession of divine revelation? Newman's answer to the first question is that we know through the experience of conscience that God exists. This appeal to conscience effectively takes the place of classical natural theology, as found, say, in Locke, a tradition which Newman did not find especially compelling or appealing.

It is indeed a great question whether Atheism is not philosophically consistent with the phenomena of the physical world, taken by themselves, as the doctrine of a creative and governing Power. But, however this may be, the practical safeguard against Atheism in the case of scientific inquirers is the inward need and desire, the inward experience of that Power, existing in the mind before and independently of their examination of His material world.[12]

The appeal to conscience is nicely stated as follows:

As from a multitude of instinctive perceptions, acting in particular instances, of something beyond the senses, we generalise the notion of an external world, and then picture the world in and according to those phenomena from which we started, so from the perceptive power which identifies the intimations of conscience with reverberations or echoes (so to say) of an external admonition, we proceed on the notion of a Supreme Ruler and Judge.[13]

More specifically and explicitly, he makes the following argument:

If, in doing wrong, we feel the same tearful, broken-hearted sorrow which overwhelms us on hurting a mother; if, on doing right, we enjoy the same sunny serenity of mind, the same soothing, satisfactory delight which follows us from receiving praise from a father, we certainly have within us the image of some person, to whom our love and veneration look, in whose smile we find our happiness, for whom we yearn, towards whom we direct our pleadings, in whose anger we are troubled and waste away. These feeling in us are such as require for their exciting cause an intelligent being.[14]

Having arrived at the existence of God, Newman's answer to the second question of the identification of special revelation is that we become aware of divine revelation through a variety of

---

[12] 'Nature of Faith', 186.
[13] *An Essay in Aid of a Grammar of Assent* (Notre Dame, Ind.: University of Notre Dame Press, 1979), 97.   [14] Ibid. 101.

signs which, taken together, constitute entirely sufficient evidence for the claim that God has spoken to us. At this point Newman assembles a complex narrative which runs all the way from the existence of the Hebrew nation and the Mosaic religion through the appearance of Jesus of Nazareth and the growth of the Church to Christianity as the fulfilment of the promise made to Abraham.[15]

Our reading of the human condition and our recognition of divine revelation within history are not formal or casual affairs. We need to have a right disposition of heart and mind to perceive God in and through the experience of conscience and in and through the signs of divine revelation. In this regard Newman is a naturalist in epistemology.[16] Right thinking and perception with regard to the divine depend on the right functioning of our cognitive faculties. Furthermore, it is not possible to provide a formal calculus of all the factors which rightly have a place in the formation of our judgement as to what constitutes divine reality or divine judgement. We can, and should, seek to analyse the various considerations which play a role in coming to relevant conclusions, but this is a hazardous process and by no means essential to good judgement. We operate according to our illative sense; this is the heart of the matter from an epistemological point of view.

There is an additional consideration of note in the case of the recognition of divine revelation. Coming to believe that Christianity indeed possesses a divine revelation rests on the exercise of the illative sense on a variety of subtle considerations. However, once we come to the point where we recognize the revelation for what it is, we reach a threshold. While the initial, foundational process is one of probability or plausibility, once we have satisfied ourselves that we are in possession of divine revelation, our commitment to the revelation is unconditional and certain.[17] We pass, as it were, a threshold from probability to infallibility because the content of the identified revelation is now

[15] Newman presents the case for this (ibid. 335–79).

[16] For a fine historical and philosophical discussion of this aspect of Newman's thought see M. Jamie Ferreira, *Scepticism and Reasonable Doubt: The British Naturalist Tradition in Wilkins, Hume, Reid, and Newman* (Oxford: Clarendon Press, 1986).

[17] Newman was fully prepared to allow for the possibility of certainty based on cumulative probabilities, but what is at stake here is a degree of certainty derived from divine infallibility.

guaranteed by God, whose Word merits unconditional and absolute assent. Of course, if the original considerations which led us to believe in the identity of revelation were to be undermined, or if we were to find decisive evidence which told against the original commitment, then the latter would also be undermined. However, in the absence of such developments, the new commitment which emerges in the course of the identification of divine revelation remains absolute and unconditional.[18]

Where, then, is divine revelation to be located? Initially it is found in conscience and in the vestiges of natural religion. However, it is finally and definitively available in the history of Israel, in Jesus Christ, and in the minds of his chosen apostles. This positive revelation is full and complete; there is no new revelation after the death of the last apostle. The whole content of divine revelation was in fact available to the minds of the apostles. In a real sense it is to be found, then, in Scripture, for it is through Scripture that we are given access to the relevant agents of revelation. Thus far Newman is a typical medieval, and even a typical Protestant, theologian.

However, that revelation is technically confined to Scripture does not mean that the truths of revelation can be read in a simple-minded manner from the content of Scripture. The truth of Scripture does not lie on the surface of Scripture; this is the error of classical Protestantism and its successors in Evangelicalism. Revelation is itself a subtle and complex reality, which, while fully available to the mind of the Church and deposited in various ways in Scripture, is subject to articulate development in the tradition of the Church across time. Hence Newman found himself drawn to those classical Anglican divines who stressed with the early Fathers of the Church the crucial role that tradition played in the interpretation of scripture. Moreover, given that divine revelation lies at the base of the Church's doctrine and morals, it is an obvious corollary of this that the

---

[18] Drawing on the work of Newman this issue is given extended attention by Basil Mitchell in *Faith and Criticism* (Oxford: Clarendon Press, 1994). See also M. Jamie Ferreira, *Doubt and Religious Commitment: The Role of the Will in Newman's Thought* (Oxford: Clarendon Press, 1980), for a very illuminating discussion. Also exceptionally interesting is Thomas D. Sullivan, 'The Problem of Certitude', in Thomas Russman (ed.), *Thomistic Papers V* (Houston: Center for Thomistic Studies, University of St Thomas, 1990), 63–77.

interpretative tradition of the Church shares in the infallibility which is a natural feature of the original revelation. Newman's eventual quarrel with Anglicanism was not that Anglicanism failed to recognize the crucial place that tradition and reason, properly interpreted, played in the life of faith, but that Anglicanism, being in a state of schism from the patristic Church, did not faithfully transmit the full apostolic revelation and its appropriate development. Anglicanism was more akin to the Arians and the Monophysites; her own principles impeded her from representing the universal consensus of the Catholic Church. And this consensus was essential to a right interpretation of divine revelation.

Once Newman had come to the conclusion that the Church was the carrier of divine revelation, and that she is divinely appointed and guided in the articulated development of that revelation, it was a relatively simple step to the doctrine of papal infallibility. Initially this was a matter of administrative arrangement. After all, the Roman tradition was the true heir of the apostles, so whatever arrangements prevailed in the Roman tradition concerning the actual guardianship and transmission of the tradition were appropriate.[19] As it happened, Rome reached a formal judgement on the nature and extent of papal infallibility at the First Vatican Council. While Newman initially held to papal infallibility as a matter of theological opinion, and while prior to the decision of 1870 he seriously doubted the prudence of formally defining the nature and extent of papal infallibility, there was next to no wavering on his part once the relevant action had been taken. This is entirely in keeping with Newman's convictions about the infallibility of the Church as the guardian and interpreter of divine revelation.[20]

Moreover, the acceptance of papal infallibility provided Newman with space to tackle the vexed question of the inspiration

---

[19] The thinking of Newman is nicely laid out by Henry Chadwick: 'Anglicans believe that the Church has reliably transmitted the word and sacraments, since "The Church has authority in matters of faith" (Art. 20). Then is it extravagant to hold that St. Peter's successor has a privileged position in articulating the faith of the universal Church and in providing an organ of decision?' ('Newman's Significance for the Anglican Church', in David Brown (ed.), *Newman: A Man for Our Time* (Harrisburg, Pa.: Morehouse, 1990), 66).

[20] Newman's views on infallibility prior to Vatican I can be found in J. Derek Holmes (ed.), *The Theological Papers of John Henry Newman on Biblical Inspiration and on Infallibility* (Oxford: Clarendon Press, 1979), 105–60.

of Scripture and the troublesome questions posed by new developments in science and historical criticism.[21] Though a conservative by temperament and conviction, he was well able to
countenance a fresh way of reconciling science, history, and faith
by insisting that until the relevant scriptural material had been
expounded in a definitive way by the Pope, there could be no
necessary clash between the contending parties. And once a definitive judgement was rendered by the Pope, then it was up to the
theologians of the tradition to work out the relevant account of
the relationship between revelation, science, and history. In principle, there could not be a clash between revelation and reason,
for both were derived from the fountain of all truth in God. The
only problem was to work out how this was to be shown with
respect to the biological and historical claims of the day.

We can now see the broad outlines of Newman's strategy for
dealing with the problems bequeathed by the Lockean heritage.
Newman rejects Locke's evidentialism, his natural theology, and
his simple-minded appeal to miracles as a sign of revelation. He
replaces these with a different ethic of belief, with a different
defence of belief in God based on conscience, and with a
complex, cumulative argument for divine revelation. In and
around these themes he articulates a comprehensive theory of
judgement, of certainty, and of doctrinal development. These in
turn create space for a reclaiming of the classical doctrines of the
tradition represented by the Trinity and the Incarnation. From his
doctrines of divine revelation and development, he then presses
on to argue for a doctrine of infallibility which is linked to a
complex doctrine of development in which the content of the
original revelation is articulated under the guidance of a divinely
directed Church. In this fashion he overturns the foundations and
consequences of liberalism within the life of the Church. He
replaces the epistemological proposals of liberalism by a competing network of proposals which underwrite the full embrace of
those dogmas he held to be constitutive of the life of faith.

Newman's conception of spiritual and intellectual formation in
the Church is incremental. Entering the Church is like entering
into a grand castle which first has to be identified and secured

---

[21] See John Henry Newman, *On the Inspiration of Scripture* (Washington:
Corpus Books, 1967).

from enemy forces. Once secured, it yields up treasures which have to be recovered from the attic, set in their right place, and given a good polishing by its present occupants and owners. Contemporary visitors and tourists are tempted to construe the current treasures as recent inventions or as crudely extended reworkings, rather than as carefully guarded heirlooms from the original builders. It takes time and intellectual dexterity to explain the theory underlying the transmission and transposition of the castle's current furniture and practices.

It is clear that Newman's epistemological alternative provides him with a fresh way of receiving the canonical heritage of the Church in the West. It is equally clear that he is deeply captive to the epistemological anxiety which has come to preoccupy the Christian tradition in the West. This is visible not just in the remarkable epistemological insights which are generated by his spiritual pilgrimage, but by four features of his work which deserve to be singled out for attention at this juncture. We shall look in turn at his positive indebtedness to the general empiricist tradition which he inherited, his strategy for overcoming scepticism within the Church, his treatment of *sola scriptura*, and the consequences of his being considered a Father or doctor of the Church. As we proceed, we shall provide an evaluative commentary on Newman's proposals.

We note, first, the general epistemological vision which is bequeathed to him by the empiricist tradition represented by Locke, Berkeley, and Hume, and which is pivotal for his ideas on development. This vision becomes most visible in his famous sermon on development, which was the seed-bed for his later work. Newman's picture of the relationship between reality, language, and intellect is entirely empiricist in orientation.

Theological dogmas are propositions expressive of the judgments which the mind forms, or the impressions which it receives of Revealed truth. Revelation sets before it certain supernatural facts and actions, beings and principles; these make a certain impression or image upon it; and this impression spontaneously, or even necessarily, becomes the subject of reflection on the part of the mind itself, which proceeds to investigate it, and to draw it forth, in successive and distinct sentences.[22]

---

[22] 'The Theory of Developments in Religious Doctrine', in *Sermons Chiefly on the Theory of Religious Belief*, 320–1.

These impressions need not be recognized by the parties possessing them. 'Nothing is of more frequent occurrence, whether in things sensible or intellectual, than the existence of such unperceived impressions.'[23] Hence a person may possess a wealth of inward knowledge without being conscious thereof, leaving this implicit material to emerge explicitly in later circumstances. This process of moving from implicit knowledge to explicit knowledge is fraught with danger; it can be arduous in the extreme. This applies to individuals in their knowledge of themselves or of the world, and it applies to the Church in its knowledge of revelation. In this latter case, 'there is no natural connection between certain dogmas and impressions; and that theological science is a matter of time, and place, and accident, though inward belief is ever and everywhere one and the same'.[24] However, given the unity of God and the uniformity of inward belief, the result at the level of dogma ought also to be unity of expression.

Surely, if Almighty God is ever one and the same, and is revealed to us as one and the same, the true inward impression of Him, made on the recipient of revelation, must be one and the same; and since human nature proceeds on fixed laws, the statement of the impression must be one and the same, so that we may as well say that there are two Gods as two Creeds.[25]

It is clear here that Newman is applying in his own way the apparatus of ideas, impressions, and images which were the stock terms of Locke, Hume, and others in the empiricist tradition.[26] God and material objects are logically parallel notions in this vision.

Material objects are real, whole, and individual; and the impressions which they make on the mind by means of the senses, are of a corresponding nature, complex and manifold in their relations and bearings, but considered in themselves integral and one. And in like manner the ideas which we are granted of divine Objects under the Gospel, from the nature of the case and because they are ideas, answer to the Originals so far as this, that they are whole, indivisible, substantial, and may be called real, as being images of what is real. Objects which are conveyed to us through the senses, stand out in our minds, as I may say, with dimensions and aspects and influences various, and all these are

[23] Ibid. 321.   [24] Ibid. 328.   [25] Ibid. 329–30.
[26] I leave aside here the place that Newman assigns to imagination in his proposals.

consistent with one another, and many of them beyond our memory or even knowledge, thus forcing upon us a persuasion of their reality from the spontaneous congruity and coincidence of these accompaniments, as if they could not be creations of our minds, but were the images of external and independent beings. This of course will take place in the case of the sacred ideas which are the objects of our faith. Religious men, according to their measure, have an idea or vision of the Blessed Trinity in Unity, of the Son incarnate in His Presence, not as a number of qualities, attributes, and actions, not as the subject of a number of propositions, but as one and individual, and independent of words, like an impression conveyed through the senses.[27]

This whole thesis rests on a dubious analogy between the cognitive life of the individual and the cognitive life of the Church as a whole. It is an analogy which Newman nowhere justifies as appropriate. Moreover, when applied to the life of the Church, it has consequences which Newman finds reprehensible. On the one side, it sails close to 'enthusiasm', for it entails the existence of appropriate senses to receive the divine impressions. On the other side, it does not fit easily with the role of revelation and Scripture in furnishing knowledge of God, for it works on a model of religious experience rather than special revelation. Not surprisingly Newman quickly noticed the difference.

. . . these religious impressions differ from those of material objects, in the mode in which they are made. The senses are direct, immediate, and ordinary informants, and act spontaneously without any will or effort on our part; but no such faculties have been given us, as far as we know, for realizing the objects of Faith. . . . The secondary and intelligible means by which we receive the impression of Divine Verities, are such as the habitual and devout perusal of Scripture, which gradually acts upon the mind; again, the gradual influence of intercourse with those who are themselves in possession of the sacred ideas; again, the study of Dogmatic Theology, which is our present subject; again, a continual round of devotion; or again, sometimes, in minds both fitly disposed and apprehensive, the almost instantaneous operation of a keen faith. This obvious distinction follows between sensible and religious ideas, that put the latter into language in order to fix, teach, and transmit them, but not the former. No one defines a material object by way of conveying to us what we know so much better by the senses, but we form creeds as a chief mode of perpetuating the impression.[28]

---

[27] Ibid. 331–2.   [28] Ibid. 334–5.

Newman is trying valiantly here to have the best of both worlds. He wants the sense of correspondence with reality which he thinks the Lockean theory of ideas and impressions supplies, but he also wants to keep intact a straight appeal to Scripture which would override any appeal to religious experience. The result is an awkward synthesis which is artificial and unconvincing. His proposal is a strange mixture of epistemological notions drawn from perception and the experience of impressions on the one hand and divine revelation on the other, which have not been fully integrated and which in the nature of the case are unlikely to be fully integrated, given the empiricist cast in which they are located. Sooner or later the tension between perception and revelation is likely to force a decision in which one or the other will be given the priority. In Newman's case revelation eventually won out over perception and experience of impressions.

The second arena in which we can see the impact of Newman's epistemological worries as they relate to the canonical life of the Church is equally interesting. In this instance epistemological concerns become the conspicuous drive to avoid theological scepticism within the Church.[29] In fact, one of his crucial arguments in support of the Church's infallibility directly speaks to the danger of scepticism in theology.

The argument is embedded in a narrative of the human condition which draws attention to the misuse of reason in matters of faith. Newman wants to know 'what must be the face-to-face antagonist, by which to withstand and baffle the fierce energy of the passion and the all-corroding, all-dissolving scepticism of the intellect in religious inquiries'.[30] Various solutions to this problem have been tried and found wanting. One solution was to rely on the political establishment; a second was to rely on education; and a third was to rely simply on Scripture. Not even the latter can

---

[29] It was common among late nineteenth-century critics of Newman to accuse him of scepticism. See esp. Leslie Stephen, 'Cardinal Newman's Scepticism', 168 (1891), 179-201, and *idem*, 'Newman's Theory of Belief', in *An Agnostic's Apology* (New York: G. P. Putnam's Sons, 1893), 168-241. Newman was not a sceptic either generally or in the case of theology. He was really an epistemological pessimist. However, he was indeed concerned to provide an antidote to theological scepticism.

[30] *Apologia pro Vita Sua* (London: Sheed and Ward, 1945), 163.

'make a stand against the wild living intellect of man, and in this day it begins to testify, as regards its own structure and contents, to the power of that universal solvent, which is so successfully acting upon religious establishments'.[31] The ground is now cleared for the appearance of an infallible institution.

Supposing then it to be the Will of the Creator to interfere in human affairs, and to make provisions for retaining in the world knowledge of Himself, so definite and distinct as to be proof against the energy of human scepticism, in such a case,—I am far from saying that there was no other way,—but there is nothing to surprise the mind, if He should think fit to introduce a power into the world, invested with the prerogative of infallibility in religious matters. Such a provision would be a direct, immediate, active, and prompt means of withstanding the difficulty; it would be an instrument suited to the need; and, when I find that this is the very claim of the Catholic Church, not only do I feel no difficulty in admitting the idea, but there is a fitness in it, which recommends it to my mind. And thus I am brought to speak of the Church's infallibility, as a provision, adapted by the mercy of the Creator, to preserve religion in the world, and to restrain the freedom of thought, which of course in itself is one of the greatest of our natural gifts, and to rescue its own suicidal excesses. . . . a power, possessed of infallibility in religious teaching, is happily adapted to be a working instrument, in the course of human affairs, for smiting hard and throwing back the immense energy of the aggressive, capricious, untrustworthy intellect.[32]

The powers granted to the Church on this scheme are both cognitive and social or juridical.

This power, viewed in its fullness, is as tremendous as the giant evil which has called for it. It claims, when brought into exercise but in the legitimate manner, for otherwise of course it is but quiescent, to know for certain the very meaning of every portion of that Divine Message in detail, which was committed by our Lord to His Apostles. It claims to know its own limits, and to decide what it can determine absolutely and what it cannot. It claims, moreover, to have a hold upon statements not directly religious, and, according to its own definitive judgment, to pronounce whether or not, in a particular case, they are simply consistent with revealed truth. It claims to decide magisterially, whether as within its own province or not, that such and such statements are or are not prejudicial to the *Depositum* of faith, in their spirit or in their consequences, and to allow them, or condemn and forbid them, accordingly.

---

[31] Ibid. 164.   [32] Ibid. 164–5.

It claims to impose silence at will on any matters, or controversies, of doctrine, which on its own *ipse dixit*, it pronounces to be dangerous, or inexpedient, or inopportune. It claims that, whatever may be the judgment of Catholics upon such acts, these acts should be received by them with those outward marks of reverence, submission, and loyalty, which Englishmen, for instance, pay to the presence of their sovereign, without expressing any criticism on them on the ground that in their matter they are inexpedient, or in their manner violent or harsh. And lastly, it claims to have the right of inflicting spiritual punishment, of cutting off from the ordinary channels of the divine life, and of simply excommunicating, those who refuse to submit themselves to its formal declarations. Such is the infallibility lodged in the Catholic Church, viewed in the concrete, as clothed and surrounded by the appendages of its high sovereignty: it is, to repeat what I said above, a supereminent prodigious power sent upon earth to encounter and master a giant evil.[33]

We see in this material how the full force of scepticism is to be countered both epistemologically and juridically. Two birds are to be killed by one stone. The right of the teaching magisterium to discipline all the members of the Church, including its scholars and intellectuals, is derived from its superior epistemic position. God has supplied not just a system of governance, but a system of governance which comes equipped with the gift of infallibility. The forces of scepticism are met by a counter-force of divine knowledge lodged in the bosom of the Church, an institution which has divine authority to back its juridical decisions.

This takes us naturally to the third place where Newman's epistemological concerns affect the canonical heritage of the Church: namely the role of infallibility in determining the meaning of Scripture. Newman, in fact, worked out a very particular doctrine of divine revelation in which papal infallibility played a key role. What is ironic is that it is also a sophisticated doctrine of *sola scriptura*. Odd as it may appear on the surface, Newman's proposal at this point is one more attempt to repair the doctrine of *sola scriptura*, and in that sense it is one more effort to reform Protestantism. This time the reform is to take place by grafting the doctrine of *sola scriptura* back into the Catholic tradition of the West. In some ways this is not really all that surprising, for this is where the theory was first fully developed.

---

[33] *Apologia pro Vita Sua*, 168.

Recall that the initial move in the process of building an epistemic vision of the canonical life of the Church was to make
Scripture the content of divine revelation. This, as we have seen,
goes right back to certain clear impulses in the Fathers of the
patristic period. However, once Scripture turned out to be not
the kind of entity which delivered clear and certain doctrine, the
next move was to make good its inadequacy in this regard by
appealing to the tradition of the Church Universal. The role of
tradition was to provide a clear and agreed interpretation of
Scripture. However, if Scripture is much too cumbersome and
complex an entity to deliver clear and certain answers, this is even
more so in the case of tradition, for tradition is itself more diverse
and complex than Scripture. If sixty-six books cannot supply an
agreed warrant for theological proposals, it is hard to see how the
hundreds of documents lodged in tradition can do the job. Hence
the drive to have some single, determinative, infallible interpreter
whose judgements are sufficiently few and definitive to be identifiable is one obvious way out of the dilemma.

. . . history and the patristical writings do not absolutely decide the truth
or falsehood of all important theological propositions, any more than
Scripture decides it. As to such propositions, all that one can safely say
is, that history and the Fathers look in one determinative direction.
They make a doctrine more or less probable, but rarely contain a statement, or suggest a conclusion, which cannot be plausibly evaded. The
definition of the Church is commonly needed to supply the defects of
logic.[34]

This is precisely what is supplied in the doctrine of papal
infallibility.[35] To those committed to epistemizing the canonical

---

[34] *Via Media of the Anglican Church*, 89, no. 1. Newman is prepared to
concede that matters of salvation may be discernible, but it is the rare Christian
who will be able to provide an adequate reading of divine revelation (*Apologia
pro Vita Sua*, 190, 195).

[35] It is important to note that the Pope is bound by Scripture and tradition
in his deliberations. In fact, Newman rightly points out that the claim he
advanced in his days as an Anglo-Catholic differs only verbally from that held by
Rome. See the important note on Lecture XI in *Via Media of the Anglican
Church*, 301. The shift from infallible Church to infallible Pope is an internal
development within Roman Catholicism which does not logically alter the role
of Scripture and tradition. The Pope is simply the designated interpreter on
certain formal occasions within the tradition.

heritage, papal infallibility will appear as the last and perhaps greatest gift of grace in the Church. To those not committed to this project, it will appear as one last-ditch effort to salvage a lost cause. It simply represents one more tortuous twist of the epistemological wheel as applied to the canonical life of the Church.

There remains a fourth area to explore briefly as we round off this discussion of the impact of epistemology on the canonical heritage of the Church: namely, the significance of Newman as a potential Father or Doctor of the Church. In taking up this issue, I am aware that Newman's deliberations, while they rightly have had enormous influence on developments in contemporary Roman Catholicism, are not in themselves canonical. At the lowest estimate, these deliberations are simply Newman's own private opinion; at the highest, they are potentially the work of a future saint, doctor, or even Father of the Roman tradition.[36] In the mean time his having been made a cardinal of the Church and given the title 'Venerable' makes it clear that his work is not that of the average theologian.[37] This raises the interesting question of the canonical status of Aquinas as a Father and Doctor of the Church.

Newman's work is clearly rooted in the tradition of the Church in the West, yet it is much more than a return to the earlier tradition of the West. It is really a radical transposition of that tradition, as a cursory comparison of Newman and Aquinas reveals. There are, to be sure, fascinating continuities between Aquinas and Newman, not least in the general attempt to provide a carefully crafted synthesis of revelation and reason. Yet it is the differences which are illuminating. Thus, while Aquinas is committed to the primacy of the literal sense, Newman is committed to the primacy

---

[36] Opinion remains divided at this point on Newman. Ker sees Newman as 'one of those comparatively few Christian thinkers whose name may be mentioned in the same breath as the Fathers of the Church' (*Newman the Theologian: A Reader* (Notre Dame, Ind.: University of Notre Dame Press, 1990), 3). For spirited opposition to the canonization of Newman as a saint see P. J. Fitzpatrick, 'Newman's *Grammar* and the Church Today', in David Nichols and Fergus Kerr (eds.), *John Henry Newman: Reason, Rhetoric and Romanticism* (Carbondale and Edwardsville, Ill.: Southern Illinois University Press, 1991), 119–28.

[37] Newman was declared 'Venerable' in 1991.

of the spiritual sense, locating theological error in the former.[38] While Aquinas is one of the great inventors of natural theology, Newman is far from convinced by its validity, and explores altogether different territory in the experience of self and conscience for the foundation of his theism. While Aquinas favours *scientia* as the paradigm of theology, Newman develops an entirely different conception which picks up a very different legacy from Aristotle: namely, *phronēsis*, or the illative sense.[39] While Aquinas has one conception of probability, Newman has an entirely different one. While Aquinas is happy to appeal to the dexterity of the interpreter to find a reading of Scripture which will be reconcilable with science, Newman is happy to await the formal pronouncements of the Pope as a crucial ingredient in the apologetic task. While Aquinas clearly favours the relatively clear deployment of deduction and proof, Newman favours the more subtle and murky world of human judgement and probability. Aquinas and Newman are seen to represent radically different epistemological projects when these considerations are taken seriously.

It is therefore not surprising that Newman has only come into his own in Roman Catholic circles in the last generation or so. Ironically, the period which saw the emergence of papal infallibility also saw the formal recognition of the crucial place of Aquinas in the canonical life of the Roman Catholic Church. It was only when the reception of Aquinas had played itself out in sufficient philosophical diversity and pluralism that there was room to hear the competing vision which Newman offered.[40]

---

[38] The crucial role of the spiritual sense is brought out in the section on 'Scripture and its Mystical Interpretation', in *An Essay on the Development of Christian Doctrine* (Notre Dame, Ind.: University of Notre Dame Press, 1989), 338–45.

[39] It has also been suggested that Thomas Reid may have had a significant role in the formation of Newman's concept of the illative sense. See Rik Achten, *First Principles and Our Way to Faith: A Fundamental-Theological Study of John Henry Newman's Notion of First Principles* (Frankfurt-on-Main: Peter Lang, 1995), 37–8.

[40] See Gerald A. McCool, *From Unity to Pluralism: The Internal Evolution of Thomism* (New York: Fordham University Press, 1989). It is of course possible to attend to Aquinas as a saint and ignore his work as a philosopher. Consider the comment of Ronald Knox: 'St Thomas was a great saint; and what we properly celebrate on the feast of a great saint are his virtues; his purity of soul, his humility, his easy converse with the other world. If he happened to be a philosopher as well, that does not really concern us; it was part of God's

The result is a fascinating dilemma. Either Aquinas is canonical, or he is not. And either Newman is potentially canonical, or he is not. If Aquinas is canonical, then those critics of Newman who reject his epistemological proposals are right to resist the move to make his work canonical. Otherwise the whole status of Aquinas becomes equivocal, or the canonical heritage with respect to epistemology becomes incoherent. Alternatively, if Newman is potentially canonical, then the position and designation of Aquinas in the canonical life of the Church will have to be renegotiated or redefined to accommodate epistemological pluralism, and the way is then open for the reception of Newman as an official philosophical mentor. For a variety of reasons, the latter would appear at present to be the more attractive option. In this instance the work of Aquinas would be seen as a significant, contingent experiment, rather than a normative model.

How things turn out will depend in part on how well Newman's proposal stands up to intellectual scrutiny, for decisions by the teaching magisterium are not taken in a vacuum, but are intimately joined to critical evaluation within the Church as a whole. This is exactly how Newman himself saw the matter, for the teaching office is not some kind of holy labour-saving device. The papal office is indeed an epistemic mechanism, but it is integrated economically into the wider life of the Church.[41] For the moment Newman's fortunes as a potential Father or doctor of the Church hang in the balance.

Having looked in some detail at how epistemological concerns play themselves out in Newman, it is worth standing back and identifying some of the difficulties inherent in his position as a whole. One obvious difficulty stems from his inability to engage seriously with the claims of the Eastern tradition. If my earlier narrative is accurate, then the Roman Catholic tradition involves

Providence that he should realize his sanctity in the life of a philosopher, just as it was part of God's Providence that St Benedict Joseph Labre should realize his sanctity in the life of a tramp covered with vermin. There is no more reason to talk about philosophy when you are celebrating the virtues of St Thomas than there is to talk about entomology when you are discussing the virtues of St Benedict Joseph Labre' (*Occasional Sermons* (New York: Sheed and Ward, 1960), 52).

[41] This is well brought out in *Apologia pro Vita Sua*, 179. Cf. *Via Media of the Anglican Church* 134 n. 3.

a deep transposition of the patristic heritage which cannot be accommodated on Newman's theory of development. As we have seen, the whole effort to canonize epistemological materials in the full and official way taken by Rome is a radical departure from the earlier tradition. Newman is too much a prisoner of this process to be able to identify any alternative option. Equally, he was much too cavalier in his treatment of the East to take it seriously.[42] This had devastating consequences for his move from Canterbury to Rome, for the whole argument turns on Rome as the only alternative. Clearly, there is more than one alternative.

It is worth dwelling on this for a moment. The division between East and West, as I have delineated it heretofore, is conspicuously visible in some of the tensions inherent in Newman's pilgrimage. This is not surprising, for Newman's initial study took him deep into the patristic material and led him to adopt an outlook which was somewhat at odds with his later Roman commitments. Thus Newman was much taken with the place of universal consensus as crucial in determining the true teaching of the Church on any issue. It was the famous phrase of Augustine, *securus judicat orbis terrarum*, which was the body blow to the Anglican claims as he had developed them for himself.[43] Also, Newman put a high premium on the place of sanctification in the healing of our cognitive capacities, a familiar theme in the epistemic suggestions of the Eastern Fathers. Moreover, he rightly insisted that the mind of the faithful laity had a significant place to play in the development and articulation of doctrine. It is no surprise that he found some of his early comments on the role of the laity in the defeat of Arianism something of an embarrassment standing in need of later qualification.[44] Nor is it a surprise that his

[42] Newman accuses the Greek tradition of being barren and lacking in internal soundness. See *An Essay on the Development of Christian Doctrine*, 181, 205. Elsewhere he accuses the Greek Church of having lost its political life. See *Via Media of the Anglican Church*, 48. For an interesting discussion of the wider relationship between the Oxford Movement and the Eastern Church see P. E. Shaw, *The Early Tractarians and the Eastern Church* (London: A. R. Mowbray & Co., 1930).

[43] Newman's own translation of this phrase was 'The universal Church is in its judgments secure of truth' (quoted in Ker, *Newman the Theologian*, 35).

[44] See the famous note 5, 'Orthodoxy of the faithful during the supremacy of Arianism', and the concluding comment in *The Arians of the Fourth Century* (London: Longmans, Green, and Co., 1895), 445–68.

work on consulting the faithful[45] and on the voice of conscience as logically prior to that of the Pope[46] constituted a real challenge to the prevailing opinion in high circles in Rome. Furthermore, it is of note that he initially accepted the decree on papal infallibility only on condition that it be received by the faithful.[47] He saw universal consensus as a real alternative to papal infallibility, and this may well have led him to construe the latter as a theological opinion which were best left alone. Indeed, Newman appealed to the infallible interpretive activity of the whole Church to resolve doubts about the meaning of papal decisions.[48] In the end, of course, Newman was able to accommodate these convictions to the new frontiers of canonization in the Roman tradition. One can surely ask if they really belong in a milieu which sets such great store by the kind of epistemic mechanism represented by papal infallibility. But having crossed the epistemological Rubicon to Rome, there was no alternative but to settle into the streets of the new city as best he could.

There are other difficulties in Newman's position. First, the idea that all revelation is given completely and fully to the early apostles is artificial and strained.[49] Newman's case at this point is, of course, a subtle and complex one. It is only implicit revelation which has been given to the apostles; this implicit material is then developed in an explicit way under appropriate circumstances. Even in this form the thesis is unconvincing. It is more fitting to

[45] See his *On Consulting the Faithful in Matters of Doctrine* (London: Collins, 1986).

[46] See his 'A Letter to the Duke of Norfolk' in Ian T. Ker (ed.), *The Genius of John Henry Newman* (Oxford: Clarendon Press, 1989), 262–7.

[47] This is well brought out in Ker, *John Henry Newman*, 655.

[48] Having asserted papal infallibility as a form of active infallibility, Newman supplements this with a form of passive infallibility in the whole body of the Catholic people. 'The active infallibility lies in the Pope and Bishops—the passive in the "universitas" of the faithful. Hence the maxim *"securus judicat orbis terrarum."* The body of the faithful can never misunderstand what the Church determines by the gift of its active infallibility.' See his letter to Miss Froude, in Appendices to Romauld A. Dibble, *John Henry Newman: The Concept of Infallible Doctrinal Authority* (Washington: Catholic University Press of America, 1955), 295.

[49] In a private letter Newman expressed this by saying that 'the Church does not know more than the Apostles knew' (quoted in Ker, *Newman the Theologian,* 37). Newman's view is well brought out in his 'Paper on Infallibility', in Dibble, *John Henry Newman,* 288–9.

allow for genuine development above and beyond what would be recognized by the apostles. The obvious explanation for Newman's convictions at this point is that they are an extension of his consistent commitment to *sola scriptura*. In the end, everything has to be traced back to one single source in the apostles as received through Scripture. Not surprisingly, various strategies must then be deployed to square this with the obvious differences between the claims of the apostles and the claims of their successors.

Second, it is historically dubious to assert that the crucial claim of papal infallibility was available to the first apostles, much less to the patristic Church. The development of ministry was much more haphazard and varied than anything that Newman can allow at this point, and it is much more plausible to see the whole idea of papal infallibility as a contingent later development.[50]

Third, it is exaggerated to claim that infallibility is essential to the canonical life of the Church in the way posited by Newman. Newman is entirely correct to claim that the voice of God is to be trusted. Leaving aside subtleties in the concept of revelation, it is platitudinous to say that divine revelation is infallible, for God does not lie. Moreover, Newman is right to insist that some kind of social authority or episcopacy is essential to the inner life of the Church if the treasures of divine revelation and their appropriate development are to be preserved across the generations. However, it is not at all clear that this requires infallibility. It is surely more than enough to claim that the transmission of the divine revelation is reliable and that there are duly appointed agents entrusted with the responsibility of guarding and preserving the riches of the Faith. To posit infallibility as essential to the reception or ongoing transmission of divine revelation is unnecessary. In fact, the potential abuses related to infallibility are all too visible in the record of the Roman Catholic tradition across the centuries. The whole quest for infallibility in all likelihood stems from a variety of motives and sources. Thus it is easily explicable by the inadmissible transfer of the infallibility of the divine

---

[50] For a compelling historical case against Newman see Paul Misner, *Papacy and Development: Newman and the Primacy of the Pope* (Leiden: E. J. Brill, 1976), ch. 13, pp. 109-18.

message to the infallibility of the divine messenger,[51] by the natural desire to project the quest for absolute certainty in matters of faith and morals on to the transmission of divine revelation,[52] and by the desire to have a single central authority in Church and State.[53]

It is worth dwelling for a moment on how it is possible to believe that the early Church was entirely right in its decisions, say, about the Trinity, without at all positing a doctrine of infallibility. Suppose we agree that the early Church got the heart of the matter right when it canonized the doctrine of the Trinity. We can think of two radically different ways of describing this situation from an epistemic point of view. One is to say that the warrant for belief in the Trinity is that the Church is infallible. If one has warrant for holding that the Church is infallible, then one is entitled to belief in the Trinity. One might, of course, go on to provide reasons for the doctrine independently of its being adopted by the Church, but this would fall into the domain of apologetics, and the original acceptance of the doctrine would not depend on any arguments produced at this point.

The other way is to say that the Church adopted the doctrine of the Trinity and that in so doing the Church was correct in its doctrine of God. Nothing would follow in this case about the infallibility of the Church. All that is needed is the assertion that the Church got the matter right when it adopted the doctrine of the Trinity. One might then, of course, go on to claim that the

---

[51] It is easy to slide from the proposition that x—say, the Church—decides that proposition p is true to the proposition that x, the Church, is the criterion for proposition p. In this case we are confusing the psychological condition of believing p with the epistemic warrant for the belief p. If x believes that p is true, then there has to be the psychological state of believing p on the part of x. But this does nothing to show that x is the criterion of p.

[52] 'The human mind wishes to be rid of doubt in religion; and a teacher who claims infallibility is readily believed on his simple word' (*Via Media of the Anglican Church*, 156).

[53] 'It is the absolute need of a monarchical power in the Church which is our ground for anticipating it. A political body cannot exist without government, and the larger the body is the more concentrated must the government be. If the whole of Christendom is to form one Kingdom, one head is essential; at least this is the experience of eighteen hundred years. As the Church grew in form, so did the power of the Pope develop; and wherever the Pope has been renounced, decay and division have been the consequence' (*Essay on the Development of Christian Doctrine*, 154).

Church on this occasion was divinely assisted in its deliberations, and one might also proceed to provide an account of why the Church was right to adopt the doctrine of the Trinity. The claim to divine assistance would signal a rejection of a Pelagian view of the Church's decisions, and the account of why the Church adopted the doctrine of the Trinity would constitute a partial case for believing the doctrine of the Trinity to be true. Whether a full case could be made for the doctrine of the Trinity would in turn depend upon developing an account of the relationship between faith and reason. The relevant point to grasp, however, is that it is entirely feasible to believe that the Church was right to adopt the doctrine of the Trinity without committing oneself to any doctrine of infallibility. One can adopt this particular doctrine, and the Church can adopt this particular doctrine, without having to hand a theory of reflective rationality of the kind constituted by papal infallibility. One can adopt it, that is, without also adopting an epistemology of theology. This was precisely how it was in the early Church, long before there was any doctrine of papal infallibility.

Fourth, and finally, while the quest for a final interpretative adjudication is intelligible psychologically, it is vulnerable logically. On the one side the quest exaggerates the extent to which Scripture and tradition lack clarity and substance. In fact, if pressed too far, insisting on the need for a locus of clear interpretation outside Scripture and tradition undercuts Scripture and tradition as genuine embodiments of the mind of God. If Scripture and tradition are essentially opaque, they do not transmit the will of God. On the other side, as Newman himself was well aware, even the formal *ex cathedra* pronouncements of the Pope themselves require interpretation, so that the quest for clear and distinct interpretation takes off in an infinite regress of further interpretation. Somewhere this whole process has to be halted, and it appears entirely arbitrary to stop with formal papal pronouncements. It is better by far, surely, to claim that God has already spoken and been heard in a sufficiently reliable way. If Newman replies that papal infallibility is a matter of divine revelation—that is, that the doctrine of papal infallibility is itself secured by divine revelation—then the rebuttal is obvious. This either begs the question by making papal infallibility depend on papal infallibility, for only papal infallibility secures the right interpretation of the Word of God, or it will have to be supported by historical arguments about doctrinal development which cannot plausibly be sustained.

Overall, then, Newman's remarkable account of papal infallibility is a brilliant but flawed attempt to rescue the epistemic vision of Scripture which was falling apart within Protestantism. Schleiermacher turned his back on the Reformed doctrine of Scripture, and sought to find an altogether different foundation for theology in religious experience. The great Princeton theologians returned to the work of the Reformers, relocating it within the contours of the Scottish Common Sense tradition, even though their commitment to this tradition faltered in the end in theology. Newman went back beyond the Reformers to the Roman Catholic tradition out of which their work emerged. We might say that he sought to heal Protestantism by returning to the fold of Roman Catholicism.

14

Ending the Great Misery of Protestantism

Once the canons of the Christian Church were transformed into epistemic norms, then it was natural that debate about canon be transformed into a debate about the epistemology of theology. Once the canons were reduced to the single canon of Scripture, then the epistemology of theology was naturally cast in terms of a foundationalism in which there was one, single foundation on which all of the Church's life and thinking could rest secure. Scripture, however, was not the only candidate for this coveted position. After all, Scripture was in part the creation of the Church. So why not appeal to the Church, or to the Church's tradition, or to the special office of the Pope, as the ultimate foundation of the Church's life and doctrine? Once it became clear through intense debate and bloody warfare that this discussion had reached an impasse, it was natural to move the whole debate about the epistemology of theology into the wider arena of general epistemology. Once several competing criteria of theology were invoked, and once the appeal to the various foundations appeared entirely arbitrary and question begging in the face of the competing alternatives, the debate was at a standstill. There was no alternative but to shift the whole discussion to another, more general level.

By this stage the debate had moved into the field of philosophy. Not surprisingly, philosophers simply adopted the fundamental structure of the epistemology of theology which they had inherited, for they themselves were Christian intellectuals who had internalized the crisis of the Christian tradition in the West. So within philosophy one turned first to reason and then to experience as a way forward in the quest for adequate foundations. These in turn were picked up by those who continued to be worried about the epistemology of theology. Thus rationalists attempted to show that the whole of Christian theology could be derived from reason. The result was the deism and natural religion of the Enlightenment. Anglicans, attracted by the appeal to reason but wanting to hold on to earlier tradition, attempted as we have seen, to patch together an epistemological quilt of Scripture, tradition, and reason. Locke, charmed by the possibility of sense experience as the only foundation of knowledge, tried to work out a synthesis of reason and revelation, but ultimately reason was posited as the last rule and guide in everything. Before long the whole Lockean project was subject to devastating criticism at the hands of Hume. Accepting Locke's initial premiss concerning the primacy of sense experience, Hume showed that even Locke's reduced version of the Christian faith was incompatible with his empiricist epistemology. Schleiermacher, dissatisfied by all forms of rational theology, turned to a special kind of religious experience as providing the appropriate foundations for faith, carefully reworking the content of the Christian tradition to fit this new foundation. In the case of Locke and Schleiermacher, because of the inevitable constraints built into their appeal to reason and experience, significant tracts of the Christian heritage were set aside as incredible, superstitious, or irrational.

The strain which these labours caused discerning intellectuals of the Christian tradition has been incalculable. It drove the great Princeton theologians of the nineteenth century back to the Confessions and Fathers of the Reformation, as they picked up and carefully developed a doctrine of divine inspiration in order to find an infallible foundation. It drove John Henry Newman to Rome, where he was convinced that he had found, in the Church initially and then in the infallibility of the Pope, that solid foundation which would stand secure for ever. In both cases they did the best they could to combine this kind of canonical foundationalism with a deep commitment to reason. Thus they kept intact a strong commitment to natural theology and to developing an appropriate apologetic for special revelation. In other words, they worked out a complex synthesis of revelation and reason.

Such a proposal is bound to be unstable in the life of the Church. The host of queries evoked by the concepts of revelation and reason inevitably calls forth worries that revelation will be swallowed up by reason. The treasures of revelation, it is feared, will be taken hostage to the demands of reason. Hence challenge is constantly waiting in the epistemic wings. Those concerned to secure the position of Scripture in the Church are likely to worry about its precarious status. One way to confront this worry is to challenge the whole idea of a cosy synthesis between revelation and reason. By far the most interesting and demanding challenge to any attempt to work out a synthesis between reason and an appeal to divine revelation in the modern period is presented in the work of Karl Barth.

At one level what Barth did was to return to the Bible and to appeal to it in stark opposition to any attempt to rely on any kind of general epistemology as a defence of Christian belief. The fact that he could even think of such a possibility reveals that he continued to think of Scripture primarily in epistemological categories. It was because he saw Scripture as representing a very particular option in the epistemology of Christian belief that he was driven to set it in opposition to the prevailing strategy which had been in place among Christian intellectuals. Scripture represented, for Barth, a single foundation for theology, which could tolerate no rival if its position were to be properly recognized.

The irony of this position is that it was an attempt to return to the very position which had in part precipitated the invention of modern epistemology in the first place. Given what has been outlined of that history heretofore, one is bound to wonder whether Barth can extricate himself from the deep hole in epistemology which Christians have dug for themselves in Western culture. We must await the exposition of Barth's position before we can tackle this question. For the moment we are content to anticipate that the complex manner in which Barth worked out his position will expose fresh dimensions of the epistemizing of the canonical heritage of the Church which would otherwise be missed by the unwary observer. Thus Barth argued for the rejection of natural theology in terms not just of *sola scriptura* but also of the significance of divine revelation, and in terms of very particular doctrines, like justification by faith through grace alone. This is an intriguing development which clearly cries out for analysis and explanation.

Moreover, it is clear that Barth developed, if only embryonically, an account of the epistemology of Christian belief which set enormous store by encounter with God. He was, in fact, a radical particularist,[1] insisting that theology had its own locus, source, and norm of knowledge. In addition, it was not long before his followers found themselves drawn back into the wider debate about epistemology. Indeed, some of them have argued at length that the epistemology of theology is no different in principle from that of the natural sciences. Hence the wheel has come full circle. We begin in the early Barth with the rejection of a universal epistemology, because this rules out precisely the kind of beliefs which are constitutive of Christianity; we end with the construction of a general epistemology which sees theology as offering a representative form of knowledge. This too cries out for analysis and explanation.

It is a commonplace that the thought of Karl Barth is internally so complex and extensive that it defies easy analysis. There is, however, considerable agreement on those features of his work which are pertinent to our project. After some preliminary observations, we shall look in turn at his recovery of the Reformed tradition, his account of divine revelation, his attitude to natural theology, and his incipient epistemology of theology. With these in place, we shall stand back and comment on the significance of the Barthian project for our understanding of the canonical heritage of the Church.

Few theologians have grasped as astutely as Barth did the significance of the debate about criterion for an understanding of the history of Protestant theology. In his characteristically long-winded fashion he resorted to this issue again and again, examining it now from this angle, now from that. Speaking of Liberal Protestantism,[2] he noted that this great tradition was rightly very concerned to pursue the proper task of dogmatics.

But it lost the proper criterion for and over against Church proclamation, as it had been put into its hand by the Reformation in particular. It was still acquainted with it, but it had ceased to regard it as a criterion, as distinct from the present state of Church activity and superior to it. It still continued to take account of it, but it had ceased to understand its dignity, its character as an authority from which there can be no appeal.

---

[1] This motif has been nicely emphasized by George Hunsinger, *How to Read Karl Barth: The Shape of his Theology* (New York: Oxford University Press, 1991), 32–5.

[2] Barth uses the term 'Modernist Protestantism', but nothing hangs on this designation as Barth was happy to deploy both terms.

It forgot its duty of looking to it alone in the question as to the Word of God, by which Church proclamation is to be measured. On this question it invariably looked another way. The place of the criterion of Reformed theology, which has as it were become empty, had to be otherwise occupied and was in fact occupied. Even if we regard as heretical this newer theology which took the lead with Pietism and the Enlightenment, we must admit that it wished to continue the critical function of theology; it wished first and last to be the conscience of a preaching church; it was also aware that a conscience must have criteria. After it had ceased to understand as such the criterion of Reformed theology, and therefore seized upon other criteria, it did so with the idea of possessing in these other criteria a full and equal substitute, in a measure representing what had been lost. Not of ill-will, but with a right good will it is as philosophical, cosmical, moral, secular, in a word as Protestantly civilised as it has become and always was becoming with ever new variations, right through the 18th and 19th centuries and up to our own. Even the golden calf (Ex. 32) was not to set forth as a strange God, but the God who led Israel out of Egypt. Even Israel acted piously in that, and even Aaron met it with the best intentions. In this way we may regard the theology of Modernist Protestantism. It had ceased to envisage the possibility of getting within sight of the Word of God as an entity distinct from Church proclamation. But it was very much in sight of other entities, likewise distinct from Church proclamation and likewise very authoritative, comprised in the modern consciousness of being civilised. This consciousness, therefore, it thrust as a substitute into the place of the Word of God, became unreal to it, volatised into an idea. And now it delivered judgment from that standpoint.[3]

The crux of Barth's criticism of the development of Protestantism across the centuries, then, was that it abandoned its own internal criterion and put in place of the Bible a whole series of other criteria as a substitute.

The obvious potential challenge to this procedure could have come from the bosom of the older Protestant orthodoxy, for orthodoxy had always stood for the authority of the Bible. The response of the older Protestant orthodoxy was, as Barth saw it, entirely inadequate to meet this challenge. The reasons for this were manifold. It did not meet the challenge of Liberal or Modernist Protestantism with a better theology, but relied instead on its gloomy conservative instincts. It operated not by spiritual conquest but by means of strong political repression. Thus it was

---

[3] Karl Barth, *Church Dogmatics* (Edinburgh: T. & T. Clark, 1936), I. I. 288.

totally unable to match the human glory and religious passion which were the mark of such figures as Troeltsch, Harnack, and Herrmann. These theologians became something akin to intellectual martyrs in their own eyes and that of the culture, for the orthodox were unable to deliver a superior message which would get to the bottom of the unrest which lay within Protestantism due to its buried commitment to its own, original criterion of dogmatics. Worst of all, the orthodox had joined with their enemies in the hunt for other criteria. Hence, by developing an apologetics which was in principle no different from that of its opponents, they played the same game as Liberal Protestantism did and could easily wake up some morning committed to the same intellectual enterprise. What prevented total collapse in both camps was the fact that the Church continued to preach from the Bible.

The Bible continued to live, for the Bible still remained for the Church, a Bible frequently relativised on historico-psychological principles and misinterpreted in the interests of philosophy of religion, a Bible whose claim and need to constitute the textual basis of Church proclamation was questioned more as a matter of fact than of insight extensively affirmed as against theological theory, a Bible to which one felt more or less bound—but nevertheless the Bible, and with the Bible the problem and with the problem the unrest over the neo-Protestant solution.[4]

It was the study of Scripture and of the Reformation material which awakened Barth from his Liberal Protestant slumbers and forced him to work out an entirely different account of the criterion of theology than that currently available. This was undergirded by his own experience and need as a preacher in the Reformed tradition. His early work, both in his commentary on the epistle to the Romans and in his shorter essays, was extraordinarily fresh, lively, and radical.[5] The very style was that of a mind and soul caught in the fires of the new discovery of an older tradition. He was absolutely resolute in his rejection of the current alternatives, yet he wrote with a candour about the finite limits of his own alternative and with a sympathy for the

---

[4] Karl Barth, *Church Dogmatics*, 291.

[5] Especially revealing are the essays collected in *The Word of God and the Word of Man* (London: Hodder & Stoughton, n.d.).

achievement of the opposition which are staggering in their realism.[6]

One way to envisage the Barthian project is to see it as a search for that criterion of truth which is internal to theology itself. There is a fruitful analogy here between the work of Thomas Reid and that of Barth. Just as Reid rejected Hume's attempt to base all his beliefs on the basis of sense experience in the name of the platitudes of Common Sense which struck him with immediate certainty, so Barth rejected all attempts to ground theological claims on the basis of a general philosophical epistemology in the name of specific theological claims which struck him with immediate certainty. Just as Reid attempted to develop a general epistemology which would accommodate the impact of Common Sense, so Barth sought to develop an epistemology of theology which would begin from the impact of Scripture on the elect within the Church.

This is the kind of revolutionary operation which comes across as intellectual suicide in the minds of all methodists in the field of epistemology. The methodist argues that there can be no knowledge without an appropriate method to secure truth. Without a method or criterion of validation, particular claims appear entirely arbitrary and unsupported. Against this, the particularist argues that all claims about method are precarious in the extreme. First, if a method is essential for securing knowledge, then one needs a method for deciding on the right method. However, this second method needs also to be secured by a third method, and so on, *ad infinitum*. Second, claims about method are themselves extremely difficult to secure, even on a relaxed scheme of requirements. The history of both of modern philosophy and modern theology make it abundantly clear that there is next to no agreement on a right method. Hence the better way to proceed is to begin from what we appear to know and modestly proceed to theories about the right method.[7]

---

[6] Nowhere is this more visible than in his remarkable, insightful treatment of Schleiermacher, who was a kind of constant, unseen partner in much of his conversation.

[7] It is also possible, of course, for the particularist to eschew the quest for the right epistemological theory as a snare. The particularist could well be an epistemological sceptic. He might say that we know certain things but will never know how we know them. What is crucial to the particularist is the claim that it is possible to have knowledge of p without knowing that one's belief in p is grounded upon some identifiable and certifiable method.

One finds clear intimations of a particularist outlook in the early work of Barth. Close attention to Scripture rendered entirely inadequate the various attempts to ground the Christian faith in morality, history, philosophy, psychology, and the like. Immersion in Scripture was like immersion in a river that carried its readers away from themselves to the sea. The content of Scripture did not fit the conventional cultural categories of morality, piety, and religion. In the early Barth, measuring God by our own measures got reversed, conceiving God by our own conceptions was overturned, and wishing ourselves a God by our own desires was arrested. Ultimately one was confronted with the strange new world of the Bible, where one was led to the very threshold of the kingdom of God. 'There one asks no longer. There one sees. There one hears. There one knows. There one no longer gives his petty, narrow little answers.'[8]

This kind of confidence was not the confidence of the cock-sure and the obstinate. One approached this new world not just in fear and trembling but in unbelief. 'It is only because of unbelief that even now I can only stammer, hint at, make promises about that which could be opened to us if the Bible could speak to us unhindered, in the full fluency of its revelations.'[9] But there was no doubt in Barth's mind but that the Bible gave us a knowledge of God, a knowledge which is the 'premise of all our life and thought'.[10] Reading Scripture was like looking out of a window and seeing people peer upwards toward the sky, shading their eyes with their hands in order to observe something hidden from us by the roof. What they saw, of course, was an airplane. Likewise, Barth was arrested by Paul: 'This man evidently hears something and sees something which is above everything, which is absolutely beyond the range of my observations and the measure of my thought'.[11] Even if Paul did not write the epistle to the Ephesians, the impact of the letter was enormous.

I seem to see within so transparent a piece of literature a personality who is actually thrown out of his course by seeing and hearing what I

---

[8] 'The Strange New World of the Bible', in *Word of God and the Word of Man*, 47.   [9] Ibid. 48.
[10] 'Biblical Questions, Insights, and Vistas', in *Word of God and the Word of Man*, 53.   [11] Ibid. 63.

for my part do not see and hear—who is, so to speak, captured, in order to be dragged as a prisoner from land to land for strange, intense, uncertain, and yet mysteriously well-planned service.[12]

If someone worried that this might be a case of self-hallucination, then:

. . . one glance at the secular events of those times, one glance at the widening circle of ripples in the pool of history, tells me of a certainty that a stone of unusual weight must have been dropped into deep water there somewhere—tells me that, among all the hundreds of peripatetic preachers and miracle-workers from the Near-East who in that day must have gone along the same Appian Way into imperial Rome, it was this one Paul, seeing and hearing what he did, who was the cause, if not of all, yet of the most important developments in that city's future. And this is only one of the Biblical company, 'Paul' by name.[13]

Barth is not here setting up an argument for the divine origin of the biblical material in the way that was so common in the apologetics of the Princeton tradition. He is simply insisting that the biblical traditions be heard on their own terms and with their own voice. In attending to that material, one encountered a turning of God towards humanity. This was and is unique. 'In the Biblical experience there is a final element to which nothing in psychology corresponds, which cannot be reproduced in feeling, which cannot be demonstrated in experience.'[14] Hence the Church must take great care to hear its content in patience and humility. Often this has been ignored, for the Church has not been able to tolerate her own relativity. 'She acts in her own lofty ecclesiastical estate as if she were in possession of a gold mine; and in the so-called "religious values" she actually pretends to give out clinking coins.'[15] What is needed by way of response to the divine aliveness present in Scripture is 'neither virtue, nor inspiration, nor love, but the *fear* of the Lord, mortal fear, the last, absolute, perfect fear'.[16]

Consequently, Scripture presents us with a crisis: The affirmation of God, man, and the world given in the New Testament is based exclusively upon the possibility of a new order absolutely beyond human thought; and therefore, as prerequisite to that

---

[12] Ibid.   [13] Ibid.   [14] Ibid. 66.
[15] Ibid. 67.   [16] Ibid. 77; emphasis original.

order, there must come a crisis that denies all human thought.'[17] Yet it is through this crisis that the Church encounters Jesus, the Son of the living God, and 'on the rock of this knowledge coming thence, out of the blue, is built the church against which the gates of hell will not prevail'.[18]

Such was the radical newness of Barth's encounter with the strange new world of the Bible, and such was the distrust of himself in interpreting the significance of his findings, that he turned to the Reformed tradition for special help in the field of doctrine. He found there plenty of material to kindle his fertile intellect. Not surprisingly, his findings were somewhat paradoxical; for what the Reformers did was to point not to themselves but back to Scripture itself. There was in fact no Reformed doctrine 'except the timeless appeal to the open Bible and to the Spirit which from it speaks to our spirit'.[19] Unlike the Lutherans, the Fathers of the Reformed tradition left only creeds, more than one of which had a proviso for future improvement. The authority lay not in the Church's dogma but in the Scriptures and in the Spirit.

The part of loyalty to the fathers, then, is to hold to the past as they themselves held to it; to look to history but to note that it points beyond itself to revelation; to guard against confusing antiquity with the primal order, and the authority which the church possesses with the authority by which it is founded; to reject every invariata and invari-abilis but *one*; to refuse to bow to any cap set up in the market place, were it even the cap of Calvin himself; to let Scripture and Spirit, and Spirit and Scripture alike, work their way to authority through criticism; and to let them do so in face of what is best in the *Reformed* theory and practice of the present day, *as* they did in our Fathers' time in face of what was best in the Christian tradition of the Middle Ages.[20]

In heeding the Reformers, one discovers not just a diversity of emphases. One finds ultimately that their doctrines were born in a place of prayer to God. They refer all doctrine to one object. They refer the enquirer not to their thought about God but to God himself and God alone, 'as he speaks his own *Word* in Scripture and in Spirit'.[21] What one ultimately meets is a revelation

---

[17] *Word of God and the Word of Man*, 80.   [18] Ibid. 83.
[19] 'The Doctrinal Task of the Reformed Church', in *Word of God and Word of Man*, 229.   [20] Ibid. 230; emphasis original.
[21] Ibid. 235; emphasis original.

witnessed to and perceived in the scriptures, which is 'the origin of all doctrine and the standard by which all doctrine is and forever must be measured'.[22]

We are by now on familiar territory, for this is not the first time that a theologian has insisted that revelation, and revelation alone, be the touchstone of doctrine. Barth was well aware of the obvious question which immediately arises: namely, how do we know that the purported revelation is indeed a revelation from God? Barth was absolutely adamant that there can be no appeal to some criterion outside revelation itself in addressing this issue. In fact, this whole question was itself called into question by the knowledge of God given in the Church. God's sovereignty governed the question of truth as much as it governed his reign over all things.

How could the statement that the Bible is his Word be proved in any other way than by an act of free grace by which he *himself* makes the proof? Would it be the Word of God if it could be verified except by him? The astonishing statement that the Bible is his Word has been called an axiom. But it is such only in its logical form. In content its certainty is wholly unlike the self-evidenced *revelation* which God gives simultaneously to his Biblical witnesses and to those who accept their witness. It expresses obedience to the *testimonium spiritus sancti internum*, to the spirit of God in which the human spirit of the writer and the reader become one in common adoration; and the truth of the statement stands or falls with the reality of this sovereign act preceding from God and authenticated by him.[23]

What gives Barth's theology a radical edge rarely seen elsewhere is the way he pressed home this claim. For him the genius of the Fathers of the Reformation lay not in any special insight or type of godliness, but in their clear understanding of the basis of things: 'They knew that their basis was God and God alone.'[24] However, things went astray when people wandered away from what God had spoken and began looking for substantiation. People began surrounding the witness of the Spirit with other reasons for belief. 'An apologetic friendly to man began to twine about the trunk of "*God is speaking*" and to rob its roots of nourishment.'[25] When historical criticism came along, the old answer

---

[22] Ibid.

[24] Ibid.

[23] Ibid. 244; emphasis original.

[25] Ibid. 245; emphasis original.

of Christian freedom and Christian reality had been forgotten, and people either fell back on dogmatic assertion or developed a guerrilla warfare in apologetics.

We lost the wonder of *God*, and now we had to learn to eke out an increasingly difficult and miserable existence by asserting the *wonder* of the world, the miracle of history and of the inner life (all equally questionable!). The great misery of Protestantism began: doctrine, parted from its life-giving origin, hardened into *Orthodoxy*; Christian experience, confusing itself with this origin, took refuge in *Pietism*; truth no longer understood and no longer understandable, shrivelled into the moral and sentimental maxims of the *Enlightenment*; and finally even Christian experience was reduced in *Schleiermacher* and his followers, both of the left wing *and* the right, to the hypothesis of being the highest expression of a religious instinct common to man.[26]

Escape from these four corner-stones of the prison in which modern Protestants were living could only be found by being absolutely clear about the basis of doctrine. Doctrine must be born in faith of the Word of God. Until that was settled, there was little use in racking our brains about what followed after. Theologians and Church teachers needed to think through the category of revelation again, and learn to read Scripture from that viewpoint. One cue for this work could be found in the Reformed, as opposed to Lutheran, attitude to the Lord's Supper. Where the Lutherans looked for a direct identity between substance and symbol, between revelation and witness, the Reformed were more reserved, insisting that revelation was in part a concealment. Thus revelation was not to be taken as a kind of miracle that began and ended on earth, a piece of direct information, a religious fact. Equally, they needed to follow the Reformed tradition in its concern both for the self-manifestation of God and for the situations of human agents in time. However, in all cases, the words of the Fathers cannot become truth and life 'unless and until they rise again out of the same premise as before'.[27]

It is abundantly clear by now that Barth was content neither to parrot the inheritance of the Reformation nor to rest in the appeal to the particular theological claims of his forebears. He

[26] *Word of God and the Word of Man*, 246; emphasis original.
[27] Ibid. 268.

may have begun his challenge to the prevailing options in theology by pitting against them the strange new world of the Bible, but this was merely an opening rocket across the bows of the sinking ships around him. He was as keen as his most earnest opponent in the modern period to build his own epistemological ship. He was as obsessed with the issues of foundations, method, and epistemic respectability as the Reformers he sought to emulate. In his own way he was as rigorous an epistemologist of theology as one could imagine. There are almost two thousand pages at the beginning of his great work in systematic theology to prove as much.

Thus far I have drawn attention to several dimensions in the Barthian account of canon and norm. First, there is a diagnosis of the current malaise in theology and the Church: people have set up alien criteria for testing the preaching of the Church. Second, there is a prescription: we need to return to the fundamental principle of the Reformation and make Scripture once again the basis of the Church's life and thought. Third, there is a promissory note: when we turn to Scripture, we shall find that the ultimate criterion of truth in theology is divine revelation, the Word of God. Unpacking this promissory note of Barth is an arduous undertaking. Yet to attempt to do so is to enter into one of the most remarkable epistemological visions ever to emerge in the history of theology.

One way into Barth's vision of divine revelation is to see it as involving a shift from an internalist to an externalist conception of knowledge of God.[28] The Princeton theologians, for the most part, were committed to an internalist conception of theology. For them, one arrived at the truth about God by taking the Bible as a divinely inspired set of propositions whose truth was guaranteed by virtue of their divine inspiration. One could only claim to have a true account of God by having access internally to the relevant propositions either given in Scripture or derived from Scripture by relevant rules of inference. In this account the role of the Holy Spirit was to clear away obstacles to the perception of the truth that Scripture was truly the Word of God. The

---

[28] For a brief but very helpful analysis of this distinction see Laurence Bonjour, 'Externalism/Internalism', in Jonathan Dancy and Ernest Sosa (eds.), *A Companion to Epistemology* (Oxford: Blackwell, 1992), 132–6.

task of the systematic theologian was to organize the exegetical material first into a biblical theology and then into a systematic theology. Once these materials were properly formulated, one had to hand a system of doctrine which was true in and of itself. Its truth was secured by the truth of the premisses from which it was derived.

Barth rejected this whole way of thinking about the justification of theological claims. Instead he saw knowledge of God in terms of a process governed from beginning to end by the sovereign working of grace. He begins with an internalist claim, that is, the claim: namely, that Scripture alone is the basis and norm of Reformed theology. Presumably this claim is to be established by appeal to certain propositions derived from the work of the Reformers and available internally to the person who accepts this position. Alternatively, it is derived from the inner witness of the Holy Spirit. The claim that Scripture alone is the norm of Reformed theology, however, is a purely formal claim. To say that Scripture is the norm of theology does not tell us how and in what way Scripture is a norm. So Barth went on to insist that Scripture itself teaches materially that knowledge of God is brought about by an encounter with God in the Church through divinely appointed media working from start to finish through the activity of the Holy Spirit. Knowledge of God is a gift of grace in which God creates knowledge of himself in the human subject through the Spirit. Thus in theology, the object of knowledge creates knowledge of itself in the human subject. Whether the knowing subject knows this does not alter how the knowledge of God is actually gained, although enormous harm can be done over time in the Christian community when Christians look to other ways of gaining knowledge of God, such as happens in the case of natural theology. In fact, turning to find God in any other way than that actually determined by God leads to idolatry. In technical terms, this is clearly an externalist conception of knowledge of God.

Perhaps the crucial claim in this proposal is that God creates in the human subject true knowledge of himself. For Barth this means that one does not first set up some general theory of knowledge and then show how theology satisfies the conditions of knowledge laid down by that theory. The Princeton theologians did this by making apologetics the foundation of their work and then moving on to, say, the doctrine of God. For Barth, the prolegomenon to any systematic theology is itself about God, about how God makes himself known in his Word, and therefore the prolegomenon is itself a part of the very substance of theology.[29] Consequently, it is not in the least surprising that one meets the great doctrines of the Christian faith, like that of the Trinity and the incarnation of God in Christ, almost in the first breath of Barth's epistemology. Early readers of Barth were so accustomed to having these doctrines established only after the basis of theology itself has been laid out that their early appearance in the very foundations of Barth's theology came as a scandalous shock to their thinking. Moreover, they were repelled by Barth's volatile and persistent hostility to providing any kind of argument for such doctrines. On the surface this appeared to be intellectually suicidal.

Yet these moves make sense within the contours of the specific version of externalism which Barth embraced. If God is known by encounter with God through the means ordained by God, then there can be no description of that knowledge without a description of the actual knowledge gained in this fashion. The epistemology on offer will involve a description of the content and form of knowledge actually specified by those who claim to know God. There is a clear analogy here to an externalist approach to the epistemology of perception or of memory. If these are taken to involve genuine knowledge claims, then the nature of those claims cannot be ascertained by setting forth, say, the epistemology of testimony or of deductive inference. All one can do is to lay out the logic of the situation as ascertained from paradigm cases of perception and memory. In similar fashion Barth totally rejected recourse to some general theory of knowledge or to some ordinary paradigm of knowledge as a way of securing knowledge of God. Knowledge of God was unique, created in the human subject by grace through the working of the Holy Spirit using the means appointed by God. The only way to develop an account of this knowledge was from within that knowledge itself. This is perhaps the key to unlocking the intelligibility of Barth's epistemology.

---

[29] 'Prolegomena to Dogmatics is the name we give to the introductory part of Dogmatics, in which it is our business to explain its particular path to knowledge' (*Church Dogmatics*, I. I. 26).

Looking at Barth's epistemology of theology in this manner explains why his account of the knowledge of God involves extended discussion of divine revelation, Scripture, the Trinity, the inner witness of the Holy Spirit, the certainty of human knowledge of God, and natural theology. These themes emerge because they are either positively or negatively constitutive of the internal grammar of coming to know God in the Christian tradition. They are not topics to be taken up after establishing a general theory of knowledge and then applying this theory to the relevant topics in theology. Rather, the specific and particular way one comes to know God cannot be delineated without providing an account of revelation, Scripture, the Trinity, and the like. These topics are essential if the full objectivity of the divine reality is to be acknowledged. It is worth pausing to note briefly how this is the case.

On Barth's analysis, knowledge of God begins with God's own objective knowledge of himself in his triune nature. This knowledge then flows from God to the human subject through media chosen and ordained by divine agency and decision.

As He certainly knows Himself first of all, God is first and foremost objective to Himself. . . . In His triune life as such, objectivity, and with it knowledge, is divine reality before creaturely objectivity and knowledge exist. We call this the primary objectivity of God, and distinguish from it the secondary, i.e., the objectivity which He has for us too in His revelation, in which He gives Himself to be known by us as He knows Himself. It is distinguished from the primary objectivity, not by a lesser degree of truth, but by its particular form for us the creature. God is objectively immediate to Himself, but to us He is mediately objective. That is to say, He is not objective directly but indirectly, not in the naked sense but clothed under the sign and veil of other objects different from Himself. His secondary objectivity is fully true, for it has its correspondence and basis in His primary objectivity. For God does not have to be untrue to Himself and deceive us about His real nature in order to become objective to us. For first to Himself, and then in His revelation to us, He is nothing but what He is in Himself. It is here that the door is shut against any 'non-objective' knowledge of God. As such it would not be knowledge of God, for God is objective to Himself. He is immediately objective to Himself—for the Father is objective to the Son, and the Son to the Father, without mediation. He is mediately objective to us in His revelation, in which he meets us under sign and veil of other objects.[30]

---

[30] *Church Dogmatics*, II. 1. 16.

As this passage makes clear, the objective reality of God is made known to the human subject through divine revelation. It is only as God speaks to us in his Word that we come to know the objective reality of God. That Word assumes a threefold form: in Jesus Christ, in Scripture, and in the proclamation of the Church.[31] Jesus Christ is the primary form of the Word of God. Strictly speaking, he is the Word of God, the criterion of all genuine revelation and the agent of reconciliation as the Word of God made flesh. Scripture, or the prophets and apostles, are the second form of the Word of God, for they bear witness to the Christ, the primary Word. The third form of the Word is Church proclamation, understood in a broad sense. As the Church proclaims the witness of Scripture to Christ, God uses that proclamation here and now as a medium of revelation. The proclamation is a sacramental veil which mediates genuine knowledge of God.

For Barth there can be no independent evidence to validate that this threefold form of the Word of God really is divine revelation. Certainly Church proclamation can and should be tested by the Word of God attested to in Scripture. Indeed, this is precisely the fundamental task of the science of dogmatics. 'As a theological discipline, dogmatics is the scientific test to which the Christian Church puts herself regarding the language about God which is peculiar to her.'[32] However, the Word attested to in Scripture cannot be subject to validation outside the inner witness of the Holy Spirit. There is no objective, independent proof of the Word of God. The ultimate truth of the reality of divine revelation is self-evident. The location of divine revelation is a matter of spiritual discernment made possible to those who have been born anew by the inner working of the Holy Spirit. Such discernment is logically tied to God's saving acts of reconciliation and the human response of obedience and trust.

In turning to the Word of God, we are confronted immediately with the triune God. It is not as if we can first establish the existence and nature of God and then go on to discover that God

---

[31] Ibid. I. I. 98–150. Barth modifies this scheme somewhat in his later writings, but the changes do not affect the point at issue here.

[32] Ibid. I. I. I. Ch. I opens with the title, 'The Word of God as the Criterion of Dogmatics' (ibid. 49).

is triune. The one who is encountered in divine revelation is none other than the triune God. It is only in meeting God in his Word that we can speak of the existence and nature of the divine reality. In meeting the Word of God, we encounter the triune God.

God's Word is God Himself in His revelation. For God reveals Himself as the Lord and that according to Scripture signifies for the concept of revelation that God Himself in unimpaired unity yet also in unimpaired difference is Revealer, Revelation, and Revealedness.[33]

Revelation is, therefore, the 'root of the doctrine of the Trinity'.[34] Given the sovereign lordship of the God of the Bible, only God can reveal himself. Analysis of the concept of revelation manifests a threefold lordship: that of the Father, that of the Son, and that of the Holy Spirit. Christ's work of reconciliation and revelation is identical to the work of the Father and made subjectively known to the human agent through the work of the Spirit. Without any 'special dialectical towering',[35] but merely by taking seriously the biblical assertions about revelation, one can arrive at the conclusion that 'God is Spirit as He is God the Father and God the Son'.[36]

Barth's proposals concerning the sovereignty of God in divine revelation lead him straightway not only to the doctrine of the Trinity, but also to exclude any appeal to natural theology. The issue at this point is not that Barth surveys the arguments for the existence of God and then finds that they are invalid or unsound. For Barth the whole appeal to any kind of evidence outside God's revelation of himself disregards the true nature and status of that revelation. Thus to seek to validate divine revelation by reason sets reason above divine revelation, putting God in the dock of human judgement. In reality, however, human judgement is in the dock and subject to divine revelation. To look for some higher ground from which to judge divine revelation is to deny divine revelation. Moreover, to look for God outside God's own self-manifestation is ultimately to create a god in our own image, an idol of our own making. The only true God is the God made known in Jesus Christ; to seek to know God outside Christ

[33] *Church Dogmatics*, I. I. 339. [34] Ibid. 349.
[35] Ibid. 534. [36] Ibid.

is to seek an idol. It is also to seek to save ourselves apart from divine grace. It is to use our own works to build ourselves a bridge to God, all the while ignoring the grace which has come to us in the Son and works within us through the Holy Spirit to enable us to believe in the first place. The truth of the matter is that the whole quest for proof is an expression of our sinful propensity to pride; it is an exercise of our fallen nature, which refuses to acknowledge the necessity and reality of divine grace; it is a rebellion against, and refusal of, the work of the Holy Spirit.

It is only by the Spirit that the truth of God incarnate in Jesus Christ and witnessed to in Scripture is brought home to our fallen minds. The Spirit supplies the very capacity to hear God's Word. Human agents in themselves do not possess a faculty for hearing God. 'It is the man who really knows the Word of God who also knows that he can bring no capacity to this knowledge, but must first receive all capacity.'[37] This capacity is not something which becomes an integral feature of the human agent as religious person; it is 'lent in the reality of the receipt of it'.[38] The Spirit also provides a certainty which cannot be matched by human argument. It is so strong that the believer is willing to put his hand in the fire for it.

The certainty with which dogmatics, Church proclamation, and the Church have to deal in the possibility of human knowledge of the Word of God cannot be great enough, and it is, of course, my opinion—and naturally not mine alone—that in the case of the single distinctive possibility under consideration here, in the case of personal assurance about the divine Word it must be emphatically an 'unheard-of' assurance.[39]

This certainty concerning the Word of God does not mean that human agents now have access to a set or system of closed propositions about God: 'The only possible system in Holy Scripture and in proclamation is revelation, i.e. Jesus Christ.'[40] In encountering revelation, one encounters a mystery. There is both an unveiling and a veiling in the experience of revelation.

---

[37] Ibid. 224.   [38] Ibid. 244.

[39] Ibid. 256. '[I]t is an assurance which bears in itself a metal which makes it superior to any other assurance: because and so far as it is the confession of God's free grace, and therefore just so far as it is submission to grace and non-grace, i.e. an appeal to God Himself' ibid. 259).   [40] Ibid. 156.

In view of this situation, acknowledgment of the Word of God must mean letting oneself continually be led, continually taking the step, continually being in movement from the experience felt at one time, from the thought grasped at one time, to the opposite experience and thought, because hearing the Word of God always consists of a simultaneous hearing of the one in the other and the other in the one. In this movement, which cannot be brought to rest by any synthesis, a man acknowledges the mystery of the Word of God and he has Christian experience.[41]

So while Barth has much to say about knowledge of God, that knowledge ends in mystery and silence.

What interests us here, of course, is whether Barth has been able to rescue Protestantism from the epistemic pit it has dug for itself over time. As we turn to this issue, we should note at the outset that one of the great attractions of Barth is his keen perception of the internal chaos which has haunted Protestantism across the centuries. One of the reasons why Barth's work was hailed with both consternation and joy stemmed from the extraordinarily fresh and even brutal way he confronted the past developments of the Protestant tradition. In Barth there was no drawing back from the truth. Moreover, he was absolutely convinced that the primary problem was epistemological. Protestantism had lost its way because it had made pivotal mistakes in its theory of knowledge. It had through its own pious efforts become sick and emaciated, subjecting itself to the prevailing norms of the culture. He was well aware that his stance would appear archaic, bizarre, and 'Catholic' to his contemporaries. In a poignant comment in the foreword to the first half-volume the *Church Dogmatics*, he hit back hard against this charge.

. . . should I rather weep over the constantly increasing barbarism, tedium, and insignificance of modern Protestantism, which has gone and lost—apparently along with the Trinity and the Virgin Birth—an entire third dimension (let us say it once for all the dimension of mystery—not to be confused with religiously moral 'seriousness'); only to be punished with every possible worthless substitute, only that it might with less check relapse into High Church, German Church, Christian Community, religious socialism, and similar miserable cliques and sects, only that in the end so-and-so many of its preachers and faithful people might learn finally how to discover religious insight in the intoxication of their Nordic blood and in their political *Führer* (Leader).[42]

---

[41] *Church Dogmatics*, 237.   [42] Ibid., p. xi.

Clearly Barth intended to change this situation for the better. His fundamental move was to return to the tradition of the Reformers and to re-establish the authority of Scripture over every other voice in the Church and in the world. It was as if he set out to put things right by making yet one more, massive, last-ditch, epistemological effort to rescue the Protestant experiment. What better way to do this than by returning to the exclusivist foundationalism of the Reformation and starting all over again? In the light of the consequences we have already traced in the wake of the shift from canon to norm, one cannot but admire the courage and thoroughness exhibited by Barth. Several matters deserve extended attention.

It is worth dwelling, initially, on the way Barth deployed the resources of the Reformation tradition. In his approach to Scripture Calvin developed both a doctrine of the divine dictation and inspiration of Scripture and a doctrine of the inner witness of the Holy Spirit. He needed the latter in order to deal with the issue of the genuine location of the Word of God, and he needed the former to secure the foundational premises which were essential to his doctrinal system. If anything, the emphasis fell on the former, for the doctrine of the inner witness of the Holy Spirit was so little developed that it is not clear whether we should read it as an appeal to divine revelation or an appeal to religious experience.

Once accepted, the doctrine of divine inspiration leads naturally into a strongly evidentialist and internalist approach to Christian doctrine. One secures the rightness of one's doctrinal claims by showing that they can be derived from proper exegesis of Scripture or by inference therefrom. The doctrine of inspiration simply secures the correctness of the initial starting point in this system. It was this aspect of the Reformers which was developed by the great Princeton theologians. In the hands of Alexander and Warfield the internalist, evidentialist side of the Reformation predominated—so much so, that in Alexander and Warfield, but not in Hodge, the appeal to the inner witness played an ancillary epistemic role. Even in Hodge, any appeal to experience, including experience of the inner witness of the Holy Spirit, had to be ultimately validated by Scripture.

What we see in Barth is precisely the opposite. Although Barth has a fully developed account of the inspiration of the

Scriptures,[43] this played a very limited role in his epistemology, whereas the doctrine of the witness and working of the Holy Spirit played a pivotal role.[44] Thus we might say that Barth developed the externalist side of the Reformation tradition. More precisely, we might interpret Barth as a reliabilist. It was because God produced knowledge of himself working by the power of the Spirit through designated media that the believer had knowledge and assurance. Even the capacity to perceive the revelation of God was momentarily given and repeatedly renewed in the human subject. So knowledge was ultimately secured by a process governed from start to finish by divine grace.[45]

Not surprisingly, this difference led in Barth to a radically different conception of divine revelation from that found in the Princeton theologians. While both are exclusivist foundationalists,

[43] Barth supplies an extended excursus on the doctrine of divine inspiration (see ibid. I. 2. 514–26). Even though he holds that every single part of Scripture is divinely inspired and therefore worthy of the utmost respect, he is resolutely opposed to the way the doctrine of inspiration developed and the status it achieved in Protestant orthodoxy. One cannot help but feel that, like the Princeton theologians, Barth used the Reformers as a kind of cipher for the propagation of his own constructive proposals.

[44] It would be difficult to underestimate the place that the working of the Holy Spirit played in Barth's theology and epistemology. Early on he rightly pointed out that his whole theology was an attempt to take seriously the work of the Spirit. 'According to the eight chapter of Romans, there is more hope when one sighs *Veni Creator Spiritus*, than when he exults as if the spirit were there already. You have been introduced to "my theology" if you have heard this sigh' ('The Need of Christian Preaching', in *Word of God and Word of Man*, 134). Moreover, it was because he was convinced that Schleiermacher was attempting to develop the significance of the third article for knowledge of God that he took him so seriously. 'What Schleiermacher constructed by means of his theology of awareness by planting himself in the centre for the Reformers had been a subsidiary centre, *could* be the pure theology of the Holy Spirit; the teaching of man brought face to face with God by God, of man granted grace by grace' (*From Rousseau to Ritschl* (London: SCM Press, 1959), 341; emphasis original).

[45] It is worth pointing out here that there is clear continuity between the ideas of Descartes and Barth at this point. Just as Descartes secured the reliability of human cognition against the possibility of demonic deception by appeal to the creative activity of God, so Barth secured the reliability of human perception of the Word of God against the possibility of deception due to fallen human nature by appeal to the immediate working of the Holy Spirit in supplying the relevant cognitive ability.

while both set the greatest possible store by the reception of the Word of God, while both are obsessed by the idea of divine speaking, they arrive at radically different positions on the nature of divine revelation. The Princeton theologians develop a doctrine in which the content of divine revelation is a set of propositions which can theoretically be held independently of faith and obedience. For Barth the content of divine revelation is ultimately a divine mystery which, while it can be witnessed to in human doctrine, can never be ultimately expressed and secured in human words. For Barth, divine revelation must ever and anew be received, believed, and obeyed.

Moreover, for the Princeton theologians the appeal to divine revelation presupposes the validity of natural theology and the deployment of relevant credentials. For Barth appeal to divine revelation rules out as sinful and wrong-headed all efforts to appeal to independent evidence in support of claims about the existence of God or the locus of divine revelation. In fact, for Barth, the development of natural theology was a heretical development. He was extremely pleased, therefore, that for the first time in history the Barmen Declaration made the rejection of natural theology a matter for official confession in the Church. In short, his personal epistemic proposals were construed in his own eyes as nothing short of canonical.

It is precisely at this juncture that we can see how little Barth has escaped from the epistemological captivity of the Church in the West. The situation is this. At one level Barth took the Bible as an epistemic norm. He agreed with the Reformers that this was the foundation of the Church's life, and that this norm stood in judgement over the tradition of the Church and over the teaching magisterium of the Roman see. Here Barth was as partisan and polemical as the most ardent follower of Luther and Calvin. Once this idea is in place, one can further develop this line of enquiry by working out how also to pit the Bible against reason and experience. However, one can also take this line as merely a formal commitment. As Luther made very clear, commitment to this formal norm may also lead to a debate about the material norm of theology. Thus Luther insisted that, while the formal norm of theology was Scripture, the material norm—that is, what Scripture itself posits as the norm of theology—was what preached Jesus

Christ.[46] What we find in Barth is a retention of the exclusive, canonical foundationalism of the Reformers; only this time what is brought front and centre is the appeal to the material norm. Barth took hold of the *sola fide*, the *sola gratia*, the *solus Christus*, of the Reformation and pitted these, rather than a merely formal appeal to the authority of Scripture, against the epistemic alternatives which were canvassed. This is the truly original and unique move that Barth made in his quest to liberate Protestantism from its enslavement to the cultural norms of the modern period.

It should be clear by now, however, that this is an illusory liberation. Despite all Barth's warnings about the need to eliminate any trace of Cartesianism from our thinking, in terms of epistemology Barth is thoroughly Cartesian in his outlook.[47] Like the Reformers who inspired him, he was wedded to an exclusivist foundationalism which sought to track every idea back to the Word of God. This affinity with Descartes should not, of course, surprise us; for Descartes may well have indirectly imbibed his exclusive foundationalism from the very Reformers to whom Barth returned for epistemic inspiration. Descartes and Barth are both totally enmeshed in the same epistemological soil. They share the same epistemic sensibilities. Once we make allowances for the fact that Barth's interests were confined to theology, while those of Descartes were more general, we can discern that they are both wedded to the same fundamental ideas. They both hold that there is only one foundation for knowledge; they both believe that this foundation must provide certainty; they both insist that every effort needs to be expended to ensure the right foundation; and they both believe that all other foundations lead to epistemic disaster. Both Barth and Descartes occupied the same epistemic territory. Differences in their material positions do nothing to undercut this claim.

Here we need only draw attention to one or two problems inherent in Barth's material epistemological proposals. To begin,

---

[46] Luther just as easily made justification by faith the material norm of theology, but of course this did not really alter the material norm, for in Luther justification by faith was another way of laying hold of the Gospel manifest in Christ.

[47] Ironically, Barth once remarked: 'we merely make the point that in theology at least thought cannot proceed along Cartesian lines' (*Church Dogmatics*, I. I. 223).

most of his objections to natural theology are wide of the mark. It is simply false to say that someone committed to the possibility of natural theology is logically committed to a denial of the potential status of divine revelation, or to the denial of justification by faith, or to a denial of the crucial significance of the witness of the Holy Spirit in the life of faith. All one is committed to in exploring the possibility of natural theology is the investigation of the soundness and validity of various arguments for the existence of God. This is a matter of the cogency of certain arguments; the arguments do not in themselves have entailments for any thesis about the availability of divine revelation, for a particular doctrine of grace, or for this or that doctrine of the inner witness of the Holy Spirit. Thus, for example, it is one thing to argue for and against the cogency of the teleological argument; it is another to argue for or against justification by faith. Barth was so enmeshed in his version of canonical foundationalism that he could not perceive this kind of obvious distinction.[48]

We can express this same point theologically. Barth simply begged crucial questions about the nature of the grace of God working in creation and in the human subject. Engaging in natural theology can be interpreted as an activity made possible by God's common grace working in creation or as an expression of the image of God in the human mind without strain. It could equally well be expressed in terms of a doctrine of creation which speaks of the working of the Holy Spirit. Natural theology can well be interpreted as one means which the Holy Spirit uses to bring people to commitment to God. It is only if one is committed to a certain doctrine of sin or to a certain pneumatology that these claims will be called into question. However,

[48] Barth generally refused to even discuss the cogency of the various arguments for the existence of God. In the one case where he provides extended commentary—namely, in the case of Anselm's version of the ontological argument—he is at pains to argue that Anselm's proof is from within faith itself. See Karl Barth, *Anselm: Fides Quaerens Intellectum* (New York: Meridian, 1962). Of course, Anselm's proof arises from meditation and prayer, and it draws on a particular conception of God developed in Christianity; but the question of the validity and soundness of the argument is logically quite independent of the question of the origin of Anselm's ideas and arguments. For a splendid assessment of Barth's account of Anselm's position see M. J. Charlesworth, *St Anselm's Proslogion* (Oxford: Clarendon Press, 1965), 40–6.

unless we want to beg the question against our opponent, these doctrines themselves need to be examined carefully in their own right, rather than posited in a dogmatic manner at the outset.

Barth's proposals are question begging in another way. Barth built fundamental doctrines of the Christian faith into the very foundations of his epistemology at the outset. He launched a network of claims about the objectivity of God and divine revelation which make it impossible for any of these proposals to be challenged. He built the existence of the triune God and the reality of the incarnation of God in Jesus Christ into the very content and analysis of divine revelation, and posited divine revelation as the sole ground of truth. On this scheme, however, the same option is available to those who would argue for a totally different set of doctrines, so long as they are prepared to adopt the same exclusivist foundationalism. Thus a similar move is available to the Roman Catholic, the Mormon, the Orthodox Jew, or the Muslim. All of these can—and some of them do—appeal to the inner witness of the Holy Spirit to secure the location of special revelation.[49] Given this inner witness, their material doctrines are secured automatically. Hence we encounter here exactly the same problem which emerged at the Reformation in debates about the location of the canon. Both Protestants and Counter-Reformation Roman Catholics appealed to the inner witness to validate their favoured source of divine truth. Consequently, their followers had to turn to the development of a more general epistemology to resolve the impasse.

It is no accident that some of the disciples of Karl Barth have been forced to move in the same direction. Thus Thomas Torrance has argued at length that Barth's epistemology represents precisely the kind of epistemology which one finds in the

[49] Given this development, it is very tempting for the Calvinist or the Barthian to posit another witness of the Spirit to determine which of the claimed witnesses is a true witness of the Spirit. However, this is the kind of desperate measure which is also open to an adherent of the competing claims, so, to resolve this debate, we will need yet another witness of the Spirit, and we are off on the road *ad infinitum*. This shows once again that, when used in this way in epistemology, the appeal to the witness of the Spirit is a moveable feast which can be relocated at will.

natural sciences.[50] Others, again apparently impressed by the significance of the natural sciences, have supplemented Barth's epistemology by appeal to the insights of Michael Polanyi, a natural scientist turned philosopher.[51] One wonders how far Barth, given the radical particularism which governed his work and the disdain he showed for developing a universal epistemology, would approve of these developments.[52] Yet one can surely sympathize with them, for without some such operation the whole Barthian project will appear arbitrary and subjective. Moreover, the choice of epistemic partner is both unsurprising and paradoxical. It is unsurprising, in that the whole modern period has been wedded to the idea of natural science as the paradigm of rationality and knowledge. It is paradoxical because the Barthian project was supposed to deliver us from bondage to the epistemic idols of modern culture; yet here again, in the very heartland of the Barthian tradition, one of them, the appeal to science as the paradigm of knowledge, suddenly reappears.[53]

Another angle on Barth is to reflect further on the way he attempted to secure some of the classical doctrines of the Christian tradition, notably the doctrine of the Trinity. In the canonical traditions of the early Church this was clearly a pivotal doctrine, for it is carefully and repeatedly expressed in the Nicene Creed, in the writings of the Fathers, in the liturgy, and in the iconography. The Church did not specify, however, how this doctrine was secured intellectually. What mattered was not so

---

[50] See e.g. Thomas Torrance, *Reality and Evangelical Theology* (Philadelphia: Westminster Press, 1982).

[51] See e.g. Colin Gunton, 'No Other Foundation: One Englishman's Reading of Church Dogmatics Chapter V', in Nigel Biggar (ed.), *Reckoning with Karl Barth: Essays on the Centenary of Karl Barth's Birth* (London: Mowbray, 1988), 61–79.

[52] There is some evidence that Barth was in favour of this line of enquiry. See the interesting report of Barth's attitude to Torrance's work in Thomas Torrance, *Karl Barth, Biblical and Evangelical Theologian* (Edinburgh: T. & T. Clark, 1990), 135.

[53] It would surely be much more promising to pursue the externalist conception of knowledge of God which I attributed to Barth in the exposition above. However, it will take great dexterity to extract this element from the wider components of Barth's comprehensive epistemology of theology. Moreover, it is not at all clear that a purely externalist epistemology will do full justice to the full contours of Christian belief as identified canonically.

much a theory of knowledge concerning how one proved the doctrine of the Trinity as the doctrine itself, together with the ramifications it entailed for life in the Church and before God. Like the Reformers, Barth wanted to assert the doctrine of the Trinity. Like the Reformers, too, he reduced the canons of the Church to the single canon of Scripture, treating it, first, as the locus of divine revelation and, second, as the sole, formal norm of theology. How, then, were these two commitments to be married? Barth achieved this marriage by insisting that the doctrine of the Trinity can be derived from an analysis of his doctrine of divine revelation. The doctrine of the Trinity is, then, analytically derivable from his epistemology.

This is a bizarre attempt to find adequate grounds for the doctrine of the Trinity, for, whatever else we may say about the doctrine of the Trinity, it surely cannot be derived from an analysis of the concept of divine revelation. One can only be amazed that the doctrine survived even in the relatively modalistic form which Barth's critics have often lamented. It is a marvel that it survived at all in this epistemological scheme. One is tempted to surmise that Barth, like the Reformers, was so taken by the Church's long-standing commitment to the Trinity that he would have found some way or other to fit it into his theology. However, given that he rejected the delicate canonical heritage of the Church which existed outside Scripture, and given that the only canon left had been turned into an item of epistemology, there was really no other place to locate the Trinity than in his doctrine of divine revelation. In fact, everything of value has to be derived from divine revelation, for this is the only live option given the premises of his exclusivist foundationalism.

What we are observing here is the way Barth's epistemology absorbed, and even determined, the content of his doctrine of the Trinity. That epistemology also had consequences for the reception and interpretation of Scripture itself. Given Barth's material epistemology, Scripture must be read in broad terms as a witness to divine revelation. The great danger with this, of course, is that it will engender the kind of mental cramp which will lead either to a forced reading or a subtle ignoring of large tracts of Scripture. Scripture is much more than a witness to divine revelation. Whole tracts, like that represented by wisdom literature, do not fit this category. Indeed, any single description will mask the great diversity and adaptability of Scripture.[54]

Likewise, any attempt to derive a particular epistemology from Scripture will flounder, either because the epistemic material is not sufficiently developed, or because this is the last concern represented by the biblical writers and editors. Yet, given the mentality of exclusivist, canonical foundationalism, these facts have to be hidden from view. For the exclusivist foundationalist, on pain of inconsistency, must locate his own foundationalist doctrine in the canon itself. Hence there arises the need to argue that Scripture teaches the precise epistemology developed by the foundationalist.[55] It is bad enough that this whole procedure involves a circularity which is rarely addressed; it is worse when it forces Scripture into a Procrustean bed to which it was never meant to be tied.

When Barth launched his great project, he clearly hoped to set modern Protestantism on a better path than it was currently pursuing. He believed with his great teacher Herrmann that faith did not need proof, that theology did not need an ancillary science for its legitimization. This doctrine became for Barth 'the rat-poison against all intellectualizing subtleties in theology'.[56] The rat poison he developed turned out to be an extraordinary exercise in epistemology. As such, it is full of interesting twists and turns, of fascinating virtues and vices. It deserves extended attention from those who are called to deal with the epistemological queries which Christian intellectuals sooner or later are forced to address. Unfortunately, Barth's poison kills off more

---

[54] A generation or so later the influence of Barth led to the slogan that the Bible is the book of the acts of God. This too led to a tendency to lose the particularity and richness of the Bible as it is.

[55] Hence the energy expounded by Barthians to prove that Scripture is opposed to natural theology and the counter-attack by their opponents to show otherwise. The fact of the matter is that Scripture at best gives us hints to be developed in various directions. We should not disparage such hints, but they need to be kept carefully in their place in the economy of the Church. The same applies to the material of the Fathers which was canonized. It is only rarely that one finds a full-blown epistemology in this material, but there are plenty of hints and suggestions to be followed up and explored.

[56] This phrase has been attributed to Barth himself. It is quoted in H. Martin Rumscheidt, *Revelation and Theology* (Cambridge: Cambridge University Press, 1972), 4.

than unwelcome philosophical vermin. If swallowed as it stands, it is also likely to destroy crucial components of the canonical heritage of the Church which Barth himself sought to preserve. The canonical heritage of the Church has something better to offer than epistemology. Its adherents should be wary of any epistemic poison, Barthian or otherwise.

15

Digging Still Deeper for Firm Ground

Karl Barth's effort to recover the canonical heritage of the Reformation, while it secured him a place of prominence and glory in the history of Protestant theology, did not win the allegiance of the tradition as a whole. Indeed, it is fascinating that the Barthian project was quickly challenged by the resurgence of lively forms of Liberal and Radical Protestantism.[1] This challenge was relatively easy to put in place because Barth himself, despite the fact that his position is constitutive of a certain kind of orthodoxy, was engaged in a penetrating exercise of self-criticism, a feature of his work which can easily be taken as one of the hallmarks of Liberal Protestantism. Hence it is not at all surprising that one of the most interesting and rigorous proponents of the renewal of Liberal Protestantism can relocate Barth's project and see it as a moment in the trajectory of that tradition. I have in mind the work of the North American theologian Schubert Ogden.[2] In this chapter we shall explore

---

[1] The deep cleavage between Liberal and Radical forms of Protestantism is easily missed by most observers, because they often find the differences between conservative and non-conservative forms of Protestantism more interesting and significant. No doubt this is partly due to the continued tendency to divide Protestants into the simple camps of fundamentalists and modernists, or conservatives and liberals. It is also due to the fact that there is indeed deep continuity in epistemology in the shift from Liberal to Radical Protestantism, as we shall see later.

[2] Ogden expresses this claim about 'neo-orthodoxy' in this fashion: 'Yet it is of the utmost importance to realize that this movement began as, and to a considerable extent continued to be, a movement of *self*-criticism from within the ranks of liberal theology. Wilhelm Pauck used to point out that this is by no means accidental, since it is not in the nature of orthodoxy to give rise to a neo-orthodoxy. In any case, it is possible to argue—and my guess is that time and distance will tend more fully to support the argument—that neo-orthodoxy for the most part is itself but a chapter in the larger history of theological liberalism'

the carefully constructed account of canon and norm which Ogden has developed.

In Ogden's case we are particularly fortunate to have at our disposal a full-dress account of his approach to the authority of scripture.[3] We note immediately that Ogden, in keeping with time-honoured practice in the Protestant tradition, prefers at times to speak of the *authority* of Scripture rather than the *canon* of Scripture. He initially approaches Scripture, therefore, first and foremost as a potential criterion of truth in theology. His immediate response to this possibility is to reject the claim outright. The argument is simple: by its very nature, any appeal to authority cannot authorize the truthfulness of any assertion.

In the nature of the case, no authority, properly so-called, can be a sufficient authorization for the truth of the assertions derived from it or warranted by it. Unless the assertions made by the authority are themselves already authorized as true by some method other than appeal to authority, no assertion derived from them or warranted by them can by that fact alone be an authorized assertion. This is not to deny, of course, that an assertion authorized by appeal to authority may well be true. The point is simply that, if it is so, the fact that it is authorized is not itself sufficient to make it so.[4]

What is fascinating about this argument is that it is purely formal. The debate about the authority of Scripture has been reduced to the merely formal issue of whether something can be true on the basis of someone's word. Hence at the outset Scripture is construed as an entirely human document from start to finish; any mention of Scripture as divinely inspired, as related to divine revelation, as the Word of God or containing the Word of God, as spoken by God, and the like, has completely disappeared from the discussion. The only ecclesial notion around is that of the canon of Scripture or the Scripture principle. Every other theological notion has simply disappeared off the map.

('A Critique of Religious Liberalism', in *Revolutionary Changes to Religious Liberalism: The Meadville/Lombard Theological School 125th Anniversary Lectures* (1971), 5–6; emphasis original).

    [3] There are two crucial essays on this issue: 'Sources of Religious Authority in Liberal Protestantism', *Journal of the American Academy of Religion*, 44 (1976), 403–16; and 'The Authority of Scripture for Theology', in *On Theology* (San Francisco: Harper and Row, 1986), 45–68.

    [4] 'Authority of Scripture', 47.

Historically this is extremely odd, for in classical Protestant discussions of the authority of Scripture, it would have been absurd to appeal to the authority of any book unless that book was already construed in terms which related it back to divine inspiration, divine revelation, the Word of God, and the like. In fact, the whole attack on the Roman see was centred in the claim that, by exalting tradition and human authority, she had put merely human authority in the place of the Word of God. That Word was to be believed on the authority of God, a claim which, given the epistemic status of God, was not subject to the negative rule that appeal to authority did not authorize truth.

However, given the terms of the discussion delineated by Ogden, he is entirely correct. Logically speaking, the mere fact that a book or a person or some authority asserts p does not in itself establish that p is true. For Ogden, any attempt to speak of Scripture in terms of traditional doctrines of divine inspiration is no longer possible, given the dismantling of traditional accounts of that doctrine in the aftermath of the rise of historical criticism. Scripture is a book like any other book, subject to the same rules which apply to the authority of any human document. Hence appeal to Scripture does not in itself establish the truth of any proposition.

Does this mean, then, that the concept of authority in general or the concept of scriptural authority in particular should be jettisoned altogether? Is there a place for the idea of authority in theology? And is there, more specifically, a place for the authority of Scripture in theology? As we pursue these questions, we shall enter into the inner sanctuary of Ogden's whole conception of theology, together with the account of canon, norm, authority, revelation, rationality, and the like related to it.

Crucial to Ogden's position is a carefully crafted account of the nature of theology. The core of his account is that theology is the critical assessment of Christian witness. We can think of witness here broadly as those acts performed by Christians or by the Church which are an expression of Christian commitment.[5] Any

[5] For a summary of Ogden's idea of witness see his 'The Service of Theology to the Servant Task of Pastoral Ministry', in Earl E. Shelp and Ronald H. Sunderland (eds.), *The Pastor as Servant* (New York: Pilgrim Press, 1986), 84–7.

act of Christian witness can be assessed ultimately in terms of three logically distinct criteria: its aptness to the situation to which it is addressed, its faithfulness to the normative content of Christian witness, and general norms of credibility.

Thus to take the case of explicit witness represented, say, by a sermon, that sermon must, first, relate to and fit precisely the situation of the hearer. Thus it would fail to satisfy this criterion if it was delivered, say, in crude, populist style when the audience was a group of sophisticated graduate students from the University of Chicago's Department of Religious Studies. It must, second, really be a form of Christian witness. It would fail in this regard if, rather than presenting the apostolic witness to Jesus Christ as the decisive representation of the universal love of God, it used the language of the Gospel to present the claim that Jesus saved us from our sins by giving us a model of morality, which by following we could earn the respect and approval of God. Third, the content of the sermon must be credible. It must be true, judged by criteria given by universal human experience. Hence it would fail if, say, it included miraculous and legendary material as if these constituted real events in human history.

It is clearly the second two criteria which are of crucial importance in articulating Ogden's approach to both the canon of Scripture and the criteria of credibility. However, the three criteria are very closely related. In fact, they can only be properly understood when their internal relations are adequately grasped.

Consider, first, the way in which Ogden interprets our current situation in the modern world. This is not just a matter of cultural style. What is at issue is a very general description of the boundaries of intelligibility. Ogden gets at this by asking the question, What precisely is our situation? His answer has two components:

In the first place, there is the fact of the ever-growing domination at all levels of the common life of the modern scientific picture of the world. Increasingly, men today are coming to understand themselves and their experience in terms of the basic conceptuality of modern science and technology. They simply take it for granted that the world in which they live is indeed the closed and lawfully ordered universe which scientific research and technological achievement alike assume it to be. And whereas previous generations were more or less uncritical in their whole attitude to the question of meaning and truth, we today commonly insist that every assertion which is put forward for serious consideration must meet very specific criteria of meaningfulness and verification.

In the second place, however, our situation is determined by the increasing prevalence of a positive or affirmative attitude toward man's various natural and cultural possibilities. Frequently, this particular phenomenon is popularly referred to as the 'this-worldliness' of modern culture. And this is indeed in many ways an appropriate designation. For what peculiarly distinguishes our period from previous ones is its insistence that 'this world' and all that it represents should be brought to its completest possible fulfillment. Whereas in earlier ages, man's self-realization was commonly restricted within rather narrow limits, modern man has declared his independence and refuses to brook any arbitrary or heteronomous interference of his own autonomous development.[6]

What has to be noted immediately about this description of our contemporary situation is that it builds into the criterion of aptness to the situation an epistemological requirement of a very particular sort. Another way to state this is to say that the concept of modernity deployed here is an epistemic rather than a temporal one. To be modern is not to fit into a particular chronological period, which is what we might ordinarily expect the term 'modern' to mean; to be modern is to be committed to a very specific set of epistemic requirements. Hence the first of Ogden's criteria of success is really a disguised form of the third, the criterion of credibility.

Ogden's second criterion for assessing prospective forms of

---

[6] 'The Situation in Contemporary Protestant Theology, II. Systematic Theology', *Perkins School of Theology Journal*, 12 (1959), 16. Elsewhere Ogden makes this same crucial point in this fashion: 'So far as I understand the matter, the conditions of reasonableness in our situation demand the unqualified acceptance both of the method and the world-picture of modern science and critical history and of the reality and significance of this world of time and change, which is the context of our lives as secular men' ('Love Unbounded: The Doctrine of God', *Perkins School of Theology Journal*, 19 (1966), 10). In his later writings Ogden develops a different account of our contemporary situation, but this has not altered the fundamental content of his account of canon and credibility. What is essential to bring out here is the crucial relationship between his earlier account of the contemporary situation and his views on canon and credibility. Ogden's later concern to work out the full logic of a theology of liberation in no way involves a repudiation of his earlier work in the epistemology of theology. On the contrary, he clearly holds that a true theology of liberation needs exactly the kind of epistemic and metaphysical foundations he has been at such pains to provide.

Christian witness leads us directly into his account of canon and Scripture. In this case the aim of critical reflection is to determine how far Christian witness is faithful to its own internal identity. In his early work Ogden, adhering in formal terms to the position of Barth, located this criterion in the message of Scripture. Thus an act of witness was Christian in so far as it represented a faithful rendering of the Scriptural message. Over time, however, he changed his mind on this, relocating the normative test of identity not in the canon of scripture or in a 'canon within the canon' but in a 'canon before the canon'.[7]

The reason for this shift was relatively simple. Ogden, following the work of Hans van Campenhausen, came to believe on historical grounds that the formal norm for Scripture was apostolicity. What really led the early Church to adopt the canon of the New Testament as we currently have it was the conviction that these books were produced by the apostles. Hence the formal norm of Christian identity in the early Church was the witness of the apostles.

While the Church has been correct about the formal norm of apostolic witness, it has been mistaken in the material identification of that norm. There was nothing dishonest or deceptive about this material identification of apostolic witness with the current canon of the New Testament. The Church of the early centuries did not have at its disposal the kind of critical historical enquiry we now have in the wake of the development of historical criticism. Hence it did the best it could with the tools at its disposal. We now know, however, on the basis of expert historical investigation, that they were wrong in attributing the books of the New Testament to the apostles. Hence our task today is to

---

[7] Ogden's earlier position can be located in 'What is Theology?,' *Perkins School of Theology Journal*, 26 (1973), 1–13. Note that the shift involves a change only in the material location of the canon, not in the conception of canon deployed by Ogden. Note also that Scripture is still the source of Ogden's canon before the canon. It is by the critical examination of the New Testament, more especially the synoptic tradition, that we get access to the content of the canon before the canon. Strictly speaking, there does not exist a canon before the canon in the same way that the current canon exists; the canon before the canon is a critical reconstruction made in the light of expert historical judgement. For a typically forthright defence of his proposal from a historical point of view see his 'The Problem of Normative Witness: A Response', *Perkins School of Theology Journal*, 41 (1988), 22–5.

revisit the matter of apostolic witness and reconstruct the record to fit the facts of the situation in the early Church.

At this point Ogden follows the findings of the modern New Testament scholar Willi Marxsen. The earliest, original apostolic witness of the Church is to be found in the Jesus kerygma of the first Palestinian Christian community.

Given our present historical methods and knowledge, the locus of the canon—in the early church's own sense of the apostolic witness—cannot be the writings of the New Testament as such but can only be the earliest traditions of Christian witness accessible to us today by historical-critical analysis of these writings. Specifically, the canon of the church, and hence also the primary authority for theology, must now be located in what form critics generally speak of as the earliest layer of the synoptic tradition, or what Marxsen in particular refers to as 'the Jesus-kerygma,' as distinct from the 'Christ-kerygma' and from 'the mixed form of the Jesus-kerygma and the Christ-kerygma' that we find expressed in the writings of the New Testament. Accordingly, the witness to which theological assertions must be appropriate is not the *scriptural* witness typically spoken of in most postliberal Protestant theology, but, rather, the *apostolic* witness which is to be discerned by critical interpretation in the earliest layer of Christian tradition or kerygma.[8]

This earliest layer of Christian tradition or kerygma must now be take as the criterion of apostolicity. This apostolic witness is 'the *norma normans, sed non normata*'.[9] It is the norm of norms which is not itself normed by anything else. Yet, strictly speaking, this has to be qualified, for, following the Reformers, Ogden holds that it is Christ alone who is the source of the authority of the original apostolic witness. So the apostolic witness 'is normed, even if not by any other norm properly so-called'.[10] As Luther expressed the matter graphically, the Christ who is Lord of the apostles is 'King of Scripture', while the Scripture is 'queen'. Luther expressed the crucial point about Scripture this way:

This queen ought to rule, and all ought to obey and be subject to her. They ought not to be masters, judges, or arbiters, but only witnesses, disciples, and confessors—whether it be the Pope, Luther, Augustine, Paul, or an angel from heaven. Nor ought any other doctrine be taught and heard in the church except the pure word of God.[11]

---

[8] 'Authority of Scripture', 64; emphasis original.   [9] Ibid. 59.
[10] Ibid.   [11] Quoted by Ogden, ibid. 60.

In Ogden's terms it is now the original apostolic witness which is queen and it is the Jesus attested in that witness who is king. The rule of the queen is strictly limited; her task is to authorize not the truth or the credibility of non-apostolic witness but its appropriateness to its own Christian identity and content.

What lies behind this fascinating transposition of Luther is a particular philosophy of authority. The crucial distinction to register is that between *de facto* and *de jure* authority. Authority exists *de facto* whenever one person recognizes another as having the right to command or to act as regards his or her action or belief. 'Thus scripture may be said to have a *de facto* authority for theology whenever a theologian recognizes that the writings of the canonical authors are entitled to function as a standard or norm for determining the appropriateness of his or her assertions to the Christian witness of faith.'[12] However, behind *de facto* authority lies *de jure* authority. It is not enough that in conventional Protestant theology Scripture happens contingently to be authoritative because theologians recognize historically that this has been so. Scripture 'by right *ought to be* thus authoritative whether they recognize its authority or not'.[13] This kind of authority is by necessity rule-governed. It exists only if there is a rule which confers the right to authorize on the part of the designated authority. Without this conferring rule, all that exists is the exercise of raw power. Moreover, it is this insight that warrants the claim that both the judge and the accused are ultimately on the same level, standing under the same laws and rules of justice. They do so because they both recognize the *de jure* authority of the law by which their actions are tried.[14]

The upshot of this for the conventional Protestant account of the authority of Scripture is twofold. First, accepting the authority of Scripture in no ways diminishes or destroys the need for the individual to control the decision as to what counts as *de jure*

[12] 'Authority of Scripture', 49. Note again the characteristic Ogdenian move to restrict the authority of Scripture to the appropriateness rather than the credibility of Christian witness.

[13] Ibid.; emphasis original.

[14] Ogden also uses here the case of teacher and student: 'the teacher no less than the student is subject to the demands of their particular discipline, which confront both of them alike in its constitutive methods of inquiry and procedures of verification' (ibid. 50).

authority on the basis of the relevant rule. Acceptance of authority is not an arbitrary, irrational matter. On the contrary, it requires that one ensure that any authority prove itself as such by those who stand under it. In technical terms the theological norm one deploys is both *norma normata* and *norma normanda*. It is both a norm normed and a norm to be normed. 'It is the former insofar as it has already proved itself to those who stand under it and have thus controlled its right to control them; and it is the latter insofar as this right does not exclude but presupposes their continuing right and responsibility to control it.'[15] It is this latter claim which provides Ogden with the warrant for reviewing the whole status of Scripture in theology and replacing it with a temporally prior 'canon before the canon'. Applying the rule that the locus of the true canon is the original apostolic witness secures this shift.

Second, accepting the authority of Scripture, even though it means that Scripture is a norm that norms but is not itself normed, does not entail that Scripture is not itself normed and is to be normed in relation to Jesus Christ. On the contrary, Scripture is normed by Christ himself. Yet this form of being normed is unlike every other kind of norming. What authorizes Scripture is not itself a theological authority in the proper sense of the words; what authorizes Scripture is its source. 'Although Christ, or God, is indeed the primal source of all authority, it is misled and misleading to say in any literal sense that (as one recent writer puts it) "Christianity recognizes only one absolute authority—that of God himself." '[16] Applying this to Ogden's reworked account of the locus of the canon, we might say that the canon before the canon, the apostolic witness, has Christ as its primal source. This canon before the canon is not normed by any other theological authority, so it retains the status of a norm which norms but is not normed, yet it itself is normed and is to be normed in its relation to Jesus Christ.

Thus far we have identified two criteria which have to be applied to any putative case of Christian witness. That witness must be apt to its situation, and it must be faithful to the original apostolic witness to Christ. The former brings success or failure with respect to the fittingness of the witness; the latter secures

---

[15] Ibid. 51.   [16] Ibid. 51–2.

success or failure with respect to its Christian identity. The former takes us into the field of practical theology; the latter draws us into the territory of historical theology. With these behind us we are on the threshold of systematic theology.

It is the threshold because we have been working throughout with mostly formal categories. We do not yet know how to understand the actual content of the original apostolic witness to Christ beyond knowing that it is the confession that Jesus is the Christ. How is this confession to be interpreted? The route into this answer is through Ogden's account of the meaning of religious language. With that in place we can then spell out how Ogden understands and deploys his criterion of credibility.

Ogden is deeply versed in the modern analytic discussion concerning the meaning of religious discourse.[17] The crucial objection which emerged in the 1920s and 1930s was that religious assertions failed the famous criterion of verifiability and falsifiability, a test which was taken to provide the demarcation between cognitive and emotive discourse. There is a vast literature on this topic, but the options relevant to the exposition of Ogden can be reduced to four. One can accept the positivist standard of meaning and applied critique and dismiss religious discourse as a disguised forms of emotive discourse. One can accept the positivist standard and show that religious language readily meets that standard. One can accept the positivist standard of meaning but argue that religious discourse is not in the business of either making assertions or expressing emotions; religious discourse has its own internal grammar which has to be understood on its own terms. Lastly, one can accept the notion that religious discourse is cognitive and that cognitive discourse does

---

[17] Ogden has written several articles in and around this debate. See esp. 'God and Philosophy: A Discussion with Anthony Flew', *Journal of Religion*, 48 (1968), 161–81; 'Falsification and Belief,' *Religious Studies*, 10 (1974), 21–43; ' "Theology and Falsification in Retrospect": A Reply', in Malcolm L. Diamond and Thomas V. Litzenburg, Jun. (eds.), *The Logic of God: Theology and Verification* (Indianapolis: Bobbs-Merrill, 1975), 290–7; 'Linguistic Analysis and Theology', *Theologische Zeitschrift*, 33 (1977), 318–25. For one who claims that 'his background and interests are shaped less by linguistic analysis than by certain forms of revisionary metaphysics', his analysis and prescriptions in this territory are at times extraordinarily incisive. For this self-description, see 'Linguistic Analysis and Theology', 320.

indeed have to meet certain standards of meaning, but insist that religious discourse has its own cognitive standard, and that Christian religious discourse as presented in the original apostolic witness fully satisfies that standard. It is this fourth option which Ogden adopts and deploys.

In developing this position, Ogden appeals to the famous revolution in Wittgenstein's philosophy wherein he shifted from a criterion of meaning as verification to a criterion of meaning as use. Religious language, in fact, has its own distinct domain of use. According to Ogden, it arises in certain boundary situations of our everyday existence where we are forced to ask certain limiting questions. In pursuing scientific questions, for example, we find ourselves not just searching out the general laws which enable us to predict various events in the world; we also find ourselves asking how there are any laws and events at all. To take another example, in pursuing moral issues, we find ourselves asking not just whether a particular action is right or wrong, but whether we should be moral at all or not. Most importantly, when faced with the uncertainty of the future, we find ourselves confronted not just with questions about this or that item in our future lives, but with the more general and distressing question of the very meaning of our existence overall. Finitude and death bring us face to face with a total threat to a meaningful existence. Religious and theological language arises in our actual life to provide answers to these boundary questions. More specifically, religious language arises in order to provide a reassurance that will not be disappointed.

What does this mean? Ogden appeals at this stage to everyday experience.

As we know from our everyday experience, to reassure someone is simply to restore to him an assurance of confidence which, for some reason or other, he seems to have lost. And this can be done only in the one way suggested by the word '*re*-assure' itself, namely, by assuring *again*, by re-presenting assurance. This would seem to indicate that religious assertions can serve to reassure us only because they themselves are the re-presentation of a confidence somehow already present prior to their being made.[18]

---

[18] *The Reality of God and Other Essays* (San Francisco: Harper and Row, 1963), 32.

402 *Digging Still Deeper for Firm Ground*

Religious assertions, on this view, have a strictly re-presenta-
tive character.

They are not so much the *cause* of our general confidence that existence
is meaningful as its *effect*. By this I mean that the various 'religions' or
'faiths' of mankind, including what may be called the 'Christian religion,' are one and all expressions or re-presentations of a yet deeper
faith that precedes them. Logically prior to every particular religious
assertion is an original confidence in the meaning and worth of life,
through which not simply all our religious answers, but even our religious questions first become possible or have any sense. Hence the
different historical religions, again including Christianity, can be thought
of only as several attempts at a more or less self-conscious understanding
of this original confidence. They are the results, one may say, of *fides
quaerens intellectum*, of that original faith itself in search for a more fully
conscious understanding of its own nature.[19]

We can now see what is at stake for Ogden in speaking of
God.

I hold that the primary use or function of 'God' is to refer to the objective ground in reality itself of our own ineradicable confidence in the
final worth of our existence. It lies in the nature of this basic confidence
to affirm that the real whole of which we experience ourselves to be
parts is such as to be worthy of, and thus in itself to evoke, that very
confidence. The word 'God,' then provides the designation for whatever it is about this experienced whole that calls forth and justifies our
original and inescapable trust, thereby meaning existentially, as William
James once said, 'You can dismiss certain kinds of fear.' From this it
follows that to be free of such fear by existing in this trust is one and the
same thing with affirming the reality of God.[20]

We can also now see how Ogden unpacks the meaning of the
assertion that Jesus is the Christ. The crucial concept is that of re-
presentation. The core claim is that Jesus, as attested in the apostolic witness, is the decisive re-presentation of God in the sense
that through him the meaning of God for us is made fully
explicit. In Jesus the gift and demand of God's love are made fully
explicit.

Even though Jesus hardly thought and spoke of himself as the Christ or
the Son of Man, he evidently did point to himself and his word as being
of decisive significance, in that already through him God was

---

[19] *The Reality of God and Other Essays*, 34.   [20] Ibid. 37–8.

confronting his hearers with the gift and demand of boundless love and thus with the possibility of authentic existence in faith. Consequently, in thinking and speaking of Jesus as the Christ or as the Son of Man, the early church but affirmed explicitly, in such terms and categories as were available for the purpose, Jesus' own implicit claim to be the decisive revelation of God's love.[21]

What this means is that in encountering the apostolic witness to Jesus, we encounter the full truth about ourselves and about God. *Ipso facto* we are called to repentance, to commit ourselves in faith to God, to live a life of freedom, and to live a life of loyalty to God and to the neighbour.[22] The real content of the core Christological assertion that Jesus is the Christ is not, then, the past person, sayings, or deeds of Jesus, but the present truth about ultimate reality and about ourselves. The Christological assertion that Jesus is the Christ is at once theological and existential; it is not some neutral, abstract remark about a past, historical figure. In the apostolic witness to Jesus in the past and the present we are presented again with the decisive truth about the meaning of authentic existence, and thereby we are given reassurance of the ultimate value of all we do. We are confronted explicitly with that truth which is implicit in our basic confidence in the significance of our daily existence.

This core claim has, of course, been clothed in a host of terms and conceptualities across the generations. It was originally clothed in the language of Jewish apocalyptic, and it has been restated in various ways since then. Early on it was cast in terms of honorific titles and of the origin, destiny, and course of the life of Jesus. Later on, this core claim was expressed in the conceptuality of Greek philosophy, as we see in the creeds of the early Church. So various mythological and other ways were found in diverse cultural settings to make the precise same point about the witness to Jesus which was made by the original apostolic witness. In some instances the core Christological assertion was bound up with political and moral claims which we now have to dismantle.

[21] *The Point of Christology* (Dallas: Southern Methodist University Press, 1982), 120.
[22] The implications of this claim for the political interpretation of the Christian message is worked out in *Faith and Freedom: A Theology of Liberation* (Nashville: Abingdon Press, 1979).

However, the crux of the claim stays the same: to assert that 'Jesus is the Christ' is to assert that Jesus is the decisive re-presentation of the meaning of ultimate reality for us.

On the surface, we seem to have come a long way from the question which has been our quarry. Our concern was to identify the criterion needed to test the truthfulness, and not just the appropriatness, of putative Christian witness. Yet our journey has surely not been in vain. If the apostolic witness re-presents the meaning of ultimate reality, then the truthfulness of that witness cannot be found other than by exploring how Ogden justifies any claim concerning the truth of ultimate reality. What the apostolic witness does is express again the truth about ultimate reality; it does not ground or warrant what is expressed in that witness. Thus a putative instance of Christian witness is faithful if it fits appropriately with the apostolic witness to Christ. Appropriateness to that witness does not, however, contribute one iota to the validation of that instance of witness as true. Ogden's characteristic way of making this claim is to say that the truth about ultimate reality is in fact grounded in universal human experience. In terms of the nature of systematic theology he formally lays it out in this fashion:

Systematic theology, including what is sometimes distinguished as moral theology, answers all questions of this type, 'What is the Christian witness of faith as decisive for human existence?'; since it therefore consists in a reflective understanding of ultimate reality, it is more or less closely related to all the other systematic inquiries of philosophy and the special sciences and is credible by the same criteria.[23]

This is a pivotal claim for Ogden. Essentially what Ogden is positing is that there is a true understanding of ultimate reality given with human existence as such. Hence the ultimate criterion of the truth of claims about ultimate reality is universal human experience. This is the foundation of theology, as it is of philosophy and any other pertinent special science. There are no special criteria to which theology may appeal: say, of special mystical experience, special revelation, or miraculous intervention. In the conventional categories of the debate about the epistemology of religious belief we are knocking on the door of classical natural

---

[23] 'What is Theology?', in *On Theology*, 10.

theology. What is intriguing about Ogden is that he knocks but refuses to enter that house.

Ogden refuses to enter because he is implacably opposed to the tenets of classical Christian theism. By classical Christian theism I mean here 'the *philosophia perennis* or "Christian philosophy", whose crowning achievement is a supernaturalistic theism uniquely combining elements of classical Greek philosophy with religious insights derived from the Hebraic-Christian Scriptures'.[24] Classical theism fails, for Ogden, on at least two counts. First, it is not appropriate to the canon of the original apostolic witness. Classical theism posits a deity who is only externally related to the world. Thus, although God radically affects all that happens, he is not in turn affected by what goes on in the world. In traditional philosophical terms God has the attributes of immutability, impassibility, and simplicity. This is not the God of unbounded love who is represented in the earliest proclamation of the Church. The God of the apostolic witness is radically affected by what goes on in the world, reacting contingently in unsurpassed love to all that happens. Hence the deity of traditional Christianity is not the God of the Gospel.

Second, the deity of classical natural theology cannot answer the question which religious discourse is logically required to answer: namely, can we have assurance that our lives are ultimately significant and meaningful? If God is impassible, what happens in the world, including the world of human action, cannot make any difference to him. Hence as a matter of strict logic, if we accept the tenets of classical theism, our life and action cannot be of ultimate significance, because ultimate reality is by definition immutable. What we do cannot make a difference to God, therefore it cannot have ultimate significance, and the deep existential question about the meaning of our lives goes unanswered.

The core of Ogden's concern can be expressed even more forcefully by saying that the deity of traditional Christian theism cannot be God, for the word 'God' 'provides the designation for whatever it is about this experienced whole which calls forth and justifies our original and inescapable trust'.[25] Formally speaking, the term 'God' functions to account for our basic confidence. By

---

[24] *Reality of God and Other Essays*, 16–17.   [25] See above.

definition, the deity of the classical Christian tradition cannot fulfil this description and must, therefore, be redescribed as an idol.

What would then call forth and justify our basic confidence? Ogden's proposal is that our confidence is justified if we accept the dipolar theism developed of late in the neo-classical, meta-physical theism of Alfred North Whitehead and Charles Hartshorne. There are three basic components to this revisionary metaphysics. There is, first, Whitehead's reformed subjectivist principle.

According to this principle, we can give an adequate answer to the metaphysical question of the meaning of 'reality' only by imaginatively generalizing 'elements disclosed in the analysis of experiences of subjects.' In other words, the principle requires that we take as the experiential basis of all our most fundamental concepts the primal phenomenon of our own existence as experiencing subjects or selves.[26]

On this view, to be anything at all is to be an instance of process or creative becoming. For an entity to be actual, for a self to be a self, it must, logically speaking, be constituted essentially by relatedness to others and by temporality. Every entity or self is dipolar. It is characterized by both passion and action, by both relatedness and absoluteness. On the passive side, the self is acted upon or affected by others. On the active side, the self creatively synthesizes the data received passively by others, including the data from the self's own past. In so doing the self constitutes itself ever anew in the present, and offers itself as data for inclusion in the actions and projects of other selves in the future. This revolu-tionary, revisionary metaphysics replaces the static categories of unchanging substance with that of creative process, and provides the foundation for a metaphysics of freedom. At its centre is the idea of a free response to the free decisions of others. 'This means that anything actual both freely creates itself by responding to the self-created others already actualized and belonging to its past and then contributes itself, along with those others, to the still other self-creations as yet unactualized and belonging to the future.'[27]

This has immediate consequences for any view of deity we care to embrace. If all reality is constituted by creative process,

---

[26] *Reality of God and Other Essays*, 57.   [27] *Faith and Freedom*, 74–5.

then God must be seen not as an exception to this metaphysical principle but as its highest expression. Conceived on analogy with our own selves, God must be seen as that Self who is unsurpassed in absoluteness and relatedness. Related to the world in a way analogous to the way the human self is related to the brain, God is active in being causally involved in absolutely everything that happens, and God is passive in receiving into his own being the effects of the actions of absolutely all other agents which exist.[28] Following Anselm's famous rule that God is that than which nothing greater can exist, this follows necessarily once God is construed as exemplifying the possible properties of any conceivable reality whatsoever. This is the second crucial component of Ogden's revisionary theism.

The third component is his conviction that the ontological argument is both sound and valid. Properly formulated, it is immune to the standard arguments deployed by Hume and Kant, for God's existence is not a contingent existence but a logically necessary existence. God is radically different from everything else we experience; and to take the measure of this is to come to see that the question of God cannot be a contingent matter.

Just this, indeed, is the real import of the famous ontological argument for God's existence first worked out by Anselm of Canterbury. The widespread notion that the purpose of this argument is merely to establish one more fallacious inference from idea to reality does as little credit to the acumen of Anselm's critics as it is unfair to the saint himself. His point was not that *any* idea provides the warrant for such an inference, but that it *is* warranted by the idea of God implicit in Christian faith. He discovered, in other words, that this idea, alone among others, has a peculiar logical character that exempts it from the law otherwise pertaining to the relation of essence and existence. To be able to conceive what God is, is also to know that he is; and from this it follows that no one can be utterly without faith in his reality, since as the necessary existent he must somehow be experienced in anything that is so much as even possible.[29]

[28] Ogden carefully explores the significance of this claim for a theory of divine agency and divine action in 'What Sense Does it Make to Say, "God Acts in History" ', in *Reality of God and Other Essays*, 164–87.

[29] *The Reality of God and Other Essays*, 21–2; emphasis original. This quotation immediately raises the problem of the existence of atheists. If no one can be utterly without faith in the reality of God, how come there are those who, with varying degrees of passion, disclaim any faith or belief in God? Ogden is well aware of this issue, and argues essentially that 'unfaith is not the absence of faith,

The import of this last move is crucial for Ogden. It secures the credibility of his basic assertions about the nature of ultimate reality which are re-presented in the apostolic witness to Jesus Christ. The theism which is most appropriate to the original apostolic witness is true because it can be properly validated. It can be shown to be true by universal human experience. We can summarize his position, then, in this way: implicit in human experience as such is a basic confidence in life; this confidence is warranted if the fundamental claim of dipolar theism is true; the fundamental claim of dipolar theism is true because the ontological argument properly formulated is sound and valid.

In one of his essays Ogden describes our situation in the modern world as one where 'we are forced to dig deeper for firm ground on which to build'.[30] Certainly, Ogden has done his fair share of digging in these resources in his quest for firm ground. It remains to explore how firm this ground really is.

Clearly Ogden's work constitutes one of the most carefully constructed accounts of authority to appear in the recent past. Few theologians have wrestled so thoroughly with the tangled issues related to canon, criterion, and the credibility of Christian theology. In the course of his work he develops *inter alia* a vision of Christian theology which distinguishes carefully between theology and witness, between apostolicity and credibility, between ideology and critical reflection, and between theology and life. He offers his work as a revisionary restatement of the intention of the Protestant tradition as a whole.[31] Indeed, it is no

---

but the presence of faith in a deficient or distorted mode. It is, as Scripture universally declares, faith in God in the perverted form of *idolatry*. "The idea of God," Henry de Lubac writes, "cannot be uprooted because it is, in essence, the Presence of God in man. One cannot rid oneself of that Presence. Nor is the atheist a man who has succeeded in doing so. He is only an idolater who, as Origen said, 'refers his indestructible notion of God to anything rather than to God Himself' " ' (ibid. 23; emphasis original).

[30] ' "The Reformation That We Want" ', *Anglican Theological Review*, 54 (1972), 261.

[31] One of the best expositions of Ogden's whole project can be found in Philip E. Devenish and George L. Goodwin, 'Christian Faith and the First Commandment: The Theology of Schubert Ogden', in Devenish and Goodwin (eds.), *Witness and Existence: Essays in Honor of Schubert M. Ogden* (Chicago: University of Chicago Press, 1989), 1–42. For an incisive defence of Ogden's position against recent criticism see Mark Lloyd Taylor, 'The Boundless Love of

exaggeration to claim that Ogden's work represents by far the most meticulously constructed vision of canon to have surfaced in Liberal Protestantism since Schleiermacher.[32] Certainly its home in the Protestant heritage of the modern Church is secure. To an astonishing degree Ogden combines in one person the transformationist piety of John Wesley,[33] the religious sensibility of Schleiermacher, the concern of Barth to be true to the internal content of the Gospel, and the intellectual relentlessness of Warfield.

The crucial areas which deserve extended evaluation for our project relate to his proposals on canon and criterion in the Christian tradition. As we proceed, we shall take up his account of canon, then look at his account of credibility, and then, finally and briefly, comment on his requirements of fittingness with respect to Christian witness in the modern situation. We shall argue that there are insuperable difficulties on every front with Ogden's position. In fact, his position precipitates a fresh crisis or turning-point in our thinking about canon deserving of the most careful attention.

One of the most significant features of Ogden's work is the clear distinction he makes between canon and credibility in Christian theology. This was in all likelihood first made in the modern period by Schleiermacher, yet in Schleiermacher it is merely made and recorded, as it were. Ogden has taken hold of this distinction and developed its implications in a way which is wholly original and thorough. For Ogden a proposal concerning canon addresses the question of the Christian identity of a claim; a proposal concerning credibility addresses the question of the truth of a claim. The former has to do with what makes a claim Christian, the latter with what makes it true.

God and the Bounds of Critical Reflection', *Journal of the American Academy of Religion*, 67 (1989), 103–47. In this essay Taylor brings out especially well the significance of Ogden's work for a theology of liberation.

[32] This judgement stands whether we locate the work of Karl Barth on canon within or outside the Liberal Protestant experiment.

[33] Ogden explicitly relates his constructive theological work to the thought of John Wesley in 'Love Unbounded: The Doctrine of God'. See also his 'Doctrinal Standards in the United Methodist Church', *Perkins School of Theology Journal*, 28 (1974), 19–27, and 'Process Theology and the Wesleyan Witness', *Perkins School of Theology Journal*, 37 (1984), 18–33.

It is this that places Ogden squarely in the tradition of Liberal Protestantism, for this tradition has characteristically insisted that theology has no special warrant for its claims in special revelation.[34] Christianity is shown to be true in virtue of its satisfying objective, public criteria of evidence. Indeed there is no special divine revelation which operates as a unique source of knowledge other than what can be gained by reason and experience generally.[35] Even if there were some kind of special warrant within theology for the truth of the Christian tradition, the truth of the claim would have to be confirmed by independent reasoning.

This observation fits with a further observation. While it is true that Ogden is at pains to develop a doctrine of divine revelation, revelation does not do any epistemic work.[36] Nor does his

[34] This is one of the central claims of 'Sources of Religious Authority in Liberal Protestantism'.

[35] This thesis is crucial to Ogden's case for theology as a genuine discipline in the modern university. See 'Theology in the University', in *On Theology*, 121–33. He argues there the case for Christian theology as a possible component in the liberal arts curriculum of a Christian university but not of a secular university. This in no way suggests that Christian theology has standards of truth different from those of religious studies or any other field of study. Christian theology does not belong in the university as such because Christian theology necessarily presupposes the specifically Christian religion, something clearly not necessary to the existence of a university.

[36] Ogden discusses the issue of revelation in 'On Revelation', in *On Theology*, 22–44. We have in that essay virtually a repetition of what Ogden has said again and again about how God is known universally and how that knowledge relates to the concrete particularities of the Christian tradition. The old notion of general revelation is replaced by that of 'original revelation', and the old notion of special revelation is replaced by 'decisive revelation'. '[F]rom the New Testament down to our own time, the primary sense of "revelation" in Christian theology has not been "original revelation" but what I call "special revelation," and, more exactly, "decisive revelation," which is to say, the representation of God that has taken place and continues to take place through the particular strand of human history of which Jesus is the center' (ibid. 29). That 'decisive revelation' does no epistemic work is emphatically asserted by Ogden: 'Not only Protestant neo-orthodoxy but, increasingly, progressive Roman Catholic theology as well, provides abundant evidence that any understanding of revelation as primarily the communication of supernatural knowledge has now been overcome' (ibid. 31). Ogden's own positive account of the necessity of 'decisive revelation' hinges on the thesis that such revelation makes explicit what was originally implicit: 'Whereas original revelation, we may say, is *immediately* and *proximately* necessary to our authenticity, decisive revelation is only *mediately*

revised canon. In traditional Protestant theology canon and revelation were inescapably epistemic notions. One appealed to the
canon of Scripture as a warrant for the truth of one's theology, and
one did this precisely because the canon was either itself divine
revelation *tout court*, or it was a unique source of divine revelation.

This brings to light a fascinating analogy between the position
of Ogden and that of the eighteenth-century deists. While meta-
physically Ogden is as far removed as one can imagine from a
deist, in epistemology he is a paradigm case of a deist. What one
encounters in the apostolic witness is a re-presentation of what is
established to be true on the basis of universal reason and experience.[37] The apostolic witness in itself offers no cognitive material
which cannot be secured independently, without it.[38] Yet, while
the canon does not act as a criterion of truth, it still functions as a
criterion. In Ogden's revised account of canon, whereas epistemology has disappeared from the scene, we can still hear the echo
of its withdrawal. If the canon is not a criterion of truth, it must
yet somehow remain as a criterion. It is neatly transposed into a

and *remotely* necessary to it, being necessary in the first instance not to the
constitution of our possibility, but to its full and adequate explication' (ibid. 41;
emphasis original).

[37] Ogden also develops the classical deistic notion that to make salvation
constitutively dependent on access to the Church's witness to Jesus Christ
creates insuperable moral problems for any form of Christian theism. See *Is there
One True Religion or are there Many?* (Dallas: Southern Methodist University
Press, 1992), 40–52, for a superb statement of his argument.

[38] This is nicely captured as follows: 'The Christian community exists in the
world for the sole purpose of bearing witness by word and deed to a truth so
ultimate and so profound that it is not simply the possession of some individual
or group, but is the truth in which all things have their beginning and end and
which "lighteneth every man that cometh into the world." Of necessity, then,
the Christian theologian, whose task it is to bear witness in the clearest and most
self-conscious form possible, labors in the conviction that the truth as it is
known in Jesus Christ is the only ultimate truth to be known anywhere and that
its congruence with man's self-knowledge, which an adequate philosophy seeks
to bring to rational consciousness, is the reason why the Christian claim is not
merely one more in the welter of claims and counterclaims to ultimate truth'
('Theology and Philosophy: A New Phase of the Discussion', *Journal of Religion*,
44 (1964), 13). Ogden differs here from the deists of the eighteenth century in
his stress on the responsibility of the Christian theologian to bear witness to Jesus
Christ, but he shares with the deist the claim that the Church's witness is essentially no more and no less than a re-publication of truths universally available to
humankind.

criterion of identity or, as Ogden prefers to speak of it, a criterion of appropriateness.

We have, then, the last possible hold-out position for treating the canon in epistemic categories. Even when the epistemic use has been abandoned, the shell of the epistemic usage remains in the continued use of the canon as a criterion. No other possible meaning of canon is considered other than that of the canon as a criterion. What was originally a complex list of books set in a network of canonical materials, persons, and practices has now been reduced materially to a single Christological assertion extracted by painstaking historical investigation from the synoptic tradition. The books of the New Testament, as we know them, have vanished from the Church's canon, while the Old Testament, with all its extraordinary richness, has been reduced to the presupposition or question which lies behind the assertion that Jesus is the Christ.[39]

To call Ogden's canon a 'canon before the canon' in these circumstances is extremely misleading. In reality there was indeed a 'canon before the canon'; it was astutely redescribed as the Old Testament by the Church Catholic. Ogden's historical revision is remarkably wide of the mark historically. The canon of Scripture was first and foremost a list of books; it was not a norm of identity; and the Church had possession of a very different canon before the canon from that recognized by Ogden. The Church had her Hebrew Scriptures which she was at pains to retain and integrate into her new, revised canon of scriptural materials.

---

[39] The place of the Old Testament in Ogden's theology is briefly explored in 'Authority of Scripture', 65–8. 'Logically speaking, then, one may say that the relation of the Old Testament to the earliest Christian witness is like that of the necessary presupposition of an assertion to the assertion itself, or, alternatively, like that of a question to its answer' (ibid. 67). Ogden deploys analogical reasoning here, so his position is subtle. Yet one cannot help but wonder how something can be both a presupposition and a question at the same time. One suspects that the actual canon of the Church has to be accommodated somewhere in the scheme as a whole, and that this whole claim constitutes a kind of intellectual stretching to make it somehow fit. It is really quite astonishing that the Church's canon has proved to be so resistant to rejection across the centuries. It is equally astonishing that Ogden feels any obligation outside a kind of filial piety to retain it at all. Given the minimal work which the canon performs, it is passing strange to worry over-much about what lies outside its proper boundaries. One suspects that Ogden does not himself worry over-much.

Allowing for the purposes of discussion the conventional Protestant claim that the only canon the Church possesses is that of Scripture, the reason why Ogden makes the shift from the canon we actually have to his historically reconstructed canon is exceptionally revealing. The real canon of the Church Catholic, according to Ogden, was not that adopted informally across the Church and then more formally in its councils, but the canon of the original apostolic witness.[40]

There is a nest of problems in this proposal. First, this apostolic witness was not formally the canon at all. The canon of Scripture was simply a list of books to be read in worship and to be used for spiritual direction and instruction in the Church. Neither the form nor the content of the apostolic witness as reconstructed by Ogden fits this description. In contrast to the actual canon adopted by the community, Ogden's canon is a short Christological assertion, whose content owes at least as much to the claims of modern existentialist philosophy as it does to the content of the synoptic tradition. This is so because he approaches the content of the Scriptures, including its Christological assertions, armed with a concern about authentic human existence and the meaning of life which is derived from the modern existentialist tradition. Both philosophy and theology are constituted by attention to the truth about human existence, a classic existentialist theme. His whole conception of hermeneutics as a way of expressing the claims of normative witness in another set of concepts and terms is his way of providing intellectual cover for this assumption.[41] Under these circumstances, the original intention of the canonical material

[40] It should be stressed that Ogden has always had the intention to be faithful to the concerns of the Church Catholic. As he put the matter as early as 1960: 'we intend to speak within and, indeed, on behalf of the catholic Christian church' ('The Lordship of Jesus Christ: The Meaning of Our Affirmation', *Encounter*, 21 (1960), 409).

[41] This comes out especially clearly in his lectures in systematic theology, where hermeneutics is given a position logically prior to validation. The very understanding of the original Christian witness is dependent on hermeneutics as Ogden describes it. Ogden is acutely aware of the risk involved: '[T]he risk, of course, is that in interpreting what is said in *this* set of concepts and terms in this *other* set, you will have lost the meaning and put something else in its place, so that it is not so much of an interpretation as it is simply a substitution of another point of view' (unpublished 'Prolegomena Lectures', Perkins School of Theology, Fall 1989).

inescapably becomes the cipher for a network of existentialist commitments.[42]

Second, even if we allow Ogden's assumption that the content of the canon is to be determined by the witness of the apostles, it is sheer assertion to insist that only the earliest or first apostolic witness is to count as its content. If canonicity is determined by apostolicity, then at the very least the whole of the apostolic witness has a right to be considered as normative. The peculiarity, if not the arbitrary nature, of Ogden's claim is manifest in the fact that the core apostolic witness says nothing about the cross.[43] To posit the Christian faith without the cross of Christ is enough to call into question Ogden's whole way of thinking about the content of Christian identity.

This brings us naturally to our third problem. While it is refreshing in the extreme to find a Liberal Protestant theologian so deeply concerned about the constitutive identity of the Christian faith, it must be acknowledged that the criteria of identity are thoroughly social in character. Scholars in religion have their own rules for drawing up identity claims, but the internal identity claims of the community are decided not by this or that individual but by the community as a whole. Individuals can, of course, make proposals on this score, and as members of the community they naturally have their say, but the issue is fundamentally social or ecclesial. Hence Ogden's material claim about the canon as a norm of identity can only work if it is in fact

---

[42] I am well aware of the objections which have been made to the concept of original intention and have addressed this issue in 'Intentions and the Logic of Interpretation', *Asbury Theological Journal*, 40 (1988), 11–25.

[43] This point is well brought home by John Deschner. 'If I understand Mr. Ogden, his criterion or his understanding of apostolic is that witness which is the earliest witness determinable by historical-critical reading of the New Testament and in particular the synoptic gospels. For my lectures I would, if pressed, be willing to accept the notion of the earliest as a criterion for the apostolic witness. But it seems to me that it must be the earliest witness concerning Good Friday, Easter, and Pentecost, that heart of the Christ Event, that heart of *kerygma* concerning Good Friday, Easter, and Pentecost. And recovering a witness which does not include Easter and Pentecost seems to me to be looking for something which the apostles themselves are not prepared to endorse' (unpublished 'Prolegomena Lectures', Perkins School of Theology, Fall 1989). Note here that I am not pressing the issue of whether the earliest is to be taken as normative simply because it is earliest.

adopted by the Church. Failing this, all it can be is an item on the agenda for pending ecclesial action or the internal identity claim of a new Protestant sect which treats Ogden canonically as one of its Fathers.[44]

The really devastating problem in Ogden's new proposal, however, cuts much deeper than any of these arguments. Following the authorities on whom he relies, Ogden has built his whole case on the fact that there was a canon before the canon of the New Testament: namely, the canon of apostolic witness. This is historically mistaken, and the consequence of this whole line of reasoning is patently absurd. What we can actually say is that many in the early Church adopted this or that book as canonical because they believed it to stem from the apostles. This is a commonplace in treatments of the history of the process of canonization. But it in no way constitutes a norm or canon of canonicity; it simply represents one of the reasons why some influential members of the Church favoured the books that made it into the canon. Moreover, a reason is not in itself a norm; it may be entirely singular in character, carrying no implications for one's general principles other than the assumption that whatever principles one adopts must be congruent with the reason deployed.

The actual historical situation in the Church across the early centuries was that there were all sorts of reasons why this or that book made it into the canon. The effort on the part of some theologians to insist on a set of necessary and sufficient conditions for canonicity failed.[45] Furthermore, their deliberations at this level were never made canonical. The matter rumbled across the face of the Church with arguments going this way and that; no single theory concerning the criteria for canonical books ever carried the day. This is altogether propitious, for if some of the reasoning deployed were to be treated in the way proposed by Ogden and his authorities, the result would be absurd. We know, for example, that some were in favour of the canon of four gospels because there are four seasons of the year. We can leave it to the imagination to invent the great numerological account of formal norm which Ogden or one of his followers might devise if

---

[44] I shall shortly suggest that this is not quite the far-fetched fantasy it may initially appear to be.   [45] See above, pp. 34–5.

we were to pick out this reason as the norm which determines this unit of the canon.

I am aware, of course, that this is a slightly ridiculous example. Ogden is perfectly right to say that in so far as there was a debate, apostolicity played a very significant role in the discussion. Hence my objection has an air of academic comedy which can be misleading. However, the crucial point deserves to be made in the strongest terms possible, if the illusory basis of Ogden's argument is to be exposed. So I repeat the crucial point at issue. Apostolicity counted as one among many reasons for the Church's decisions concerning the content of the canon, but it was not the only one, or the one that always prevailed in the deliberations related to the actual list of books eventually selected. Nor was it the reason that the Church in any way adopted as canonical, for it adopted none.

There is a fascinating parallel between Ogden and his conservative opponents at this juncture. Both are interested in making a process behind the canon more canonical than the actual canon the Church produced. Conservatives want a theory of revelation to be paramount; Ogden wants a theory of apostolicity to occupy this coveted position. Both misread the subtlety of the situation historically. Because of their obsession with the concept of canon as a criterion, they insist on tilting the history to fit their predilections. They will only be satisfied if the canon is a norm. To treat it primarily as a unique means of grace which the Church contingently, under the guidance of the Spirit, adopted is somehow not to give the canon its proper due. So conservatives turn the canon into a norm of truth; Ogden, determined Liberal Protestant that he is, rejects this on epistemic grounds, and turns it into a norm of identity. Both have overlooked the possibility of a third option.

There is a fifth and final problem worth mentioning before we change direction. Even though the original apostolic witness is the ultimate norm of appropriateness for Ogden, it is intriguing that he can still posit something else lying behind that norm which actually norms it. It is Christ alone, says Ogden, who norms the apostolic norm. If we were to follow through on the logic of this claim, the only conclusion we could reach is that the ultimate norm of all norms is Christ. Yet Ogden draws back from this position, equivocating between whether Christ is the *source* of the original apostolic witness or the *norm* of apostolic authority. What is lurking in the neighbourhood, of course, is the claim that the ultimate authority belongs to God; for in traditional Christian teaching Christ is authoritative or normative precisely because he is seen as divine. Yet Ogden immediately cuts off this possibility by rejecting outright the claim that 'Christianity recognizes one absolute authority—that of God himself'.[46] For if God were in any way the source of the apostolic witness, as would be the case were Christ divine, Ogden's whole case would immediately collapse not just in one but in two ways. The norm of the original apostolic witness would have been replaced by that of Christ; and, as a norm, it would function no longer as a norm of identity but as a norm of credibility.[47]

For a host of reasons, then, Ogden's position on the canon before the canon should be rejected. What can be salvaged is his concern to ensure that Christian theologians take responsibility for the Christian identity of their claims. Yet even here it is doubtful if the best way to proceed is by arguing for the adoption of a single criterion of appropriateness. What we really need is a proposal which will come to terms with the internal complexity of the debate as to what is constitutive of the Christian tradition. We can bring this out in several ways. Thus we can see Ogden's norm of appropriateness as his way of addressing the old question of the demarcation between orthodoxy and heresy. It can also be seen as another way of addressing the nineteenth century question of the essence of Christianity. Again, it can be seen as an attempt to come to terms with the contested character of the Christian tradition. None of these three closely related enterprises is likely to be resolved by appeal to a single criterion of adequacy. Or, if one argues at the outset that they must be resolved in this manner, crucial questions of a foundational nature will be begged early on in the debate. So we can salvage Ogden's concern to

[46] See above, p. 399.

[47] Given who God is, it would be impossible to say both that p was authorized by God as its source and that p is false. Given Ogden's Anselmic conception of deity, it is surely odd in the extreme that he rejects the epistemic authority of God; but the issues are too tangled to pursue here, as they would take us deep into discussions of autonomy and heteronomy. We are content at this point to draw attention to the equivocation of Ogden on the locus of his norm of appropriateness to Christian witness.

provide an account of Christian identity, but it is not likely that we can salvage his approach to the issue without extensive repair.[48]

There is a sense in which this whole debate is a verbal affair. It resolves around how to conceive of the identity of the Christian tradition. Not much hangs on it, so long as we keep a clear head about the precise issues being pursued and appropriate ways to deal with them. At least, this is how it is if we work with it in terms of identity, as Ogden does. The really deep issue for Ogden is the truth of the Christian tradition. It is in part because of his concern to be faithful to truth that he is convinced that the Liberal Protestant tradition was correct to reject prior expositions of the content of the Faith.[49]

Given this conviction, it is pointless to appeal to the canonical heritage of the Church to challenge his material, revisionary claims about, say, the person of Jesus Christ, his resurrection, or the doctrine of the Trinity. Ogden clearly rejects the whole idea of a miraculous resurrection as mythological, interpreting such language as a symbolic way of speaking about our resurrection to authentic existence by grace through faith. While he retains trinitarian language, he tends to see his doctrine of God as binitarian, even though it is probably best seen as simply unitarian in structure.[50] Moreover, he is thoroughly agnostic concerning the actuality of personal survival beyond death. Many Christians formed

[48] In my judgement the issue of orthodoxy and heresy is indirectly a canonical matter. Identifying a body of canonical material contributes to the discussion of what counts as orthodoxy or heresy, even though this is not the primary impulse behind the development of a canonical heritage. As to the debate about the essence of Christianity or its true identity, by far the most useful approach to this is by way of the idea of essentially contested concepts.

[49] I say 'in part' because we must never lose sight of the fact that Christian identity is crucial to the content of Christian witness, as Ogden sees it. The criteria of appropriateness and credibility both deserve to be satisfied in any constructive theology we adopt. He is ever the strict professional on both these standards.

[50] See 'On the Trinity', *Theology*, 83 (1980), 97–102. As in the case of the canon of the Old Testament, it is plausible to maintain that this language is retained as an act of pious loyalty to the discourse of the tradition. Ogden is clear that there is no room in his position as a whole for the canonical doctrine of the Trinity. Under these circumstance the best way to avoid confusion would be to drop this language entirely and find another way to speak about God.

in the conventional catechesis of the Church will find these moves shocking to their sensibilities, for they tend to see the doctrines Ogden rejects both as true and as constitutive of the Christian tradition.[51] Like the person hearing the sounds of a burglar in the middle of the night, they will be tempted to turn to the first weapon at hand to ward off such radical revision of the Faith. Hence they will reach for the canonical heritage of the Church as the nearest weapon. Such a move, however, is a futile exercise.

To argue, for example, that the Church has canonized a particular rendering of the Resurrection or of the Trinity, and that canonization provides warrant for either the identity or the truth of these claims, simply begs the question against Ogden. For Ogden, only the canon of the original apostolic witness can be a norm of identity. Furthermore, if these doctrines are to be defended as true, then they must be shown to be true by the criterion of general human experience. On Ogden's analysis, to appeal to Scripture, or to the wider canonical heritage of the Church, is merely to repeat what various human agents have said. This involves a complete abdication of intellectual responsibility. Moreover, he holds that there is no special divine revelation behind the Church's teaching or particular form of divine superintendence guiding its adoption. Even if there were such divine revelation or guidance, these claims themselves would have to be shown to be true by general human experience. All that this appeal could possibly be is an appeal to authority, and any such appeal is ruled out by his philosophy of authority. Particular authorities have *de jure* authority only if they stand under a rule or method which shows that they can be applied. Neither the rule governing identity nor that governing credibility have been satisfied in this case. Any attempt to challenge Ogden's material proposals on credibility, therefore, will have to go much deeper.

---

[51] This explains why Ogden's work has failed to find its way into much of the general Church. There has been considerable informal hostility to his whole approach to canon within his own United Methodist tradition. Accommodating a position like Ogden's within the tradition has led to massive attempts to develop a meta-doctrine of doctrinal pluralism in order to try and relieve the internal strain involved. How far such pluralism is a coherent possibility cannot be pursued here. Suffice it to say that in the last decade the language of pluralism has been officially replaced by the language of diversity.

My concern here is to argue that his account of credibility is thoroughly questionable. I also want to make manifest the significance of the adoption of his epistemology for the life of the Church. At this level, Ogden's project is subject to the same fate which we have encountered again and again in the great Protestant experiment in epistemology. Having dismantled the canonical heritage of the Church, he offers us a curious alternative. We are given a combination of a short apostolic assertion that Jesus is the Christ, reconstructed by means of expert historical investigation, coupled with a network of speculative philosophical proposals. The whole complex of canonical tradition is replaced by a blend of original, apostolic confession attached to a substantial body of epistemic theory. The bread of life is reduced to a big crumb housed in the foundation stones of a complex philosophical theory. The stones turn out to be surprisingly brittle.

Consider Ogden's account of the meaning of religious language. The obvious difficulty with it is his claim that there is somehow a single function which religious language must perform. Rather than there being a religious use of language, language within religion is used in a host of ways. Moreover, if we focus on assertion within just the Christian religion, leaving aside other religions entirely, it is false to claim that such assertions function fundamentally to give reassurance. Some assertions—namely, those about divine judgement—do quite the opposite. At least, this is how it is if we follow actual usage.

Ogden does not in act follow usage, as he claims. Built into his doctrine of reassurance is the notion that religious assertions represent 'a confidence somehow already present prior to their being made'. Hence they logically presuppose a confidence in the meaning and worth of life. The different world's religions 'can be thought of only as several attempts at a more or less self-conscious understanding of this original confidence'.[52] This is not a description of what we find in the great variety of assertions which actually crop up in religion, Christian or otherwise; it is a prescription Ogden has brought to the investigation at the outset. This doctrine about meaning betrays a certain philosophical theory imposed on the interpretation of language in religion. In its own

---

[52] See above, p. 401.

way it is as restrictive as the strictures he rightly excoriates in the whole positivist approach to religious discourse.

His convictions about the meaning and worth of life are also mistaken. The claim advanced is that everyone implicitly must be a theist, for, without theism, they could never invest their actions with meaning or worth. Aside from not giving genuine atheists the intellectual respect due to them in this debate,[53] the argument fails to reckon with the clear possibility that our actions can have all sorts of meaning and worth, whether or not theism is true. To be sure, it may not have the ultimate meaning and worth which Ogden posits. If one defines meaning and worth so that they only make sense on theistic terms, then life will be meaningless if atheism is true. However, this sort of linguistic imperialism ignores the great variety of genuine ways in which meaning and worth may be posited if theism is false.[54]

As to the specific version of theism proposed by Ogden, then the following observations are suggestive. First, it is not the case that only the tenets of neo-classical theism will provide the kind of ultimacy depicted by Ogden. Ogden makes life relatively easy for his argument on this score by taking as the only alternatives 'classical theism', as represented, say, by Aquinas, and the 'neo-classical theism', say, of Whitehead and Hartshorne. Thus a form of contingent theism which rejected Anselm's rule that theism is necessarily either true of false, which posited universal salvation, and which was not wedded to the doctrine of impassibility

---

[53] The whole idea, borrowed in part from John Baillie, that the atheist deep down really does believe in God is extremely distasteful. It begs the argument against the atheist either by positing a necessary confusion in his or her mind or by accusing him or her of idolatry. This last accusation is especially otiose, for it makes a disagreement about the modal property of certain sentences into the altogether different and more serious religious charge of idolatry.

[54] For an excellent set of essays along this line see E. D. Klemke, *The Meaning of Life* (New York: Oxford University Press, 1981), part II. All that is needed to provide an atheistic alternative to Ogden's account of the significance of our actions is: (1) a notion of intrinsic value, i.e. the concept that certain states of affairs are worthwhile in themselves; and (2) a theory of moral intuition which provides an epistemology undergirding our judgements of intrinsic value. Theories along both these lines have long been available in the history of theology and philosophy. Note that for the moment I am not challenging the evidentialist cast of Ogden's requirements.

embraced by Aquinas would equally well invest our lives with everlasting meaning and worth.[55]

Equally, there are various metaphysical principles which we might want to consider outside the reformed subjective principle posited by Whitehead. In fact, there is no necessity to think of all reality as somehow consisting of instances of creative becoming. Indeed, the pan-psychism which naturally accompanies this doctrine should give us pause.[56] The history of philosophy is littered with various metaphysical schemes which would invite us to conceive of all reality in terms merely, say, of form, being, matter, mind, monads, ideas, sense-data, and the like, with consequent difficulties in coping with various features of existence as they appear *prima facie* to us. It is certainly understandable if we confess that, after pondering the options, we are not all that much the wiser than when we started. We may well want even to stay clear of the whole metaphysical enterprise, as Ogden envisages it.[57]

The same applies to discussion about the soundness and validity of the ontological argument for any form of theism. This is an extraordinarily beautiful argument, and Ogden is entirely correct to call for a careful revisit of this old debate, but it is precarious to

[55] Note that I am not here arguing for or against such a form of theism. My point is that Christians, given the canonical heritage of the Church, are free to embrace forms of theism which see the assertion 'God exists' as contingent. There are perfectly respectable versions of such theism available in the history of philosophy and theology.

[56] Frankly, I find this whole element of the Process tradition wholly unconvincing. Ogden himself has had second thoughts in the neighbourhood of this concern: 'as deeply convinced as I still am that metaphysical theism is necessarily implied by any adequate Christological formulation, I have become increasingly skeptical of all formed of categorical metaphysics, neoclassical as well as classical' (*Point of Christology*, 135). Ogden's worries stem from problems which crop up in a theory of analogy. Mine crop up simply from counter-intuitions about certain features of the physical universe.

[57] In a certain sense I agree entirely with Ogden that what we might call metaphysical commitments are inescapable. We cannot escape very general beliefs about the world, nor should we try to do so. However, I am not at all convinced that the kind of metaphysical enterprise embraced by Ogden is inescapable; that is, I am sceptical that we must be committed to some theory of how reality necessarily is if we are to engage in metaphysics. The debate on what counts as metaphysics only exposes how tangled the issues are in this domain. My major concern, of course, is to challenge the claim that metaphysical schemes of the sort required by Ogden are essential for the Christian theist or for the welfare of the Church. They strike me as often doing more harm than good.

make the fortunes of the Church depend on the outcome of this discussion.

Everything depends at this point on the precise status we give to the place of evidence and argument in the life of the Church. Ogden's position is a subtle one. He certainly suggests that getting the intellectual foundations right is crucial to the reformation which he thinks is needed in the Church. Given the growth in secularism in the culture and the consequent challenge to conventional theological ideas, Ogden insists that we are forced to dig much deeper for firm ground on which to build. Moreover, he believes that there is a strict interrelation between the goal of reformation and the task of theological reflection.[58] So finding the right way ahead in theology is essential to the future of the Church. Further, as we have seen, essential to theological reflection is adhering strictly to Ogden's criterion of credibility. Hence Ogden sets enormous store by his whole epistemological enterprise as part of a wider renovation in the life of the Church.

The question to be determined is precisely how much store he sets by it. Certainly, providing evidence is essential for doing theology as Ogden conceives it. Generally speaking, Ogden is a foundationalist and an evidentialist. 'We have slowly learned through our actual history that no assertions are to be judged true, unless, in addition to being logically consistent, they are somehow warranted by our common experience, broadly and fairly understood.'[59] Given that religious claims are thoroughly contested, Ogden insists that there is a certain duty to show them to be true: 'my position is that there must be a general justification of religious or theological claims and that there cannot be any such justification unless there can be (1) a justification of religion as such as true; and (2) a justification of any and all particular religious claims to be true.'[60] In Ogden's account, to be warranted

---

[58] 'Reformation that We Want', 261.

[59] *Reality of God and Other Essays*, 20.

[60] 'Linguistic Analysis and Theology', 324. The alternative discussed and rejected in this paper is the Wittgensteinian fideism of D. Z. Phillips. Ogden also expresses this point in terms of what we might call an epistemology of speech acts. 'There is one further respect in which the act of witnessing is like other speech acts. Once the claims to validity that it necessarily involves have been rendered problematic, there is nothing to be done if it is still to be performed except to validate its claims by way of critical reflection. The reason

in one's assertions, or to provide justification for them, is to bring forth the relevant evidence or argument for them.[61]

It is crucial to note that Ogden is intensely aware of how complex this matter is. At heart he wants not just to have his assertions justified by appropriate criteria; he wants to make sure that the criteria themselves have been critically established.[62] Yet he is acutely aware of how contested these sorts of claims have been and continue to be.

. . . it is not only that we disagree with one another in our opinions about the truth; it is that we disagree with one another even concerning the criteria by which we try to adjudicate the difference between our opinions. In fact, the most intractable of all human differences have to do with these questions of criteria. If we could just agree on what the rules are, we might just be able to play the game. The problem is, we cannot agree on the criteria. There is a radical pluralism with respect to criteria of truth as well as respect to the various views that claim in one way or another to satisfy those criteria.[63]

This is a rare confession for a theologian of Ogden's stature to make. The temptation is to finesse the matter by ignoring the

for this is that one cannot make such claims in good faith except by assuming the obligations to validate them if and when they are seriously questioned. Consequently, to perform the act of witnessing *obligates one to give reasons for its claims* to be both adequate to its content, and so credible as well as appropriate, and fitting to its situation' ('Service of Theology to the Servant Task of Pastoral Ministry', 90; emphasis added).

[61] This requirement in Ogden's mind also commits him to a further requirement of clarity. 'Since any term or assertion that is vague enough can always escape the verdict that it is inconsistent or not experientially significant, compliance with the demands of reason requires that its meaning be sufficiently clear so that its consistency and application be fairly determined.' In the context Ogden is speaking of 'the very nature of cognitive meaning' and 'the unconditionally necessary conditions of any and all rational inquiry' ('God and Philosophy', 171). It hardly needs to be said that this principle will wreak havoc on the subtleties and mysteries of the canonical heritage of the Church. With one swipe it removes the whole apophatic dimension of the tradition.

[62] Thus, speaking of the validity of the claims of Christian witness with respect to their credibility, he wants to validate their truth 'in accordance with completely general criteria, *themselves critically established*' ('On Revelation', in *On Theology*, 24; emphasis added).

[63] Unpublished 'Prolegomena Lectures'. Ogden goes so far as to say that: 'The difficulties here are so formidable that I am not sure that they can be surmounted. And yet, if they cannot be, then, to that extent, systematic theology is not possible' (ibid.).

consequences of evidentialism. Paradoxically the problem is both doubly worse, yet also not quite as bad, as Ogden suggests. It is worse, first, because Ogden's proposal propels us into an infinite regress. If the criteria for criteria have to be critically established, then we must surely say the same for the criteria for these criteria, and so on *ad infinitum*. To know p fully reflectively, we have to have a method for knowing p, but then we need a method for knowing the right method, and so on, and on.[64] There does not seem to be any way on this scheme to stop the infinite regress other than by just stopping somewhere arbitrarily. Ogden stops it by insisting that the final foundation is universal human experience. However, the problem with this claim is that it is not clearly warranted by universal human experience,[65] or if it is, the whole argument is circular.[66]

[64] It is worth noting here that Ogden is very sympathetic to Hartshorne's thesis that the crucial arguments for theism really rest on basic insights rather than on demonstration. He commends Hartshorne in that 'he has always insisted that all philosophical arguments, including the arguments for the existence of God, are but ways of understanding more clearly and self-consciously what no rational argument as such either could or need provide' ('Theology and Philosophy', 13). Crucial to the integration of this thesis into his epistemology is that critical reflection makes explicit what is already implicit. This really needs further elaboration to be satisfactory. What appears to be said here is that certain crucial beliefs can be held without any evidence at all. This cuts clean across the repeated insistence on giving good reasons according to relevant criteria, if our beliefs are to be held as true.

[65] Part of our difficulty here is that the appeal to universal human experience seems transparent to Ogden. It has clear and immediate significance for him. Yet one wonders about this notion of universal human experience. Experiences generally come already couched in the terms of some conceptuality or other. It would be cavalier to claim that there may not be certain experiences which require one to think of the world in a certain way, even though this claim has been deeply contested in the wake of the work of the later Wittgenstein. I simply flag here a major piece of unfinished business in Ogden's project related to the relationship between our deep conceptual schemes and the identification of our experience.

[66] It is intriguing that Ogden seems to prefer the circularity option here. Rejecting the hypothesis that there is a presumption in favour of atheism, he writes: 'My own advice, quite frankly, is that we do well to abjure any such hypothesis, acknowledging instead that each position must take full responsibility for its particular claims in face of the counterclaims of all other positions. There are various reasons for this, but what they all come to, I think, is that experience has shown that there is very little of importance in matters philosophical and theological that is not in some way or other controversial. *At this*

426 Digging Still Deeper for Firm Ground

The problem is worse, second, in that Ogden appears to confine the disagreements to disputes as to what should count as adequate and relevant *criteria* to validate our truth-claims. In fact, the disputes in epistemology cut much deeper, for it is not at all clear that a theory of knowledge should be cast in terms which make the search for criteria the relevant goal. Nor is there agreement on what constitutes a fully successful theory of truth, justification, knowledge, and the like. Yet the situation may not be quite as grim as Ogden proposes, for some theories of knowledge reject the assumption that all validation, to use Ogden's term, is a matter of providing evidence according to some critically established criterion.[67] According to some accounts of knowledge, one can really know p in certain instances without knowing how one knows p. If this is the case in theology, then Ogden's worries can be set aside. However, the likelihood is that we will not only sweep away his worries with this move, but we will also sweep away his whole conception of theology.

Yet it would be mistaken, on Ogden's view, to insist that every Christian must be a theologian or to require that theology be made primary either in life or in the Church. This emerges, for example, in his account of the place of proofs in the wider scheme of things.

---

absolutely radical level of human reflection, there can be no adequate starting point simply because all starting points are in a way also conclusions, the movement of such reflection being in the very nature of the case circular rather than linear.' ' "Theology and Falsification" in Retrospect', 296; emphasis added.

[67] Ogden himself appears to relieve the pressure to have all the relevant evidence and criteria at hand by settling for a minimalist theory of rationality. '[T]he real mark of a rational mind is how one behaves after one has come to one's conclusion. How do you treat the conclusions at which you have arrived? Do you treat them as having closed the discussion of which you have been a part? Or do you treat them as new ways of carrying on that discussion? Do you treat them as something fixed and final that now settles everything, or do you treat them as something that is indefinitely open to correction by alternative points of view, pending entering into discussion with all those others whom we so easily ignore in our attempts to make our conversation simple, to reduce them to domesticated dimensions where we do not have to take into account all the others whose claims run counter to our own?' ('Prolegomena Lectures'). The problem with this, of course, is the word 'all'. At best this can be a regulative ideal rather than a serious workable suggestion. One can see here again the classical Protestant opposition to tradition as an integral component of the life of the mind.

On the matter of the proofs of God's existence as they may be developed by the philosopher or the theologian, I would add that I consider such proofs to be both necessary and important—in their proper place. That place, as I see it, is the secondary place of reason and reflection generally, whether in philosophy or theology.[68]

Life is more than theory, so theology renders an indirect rather than a direct service to the life of the mind and to the Church.[69] It is one of 'the works of love' to which the Christian is called.[70]

The crux of the matter, however, is that Ogden's proposals are clearly meant to have profound effects in the life of the Church. Whether these are direct or indirect effects is an entirely secondary matter. They are constitutive of the reformation he considers essential in our modern situation. His work is not a neutral exercise for the academy; it calls for wholesale changes in the canon, the creeds, in ethics, and in the whole range of activity sheltering under the banner of practical theology.[71] Hence we cannot escape the judgement that if we adopt Ogden's proposals, the Church will find itself landed with the whole network of speculative metaphysical and epistemological theory he has devised. Once again, the canons of the Church will be totally enmeshed in yet another round of epistemological theorizing.

We can make this point by noting how Ogden handles the place of 'classical theism' in the Church. He sees it more or less as constitutive of the whole sweep of Christianity from the patristic period onwards. What is missing here is the more modest, but no less substantial, notion of canon which we have been at pains to identify in the early Church, and which has been systematically neglected in theories of canon which have been the rule in the West. On this analysis, Aquinas's views on, say, impassibility, simplicity, and the like may be classical, traditional, conventional,

---

[68] *Reality of God and Other Essays*, 42 n. 71.

[69] This is an important theme in 'The Service of Theology to the Servant Task of Pastoral Ministry', esp. 93–101.

[70] This is nicely brought out in 'Theology and Philosophy', 14.

[71] For Ogden practical theology is logically dependent on foundational work in systematic theology. For an extended discussion see his 'Prolegomena to Practical Theology', in *On Theology*, 94–101. I should add that the crucial point that Ogden makes about practical theology, i.e. that it is directed primarily to the fittingness of Christian witness or action, is extraordinarily suggestive and helpful.

or customary. But, they are most certainly not canonical *tout court*. They represent one way of articulating the theistic commitments embedded in the canonical heritage of the Church. They are by no means obligatory.

They may be canonical in the Roman Catholic Church, for in that tradition Aquinas counts as a Father of the Fathers. To what degree they are canonical is, of course, a matter for adjudication by the Pope or others in appropriate circumstances. The Roman tradition has its own way of identifying the scope and meaning of its canonical heritage. Yet, this is but one option in the development of the canonical tradition of the early Church. The tradition in the East took a much more cautious attitude to all philosophical developments. Discerning just how far it is committed to the concept of God captured in the term 'classical theism' is a matter for careful judgement within that tradition.

We might say here that Ogden and Rome share a common attitude to the place of philosophy in theology. They see it as indispensable, and they are forever in search of the philosophy which will be the foundation of the Faith. If not Plato, then Aristotle, or Wittgenstein, or Whitehead, or whoever. There is, however, a clear alternative to this way of conceiving the relationship between theology and philosophy. We can take a much more circumspect attitude towards all metaphysical and epistemological speculation. Rather than simply adopt some philosophy, we can seek to sift and transfigure it in appropriate ways. We cannot say in advance how things will turn out. We may even want to explore, as Ogden does, the tradition of Whitehead and Hartshorne in search of suitable treasures. Yet the whole cast of this difficult work will have a different tone and a more nuanced place in the interpretation of the Christian faith than either Aquinas or Ogden can tolerate.[72]

The reference to Aquinas provides a clue to the possible status

---

[72] Ogden will no doubt want to know if we are still saddled with a doctrine of divine impassibility. Here I can only express an unconventional opinion. It is not at all clear to me that the canonical Fathers of the Church were committed to the crude doctrine of impassibility which has for generations been attributed to them. Once we realize that Aquinas is merely a Father of the Church in the West and that the canon of Fathers in the West is but one way to read the canonical heritage of the Church, this whole debate has to be revisited on its own terms.

of Ogden's views in the modern Church. If we take Aquinas's 'classical theism' for what it really is—namely, as canonical for the Roman Church of the West—then we can read Ogden's 'neo-classical theism' as a massive bid for canonical status in the Protestant Church of the West. The difficulty with this suggestion, of course, is that, formally speaking, Protestants do not have any Fathers. All they have is Scripture. We need hardly say that by now this myth has been totally exploded. Protestant theologians and intellectuals have turned Scripture into a criterion in epistemology or, as in the case of Ogden, a norm of identity. Under the guise of philosophy, broadly conceived, they smuggle *de facto* a host of Fathers into the tradition, for it is upon this or that philosopher that they depend for their epistemology.

In truth, we can extend the analysis further. What Ogden has given us is a new scripture, a hermeneutic to go with it, a new creed, and a new evidentialist epistemology to secure appropriate foundations. His 'neo-classical theism' can be equally well explicated by saying that he is proposing that we give Whitehead and Hartshorne canonical status as Fathers of the Church. All that is missing to give us a complete new religion is a new liturgy, a new iconography, and a new system of canonical oversight.

If this is the case, we have surely reached in Ogden the end of the line in the epistemizing of the canons of the Church. What began initially as an understandable effort to add epistemology to the canonical life of the Church has ended with the radical reworking of the canonical heritage as that relates to Scripture, Creed, and Fathers. The cuckoo has truly taken over the nest, even to the point of producing her own offspring within it. It looks as if we shall have to either get rid of the cuckoo or put her firmly in her place. The only real alternative is the full, self-conscious development of the whole range of canonical material and the consequent invention of a new religion. It is precisely this option which has emerged with the arrival of gender feminists on the ecclesial and epistemological scene.

Ogden might no doubt reply that we have neglected the criterion of fittingness to our modern situation as essential to proper theological work in our day and generation. If all else fails, can he not fall back on this to salvage his project? The answer is simple. As we noted earlier, the criterion of fittingness is itself not a temporal notion but an epistemic one. It attempts to capture what is credible to modern agents who have embraced the modern scientific picture of the world and who are unconditionally committed to their autonomy. If Ogden's account of credibility collapses, then the criterion of fittingness *mutatis mutandis* also collapses. It would be redundant to repeat the relevant epistemic queries to show this all over again. We can only add that, in any case, any criterion of fittingness envisaged in this way is liable to take the form of shifting sand. To make the Christian tradition captive to what is credible to the culture is liable to make the criterion of credibility thoroughly relative, a temptation which Ogden has fought long and valiantly to overcome.

16

Feminism and the Transgressing of Canonical Boundaries

One of the truly surprising developments in recent work on the authority of Scripture is the interest shown in the subject by feminist theologians and scholars.[1] Such work is surprising in at least two ways. First, it represents a radical break from the past which few anticipated. For many scholars, trained in the days when it was *de rigueur* to deal with the intellectual problems thrown up by modernity, there was a definitive set of problems to address. Thus one had to deal with the challenge of meaning posed by the positivists and analytical philosophers, and one had to become acquainted with the demands of historical criticism. Once these two sets of concerns were met, then one was ready to proceed with one's constructive proposals. Thus the whole issue of the rationality of religious belief, for example, could be pursued with care.[2] Few anticipated that a whole new network of objections would arise to displace worries about the cognitive nature of religious language and would challenge the legitimacy of conventional forms of historical criticism. Yet this is precisely what has arrived with the feminist exploration of the Christian tradition.[3]

[1] It has become important to distinguish between equity and gender feminists in some of the recent literature. In what follows I am especially interested in the work of gender feminists: that is, those who insist that there is more to feminism than a moral crusade to rid the world of inequity related to gender.

[2] This is precisely what has happened in the revival of philosophy of religion as a discipline in the last twenty years. There has been a veritable revolution in debates concerning the epistemology of Christian belief. Yet these debates are marginal in the debates which currently detain Christian theologians.

[3] The depth of the challenge constituted by feminism is nicely expressed by Borresen: 'The contemporary collapse of androcentricity in European and North American civilization is already perceived as more threatening by Roman Catholic ecclesiastical institutions than the previous geocentric (Kepler) and

The second, and deeper, surprise is that feminist theologians have been very concerned to take the canon of Scripture with the utmost seriousness. It has become something of a refrain in recent theology to catalogue the reasons why any notion of the authority of Scripture is problematic. Most conspicuously, writers have drawn attention to the patriarchal culture in which the books of the Bible were written, to the marginal status of women in the various narratives, to the negative passages about women, and to the use of these passages to prevent women from playing a full part in the life of the Church and of society. Yet, despite these factors, and despite a strong group of feminists who have rejected any hope of reconciling the demands of feminism to the continued use of Scripture,[4] feminists have taken Scripture so seriously that they have produced a wealth of material discussing its significance and status for the life of the Church. This is an extraordinary development, given the passions which have been visible in the debate as a whole.

So rich is the current body of material that it would be quite impossible to provide even a brief survey of the field.[5] However,

anthropocentric (Darwin) breakdowns which left traditional doctrines and symbolism nearly intact. The insertion of female human beings into fully God-like humanity is a radically new phenomenon in Christian history' (Kari Elizabeth Borresen, 'Women's Studies in the Christian tradition', in Ursula King (ed.), *Religion and Gender* (Oxford: Blackwell, 1995), 252).

[4] See e.g. Mary Daly, *Beyond God the Father* (Boston: Beacon Press, 1973), and Daphne Hampson, *Theology and Feminism* (Oxford: Blackwell, 1990). For a spirited critique of Hampson see Rosemary Ruether, 'Is Feminism the End of Christianity? A Critique of Daphne Hampson's Theology and Feminism', *Scottish Journal of Theology*, 43 (1990), 390–400.

[5] For a valuable survey of the field see Ellen K. Wondra, 'By Whose Authority? The Status of Scripture in Contemporary Feminist Theologies', *Anglican Theological Review*, 75 (1993), 83–101. See also Mary Ann Tolbert, 'Defining the Problem: The Bible and Feminist Hermeneutics', *Semeia*, 28 (1983), 113–26; id., 'Protestant Feminists and the Bible: On the Horns of a Dilemma', *Union Seminary Quarterly Review*, 43 (1989), 1–17; Elizabeth Achtemeier, 'The Impossible Possibility: Evaluating the Feminist Approach to Bible and Theology', *Interpretation*, 42 (1988), 45–57; Jean C. Lambert, 'An "F Factor"? The New Testament in Some White, Feminist, Christian Theological Constructions', *Journal of Feminist Studies in Religion*, 1 (1985), 93–113; Kwok Pui Lan, 'Discovering the Bible in the Non-Biblical World', *Semeia*, 47 (1989), 25–42; Carolyn Osiek, 'The Feminist and the Bible: Hermeneutical Alternatives', in Adela Yarbo Collins (ed.), *Feminist Perspectives in Biblical Scholarship* (Chico, Calif.: Scholars' Press, 1985), 93–105; id., 'Reading the Bible as Women', in Leander E. Keck *et al.*, (eds.), *New Interpreter's Bible*

it is possible to develop the kind of selective review which permits some of the crucial developments in the thinking about canon and norm which have already surfaced to come to light. Hence we shall look in turn at the work of Rosemary Ruether, Elizabeth Schüssler Fiorenza, and Mary McClintock Fulkerson. What is especially interesting is the way in which epistemological debate continues to haunt the discussion about the nature of canon. Crucial differences within current feminist accounts of Scripture are clearly derivable from deeper differences in epistemic theory. Most conspicuously, the shift from a 'modern' to a 'postmodern' vision of epistemology has far-reaching consequences both for feminism and for any feminist account of Scripture.

What is also fascinating is that buried in the debate evoked by feminist criticism lies the possibility of developing a much more adequate interpretation of canon. I shall suggest at the outset that feminist theologians have stumbled on to a vision of canon which has long been lost in the theories of the West. Yet feminist theologians rarely notice this, partly because of long-standing feminist objections to Scripture and partly because this account still remains overshadowed by concerns about epistemology. Sorting out the wheat from the chaff in these developments will be close to the core of our work in this chapter.

From the beginning, feminist theologians were ambivalent about any appeal to Scripture in their quest to reform the Church and make it more hospitable to the experience and service of women. Arriving in the wake of the African American theology, which had made strong appeal to themes of liberation in the biblical narrative,[6] it was able to appeal to the liberation themes of Scripture without too much strain. Indeed, most versions of feminist theology have been cast in the form of a theology of

---

(Nashville: Abingdon Press, 1994), i. 181–7; Claudia V. Camp, 'Feminist Theological Hermeneutics: Canon and Identity', in Elizabeth Schüssler Fiorenza (ed.), *Searching the Scriptures, A Feminist Introduction* (New York: Crossroad, 1993), 154–71.

   [6] The classic expression of this is still James H. Cone, *A Black Theology of Liberation* (Maryknoll, NY: Orbis, 1986, 1990). The most significant treatment of the epistemology of theology available in liberation theology is that of Clodovis Boff, *Theology and Praxis: Epistemological Foundations* (Maryknoll, NY: Orbis, 1987).

liberation, and they have made common cause with other forms of liberation theology both politically and intellectually. Hence there was a natural affinity with the liberationist appeal to Scripture.

Over against this, however, feminists set the quest for liberation in the context not just of slavery and racism but in a much more historically pervasive form of oppression: namely, patriarchy or androcentrism. While slavery and racism are ascribed to a particular culture, most notably North America, patriarchy is construed as an oppressive phenomena which is much more ancient and universal, and thus stretches right back to the origins of Christianity and Judaism. In the light of this, any appeal to Scripture will involve appeal to material which came to birth in an irremediably patriarchal context. Hence, the difficulty of appealing to Scripture is much more acute for feminists than it is for liberation theologians generally. We can see this in the fascinating debate which has gradually unfolded.

The crucial concern which governs feminist interest in Scripture initially is that any relevant canon must be a means of liberation. We might say that this is the fundamental conception of canon which governs the initial approach of feminist theology to Scripture. Any material which is to function as canonical must be such that it liberates the oppressed, heals those abused by patriarchy, and empowers those who are victims. It must mediate a salvation which genuinely transforms the personal and social world of the oppressed, the marginalized, and the abused. Failure to achieve these ends signifies that the designated canon has failed to be truly canonical. Success in achieving these ends brings the designated material into the domain of the canonical.

This vision is clearly a transposition of an older conception of the function of canonical material: namely, that Scripture is intended to make people wise unto salvation. This conception, in both its older and its newer forms, is not an epistemic conception of canon. It sees Scripture as a means of healing and liberation rather than as a criterion of justification and knowledge. The focus is on Scripture as a body of literature whose content reshapes the identity and life of the reader so that he or she is enabled to live a very different kind of life from that to which they have been accustomed. This focus does not preclude that Scripture advance significant truth-claims about the human situation and the conditions of radical transformation. On the contrary, one of the ways in which salvation is mediated through Scripture is by depicting human bondage and by transmitting a message of hope and rescue. Knowledge is mediated through the canon; but to transmit knowledge is not in itself to transmit a theory of knowledge. The knowledge transmitted is knowledge related to salvation and liberation; it is not knowledge about knowledge. Hence the primary conception of canon deployed in this proposal is soteriological rather than epistemological.

This judgement on the concept of canon at work in much feminist theology can easily be missed for several reasons. This is the case, first, because feminists rarely outline explicitly the concept of canon with which they are working; the idea of canon deployed has to be arrived at indirectly by looking carefully at why they receive or reject putative canonical material. It is so, second, because feminist theologians are often more interested in using canonical material than analysing how it is constituted. The actual liberation of persons matters more than detailed discussion about the boundaries, content, and nature of canon. It is so, third, because much feminist theology is taken up with an aggressive critique of the Christian Scriptures. Hence it is easy to gain the impression that feminist theologians are opposed to the very idea of canon itself. However, the sharp criticism of Scripture is invariably on application of the claim that Scripture ought to be a liberating document. It is precisely because Scripture is supposed to mediate a certain kind of salvation that it is criticized so sharply. Equally, efforts to find or invent new canonical material are governed by the conviction that truly canonical material ought to be liberating for the reader. The fourth and final reason why it is easy to miss this tacit conception of canon within much feminist theology is because it does not take long for this conception of canon to be overshadowed by epistemological concerns. What starts out as a soteriological concern quickly becomes an epistemological one.

These features of the discussion are richly illustrated initially in the work of Rosemary Ruether. She begins her major work in systematic theology, *Sexism and God-talk*, not with a discussion of methodology, sources, and norms, but with a section entitled 'The Kenosis of the Father, A Feminist Midrash on the Gospel in Three Acts'. To anyone acquainted with the conventional rules of systematic theology, this is a strange way to begin a serious text in systematic theology. On first reading it comes across as a comic parody which dislodges the standard rules of the theological game. Closer inspection of the content and placement, however, tells another story.

What is really presented is a carefully crafted narrative which subverts the traditional rendering of the basic Christian narrative of creation and redemption. Ruether weaves together a story with three moments. In the first, God the Father acknowledges a Queen of Heaven and repents of his hierarchical ways. In the second, Jesus transmits a message of the iconoclastic subverting of all hierarchy by insisting on a life of service. Standing by this message leads to his crucifixion at the hands of the authorities, where he is deserted by his male disciples but observed to the end by his female disciples, especially Mary Magdalaene. In the third moment, Mary Magdalaene encounters an apparition who commissions her to continue the work of redemption of the world.[7] Mary's witness and message are rejected by the male disciples, who subvert the true message of Jesus by reworking it to legitimize their own position of power and authority. Mary, in the mean time, treasures her access to the secret made known through Jesus, and anticipates a new day when women like her will glimpse the truth through the distortion and recognize her as a sister.

What Ruether is clearly doing here is engaging in the formation of a new canonical heritage.[8] To begin, she is clearly displacing the canonical Creed which has formed the internal structure of Christian systematic theology with a radically different narrative. The basic content of the Creed has been turned on its head by using various components of the original Christian story. Thus the themes of the self-emptying of God, the proclamation of the reign of God by Jesus, the rejection of Jesus by the authorities, the fumbling incomprehension of the disciples, the presence of

----

[7] Ruether has an apparition of Christ appear to Mary, but it is a vision which speaks to her. See *Sexism and God-Talk* (Boston: Beacon Press, 1983), 8.

[8] What marks this as significantly different from the work of Mary Daly is that Ruether works intentionally with components drawn from the Christian tradition, whereas Daly prefers wholesale rejection. Moreover, Daly engages in an extended and lively send-up of the Christian faith, whereas Ruether seeks to rescue what she can in the wake of the feminist critique.

women in the circle close to Jesus, and the witness of Mary Magdalene are kept, but they are now used to transmit a message of redemption from patriarchy. This is accomplished by setting the whole narrative in a context where ultimate reality is construed as the Queen of Heaven, the 'Creatrix of all things', by having God recover older ways of being God and extending release to 'slaves, to Gentiles, perhaps even to women', by portraying Jesus as an iconoclastic prophet of patriarchy, and by portraying Mary Magdalene as the true successor to the life and work of Jesus.

The portrayal of Mary in this fashion provides the warrant for a different vision of episcopal succession from the conventional one. Hence a whole new vision of the canonical practice of oversight is created. Its form is radically Protestant, for it posits a succession of accurate witness over against a historical succession of lineage. Mary, with her true confession of the significance of the message of Jesus, becomes the new Peter, whose patriarchal interpretation of the significance of Jesus is rejected as corrupt. This version of early Christian history embodies a Protestant conviction of a radical falling away from the true Faith in the Church. In fact, this version is so radical that it posits a falling away with the first male disciples of Jesus, rather than with the Constantinian Church.

It should come as no surprise after these developments that Ruether also engages in a fundamental reworking of the biblical canon by drawing on those biblical materials which are amenable to her interests and adding to them tracts of other material which cohere with her conception of canon. Her primary concern is to find usable material which will liberate. She finds such material in:

(1) Scripture, both Hebrew and Christian (Old and New Testament); (2) marginalized or 'heretical' Christian traditions, such as Gnosticism, Montanism, Quakerism, Shakerism; (3) the primary theological themes of the dominant stream of classical Christian theology—Orthodox, Catholic, and Protestant; (4) non-Christian Near Eastern and Greco-Roman religion and philosophy; and (5) critical post-Christian views such as liberalism, romanticism, and Marxism.[9]

It is these materials which are drawn on to carry the exposition of the loci of her systematic theology.

---

[9] *Sexism and God-Talk*, 21–2.

This practice fits neatly with three other features of Ruether's work. First, it fits, very naturally with her attempt to provide some initial resources for an alternative canon to that of the Christian Scriptures. This material is collected together in *Womanguides, Readings toward a Feminist Theology.*[10] She is very clear in her intentions for this volume.

Feminist theology must create a new textual base, a new canon. However, this collection is not the new canon. This will have to emerge from a longer process of community building and a larger consensus of such an emerging community. This work is a handbook from which such a new canon might emerge, much as early Christians collected stories about their experience from which they preached the 'good news' and from which, eventually, fuller texts were developed and ratified as the interpretive base for the new community.[11]

As this quotation makes clear, this practice also fits with the creation of a new community in which women's experience of bondage and liberation are at the centre. Other feminists may emphasize the creation of a new community more than Ruether, and may be more separatist in their outlook, but clearly she looks for the creation of new communities which will embody an explicit adherence to liberation as the mark of the true Church. While she does not outright reject the separatist alternative, her preferred vision of the Church is furnished by the model of base communities. This model permits a dialectical relationship between base communities committed to liberation from patriarchy and the traditional institutional Churches.[12] Clearly the creation of a new canon and a new community go together.

The third component which fits with Ruether's canonical proposals is constituted in a much more fragmentary fashion, but

---

[10] Rosemary Reuther, *Womanguides: Readings toward a Feminist Theology* (Boston: Beacon, 1985).

[11] Ibid., p. ix. Not surprisingly, Ruether insists that 'Feminist theology cannot be done from the existing base of the Christian Bible. The Old and New Testaments have been shaped in their formation, their transmission, and, finally, their canonization to sacralize patriarchy. They may preserve, between the lines, memories of women's experience. But in their present form and intention they are designed to erase women's existence as subjects and to mention women only as subjects of male definition' (ibid.).

[12] See *Sexism and God-Talk*, 205–6.

is equally illuminating: namely, the creation of a new iconography. Thus *Womanguides* is sprinkled liberally with thirteen iconographic or artistic reproductions which express in various ways her theological vision of liberation. The first sets the tone of the volume which follows. In a scene set at the tomb of Queen Nefertari at Thebes, the Goddess Isis leads Queen Nefertari by the hand. Ruether observes: 'Hand in hand, women guide each other as they claim their buried past and journey to the place of the death of patriarchy and the beginning of new possibilities of womanbeing.'[13] The last is equally revealing. It depicts a duel between a woman and a Dominican friar from a text of the codex of Lancelot du Lac. Ruether's commentary provides the relevant moral admonition: 'To create new texts for Womanchurch, we must draw from our own experience and also learn to joust the guardians of male texts and break their lances.'[14]

The central reality made visible by these developments is that Ruether is engaged in the creation of a whole new reworking of the Christian religion which goes beyond what we have encountered in the development of Liberal Protestantism. While the latter movement clearly reduces the existing canon to either a 'canon within the canon' or a 'canon before the canon', Ruether explicitly sets out to develop new canonical material. This is in keeping with the initial move to work out of a soteriological vision of canon. Clearly Ruether is very concerned to make available a body of material and practices which can be a means of liberation, rather than simply an item in epistemology or a criterion of identity. What has emerged is a new body of literature which is set aside as Scripture; a new creed providing an overall account of creation and redemption, which acts as a hermeneutical lens for the reading of Scripture; a new iconography; a new community of Women-church which embodies the new vision; a new form of apostolic succession which makes the witness Mary Magdalene the new Peter; and a new rendering of the traditional loci of systematic theology to express the new vision intellectually. Not surprisingly, there have emerged in and around Ruether's general proposals new forms of liturgy, a new lectionary, new practices of spiritual direction, a new homiletics,

---

[13] *Womanguides*, p. ii.   [14] Ibid. 246.

a new interpretation of the sacraments,[15] a new pastoral care, and new proposals on ethics, on episcopal administration, and the like. There is, then, overall, a new creed, a new cult, and a new moral code. This is a form of canonical reformation which is likely to engender intense reaction on all sides.

This reaction will not surprise those who have grasped the crucial significance which is attached to changes in canon across the centuries. To reject the prevailing canons, or to rework them—or to reconstrue the nature of the canonical heritage—any or all of these will in themselves lead initially to turmoil within the Christian tradition, and then either to division or to the creation of new communities. They will also in all likelihood precipitate intense epistemic work, in order to provide intellectual backing for the proposed canonical changes. Ultimately, proponents of change will be challenged to explain their new canons, and this in turn will require extended work in epistemology in order to deal with the deep questions which will arise. This is even more acutely the case when the canonical material itself is seen in both soteriological and epistemic terms. This is clearly visible in the ongoing development of feminist theology as we can see immediately in the epistemological work of Ruether.

Ruether's epistemic suggestions are relatively underdeveloped and unoriginal. They constitute a reworking of the Liberal Protestant appeal to experience as the ultimate warrant for the truth of all theological claims.

It has frequently been said that feminist theology draws on women's experience as a basic source of content as well as a criterion of truth. There has been a tendency to treat this principle of 'experience' as unique to feminist theology (or, perhaps, to liberation theologies) and to see it as distant from 'objective' sources of truth of classical theologies. This seems to be a misunderstanding of the experimental base of all theological reflection. What have been called the objective sources of theology, Scripture and tradition, are themselves codified collective human experience.[16]

---

[15] An emerging standard text related to these topics is Marjorie Procter-Smith, *In Her Own Rite* (Nashville: Abingdon Press, 1990). See also her *Praying with Our Eyes Open: Engendering Feminist Liturgical Prayer* (Nashville: Abingdon Press, 1995).

[16] *Sexism and God-Talk*, 12.

The uniqueness of feminist theology lies not in its use of the criterion of experience but rather in its use of *women's* experience, which has been almost entirely shut out of theological reflection in the past. The use of women's experience in feminist theology, therefore, explodes as a critical force, exposing classical theology, including its codified tradition, as based on *male* experience rather than on universal human experience. Feminist theology makes the sociology of theological knowledge visible, no longer hidden behind the mystification of objectified divine and universal authority.[17]

This proposal, despite its polemical posture towards the past, adopts the epistemic claim that experience is the ultimate warrant for theology. What separates feminist theology from its perceived predecessors is not the appeal to experience but the favoured location of that experience. Where before it was male experience, it is now women's experience. In either case the epistemic pedigree is clearly that of classical Liberal Protestantism.[18]

Ruether's position also differs from Liberal Protestantism in seeking to accommodate almost all other epistemic notions related to theology to her fundamental epistemic vision. Hence revelation is related to experience by being construed as 'breakthrough experiences beyond ordinary fragmented consciousness that provide interpretive symbols illuminating the *whole* of life'.[19] These revelatory experiences in turn provide the raw material for the formation of a canon of Scripture. This material and the accompanying interpretative traditions are constantly tested by the ongoing experience of individuals and the community. In the current situation, the past canon and tradition of the Church, expressive of past forms of oppressive patriarchy, are now being called into question by women's experience. Such experience provides a place to stand, from where one can wield the lever of criticism. It provides the critical principle of feminist theology.

The critical principle of feminist theology is the promotion of the full humanity of women. Whatever denies, diminishes, or distorts the full humanity of women is . . . appraised as not redemptive. Theologically

[17] Ibid. 13; emphasis original.
[18] The complex relation between the appeal to experience in liberation theology and its Roman Catholic and Protestant predecessors is well brought out in Monika Hellwig, *Whose Experience Counts in Theological Reflection?* (Milwaukee: Marquette University Press, 1982).
[19] Ibid. 13; emphasis original.

speaking, whatever diminishes or denies the full humanity of women
must be presumed not to reflect the divine or an authentic relation to
the divine, or to reflect the authentic nature of things, or to be the
message or work of an authentic redeemer or a community of redemption.

The negative principle also implies the positive principle: whatever
does promote the full humanity of women is of the Holy, it does reflect
the true relation to the divine, it is the true nature of things, the authentic message of redemption and the mission of redemptive community.
But the meaning of this positive principle—namely, the full humanity of
women—is not fully known. It has not existed in history. What we
have known is the negative principle of the denigration and marginal-
ization of women's humanity. Still, the humanity of women, although
diminished, has not been destroyed. It has constantly affirmed itself,
often in only limited and subversive ways, and it has been the touchstone against which we test and criticize all that diminishes us. In the
process we experience our larger potential that allows us to begin to
imagine a world without patriarchy.[20]

I noted earlier that Ruether's epistemic proposals are relatively
unoriginal and underdeveloped. They are unoriginal because they
reproduce the basic slogan of much of classic Liberal
Protestantism. They are underdeveloped because it is not clear
why experience should be construed as the fundamental warrant
for all theological claims. Ruether relies for the most part on an
ad hominen and dogmatic claim that this is the way theology has
always worked. The tangled history of the epistemology of theology does not support this historical proposal. Her position does
not do justice to the long debate on the place of revelation and
natural theology in the justification of religious belief. The appeal
to religious experience is a relatively late development in the
epistemology of theology, emerging first as an exclusive warrant
for religious belief in Schleiermacher.

Nor does her exposition indicate how the appeal to experience
is to be construed. Should it be interpreted as an appeal to awareness of the divine? This seems unlikely, for Ruether's proposal
focuses not on the religious experience of women but on
women's experience *simpliciter*. So, should it be seen as a form of
reliabilism in which certain experiences should be taken as veridical because they are brought about by a reliable process? Or

[20] Monika Hellwig, *Whose Experience Counts in Theological Reflection?*, 18–19.

should it be taken instrumentally to mean that whatever causally leads to the full humanity of women is somehow real or authentic? Or should it be taken as the claim that certain kinds of experience put one in a better position to perceive certain truths which one would otherwise not perceive? The problem with these options is that we do not really know if they fit what Ruether proposes epistemologically. In this respect her work is remarkably similar to Schleiermacher's in its opacity.

Perhaps it would be more apt to describe the appeal to experience as confused, rather than underdeveloped; for it is not clear how her appeal fits with her formal critical principle for feminist theology. What promotes the full humanity of women does not prima facie appear to count as an appeal to experience at all. It suggests, on the contrary, a thoroughly pragmatic criterion which looks to what works to bring about certain ends as the criterion of truth.[21] The relativist or agnostic flavour of Ruether's proposals would also support this contention, for generally appeals to experience have been taken as providing some kind of certain knowledge. To find out what works, we may simply have to wait and see what emerges out of various experimental communities. Moreover, it may be extremely difficult to reach a consensus.

Our queries about the confused character of her appeal are compounded when we note that it is quite impossible for experience to provide a warrant for the old-fashioned, objectivist moral claim embedded in Ruether's theology. Commitment to the full humanity of women is a moral endeavour as much as it is a theological principle. Yet this moral principle is surely not something derived from experience, but something brought to experience. Certain kinds of experience may, of course, make us psychologically more committed to this principle; but this does nothing to show that this principle is grounded or based on experience. That we ought to be committed to the liberation of women is taken as

---

[21] It is worth noting that on this analysis atheism may well be the truth, for, after all, maybe an atheistic world-view would be much better at bringing about the full humanity of women than any theistic proposal. Whether atheism is or is not effective in bringing about the full humanity of women is clearly a matter for future observation; one can not dogmatically assert in advance that any version of theism will have the desired outcome. It may well be that what Ruether means by experience is simply what works in the long run. In this case her appeal to experience is really a form of pragmatism.

a kind of basic, bedrock claim which is presumed throughout to be epistemically primitive. Nothing whatsoever would be permitted to call it into question.

In the light of these difficulties, it is not surprising that other leading feminist theologians should seek to ground the new feminist faith in a very different epistemic vision. The fact that Ruether's position is logically on a par with that of Liberal Protestantism is liable to render it suspect; for Liberal Protestantism is in part a product of a white, male, European culture, and thus, on Ruether's own analysis, shaped, if not determined, by patriarchy. Equally, Ruether's position on the canon of Scripture has affinities with the move to work with a 'canon within the canon', another position closely associated with the Protestant experiment in the West.

We can see the beginnings of a move away from Ruether's position in the work of Elizabeth Schüssler Fiorenza. Schüssler Fiorenza shares Ruether's commitments to liberation, to the creation of 'Women-church', to working within the current structures of the Church, to revision of the scriptural canon, and to the creation of a whole new range of canonical material related to liturgy, spirituality, homiletics, and the like. In one crucial respect—in the appeal to experience—Schüssler Fiorenza's position is virtually identical with that of Ruether. 'The Christian canon represents the collective experience of the early church whose boundaries it defines. Hence, it is clear that the canon is a normative social symbol system of the patristic church; it does not represent the collective experience of early Christian women.'[22] Clearly such a canon cannot be authoritative for women-church.

The spiritual authority of women-church rests on the experience of God's sustaining grace and liberating presence in the midst of struggles for justice, freedom and wholeness for all. It rests not simply on the 'experience of women' but on the experience of women struggling for liberation from patriarchal oppression.[23]

Appeal to such experience is the critical norm for evaluating all visions of reality. It constitutes the foundation for normative

[22] 'Introduction: Transgressing Canonical Boundaries', in Elizabeth Schüssler Fiorenza (ed.), *Searching the Scriptures*, vol. ii: *A Feminist Commentary* (New York: Crossroad, 1994), 13 n. 11.
[23] *Bread Not Stone* (Boston: Beacon Press, 1984), p. xvi.

evaluation within feminist theology. Such a foundation provides a
basis for common identity across class and race lines. Such a foundation, moreover, is itself to be understood as grounded in and
responsive to the liberating presence of God. It is God's presence
which engenders the transformative experience which is at the heart
of women-church. The struggle for liberation is itself the experience of divine grace; in that experience God is truly made known.
In truth, this experience is a form of divine revelation: 'The locus or
place of divine revelation and grace is therefore not the Bible or the
tradition of a patriarchal church but the *ekklesia* of women and the
lives of women who live the "option for our women selves." '[24]

There are, however, significant differences in emphasis
between Ruether and Schüssler Fiorenza. First, Schüssler
Fiorenza is very uneasy with any move to work with a 'canon
within the canon'.[25] All of Scripture is formed and shaped by its

[24] 'The Will to Choose or to Reject: Continuing Our Critical Work', in
Letty M. Russell (ed.), *Feminist Interpretation of the Bible* (Philadelphia:
Westminster Press, 1985), 128. Compare: 'Moreover, African-American women
such as Sojourner Truth, Amanda Berry Smith, Jarena Lee, Julia Foote, Maria
Stewart, or the Quaker Elizabeth (of whom we know only her baptismal name)
derived their authority for biblical interpretation and preaching first of all from a
mystical experience in which they encountered God or Jesus directly. It was this
confidence in the privileged nature of their relationship with the divine that
compelled African-American women to transcend the limits imposed by the
patriarchal gender-race system' ('Transforming the Legacy of the Women's
Bible', in Schüssler Fiorenza (ed.), *Searching the Scriptures*, i. 6). There are times
when Schüssler Fiorenza speaks as if the criterion of feminist theology arises out
of the community of Women-church rather than being itself the experience of
those in Women-church. 'The evaluative "canon" or criterion must be a
contemporary feminist criterion—ending relations of patriarchal domination and
exploitation—which is articulated in the contemporary struggle of women for
liberation and systematically elaborated by the discipline of feminist studies'
('Author's Response', *Horizons*, 11 (1984), 154). One detects here a move
towards the pragmatism which we can also detect in Ruether.
[25] For a succinct summary of her arguments against the notion of a canon
within the canon see 'Emerging Issues in Feminist Biblical Interpretation', in
Judith L. Weidman (ed.), *Christian Feminism: Visions of a New Humanity* (San
Francisco: Harper and Row, 1984), 43–6. Ruether provides a rejoinder to
Schüssler's Fiorenza criticism of her use of Scripture in 'Review Symposium' of
In Memory of Her: A Feminist Theological Reconstruction of Christian Origins,
Horizons, 11 (1984), 146–50. Schüssler Fiorenza's original criticisms of Ruether
can be found in *In Memory of Her. A Feminist Theological Reconstruction of Christian
Origins* (New York: Crossroad, 1983), 16–19.

patriarchal origins, hence there is no uncontaminated core or stream which can be singled out as a theological norm. Any material which can be used positively must be used not as an archetype but as a prototype which will need suitable critical transposition in the quest for liberation.

A dictionary definition reveals the significant distinction between the words. While both the archetype and the prototype 'denote original models,' an archetype is 'usually construed as an ideal form that establishes an unchanging pattern . . . ' However . . . a prototype is not a binding, timeless pattern, but one critically open to the possibility, even the necessity of its own transformation. Thinking in terms of prototypes historicizes myth.[26]

More specifically, what is needed is a hermeneutic which will cleanse the Scriptures of their negative content and use and release their liberating traces. There are four structural components embedded in this hermeneutic.

Since all biblical texts are formulated in androcentric language and reflect patriarchal societal structures, a feminist critical interpretation begins with a *hermeneutics of suspicion* rather than with a hermeneutics of consent and affirmation. It develops a *hermeneutics of proclamation* rather than a hermeneutics of historical factuality because the Bible still functions as holy scripture in Christian communities today. Rather than reduce the liberating impulse of the Bible to a feminist principle of one feminist biblical tradition, it develops a *hermeneutics of remembrance* that moves from biblical texts about women to the reconstruction of women's history. Finally, a feminist model of critical interpretation moves from a hermeneutics of disinterested distance to a *hermeneutics of creative actualization* that involves the church of women in the imaginative articulation of women's biblical story and its ongoing history and community.[27]

In Schüssler Fiorenza's more recent writings she develops what she calls a 'transgressive approach' to Scripture. She suggests that the very formation of the canon was an exclusionary political

---

[26] Quoted from Rachel Blau DuPlessis by Elizabeth Schüssler Fiorenza, 'Toward a Feminist Biblical Hermeneutics: Biblical Interpretation and Liberation Theology', in Brian Mahan and L. Dale Richesin (eds.), *The Challenge of Liberation Theology: A First World Response* (New York: Crossroad, 1981), 108.

[27] 'Emerging Issues', 47; emphasis original.

event which was intimately related to attempts to ensure the unity of the Roman Empire under Constantine.[28] After reviewing several accounts of canon, she effectively rejects all conventional ideas of canon on the ground that they posit the notion of an exclusive wall of separation between canonical and non-canonical material.[29] Thus the idea of canon has suggested to some interpreters the image of a garden enclosed by a wall. It is precisely this image of a wall of separation which needs to be rejected.

. . . the image of the enclosed garden brings into focus the need for a deconstructive, transgressive method of interpretation; however, it is not able to articulate a positive image for the function of scripture in feminist struggles to transform religion and society. Such an image, I suggest, is found in the scriptures. It is the open, cosmic house of divine Wisdom. Her indwelling of cosmic dimensions has no walls; she permeates the whole world. Her inviting table, with the bread of sustenance and the wine of celebration, is set between seven cosmic pillars that allow the spirit of fresh air to blow where it will. This image does not allow for an understanding of canonical authority as exclusive and commanding. Rather, it grasps the original Latin meaning of *augere/auctoritas* as nurturing creativity, flowering growth, and enhancing enrichment. Biblical authority should foster such creativity, strength, and freedom.[30]

We might say, then, that Schüssler Fiorenza systematically chips away at the concept of canon in a way which is even more revisionary than what we find in Ruether. Equally, she develops epistemic dimensions of the appeal to experience which are more muted or less developed in Ruether. This represents the second way in which Schüssler Fiorenza moves beyond the position of Ruether.

Consider, for example, the way Schüssler Fiorenza emphasizes the subjective, located nature of knowledge claims. This is especially clear in her call for a new paradigm of biblical interpretation.

---

[28] Schüssler Fiorenza systematically plays down theological and pastoral considerations at this point in order to press her case. See 'Introduction: Transgressing Canonical Boundaries', 6–8. She follows here much of the position laid out in Helmut Koester, 'Writings and the Spirit: Authority and Politics in Ancient Christianity', *Harvard Theological Review*, 84 (1991), 353–72.

[29] Schüssler Fiorenza shares the misgivings about canon developed by Cornel West in 'Minority Discourse and the Pitfalls of Canon Formation', *Yale Journal of Criticism*, 1 (1987–8), 193–201.

[30] 'Introduction: Transgressing Canonical Boundaries', 11.

The crucial point to be heeded initially is that 'what we see depends on where we stand. One's social location or rhetorical context is decisive of how one sees the world, constructs reality, or interprets biblical texts.'[31]

She believes that much conventional biblical scholarship has rejected this notion. Scholars have seen themselves as objective, neutral, and critically detached from the interests of this or that community. They have sought to be emotionally detached, intellectually dispassionate, and rationally value-neutral. They have been committed to an ideal of scientific, critical scholarship, free from prejudice, presupposition, and bias. They have eschewed the advocacy of partisan political or theological agendas, seeking to follow the evidence wherever it leads, oblivious to the consequences of their scholarly conclusions for the Church or the group to which they belong.

Schüssler Fiorenza rejects this account of biblical scholarship either as an adequate description of its practices or as an ideal to be followed. Interpretive communities, including the community of biblical scholars, are authoritative communities: 'They possess the power to ostracize or to embrace, to foster or to restrict membership, to recognize or define what "true scholarship" entails.'[32] The dominant ethos of biblical scholarship has to be decentred 'by recentering it in a critical interpretative praxis for liberation'.[33] The claim to be detached, objective, value-neutral, and the like is a pretension. It is a rhetorical strategy which in its own way serves various social and political interests.

Critical theory of rhetoric or discursive practices, as developed in literary, political, and historical studies, seeks to decenter the objectivist and depoliticized ethos of biblical studies with an ethos of rhetorical inquiry that could engage in the formation of a critical historical and religious consciousness. The reconceptualization of biblical studies in rhetorical rather than scientist terms would provide a research framework not only for integrating historical, archaeological, sociological, literary, and theological approaches as perspectival readings of texts but also for raising ethical-political and religious-theological questions as constitutive of the interpretative process. A rhetorical hermeneutic does not assume that the text is a window to historical reality nor does it operate with a

---

[31] Schüssler Fiorenza 'The Ethics of Biblical Interpretation: Decentering Biblical Scholarship', *Journal of Biblical Literature*, 107 (1988), 5.

[32] Ibid. 8.   [33] Ibid. 9.

correspondence theory of truth. It does not understand historical sources as data and evidence but sees them as perspectival discourse constructing their worlds and symbolic universes.[34]

Consequently, interpretation of the biblical text requires an ethics of historical reading and an ethics of accountability. The former 'changes the task of interpretation from finding out "what the text meant" to the question of what kind of readings can do justice to the text in its historical contexts'.[35] In this process the text is still given its due by asserting its original meanings over against later dogmatic usurpations. Yet the illumination of the ethical-political dimensions of the biblical text in its historical context allows a relativization of the values and authority claims of the text through contextualization. It also opens up and permits the critical assessment of those texts. The ethics of accountability, for its part, requires that the reader attend to the consequences of biblical interpretation and evaluate the various historical worlds and symbolic universes constructed from the text 'in terms of a religious scale of values'.[36]

If the Bible has become a classic of Western culture because of its normativity, then the responsibility of the biblical scholar cannot be restricted to giving 'the reader of our time clear access to the original intentions' of the biblical writers. It must also include the elucidation of the ethical consequences and political functions of biblical texts in their historical as well as in their contemporary sociopolitical contexts.[37]

In other words, scholars must engage in disciplined reflection on the societal and public values promoted by their intellectual disciplines.

[34] Ibid. 13–14. Even though there is a tradition of writing in the analytical philosophy of history which would argue for a similar position to that developed by Schüssler Fiorenza, one cannot avoid the judgement that she has never really taken the measure of a figure like Troeltsch. Troeltsch never denied that interests had a crucial role to play in the writing of historical narrative, but insisted that it was important to distinguish between interests which were directed towards gaining the truth and those which were not. Schüssler Fiorenza's depiction of the opposition is something of a caricature. For mild criticism of her position and its consequences for historical investigation see Averil Cameron, 'Response', in Elizabeth Schüssler Fiorenza, 'Theological Criteria and Historical Reconstruction: Martha and Mary, Luke 10: 38–42' , in *Protocol of the Fifty-third Colloquy* (Berkeley: Center for Hermeneutical Studies in Hellenistic and Modern Culture, 1987), 21–5.

[35] 'Ethics of Biblical Interpretation', 14.   [36] Ibid. 15.

[37] Ibid. The reference to original intentions is from a paper by Krister Stendahl.

Ultimately they must move from a form of neutral scholarship to a form of advocacy scholarship. They must use their work to promote justice and well-being for all.

There is a profound ambivalence at the heart of the epistemology advocated by Schüssler Fiorenza. On the one hand, she holds that the text constitutes an objective reality which can challenge our contemporary assumptions, world-views, and practices; on the other hand, she believes that there is no objective, scientific rendering of the text which is not shot through with social and political interests. On the one hand, one can appeal to experience, to divine grace, even to divine revelation; on the other hand, no account of experience, grace, or divine revelation can logically be allowed to call into question the moral commitment to liberation. On the one hand, her whole position rests on a causal and historical analysis of the way in which patriarchal oppression has worked to keep women and minorities out of the centres of power; on the other hand, she rejects a correspondence theory of truth and construes historical sources and texts not as windows on reality but as forms of perspectival discourse which construct various worlds and symbolic universes. On the one hand, she wants to speak of the original intentions of the text and even of the divine intention lying behind the text; on the other hand, the texts are seen overall as expressions of interest and power which perpetuate oppressive social and political institutions.

This is a thoroughly unstable epistemic vision. Hence it is not surprising that a new generation of feminists have emerged who pick up the deconstructionist element in Schüssler Fiorenza's work and expand its consequences for feminist theology. This is precisely what we find in the thorough and provocative vision developed by Mary McClintock Fulkerson.[38] Fulkerson's work constitutes a further revisionary development which dismantles any idea of an objective criterion which might serve as the foundation of theology. Neither a text, or set of texts, or even the experience of Women-church can serve as a

[38] Mary McClintock Fulkerson, *Changing the Subject: Women's Discourses and Feminist Theologies* (Minneapolis: Fortress Press, 1994). A similar shift is visible in the work of Susan Brooks Thistlethwaite. See her 'Christology and Postmodernism', *Interpretation*, 49 (1995), 267–80.

foundation.[39] The reason for this is that the very idea of a foundation has been jettisoned. So too has the idea of authorial intention,
the idea of the meaning of a text, and the idea of language functioning to reflect or represent either reality or individual experience. This network of ideas is replaced by a whole new way of
thinking about meaning, language, knowledge, and interpretation.

A valuable point of entry into Fulkerson's position is to see it
as an attempt to include the voices of women who are often
excluded by conventional feminist readings of history. From the
beginning this was an embarrassment because, after the initial
development of feminist theology, various groups of women very
quickly arose to challenge the right of white, North American,
academic women to speak for African-American, Hispanic-
American, and Third World women. The solution to this challenge was to try and hold on to some notion of generic women's
experience, all the while stressing the importance of diversity and
disclaiming the making of essentialist claims about women's experience. In other words, the appeal to a foundation in women's
experience was complemented by great stress on the social location of all claims by oppressed minorities.[40]

[39] We shall be concerned here with the work of Fulkerson, but see also
Sheila Greeve Daveney, 'The Limits of the Appeal to Women's Experience,' in
Clarissa W. Atkinson, Constance H. Buchanan and Margaret R. Miles (eds.),
Shaping New Vision, Gender and Values in American Culture (Ann Arbor: UMI
Research Press, 1987), 31–50. '[A]lthough we must oppose oppressive systems,
we cannot do so by appeal to either universal female experience nor to some
cosmic or divine perspective. We can do so only in the name of our particular
location in history and with the recognition that our Gods and Goddesses are
the articulation of our values and hopes, not the foundation of certitude nor the
promise of victory' (ibid. 48). Note the echoes of Feuerbach's analysis of religion in the closing sentence.
[40] This is nicely captured by Schüssler Fiorenza. 'I would therefore suggest
that the revelatory canon for theological evaluation of biblical androcentric
traditions and their subsequent interpretations cannot be derived from the Bible
itself but can only be formulated in and through women's struggle for liberation
from all patriarchal oppression. It cannot be universal but must be specific since
it is extrapolated from a particular experience of oppression and liberation. The
"advocacy stance for the oppressed" must be sustained at the point of feminist
critical evaluation of biblical texts and traditions and their authority claims.
The personally and politically reflected experience of oppression and liberation
must become the criterion of appropriateness for biblical interpretation and evaluation of biblical authority claims' (*In Memory of Her*, 32).

This move was something of a stopgap arrangement, for the former was liable to be swallowed up in the latter.[41] What is intriguing about Fulkerson is that she noticed that some groups of women did not make it on to the expanded list of liberated and engaged victims who were generally accepted by feminist theologians as privileged interpreters. Yet these women, constituted, for example, by Pentecostals, who were generally dismissed as having internalized the oppression of a patriarchal culture and Church, found a way to read the Scriptures in a manner which brought liberation to their lives. It is in part to accommodate the reading practices of such women that Fulkerson jettisons the appeal to experience, the idea of the meaning of the text, and other related notions. More importantly, at the outset of her project Fulkerson finds herself compelled to construct a feminist liberation epistemology, for only by so doing can she develop the kind of inclusivism required by a feminist theology which listens to all the voices which must be heard.

It quickly becomes clear, however, that Fulkerson has a further reason for rejecting the appeal to experience. Retaining such an appeal to experience is inconsistent with the rejection of foundationalism in epistemology.

Because the oppressed subject continues to be multiplied, it becomes more and more difficult to valorize 'women.' The basis for feminist theology—or any theology—as an academic theology dissolves. Dissolution of the basis of theology is not a bad thing for an antifoundationalist theology, that is, a theological proposal that understands the located character of all theological discourse. But this loss is bad news for a feminist theology that understands itself as legitimated by women's experience.[42]

---

[41] This point is very well made by Sheila Greeve Daveney: '[W]hen the claims for the social character of experience and knowledge are pushed further, we must confront the possibility that *no* perspective offers a privileged access to the "way things really are"; all we have are alternative ways of conceiving of reality. In a thoroughly social view, we have no access to a world which is separate from our interpretations of it, nor is there a basis for claiming that one socially-derived perspective resonates and corresponds to "reality as it really is." From this perspective, Ruether's and Schüssler Fiorenza's tendency to claim not only historical adequacy but ontological validity appears as special pleading, a failure to carry through the insights of the historicism that informs so much of their work' ('Limits of the Appeal to Women's Experience', 43).

[42] Fulkerson, *Changing the Subject*, 16.

The tension between the appeal to experience and the appeal to located perspective is here dissolved by dropping the appeal to experience and developing an entirely new way to look at epistemology.

Feminist theology needs a liberation epistemology if it is to move beyond or radicalize inclusionary strategies and respect difference. Such an epistemology is not about the problem of how a subject knows but about the relation between social relations, discourses, interests, and oppression-liberation. Its purpose is to investigate how certain kinds of subjects are produced that make objects of others. A liberation epistemology is nothing new to feminist theology, which virtually began with something like ideology critique as feminist theologians identified formulations of Christian secular traditions—language and ideas—as oppressive to women. My wish is to expand this feminist recognition of the relation of interest to language and ideas and to connect them to social situations.[43]

One way to conceptualize this kind of epistemology is to see it as an epistemology of negative or failed perception. Such an epistemology seeks to show how there has been massive self-deception and blindness, and the accompanying legitimation of violence. Equally, it seeks to show how certain groups have managed to struggle against oppression and for liberation. It does not pursue the issue of whether God exists, but the issue of 'what kind of God is practiced'.[44] The aim is to explore the social effects and the utopian possibilities of faith, to delineate the obscuring and pernicious effects of interest, all the while rejecting any claim to knowledge of an essential humanness.

Such an epistemology has five characteristics. First, it posits that theology has ideological or oppressive possibilities.

. . . we are to understand that the beliefs of and official discourse that constitute theological systems and define truth are not impervious to the impact of human interest in its pernicious forms. Nor are we to understand that the opposite is necessary, that by virtue of being situated and interested, a tradition is essentially pernicious. Knowledge is not *tainted* by interest; it *is* interest.[45]

Second, interests are connected to social conditions. These conditions include 'the economic, political, and civil or cultural

---

[43] Ibid. 18–19.   [44] Ibid. 20.
[45] Ibid. 25; emphasis original.

aspects of asocial formation'.[46] Such conditions are related to systems of meaning. Third, relating social conditions and meaning entails that the crucial concepts for the articulation of a liberation epistemology are those of 'making' and 'practice', rather than 'disclosure' or 'correlation'. Here Fulkerson qualifies, if not rejects, her earlier concern with perception.

Contrasted with the epistemological image of vision and the implied passivity of knowers, a production model is important for attending to social location. Vision, however compelling aesthetically, too often invites a way of knowledge that is unsituated. A production model reminds us that a liberation perspective must examine the effects of dominant codes and systems of meaning it brings into being, those that produce it as well as those it consciously employs.[47]

Fourth, focusing on the inextricable relationship between knowledge and social relations encourages the recognition of the multiple ways in which social forces may work 'to overdetermine, or to converge in multiple ways on women, so that oppressions and possibilities for emancipation are signified in women's discourse in multiple ways'.[48] This observation dovetails with a theological grammar of sin, for it highlights the role of desire, fear, and pleasure in a way which is necessarily neglected by a reflection theory of knowledge. Fifth, this approach to epistemology allows for the respecting of difference that attends to the production of women by stressing the social character of the subject. Hence it avoids the pitfalls of the kind of reflective theory of the self associated with Descartes.

It would be tempting to infer that this account of knowledge leads automatically into a reductionist account of theology, long made familiar in criticisms of a reductive sociology of knowledge. While Fulkerson is happy to describe her position as 'constructionism', she still insists that theological claims can be construed as linked to divine reality: 'I operate with a social conception of finitude that gestures at what cannot be caused or proven but only witnessed to: its ultimate conditions, God's redemptive reality.'[49] Yet she is severely critical of those theologians, like

---

[46] Fulkerson, *Changing the Subject*, 25.   [47] Ibid. 26.
[48] Ibid.
[49] Ibid. 29. This coheres with a later claim that theology be seen as testimony. See ibid. 372.

Ruether and Schüssler Fiorenza, who by deploying an epistemology of experience have seen texts and traditions as constitutively oppressive or liberating. Such a theory cannot account for the way that texts which are supposed to be essentially oppressive are in fact liberating for some readers in certain social locations. 'If we took those particular "sexist texts" and contents and their pernicious working to be adequate to the work of patriarchy in all women's lives, we would have to assume that women who do not agree with such accounts are lobotomized by distorted discourse.'[50] Hence a different kind of liberation epistemology is called for which moves beyond the expressivist appeal to experience.

This liberation epistemology provides for a different way of construing Scripture. There is now no such entity as an objective text waiting out there in free space to be interpreted. There exists instead a host of different reading practices constituted by the diverse social relations which obtain. Readings are complex productions. For a time these productions remain stable in a particular community; hence they are not arbitrary in the sense that any reading is possible. The boundaries of possible reading are effectively determined by the communities in which they are embedded. So there are no transcendental contents to be mined, no original situation of origin with a self-contained meaning independent of its rendering to be located, and no original intention to be sought. There are no foundational facts; all claims, including those about the past, are read through a grid of interest which makes the identified features outstanding. The grid of interest 'grants them their being'.[51] Automatically the text is multiplied, for there is no text apart from productive practices, and different practices—say, by different women—entail that there cannot any longer be one text. Moreover, there is no way to privilege one reading—say, that produced in the academy over that produced by Pentecostal hill-billy women. What matters from a Christian point of view is the production of 'Christian practices that create emancipatory space and widen the realm of God's kingdom'.[52]

These practices are part of a canonical system created by a community and its religious traditions. That system includes such

---

[50] Ibid. 57.   [51] Ibid. 128.   [52] Ibid. 164.

matters as the rules for reading Scripture, taking the text as a certain kind of thing, the institutional supports for the text's existence and dissemination, the rules of access and authorization for its readers, and the goal of the community's practice of reading. The canonical system generates its own ideal regime of reading or an ideal reading performance. It also allows for the possibility of a women's resisting regime which challenges, say, oppressive readings by working from within the canonical system and subverting them. In some cases it is possible to produce liberating readings which transgress the canonical system itself. The relationship between these practices and social location is so important that it is given a special, technical name: 'register' or 'discursive genre'.

A register or discursive genre can be as contained an utterance as a prayer. A type of literature can be identified as a genre containing within it a number of subgenres or registers. What connects these examples is their susceptibility to analysis by three variables that create unity out of a situation of utterance (i.e. make it a register); (1) field or subject matter; (2) tenor or quality of social relations; and (3) mode, the linguistic symbolic organization or channel of communication. Correlating to semiotic functions, the variables suggest how the content function of language, its interpersonal or social function, and its rhetorical or textual function are all constitutive of situational meaning and must be looked at together to suggest what meaning is generated.[53]

This third category, that of mode, is especially interesting from an epistemic point of view.

The final category, the impact of social formation on an intertextual economy, is a necessary part of the analysis because of our shift away from cognitive notions of oppression. If language does not represent or reflect reality or individual experience, neither is it a reflection of group experience. The poor do not have their common reality expressed in language; neither do women. Only the particular relation of discourses in a setting produce the truth.[54]

Fulkerson is fully aware that this entails the rejection of any correspondence theory of truth. She goes so far as to claim that theology, on this view, is 'an odd kind of noetic practice, and it sponsors what to some will appear to be an odd kind of truth'.[55] Her position would appear to be a variation on one recently

---

[53] Fulkerson, *Changing the Subject*, 178.   [54] Ibid. 180.

[55] Ibid. 376.

developed by Richard Rorty. She claims to embrace epistemological nihilism, that is, 'problematize knowledge'—without embrac-
ing alethiological nihilism—that is, denying the claim that there is
truth.[56]

I have refused a nihilist position with regard to whether there is a reality
outside of discourse. I have argued that reality only becomes intelligible
as discourse. It remains to me to clarify the way in which I deny our
access to 'truth' with my position.

The option I refuse is one that distinguishes knowledge and truth in
such a way that truth is accessed outside of our community based practices. These community based knowledges are sufficient, as non-foundationalist Richard Rorty says, for justified belief. They are, as it were, all
that we have; it is community based discourse 'all the way down.' This
position, one that is inevitable from my account of discourse, does not
lead to a vicious relativism (the conclusion that one thing is as good as
another). Nor does this position require the absolutizing of our communal values and beliefs. The loss is not of values, but of a God's-eye view
of discourses. As Donna Haraway says, 'relativism and totalization are
both "god-tricks" promising vision from everywhere and nowhere
equally and fully.' Constructively, then, Haraway is right that 'only
partial perspectives promise objective vision.' The fear that 'mere'
communal values will be absolutized is misplaced when the restriction
to communal discourses simply allows us as Christians to commit
passionately to a particular, finite situation that is God's.[57]

Although Fulkerson does not use the term, she is materially
committed to an epistemic, as opposed to a realist, conception of
truth. The counter-argument to her position would require

an account of truth that is distinguishable from those reasons, rules,
values, and beliefs that have their only foundation in communities and
their traditions. Such a separate site of access, as I have argued, seems to
beg the problematic question of who occupies it—the issue I find most
important. That, as I have implied all along, is some kind of 'community' not exempt from the productive work of power.[58]

We have now arrived back full circle at the vision of knowledge
not as tainted by interest, but as identical with interest.

At this point we should pause and reflect on the various tensions
in Fulkerson's position. At one moment she embraces the language
of perception; at the next she rejects it. At one moment she adopts

what appears to be a realist account of truth; at the next she retreats to a constructionist account of truth. At one moment she makes knowledge identical with interest; at the next she retreats to a position which distinguishes but relates knowledge and interest. At one moment she rejects a foundationalist account of knowledge; at the next she embraces a position which makes the reasons and values of a community the foundation of truth.

Furthermore, one might query the dogmatism which simply asserts or relies on authority to carry the day on the validity of a non-realist account of truth, all the while failing to distinguish between the issue of how we are to analyse the concept of truth—that is, deal with the question of the meaning of truth—and the way we are to delineate criteria of truth—that is, deal with the problem of the justification of truth-claims. Equally, one might legitimately wonder how she can reject the so-called universal claim that language does not represent or reflect reality, all the while proposing her own universal 'theory' of discourse which depends crucially on the depiction of causal claims about the relationship between language, interests, and power. Moreover, one might legitimately ponder whether any attempt at criticism would be worth the trouble, for the very idea of criticism will be encoded in terms of discursive practices which are likely to be construed as expressions of interest and power. The whole proposal is guarded by defensive devices and apologetic strategies which may make her position impervious to scrutiny.[59] One might also question the implied argument at the base of Fulkerson's proposal that somehow her overall position is to be recommended because it makes room for those voices which have recently been excluded from Women-church. This is a debatable claim, for there is more than one way to make room for such voices from an epistemic point of view.[60]

Interesting as pursuing these lines of investigation might be,

[59] One suspects that this is even more so in the case of Schüssler Fiorenza. See her failure to deal with a network of substantial objections raised by Sandra Ely Wheeler, Leander E. Keck, and Nicholas Lash at a conference at Duke University in April 1995, in 'The Author is Dead? Is She? Practicing the Ethics of Interpretation'.

[60] Thus one could well do so from an old-fashioned Liberal Protestant appeal to experience. The technical fallacy to which Fulkerson is prone is that of the fallacy of affirming the consequent.

they do not begin to capture the crucial observation which needs to be made as we pursue the more general topic of canon and criterion in the Christian tradition. It is worth providing a sharp reminder of the speculative, contested, and debatable nature of Fulkerson's liberation epistemology because it takes us back to where we have been again and again in the history of the Protestant tradition. The canonical traditions of the Church have once more been taken captive to the demands of an epistemological tradition. Modern Protestantism, like its earlier incarnations, appears to have no way of resisting the deployment of one epistemic proposal after another. Its divisions now fall not along lines dictated by the identity of the canon—say, Scripture or tradition—but along lines dictated by rival epistemic commitments.[61] Even the feminist tradition, despite its core commitment to women's liberation, is not likely to avoid internal division, and there are signs that this is already happening.

In this particular case the epistemic tradition is still in the making. Hence Fulkerson's position could easily be dismissed as a scissors-and-paste job; such a description would account, for example, for the list of difficulties cited above. However, this would be inappropriate criticism, for the details of a postmodernist account of knowledge, truth, justification, and related notions are still in the making. A full-dress assessment at this stage would be premature. The point to grasp is that this new position in modern Protestantism is an old and stale orthodoxy. While a feminist theology of liberation presents itself as a revolutionary undertaking, it is in reality a profoundly conservative affair, indebted to a tradition whose pedigree stretches back for centuries. It conserves the idea that the heart of the matter in the end rests in a theory of knowledge. In these circumstances there

---

[61] This observation is in keeping with the following comment of Daniel Maguire: 'Feminism is concerned with the shift in roles and the question of rights that have been unjustly denied women. But all of that, however important and even essential, is secondary. The main event is epistemological. Changes in *what* we know are normal; changes in *how* we know are revolutionary. Feminism is a challenge to the way we have gone about *knowing*. The epistemological *terra firma* of the recent past is rocking, and, as the event develops, it promises to change the face of the earth' (quoted in June O'Connor, 'The Epistemological Significance of Feminist Research in Religion', in King (ed.), *Religion and Gender*, 45; emphasis original).

is little likelihood that the canonical heritage of the Church will ever get the careful hearing and use it deserves.

We are now in a position to summarize the most important conclusions which have emerged from our review of this stream of feminist theology, as it explores the nature of canon and criterion in the Christian tradition.

1. The feminist tradition as a whole has approached the debate about canon by looking at canon as a means of healing and transformation. This represents a radically different way of construing canon from that which has been standard in the Church in the West since 1054. However, when evaluated in these terms, virtually all of the canonical heritage, aside from a selected 'canon within the canon' of Scripture, has been judged to be a failure. Whereas the whole canon of Scripture has been deemed to be inherently patriarchal and oppressive, selected readings have been judged to be liberating and redemptive. This interpretation of the canonical heritage as essentially salvific and transformative captures a way of thinking about canon which has ancient precedent in the Church and deserves the most careful exploration. It is clearly a soteriological concept of canon.

2. While two out of the three theologians we have looked at are Roman Catholic by profession, all of them focus on Scripture as the primary, if not exclusive, canon of the Church's heritage. In all three cases, then, we have a thoroughly Protestant orientation with respect to the initial identification of canonical material.[62] While in practice there is perhaps an implicit recognition that Scripture does not and cannot stand alone, there is no sense that any other material can truly count as canonical. At best there is an intellectual ambivalence about such a proposal. It is simply taken for granted that the debate about canon is really a debate about the authority of Scripture.

---

[62] Even then one cannot help but believe that the use of the Bible is a political act. It is because the Bible is such a crucial document of Western culture that it must be either neutralized in the struggle for emancipation or, better still, co-opted to serve the interests of the favoured feminist cause. In this respect one suspects that some feminist theologians practise very well what they preach as a matter of epistemic theory. If knowledge is interest, then any text or tradition is fair game to be used in the struggle. The whole point of the surrounding hermeneutical and epistemic theory is to legitimize this practice.

3. While this claim is true as it stands, and represents what is at issue *de jure*, the *de facto* situation is entirely different. Fulkerson, for her part, is extremely sensitive to the way in which Scripture is part of a wider canonical system. Ruether and Schüssler Fiorenza are committed to the imaginative development and creation of other sorts of material, which clearly replaces the wider canonical heritage which was developed by the early Church. This turn of events is extremely significant. As we noted, we ended up in Reuther's case with not just a new 'canon within the canon', but the beginnings of new scriptural material which could be put alongside her selections from the Old and New Testament. Equally, she and others are in search of a new creed, a new iconography, a new lectionary, a new form of episcopacy or oversight, a new liturgy, and so on.

What does this mean? I suggest that it may mean the creation of a new post-christian religion. There is the creation of a new creed, a new cult, and a new moral code. In this case the canonical reformation has become so radical that it may best be seen as the emergence of a new religion. If I am right about this, we have to hand a ready explanation for the intense turmoil which the work of Ruether and those committed in broad terms to her project has precipitated. Reuther, of course, will see a negative reaction to her proposals as either an expected response on the part of the patriarchial tradition or a sophisticated backlash. It may be accurate, in turn, to see this redescription of the turmoil in the Church as an apologetic device designed to keep penetrating criticism of her position at bay. This, of course, is masked by the use of Christian material and by various explicit avowals which insist that what is at stake is really a recovery of the original truth of the Christian tradition. However, as Ellen Charry has rightly observed, one cannot dispose of the radical consequences of the relevant canonical changes for the identity of the Christian tradition so lightly.[63] One can tamper here and there, one can make this or that alteration in the reception of the canonical heritage, and the community will find ways to adjust appropriately.

---

[63] See Ellen T. Charry, 'Literature as Scripture: Privileged Reading in Current Religious Reflection', *Soundings*, 74 (1991), 65–99. This is a profound essay on the significance of the creation of new canonical material which focuses in broad terms on the creation of a new scripture.

However, one cannot engage in a comprehensive and radical overhaul of the whole canonical system of the kind explicitly proposed here so easily. The development of canonical material has immediate consequences for the life of the Church as a whole. Hence the response of rank and file Christians, as much as that of those who study these matters carefully, is profoundly indicative of the issues at stake. What may be at stake is the creation of a whole new post-christian religion which will not merely reform the standard canonical material but effectively replace it.

4. This orientation, or perspective, explains a remarkable feature of the work we have examined: namely, the scant treatment given to such central doctrines as the Trinity and the Incarnation. Once we see that the Creed and the Chalcedonian Definition were crucial canonical materials, intended to be used alongside the canon of Scripture, the tendency to develop a message Christology and to ignore the whole Trinitarian tradition of the Church becomes especially conspicuous. More positively, the tendency to reduce the central themes of Christianity to talk about grace and redemptive presence betrays a modern Protestant sensibility which has systematically dismantled its own rich commitments. The drive to find replacement material to fill the gap created by the erosion of Trinitarian and Christological material only highlights the extent to which much feminist theology is committed to the intentional creation of a new body of canonical material. Especially interesting within this is the replacement of a general doctrine of sin with an anthropology which lifts up the particular sin of patriarchy as the fallen condition from which we must be rescued. Not surprisingly, there is a tendency, given the soteriology which matches this vision, to ignore the concepts of justification, forgiveness, reconciliation, assurance, new birth, faith, humility, and the quest for a sanctification of perfect love. In all, we can detect the distant and impoverished echo of a Protestant tradition which has long been in the process of losing its own distinctive voice.

5. Even though much feminist theology begins by deploying implicitly a soteriological concept of the canon of Scripture, this is very quickly transformed into epistemic categories. In the case of Ruether and Schüssler Fiorenza, the true canon becomes a criterion, and is identified as an appeal to women's experience,

which is simultaneously interpreted as the medium of divine grace, divine revelation, and cosmic wisdom. In time this kind of foundationalist appeal so reminiscent of Liberal Protestantism is dismantled by Fulkerson in the name of a deconstructionist epistemology which controls the interpretation and appropriation of Scripture. In this latter case the canon of Scripture has been made captive to the demands of a particular epistemology every bit as much as it was at the hands of Aquinas.

6. What remains intact across these changes is a moral and political agenda constituted by the quest for equality and the liberation of women. Feminist theology faces an acute dilemma at this juncture. Given its epistemic predilections, the obvious question which emerges is this: How is this agenda to be grounded? The agenda could, of course, be taken simply as a given, as basic, as a bedrock foundation. But, this does not fit the appeal to experience as the sole foundation of feminist theology; nor does it fit the rejection of all talk of foundations. Hence the options would appear to be these. The commitment to liberation can be grounded in the appeal to experience, or it can be construed as the discursive practice of a contemporary feminist community. The latter reduces it to the preferential option of a community in the West at the end of the twentieth century, and thereby any claim to objectivity above and beyond the interests of a particular community is lost. At best it is the arbitrary commitment of a designated group.[64] The former keeps intact the claim to present an objective moral demand, but it does not begin to show how it can be adequately grounded in experience. At best it is a piece of unfinished business in moral philosophy.

7. A further dilemma arises with respect to the causal analysis which is essential to any feminist proposal. By 'causal analysis' here, I mean the recurring claim that past history has been marked by the systematic oppression of women and various minorities. This is a causal claim about the activity of certain agents and the impact of those agents on others. The dilemma is as follows. On the one hand, we can keep intact the causal

---

[64] This criticism does not beg the question against Fulkerson, for it is perfectly possible to identify a difficulty in an epistemic proposal without having an alternative at hand to replace it. This is precisely why the discipline of epistemology has emerged within philosophy; it arose because of dissatisfaction with scepticism before it became a sub-discipline in its own right.

analysis, deploy a correspondence theory of truth to preserve its relation to the world, and, presumably, provide some kind of non-person-relative evidence to support such a causal claim. So we can keep the causal claim afloat only by preserving some kind of claim to describe reality objectively. On the other hand, if we either drop a correspondence conception of truth or we abandon the claim to objective description, then the crucial causal claim which permeates the whole enterprise collapses. Equally, if we deploy a theory of language which does not permit the occurrence of speech acts which genuinely picture the world, the claim that patriarchy exists as a system of oppression will have to be taken, not as a description of reality, but as an attempt to express certain interests and bring about certain changes in the world. Ruether would appear to take the first option, and Fulkerson the second; Schüssler Fiorenza oscillates between the two.

8. Whatever we may say about the relative merits of these proposals, all three remain deeply embedded and embroiled in the epistemological obsessions of the Enlightenment. The results of this entanglement are substantial. First, any potential insights available for the construction of a more adequate interpretation of the canonical heritage of the Church are smothered and lost. Second, this tradition as a whole cannot remain stable, for it is immediately at the mercy of rival epistemic schemes, none of which adequately supports the moral quest for equality which is so close to the core of the intended theological experiment. Third, while the feminist tradition, as represented here, can make a spirited criticism of the Christian tradition, it cannot launch a deep healing of the practices of the Church and society because it is drowned in a sea of epistemic issues and problems which nobody has yet resolved satisfactorily. Hence it is likely to lead to further division even among those groups it seeks to liberate, as the rival epistemological proposals gather momentum.

9. The challenge to the Christian tradition posed by this stream of feminist criticism can be expressed in this fashion. Does the complex canonical heritage of the Church, when it is rightly used, provide healing for the sins of patriarchy and androcentrism? This is not an epistemological issue. Translating it into an epistemological problem merely ensures that its resolution will be dependent on the addressing of philosophical questions which yet await an adequate answer. It is a soteriological and moral problem, one of

the many such problems which the Christian tradition has had to resolve in its long pilgrimage through history.

It would be inappropriate to claim here that this soteriological problem can be resolved, but we can identify what is needed. The problem, if it is to be resolved, can be addressed in part by articulating a comprehensive vision of the canonical heritage of the Church which shows that the doctrine of the Trinity is good for all of us, which shows that salvation from all sin, including salvation from male oppression, can be found in Christ, and which shows that the Holy Spirit works through the whole canonical heritage to re-create in all repentant sinners the mind of God in Christ. In short, this problem can be solved by showing that the salvation brought by Christ through the working of the Holy Spirit saves all humankind to the uttermost. Clearly, such a challenge is likely to evoke in time the full, self-critical response it so richly deserves.[65]

[65] Various efforts along these lines are already under way with respect to the appropriation of the biblical canon. See e.g. Gayle Gerber Koontz, 'The Trajectory of Scripture and Feminist Conviction', *Conrad Grebel Review: A Journal of Christian Inquiry*, 5 (1987), 201–20; Marti Steussy, *Setting the Table: Women in Theological Conversation* (St Louis: Chalice Press, 1995); Roberta Bondi, *Memories of God* (Nashville: Abingdon Press, 1995); Ellen T. Charry, *By the Renewing of Your Minds: The Pastoral Function of Christian Doctrine* (New York: Oxford University Press, 1997).

17

The Canonical Heritage and the Epistemology of Theology

It is now time to gather together the core of the argument which has been developed cumulatively across the history of theology on the nature and status of canon. My aim has not been to develop a comprehensive history of canon and criterion in Christian theology, but to provide sufficient information to show the crucial twists and turns in the journey. Within this the aim has been to recover a way of thinking about canon which is soteriological rather than epistemological in outlook, and to pave the way for a fresh approach to the epistemology of theology. The salutary essentials of the argument are as follows.

The early Church did not formally offer any reflective theory of its message and its theology. Long before Christians got around to developing epistemologies of theology, they cultivated a very rich canonical heritage. Before they did that, they were constituted as a community of living faith. Leaders and members of this community were convinced that the kingdom of God had drawn near and was present in the person of Jesus Christ through the working of the Holy Spirit. The heart of the Faith was a message of salvation geared to a complex vision of creation and of the human situation. So before there was any epistemology, any canon, and any community, there was Pentecost, and before Pentecost there was the work and ministry of Jesus Christ. It is, therefore, profoundly mistaken to see early Christianity as a theory of knowledge, or as a collection of books, or as a religious community. It was first and foremost a response to a series of acts of God, arising in and around Jesus Christ, crucified and risen, through the working of the Holy Spirit. The womb in which the community and its canonical traditions arose was the life of the triune God manifest and present as real in human history.

Christianity was first a pneumatological event which disrupted the way of death and opened up a radically different way of life for those who were initiated into new life in Christ.

Once the Christian community came into existence and became a missionary movement, it had to hand from the beginning a Gospel, a network of canonical practices, like preaching and sacraments, and a system of canonical oversight represented by episcopal succession and apostolic councils. It was a messianic movement deeply rooted in Judaism, focused on Jesus Christ as saviour and lord, and swept along by the power and presence of the Holy Spirit. It won converts by its preaching, by the mighty acts of the Holy Spirit, by its uncompromising zeal, and by its aggressive gossiping about the good news of the kingdom of God. In time there emerged a body of literature, most conspicuously a body of gospel writings and the letters of Paul, which were generally received as essential to preserving the extraordinary treasures which had been made available in Jesus Christ. Under pressure from various groups and individuals within and outside the Church, these were collected together and recognized as a gift from God to be used in worship and teaching. Alongside these there arose a creed which provided a memorable, portable summary of the intellectual backbone of the tradition. Initially used in catechesis, it became a minimal summary of the core of the Church's beliefs. Over time there developed a detailed definition related to the person of Christ, a canonical liturgy, canonical forms of iconography, and a list of pertinent teachers and saints. Over time canonical regulations were introduced for ordering the life of the community, as the community streamlined its practices of episcopal oversight.

These canonical materials, persons, and practices were received as gifts of the Holy Spirit. Taken together and working in harmony, their purpose was to initiate new believers into the life of God, returning them to the original intention of their creation. They were to mediate salvation, make possible the creation of the mind of Christ, equip Christians to be servants of God, and bring about profound transformation. Such goals could not be attained without repentance, faith, obedience, humility, and constant dependence on God. Nor could these goals be reached without a deep immersion in the life of the Holy Spirit. In an appropriate manner the canonical materials, persons, and practices mediated the revelation of God accomplished in his mighty acts in Jesus Christ. Yet they were themselves also a response to that revelation. They were brought into existence through human activity inspired by the Holy Spirit. Moreover, initiation involved encountering a mystery which could not be adequately expressed in language. It entailed immersion in a divine love beyond human knowledge, which was beyond human discourse to describe fully.

On conventional understandings of rationality the content of the Christian faith was incredible and foolish. Christian believers were rejected from the womb of Judaism, dismissed as atheists, derided for their convictions about God's saving activity in Jesus Christ, and persecuted as a standing threat to the political orders of the day. Yet their lives were marked by a commitment, and at times a certainty, which made possible faithfulness to death. They were deeply convinced of the truth of their faith, and had an assurance of their own acceptance and transformation by God which they attributed to the working of the Holy Spirit in their lives. Falling away, returning to their former ways, and yielding to government pressure were acts which entailed both a departure from the truth and a betrayal of their commitment to God.

This does not mean that Christianity was marked from the beginning by harmony. On the contrary, from its earliest days there were internal tensions aplenty, for disputes arose on a host of issues which few could have predicted. Preserving the riches of the Gospel and of the community, ordering the internal life of a new faith which welcomed all and sundry, coping with the ideas and practices which converts brought with them to baptism, and responding to new developments in the culture—these were a constant source of both stimulus and tension. They prompted both the preservation and the creation of new canonical tradition.

None of this tradition was constituted by the possession of an epistemology of theology, not to speak of a general epistemology. Christians claimed to know the true and living God without claiming officially or formally to know definitively how they knew that they knew the living and true God. They had no canonical account of reflective rationality, nor did they insist on unanimity in the epistemology of theology. This was a relatively esoteric, philosophical matter which could be left to the discretion of its members so long as their commitments in this domain did not undermine the emerging canonical heritage of the Church. Opinion ranged all the way from outright hostility to any alliance with any philosophical theory to the welcoming embrace of philosophical speculation. In between there was a mediating position which was prepared to use philosophical argument in an *ad hoc*, creative manner.

The vast majority of Christian believers and leaders paid little attention to such matters. However, the canonical material itself clearly raised epistemological questions. One has only to read the Creed to realize that it is natural to ask how we can justify the doctrines contained within it. Or one has only to think of various theological positions associated with the Eucharist to find oneself wondering which, if any, is true. That quest in turn easily leads into a deeper quest for a general theory of rationality, justification, and knowledge which will fit the enterprise in hand. So epistemological questions naturally arise once one begins thinking about the canonical heritage of the Church in a certain way.

Moreover, the canonical material itself clearly contains epistemic suggestions and proposals. Thus Paul insisted that the reality and nature of God were made known in creation, and that the law of God was inscribed in the human heart, with conscience bearing supporting witness.[1] He claimed that the Christian faith did not rest on clever arguments or human wisdom, but on the power of God. Understanding the truth of the Gospel involved a revelation of the Spirit, and human agents naturally refuse what belongs to the Spirit because of their passions and pride.[2] Hence coming to know the truth about God involved a healing of human cognitive capacities. Without such inner illumination it was not possible to perceive the revelation of God made visible in the life and work of Jesus Christ, and hence not possible to confess him as the Son of God and the saviour and lord of the world. These scattered teachings of Paul were amply repeated and extended in other parts of the Christian Scriptures. It was, and is, entirely legitimate, therefore, to explore the host of epistemic issues raised by and within the canonical heritage of the Church.

On this interpretation of canonical development, however, to possess a canon of Scripture was not in itself to possess an epistemology of theology. To be sure, Scripture was appealed to as a

---

[1] Rom. 1–2.   [2] 1 Cor. 1–2.

ground for argument. At times this strategy was in turn grounded in the claim that Scripture was inspired, or dictated, or authored by God, and hence reliable in its content. Moreover, Christians often deployed an implicit doctrine of divine revelation which entailed that to appeal to Scripture was to appeal to a criterion of truth. In this instance, however, it is revelation, rather than Scripture or canon, which is the relevant epistemic notion being deployed. Furthermore, given their convictions about the nature and person of Jesus Christ as the Son of God and about the role of the Spirit, say, in the life of the apostles, it was entirely natural to identify and rely on this or that piece of divine discourse or inspired tradition. What God spoke or revealed or inspired was true because, given who God is, he does not lie. Even then, as the case of Origen clearly shows, God acted in divine revelation as an astute tutor who worked with the grain of human learning, communicating with human agents in ways which drew them into the appropriation of divine truth, rather than allowing them to settle for a simple, flat-footed reception.[3]

However, much as it had the opportunity to do so, the early Church did not canonize these epistemic proposals. They were left informally present in the canonical heritage of the Church. Some of the pertinent insights about how they knew that their knowledge of God was genuine knowledge were discussed and debated in the writings of those who were later canonized as teachers, but no theory of revelation or inspiration was set apart as canonical.

The canonical heritage functioned, then, soteriologically. Taken as a whole, it was constituted by a network of materials, persons, and practices which mediated divine revelation, encounter with the living God, the bread of heaven and wine of fellowship, forgiveness of sins, instructions in holy living, directions for the corporate life of the Church, a host of insights for the life of obedience to God, and various epistemic suggestions. In time, Christians developed full-blown theories of knowledge which sought to explain by means of a theory of reflective rationality how they could claim to possess genuine knowledge of the God they worshipped and served. In short, they developed various epistemologies of theology.

[3] Origen goes so far as to say that Scripture contains stumbling-blocks. See *On First Principles* (Gloucester, Mass.: Peter Smith, 1973), 285.

The first really deep schism in the Church, while it had a host of causes, ultimately became demarcated by contested accounts of the canonical heritage developed in the patristic period. Crucial to the division were changes in the Nicene Creed in the article on the Holy Spirit and changes in the conception and location of canonical oversight. The Western half of the tradition added the *filioque* clause to the Creed, and elaborated a theory of papal infallibility which interpreted the episcopate of Rome as being in an epistemically privileged position. With the canonization of the work of Thomas Aquinas, the Western half of Christendom also expressed partiality towards a single epistemology of theology which elaborated an extremely sophisticated doctrine of biblical inerrancy, even though the precise status of this epistemology is difficult to determine. These developments involved the canonization of specific epistemic proposals which were never adopted by the Eastern half of the tradition. By contrast, the East systematically eschewed the canonization of any specific epistemology of theology, arguing, as it did through the writings of Gregory of Palamas and other teachers, that knowledge of God could not be conceptualized within the contours of any secular epistemology.

In the course of time the canonical heritage of the West was systematically epistemized; that is, canonical materials, persons, and practices were treated as items in a theory of knowledge. This is most conspicuous in the epistemology of Aquinas and in the teachings of the Council of Trent. The canon of Scripture and the tradition of the Church were interpreted as divinely dictated, and the office of the papacy was interpreted as having, under the right circumstances, a special access to the mind and will of God. Thus Scripture, tradition, and that section of the Church joined to the Roman see were formally identified as sites of divine revelation. This reading of the canonical tradition began to overshadow any soteriological vision of the canonical heritage, even though soteriological considerations were never abandoned or ignored. The canonical heritage was subject to a kind of inversion. Epistemic considerations became primary, with the result that the whole tradition was reconceived to fit the primacy of epistemology. Within the Church in the West, how one knew that one knew the truth about God overshadowed knowing God.

At least, this is how it eventually came to appear to many of those who revolted against the Roman see at the Reformation.

Driven by soteriological interests and obsessed by what they took to be a corruption of the life of the primitive and patristic Church, the Reformers sought to reform and then to rebuild the Church virtually from scratch. In doing so, they quickly adopted a thoroughly epistemic conception of the canon of Scripture. Drawing on epistemic tools already developed informally by some of the early Fathers and more formally by teachers like Aquinas, they turned to a doctrine of *sola scriptura* as the strategy for comprehensive reform. Hence their captivity to an epistemic conception of canon was built into their efforts at the outset. Their disputes with the brilliant leaders of the Counter-Reformation only deepened the epistemizing of the canonical heritage of the Church.

Fortunately, *de facto* they more often failed than succeeded in executing the *de jure* programme to which they were committed; for they borrowed lavishly from the full canonical heritage of the Church without there being any warrant in their canonical foundationalism to do so. No doubt one reason for this providential and splendid failure of nerve stemmed from the soteriological needs which could only be met in the wider canonical life of the Church. The success of the Reformers was rooted less in their epistemology of theology, for this was in trouble from the outset, than in the working of the Holy Spirit to save and liberate hungry and needy sinners. It is not at all surprising that the Reformers recovered the canonical practice of preaching Scripture, for precisely this practice was essential in the economy of the Church to bring home the meaning of the Gospel. Nor is it surprising that they loved the Fathers of the Church, for they found in them a body of extraordinarily helpful material for renewing and rebuilding the corporate life of believers. Happily, then, epistemic theory was often overshadowed by a recovery of canonical materials, persons, and practices which had been lost or neglected in the Church.

Happily, too, they were well aware that there could be no Christian existence without the life-giving work of the Holy Spirit. At times they were entirely convinced that the working of the Holy Spirit had a profound role in coming to a knowledge of the triune God, even though their explicit epistemic proposals tended towards the development of an exclusivist theological foundationalism which insisted that proposals concerning the detailed life of the Church must be grounded solely, clearly, and explicitly on the text of Scripture understood to be dictated by God, or, alternatively, that they be derived by valid inference from clear and explicit texts of Scripture.

The debate precipitated among Christian intellectuals and leaders in the West by the Reformation was extraordinarily fruitful from an epistemic point of view. Joined to the recovery of ancient texts, the revival of scepticism, and the rise of natural science, the Reformation debates about canon were transposed into a debate about the criterion of truth. Descartes recognized, if only unconsciously, that the debates about canon after the Reformation could no longer be resolved within the framework in which they were located. His attempt to raise everything on universally indubitable foundations, while it rejected the material proposals of the Reformers and the Counter-Reformers, kept intact the intellectual structure of the epistemology of theology worked out by the Reformers. The work of John Locke, which in turn repudiated the material proposals of Descartes, kept intact the classical foundationalist structure of Descartes's general epistemology. Locke heightened the crisis which this entailed for the canonical heritage of the Church by requiring as a condition of rationality that all theological claims be subject to the rule of reason. On this reading, the Enlightenment, in so far as it is expressed in the thought of Descartes and Locke, was the invention of Christian intellectuals intent on resolving the epistemic crises precipitated in part by the internal divisions of Western Christendom. Its version of classical foundationalism is the transposition and secularization of the epistemized canonical heritage of the Protestant Reformation.

The net result of this process was a heightened interest in the epistemology of theology within Western forms of Christianity. In time, three crucial themes emerged as the exclusive foundations for Christian theology: natural theology, special revelation, and religious experience. Deists opted for natural theology; Locke and his followers argued for a combination of natural theology and special revelation; Schleiermacher and Liberal Protestantism rejected these in favour of appeal to religious experience. Given the Protestant background, the canonical heritage of the Church was reduced to Scripture in all of these traditions. None of them succeeded in sustaining the place of Scripture in the life of the

Church without enormous strain. Even Locke, who came closest to the classical position of the Reformation, could make room for appeal to Scripture only within the bounds of appeal to reason alone. For the most part deists and Liberal Protestants made use of Scripture in so far as it republishes the truths which could be garnered either from natural theology or from religious experience. Not surprisingly, the wider canonical material represented, say, by the doctrine of the Trinity laid out in the Nicene Creed or in the high Christological commitments expressed in the Chalcedonian Definition, were systematically marginalized or eroded in these trajectories.

Given the epistemizing of the canonical heritage of the Church and the creation of a lively sub-discipline of epistemology within philosophy, it is natural that attempts were made to combine elements from both fields. The most conspicuous of these can be found among Anglicans and United Methodists. The Anglican tradition, inspired by Richard Hooker, made a serious effort to develop an epistemology which combined an appeal to Scripture, tradition, and reason. Much later, the United Methodist tradition, inspired by Albert Outler, sought to reconstitute itself on the basis of the Methodist quadrilateral: that is, an appeal to Scripture, tradition, reason, and experience. In both cases these constitute a kind of scissors-and-paste epistemology which tends to displace those canonical doctrinal traditions which were pivotal at the beginnings of both communions. Doctrinal and theological pluralism have in both cases become the *de facto* orthodoxy of the tradition. Unity is sought in terms of commitment to a particular epistemology of theology. The consequences for doctrinal commitment are predictable: each tradition is a constellation of doctrinal parties at odds with each other. Combining ecclesial canons and epistemic concepts has not, then, been successful. It is a form of amateur epistemology, and it is ultimately damaging from a spiritual point of view.

Over the centuries various protests against the epistemizing of the canonical heritage of the Church have surfaced within Protestantism. Pietism, early Methodism, and Pentecostalism represent a Protestant underworld of protest which has sought to return to a soteriological vision of the Scriptures. Uneasy with a purely cognitive approach to the Christian faith, its inhabitants have searched the Scriptures for salvation, and have been remarkably successful for a time as agents of evangelization. Beginning as movements of piety which arose as quests for the life of the Spirit, they quickly became ecclesial institutions which were constituted by various components of the canonical heritage of the Church. They instituted sacraments, creeds, forms of oversight and ministry, adaptable liturgies, and their own equivalent of ancient canon law. Invariably they moved to a Protestant conception of Scripture, complete with its epistemic categories, even though this often sat uneasily with their usage and their original intention. As they matured over the years, they were readily drawn into adopting the prevailing epistemological strategies of their elder brothers and sisters in the Christian family. Ironically, as a result, they became the forebears of Liberal Protestantism, and have constantly succumbed to its temptations.

At a much more sophisticated level, protest took the form of a rejection of the prevailing epistemic orthodoxy in the name of an alternative epistemology. Thus the great Princeton theologians skilfully drew on the work of Thomas Reid to provide a bulwark against the attack on the Faith they saw arising both within and outside the Church. In the end the attachment to the Common Sense tradition had its limitations; under no circumstances would they allow the old doctrine of *sola scriptura* to be jettisoned. A very different way to salvage the commitment to *sola scriptura* was developed by John Henry Newman. Newman found a way to combine a return to Rome with his own original epistemological proposals. He relocated the canon of Scripture back in the life of the Western Church, accepted the doctrine of papal infallibility as a way of banishing doubt about its meaning, and found a way to provide a case for both the existence of God and the identity of divine revelation.

Yet another way to rescue Protestantism from the clutches of epistemology can be found in the work of Karl Barth. His aim was to let the Christian heritage be itself, unencumbered by epistemic theory borrowed from philosophy. The Christian heritage had to be given its full right to speak for itself, without having first to be expressed or translated into the idiom of an alien intellectual framework. The intellectual scandal and foolishness of the Gospel were fully acknowledged, the illuminating work of the Holy Spirit was celebrated, the internal paradoxes of the Faith were highlighted, and every effort was made to avoid an alliance with philosophy.

Alas, success on this score remained illusory. The protest against epistemology became so vehement that the response was itself shaped by the prevailing epistemology. The great doctrines of grace and justification by faith were transformed into epistemic doctrines, in order to keep any appeal to natural theology or religious experience at bay. An echo of the Protestant appeal to *sola scriptura* remained in the form of an appeal to divine revelation as the foundation of faith. Within a generation Christian theology in the Barthian tradition was once again presented as a technical species of knowledge, this time modelled on the natural sciences.

In the recent past a fascinating attempt to recover a soteriological vision of the canonical heritage has surfaced in the work of feminist theologians. To date this has mostly been a negative exercise, for the actual canonical heritage is rejected in the name of liberation, and a whole new network of canonical materials and practices are being created. Yet even before this process has matured, the epistemizers have appeared once again. This time they come equipped with post-modernist theories of discourse and truth to provide a thoroughly epistemic account of the old and new heritage. Meanwhile, the descendants of the great Princeton theologians and their Liberal Protestant rivals are waiting in the wings with their alternative epistemology of theology, should the quest for a feminist epistemology falter.

This is occurring at a time when a quiet revolution has been under-way in epistemology itself. Within philosophy epistemology has flourished over the last half century. The impact within philosophy of religion has been extraordinary. Consider some of the major options which are currently on offer. There is the suggestion that theism be interpreted as a large-scale explanatory hypothesis to be judged probabilistically on the basis of all the relevant evidence and according to Bayes' theorem.[4] There is the suggestion that belief in God is a basic belief, no more in need of evidence than belief in the existence of the external world.[5]

---

[4] Richard Swinburne, *The Existence of God* (Oxford: Clarendon Press, 1979).

[5] Alvin Plantinga, 'Reason and Belief in God', in Alvin Plantinga and Nicholas Wolterstorff (eds.), *Faith and Rationality: Reason and Belief in God* (Notre Dame, Ind.: University of Notre Dame Press, 1983),16–93; Nicholas Wolterstorff, *Reason within the Bounds of Religion* (Grand Rapids, Mich.: Eerdmans, 1976).

There is the suggestion that theism is based on various perceptual practices which should be taken as reliable until proved otherwise.[6] There is the suggestion that Christian belief should be seen as based not on some single proof or argument, but on a whole network of evidence and argument which cannot be captured in a formal calculus.[7] There is the suggestion that the passion of the heart may be essential to seeing the force of the deliverances of objective reason in theology.[8]

What is fascinating about these developments is that there is virtually no mention of the canonical heritage of the Church in them. These theories have no obvious entailments, for example, for this or that interpretation of the canon of scripture or of the Nicene Creed. What is significant is that the various proponents of the options I have just rehearsed can all whole-heartedly assent to the Nicene Creed or to Scripture as a canon of the Church, even as they disagree about the epistemology they deploy in their attempts to show that the doctrines of theism or of Christianity are true, rational, properly justified, or constitute knowledge. Were we to pursue what is said or might be said about divine revelation, the same fundamental point holds: no modern proponent of a philosophical account of divine revelation would propose for one moment that his or her theory be received as canonical.

These developments in the epistemology of theology do not mandate, then, the adoption of any position on the interpretation and content of the canonical heritage of the Church. They do, however, permit the retrieval of the kind of position I have been at pains to emphasize throughout the narrative and critical assessment pursued here. On this analysis, the canonical heritage should be seen as a network of means of grace given by God to be received through the working of the Holy Spirit. Thus the canon of Scripture is not an item in a theory of knowledge, like a criterion of justification; it is a body of literature inspired by God and adopted over time in the Church to make us wise unto salvation.

[6] William P. Alston, *Perceiving God* (Ithaca, NY: Cornell University Press, 1991).

[7] Basil Mitchell, *The Justification of Religious Belief* (London: Macmillan, 1973).

[8] William J. Wainwright, *Reason and the Heart* (Ithaca, NY: Cornell University Press, 1995).

Furthermore, it is one element in a rich tapestry of materials, persons, and practices which are to function together in harmony for the welfare of the Church and for the salvation of the world. Repairing this canonical heritage of the Church, or rescuing it from chronic dysfunction, will not be achieved by the discovery of a new epistemology. It will be brought about by patient renewal and retrieval inspired by the Holy Spirit. The best that philosophy can do in this activity is to ensure that relevant distinctions are observed and to ensure that the epistemology of theology be pursued with rigour and thoroughness.

The latter end will be usefully furthered when the epistemic proposals, insights, and suggestions embedded in the canonical heritage are carefully explored. This would in no way displace the importance of the range of questions which have been pursued in debates about the justification of theistic belief of late. The perennial questions which swirl around the validity of the classical arguments for the existence of God, the nature and grounds for belief in divine revelation, and the nature and force of the evidential force of religious experience are as pertinent as ever. These too crop up in the canonical heritage within and outside of Scripture. Moreover, new work in the epistemology of religious belief may well alert the perceptive student to epistemic components in the tradition which have been ignored, neglected, or not formulated adequately. Thus recent work on virtue epistemology may well help to identify epistemic materials in the canonical heritage which stress the importance of conversion and transformation for knowledge of God. Ongoing work on the nature of perception may throw invaluable light on ways of thinking about perception of the divine. The whole range of discussion on the nature of justification, rationality, truth, knowledge, explanation, evidence, inference, and the like continues to be pertinent to claims about the grounding of Christian theism and of specific Christian doctrines. Equally, careful study of the canonical teachers of the Church may bring to light material which is neglected in current discussions of the epistemology of theology. To take but one example, the work of Gregory of Palamas on the limits of all epistemological work in articulating knowledge of God deserves the closest examination.

It will be clear by now that the canonical heritage of the Church encourages, rather than inhibits, the pursuit of epistemic questions. Some Christian communions have in fact canonized particular epistemic proposals or traditions. Roman Catholics clearly give a status to the work of Aquinas which is not accorded to others. Eastern Orthodoxy has a way of reflecting on the nature of knowledge of God which is only now receiving the attention it deserves. Reformed thinkers have been keen in recent years to develop a Reformed account of rationality and justification which draws heavily on its founding teachers. Anglicans and United Methodists have sought in their own way to articulate ways of thinking about the relationship between faith and reason which can be recognized as characteristic of their traditions.

Given the account of the nature of the canonical heritage of the Church, such moves are entirely appropriate, formally speaking. Different Christian communities are entirely at liberty to develop and even canonize this or that epistemology. They are not, however, at liberty to ignore the consequences of their actions in this area. Problems emerge on three fronts. First, too often, crucial canons of the Church, especially the canon of Scripture, are taken to be proposals in epistemology, when they were never intended to be items in an epistemic theory. Second, epistemic proposals are sometimes adopted which are at odds with the canonical heritage already in place, or which create accounts of the canonical heritage which prevent it from functioning as it ought. Third, epistemic proposals are developed which effectively replace the canonical heritage of the Church, and hence make the Church captive to the fortunes of epistemology as it develops across the centuries. The solution to these difficulties is not to abandon the epistemology of theology, but to be clear about the content and nature of the canonical heritage of the Church and to be equally clear about the nature and limits of epistemology in the economy of faith. Once that clarity has been developed in theology and in the Church, we may well make additional progress on the epistemology of theology. Even then, there is no guarantee that we shall be able to develop the kind of comprehensive theory which has so often been the goal of the epistemology of theology. We may have to be content with epistemic proposals which illuminate crucial tracts of Christian theology, rather than provide a single theory which will cover the whole terrain. It may even be the case that the best way ahead in the epistemology of theology is to be epistemically agnostic, cautious about the success of any general epistemological theory as applicable to theology. As in many other areas of life, it may be that in theology we know much more than we can either explain or show that we know.

BIBLIOGRAPHY

AARSLEFF, HANS, 'Locke's Influence', in Vere Chappell (ed.), *The Cambridge Companion to Locke* (Cambridge: Cambridge University Press, 1994).

ABRAHAM, WILLIAM J., *The Coming Great Revival: Recovering the Full Evangelical Tradition* (San Francisco: Harper and Row, 1984).

—— *The Divine Inspiration of Holy Scripture* (Oxford: Oxford University Press, 1981).

—— *Divine Revelation and the Limits of Historical Criticism* (Oxford: Oxford University Press, 1982).

—— 'Intentions and the Logic of Interpretation', *Asbury Theological Journal*, 40 (1988), 11–25.

—— *An Introduction to the Philosophy of Religion* (Englewood Cliffs, NJ: Prentice-Hall, 1985).

—— *Waking from Doctrinal Amnesia: The Healing of Doctrine in The United Methodist Church* (Nashville: Abingdon Press, 1995).

—— 'The Wesleyan Quadrilateral', in Ted Runyon (ed.), *Wesleyan Theology Today: A Bicentennial Theological Celebration* (Nashville: Kingswood Books, 1985), 119–26.

ACHTEMEIER, ELIZABETH, 'The Impossible Possibility: Evaluating the Feminist Approach to Bible and Theology', *Interpretation*, 42 (1988), 45–57.

ACHTEN, RIK, *First Principles and Our Way to Faith: A Fundamental-Theological Study of John Henry Newman's Notion of First Principles* (Frankfurt-on-Main: Peter Lang, 1995).

AFANASIEV, NICHOLAS N., 'The Canons of the Church: Changeable or Unchangeable?', *St Vladimir's Seminary Quarterly*, 11 (1967), 54–68.

AHLSTROM, SYDNEY, 'The Scottish Philosophy and American Theology', *Church History*, 24 (1955), 257–72.

ALEXANDER, ARCHIBALD, *Evidences of the Authenticity, Inspiration and Canonical Authority of the Holy Scriptures* (Philadelphia: Presbyterian Board of Publication, 1836).

—— *Thoughts on Religious Experience* (Philadelphia: Presbyterian Board of Publication, 1844).

ALLEN, DIOGENES, 'The Paradox of Freedom and Authority', *Theology Today*, 36 (1979), 167–75.

ALSTON, WILLIAM P., 'Emotion and Feeling', in Paul Edwards (ed.),

The Encyclopedia of Philosophy (New York: Macmillan, 1967), ii. 479–86.

—— *Perceiving God* (Ithaca, NY: Cornell University Press, 1991).

—— 'Reid on Perception and Conception', in Melvin Dalgarno and Eric Matthews (eds.), *The Philosophy of Thomas Reid* (Boston: Academic Publishers, 1989), 35–48.

AQUINAS, ST THOMAS, *Summa Contra Gentiles*, trans. C. J. O'Neil (Notre Dame, Ind.: University of Notre Dame Press, 1957).

—— *Summa Theologiae* (Garden City, NY: Image Books, 1969).

ARIEW, ROGER, 'Descartes and Scholasticism', in John Cottingham (ed.), *The Cambridge Companion to Descartes* (Cambridge: Cambridge University Press, 1992), 58–90.

ARMSTRONG, A. H., 'Pagan and Christian Traditionalism in the First Three Centuries', *Studia Patristica*, 15 (1984), 414–31.

ARNDT, WILLIAM F., and GINGRICH, F. WILBUR (eds.), *A Greek–English Lexicon of the New Testament and Other Early Christian Literature* (Chicago: University of Chicago Press, 1957).

AUGUSTINE, ST, *Confessions* (Oxford: Oxford University Press, 1991).

—— *Soliloquies* (Warminster: Aris and Phillips, 1990).

AVIS, PAUL, *Anglicanism and the Christian Church* (Edinburgh: T. & T. Clark, 1989).

BABCOCK, WILLIAM S., 'A Changing of the Christian God: The Doctrine of the Trinity in the Seventeenth Century', *Interpretation*, 45 (1991), 133–46.

BANNER, MICHAEL C., *The Justification of Science and the Rationality of Religious Belief* (Oxford: Clarendon Press, 1990).

BARNES, LAURENCE PHILIP, 'Religious Experience, Philosophical Foundationalism and the Quest for Certainty in Modern Theology' (Ph.D. thesis, Trinity College, Dublin, 1992).

BARR, JAMES, *Biblical Faith and Natural Theology* (Oxford: Clarendon Press, 1993).

—— *Holy Scripture: Canon, Authority, and Criticism* (Oxford: Clarendon Press, 1983).

BARRES, OLIVER, *One Shepherd, One Flock* (New York: Sheed and Ward, 1956).

BARTH, KARL, *Anselm: Fides Quaerens Intellectum* (New York: Meridian, 1962).

—— *Church Dogmatics* (Edinburgh: T. & T. Clark, 1936).

—— *From Rousseau to Ritschl* (London: SCM Press, 1959).

—— *Protestant Theology in the Nineteenth Century* (London: SCM Press, 1972).

—— *Protestant Thought from Rousseau to Ritschl* (London: SCM Press, 1959).

—— *The Word of God and the Word of Man* (London: Hodder & Stoughton, n.d.).

BASIL, ST, *On the Holy Spirit* (Crestwood, NY: St Vladimir's Seminary Press, 1980).

BEATTIE, FRANCIS R., *Apologetics or the Rational Vindication of Christianity* (Richmond, Va.: Presbyterian Committee of Publications, 1903).

BEHRENS, GEORGE, 'Schleiermacher *contra* Lindbeck on the Status of Doctrinal Sentences', *Religious Studies*, 30 (1994), 399–417.

BEISER, FREDERICK C., *The Fate of Reason: German Philosophy from Kant to Fichte* (Cambridge, Mass.: Harvard University Press, 1987).

BENTIVEGNA, J., 'The Times of the Christian Fathers: Theological Attempts at an Ecumenical Definition', *Studia Patristica*, 15 (1984), 268–77.

BERLIN, ISAIAH, *The Age of Enlightenment* (New York: Mentor, 1956).

—— *The Magus of the North, J. G. Hamann and the Origins of Modern Irrationalism* (New York: Farrar, Straus & Giroux, 1993).

BEVENOT, MAURICE, 'Tradition, Church, and Dogma', *Heythrop Journal*, 1 (1960), 34–47.

BIGGAR, NIGEL (ed.), *Reckoning with Karl Barth: Essays on the Centenary of Karl Barth's Birth* (London: Mowbray, 1988).

BOFF, CLODOVIS, *Theology and Praxis: Epistemological Foundations* (Maryknoll, NY: Orbis, 1987).

BOHLMANN, RALPH ARTHUR, 'The Criteria of Biblical Canonicity in Sixteenth-Century Lutheran, Roman Catholic, and Reformed Theology' (Ph.D. thesis, Yale University, 1968).

BONDI, ROBERTA, *Memories of God* (Nashville: Abingdon Press, 1995).

BONJOUR, LAURENCE, 'Externalism/Internalism', in Jonathan Dancy and Ernest Sosa (eds.), *A Companion to Epistemology* (Oxford: Blackwell, 1992), 132–6.

BORRESEN, KARI ELIZABETH, 'Women's Studies in the Christian Tradition', in Ursula King (ed.), *Religion and Gender* (Oxford: Blackwell, 1995), 245–56.

BOUYER, LOUIS, *Newman: His Life and Spirituality* (New York: Meridian, 1988).

BRANDT, RICHARD, *The Philosophy of Schleiermacher: The Development of His Theory of Scientific and Religious Knowledge* (New York: Harper and Row, 1941).

BRUCE F. F., *The Canon of Scripture* (Downers Grove, Ill.: InterVarsity Press, 1988).

—— *Tradition Old and New* (Exeter: Paternoster Press, 1970).

BUTTS, R. E., and DAVIS, W., (eds.), *The Methodological Heritage of Newton* (Oxford: Blackwell, 1970).

BYRNE, EDMUND F., *Probability and Opinion: A Study in the Medieval Presuppositions of Post-Medieval Theories of Probability* (The Hague: Martinus Nijhoff, 1968).

CALLAHAN, DANIEL J. et al. (eds.), *Christianity Divided* (New York: Sheed and Ward, 1961).

CALVIN, JOHN, *Institutes of the Christian Religion*, ed. John T. McNeill (2 vols., Philadelphia: Westminster Press, 1960).

CAMERON, AVERIL, 'Response', in Elizabeth Schüssler Fiorenza, 'Theological Criteria and Historical Reconstruction: Martha and Mary, Luke 10: 38–42', in *Protocol of the Fifty-Third Colloquy* (Berkeley: Center for Hermeneutical Studies in Hellenistic and Modern Culture, 1987), 21–5.

CAMP, CLAUDIA V., 'Feminist Theological Hermeneutics: Canon and Identity', in Elizabeth Schüssler Fiorenza (ed.), *Searching the Scriptures*, vol. i: *A Feminist Introduction* (New York: Crossroad, 1993), 154–71.

CAMPENHAUSEN, H. F. VON, *The Formation of the Christian Bible* (Philadelphia: Fortress Press, 1972).

CARTER, STEPHEN, 'The Protestant Doctrine of Scripture in the Church of England, 1547–1553' (M.Phil. thesis, University of Oxford, 1990).

CARY, PHILIP, 'On Behalf of Classical Trinitarianism: A Critique of Rahner on the Trinity', *Thomist*, 56 (1992), 365–406.

CHADWICK, HENRY, *Early Christian Thought and the Classical Tradition* (Oxford: Clarendon Press, 1966).

—— 'Newman's Significance for the Anglican Church', in David Brown (ed.), *Newman: A Man for Our Time* (Harrisburg, Pa.: Morehouse, 1990), 52–74.

CHARLESWORTH, M. J., *St Anselm's Proslogion* (Oxford: Clarendon Press, 1965).

CHARRY, ELLEN. T., *By the Renewing of Your Minds: The Pastoral Function of Christian Doctrine* (New York: Oxford University Press, 1997).

—— 'Literature as Scripture: Privileged Reading in Current Religious Reflection', *Soundings*, 74 (1991), 65–99.

CHILDS, BREVARD S., *Introduction to the Old Testament as Scripture* (Philadelphia: Fortress Press, 1979).

—— *The New Testament as Canon: An Introduction* (Philadelphia: Fortress Press, 1985).

CHISHOLM, RODERICK M., 'The Problem of the Criterion', in *The Foundations of Knowing* (Minneapolis: University of Minnesota Press, 1982), 61–75.

CLARK, J. C. D., *English Society, 1688–1832: Ideology, Social Structure and Political Practice during the Ancien Regime* (Cambridge: Cambridge University Press, 1985).

CLARKSON, JOHN. F., *et al.*, *The Church Teaches* (St Louis: Herder, 1955).

CLEMENT OF ALEXANDRIA, *Stromateis* (Washington: Catholic University of America Press, 1991).

CONE, JAMES H., *A Black Theology of Liberation* (Maryknoll, NY: Orbis, 1986, 1990).

COPLESTON, FREDERICK, *A History of Philosophy* (New York: Image Books, 1964), vol. v.

COTTINGHAM, JOHN, *Descartes* (Oxford: Blackwell, 1986).

CURLEY, E. M., *Descartes against the Skeptics* (Cambridge, Mass.: Harvard University Press, 1978).

DALY, MARY, *Beyond God the Father* (Boston: Beacon Press, 1973).

DAVENEY, SHEILA GREEVE, 'The Limits of the Appeal to Women's Experience', in Clarissa W. Atkinson, Constance H. Buchanan, and Margaret R. Miles (eds.), *Shaping New Vision: Gender and Values in American Culture* (Ann Arbor: UMI Research Press, 1987), 31–50.

DAVIES, BRIAN, *The Thought of Thomas Aquinas* (Oxford: Clarendon Press, 1992).

DAVIES, W. D., 'Canon and Christology', in L. D. Hurst and N. T. Wright (eds.), *The Glory of Christ in the New Testament* (Oxford: Clarendon Press, 1987), 19–36.

D'AVRAY, DAVIS L., 'Papal Authority and Religious Sentiment in the Late Middle Ages', in Diana Wood (ed.), *The Church and Sovereignty c. 590–1915* (Oxford: Blackwell, 1991), 393–408.

DE GEORGE, RICHARD T., *The Nature and Limits of Authority* (Lawrence, Kan.: University Press of Kansas, 1985).

DESCARTES, RENÉ, *Discourse on Method* (London: Penguin, 1968).

—— *The Meditations* (London: Penguin, 1968).

DEVENISH, PHILIP E., and GOODWIN, GEORGE L., 'Christian Faith and the First Commandment: The Theology of Schubert Ogden', in Philip E. Devenish and George L. Goodwin (eds.), *Witness and Existence: Essays in Honor of Schubert M. Ogden* (Chicago: University of Chicago Press, 1989), 1–42.

DIBBLE, ROMAULD A., *John Henry Newman: The Concept of Infallible Doctrinal Authority* (Washington: The Catholic University Press of America, 1955).

DICKER, GEORGE, *Descartes: An Analytical and Historical Introduction* (New York: Oxford University Press, 1993).

DIONNE, ROBERT J., *The Papacy and the Church* (New York: Philosophical Library, 1987).

DÖLLINGER, J. J. I. VON, *The Pope and the Council* (Boston: Robert Brothers, 1870).

DUPRÉ, LOUIS, 'Towards a Revaluation of Schleiermacher's *Philosophy of Religion*', *Journal of Religion*, 44 (1964), 97–112.

DVORNIK, FRANCIS, *The Photian Schism: History and Legend* (Cambridge: Cambridge University Press, 1948).

ERICKSON, JOHN. H., *The Challenge of the Past* (Crestwood, NY: St Vladimir's Seminary Press, 1991).

EUSEBIUS PAMPHILIUS, *The Ecclesiastical History* (Grand Rapids, Mich.: Baker Book House, 1955).

EVANS, G. R. (ed.), *Christian Authority: Essays in Honour of Henry Chadwick* (Oxford: Clarendon Press, 1988).

FARMER, W. R., and FARKASFALVY, D., *The Formation of the New Testament Canon* (New York: Paulist Press, 1983).

FERREIRA, M. JAMIE, *Doubt and Religious Commitment: The Role of the Will in the Newman's Thought* (Oxford: Clarendon Press, 1980).

—— *Scepticism and Reasonable Doubt: The British Naturalist Tradition in Wilkins, Hume, Reid, and Newman* (Oxford: Clarendon Press, 1986).

FIERING, NORMAN, 'The Rationalist Foundations of Jonathan Edwards's Metaphysics', in Nathan O. Hatch and Harry S. Stout (eds.), *Jonathan Edwards and the American Experience* (New York: Oxford University Press, 1988), 73–101.

FILSON, FLOYD V., *Which Books Belong in the Bible* (Philadelphia: Westminster Press, 1957).

FITZPATRICK, P. J., 'Newman's *Grammar* and the Church Today', in David Nichols and Fergus Kerr (eds.), *John Henry Newman: Reason, Rhetoric and Romanticism* (Carbondale and Edwardsville, Ill.: Southern Illinois University Press, 1991), 119–28.

FRASER, A. C., *Thomas Reid* (Edinburgh: Oliphant, Anderson, and Ferrier, 1898).

FULKERSON, MARY MCCLINTOCK, *Changing the Subject: Women's Discourses and Feminist Theologies* (Minneapolis: Fortress Press, 1994).

FULLER, DANIEL P., 'Benjamin B. Warfield's View of Faith and History', *Journal of the Evangelical Theological Society*, 11 (1968), 75–83.

GALLIE, W. D., 'Essentially Contested Concepts', in *Philosophy and the Historical Understanding* (London: Chatto & Windus, 1964), 157–91.

GAMBLE, HARRY Y., *The New Testament Canon: Its Meaning and Making* (Philadelphia: Fortress Press, 1985).

GEISELMANN, JOSEPH RUPERT, 'Scripture, Tradition, and the Church: An Ecumenical Problem', in Daniel J. Callahan *et al.* (eds.), *Christianity Divided* (New York: Sheed and Ward, 1961), 39–72.

GEISLER, NORMAN, *Thomas Aquinas: An Evangelical Appraisal* (Grand Rapids, Mich.: Baker Book House, 1991).

General Assembly of the Presbyterian Church in the USA, *The Plan of the Theological Seminary* (Philadelphia: Aitken, 1816).

GERRISH, B. A., *The Old and New Protestantism* (Edinburgh: T. & T. Clark, 1982).

—— *A Prince of the Church: Schleiermacher and the Beginnings of Modern Theology* (London: SCM Press, 1984).

GERSTNER, JOHN H., 'The Contributions of Charles Hodge, B. B. Warfield, and J. Gresham Machen to the Doctrine of Inspiration', in Gordon R. Lewis and Bruce Demarest (eds.), *Challenges to Inerrancy: A Theological Response* (Chicago: Moody Press, 1984), 347–82.

GIBSON, JAMES, 'John Locke', *Proceedings of the British Academy*, 19 (1933), 13–30.

—— *Locke's Theory of Knowledge* (Cambridge: Cambridge University Press, 1968).

GILLEY, SHERIDAN, *Newman and His Age* (London: Darton, Longman and Todd, 1990).

GRECO, JOHN, 'Virtue Epistemology', in Jonathan Dancy and Ernest Sosa (eds.), *A Companion to Epistemology* (Oxford: Blackwell, 1992), 520–2.

GREGORY OF NYSSA, *The Life of Moses* (New York: Paulist Press, 1978).

—— 'Theological Orations', in E. R. Hardy (ed.), *Christology of the Later Fathers* (Philadelphia: Westminster Press, 1954), 128–214.

GREGORY PALAMAS, *The Triads* (New York: Paulist Press, 1983).

GRYSON, ROGER, 'The Authority of the Teacher in the Ancient and Medieval Church', *Journal of Ecumenical Studies*, 1912 (1982), 176–87.

GUNTON, COLIN, 'No Other Foundation: One Englishman's Reading of Church Dogmatics Chapter V', in Nigel Biggar (ed.), *Reckoning with Karl Barth: Essays on the Centenary of Karl Barth's Birth* (London: Mowbray, 1988), 61–79.

HACKING, IAN, *The Emergence of Probability: A Philosophical Study of Early Ideas about Probability, Induction, and Statistical Inference* (Cambridge: Cambridge University Press, 1975).

HAHNEMAN, GEOFFREY MARK, *The Muratorian Fragment and the Development of the Canon* (Oxford: Clarendon Press, 1992).

HALDANE, JOHN J., 'Reid, Scholasticism and Current Philosophy', in Melvin Dalgarno and Eric Matthews (eds.), *The Philosophy of Thomas Reid* (Boston: Academic Publishers, 1989), 285–306.

HAMPSON, DAPHNE, *Theology and Feminism* (Oxford: Blackwell, 1990).

HANSON, R. P. C., *Tradition in the Early Church* (London: SCM Press, 1962).

HARDY, EDWARD, R. (ed.), *Christology of the Later Fathers* (Philadelphia: Westminster Press, 1954).

HARRIS, HARRIETT ANNE, 'The Banner of Truth: Fundamentalism and its Influence on Evangelicalism' (D.Phil. diss., University of Oxford, 1994).

HARVEY, VAN AUSTIN, 'On the New Edition of Schleiermacher's *Addresses on Religion*', *Journal of the American Academy of Religion*, 39 (1971), 488–512.

—— 'A Word in Defence of Schleiermacher's Theological Method', *Journal of Religion*, 42 (1962), 151–70.

HAVGAARD, WILLIAM P., *Elizabeth and the English Reformation: The Struggle for a Stable Settlement of Religion* (Cambridge: Cambridge University Press, 1968).

HELLWIG, MONIKA, *Whose Experience Counts in Theological Reflection?* (Milwaukee: Marquette University Press, 1982).

HELM, PAUL, 'Faith, Evidence, and the Scriptures', in D. A. Carson and John D. Woodbridge (eds.), *Scripture and Truth* (Grand Rapids, Mich.: Zondervan, 1983), 303–20.

—— 'Thomas Reid, Common Sense and Calvinism', in Hendrik Hart, Johan Van Der Hoeven, and Nicholas Wolterstorff (eds.), *Rationality in the Calvinian Tradition* (Boston: University Press of America, 1983), 71–92.

HENRY, A. M. (ed.), *Introduction to Theology* (Chicago: Fides Publishers Association, 1954).

HERON, ALISDAIR, 'The Filioque Clause', *Reformed World*, 39 (1987), 842–52.

HODGE, A. A., *Life of Charles Hodge* (New York: Charles Scribner, 1880).

HODGE, CHARLES, *Essays and Reviews* (New York: Robert Carter and Brothers, 1856).

—— *Systematic Theology* (3 vols., Grand Rapids, Mich.: Eerdmans, n.d.).

—— *The Way of Life* (Philadelphia: American Sunday School Union, 1841).

HOLMES, J. DEREK (ed.), *The Theological Papers of John Henry Newman on Biblical Inspiration and on Infallibility* (Oxford: Clarendon Press, 1979).

HOOKER, RICHARD, *The Works of Richard Hooker* (Oxford: J. Vincent, 1843).

HUNSINGER, GEORGE, *How to Read Karl Barth: The Shape of his Theology* (New York: Oxford University Press, 1991).

IRENAEUS, *Against the Heresies* (New York: Paulist Press, 1992).

JOHN OF DAMASCUS, *Writings*, trans. Frederick H. Chase (Washington: Catholic University of American Press, 1958), 3–110.

JOLLEY, NICHOLAS, 'The Reception of Descartes' Philosophy', in John Cottingham (ed.), *The Cambridge Companion to Descartes* (Cambridge: Cambridge University Press, 1992), 393–423.

JORDAN, MARK D., *The Alleged Aristotelianism of Thomas Aquinas* (Toronto: Pontifical Institute of Medieval Studies, 1992).

KANT, IMMANUEL, *Prolegomena to Any Future Metaphysic of Morals* (Indianapolis: Bobbs-Merrill, 1950).

KAUFMAN, FRANZ-XAVER, 'The Sociology of Knowledge and the Problem of Authority', *Journal of Ecumenical Studies*, 19/2 (1982), 18–31.

KEELING, S. V., *Descartes* (Westport, Conn.: Greenwood Press, 1970).

KELLY, J. N. D., *Early Christian Creeds* (London: Longmans, Green & Co., 1950).

KELSEY, DAVID, *The Uses of Scripture in Recent Theology* (London: SCM Press, 1921).

KER, IAN T., *John Henry Newman* (Oxford: Clarendon Press, 1988).

—— (ed.), *Newman the Theologian: A Reader* (Notre Dame, Ind.: University of Notre Dame Press, 1990).

KHOMIAKOV, ALEKSEY STEPANOVICH, 'On the Western Confessions of Faith', in Alexander Schmemann (ed.), *Ultimate Questions* (New York: Holt, Reinhart, and Winston, 1965), 31–69.

KLEMKE, E. D., *The Meaning of Life* (New York: Oxford University Press, 1981).

KNOX, RONALD, *Occasional Sermons* (New York: Sheed and Ward, 1960).

KOESTER, HELMUT, 'Writings and the Spirit: Authority and Politics in Ancient Christianity', *Harvard Theological Review*, 84 (1991), 353–72.

KOONTZ, GAYLE GERBER, 'The Trajectory of Scripture and Feminist Conviction', *Conrad Grebel Review: A Journal of Christian Inquiry*, 5 (1987), 201–20.

KÜNG, HANS, *Infallible?* (London: Collins, 1971).

—— (ed.), *Papal Ministry in the Church* (New York: Herder and Herder, 1971).

LAMBERT, JEAN C., 'An "F Factor"? The New Testament in Some White, Feminist, Christian Theological Constructions', *Journal of Feminist Studies in Religion*, 1 (1985), 93–113.

LAN, KWOK PUI, 'Discovering the Bible in the Non-Biblical World', *Semeia*, 47 (1989), 25–42.

LAUDAN, L. L., 'Thomas Reid and the Newtonian Turn of British Methodological Thought', in A. Koyre (ed.), *Newtonian Studies* (Chicago: University of Chicago Press, 1968), 103–31.

LAYMON, RONALD, 'Transubstantiation: Test Case for Descartes's Theory of Space', in Thomas M. Lennon, John M. Nicholas, and John W. Davis (eds.), *Problems of Cartesianism* (Kingston and Montreal: McGill–Queen's University Press, 1982), 149–70.

LEHRER, KEITH, 'Reid's Influence on Contemporary American and British Philosophy', in Stephen F. Barker and Tom L. Beauchamp (eds.), *Thomas Reid: Critical Interpretations* (Philadelphia: Philosophical Monographs, 1976), 1–7.

—— 'Scottish Influences on Contemporary American Philosophy', *Philosophical Journal*, 5 (1968), 34–42.

LEITH, JOHN H., *Creeds of the Church* (Louisville, Ky.: John Knox Press, 1982).

LEMCIO EUGENE E., and WALL, ROBERT W. (eds.), *The New Testament as Canon: A Reader in Canonical Criticism* (Sheffield: JSOT Press, 1992).

LINDBECK, GEORGE, *The Nature of Doctrine* (Philadelphia: Westminster Press, 1984).

LINDSAY, THOMAS, 'The Doctrine of Scripture: The Reformers and the Princeton School', *Expositor*, 14 (1895), 278–93.

LINDSELL, HAROLD, *The Battle for the Bible* (Grand Rapids, Mich.: Zondervan, 1976).

LOCKE, JOHN, *An Essay Concerning Human Understanding*, ed. P. H. Nidditch (Oxford: Clarendon Press, 1975).

—— *The Reasonableness of Christianity as Delivered in the Scriptures*, ed. with an introduction by George E. Ewing (Washington: Regnery Gateway, 1965).

—— *The Works of John Locke* (London: Rivington Press, 1824).

LORTZ, JOSEPH, *How the Reformation Came* (New York: Herder and Herder, 1964).

LOTZ, DAVID W., 'Sola Scriptura: Luther on Biblical Authority', *Interpretation*, 35 (1981), 258–73.

LUTHER, MARTIN, *Briefe* (Weimar: H. Böhlau, 1883).

—— *Luther's Works* (St Louis: Concordia Press, 1955).

—— *Werke* (Weimar: H. Böhlau, 1883).

McCOOL, GERALD A., *From Unity to Pluralism: The Internal Evolution of Thomism* (New York: Fordham University Press, 1989).

MACDONALD, SCOTT, 'Theory of Knowledge', in Norman Kretzmann and Eleonore Stump (eds.), *The Cambridge Companion to Thomas Aquinas* (Cambridge: Cambridge University Press, 1993), 160–95.

McDONALD, L. M., *The Formation of the Christian Biblical Canon* (Nashville: Abingdon Press, 1988).

McDONNELL, KILLIAN, and MONTAGUE, GEORGE T., *Christian Initiation and Baptism in the Holy Spirit* (Collegeville, Minn.: The Liturgical Press, 1991).

McGRATH, ALISTAIR, 'Forerunners of the Reformation? A Critical Examination of the Evidence for Precursors of the Reformation Doctrines of Justification', *Harvard Theological Review*, 75 (1982), 219–42.

McIRNERNY, RALPH, 'Second-Hand Straw', *Crisis*, 11 (1993), 15–17.

MACHEN, H. GRESHAM, 'The Relation of Religion to Science and Philosophy', *Princeton Theological Review*, 24 (1926), 38–66.

MACKINTOSH, H. R., *Types of Modern Theology* (London: Collins, 1937).

MANDROU, ROBERT, *From Humanism to Science, 1480–1700* (New York: Penguin, 1978).

MANNING, H. E., *The Oecumenical Council and the Infallibility of the Roman Pontiff* (London: Longmans, Green, 1863).

MARITAIN, JACQUES, *Three Reformers: Luther – Descartes – Rousseau* (New York: Charles Scribner's Sons, n.d.).

MARSDEN, GEORGE, 'J. Gresham Machen, History, and Truth', *Westminster Theological Review*, 42 (1979), 157–75.

MARSHALL, JOHN, *John Locke in Context: Religion, Ethics, and Politics* (Cambridge: Cambridge University Press, 1994).

MATTHEWS, REX D., ' "Religion and Reason Joined": A Study in the Theology of John Wesley' (Th.D. thesis, Harvard University, 1986).

MAVRODES, GEORGE I., *Revelation in Religious Belief* (Philadelphia: Temple University Press, 1988).

MEETER, JOHN E. (ed.), *Selected Shorter Writings of Benjamin B. Warfield* (2 vols., Phillipsburg, NJ: Presbyterian and Reformed Publishing Company, 1970).

MERCIER, CARDINAL, *A Manual of Modern Scholastic Philosophy*, trans. T. L. Parker and S. A. Parker (St Louis: Herder, 1953).

METZGER, B. M., *The Canon of the New Testament: Its Origin, Development, and Significance* (Oxford: Clarendon Press, 1987).

MEYENDORFF, JOHN, 'Rome and Orthodoxy', in Peter J. McCord (ed.), *A Pope For All Christians* (New York: Paulis Press, 1976), 129-47.

——*A Study of Gregory Palamas* (Crestwood, NY: St Vladimir's Seminary Press, 1964).

MILLER, J. MICHAEL, *What are they Saying about Papal Primacy?* (New York: Paulist Press, 1982).

MISNER, PAUL, *Papacy and Development: Newman and the Primacy of the Pope* (Leiden: E. J. Brill, 1976).

MITCHELL, BASIL, *Faith and Criticism* (Oxford: Clarendon Press, 1994).

—— *The Justification of Religious Belief* (London: Macmillan, 1973).

—— 'Newman as a Philosopher', in Ian T. Ker and Alan G. Hill (eds.), *Newman after a Hundred Years* (Oxford: Clarendon Press, 1990).

MORE, PAUL ELMER, and CROSS, FRANK LESLIE (eds.), *Anglicanism* (London: SPCK, 1951).

MULLER, RICHARD A., *Post-Reformation Reformed Dogmatics*, vol. i: *Prolegomena to Theology* (Grand Rapids, Mich.: Baker Books, 1987).

—— *Post-Reformation Reformed Dogmatics*, vol. ii: *Holy Scripture: The Cognitive Foundation of Theology* (Grand Rapids, Mich.: Baker, 1993).

NEWMAN, JOHN HENRY, *Apologia pro Vita Sua* (London: Sheed and Ward, 1945).

—— *The Arians of the Fourth Century* (London: Longmans, Green, & Co., 1895).

——*An Essay in Aid of a Grammar of Assent* (Notre Dame, Ind.: University of Notre Dame Press: 1979).

NEWMAN, JOHN HENRY, *An Essay on the Development of Christian Doctrine* (Notre Dame, Ind.: University of Notre Dame Press, 1989).

—— 'Holy Scripture in its Relation to the Creed', in *Discussion and Arguments on Various Subjects* (New York: Confucian Press, 1981), 109–253.

—— 'The Introduction of Rationalistic Principles into Revealed Religion', in *Essays Critical and Historical* (2 vols., London: Longmans, 1910), i. 30–99.

—— *Lectures on Justification* (London: Rivington Press, 1940).

—— 'A Letter to the Duke of Norfolk', in Ian T. Ker (ed.), *The Genius of John Henry Newman* (Oxford: Clarendon Press, 1989), 262–8.

—— *On Consulting the Faithful in Matters of Doctrine* (London: Collins, 1986).

—— *On the Inspiration of Scripture* (Washington: Corpus Books, 1967).

—— *Sermons Chiefly on the Theory of Religious Belief Preached before the University of Oxford* (London: Rivington Press, 1844).

—— *The Via Media of the Anglican Church*, ed. H. D. Weidner (Oxford: Clarendon Press, 1990).

NICHOLS, AIDAN, *The Shape of Catholic Theology* (Collegeville, Minn.: The Liturgical Press, 1991).

NOLL, MARK A. (ed.), *The Princeton Theology, 1812–1921* (Grand Rapids, Mich.: Baker, 1983).

NOONAN, JOHN T., 'The Protestant Philosophy of John Locke', in John K. Ryan (ed.), *Philosophical Studies in Honor of The Very Rev. Ignatius Smith, O. P.* (Westminster, Md.: Newman Press, 1952), 92–126.

OBERMAN, HEIKO AUGUSTUS, *The Dawn of the Reformation* (Edinburgh: T. & T. Clark, 1986).

—— *Forerunners of the Reformation: The Shape of Medieval Thought, Illustrated by Key Documents* (New York: Holt, Rinehart and Winston, 1966).

—— *The Harvest of Medieval Theology* (Durham, NC: Labyrinth Press, 1983).

O'CONNELL, MARVIN R., 'Newman and Liberalism', in Stanley L. Jaki (ed.), *Newman Today* (San Francisco: Ignatius Press, 1989), 79-93.

O'CONNOR, JUNE, 'The Epistemological Significance of Feminist Research in Religion', in Ursula King (ed.), *Religion and Gender*, (Oxford: Blackwell, 1995), 45–64.

OGDEN, SCHUBERT, 'A Critique of Religious Liberalism', in *Revolutionary Challenges to Religious Liberalism: The Meadville/Lombard Theological School 125th Anniversary Lectures* (1971), 1–19.

—— 'Doctrinal Standards in the United Methodist Church', *Perkins School of Theology Journal*, 28 (1974), 19–27.

—— *Faith and Freedom: A Theology of Liberation* (Nashville: Abingdon Press, 1979).

—— 'Falsification and Belief', *Religious Studies*, 10 (1974), 21–43.

—— 'God and Philosophy: A Discussion with Anthony Flew', *Journal of Religion*, 48 (1968), 161–81.

—— *Is there One True Religion or are there Many?* (Dallas: Southern Methodist University Press, 1992).

—— 'Linguistic Analysis and Theology', *Theologische Zeitschrift*, 33 (1977), 318–25.

—— 'The Lordship of Jesus Christ: The Meaning of Our Affirmation', *Encounter*, 21 (1960), 408–22.

—— 'Love Unbounded: The Doctrine of God', *Perkins School of Theology Journal*, 19 (1966), 5–17.

—— *On Theology* (San Francisco: Harper and Row, 1986).

—— 'On the Trinity', *Theology*, 83 (1980), 97–102.

—— *The Point of Christology* (Dallas: Southern Methodist University Press, 1982).

—— 'The Problem of Normative Witness: A Response', *Perkins School of Theology Journal*, 41 (1988), 22–6.

—— 'Process Theology and the Wesleyan Witness', *Perkins School of Theology Journal*, 37 (1984), 18–33.

—— *The Reality of God and Other Essays* (San Francisco: Harper and Row, 1963).

—— ' "The Reformation that We Want" ', *Anglican Theological Review*, 54 (1972), 260–73.

—— 'The Service of Theology to the Servant Task of Pastoral Ministry', in Earl E. Shelp and Ronald H. Sunderland (eds.), *The Pastor as Servant* (New York: Pilgrim Press, 1986), 81–101.

—— 'The Situation in Contemporary Protestant Theology, II. Systematic Theology', *Perkins School of Theology Journal*, 12 (1959), 13–20.

—— 'Sources of Religious Authority in Liberal Protestantism', *Journal of the American Academy of Religion*, 44 (1976), 403–16.

—— ' "Theology and Falsification" in Retrospect: A Reply', in Malcolm L. Diamond and Thomas V. Litzenburg, Jun. (eds.), *The Logic of God: Theology and Verification* (Indianapolis: Bobbs-Merrill, 1975), 290–7.

—— 'Theology and Philosophy: A New Phase of the Discussion', *Journal of Religion*, 44 (1964), 1–16.

—— 'What is Theology?', *Perkins School of Theology Journal*, 26 (1973), 1–13.

ORIGEN, *On First Principles* (Gloucester, Mass.: Peter Smith, 1973).

ORR, ROBERT, *Reason and Authority: The Thought of William Chillingworth* (Oxford: Clarendon Press, 1967).

OSIEK, CAROLYN, 'The Feminist and the Bible: Hermeneutical

Alternatives', in Adela Yarbo Collins (ed.), *Feminist Perspectives in Biblical Scholarship* (Chico, Calif.: Scholars' Press, 1985), 93–105.

—— "Reading the Bible as Women", in Leander E. Keck *et al.* (eds.), *New Interpreter's Bible* (Nashville: Abingdon Press, 1994), i. 18–7.

OUSPENSKY, LEONID, *The Theology of Icons* (Notre Dame, Ind.: Ave Maria Press, 1987).

OZMENT, STEVEN, *Protestants: The Birth of a Revolution* (New York: Doubleday, 1992).

PASSMORE, J. A., 'Locke and the Ethics of Belief', in Anthony Kenny (ed.), *Rationalism, Empiricism, and Idealism* (Oxford: Clarendon Press, 1986), 23–46.

PATTISON, ROBERT, *The Great Dissent: John Henry Newman and the Liberal Heresy* (Oxford: Oxford University Press, 1991).

PEARSON, JOHN, *An Exposition of the Creed* (Oxford: Oxford University Press, 1847).

PELIKAN, JAROSLAV, *Christianity and Classical Culture: The Metamorphosis of Natural Theology in the Christian Encounter with Hellenism* (New Haven: Yale University Press, 1993).

—— ' "Council or Father or Scripture": The Concept of Authority in the Theology of Maximus the Confessor', in David Nieman and Margaret Schatkin (eds.), *The Heritage of the Early Church* (Rome: Pontifical Institute of Oriental Studies, 1973), 277–88.

PLANTINGA, ALVIN, and WOLTERSTORFF, NICHOLAS (eds.), *Faith and Rationality: Reason and Belief in God* (Notre Dame, Ind.: University of Notre Dame Press, 1983).

PLASS, EWALD M., *What Luther Says* (St Louis: Concordia Press, 1959).

POPKIN, RICHARD H., *The History of Skepticism from Erasmus to Spinoza* (Berkeley: University of California Press, 1979).

PROCTER-SMITH, MARJORIE, *In Her Own Rite* (Nashville: Abingdon Press, 1990).

—— *Praying with Our Eyes Open: Engendering Feminist Liturgical Prayer* (Nashville: Abingdon Press, 1995).

PROUDFOOT, WAYNE, *Religious Experience* (Berkeley: University of California Press, 1985).

QUASTEN, JOHANNES, *Patrology* (Utrecht and Brussels: Spectrum, 1950).

RACK, HENRY, *Reasonable Enthusiast: John Wesley and the Rise of Methodism* (Nashville: Abingdon Press, 1993).

REDEKER, MARTIN, *Schleiermacher: Life and Thought* (Philadelphia: Fortress Press, 1973).

REDWOOD, JOHN, *Reason, Ridicule and Religion* (London: Thames & Hudson, 1970).

REID, THOMAS, *Essays on the Intellectual Powers of Man*, in *Works*, ed. Sir William Hamilton (2 vols., Edinburgh: James Thin, 1895).

——*An Inquiry into the Human Mind*, in *Works*, ed. Sir William Hamilton (2 vols., Edinburgh: James Thin, 1895).

—— *The Philosophical Orations of Thomas Reid* (Carbondale and Edwardsville, Ill.: Southern Illinois University Press, 1989).

REITH, HERMAN R., *René Descartes: The Story of a Soul* (Lanham, Md.: University Press of America, 1986).

REUSS, EDWARD, *History of the Canon of Holy Scriptures in the Christian Church* (Edinburgh: R. W. Hunter, 1891).

ROGERS, JACK B., and McKIM, DONALD K., *The Authority and Interpretation of the Bible* (San Francisco: Harper and Row, 1979).

ROMANIDES, JOHN S., *Franks, Romans, Feudalism, and Doctrine* (Brookline, Mass.: Holy Cross Orthodox Press, 1982).

RUETHER, ROSEMARY, 'Is Feminism the End of Christianity? A Critique of Daphne Hampson's *Theology and Feminism*', *Scottish Journal of Theology*, 43 (1990), 390–400.

—— ' "Review Symposium" of *In Memory of Her: A Feminist Theological Reconstruction of Christian Origins*', *Horizons*, 11 (1984), 146–50.

—— *Sexism and God-Talk* (Boston: Beacon, 1985).

—— *Womanguides: Reading toward a Feminist Theology* (Boston: Beason Press, 1985).

RUMSCHEIDT, MARTIN, *Revelation and Theology* (Cambridge: Cambridge University Press, 1972).

RUNCIMAN, STEVEN, *The Eastern Schism* (Oxford: Clarendon Press, 1955).

RUSSELL, LETTY M., *Household of Freedom: Authority in Feminist Theology* (Philadelphia: Westminster Press, 1987).

RYLE, GILBERT, *John Locke on the Human Understanding* (Oxford: Oxford University Press, 1933).

SANDERS, JAMES A., *Canon and Community: A Guide to Canonical Criticism* (Philadelphia: Fortress Press, 1984).

—— *Torah and Canon* (Philadelphia: Fortress Press, 1972).

SCHLEIERMACHER, FRIEDRICH, *Brief Outline on the Study of Theology* (Richmond, Va.: John Knox Press, 1966).

—— *The Christian Faith* (Edinburgh: T. & T. Clark, 1928).

—— *Christmas Eve: Dialogue on Incarnation* (Richmond, Va.: John Knox Press, 1967).

—— *On Religion: Speeches to its Cultural Despisers* (Cambridge: Cambridge University Press, 1988).

—— 'On the Discrepancy between the Sabellian and Athanasian Method of Representing the Doctrine of the Trinity in the Godhead', *Biblical Repository and Quarterly Observer*, 5 (April and July 1835), 1–116.

—— *Servant of the Word* (Phildelphia: Fortress Press, 1987).

SCHOULS, PETER A., *The Imposition of Method: A Study of Descartes and Locke* (Oxford: Clarendon Press, 1980).

SCHULTHESS, DANIEL, 'Did Reid Hold Coherentist Views?', in *The Philosophy of Common Sense*, 193–204.

SCHÜSSLER FIORENZA, ELIZABETH, 'Author's Response', *Horizons*, 11 (1984), 154–7.

—— *Bread not Stone* (Boston: Beacon Press, 1984).

—— 'Emerging Issues in Feminist Biblical Interpretation', in Judith L. Weidman (ed.), *Christian Feminism: Visions of a New Humanity* (San Francisco: Harper and Row, 1984), 33–54.

—— 'The Ethics of Biblical Interpretation: Decentering Biblical Scholarship', *Journal of Biblical Literature*, 107 (1988), 3–17.

—— *In Memory of Her: A Feminist Theological Reconstruction of Christian Origins* (New York: Crossroad, 1983).

—— 'Introduction: Transgressing Canonical Boundaries', in Elizabeth Schüssler Fiorenza (ed.), *Searching the Scriptures*, vol. ii: *A Feminist Commentary* (New York: Crossroad, 1994), 1–14.

—— 'Toward a Feminist Biblical Hermeneutics: Biblical Interpretation and Liberation Theology', in Brian Mahan and L. Dale Richesin (eds.), *The Challenge of Liberation Theology: A First World Response* (New York: Crossroad, 1981), 91–112.

—— 'Transforming the Legacy of the Women's Bible', in Elizabeth Schüssler Fiorenza (ed.), *Searching the Scriptures*, i: *A Feminist Introduction* (New York: Crossroad, 1993), 1–24.

—— 'The Will to Choose or to Reject: Continuing Our Critical Work', in Letty M. Russell (ed.), *Feminist Interpretation of the Bible* (Philadelphia: Westminster, 1985), 125–36.

SCOTT, CHARLES E., 'Schleiermacher and the Problem of Divine Immediacy', *Religious Studies*, 3 (1968), 449–512.

SEBBA, GREGOR, *The Dream of Descartes* (Carbondale, Ill.: University of Illinois Press, 1987).

SHAW, P. E., *The Early Tractarians and the Eastern Church* (London: A. R. Mowbray & Co., 1930).

SHERIDAN, THOMAS L., *Newman on Justification: A Theological Biography* (New York: Alba House, 1967).

SHERRARD, PHILIP, *The Greek East and the Latin West* (London: Oxford University Press, 1959).

SHIMIZU, MITSUO, 'Epistemology in the Thought of John Wesley' (Ph.D. diss., Drew University, 1980).

Society for Promoting Christian Knowledge, *Certain Sermons or Homilies Appointed to be read in Churches in the Time of Queen Elizabeth of Famous Memory* (London: SPCK, 1890).

STANIFORTH, MAXWELL, *Early Christian Writings: Apostolic Fathers* (New York: Penguin, 1982).

STEINMETZ, DAVID C., 'Luther and Calvin on Church and Tradition', in *Luther in Context* (Bloomington, Ind.: Indiana University Press, 1986), 85–97.

STEPHEN, LESLIE, 'Cardinal Newman's Scepticism', *Nineteenth Century*, 168 (1891), 179–201.

—— 'Newman's Theory of Belief', in *An Agnostic's Apology* (New York: G. P. Putnam's Sons, 1893), 168–241.

STEUSSY, MARTI, *Setting the Table: Women in Theological Conversation* (St Louis: Chalice Press, 1995)

STEWART-ROBERTSON, CHARLES, 'Thomas Reid and Pneumatology: The Text of the Old, the Tradition of the New', in Melvin Dalgarno and Eric Matthews (eds.), *The Philosophy of Thomas Reid* (Boston: Kluwer Academic Publishers, 1989), 389–412.

STICKLER, ALFONS M., 'Papal Infallibility—A Thirteenth-Century Invention? Reflections on a Recent Book', *Catholic Historical Review*, 60 (1974), 427–41.

—— 'A Rejoinder to Professor Tierney', *Catholic Historical Review*, 61 (1975), 274–9.

STOUT, JEFFREY, *The Flight from Authority: Religion, Morality, and the Quest for Autonomy* (Notre Dame, Ind.: University of Notre Dame Press, 1981).

STUMP, ELEONORE, 'Aquinas and the Foundations of Knowledge', *Canadian Journal of Philosophy*, supp. vol. 17 (19), 125–58.

—— 'Intellect, Will, and the Principle of Alternative Possibilities', in Michael D. Beatty (ed.), *Christian Theism and the Problems of Philosophy* (Notre Dame, Ind.: University of Notre Dame Press, 1990), 254–85.

—— 'Revelation and Biblical Exegesis: Augustine, Aquinas, and Swinburne', in Alan G. Padgett, (ed.), *Reason and the Christian Religion* (Oxford: Clarendon Press, 1994.

SULLIVAN, THOMAS D., 'The Problem of Certitude', in Thomas Russman (ed.), *Thomistic Papers V* (Houston: Center for Thomistic Studies, University of St Thomas, 1990), 63–77.

SUNBERG, ALBERT C., Jun., 'The Old Testament of the Early Church', *Harvard Theological Review*, 51 (1958), 205–26.

SWETE, H. B. (ed.), *Essays on the Early History of the Church and the Ministry* (London: Macmillan, 1918).

SWINBURNE, RICHARD, *The Existence of God* (Oxford: Clarendon Press, 1979).

—— *Revelation* (Oxford: Clarendon Press, 1992).

SYKES, STEPHEN, and BOOTY, JOHN (eds.), *The Study of Anglicanism* (London: SPCK, 1988).

SYMEON THE NEW THEOLOGIAN, *The Discourses* (New York: Paulist Press, 1980).

SYMEON THE NEW THEOLOGIAN, *The Practical and Theological Chapters and the Three Theological Discourses* (Kalamazoo, Mich.: Cistercian Publications, 1982).

SYNAVE, PAUL, and BENOIT, PIERRE, *Prophecy and Inspiration* (New York: Desclee Company, 1961).

TANNER, NORMAN (ed.), *Decrees of the Ecumenical Councils*, vol. ii: *Trent to Vatican II* (Washington: Georgetown University Press, 1990).

TAPPERT, THEODORE G. (ed.), *Selected Writings of Martin Luther, 1517–1520* (Philadelphia: Fortress Press, 1967).

—— *Selected Writings of Martin Luther, 1539–1546* (Philadelphia: Fortress Press, 1967).

TAVARD, GEORGE, *Holy Writ or Holy Church* (London: Burns and Oates, 1959).

TAYLOR, CHARLES, 'Philosophy and its History', in Richard Rorty, J. B. Schneewind, and Quentin Skinner (eds.), *Philosophy in History* (Cambridge: Cambridge University Press, 1984), 17–30.

TAYLOR, MARK LLOYD, 'The Boundless Love of God and the Bounds of Critical Reflection', *Journal of the American Academy of Religion*, 57 (1989), 103–47.

THISTLETHWAITE, SUSAN BROOKS, 'Christology and Postmodernism', *Interpretation*, 49 (1995), 267–80.

THOMAS, STEPHEN, *Newman and Heresy: The Anglican Years* (Cambridge: Cambridge University Press, 1991).

TIERNEY, BRIAN, 'Origins of Papal Infallibility', *Journal of Ecumenical Studies*, 9 (19), 841–64.

—— *Origins of Papal Infallibility, 1150–1350* (Leiden: E. J. Brill, 1988).

TOLBERT, MARY ANN, 'Defining the Problem: The Bible and Feminist Hermeneutics', *Semeia*, 28 (1983), 113–26.

—— 'Protestant Feminists and the Bible: On the Horns of a Dilemma', *Union Seminary Quarterly Review*, 43 (1989), 1–17.

TORRANCE, THOMAS, *Karl Barth, Biblical and Evangelical Theologian* (Edinburgh: T. & T. Clark, 1990).

—— *Reality and Evangelical Theology* (Philadelphia: Westminster Press, 1982).

TOULMIN, STEPHEN, *Cosmopolis* (Chicago: University of Chicago Press, 1990).

TOVEY, W. A. C., 'Forms of Authority in the Theology of the Elizabethan Separatists' (BD thesis, University of Oxford, 1991).

TURRETIN, FRANCIS, *Institutes of Elenctic Theology* (Phillipsburg, NJ: Presbyterian and Reformed Publishing Company, 1992).

VAN DER PLOEG, J., 'Holy Scripture in the Theology of St. Thomas', *Thomist*, 10 (1947), 398–442.

VANDER STELT, JOHN C., *Philosophy and Scripture* (Marlton, NJ: Mack, 1978).

VAN DER WALL, ERNESTINE, 'Orthodoxy and Skepticism in the early Dutch Enlightenment', in Richard Popkin and Arjo Vanderjagt (eds.), *Skepticism and Irreligion in the Seventeenth and Eighteenth Centuries* (Leiden: E. J. Brill, 1993), 121–41.

VAN LEEUWEN, HENRY, *The Problem of Certainty in English Thought, 1630–1690* (The Hague: Martinus Nijhoff, 1963).

VENDLER, Z., 'Descartes' Exercises', *Canadian Journal of Philosophy*, 19 (1989), 193–224.

VERNIER, PAUL, 'Thomas Reid on the Foundations of Knowledge and his Answer to Skepticism', in Stephen F. Barker and Tom L. Beauchamp (eds.), *Thomas Reid: Critical Interpretations* (Philadelphia: Philosophical Monographs, 1976), 14–24.

WACE, HENRY, and SCHAFF, PHILIP (eds.), *A Select Library of Nicene and post-Nicene Fathers of the Christian Church* (New York: Christian Literature Company, 1890), vol. vi.

WAINWRIGHT, GEOFFREY, 'The New Testament as Canon', *Scottish Journal of Theology*, 28 (1975), 551–71.

WAINWRIGHT, WILLIAM J., *Reason and the Heart* (Ithaca, NY: Cornell University Press, 1995).

WARFIELD, BENJAMIN BRECKENRIDGE, *Counterfeit Miracles* (London: Banner of Truth, 1972).

—— *The Idea of Systematic Theology as a Science* (New York: Anson Randolph & Co., 1888).

—— *The Inspiration and Authority of the Bible* (Philadelphia: The Presbyterian and Reformed Publishing Company, 1970).

—— *Studies in Tertullian and Augustine* (New York: Oxford University Press, 1930).

—— *Studies in Theology* (New York: Oxford University Press, 1932).

WATSON, RICHARD A., 'Transubstantiation among the Cartesians', in Thomas M. Lennon, John M. Nicholas, and John W. Davis (eds.), *Problems of Cartesianism* (Kingston and Montreal: McGill-Queen's University Press, 1982), 127–48.

WEINANDY, THOMAS G., *The Father's Spirit of Sonship: Reconceiving the Trinity* (T. & T. Clarke, 1995).

WEST, CORNEL, 'Minority Discourse and the Pitfalls of Canon Formation', *Yale Journal of Criticism*, 1 (1987–8), 193–201.

WESTCOTT, BROOKE FOSS, 'On the Primitive Doctrine of Inspiration', repr. in Everett Ferguson (ed.), *The Bible in the Early Church* (New York and London: Garland Publishing Co., 1993), 2–45.

WHEDER, SANDRA ELY, KECK, LEANDER E., and LASH, NICHOLAS, 'The Author is Dead? Is She? Practicing the Ethics of

Interpretation' (paper read at a conference at Duke University in April 1995).

WOLTERSTORFF, NICHOLAS, 'Locke's Philosophy of Religion', in *The Cambridge Companion to Locke* (Cambridge: Cambridge University Press, 1994), 172–98.

—— 'The Migration of the Theistic Arguments: From Natural Theology to Evidentialist Apologetics', in Robert Audi and William J. Wainwright (eds.), *Rationality, Religious Belief, and Moral Commitment* (Ithaca, NY: Cornell University Press, 1986), 38–81.

—— *Reason within the Bounds of Religion* (Grand Rapids, Mich.: Eerdmans, 1976).

WONDRA, ELLEN K., 'By Whose Authority? The Status of Scripture in Contemporary Feminist Theologies', *Anglican Theological Review*, 75 (1993), 83–101.

WOODBRIDGE, JOHN D., and BALMER, RANDALL H., 'The Princetonians and Biblical Authority: An Assessment of the Ernest Sandeen Proposal', in D. A. Carson and John D. Woodbridge (eds.), *Scripture and Truth* (Grand Rapids, Mich.: Zondervan, 1983), 251–79.

WORTLEY, J., 'The Sixtieth Canon of the Council in Troullo', *Studia Patristica*, 15 (1984), 255–60.

ZOPPI, JOHN J., 'The Correspondence of 1573–1581 between the Lutheran Theologians at Tübingen and the Eastern Orthodox Patriarchiate at Constantinople, and the Dispute concerning Sacred Tradition', *Patristic and Byzantine Review*, 4 (1985), 175–95; 5 (1986), 5–18, 139–46, 207–21.

INDEX